Complete one 3-minute timing on the timing text below. *Note: With this session, the default WPM goal for 3-minute timings has been increased by 5 WPM in the Online Lab. However, your instructor may have customized this goal.*

3-Minute Timing

Timing 86.3

Sometimes it seems we have complicated our lives so much through necessity and technology that we have lost one of the greatest pleasures of all, which is simply sitting and enjoying the satisfaction of making something of lasting beauty with our hands. Woodcarving provides this pleasure. Of all the artistic mediums available today, wood is the most expressive and sensitive, and yet the least understood and perhaps the most neglected.

Woodcarving is a solitary pursuit, but it is an experience that goes beyond just shaping a piece of wood. Wood is a living material. Each piece has its own beauty and individuality, and you must develop a feeling for working in cooperation with it. A person working with clay or metal can force it into any shape desired, but not with wood. A carver must work along with the character of each piece.

A person does not have to be an experienced artist or crafter to enjoy woodcarving. All that is required is a natural curiosity, a desire to learn, and a little time. This hobby does not require a lot of tools and equipment. All you need to get started is a small pocketknife and a piece of wood.

 Ergonomic Tip

Position your keyboard so that your body is centered on the B key. This position provides you with a more direct reach to the keys in the various rows of the keyboard.

Inserting Symbols

Microsoft Word offers a wide variety of symbols that can be inserted into documents. Some symbols are used to enhance a document, whereas other symbols are necessary based on the content of the document. For example, you have to use certain symbols when preparing legal documents. In this session, you will insert several of the symbols available in Word.

One method of inserting symbols is to use the Symbol button in the Symbols group on the Insert tab. Available symbols include ©, ¶, ♣, ☺, and æ; letters from non-Latin alphabets such as ß, ¿, and ϖ; mathematical symbols such as ∫, ∞, and ‰; and many more. Click the Symbol button to display a drop-down list of the most recently used symbols on the computer on which you are working (see Figure 86.1). Click a symbol to insert it into the document. If the symbol you are looking for does not appear in the drop-down list, click *More Symbols* to display the Symbol dialog box.

Session 86

Inserting Symbols and Borders

Session Objectives

- **Insert symbols**
- **Resize symbols**
- **Apply vertical and horizontal borders**
- **Create a customized letterhead**
- **Efficiently produce documents in mailable form**

Getting Started

Exercise 86.1 If you are continuing immediately from Session 85, you may skip the Exercise 86.1 warm-up drill. However, if you exited the Online Lab at the end of Session 85, warm up by completing Exercise 86.1.

Exercise 86.2 Begin your session work by completing Exercise 86.2, a timed short drill, in the Online Lab.

Assessing Your Speed and Accuracy

Complete Timings 86.1 through 86.3 in the Online Lab. At the end of each timing, the Online Lab will display your WPM rate and any errors. Results will be saved in your Timings Performance report. If you have been surpassing the speed and accuracy goals identified in the Online Lab, set slightly more challenging personal goals and strive to exceed them.

Complete two 1-minute timings on the timing text below. If you do not key at or above the WPM rate identified in the Online Lab on Timing 86.1, concentrate on speed on Timing 86.2. If you meet the Online Lab's WPM goal but make more errors than the goal set in the Online Lab on Timing 86.1, concentrate on accuracy on Timing 86.2. However, if you meet or exceed both goals for Timing 86.1, push for greater speed on Timing 86.2.

1-Minute Timings

Timings 86.1–86.2 Communication systems cannot be set up without careful thought. It is best when firms assign who is to be in charge of communications and prepare well-designed plans and guidelines for this area. The trend to digitize all communications such as voice, data, and video simplifies how the transmission works. Thus, communications can be managed better by just one person, group, or unit. For smaller firms or those without internal expertise, assistance in writing these plans can be obtained from consultants and vendors.

Figure 86.1 Symbol Button Recently Inserted Symbols List

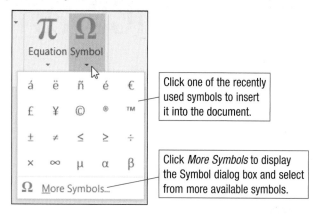

Click one of the recently used symbols to insert it into the document.

Click *More Symbols* to display the Symbol dialog box and select from more available symbols.

Figure 86.2 shows the Symbol dialog box with the Symbols tab selected. The *(normal text)* option is selected in the *Font* option box, and the symbols shown in the gallery all belong to that font. To change the font, and therefore the symbols available in the gallery, click the *Font* option box arrow and then click the desired font name. Use the scroll bar at the right side of the gallery to scroll through all of the symbols in all of the available fonts, click the symbol to select it, and then click the Insert button to insert the symbol into the active document. Another method for selecting a symbol at the Symbol dialog box is to type the symbol code in the *Character code* text box.

Some symbols can be inserted by using keyboard shortcuts. For example, when you key (c), the copyright symbol © will replace the keyed text. If you do not want to accept the replacement, press the Backspace key immediately after the replacement is made. The AutoCorrect tab in the AutoCorrect dialog box shows a list of all of the keyboard shortcuts that can be used to create symbols. To display this dialog box, click the File tab, click *Options*, click *Proofing* in the left panel of the dialog box, click the AutoCorrect Options button, and then click the AutoCorrect tab.

Practice keying a memo that contains symbols in the following document activity.

Figure 86.2 Symbol Dialog Box with the Symbols Tab Selected

Use the *Font* option box to display the desired set of symbols.

Click this tab to display a list of special characters and the keyboard shortcuts to create them.

Quickly select a symbol by typing its code in this text box.

Symbol															? ✕

Symbols   Special Characters

Font: (normal text)   Subset: Latin-1 Supplement

á	â	ã	ä	å	æ	ç	è	é	ê	ë	ì	í	î	ï	ð
ñ	ò	ó	ô	õ	ö	÷	ø	ù	ú	û	ü	ý	þ	ÿ	Ā
ā	Ă	ă	Ą	ą	Ć	ć	Ĉ	ĉ	Ċ	ċ	Č	č	Ď	ď	Đ
đ	Ē	ē	Ě	ě	Ė	ė	Ę	ę	Ě	ě	Ĝ	ĝ	Ğ	ğ	Ġ

Recently used symbols:

á	ë	ñ	é	€	£	¥	©	®	™	±	≠	≤	≥	÷	×

Unicode name:

Latin Small Letter A With Acute

Character code: 00E1   from: Unicode (hex)

AutoCorrect...   Shortcut Key...   Shortcut key: Ctrl+',A

Insert   Cancel

Unit
18 Graphics and Imagery

Document 86.1 Memo with Symbols

Read all instructions below before starting this document activity.

1 Navigate to the Document 86.1 launch page in the Online Lab and then click the Launch Activity button to open **Doc086.01** in the activity window.

2 Key the memo text shown in Figure 86.3 and apply the following instructions as you key the document.

   a Turn on the display of nonprinting characters and then position the insertion point immediately to the right of *TO:*. Turn off bold formatting and then press Tab twice. Key all of the memo header information, pressing Tab twice after the first three guide words and once after the fourth, remembering to turn off bold formatting. Position the insertion point before the last paragraph mark in the document and then key the body of the memo.

   b To insert the © and ™ symbols, key (c) and (tm) and allow Word to AutoCorrect to replace the keyed text with the corresponding symbols. To undo Word's automatic formatting where the replaced symbols are not desired, press the Backspace key immediately after Word replaces the text.

   c The content of the memo will indicate the font that corresponds to each symbol. Select the font from the *Font* option box in the Symbol dialog box and then click the symbol shown in the figure. The last symbol in the memo, the smiley face, is from the Wingdings font. *Hint: The Wingdings 2 font contains two scissors symbols. Select the one that most closely resembles the scissors symbol in Figure 86.3.*

   d Insert only one space before and after each symbol character, but do not insert a space between a symbol and a comma. *Hint: Do not insert a space after the smiley face at the end of the memo.*

   e At the bottom of the memo, key the reference initials ktm and the file name.

3 Proofread the document and correct any errors.

4 Save the document.

5 Click the Check button to upload the document for checking.

6 If errors are reported by the Online Lab, view the results document, correct the errors in the submitted document, save the document, and then click the Check Again button.

Figure 86.3 Memo Content for Document 86.1

> **TO:** [Tab] [Tab] Jeremy McBee ¶ **FROM:** [Tab] [Tab] Phillip J. Forrest ¶ **DATE:** [Tab] [Tab] April 22, 2020 ¶ **SUBJECT:** [Tab] Copyright and Other Symbols ¶
>
> In response to your questions concerning the correct use of symbols, the following shows two symbols and what each represents. These appear frequently in published text, product names, and company names. ¶
>
> [Tab] © [Tab] Copyright [Tab] Shortcut: key (c) [Shift + Enter]
>
> [Tab] ™ [Tab] Trademark [Tab] Shortcut: key (tm) ¶
>
> The copyright symbol © is used in creative works that have been copyrighted. The symbol means you are not allowed to reproduce, perform,

continues

Figure 85.4 Footnote Content for Document 85.2

Footnote 1: Michael Farr, *The Quick Resume and Cover Letter Book: Write and Use an Effective Resume in Only One Day* (St. Paul: JIST Publishing, 2011), 65.

Footnote 2: Louise Kursmark and Michael Farr, *The 15-Minute Cover Letter* (St. Paul: JIST Publishing, 2012), 35.

Footnote 3: Carolyn Forrest, "The Art of Keywords," *Career Finders*, accessed April 6, 2020, http://ppi-edu.net/TheArtOfKeywords.

Ending the Session

The Online Lab automatically saved the work you completed for this session. You may continue with the next session or exit the Online Lab and continue later.

Figure 86.3 Memo Content for Document 86.1—continued

display, or disseminate the work without permission of the owner. You will frequently find the copyright symbol inside the front of a textbook. ¶

The trademark symbol ™ is the symbol used by manufacturers or businesses to identify their goods and distinguish them from those made or sold by others. It identifies the source of a product and fixes responsibility for its quality. ¶

Additional symbols are available in other font faces, which you can access in the Symbol dialog box. In the Symbol dialog box with the Symbols tab selected, click the *Font* option box arrow and then click the desired font name. Some of the interesting symbols available include: 🚒, the fire truck in the Webdings font; ✄, the scissors in the Wingdings 2 font; ➜, the boldfaced, right arrow in the Wingdings font; and ☹, the not-so-smiley face in the Wingdings font. ¶

Some other special symbols that are available in Microsoft Word are found in the Symbol font. Σ is used in spreadsheets for totaling, Ω is the Greek letter Omega, and ♥ is the symbol for one of the suits from a deck of cards. ¶

As you can see, there are many available symbols that can be used to enhance your documents. Remember that some of these symbols may not print properly, depending on the printer you are using. I hope this has helped you. ☺

Changing the Size of Symbols

Symbols, like letters, are characters with a specific font. Therefore, the font size of symbols can be adjusted just as you would adjust the font size of text. To change the size of a symbol, select the symbol and then click the Increase Font Size button or the Decrease Font Size button in the Font group on the Home tab. Alternatively, click the *Font Size* option box arrow in the Font group and then select the font size from the drop-down gallery. You can also click in the *Font Size* option box, type a font size, and then press Enter.

Practice inserting symbols and changing their font size in the following document activity.

Document 86.2 **Informational Document with Symbols**

Read all instructions below before starting this document activity.

1 Navigate to the Document 86.2 launch page in the Online Lab and then click the Launch Activity button to open **Doc086.02** in the activity window.

2 Set left tabs at 2 inches and 3.5 inches on the horizontal ruler.

3 Press Enter three times to position the insertion point approximately 2 inches from the top of the document.

steps continue

Figure 85.3 Manuscript Content for Document 85.2—continued

use it, open the file, select and copy the text, and paste it into the online application or email message. ¶ Test your electronic resume by emailing it to a friend or two. Paste the electronic resume into the body of the email instead of sending it as an attachment. That way, they will be able to tell you how it looks when it shows up in their email system and whether it is legible. After getting their feedback, make any adjustments necessary. ¶ **The Importance of Keywords** ¶ Creating an electronic resume is more than just putting it into a plain text format. Employers look for qualified applicants in a resume database by searching for keywords—various skills and attributes that they seek. When you add keywords to your electronic resume, your chance of being selected for appropriate jobs increases. ¶ When your resume is scanned into an employer's database, the database looks for specific keywords that the employer has defined ahead of time. The database extracts your relevant keywords and characteristics into a profile. The Human Resources Department then searches the profiles for the best matches, allowing an employer to search thousands of resumes to find ones that meet specific criteria. ¶ For example, an employer could start with major criteria and then use it to sort for people with specific skills. The database would then search for profiles that met these criteria (often passing over good applicants not including the right words). ¶ **Selecting Keywords to Include in Your Resume** ¶ You probably already have many terms in your resume that can be used in a keyword section in your electronic resume.[Insert Footnote 3] Leave them where they are, but repeat some of the most important ones in a *Key Skills* section near the top of your resume. ¶ **Think Like a Prospective Employer.** Think of the jobs you want and include keywords an employer would use to find someone with your skillset. Emphasize technical terms, specific equipment or software names, certifications, and other specific terms an employer might use to fill the position. Read job ads on the Internet or in newspapers to determine keywords employers value. ¶ **Review Job Descriptions from Major References.** Read the descriptions for jobs in major references like the *Occupational Outlook Handbook* or the *O*NET Dictionary of Occupational Titles.*

4 Key the main title and subtitle by completing the following steps:

   a Change the paragraph alignment to center alignment, turn on bold formatting, key RESIZING SYMBOLS, and then press Enter.

   b Key Wingdings, turn off bold formatting, and then press Enter.

5 Change the paragraph alignment to left alignment.

6 Turn off automatic formatting of bulleted and numbered lists. Key the content shown in Figure 86.4. All the symbols are available in the Wingdings font. Leave the symbols in the default font size for now—you will adjust them in the next step. *Hint: Refer to Session 79 if you are unsure of how to turn off automatic formatting of lists.*

7 Resize the symbols so that they appear in the sizes indicated in the corresponding text. For example, set the mouse symbol at 16 points. Do not resize the nonprinting tab characters that appear on either side of the symbols.

8 Proofread the document and correct any errors.

9 Save the document.

10 Click the Check button to upload the document for checking.

11 If errors are reported by the Online Lab, view the results document, correct the errors in the submitted document, save the document, and then click the Check Again button.

Figure 86.4 Content for Document 86.2

Research shows that visual images improve the clarity of a document. In addition, readers are more likely to be interested in a document if images are present. This fact is well demonstrated by the use of icons in computer software today. This concept is referred to as *being user-friendly.*

The following are examples of four symbols selected from the Wingdings font. Each symbol has been resized from its default size. ¶

[Tab] ⌖ [Tab] Mouse symbol set at 16 points ¶

[Tab] ↘ [Tab] Arrow symbol set at 24 points ¶

[Tab] ▱ [Tab] Open folder symbol set at 36 points ¶

[Tab] ✉ [Tab] Envelope symbol set at 72 points ¶

Any available symbols can be easily inserted into a document and resized as desired. Think about how symbols can help to improve the readability and visual impact of your document.

Figure 85.3 Manuscript Content for Document 85.2

[Tab] More people are looking for jobs online and posting their resumes on the Web for employers to view. This technology requires you to have an electronic version of your resume to make your credentials available to employers. Resumes on the Web are stored in databases designed to save space and will be viewed by employers with many variations in computers and software. Most resumes are not stored as graphic images but as text files.[Insert Footnote 1] Simple text files take up less space than graphic files and can be read easily by any word processing program or searched for keywords. ¶ Before, employers took paper resumes and scanned them into electronic form. This enabled employers to put resume information into their own searchable databases. Scanning can introduce text errors and odd formatting due to the imperfect science of scanning technology, so you are better off making the modifications if you know your resume will be scanned, submitted to resume banks, or emailed. ¶ **Applying Directly to Employers Online** ¶ You may be asked to send your resume online. Pay attention to the instructions—they will probably specify if you should send your Word file as an email attachment, a PDF file, or plain-text via email or their website. ¶ Many employers enable applicants to put resumes directly into their website databases, saving them time and money. Larger employers get thousands of resumes, so it is impractical for them to store and retrieve paper resumes as jobs open up. Yet employers want to retrieve resumes as positions become available and may want to consider applicants who submitted resumes weeks or even months in the past. ¶ **Adapting Your Resume for Electronic Use** ¶ Louise Kursmark, coauthor of *The 15-Minute Cover Letter*, provides pointers for converting your resume to plain text. She suggests you save the resume with a different name, select *Plain Text (*.txt)* in the *Save as type* option box, and then reopen the file. Word automatically reformats your resume into a Courier font, removes all formatting, and left-justifies the text. Reset the margins to 2 inches left and right and adjust line lengths to fit within the narrow margins by adjusting hard returns.[Insert Footnote 2] ¶ Fix any glitches such as odd characters that may have been inserted to take the place of curly quotes, dashes, accents, or other nonstandard symbols. At this point, remove any tabs and adjust the spacing as necessary. You might add a few extra blank spaces or lines for readability. ¶ When you close the file, it will be saved with the .txt file extension. When you are ready to

continues

Inserting Horizontal and Vertical Borders

One way to insert horizontal and vertical lines into a document is by using options in the Borders and Shading dialog box with the Borders tab selected. To display the Borders and Shading dialog box, complete the following steps:

1   Click the Home tab, if necessary.

2   Click the Borders button arrow in the Paragraph group. (Note that the image on the button changes depending on the last border style selected.)

3   Click *Borders and Shading* at the drop-down gallery. This displays the Borders and Shading dialog box.

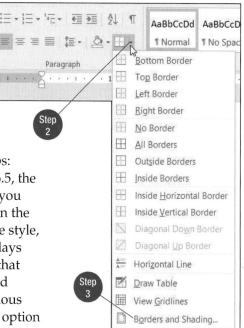

The Borders and Shading dialog box contains three tabs: Borders, Page Border, and Shading. As shown in Figure 86.5, the Borders tab of the Borders and Shading dialog box allows you to choose from various border types in the *Setting* section in the left panel of the tab. In the center panel of the tab, select the style, color, and width (thickness) of the border. A preview displays in the right panel. Click the preview image or the buttons that surround it to indicate where the borders should be applied in the document. The *Apply to* option box may contain various options, so confirm that you have selected the appropriate option before clicking OK to apply the border(s) to the document and close the dialog box.

In the following document activity, you will create a document that includes horizontal borders with options at the Borders and Shading dialog box with the Borders tab selected.

Figure 86.5 Borders and Shading Dialog Box

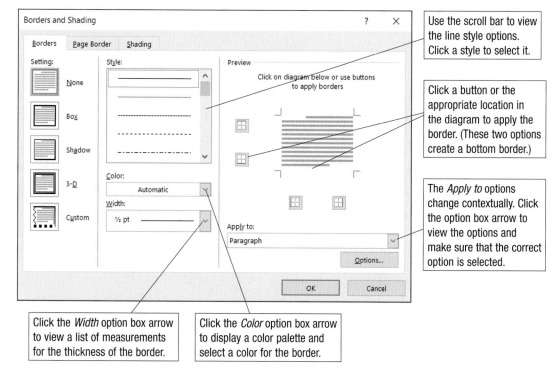

Document **Unbound Manuscript in Chicago Style with Footnotes**

85.2   Read all instructions below before starting this document activity.

1   Navigate to the Document 85.2 launch page in the Online Lab and then click the Launch Activity button to open **Doc085.02** in the activity window.

2   Change the document's default formatting by completing the following steps:

   a   Change the document's default line spacing to double spacing with no spacing after paragraphs.

   b   Change the document's default font to 12-point Times New Roman.

3   Key the main heading of the document by completing the following steps:

   a   Change the paragraph alignment to center alignment and then turn on bold formatting.

   b   Key DEVELOP AN ELECTRONIC RESUME, turn off bold formatting, and then press Enter.

   c   Change the paragraph alignment back to left alignment.

4   Key the text shown in Figure 85.3. Consider the following as you key the text:

   a   Begin all paragraphs with a 0.5-inch tab indent.

   b   When keying the side headings, turn off bold formatting before pressing Enter at the end of the heading.

   c   When keying the paragraph headings, press Tab before turning on bold formatting and turn off bold formatting after keying the period at the end of the heading. (Do not format the space following the period in bold.)

   d   When formatting words in italics, do not set the space before or after the word in italics and do not set the punctuation following the italic word in italics. Do italicize the parentheses in the expression *Plain Text (*.txt)*. Spaces between italic words should be formatted in italics.

5   Key the footnotes shown in Figure 85.4, locating the reference numbers in the document according to the placement instructions in Figure 85.3. Each reference number should appear immediately after the period at the end of the sentence. Do not press Enter at the end of the footnotes.

6   Format the page numbers in the document by completing the following steps:

   a   Format the document so that it has a different first page header and footer.

   b   On the first page, insert a *Plain Number 2* style page number at the bottom of the page.

   c   On the second page, insert a *Plain Number 3* style page number at the top of the page.

7   Proofread the document and correct any errors.

8   Save the document.

9   Click the Check button to upload the document for checking.

10   If errors are reported by the Online Lab, view the results document, correct the errors in the submitted document, save the document, and then click the Check Again button.

Document Form with Horizontal Borders

86.3 Read all instructions below before starting this document activity.

1 Navigate to the Document 86.3 launch page in the Online Lab and then click the Launch Activity button to open **Doc086.03** in the activity window.

2 Begin creating the form shown in Figure 86.6 by changing the default line spacing for the document to single spacing with no spacing after paragraphs. Change the default font size for the document to 12 points. Change the paragraph alignment to center alignment, turn on bold formatting, and then key the title Pontiac Township High School.

3 Press Enter and then key Permission Slip.

4 Turn off bold formatting, press Enter, change the paragraph alignment to left alignment, and then press Enter again.

5 Insert a table with two columns and four rows and then complete the following steps:

   a Key Student Name in cell A1 and then press Tab.

   b Key Group Name in cell B1 and then press Tab.

   c Merge cells A2 and B2, key Event Date, and then press Tab. *Hint: Refer to Session 72 if you are unsure of how to merge cells.*

   d Merge cells A3 and B3, key Event Location, and then press Tab.

   e Key Parent/Guardian Name (printed) and then press Tab.

   f Key Parent/Guardian Signature.

6 Select the table and then change the line spacing to double spacing.

7 Insert the orange border above the table by completing the following steps:

   a Click the Show/Hide ¶ button to turn on the display of nonprinting characters and then position the insertion point to the left of the paragraph mark that appears immediately above the table.

   b Click the Borders button arrow in the Paragraph group on the Home tab and then click *Borders and Shading* at the drop-down gallery.

   c At the Borders and Shading dialog box, click the Borders tab, if it is not already selected, and then click *Custom* in the *Setting* section.

   d Scroll down the *Style* list box and then click the option that appears as a thick line above a thin line (ninth option). Refer to Figure 86.6 to see what the border style should look like.

   e Click the *Color* option box arrow and then click *Orange, Accent 2* (sixth column, first row in the *Theme Colors* section).

   f Click the *Width* option box arrow and then click *3 pt* at the drop-down list.

   g In the *Preview* section, click the top border in the diagram to apply the border to the top of the paragraph. *Note: If the thick-thin border line appears on the bottom or side borders in the diagram, click the border line to remove it.*

   h Confirm that *Paragraph* is selected in the *Apply to* option box and then click OK to close the dialog box.

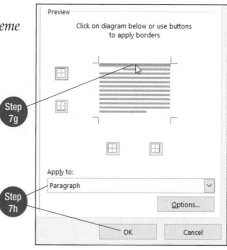

steps continue

Figure 85.2 Sources Content for Document 85.1

First Citation

Type of Source: Book

Author: Constantine, Johann

Title: The Antique Art of Making Rubber Dolls

Year: 2015

City: New York

Publisher: Phantom

Medium: Print

Second Citation

Type of Source: Article in a Periodical

Author: Latimer, Angel

Title: Creating Wooden Dolls: A Unique Skill

Periodical Title: Antique Digest

Year: 2019

Month: March/April

Pages: 72-78

Medium: Print

Third Citation

Type of Source: Web site

Author: Liu, Braylin

Name of Web Page: Doll Making from the Past

Name of Web Site: Antique Toys

Year: 2018

Year Accessed: 2020

Month Accessed: April

Day Accessed: 28

URL: http://ppi-edu.net/dolls/antique/20/8

Medium: Web

8 Insert the border below the table by completing the following steps:

   a Press Ctrl + End to move the insertion point to the end of the document.

   b Display the Borders and Shading dialog box with the Borders tab selected and then click *Custom* in the *Setting* section.

   c In the *Style* list box, scroll down and then click the candy-cane-stripe option (the 20th option, immediately following the double wavy line). Refer to Figure 86.6 to see what the border style should look like.

   d Click the *Color* option box arrow and then click *Orange, Accent 2* (sixth column, first row in the *Theme Colors* section).

   e Click the *Width* option box arrow and then click *3 pt* at the drop-down list.

   f In the *Preview* section, click the bottom border in the diagram to apply the border to the bottom of the paragraph. *Note: If the candy-cane-stripe border line appears on the top or side borders of the diagram, click the border line to remove it.*

   g Confirm that *Paragraph* is selected in the *Apply to* option box and then click OK to close the dialog box.

9 Insert a revision date at the bottom of the form by completing the following steps:

   a Double-click in the left margin directly under the second border to move the insertion point immediately below it.

   b Change the paragraph alignment to right alignment and then change the font size to 8 points.

   c Key Rev 1/10/20 and then delete any extra returns before or after the date line. *Hint: The date should display immediately below the bottom orange border, as shown in Figure 86.6.*

10 Format the document to include three copies of this form by completing the following steps:

   a Press Ctrl + A to select all of the text and then press Ctrl + C to copy it.

   b Press Ctrl + End to move the insertion point to the end of the document.

   c Press Enter three times and then paste the first copy of the form by pressing Ctrl + V.

   d Press Enter twice and then paste the second copy of the form by pressing Ctrl + V.

11 Delete any extra returns at the end of the document.

12 Proofread the document and correct any errors.

13 Save the document.

steps continue

Figure 86.6 Content for Document 86.3

Pontiac Township High School
Permission Slip

Student Name	Group Name
Event Date	
Event Location	
Parent/Guardian Name (printed)	Parent/Guardian Signature

Rev 1/10/20

   c   Change the paragraph alignment to left alignment.

   d   Click the Bibliography button in the Citations & Bibliography group on the References tab.

   e   Click *Insert Bibliography* at the drop-down list.

9   Proofread the document and correct any errors.

10   Save the document.

11   Click the Check button to upload the document for checking.

12   If errors are reported by the Online Lab, view the results document, correct the errors in the submitted document, save the document, and then click the Check Again button.

Figure 85.1 Manuscript Content for Document 85.1

Recently, ~~many~~ people have begun collecting ~~E~~arly American toys. This can be an expensive, challenging hobby. ~~Being able to find these toys is an interesting task with a variety of alternatives.~~ Looking at antique catalogs and magazines, visiting antique shops, going to estate sales, and searching the Internet help you locate what you are seeking. ¶ The earlier makers of dolls usually made only the heads, and the customer added the body. Thus, there were no two dolls the same—except for the ~~bodies~~ heads. These dolls are sought after because of their age and uniqueness. ¶ Rubber dolls have been in existence for over 100 years. Rubber dolls didn't break when thrown or dropped, but the rubber deteriorated with age. Then dollmakers began to design different dolls and take out patents on them. ¶ Wooden dolls were usually crudely jointed and easily broken; manufacturers learned to make sturdier ball joints and walking and talking dolls. Those most sought after are those that were hand carved. ~~This design was~~ probably the most loved, rag dolls were soft and could be squeezed and cuddled. Often these dolls were made at home and were unique. Material used in making them was not usually as sturdy as that used in other dolls and didn't last. ¶ Old mechanical toys display amazing artistry and ingenuity. One special feature of the mechanical toys that attracts collectors' interests is the ability for the toy to move. ¶ Mechanical toys and dolls hold a terrific attraction for modern-day collectors. The most desired are those which contain extensive detail and the capacity to move in a variety of ways. ¶ The tin toys were usually painted and were not too durable, making them very rare today. Tin toys included covered wagons, windmills that revolved, ~~and so on~~ etc. ¶ Some of the more interesting toys were made out of iron. These toys were very durable and were usually quite detailed in design, color, and artistry. ¶ Usually a mechanical bank would consist of a figure or design that would move when a coin was dropped in. This type of toy created utter fascination for a child.

citation 1 page 89

citation 2 page 72

citation 3

14 Click the Check button to upload the document for checking.

15 If errors are reported by the Online Lab, view the results document, correct the errors in the submitted document, save the document, and then click the Check Again button.

Reinforcing Formatting Skills

A customized letterhead can save time and enhance the content of your document. Now that you have worked through Session 86, you have the skills needed to create a custom letterhead. When creating a letterhead, include it in the document's first page header (and footer, if desired). Do not include the letterhead content on the pages following the first page.

To be effective, a letterhead should include the name of the organization and the appropriate contact information (mailing address, phone number(s), and/or web address). Besides providing the necessary information, a well-designed letterhead will be visually appealing and reflect the personality or mission of the organization it represents. Figure 86.7 provides an example of a customized letterhead.

Develop a customized letterhead in the following document activity.

Figure 86.7 Customized Letterhead Example   *Note: Do not key this document.*

Pontiac Township High School

8583 N. School Road ✪ Pontiac, IL ✪ 61764
http://PTHS.ppi-edu.net

Document 86.4

Creating a Customized Letterhead

1 Navigate to the Document 86.4 launch page in the Online Lab and then click the Launch Activity button to open **Doc086.04** in the activity window.

2 Format the document so that the file has a different first page header.

3 In the document, create a customized header for an organization in which you are involved, either personally or professionally. The letterhead should be attractive and include a border, appropriate contact information, and at least one symbol or visual element.

4 Proofread the document and correct any errors.

5 Save the document.

6 Click the Submit button to upload the document for instructor review.

Ending the Session

The Online Lab automatically saved the work you completed for this session. You may continue with the next session or exit the Online Lab and continue later.

Checking Production Progress: Manuscripts

Sessions 81 through 84 discussed the procedures for preparing and formatting manuscripts and research papers. In this session, you will be assessed on how accurately you can key these types of documents. In the following document activities, each completed manuscript is to be "mailable," which means that it contains no errors. A document that requires corrections is not considered *mailable*.

Your goal is to key each email and memo in mailable form. If a document contains uncorrected errors or your instructor believes you can work more efficiently, he or she may ask you to repeat document activities. To help you succeed, carefully review the document instructions and the content of each document before keying. *Note: Before you begin these documents, review the content of Sessions 81 through 84 if you are unsure how to complete a specific formatting or software task.*

Document 85.1 Unbound Manuscript in MLA Style with In-Text Citations and a Works Cited Page

Read all instructions below before starting this document activity.

1. Navigate to the Document 85.1 launch page in the Online Lab and then click the Launch Activity button to open **Doc085.01** in the activity window.

2. Change the document's default formatting by completing the following steps:

   a. Change the document's default line spacing to double spacing with no spacing after paragraphs.

   b. Change the document's default font to 12-point Palatino Linotype.

3. Set the document style reference to MLA.

4. Insert a Plain Number 3 style page number in the top right corner of the header, following the last name of the manuscript author, *Nea-Everton*. **Hint: Insert the page number first and then key the last name and a space preceding the page number. If you use a different method, the document checker may mark it as an error.**

5. Key the information about the manuscript at the top of the document. The information should indicate that the manuscript is being prepared by Jocelyn Nea-Everton for her instructor Patti Kunkle in the course English Composition. The paper date is 11 May 2020. The title of the report is *Collecting Early American Toys*. **Hint: Reference Figure 83.1 for formatting this information.**

6. Key the text shown in Figure 85.1, implementing the proofreading marks. Begin all paragraphs with a 0.5-inch tab indent. Key the entire manuscript before inserting the citations.

7. Key the source information shown in Figure 85.2, inserting the citation references in the document according to the placement instructions in Figure 85.1. Include page references for the in-text citations according to the proofreading marks. **Hint: Make sure you do not press the spacebar before inserting a citation into the document. Word will automatically insert the space before the citation.**

8. Insert a Works Cited page at the end of the document by completing the following steps:

   a. Position the insertion point at the end of the document and then insert a hard page break.

   b. Change the paragraph alignment to center alignment and key Works Cited and then press Enter.

steps continue

Creating WordArt and Shapes

Session Objectives

- Create WordArt
- Create shapes
- Apply effects to WordArt and shapes
- Create an award certificate
- Efficiently produce documents in mailable form

Getting Started

Exercise 87.1 If you are continuing immediately from Session 86, you may skip the Exercise 87.1 warm-up drill. However, if you exited the Online Lab at the end of Session 86, warm up by completing Exercise 87.1.

Exercise 87.2 Begin your session work by completing Exercise 87.2, a timed short drill, in the Online Lab.

Assessing Your Speed and Accuracy

Complete Timings 87.1 through 87.3 in the Online Lab. At the end of each timing, the Online Lab will display your WPM rate and any errors. Results will be saved in your Timings Performance report. If you have been surpassing the speed and accuracy goals identified in the Online Lab, set slightly more challenging personal goals and strive to exceed them.

Complete two 1-minute timings on the timing text below. If you meet or exceed both speed and accuracy goals for Timing 87.1, push for greater speed on Timing 87.2.

1-Minute Timings

Timings 87.1–87.2

A recent fashion show produced by Pitti Immagine utilized computers to generate images of undersea creatures. The audience could view this from both sides of the runway. Models could even interact with these images as they showed the latest fashions. Meanwhile, Philips has produced an interactive window for hotels where guests can modify the lighting and patterns. Guests might choose to make an image of a tree outside the window by selecting a sycamore tree pattern. The image is placed by moving a hand across the window.

Complete one 5-minute timing on the timing text below.

5-Minute Timing

**Timing
85.3**

In the 1840s, our nation was growing rapidly. In the East, many people were concerned about the impact of industry on their own lives. Discussions centered around a movement for better compensation and better conditions for every worker. The great reform movement had now begun to propagate. Thousands of immigrants were arriving in the new nation to begin lives anew. The influx of citizens opened new frontiers.

Because of expanding population, the quest for additional land became increasingly urgent. At that time, a unique collection of workers, burdened with many obstacles, confronted a critical task which would require three decades to complete. This early contingent, the land surveyors, activated a vital project. They were to establish boundary lines that could not be disputed in future years.

The first land survey was begun in the territory during the late 1700s. The first surveyors were compensated only three dollars per mile. This salary not only had to cover all expenses incurred but also included wages for any helpers needed. At times, survival was at stake. In one perilous segment, the men were required to establish the basic groundwork by laying a line through the center of a northern state. The initial zest and zeal for the project quickly disappeared as they confronted 200 damp and rainy miles.

Personal possessions were limited to each worker's personal backpack. The solar compass was the primary instrument; sunshine was vital. The weather failed the tired and miserable workers. Heavy deluges fell on the area encampment, and workers wore wet clothing for a week.

Humidity levels were another reason for discomfort; the moisture brought out bevies of pesky insects. At times, the workers had to wade in disagreeable muck that hampered all movement. Because their line of direction was confined, the only alternative was to plunge ahead through the swampy property. To add insult to injury, their provisions were exhausted. The tired and ravenous workers struggled through three entire days without food.

Because of the earlier work of the surveyors, a major system of schools, city government, and roads was developed. The land was plotted into six-mile squares, providing for a township method of government.

Complete one 3-minute timing on the timing text below.

3-Minute Timing

Timing
87.3

Glide across the marble floor. Brush against marble wainscoting that climbs approximately six feet up the concourse walls. Note the cherry wood paneling, shiny brass accents, and elevator doors that shimmer like gold.

It seems that you are in a theater, but instead you are in an arena. People are eager to attend events, including sports, music, and ice shows, in a building created with abundant attention to detail. Some arenas are built to create the feeling of luxury.

Service is a large part of customer satisfaction for people attending events in arenas. Most operators promise a high level of service to help attract patrons and help the arena's developers protect their investment.

The current philosophy in building arenas is to make them more than just a place to see an event. The building should be a place to entertain the family and your business clients. It should project a certain image. Food operators don't expect many lines because the arenas have been developed so that each level (floor) of the building has its own restrooms and concession area.

Ergonomic Tip

You know you have the proper distance between your body and the keyboard when your elbows are even with your sides as your fingers rest on the home row keys.

Using WordArt

The WordArt feature uses regular text to create attention-grabbing effects. WordArt is often used to enhance the appearance of documents such as advertisements and flyers. Use WordArt to create text with effects such as color, outline, shadow, reflection, and glow. WordArt text can also be distorted to conform to a variety of shapes. However, it is important not to overuse these effects, as they have the potential to become overwhelming.

Use the WordArt button in the Text group on the Insert tab to create WordArt. Clicking the WordArt button will display a drop-down list of options. Click an option to insert it into the document. When a WordArt text box is active, the contextual Drawing Tools Format tab becomes available. You can format the color, effects, and other aspects of the WordArt using the options on this tab.

You will create and format a letterhead containing WordArt in the following document activity.

Session 85
Production Progress Check: Manuscripts and Research Papers Part II

Session Objectives

- Apply features presented in Sessions 81–84
- Efficiently produce documents in mailable form

Getting Started

Exercise 85.1 If you are continuing immediately from Session 84, you may skip the Exercise 85.1 warm-up drill. However, if you exited the Online Lab at the end of Session 84, warm up by completing Exercise 85.1.

Exercise 85.2 Begin your session work by completing Exercise 85.2, a timed short drill, in the Online Lab.

Assessing Your Speed and Accuracy

Complete Timings 85.1 through 85.3 in the Online Lab. At the end of the timing, the Online Lab will display your WPM rate and any errors. Results will be saved in your Timings Performance report. If you have been surpassing the speed and accuracy goals identified in the Online Lab, set slightly more challenging personal goals and strive to exceed them.

Complete two 1-minute timings on the timing text below. If you meet or exceed both speed and accuracy goals for Timing 85.1, push for greater speed on Timing 85.2.

1-Minute Timings

Timings 85.1–85.2
Safe and secure--that's what we desire. We think about things such as walking to the car in clusters, having keys in our hands, taking self-defense classes, and being aware of our surroundings. Are we as vigilant with our computer data collections? Do we exercise the precautions necessary to protect ourselves from identity theft? When mail arrives, care should be taken to shred anything containing personal information--even junk mail. Bills that have been remunerated should also be shredded. With a modicum of precaution, we can retain our protected identity.

Document **Letterhead with WordArt**

87.1 Read all instructions below before starting this document activity.

1 Navigate to the Document 87.1 launch page in the Online Lab and then click the Launch Activity button to open **Doc087.01** in the activity window.

2 Set the top margin of the document to 2 inches.

3 Open the header pane of the document, insert a check mark in the *Different First Page* check box, and then set the header 0.7 inch from the top of the page.

4 Insert the WordArt text box into the header pane by completing these steps:

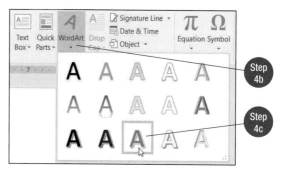

   a With the insertion point positioned in the first-page header pane, click the Insert tab.

   b Click the WordArt button in the Text group.

   c Click the blue WordArt style in the third column, third row of the drop-down list.

   d With the WordArt placeholder text selected (appears with a gray background), key JD Consulting.

5 Change the fill color of the WordArt by completing the following steps:

   a Select the WordArt text box by clicking on the dashed border so it becomes a solid border.

   b Click the Text Fill button arrow in the WordArt Styles group on the Drawing Tools Format tab.

   c Click *Blue, Accent 1, Darker 50%* (fifth column, last row in the *Theme Colors* section).

6 Apply text effects to the WordArt by completing the following steps:

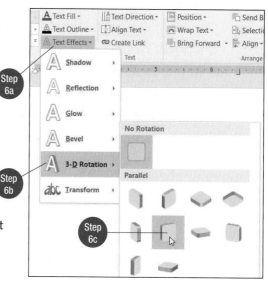

   a With the WordArt text box still selected, click the Text Effects button in the WordArt styles group.

   b Point to *3-D Rotation*.

   c Click the *Off Axis 1: Right* option (second column, second row in the *Parallel* section).

   d Click the Text Effects button.

   e Point to *Transform*.

   f Click *Chevron: Up* (first column, second row in the *Warp* section).

7 Click in the header pane outside of the WordArt text box to deselect the WordArt text box.

8 Change the paragraph alignment to right alignment, key 2329 N. Center Road, and then press Enter.

steps continue

Reinforcing Writing Skills

In the "Reinforcing Writing Skills" section of Session 81, eight steps were presented for preparing a manuscript, and seven of the steps were used to complete the Document 81.4 activity, Document 82.3 activity, and Document 83.2 activity. In the following document activity, you will create a title page and key an abstract for the report you created in the previous sessions in this unit. Use the APA style guidelines provided in this session when formatting these pages.

Document 84.3

Creating a Title Page and Writing an Abstract

Read all instructions below before starting this document activity.

1 Navigate to the Document 84.3 launch page in the Online Lab and then click the Launch Activity button to open **Doc084.03** in the activity window.

2 Change the document's default formatting to double spacing with no spacing after paragraphs and change the document's default font style to 12-point Times New Roman.

3 Key the content of the title page for the report you developed in the previous sessions of this unit.

4 Insert a page break and then key the content of the abstract. The abstract content should be an engaging and interesting one-paragraph summary of the main ideas of the report. When keying the paragraph, do not press Tab at the beginning and key only one space after each sentence within the paragraph.

5 Use Find and Replace to change the single spaces after the sentences within the paragraph to double spaces.

6 Key a list of keywords for the report on the Abstract page.

7 Create and format appropriate headers for the document.

8 Proofread the document and correct any errors.

9 Save the document.

10 Click the Submit button to upload the document for instructor review.

Ending the Session

The Online Lab automatically saved the work you completed for this session. You may continue with the next session or exit the Online Lab and continue later.

9   Key Hebron, OH 43025-5791 and then press Enter.

10 Key 740.555.6919, press Enter, key http://jdconsulting.ppi-edu.net, and then close the header pane.

11 Proofread the document and correct any errors.

12 Save the document.

13 Click the Submit button to upload the document for instructor review.

Creating Shapes

Like WordArt, shapes can enhance the appearance of documents. The Shapes button in the Illustrations group on the Insert tab provides a drop-down list of different shape options, some of which can hold text. Use these options to insert shapes or to draw lines.

Word contains a variety of options for drawing lines in a document. You can create straight lines, curved lines, diagonal lines, and even freeform scribbles. To draw a straight line, press and hold down the Shift key as you click and drag the mouse to create the line. Whether your line is vertical, horizontal, or at a 45-degree angle, this ensures that it will be precisely straight.

The following document activity provides the steps involved in creating and formatting shapes in a document.

Document 87.2

Document with Shapes

Read all instructions below before starting this document activity.

1 Navigate to the Document 87.2 launch page in the Online Lab and then click the Launch Activity button to open **Doc087.02** in the activity window.

2 Display the horizontal and vertical rulers if they are not displayed.

3 Insert a 4.5-inch line in the document by completing the following steps:

   a Click the Insert tab.

   b Click the Shapes button in the Illustrations group.

   c Click the *Line* shape (first shape in the *Lines* section of the drop-down list).

   d Position the insertion point (which will display as crosshairs) in the document at the intersection of the 0-inch mark on the vertical ruler and the 1-inch mark on the horizontal ruler. Click and hold down the left mouse button, press and hold down the Shift key, and then draw a line to the 5.5-inch mark on the horizontal ruler. After drawing the line, release the mouse button and the Shift key.

   e If necessary, click the Drawing Tools Format tab. If the *Shape Width* measurement box in the Size group displays any measurement other than *4.5"*, select the existing measurement, key 4.5, and then press Enter.

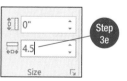

steps continue

Figure 84.7 Report Content for Document 84.2—continued

iStorage. ¶ **Hard Disks** ¶ → The first place most of us save a copy of our work is on our computer hard disk. When you save a file to your Documents folder in Windows 10, for example, it is saved to your hard disk drive. This is the disk drive that is built into your computer. The platters or disks in the drive rotate and one or more so-called "heads" read and write data to them. ¶ → Because all hard disks eventually fail, the wise person uses other media storage or cloud storage to make backup copies. ¶ **Optical Drives** ¶ → Your computer is likely to have a built-in drive where you can place a CD or DVD to read content stored there or store data of your own. Another type of storage drive that is built into some computers is a Blu-ray disc drive, mostly used for high-definition movies and games. This type of drive is called an *optical drive*. Discs placed in optical drives are covered with tiny variations, or bumps, that can be read as data by a laser beam in the drive. Optical drives use these optoelectronic sensors to detect changes in light caused by the irregularities on the disc's surface. In addition to built-in optical drives, you can purchase external optical drives; these are handy for devices such as netbooks that have no optical drive in order to keep their size and weight small. ¶ **External Hard Drives** ¶ → If you'd like additional storage, you might consider buying an external hard drive. These typically connect to your computer via a USB, FireWire, Thunderbolt, or Serial ATA cable. Select high-capacity models can connect to a network via a wired or wireless connection. Some call these devices *networked external hard drives* while others refer to them as *network attached storage (NAS)*. Some portable models don't need a separate power source. Networked models can provide centralized storage for multiple teammates or family members or can serve as a "jukebox" for storing various forms of media such as music or videos. ¶ → External hard drives are useful to back up your entire computer system, or for portable devices that have a smaller amount of internal storage. ¶ **Flash Drives** ¶ → Call them "flash drives," "USB sticks," or "thumb drives," these conveniently small devices are a great way to store your data and take it with you. As of this writing, they come with capacities as big as one terabyte (bigger than most hard drives just a few years ago), and this amount will have probably changed by now, as the capacity grows fast. ¶ → Flash drives use flash memory to record and erase stored data and to transfer data to and from your computer. Flash memory is also used in tablets, mobile phones, and digital cameras because it is much less expensive than other types of memory. Flash memory is also non-volatile, meaning that it retains information even in a powered-off state.

4 Apply a shape outline to the line by completing the following steps:

  a Make sure that the line is selected.

  b If necessary, click the Drawing Tools Format tab.

  c Click the Shape Outline button arrow in the Shape Styles group.

  d Point to *Weight* at the drop-down gallery.

  e Click *6 pt* at the side menu.

5 Apply a shape effect to the line by completing the following steps:

  a With the line still selected, click the Shape Effects button in the Shape Styles group.

  b Point to *Reflection* at the drop-down list.

  c Click *Full Reflection: 8 point offset* (third column, third row in the *Reflection Variations* section).

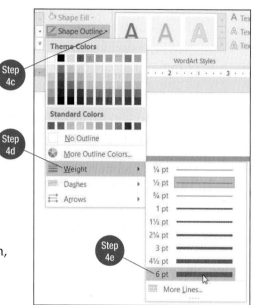

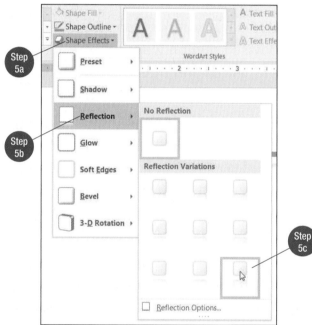

6 Insert a banner into the document by completing the following steps:

  a Click the Insert tab.

  b Click the Shapes button in the Illustrations group.

  c Click *Double Wave*, the last banner in the *Stars and Banners* section.

  d Position the insertion point in the document at the intersection of the 1-inch mark on the horizontal ruler and the 1-inch mark on the vertical ruler, click and hold down the left mouse button, draw a shape that is approximately 1-inch tall and 4.5 inches wide, and then release the mouse button.

  e Select the number in the *Shape Height* measurement box in the Size group on the Drawing Tools Format tab and then key 1.

  f Select the number in the *Shape Width* measurement box in the Size group on the Drawing Tools Format tab, key 4.5, and then press Enter.

steps continue

Figure 84.6 Abstract Content for Document 84.2

Data storage is important whatever type of computer is used. Hard disks, optical drives, external hard drives, flash drives, etc., are supplemented with cloud storage. The ability to access any data from your location has much appeal in today's mobile community. The hard drive is an integral part of most computers for day-to-day use. Other common ways to back up data are CD or DVD drives, Blu-ray disc drives, external hard drives, flash drives (USB sticks or thumb drives), and cloud storage. These also make data more mobile. It is wise to have a backup of any vital information since any disk drive may fail without warning. ¶ → *Keywords:* storage, hard drives, optical drives, flash drives

Figure 84.7 Report Content for Document 84.2

→ Because saving the work you've done on your computer is so important, computer manufacturers have devised several ways to store all kinds of data, from numbers and images to words and music. All storage media have methods for reading the data from the media (input) and for writing the data to the media (output). ¶ → The various storage media used on a computer are accessed using drives, which are identified on a Windows-based computer by a unique letter. For example, your computer's hard disk is typically identified as your C drive, while a DVD or USB stick drive might be labeled E, F, or G. Mac computers give each drive a name such as Mac HD for the hard drive and DVD_VIDEO for a DVD drive in which you have inserted a video disk. If you are connected to a network, you may also be able to access shared network drives. ¶ **Cloud Storage** ¶ → In addition to using physical storage, many users increasingly rely on cloud storage. Cloud storage refers to the storage of data on a web-connected server operated by a third party. You can access your files stored in the cloud from any location using any computer with an Internet connection. Cloud storage may be used for backing up information as well as sharing files with others. If you've ever lost or damaged your flash drive, you can appreciate how valuable it would be to have backup copies of your information that you could access via the Web from your school, on a trip, or in your office. Depending on your needs, you can choose either a fee-based cloud storage service, or free services such as Microsoft OneDrive. Some of the most popular cloud storage services today are Dropbox, Google Drive, Amazon S3, Box, Carbonite, iCloud, and

continues

7   With the banner shape selected, key Winner and then select the word.

8   Format the text in the banner by completing the following steps:

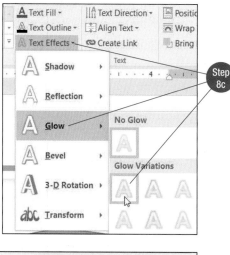

a   Change the text to 36-point Lucida Calligraphy.

b   Click the Drawing Tools Format tab.

c   Click the Text Effects button in the WordArt Styles group, point to *Glow*, and then click *Glow: 5 point; Blue, Accent color 1* (first option in the *Glow Variations* section).

d   Click the Text Fill button arrow in the WordArt Styles group and then click *Red* (second option in the *Standard Colors* section).

e   Click the More Shape Styles button in the Shape Styles group.

f   Click *Subtle Effect - Blue, Accent 1* (second column, fourth row in the *Theme Styles* section).

g   Click the More Shape Styles button in the Shape Styles group.

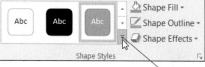

h   Point to *Other Theme Fills* and then click *Style 10* (second column, third row) at the side menu.

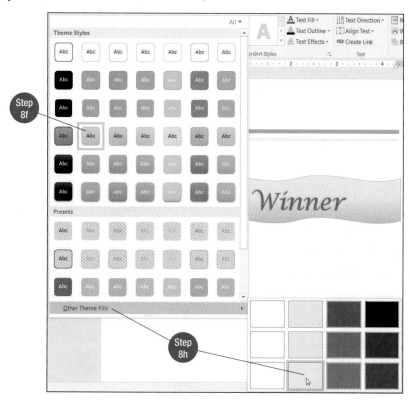

9   Compare your document to Figure 87.1 and make any necessary adjustments.

10 Save the document.

11 Click the Submit button to upload the document for instructor review.

d In the Create Source dialog box, click the *Type of Source* option box arrow and then click *Electronic Source* at the drop-down list.

e Click the *Show All Bibliography Fields* check box to insert a check mark.

f Key the following source information, being careful to key the spaces, punctuation, and capitalization as shown below:

> *Author:* Moses, Alonso
>
> *Title:* The history of computer storage
>
> *City:* St. Paul
>
> *State/Province:* Minnesota
>
> *Country/Region:* United States of America
>
> *Year:* 2019
>
> *DOI:* 10.37090/926069887

g Proofread the source and then click OK.

14 Add the second source and in-text citation by completing the following steps:

a Position the insertion point before the period at the end of the last sentence in the *Cloud Storage* section, following the words *and iStorage*.

b Direct Word to add a new source.

c At the Create Source dialog box, click the *Type of Source* option box arrow and then click *Book* at the drop-down list.

d Key the following source information, being careful to key the spaces, punctuation, and capitalization as shown below:

> *Author:* Hmun, Yi
>
> *Title:* Apples don't fall far from the tree
>
> *Year:* 2020
>
> *City:* St. Paul
>
> *Publisher:* Paradigm Publishing, Inc.

e Proofread the source and then click OK.

15 Create a References page by completing the following steps:

a Position the insertion point at the end of the document and then insert a hard page break.

b Change the paragraph alignment to center alignment and then key References. **Note: Do not format the heading in bold, per APA style.**

c Press Enter and then change the paragraph alignment to left alignment.

d Click the Bibliography button in the Citations & Bibliography group on the References tab.

e Click *Insert Bibliography* at the drop-down list. **Note: Do not delete the blank line at the end of the inserted citations.**

16 Proofread the document and correct any errors.

17 Save the document.

18 Click the Check button to upload the document for checking.

19 If errors are reported by the Online Lab, view the results document, correct the errors in the submitted document, and then click the Check Again button.

Figure 87.1 Completed Document 87.2

Reinforcing Formatting Skills

WordArt and shapes can be particularly effective in creating specialized documents such as award certificates. In the following document activity, use your imagination and the skills you learned in this and previous sessions to create a document acknowledging an accomplishment. Examples could include a perfect-attendance award or a certificate for achieving a certain keying speed.

Document 87.3

Creating an Award Certificate

1 Navigate to the Document 87.3 launch page in the Online Lab and then click the Launch Activity button to open **Doc087.03** in the activity window.

2 Create an award proclamation or certificate using both WordArt and shapes. Be creative!

3 Proofread the document and correct any errors.

4 Save the document.

5 Click the Submit button to upload the document for instructor review.

Ending the Session

The Online Lab automatically saved the work you completed for this session. You may continue with the next session or exit the Online Lab and continue later.

4 Key the Abstract page by completing the following steps:

    a With the insertion point centered at the top of the second page of the document, key Abstract and then press Enter.

    b Change the paragraph alignment to left alignment.

    c Key the text shown in Figure 84.6. *Note: Key one space after all sentences except the last sentence in the paragraph. Set the word* **Keywords** *and the colon that follows it in italic.*

5 Insert the headers in the document by completing the following steps:

    a Double-click the header area of the first page of the document to display the header pane and the Header & Footer Tools Design tab.

    b Click the *Different First Page* check box in the Options group to insert a check mark.

    c With the insertion point positioned at the left margin of the first page header pane, key Running head: COMPUTER STORAGE and then press Tab twice.

    d Click the Page Number button in the Header & Footer group on the Header & Footer Tools Design tab, point to *Current Position*, and then click *Plain Number*.

    e Click the Next button in the Navigation group to move to the second page header pane.

    f With the insertion point positioned at the left margin of the second page header pane, key COMPUTER STORAGE and then press Tab twice.

    g Click the Page Number button in the Header & Footer group on the Header & Footer Tools Design tab, point to *Current Position*, and then click *Plain Number*.

    h Click the Close Header and Footer button in the Close group or double-click in the body of the document.

6 Position the insertion point at the end of the document and insert a page break.

7 Change the paragraph alignment to center alignment, key Computer Storage, press Enter, and then change the paragraph alignment back to left alignment. *Hint: Because this is the manuscript title and not a heading, do not format it in bold.*

8 Key the text shown in Figure 84.7. Press Tab at the start of each paragraph and key one space after all sentences except the last sentence in a paragraph. Format headings bold and centered. *Hint: Remember to turn off bold formatting before pressing Enter at the ends of the headings.*

9 Keep the heading *Hard Disks* with the paragraph of text that follows it.

10 Save the document.

11 Use the Find and Replace feature to replace single spaces after sentences within paragraphs with double spaces.

12 Set the document style reference to APA.

13 Add the first source and in-text citation by completing the following steps:

    a Position the insertion point before the period at the end of the last sentence in the first paragraph on page 3, following the words *data to the media (output)*. *Hint: Use Find to locate this phrase quickly.*

    b Click the Insert Citation button in the Citations & Bibliography group on the References tab.

    c Click *Add New Source* at the drop-down list.

steps continue

Session
88

Using SmartArt

Session Objectives

- Use SmartArt to create a list
- Use SmartArt to create an organizational chart
- Use SmartArt to create a graphic
- Efficiently produce documents in mailable form

Getting Started

Exercise 88.1 If you are continuing immediately from Session 87, you may skip the Exercise 88.1 warm-up drill. However, if you exited the Online Lab at the end of Session 87, warm up by completing Exercise 88.1.

Exercise 88.2 Begin your session work by completing Exercise 88.2, a timed short drill, in the Online Lab.

Assessing Your Speed and Accuracy

Complete Timings 88.1 through 88.3 in the Online Lab. At the end of each timing, the Online Lab will display your WPM rate and any errors. Results will be saved in your Timings Performance report. If you have been surpassing the speed and accuracy goals identified in the Online Lab, set slightly more challenging personal goals and strive to exceed them.

Complete two 1-minute timings on the timing text below. If you meet or exceed both speed and accuracy goals for Timing 88.1, push for greater speed on Timing 88.2.

1-Minute Timings

Timings 88.1–88.2
In the 1970s, businesses in the United States had taken on a new look. Firms were bigger and more powerful, and computer and communications technology grew at an unheard of rate. During the latter part of that decade, the first personal computer entered the market. Local area networks became an important part of computing systems. Optical fiber technology was developed and sold, which brought sweeping changes to long-distance telephone service. By the end of the decade, 93 million television sets were in operation in the United States. Two-way cable TV was also introduced during this time frame.

Figure 84.5 Create Source Dialog Box Showing the *DOI* Text Box Field

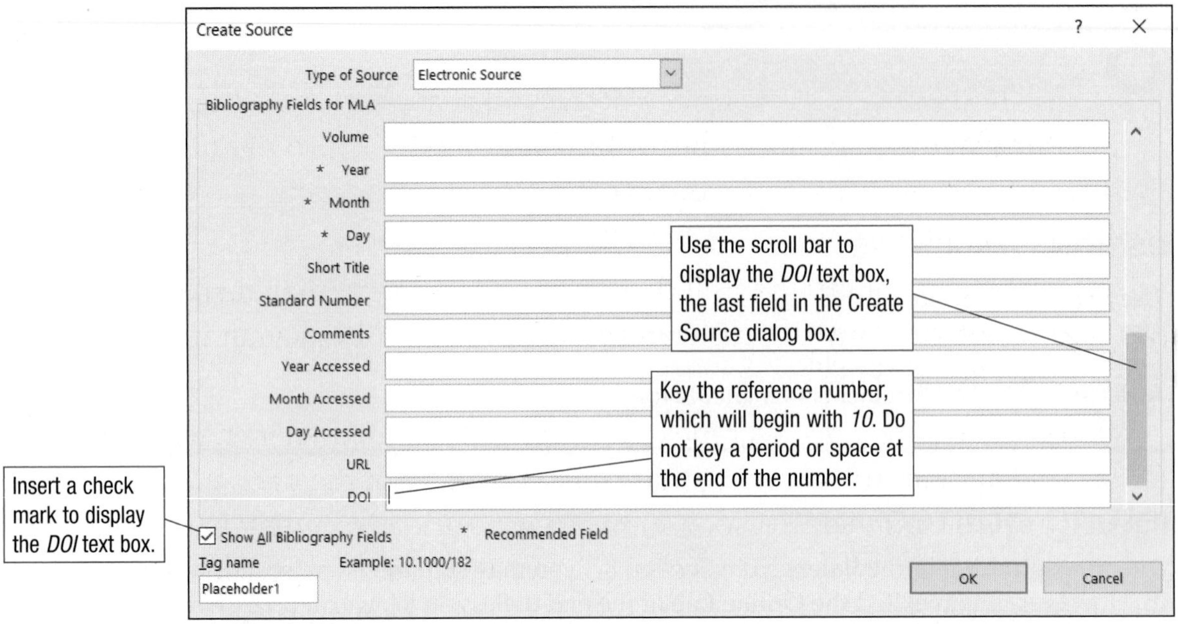

Insert a check mark to display the *DOI* text box.

Use the scroll bar to display the *DOI* text box, the last field in the Create Source dialog box.

Key the reference number, which will begin with *10*. Do not key a period or space at the end of the number.

🎓 Success Tip

In APA style, book titles are keyed with only the first word capitalized. If the title includes a subtitle, capitalize the first word of the subtitle as well.

Document 84.2

Title Page, Abstract, Manuscript Body, and References in APA Style

Read all instructions below before starting this document activity.

1 Navigate to the Document 84.2 launch page in the Online Lab and then click the Launch Activity button to open **Doc084.02** in the activity window.

2 Change the document's default formatting by completing the following steps:

   a Change the document's default line spacing to double spacing with no spacing after paragraphs.

   b Change the document's default font to 12-point Times New Roman.

3 Key the title page by completing the following steps:

   a Press Enter three times to move the insertion point approximately 2 inches from the top of the document.

   b Change the paragraph alignment to center alignment.

   c Key the title of the report, Computer Storage, and then press Enter.

   d Key the author's name, Stefan Romerez, and then press Enter.

   e Key the school affiliation, Rock Valley Community College, and then insert a page break (Ctrl + Enter).

steps continue

Complete one 3-minute timing on the timing text below.

3-Minute Timing

Timing
88.3

Many houses have some type of decking attached to the outside of them. Many of these decks are beautiful; however, they also require proper maintenance. Preventive maintenance is also very important.

Decks should be waterproofed. Climate, use, type of wood, and the waterproofing agent quality will dictate how often particular surfaces must be waterproofed. Many people waterproof annually; others wait until the appearance dictates the need.

In order to give a deck a renewed, fresh look, homeowners need to look for several appearance-marring things. First, do any of the deck planks have "cupping" on them? If so, it may be necessary to completely replace the plank, or it may be possible to simply turn the plank over. Warped and fragmented planks are also hazards. If possible, replace only the damaged section of the plank. Popped nails can be hammered back in, but they may pop up again later. It is much better to pull the popped nails and insert galvanized decking screws.

In order to regain as much "new" appearance as possible, it may be necessary to stain the planks before waterproofing. Make certain that the stain is designed for the variety of wood in the deck.

Ergonomic Tip

Rather than trying to stretch your fingers beyond their comfortable range, use your whole arm to reach for keys not located near the home row.

Using SmartArt

SmartArt allows you to create graphics that present information and ideas in a visual format. SmartArt graphics can be created in many different layouts to portray different types of information, including hierarchical data; lists of data; data processes, cycles, and relationships. You can also add colors and designs to enhance your message.

To create a SmartArt graphic, click the SmartArt button in the Illustrations group on the Insert tab. Clicking this button displays the Choose a SmartArt Graphic dialog box, which contains three panels, shown in Figure 88.1. The left panel lists the categories of preformatted graphics that are available. By default, *All* is selected, so all of the graphic options provided in Word are shown in the middle panel. To filter the options in the middle panel, click a category in the left panel. If necessary, scroll to see all of the graphic options in the middle panel.

Table 84.2 Heading Formatting for Research Papers according to APA Style

Heading Level	Formatting Style
main/first level	centered, bold, main words capitalized, press Enter once before and after
side/second level	left aligned, bold, main words capitalized, press Enter once before and after
paragraph/third level	indented on paragraph indent (0.5 inch), bold, only first word of heading capitalized, end with a bold period, and followed by a space (not bold)
fourth level	indented, bold, italic, only first word capitalized, end with a bold and italic period, and followed by a space (not bold or italic)
fifth level	indented, italic, only first word capitalized, end with an italic period, and followed by a space (not italic)

Figure 84.4 Sample Headings in APA Format   *Note: Do not key this document.*

planning law. The reasons for estate planning include protecting assets from taxes, making sure

that survivors are properly cared for, and establishing a wealth-management plan.

> main heading: centered, bold, main words capitalized

Common Estate Planning Documents

There are two typical estate planning documents; however, each type has a variety of

options and specialty clauses.

> side heading: aligned at left margin, bold, main words capitalized

Types of Wills

Different types of wills are available depending on the personal circumstances of the

individual making the will.

> The space following the paragraph heading's period is not bold.

> paragraph headings: aligned at the paragraph indent, bold, only first word capitalized, ends with a bold period

Simple will. A simple will leaves the entire estate (the testator's property covered by the

will) to one or more named beneficiaries.

Joint or mutual will. A joint will (also called a mutual will) distributes the property of

two or more people. A joint will is a single document signed by each testator and leaving all

assets to the other. It stipulates what will happen with the assets when the second person dies.

Creating Citations in APA Style

In Word, in-text citations in APA style are created in the same manner as those in MLA style, but the sources will be listed in a different order on the references page.

A digital object identifier (DOI) is often used with online articles to identify the object as unique—similar to a Social Security number. The DOI is created for online publications only (intellectual property), and not all online publications currently include them. With the reference style set to *APA*, enter a source DOI by inserting a check mark in the *Show All Bibliography Fields* check box in the Create Source dialog box for a journal article and then keying the DOI in the *DOI* field, which is the last field in the dialog box (see Figure 84.5). The DOI will always start with *10* and may be made up of letters and numbers or just numbers. The DOI is not followed by a period.

Figure 88.1 Choose a SmartArt Graphic Dialog Box

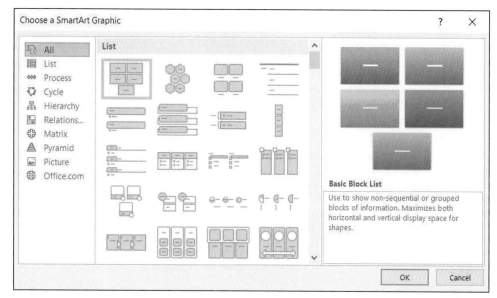

When a graphic is selected in the middle panel, a preview and description of that graphic display in the right panel. Once you have selected a graphic, click OK to insert it into the active document. After a graphic has been inserted into a document, a text pane may display next to the graphic. You can key text in this text pane or directly in the graphic.

Two contextual tabs are available when SmartArt is active in a document: the SmartArt Tools Design tab and the SmartArt Tools Format tab. The SmartArt Tools Design tab, shown in Figure 88.2, contains options that allow you to customize SmartArt by adding objects to the graphic or changing the layout or style of the graphic. You can also reset the graphic to its original format by clicking the Reset Graphic button in the Reset group on this tab.

The SmartArt Tools Format tab, shown in Figure 88.3, contains options for changing shapes and sizes within a SmartArt graphic as well as setting WordArt styles and text effects.

Practice working with SmartArt in the following document activities. In Document 88.1, you will create a SmartArt graphic using one of the options in the *List* category. In Document 88.2, you will create an organizational chart using a graphic from the *Hierarchy* category.

Figure 88.2 SmartArt Tools Design Tab

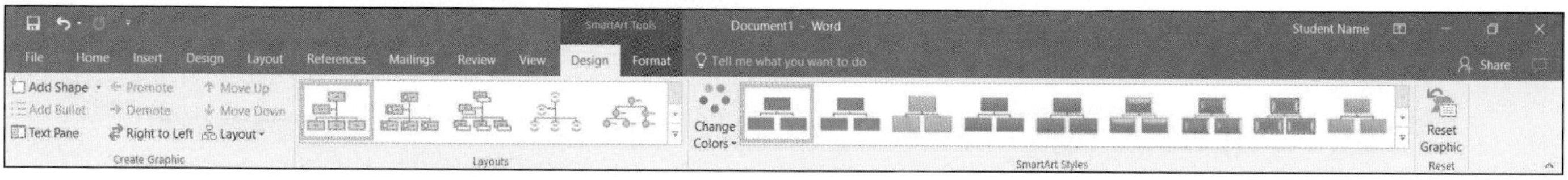

Figure 88.3 SmartArt Tools Format Tab

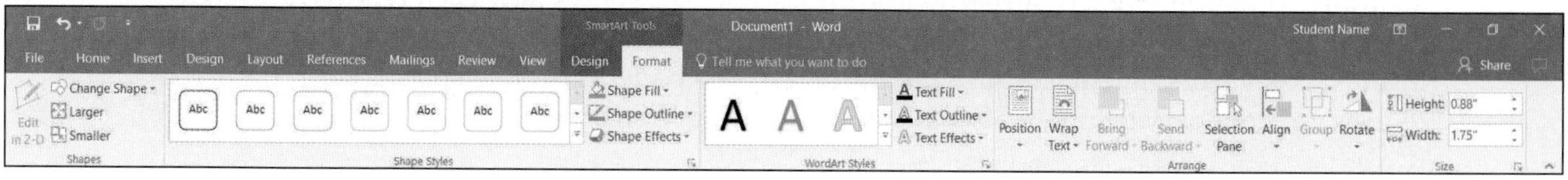

    d Click the Page Number button in the Header & Footer group on the Header & Footer Tools Design tab, point to *Current Position*, and then click *Plain Number*.

    e Click the Next button in the Navigation group to move to the second page header pane.

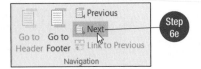

    f With the insertion point positioned at the left margin of the second page header, key ERGONOMIC CONSIDERATIONS and then press Tab twice to move the insertion point to the right margin. *Note: It is necessary to press Tab twice because the running head is shorter on the second page.*

    g Click the Page Number button in the Header & Footer group on the Header & Footer Tools Design tab, point to *Current Position*, and then click *Plain Number*.

    h Click the Close Header and Footer button in the Close group or double-click in the body of the document to make the document body active.

  7 Proofread the document, checking the format against the format shown in Figures 84.1 and 84.2.

  8 Save the document.

  9 Click the Check button to upload the document for checking.

 10 If errors are reported by the Online Lab, view the results document, correct the errors in the submitted document, save the document, and then click the Check Again button.

Figure 84.3 Abstract Content for Document 84.1

Ergonomics is concerned about understanding interactions among human beings and system elements. It is known as the science of work and is studied to make work more efficient and healthier for the user. The study of ergonomics has helped cut down on the instances of repetitive stress injuries for machinists as well as for keyboardists. The design of equipment, furniture, and actions taken all enter in when ergonomics is being discussed. ¶ → *Keywords:* ergonomics, science of work, efficiency, RSI, carpal tunnel syndrome

set the colon in italic but not the space after it

Formatting Headings in APA Research Papers

As mentioned in previous sessions, the main purpose of headings in a report, manuscript, or research paper is to help readers find the important ideas within the document. APA style identifies formatting for five levels of headings. Table 84.2 shows how each type of heading is formatted. Figure 84.4 shows examples of the first three heading levels as they would be formatted in an APA-style document. Because the entire research paper is double-spaced, no extra hard returns are necessary before or after any of the heading levels.

Document **SmartArt List**

88.1 Read all instructions below before starting this document activity.

1 Navigate to the Document 88.1 launch page in the Online Lab and then click the Launch Activity button to open **Doc088.01** in the activity window.

2 Key Places to Visit in the Phoenix Area and then select the text, change the paragraph alignment to center alignment, change the font size to 18 points, and apply bold formatting.

3 Insert a Basic Block List graphic into the document by completing the following steps:

   a Position the insertion point at the end of the title and then press Enter.

   b Click the Insert tab.

   c Click the SmartArt button in the Illustrations group.

   d With the *Basic Block List* thumbnail selected in the middle panel (first option in the *List* section with *All* selected in the left panel), click OK to insert the SmartArt graphic into the document.

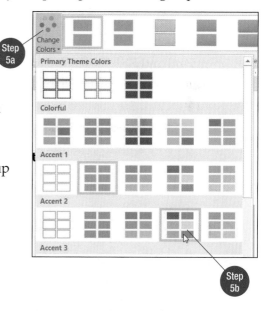

4 Add text to the SmartArt graphic by completing the following steps:

   a Click in the left box in the top row and then key Tuzigoot.

   b Click in the middle box in the top row and then key Saguaro Lake.

   c Click in the right box in the top row and then key Apache Trail.

   d Click in the left box in the second row and then key Scottsdale Museum of Modern Art.

   e Click in the right box in the second row and then key Usery Pass.

5 Change the colors used in the SmartArt graphic by completing the following steps:

   a Click the Change Colors button in the SmartArt Styles group on the SmartArt Tools Design tab.

   b Click *Gradient Loop - Accent 2* (fourth option in the *Accent 2* section).

6 Change the page layout to landscape orientation by completing the following steps:

   a Click the Layout tab.

   b Click the Orientation button in the Page Setup group.

   c Click *Landscape*.

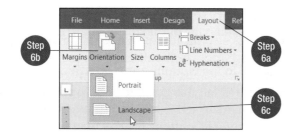

7 Vertically center the contents on the page. *Hint: Review Session 66, if necessary.*

8 Proofread the document and correct any errors.

9 Save the document.

10 Click the Submit button to upload the document for instructor review.

Document **Title Page and Abstract in APA Style**

84.1   Read all instructions below before starting this document activity.

1   Navigate to the Document 84.1 launch page in the Online Lab and then click the Launch Activity button to open **Doc084.01** in the activity window.

2   Change the document's default formatting by completing the following steps:

a   Change the document's default line spacing to double spacing with no spacing after paragraphs.

b   Change the document's default font to 12-point Times New Roman.

3   Key the title page by completing the following steps:

a   Press Enter three times to move the insertion point approximately 2 inches from the top of the document. *Hint: The insertion point should be 2.1 inches from the top of the page.*

b   Change the paragraph alignment to center alignment.

c   Key the title of the report, Ergonomic Considerations, and then press Enter.

d   Key the author's name, Stephanie Embraerson, and then press Enter.

e   Key the school affiliation, Elgin Community College—Central Campus, and then insert a page break (Ctrl + Enter).

4   Key the Abstract page by completing the following steps:

a   With the insertion point centered at the top margin of the second page of the document, key Abstract and then press Enter.

b   Change the paragraph alignment to left alignment.

c   Key the text shown in Figure 84.3. *Note: Key only one space after sentences, except the last sentence in the paragraph, and do not press Enter at the end of the last sentence. Format the colon after the word* **Keywords** *in italic, but do not format the space following the colon in italic.*

5   Because the APA style specifies that sentences end with two spaces after a period, use the Find and Replace feature to insert the double spaces by completing the following steps:

a   Position the insertion point at the beginning of the document (Ctrl + Home).

b   Click the Replace button in the Editing group on the Home tab.

c   Key a period and one space in the *Find what* text box.

d   Key a period and two spaces in the *Replace with* text box.

e   Click the Find Next button and then click the Replace button until all instances have been replaced.

f   Click OK and then close the Find and Replace dialog box.

6   Insert the headers in the document by completing the following steps:

a   Double-click in the header area of the first page of the document to display the header pane and the Header & Footer Tools Design tab.

b   Click the *Different First Page* check box in the Options group to insert a check mark.

c   With the insertion point positioned at the left margin of the first page header, key Running head: ERGONOMIC CONSIDERATIONS and then press Tab once to move the insertion point to the right margin. *Note: The running head is long enough that it is necessary to press Tab only once.*

steps continue

Document SmartArt Organizational Chart

88.2

Read all instructions below before starting this document activity.

1 Navigate to the Document 88.2 launch page in the Online Lab and then click the Launch Activity button to open **Doc088.02** in the activity window.

2 Key XFT Supply Company and then select the text, change the paragraph alignment to center alignment, change the font to 18-point Tahoma, and apply bold formatting.

3 Insert a Name and Title Organization Chart graphic into the document by completing the following steps:

   a Position the insertion point at the end of the title and then press Enter.

   b Click the Insert tab.

   c Click the SmartArt button in the Illustrations group.

   d Click *Hierarchy* in the left panel.

   e Click the *Name and Title Organization Chart* thumbnail (third column, first row in the middle panel).

   f Click OK to insert the SmartArt graphic into the document.

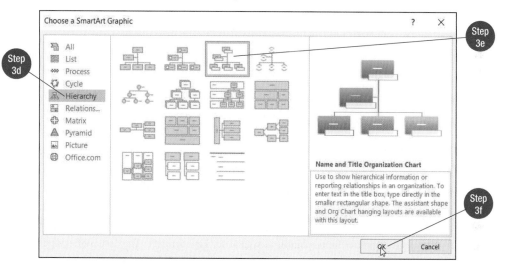

4 Edit the SmartArt graphic by completing the following steps:

   a Select the second blue box from the top. When the box is selected, the outer border will be a solid (rather than dashed) line.

   b Press the Delete key.

   c Select one of the blue boxes in the last row of the graphic and then press the Delete key.

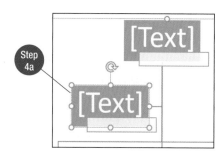

5 Add text to the SmartArt graphic by completing the following steps:

   a Click in the top blue box and then key Jill Xavier.

   b Click in the white box at the bottom of the top blue box and then key President.

   c Key Sylvia Forrest in left blue box in the second row.

   d Key Vice President in the white box below *Sylvia Forrest*.

   e Key Jose Tejada in the right blue box in the second row.

   f Key Vice President in the white box below *Jose Tejada*.

steps continue

Figure 84.1 Research Paper Title Page in APA Style

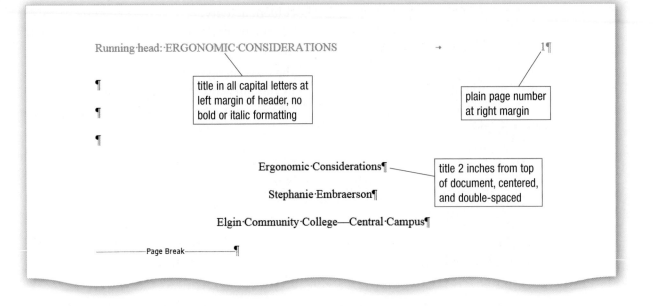

Running head: ERGONOMIC CONSIDERATIONS → 1¶

¶

¶

¶

title in all capital letters at left margin of header, no bold or italic formatting

plain page number at right margin

Ergonomic Considerations¶

Stephanie Embraerson¶

Elgin Community College—Central Campus¶

title 2 inches from top of document, centered, and double-spaced

Page Break ¶

Figure 84.2 Abstract Page in APA Style

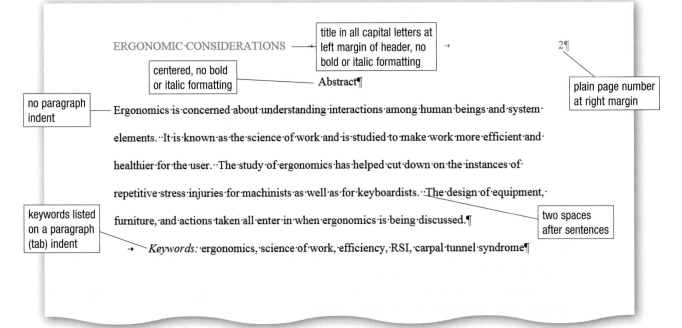

ERGONOMIC CONSIDERATIONS → 2¶

title in all capital letters at left margin of header, no bold or italic formatting

centered, no bold or italic formatting

Abstract¶

plain page number at right margin

no paragraph indent

Ergonomics is concerned about understanding interactions among human beings and system elements. It is known as the science of work and is studied to make work more efficient and healthier for the user. The study of ergonomics has helped cut down on the instances of repetitive stress injuries for machinists as well as for keyboardists. The design of equipment, furniture, and actions taken all enter in when ergonomics is being discussed.¶

→ *Keywords:* ergonomics, science of work, efficiency, RSI, carpal tunnel syndrome¶

two spaces after sentences

keywords listed on a paragraph (tab) indent

Success Tip

When keying the list of keywords in an abstract, press the Tab key, press Ctrl + I to turn on italic formatting, key Keywords:, press Ctrl + I to turn off italic formatting, and then press the spacebar.

6   Add a box to the organizational chart by completing the following steps:

a   Select the *Sylvia Forrest* box and then click the Add Shape button arrow in the Create Graphic group on the SmartArt Tools Design tab.

b   Click *Add Shape Below* at the drop-down list.

c   Key Buck Greene in the new blue box and then key Maintenance Manager in the new white box.

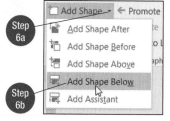

7   Add a box to the right of the *Buck Greene* box by completing the following steps:

a   Select the *Buck Greene* box and then click the Add Shape button arrow in the Create Graphic group on the SmartArt Tools Design tab.

b   Click *Add Shape After* at the drop-down list.

c   Key Barbara Tuffs in the new blue box and key Marketing Manager in the new white box.

8   Add a box to the organizational chart below the *Jose Tejada* box. Key Raj Papadakis in the new blue box and key Engineering Manager in the new white box.

9   Change the SmartArt style by completing the following steps:

a   Click the More SmartArt Styles button in the SmartArt Styles group on the SmartArt Tools Design tab.

b   Click *Cartoon* (third column, first row in the *3-D* section).

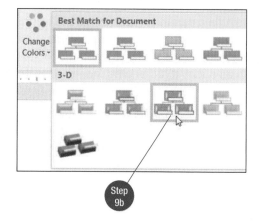

10   Change the colors used in the SmartArt graphic to Transparent Gradient Range - Accent 6 (fifth option in the *Accent 6* section).

11   Change the font color of the title *XFT Supply Company* to Green, Accent 6, Darker 50% (last column, last row in the *Theme Colors* section).

12   Change the page orientation to landscape and vertically center the contents on the page.

13   Compare the file against the image shown in Figure 88.4. Proofread the document and correct any errors.

14   Save the document.

15   Click the Submit button to upload the document for instructor review.

Table 84.1 APA Formatting Guidelines for Research Papers—continued

Paper Element	Formatting Guidelines
header/page numbers	
title page	header set 0.5 inch from top of document and includes the text *Running head: TITLE OF RESEARCH PAPER* (in plain text, no bold or italic formatting) beginning at left margin; page number (digits only) is set at right margin
remaining pages	header set 0.5 inch from the top of the document and includes *TITLE OF RESEARCH PAPER* in plain text (no bold or italic formatting) beginning at left margin; page numbers (digits only) are set at right margin
abstract	contains a brief summary of the research paper, appears on page 2, and includes the required header; the heading *Abstract* is centered at top margin in plain text (no bold or italic formatting) and paragraph is not indented
keywords	words or phrases that identify the important ideas of the paper and are used to help researchers locate the paper in database search results; listed one line below the paragraph on the Abstract page; *Keywords* and the colon that follows are set in italic formatting; indented on paragraph indent (0.5 inch)
citations	appear in-text and include author and date
references	begin on a separate page at the end of the document; the heading *References* is centered at the top margin in plain text (no bold or italic formatting); list should be double-spaced with no extra spacing between entries and with a hanging indent; allow Word to generate References page automatically from sources you have entered
tables	when included, placed on separate pages after the References page (unless otherwise requested by the instructor assigning the paper or the journal editor requesting manuscripts for publication)

Success Tip

Rather than trying to remember to key two spaces after every period when keying a document in APA style, key one space after every period and then use the Find and Replace feature to replace all periods followed by one space with a period followed by two spaces.

Figure 88.4 Completed SmartArt Organizational Chart for Document 88.2

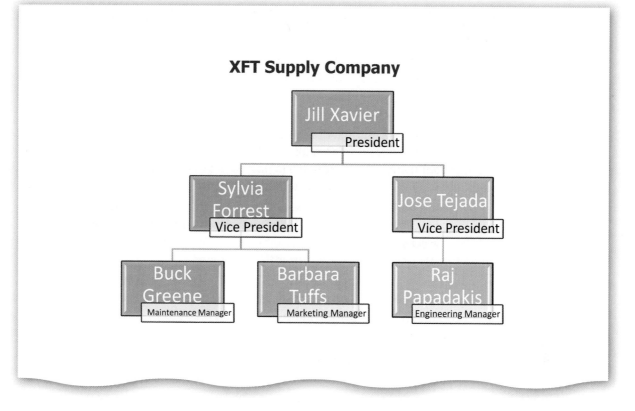

Reinforcing Formatting Skills

SmartArt graphics can be useful in a variety of scenarios. In previous activities, you used them to create lists and charts, and in this activity, you will create a diagram. Use the description information in the right panel of the Choose a SmartArt Graphic dialog box as a guide to select and create your own SmartArt graphic diagram as described in the following document activity.

Document 88.3 Using SmartArt to Create a Diagram

1 Navigate to the Document 88.3 launch page in the Online Lab and then click the Launch Activity button to open **Doc088.03** in the activity window.

2 Create a SmartArt graphic diagram in a document using the following criteria:

a Choose a SmartArt graphic from the *Process, Cycle, Relationship, Matrix,* or *Pyramid* categories. Make sure the selected category is appropriate for your content.

b Use at least six elements (names, items, categories) in your diagram.

3 Insert a title for the diagram. Use WordArt or a font that is larger than 14 points. Do not use Calibri as the font type.

4 Proofread the document and correct any errors.

5 Save the document.

6 Click the Submit button to upload the document for instructor review.

Ending the Session

The Online Lab automatically saved the work you completed for this session. You may continue with the next session or exit the Online Lab and continue later.

Formatting in APA Style

The American Psychological Association (APA) provides a guide for writers, editors, students, and educators writing for the social and behavioral sciences. The *Publication Manual of the American Psychological Association*, currently in its sixth edition, includes an easy-to-use reference and citation system as well as guidelines for using headings, tables, and figures in reports.

Research papers created in APA style require a title page and, commonly, an abstract. The abstract is a short summary (120 to 250 words) of the key points included within the paper. The abstract should contain just one double-spaced paragraph (with no tab indent at the start), and it should appear on a separate page immediately after the title page.

APA style uses parenthetical in-text citations to give credit to sources, with a full list of references at the end of the document. The format of the in-text citations is the author's last name followed by a comma and then the date; for example, (Forrest, 2019). Footnotes and endnotes are used to communicate any necessary explanatory notes for the document.

Table 84.1 provides some key formatting guidelines for the APA Style. Figure 84.1 shows an example of a title page and Figure 84.2 shows an example of an Abstract page, both applying the formatting guidelines listed in Table 84.1.

Table 84.1 APA Formatting Guidelines for Research Papers

Paper Element	Formatting Guidelines
paragraph alignment	left aligned, paragraphs begin with 0.5-inch tab (except Abstract page)
font	12-point serif font such as Cambria, Constantia, Times New Roman, or Palatino Linotype
margins	1-inch top, bottom, left, and right (default)
line spacing	double line spacing (with 0 points of spacing before and after paragraphs) throughout document, including References page
spacing after sentences	two spaces at the end of each sentence
title page	includes title of research paper, author's name, and institutional affiliation double-spaced in the top half of the page; text is centered and title is positioned 2 inches from top of document; include header as specified in this table

continues

Session 89

Inserting Images

Session Objectives

- Insert an image from a file into a document
- Insert an online image into a document
- Create an event flyer with images
- Efficiently produce documents in mailable form

Getting Started

Exercise 89.1 If you are continuing immediately from Session 88, you may skip the Exercise 89.1 warm-up drill. However, if you exited the Online Lab at the end of Session 88, warm up by completing Exercise 89.1.

Exercise 89.2 Begin your session work by completing Exercise 89.2, a timed short drill, in the Online Lab.

Assessing Your Speed and Accuracy

Complete Timings 89.1 through 89.3 in the Online Lab. At the end of each timing, the Online Lab will display your WPM rate and any errors. Results will be saved in your Timings Performance report. If you have been surpassing the speed and accuracy goals identified in the Online Lab, set slightly more challenging personal goals and strive to exceed them.

Complete two 1-minute timings on the timing text below. If you meet or exceed both speed and accuracy goals for Timing 89.1, push for greater speed on Timing 89.2.

1-Minute Timings

Timings 89.1–89.2   Ubiquitous computing (also called ambient intelligence) places computing power in your environment. That means the walls of your house might have the ability to sense your body's temperature and turn up the heat, or sense that you have fallen asleep on the couch and turn down the lighting.

What would you think about the ability to do this? Would you consider it an invasion of privacy or an efficient monitoring device? There could be applications for parents. Would it be right to monitor a family with such technology? Could there be implications for a family trying to have less ecological impact on the world?

Complete one 5-minute timing on the timing text below.

5-Minute Timing

Timing 84.3

Sailing has played an important part in this country's heritage, both in commerce and in sport. Naval architects and shipbuilders are recognized because of the beautiful and speedy ships that have sailed the oceans of the world. Full-rigged clipper ships such as the great "Flying Cloud" have set many speed records on the water route between San Francisco and East Asia. Building speedy ships has been a major objective of American yacht designers. A number of the designers of yachts have netted considerable recognition, praise, and popularity for their magnificent designs of winning yachts.

Enthusiasm for sailing as a new hobby progressed fast during the thirties; amateur sailors from England and America have competed in a series of races for many years. The vessels used in earlier races were class sloops measuring up to 135 feet in length. Today, the big competitions are run in 12-meter sloops averaging 70 feet in length. The ships are fine-precision machines designed for closed-course match racing.

Until 1945, sailboats were very limited in number, when compared with the total ownership of sailboats today. Within the past few decades, many new materials have allowed boats to be made more easily and less expensively. Fiberglass was the fabric that revolutionized the boat industry. Fiberglass has made the task of molding the hull of a boat easier and very efficient. A builder no longer has to utilize wooden timbers in boat construction. Mass production of many boats is now an economical procedure. A number of boat owners prefer the fiberglass as it requires less upkeep and is not expensive to maintain.

Every year, many kinds of sailboats are designed for sailing enthusiasts. The boats are all sizes and styles, from dinghies to large cruising sailboats on which entire families can gather. Sailors can select from elegant styles and a wide variety of sizes of new designs in sailboats.

The number of people taking part in sailing in the United States is expanding quite rapidly; the estimated number of boat owners is multiplying at an equal pace. The hobby of sailing is a family and group affair; various boating organizations are very popular and appeal to different interest groups.

Complete one 3-minute timing on the timing text below.

3-Minute Timing

**Timing
89.3**

Lightning, a spectacle glowing in the sky, is something that all people have watched. We have observed the many furious clouds, rapid flashes of brilliant light, and the crashing thunder. On our planet, this basic natural phenomenon strikes earth over 2,000 times annually. Lightning has forever been a marvel and a mystery to people. In some cases, lightning has even been thought of as an eminent power or mysterious force. The force was looked upon as an omen or warning of punishment facing them. Some even considered lightning a sign of good fortune. If an area was struck by lightning, it was considered quite sacred by certain people.

The old mystery of lightning remained until that famous kite and metal key experiment took place. Our study of lightning is much more impressive today. There are still many of us, however, who feel anxiety and admiration when lightning crackles and sparkles around us. Many persons count the seconds between the lightning and thunder to determine just how close the danger above really is. A factor that very few people realize is that the torrid flash of brilliant light changes the upper atmosphere into fertilizer for the vegetation on earth.

Ergonomic Tip

If your chair has arm rests, be sure they are adjusted so that your shoulders are relaxed and your wrists are straight. However, do not "plant" your arms on the rests—they are for occasional use only.

Inserting and Formatting Images

Insert an image, such as a picture or clip art, in a Word document with buttons in the Illustrations group on the Insert tab. Click the Pictures button to display the Insert Picture dialog box and then select a file from your computer or storage media, or click the Online Pictures button and search online for images.

Inserting an Image

To insert an image in a document, click the Insert tab and then click the Pictures button in the Illustrations group. At the Insert Picture dialog box, navigate to the folder containing the image and then double-click the image file. When you insert an image into a document, the Picture Tools Format tab will appear. Use options on this tab to customize and format the inserted image.

Practice inserting an image into a document and formatting the image using tools on the Picture Tools Format tab in the following document activity.

Session Objectives

- **Prepare a research paper according to APA style**
- **Format a title page and an Abstract page**
- **Format headings**
- **Insert sources and in-text citations**
- **Create a References page**
- **Compose a title page and an Abstract page**
- **Efficiently produce documents in mailable form**

Getting Started

Exercise 84.1 If you are continuing immediately from Session 83, you may skip the Exercise 84.1 warm-up drill. However, if you exited the Online Lab at the end of Session 83, warm up by completing Exercise 84.1.

Exercise 84.2 Begin your session work by completing Exercise 84.2, a timed short drill, in the Online Lab.

Assessing Your Speed and Accuracy

Complete Timings 84.1 through 84.3 in the Online Lab. At the end of each timing, the Online Lab will display your WPM rate and any errors. Results will be saved in your Timings Performance report. If you have been surpassing the speed and accuracy goals identified in the Online Lab, set slightly more challenging personal goals and strive to exceed them.

Complete two 1-minute timings on the timing text below. If you meet or exceed both speed and accuracy goals for Timing 84.1, push for greater speed on Timing 84.2.

1-Minute Timings

Timings 84.1–84.2 A fiber-optic cable, also identified as a light-guide, is a glass filament approximately the thickness of a hair. The glass filaments are made from extremely fine sand. They are exceptionally lightweight (80 pounds per 1,000 feet of cable), have a comparatively high tensile strength, and are surprisingly flexible. Instead of transmitting electricity, the fiber cable transmits light indicators. A laser can be used to convert an electrical signal to a light signal. The light is then passed through the glass fiber. Also, lasers can be used to transmit and receive the light signals at both ends of the fiber-optic cable.

Document Garden Tour Invitation

89.1

Read all instructions below before starting this document activity.

1 Navigate to the Document 89.1 launch page in the Online Lab and then click the Launch Activity button to open **Doc089.01** in the activity window.

2 Change the font to 18-point Comic Sans MS and then change the paragraph alignment to center alignment.

3 Key the text shown in Figure 89.1. *Note: Undo the automatic capitalization as necessary to match the text.*

4 Select the text *Neighborhood Garden Tour!* and then change the font size to 24 points and the font color to Green, Accent 6 (last column, first row in the *Theme Colors* section).

5 Position the insertion point immediately after the last sentence in the document and then insert an image by completing the following steps:

   a Click the Insert tab.

   b Click the Pictures button in the Illustrations group.

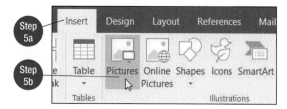

   c Click the *Documents* folder in the Navigation pane in the Insert Picture dialog box.

   d In the Content pane of the Insert Picture dialog box, double-click the *Paradigm* folder, double-click the *Keyboarding* folder, and then double-click the *DocumentActivityFiles* folder.

   e Double-click **Doc089.01_IrishDaisy.jpg**.

steps continue

Figure 89.1 Invitation Content for Document 89.1

> You are invited ¶ to a ¶ Neighborhood Garden Tour! ¶ We have some prize-winning gardens on our block. ¶ Join us on June 1, 3, or 6 at 2 p.m. ¶ We will start our walk at the Jeffers' home (#97). ¶¶ Wear comfortable shoes. ¶ Coffee and tea will be provided after the walk.

Reinforcing Writing Skills

In Session 81, the "Reinforcing Writing Skills" section presented eight steps for preparing a manuscript. You completed the first three steps in the Document 81.4 activity. These initial steps included identifying a topic, researching the topic, and taking notes. In the Document 82.3 activity, you completed Step 4, which involved the preparation of an outline to complete the manuscript. In this activity, you will complete Step 5 in the process, which is to prepare a rough draft of the manuscript; Step 6, which is to make any revisions to the document and edit the document for punctuation, spelling, grammar, word choice, and capitalization errors; and then Step 8, which is to create a Works Cited page for the sources used in the manuscript.

Before beginning the Document 83.2 activity, print a copy of the previously created files, **Doc081.04** and **Doc082.03**. Using these two documents as guides, compose a rough draft of the body of the manuscript. Be sure to include any quoted information that you found. Insert in-text citations to credit your sources. In preparing your rough draft, concentrate on composing; do not be concerned with errors in punctuation and spelling. You can fix these issues when you go through the document again (in Step 3 on the next page).

Document 83.2 — Composing a Report, Editing the Report, and Creating a Works Cited Page

Read all instructions below before starting this document activity.

1 Navigate to the Document 83.2 launch page in the Online Lab and then click the Launch Activity button to open **Doc083.02** in the activity window.

2 Compose your manuscript in the document based on the content developed in the Document 81.4 and Document 82.3 activities. Key the in-text citations as you key the document.

3 Save the document and then read through the content, making any necessary revisions or edits that will improve the document. Make sure to fix any errors in punctuation, spelling, grammar, and capitalization.

4 Create a Works Cited page with the full source information for the in-text citations.

5 Proofread the document and correct any errors.

6 Save the document.

7 Click the Submit button to upload the document for instructor review.

Ending the Session

The Online Lab automatically saved the work you completed for this session. You may continue with the next session or exit the Online Lab and continue later.

6 With the image selected, format the image by completing the following steps:

  a Select the number in the *Shape Height* measurement box in the Size group, key 2.5, and then press Enter. ***Note: The number in the* Shape Width *measurement box will automatically change to 3.33".***

  b Click the Position button in the Arrange group.

  c Click *Position in Middle Right with Square Text Wrapping* (third column, second row in the *With Text Wrapping* section).

7 Vertically center the invitation on the page. **Hint: Review Session 66, if necessary.**

8 Proofread the document and correct any errors.

9 Save the document.

10 Click the Submit button to upload the document for instructor review.

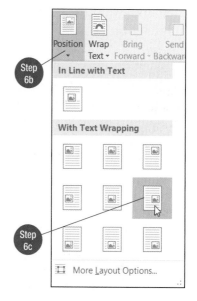

Inserting an Online Image

Use the Bing Image Search feature to search for specific images online, including pictures and clip art. To use this feature, click the Insert tab and then click the Online Pictures button in the Illustrations group to display the Insert Pictures window, shown in Figure 89.2.

Figure 89.2 Insert Pictures Window

Insert Pictures

×

Bing Image Search
Search the web

Search Bing

To search for online images, type a search word or phrase in this search text box and then press Enter.

OneDrive - Personal
studentname02@hotmail.com Remove

Browse ▶

Also insert from:

Figure 83.7 Source Content for Document 83.1

First Citation

Type of Source: Book

Author: Gordon, Jon; Lankisch, Karen; Muir, Nancy; Seguin, Denise; Verno, Anita

Title: Our Digital World: Introduction to Computing, 4th ed.

Year: 2017

City: St. Paul

Publisher: Paradigm Publishing, Inc.

Medium: Print

Second Citation

Type of Source: Web site

Author: Planque, Bo

Name of Web Page: Did I Miss Something?

Name of Web Site: What is New in Information Technology

Year: 2019

Month: January

Day: 19

Year Accessed: 2020

Month Accessed: March

Day Accessed: 20

Medium: Web

URL: http://ppi-edu.net/WhatIsNewInIT/20/2

Third Citation

Type of Source: Journal Article

Author: Pedersen, Tiger

Title: FireWire Ports Are Important

Journal Name: IT News

Year: 2020

Month: March

Day: 17

Pages: B19

Medium: Print

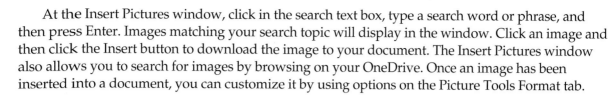

At the Insert Pictures window, click in the search text box, type a search word or phrase, and then press Enter. Images matching your search topic will display in the window. Click an image and then click the Insert button to download the image to your document. The Insert Pictures window also allows you to search for images by browsing on your OneDrive. Once an image has been inserted into a document, you can customize it by using options on the Picture Tools Format tab.

When selecting online images to use in documents, be aware that many images are copyrighted and thus may not be available for use without permission. Always review the specific license for any image you want to use to ensure you can comply with the specific requirements for that image.

Practice creating a document with an online image and formatting that image in the following document activity.

Document 89.2 **Coffee Announcement**

Read all instructions below before starting this document activity.

1 Navigate to the Document 89.2 launch page in the Online Lab and then click the Launch Activity button to open **Doc089.02** in the activity window.

2 Change the font to 16-point Lucida Sans.

3 Key the text shown in Figure 89.2 and apply bold and italic formatting as shown. *Note: The word* **is** *should be bold and italic in the second paragraph.*

4 With the insertion point positioned at the end of the text, insert an online image by completing the following steps:

   a Click the Insert tab.

   b Click the Online Pictures button in the Illustrations group.

   c At the Insert Pictures window, key donuts, and then press Enter.

   d Click to select an image of donuts, such as the one shown selected below, and then click the Insert button.

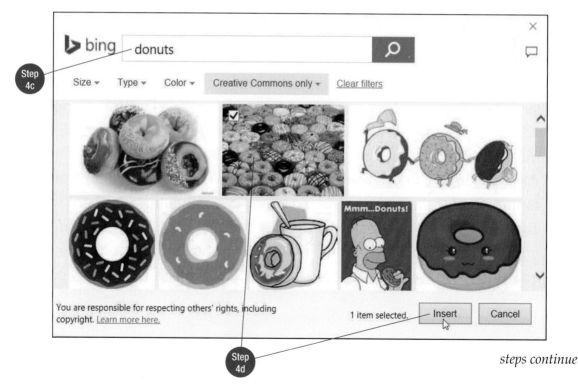

steps continue

Figure 83.6 Report Content for Document 83.1—continued

came out in version 1.0, which supported a 21 megabits per second (Mbps) data rate (the measurement of the speed at which data can be transmitted). USB 3.0 became available in 2010, providing a transfer rate of up to 5 Gbps,

insert Planque citation,

and USB 3.1 introduced an even faster transfer, called *SuperSpeed*, with a data rate of 10 Gbps. USB-C, introduced in 2014, provides a small, reversible plug connector. ¶ Usually a computer has two to four USB ports that you can use to attach peripheral devices. Often users need more ports. You can add a hub that increases the number of available USB ports. Plug the USB hub into one of your computer's USB sockets, and then you can plug USB devices into the ports on the hub. Most USB hubs offer four ports, but some offer more. ¶ FireWire Ports ¶ A FireWire port is based on the same serial bus architecture as a USB port. (A bus is essentially a subsystem of your computer that transfers data between the various components inside your computer). FireWire provides a high-speed serial interface for peripheral

insert Pederson citation, page B19

devices such as digital cameras, camcorders, or external hard drives. The newest version of FireWire supports an 800 Mbps data rate. ¶ Thunderbolt Ports ¶ The Thunderbolt port, introduced on Apple's MacBook Pro in 2011, was developed by Intel and Apple to provide a peripheral connection standard that combines data, audio, video, and power within a single high-speed connection. The newest version of Thunderbolt, Thunderbolt 3 doubled bandwidth and cut power consumption in half. Thunderbolt's high-speed connection supports high-resolution displays and other devices that require a lot of bandwidth, such as high-end video cameras or data storage devices, and is generally expected to replace FireWire. Originally added to Apple devices, Thunderbolt is now being added to some PCs, making the port no longer strictly an Apple favorite. ¶ Infrared Data Association Port ¶ An Infrared Data Association (IrDA) port allows you to transfer datum from one device to another using infrared light waves. Today the ability to transmit wirelessly between devices using Bluetooth (a wireless communications standard) is making IrDA ports obsolete. You can add Bluetooth connectivity via a device that connects to the USB port.

5 Add an effect to the image by completing the following steps:

    a Click the Picture Effects button in the Picture Styles group on the Picture Tools Format tab.

    b Point to *Bevel* and then click *Round* at the side menu (first column, first row in the *Bevel* section).

6 Click in the *Shape Width* measurement box in the Size group, type 1.7, and then press Enter.

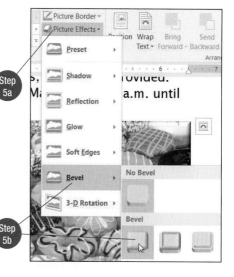

7 Click the Position button in the Arrange group and then click *Position in Top Left with Square Text Wrapping* (first column, first row in the *With Text Wrapping* section).

8 Select the text, *Saturday Social!*, and then change the font size to 24 points.

9 Vertically center the invitation on the page.

10 Proofread the document and correct any errors.

11 Save the document.

12 Click the Submit button to upload the document for instructor review.

Figure 89.2 Announcement Content for Document 89.2

> **Saturday Social!** ¶ We are having a coffee and donuts gathering at the picnic area by the pool on Saturday beginning at 9 a.m. ¶ All residents are welcome. We have six new families in the neighborhood, so let's greet them and get to know everyone better. After all, this *is* Good Neighbor Week. ¶ Coffee and donuts (and name tags, too) will be provided. Mark your calendar for Saturday, May 21, from 9 a.m. until 11 a.m. and plan to join us!

Reinforcing Writing Skills

You can use Word to easily create flyers and newsletters. These types of documents can be useful in both your work and personal lives.

Document 89.3

Creating an Event Flyer

1 Navigate to the Document 89.3 launch page in the Online Lab and then click the Launch Activity button to open **Doc089.03** in the activity window.

2 Create an interesting, attention-getting flyer for an event.

    a Include the date, time, and place for the event.

    b Use at least two images in the flyer. Resize each image to fit on the page and alter the picture border, effect, or style.

3 Proofread the document and correct any errors.

4 Save the document.

5 Click the Submit button to upload the document for instructor review.

Ending the Session

The Online Lab automatically saved the work you completed for this session. You may continue with the next session or exit the Online Lab and continue later.

7 Insert the second in-text citation into the document, using the location information shown in Figure 83.6 and the source content shown in Figure 83.7. Click the *Show All Bibliography Fields* check box to insert a check mark and expand the Create Source dialog box to allow you to key the URL address for the source. There is no page reference for the second citation.

8 Insert the third in-text citation into the document, using the location information shown in Figure 83.6 and the source content shown in Figure 83.7. Click the *Show All Bibliography Fields* check box to display the additional fields. Include the page reference *B19* in the in-text citation.

9 Insert a Works Cited page at the end of the document by completing the following steps:

    a Position the insertion point at the end of the document (Ctrl + End) and then insert a hard page break (Ctrl + Enter).

    b Change the paragraph alignment to center alignment and then key Works Cited.

    c Press Enter and then change the paragraph alignment to left alignment.

    d Click the Bibliography button in the Citations & Bibliography group on the References tab.

    e Click *Insert Bibliography* at the bottom of the drop-down list. *Note: Do not delete the blank line at the end of the inserted text.*

10 Proofread the document and correct any errors.

11 Save the document.

12 Click the Check button to upload the document for checking.

13 If errors are reported by the Online Lab, view the results document, correct the errors in the submitted document, save the document, and then click the Check Again button.

Figure 83.6 Report Content for Document 83.1

Jorge Begall ¶ Joel Neek, PhD ¶ Business Communications 101 ¶ 3 April 2020 ¶ Computer Ports ¶ A computer uses a port to connect with a peripheral device such as a monitor or printer or to connect to a network. There are several different types of ports. A physical port connects a computer to another device, sending a signal via a cable (as for a USB *port*), infrared light (as with an infrared port), or a wireless transmitter (as with a wireless device). Some types of ~~fiscal~~ *physical* ports (commonly called just *ports*) in use today are serial, USB, FireWire, Thunderbolt, and infrared. ¶ Serial Ports ¶ A serial port is a port, built into the computer, used to connect a peripheral device to the serial bus, typically by means of a plug with ~~9~~ *nine* pins. Network routers use serial ports for administration, although they are replaced by web-based administration interfaces. ¶ Universal Serial Bus Ports ¶ A universal serial bus (USB) port is a small rectangular sl~~i~~*ot* that has quickly become the most popular way to attach everything from wireless mouse and keyboard ~~toggles~~ *dongles* (the small devices that transmit wireless signals to wireless devices) to USB flash drives for storing data. USB first

insert Gordon citation, page 68

continues

Session 90

Production Progress Check: Graphics and Imagery

Session Objectives

- Demonstrate proficiency with graphic elements
- Efficiently produce documents in mailable form

Getting Started

Exercise 90.1 If you are continuing immediately from Session 89, you may skip the Exercise 90.1 warm-up drill. However, if you exited the Online Lab at the end of Session 89, warm up by completing Exercise 90.1.

Exercise 90.2 Begin your session work by completing Exercise 90.2, a timed short drill, in the Online Lab.

Assessing Your Speed and Accuracy

Complete Timings 90.1 through 90.3 in the Online Lab. At the end of each timing, the Online Lab will display your WPM rate and any errors. Results will be saved in your Timings Performance report. If you have been surpassing the speed and accuracy goals identified in the Online Lab, set slightly more challenging personal goals and strive to exceed them.

Complete two 1-minute timings on the timing text below. If you meet or exceed both speed and accuracy goals for Timing 90.1, push for greater speed on Timing 90.2.

1-Minute Timings

Timings 90.1–90.2 Air traffic controllers monitor planes traveling worldwide. This takes considerable coordination on the part of the various air traffic controllers as planes go from one controller's area of responsibility to another's. Air traffic control is not just a person in an airport tower--it's more intricate than that! These controllers are responsible for keeping the air space safe as they monitor thousands of aircraft and attempt to keep them safe. Each plane must be directed so that it stays away from other aircraft in the area, advised as to potential weather problems and ways around those situations, and kept as close to on time as possible.

Report with Citations and Works Cited Page in MLA Style

Read all instructions below before starting this document activity.

1 Navigate to the Document 83.1 launch page in the Online Lab and then click the Launch Activity button to open **Doc083.01** in the activity window.

2 Change the default formatting for the document by completing the following steps:

    a Change the default line spacing for the document to double spacing with no spacing after paragraphs.

    b Change the default font for the document to 12-point Palatino Linotype.

3 Create a header on all pages of the document by completing the following steps:

    a Click the Insert tab.

    b Click the Page Number button in the Header & Footer group.

    c Point to *Top of Page* and then click *Plain Number 3*.

    d With the insertion point positioned immediately to the left of the plain page number, key Begall and then press the spacebar.

    e Click the Close Header and Footer button in the Close group to close the header pane.

4 Set the document's style reference to *MLA* by completing the following steps:

    a Click the References tab.

    b Click the *Style* option box arrow in the Citations & Bibliography group.

    c Click *MLA* at the drop-down list.

5 Key the report shown in Figure 83.6, implementing the changes indicated by the proofreading marks as you go. Center the title of the manuscript and set the other headings at the left margin. Press Tab at the start of each paragraph. If necessary, use Figure 83.5 for reference. ***Hint: Type the entire report and then insert the in-text citations to ensure Online Lab grades the citations properly.***

6 Insert the first in-text citation noted in Figure 83.6 and then key the source information shown in Figure 83.7 into the document by completing the following steps:

    a Position the insertion point at the end of the first paragraph under the *Serial Ports* side heading, after *administration interfaces* and before the period at the end of the sentence.

    b Click the Insert Citation button in the Citations & Bibliography group on the References tab.

    c Click *Add New Source* at the drop-down list.

    d In the Create Source dialog box, click the *Type of Source* option box arrow and then click *Book* at the drop-down list.

    e Key the information for the first citation shown in Figure 83.7 in the fields in the *Bibliography Fields for MLA* section at the Create Source dialog box.

    f Proofread the keyed information and then click OK.

    g Insert the page reference for the Gordon citation by completing the following steps:

        1) Click the Gordon citation in the document.

        2) Click the Citation Options arrow that displays at the right of the citation placeholder and then click *Edit Citation* at the drop-down list.

        3) Key 73 in the *Pages* text box.

        4) Click OK or press Enter.

steps continue

Complete one 3-minute timing on the timing text below.

3-Minute Timing

Timing 90.3

Most people consider homegrown popcorn a real delight. If you have the space, popcorn is something that is fun to produce. Children in particular are fascinated by growing their own popcorn and, of course, eating it also. If popcorn is grown properly, the flavor is usually superior to commercially packaged products.

Popcorn has growing requirements similar to those of sweet corn except that it requires a lengthier growing period. The seed must be planted in a hot, sunny area. The soil must be cultivated and organic materials added; it may also be necessary to include some general-purpose vegetable fertilizer. The popcorn should be planted about one inch deep with four inches between seeds. Rows should be planted two to three feet apart.

To ensure pollination, popcorn should be planted in blocks of at least four rows standing side by side. Never plant popcorn adjoining sweet corn as the two corn types will cross-pollinate, and the popcorn will not pop. Popcorn is ready to harvest when the stalks and leaves are completely dry. This will typically take approximately 100 to 110 days.

 Ergonomic Tip

Avoid resting your hands and wrists on sharp edges while typing. Doing so may apply pressure to areas of your hands and wrists that contain nerves and tendons, which can increase your risk of injury.

Checking Production Progress: Graphics and Imagery

Sessions 86 through 89 discussed the procedures for inserting graphics and images into documents. In this session, you will be assessed on how quickly and accurately you can key documents containing these elements. In the following document activities, each completed document is to be "mailable," which means that it contains no errors. A document that requires corrections is not considered *mailable*.

In this session's document activities, you will create materials to help promote an upcoming event at the Aldeen Golf Club. Your goal is to key each email and memo in mailable form. If you are missing errors that should have been corrected or your instructor believes you can work more efficiently, he or she may ask you to repeat document activities. To help you succeed, carefully review each document's instructions and content before keying. *Note: Before you begin these documents, review the content of Sessions 86 through 89 if you are unsure of how to complete a specific task.*

If the document's default line spacing has been changed to double spacing with no spacing before or after paragraphs, then the references list that Word generates from the document's sources will have the same line and paragraph spacing. In the following document activity, you will key a report, add citations and sources, and then use Word to generate the Works Cited page at the end of the document. Figure 83.5 shows thumbnails of the final document pages. Notice that the author's name and page number appear in the header on all of the pages of the document.

Figure 83.5 Completed Report for Document 83.1

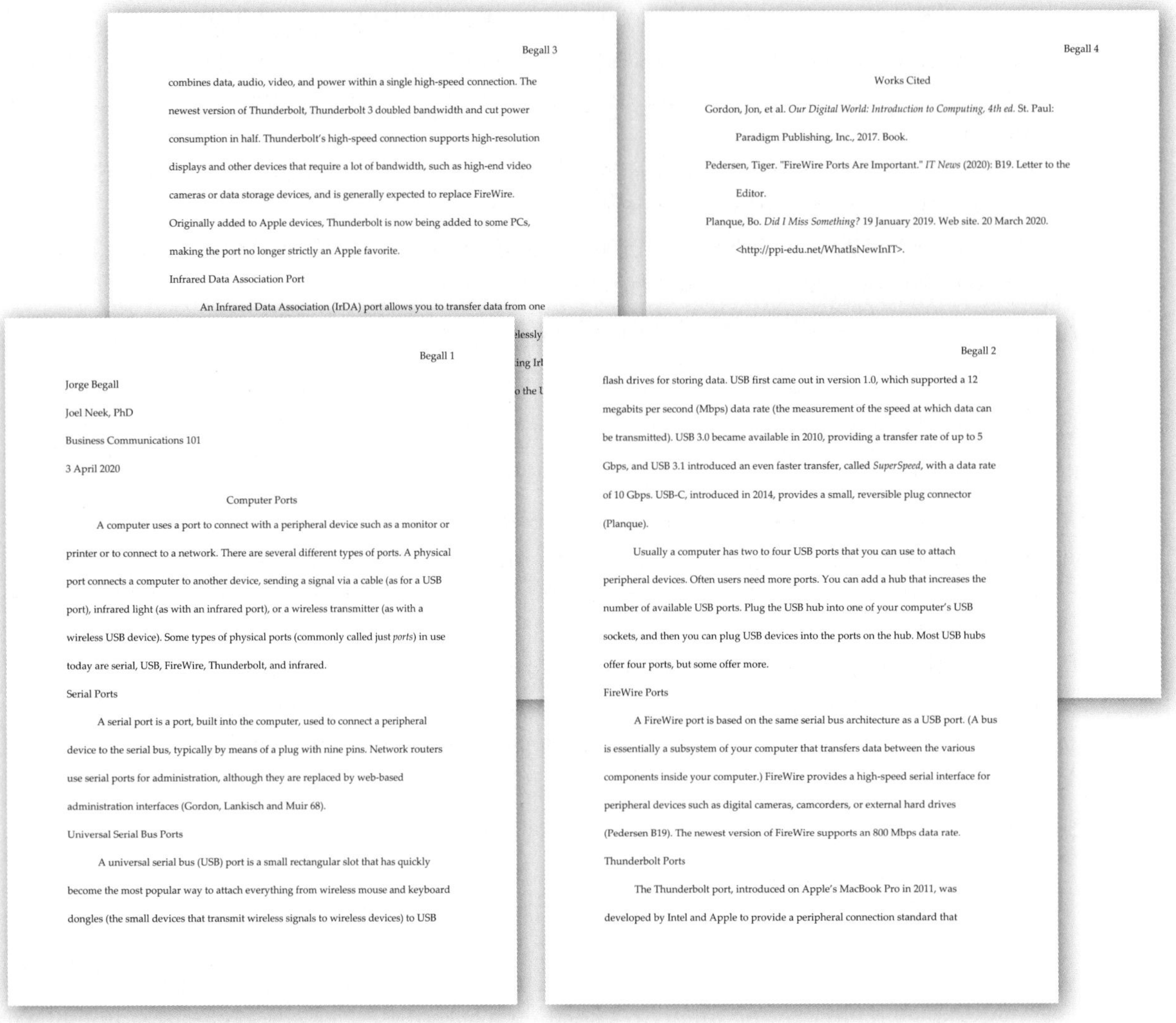

Begall 1

Jorge Begall

Joel Neek, PhD

Business Communications 101

3 April 2020

Computer Ports

A computer uses a port to connect with a peripheral device such as a monitor or printer or to connect to a network. There are several different types of ports. A physical port connects a computer to another device, sending a signal via a cable (as for a USB port), infrared light (as with an infrared port), or a wireless transmitter (as with a wireless USB device). Some types of physical ports (commonly called just *ports*) in use today are serial, USB, FireWire, Thunderbolt, and infrared.

Serial Ports

A serial port is a port, built into the computer, used to connect a peripheral device to the serial bus, typically by means of a plug with nine pins. Network routers use serial ports for administration, although they are replaced by web-based administration interfaces (Gordon, Lankisch and Muir 68).

Universal Serial Bus Ports

A universal serial bus (USB) port is a small rectangular slot that has quickly become the most popular way to attach everything from wireless mouse and keyboard dongles (the small devices that transmit wireless signals to wireless devices) to USB

Begall 2

flash drives for storing data. USB first came out in version 1.0, which supported a 12 megabits per second (Mbps) data rate (the measurement of the speed at which data can be transmitted). USB 3.0 became available in 2010, providing a transfer rate of up to 5 Gbps, and USB 3.1 introduced an even faster transfer, called *SuperSpeed*, with a data rate of 10 Gbps. USB-C, introduced in 2014, provides a small, reversible plug connector (Planque).

Usually a computer has two to four USB ports that you can use to attach peripheral devices. Often users need more ports. You can add a hub that increases the number of available USB ports. Plug the USB hub into one of your computer's USB sockets, and then you can plug USB devices into the ports on the hub. Most USB hubs offer four ports, but some offer more.

FireWire Ports

A FireWire port is based on the same serial bus architecture as a USB port. (A bus is essentially a subsystem of your computer that transfers data between the various components inside your computer.) FireWire provides a high-speed serial interface for peripheral devices such as digital cameras, camcorders, or external hard drives (Pedersen B19). The newest version of FireWire supports an 800 Mbps data rate.

Thunderbolt Ports

The Thunderbolt port, introduced on Apple's MacBook Pro in 2011, was developed by Intel and Apple to provide a peripheral connection standard that

Begall 3

combines data, audio, video, and power within a single high-speed connection. The newest version of Thunderbolt, Thunderbolt 3 doubled bandwidth and cut power consumption in half. Thunderbolt's high-speed connection supports high-resolution displays and other devices that require a lot of bandwidth, such as high-end video cameras or data storage devices, and is generally expected to replace FireWire. Originally added to Apple devices, Thunderbolt is now being added to some PCs, making the port no longer strictly an Apple favorite.

Infrared Data Association Port

An Infrared Data Association (IrDA) port allows you to transfer data from one

Begall 4

Works Cited

Gordon, Jon, et al. *Our Digital World: Introduction to Computing, 4th ed.* St. Paul: Paradigm Publishing, Inc., 2017. Book.

Pedersen, Tiger. "FireWire Ports Are Important." *IT News* (2020): B19. Letter to the Editor.

Planque, Bo. *Did I Miss Something?* 19 January 2019. Web site. 20 March 2020. <http://ppi-edu.net/WhatIsNewInIT>.

Success Tip

If you make changes to a source at the Edit Source dialog box after the Works Cited page has been generated, right-click the source list and then click *Update Field* to incorporate the changes.

Document 90.1

Aldeen Golf Club Letterhead

Read all instructions below before starting this document activity.

1 Navigate to the Document 90.1 launch page in the Online Lab and then click the Launch Activity button to open Doc090.01 in the activity window.

2 Change the top margin of the document to 2 inches.

3 Display the document header pane, place a check mark in the *Different First Page* check box, and then set the header 0.7 inch from the top of the page.

4 Insert WordArt into the document by selecting the black WordArt option in the first column, third row of the drop-down list. Change the text fill color to *Green, Accent 6, Darker 25%* (last column, fifth row in the *Theme Colors* section) and then key Aldeen Golf Club in the text box.

5 Apply a transform text effect to the WordArt using the *Double Wave: Down-Up* option (third column, fifth row in the *Warp* section).

6 Deselect the WordArt by clicking in the header pane outside of the WordArt text box. Change the paragraph alignment to right alignment.

7 Key 7605 Shady Hill Drive and then press Enter.

8 Key Gulf Shores, AL 36542 and then press Enter.

9 Key (251) 555-6919 and then press Enter.

10 Turn on italic formatting, key Best Golf on the Gulf, turn off italic formatting, press Enter, and change the paragraph alignment to left alignment.

11 Starting at the left margin of the header (turn on the display of the horizontal ruler if necessary) and below the text, insert a straight line shape that is 6.5 inches wide. *Hint:* **Check the width of the line in the Shape Width *measurement box in the Size group on the Drawing Tools Format tab.***

12 Change the shape outline color of the line to *Green, Accent 6, Darker 25%* (last column, fifth row in the *Theme Colors* section) and then change the weight of the line to 3 points.

13 Compare the document header to the image shown in Figure 90.1 and correct any errors.

14 Save the document.

15 Click the Submit button to upload the document for instructor review.

Figure 90.1 Letterhead Design for Document 90.1

Creating a Works Cited Page according to MLA Style

Once the citations and source information have been entered into a report, Word provides tools to help you compile the cited sources in a list at the end of the document. In Session 82, you created a bibliography according to *The Chicago Manual of Style*, Sixteenth Edition's format. In this session, you will create a listing of sources according to the MLA style. In MLA style, the list of sources is placed on a separate page at the end of the report and is titled *Works Cited*. The title is centered and, like the other headings in the report, is not set in bold. The text on the Works Cited page is double-spaced with no spacing before or after paragraphs, to match the format of the body of the report. The list is formatted with a hanging indent.

To create the Works Cited page for a report that contains citations, complete the following steps:

1 Position the insertion point at the end of the document (Ctrl + End) and then insert a hard page break (Ctrl + Enter).

2 With the insertion point positioned at the top of the new page, change the paragraph alignment to center alignment (Ctrl + E) and then key Works Cited.

3 Press Enter and then set the paragraph alignment back to left alignment (Ctrl + L).

4 Click the References tab.

5 Click the Bibliography button in the Citations & Bibliography group.

6 Click *Insert Bibliography* at the drop-down list.

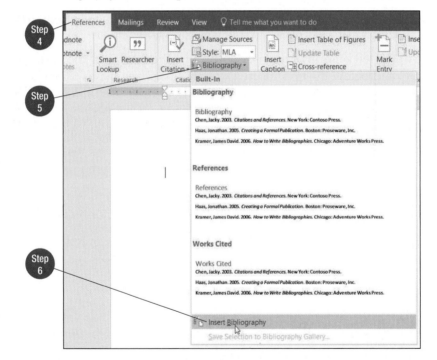

Success Tip

A quick way to insert a hard page break at the end of a document (for example, to create the Works Cited page) is to press Ctrl + End to move the insertion point to the end of the document and then press Ctrl + Enter to insert the page break.

Document Golf Play Day Memo
90.2
Read all instructions below before starting this document activity.

1 Navigate to the Document 90.2 launch page in the Online Lab and then click the Launch Activity button to open **Doc090.02** in the activity window.

2 Key the memo using the content provided in Figure 90.2. *Hint: Remember to turn off bold formatting before pressing Tab after each of the guide words. Press Tab twice after the first three guide words and once after the fourth.*

3 Replace the words in the last paragraph of the memo with the symbols shown in Table 90.1.

   a Select the word *love* and replace it with the heart symbol from the Symbol font list.

   b Select the word *golf* and replace it with the symbol of a swinging golfer from the Webdings font list.

   c Select the words *in the hole* and replace them with the dot-inside-a-circle symbol from the second row of the Wingdings 2 font list.

   d Select the word *trophy* and replace it with the trophy symbol from the Webdings font list.

4 Change the font size of the symbols in the memo to 20 points. *Hint: Do not change the size of the spaces or the punctuation marks surrounding the symbols.*

5 At the end of the memo, key the initials jam, the file name, and a reference to the enclosure.

6 Proofread the document and correct any errors. *Hint: With nonprinting characters displayed, check to make sure there is a single space (set in 11 pt font size) following the symbols that are not followed by a punctuation symbol.*

7 Save the document.

8 Click the Check button to upload the document for checking.

9 If errors are reported by the Online Lab, view the results document, correct the errors in the submitted document, save the document, and then click the Check Again button.

Figure 90.2 Memo Content for Document 90.2

TO: Kiwanis Club ¶ **FROM:** Dale Kingsly, Manager ¶ **DATE:** July 20, 2020 ¶ **SUBJECT:** Golf Play Day for Schools, August 31 ¶ Our schools are having many financial problems. Golf teams are being dropped from curriculums everywhere. Let's face it, you don't get a lot of people willing to pay to watch high school or college golf. And would you really want to try keeping a stadium-size audience quiet during play? ¶ We think that golf is important to keep in the curriculum. Golf teaches integrity, honesty, team and individual performance, hand-eye coordination, and estimations of distance and speed. Golf allows the players to have a good time at a game that may be enjoyed for a lifetime. ¶ Because we believe in the importance of having golf instruction available to the students in our community, we have decided to sponsor a Golf Play Day to help fund their golf programs. Details are provided in the enclosed flyer. Please encourage your members to participate. ¶ If you love to golf and help others learn to get the ball in the hole, join us and take a swing at winning the trophy!

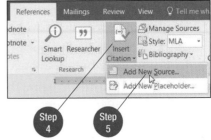

4. Click the Insert Citation button in the Citations & Bibliography group on the References tab.

5. Click *Add New Source* to display the Create Source dialog box.

6. Click the *Type of Source* option box arrow and then click the type of source at the drop-down list.

7. Key the necessary information in the *Bibliography Fields for MLA* section of the Create Source dialog box. If necessary, click the *Show All Bibliography Fields* check box to expand the Create Source dialog box and display more fields for the source.

8. Click OK to insert the citation in the document.

Once you have entered source information into the Create Source dialog box and inserted a citation in the document, add a page reference to the citation by completing the following steps:

1. Click the in-text citation in the document to select it.

2. Click the Citation Options arrow that displays at the right side of the selected citation and then click *Edit Citation* at the drop-down list.

3. Key the page reference in the *Pages* text box in the *Add* section of the Edit Citation dialog box.

4. Click OK.

5. To continue keying, click outside the citation.

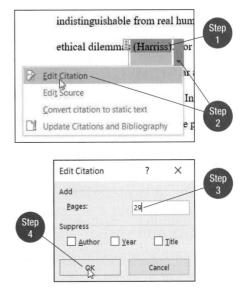

The complete citation should now appear in the body of the document, with no comma between the author's last name and the page reference. This is consistent with MLA style.

If, after inserting source information and creating a citation, you find that a change or correction needs to be made to the source, click the citation to select it, click the Citation Options arrow that displays at the right side of the selected citation, and then click *Edit Source* to display the Edit Source dialog box. The previously keyed source information displays and can be edited.

Table 90.1 Symbols Used in Document 90.2

Word(s) Replaced	Symbol Image	Font List	Character Code
love	♥	Symbol	169
golf	🏌	Webdings	137
in the hole	⊙	Wingdings 2	157
trophy	🏆	Webdings	56

Document 90.3 **Golf Play Day Flyer**

Read all instructions below before starting this document activity.

1 Navigate to the Document 90.3 launch page in the Online Lab and then click the Launch Activity button to open **Doc090.03** in the activity window.

2 Change the font size to 16 points.

3 Key the text shown in Figure 90.3. *Hint: Do not format the space following each bold colon in the bulleted list in bold. If Word formats the email address as a hyperlink, remove the formatting.*

4 Select the title (*Join us for a Benefit Play Day!*) and then change the font size to 24 points, the font color to Red (second option in the *Standard Colors* section), and make sure bold formatting is applied.

5 Position the insertion point immediately at the end of the paragraph that reads *And stay on the fairways and greens!*, display the Insert Picture dialog box, and then insert an image by completing the following steps:

   a Click the *Documents* folder.

   b Double-click the *Paradigm* folder, double-click the *Keyboarding* folder, and then double-click the *DocumentActivityFiles* folder.

   c Double-click **Doc090.03_InTheBunker.jpg**.

6 Format the image as follows:

   a Change the height of the image to 2 inches.

   b Change the position of the image to Position in Bottom Center with Square Text Wrapping (second column, third row in the *With Text Wrapping* section).

7 Position the insertion point at the beginning of the document, and using the Insert Picture dialog box, insert the **Doc090.03_GolfClubs.jpg** file located in the *DocumentActivityFiles* folder.

8 Format the golf clubs image as follows:

   a Change the height of the image to 1.8 inches.

   b Change the position of the image to Position in Top Left with Square Text Wrapping (first option in the *With Text Wrapping* section).

9 Position the insertion point on the blank line above the last paragraph and then insert a SmartArt graphic using the Vertical Box List style. Click in any of the three blue, rounded-rectangle shapes and then add another shape below so that there are four shapes total in the graphic.

10 Key Player 1, Player 2, Player 3, and Player 4 in the boxes in the SmartArt graphic as shown in Figure 90.4. You will format the graphic in the next step.

steps continue

Figure 83.4 Template Preview Window

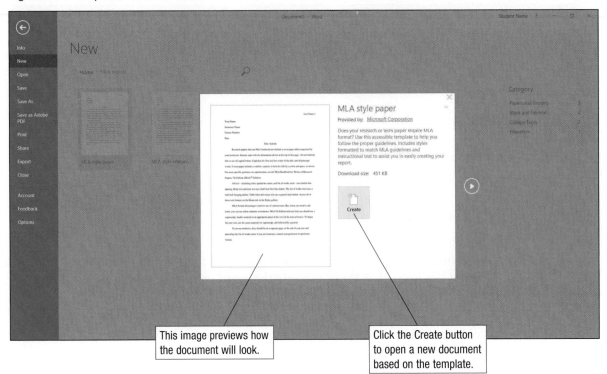

This image previews how the document will look.

Click the Create button to open a new document based on the template.

Inserting In-Text Citations according to MLA Style

In-text citations created in MLA style should include the author's last name and the page number where the information can be found in the source. The author's name might appear either in the sentence itself or in parentheses following the quote or paraphrase, but the page number(s), if included, should always appear in parentheses. A corresponding complete reference should also appear on the Works Cited page at the end of the manuscript or research paper.

Word automates the formatting process for inserting in-text citations and stores the source information so that you can insert it into a Works Cited page at the end of the report. To insert the first in-text citation for a source in a report using MLA (Seventh Edition) style, complete the following steps:

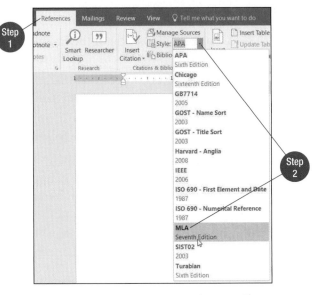

1. Click the References tab.
2. Click the *Style* option box arrow and then click *MLA* at the drop-down list.
3. Position the insertion point at the place in the report where you want the citation to appear. For example, click just before the period at the end of the sentence that is being credited.

steps continue

11 Format the SmartArt graphic as follows:

    a Use the Change Colors button to change the colors in the graphic to Colored Outline - Accent 6 (first option in the *Accent 6* section).

    b Select the entire SmartArt graphic (make sure the entire graphic is selected rather than an individual part within the graphic) and then format the height of the graphic to 2 inches and the width to 6.5 inches.

12 Proofread the document and correct any errors.

13 Save the document.

14 Click the Submit button to upload the document for instructor review.

Figure 90.3 Flyer Content for Document 90.3

Join us for a Benefit Play Day!

- **Where:** Aldeen Golf Course
- **When:** Monday, August 31, 2020
- **Sign In:** Beginning at 9:15 a.m.
- **Tee Off:** 10 a.m.
- **Meal:** Steak, baked potato, salad, dessert
- **Cost:** $60 per player or $200 per foursome
- **Benefit:** Area schools' golf teams

Bring your clubs for a day of golf and fun and an opportunity to support golf teams at our area schools! ¶ Sign up by August 17 either by calling Andy in the Pro Shop at 555-6916 or by sending an email including the names of your team members to aldeengolfclub@ppi-edu.net. ¶¶ And try to stay on the fairways and greens!

Figure 83.2 New Backstage Area

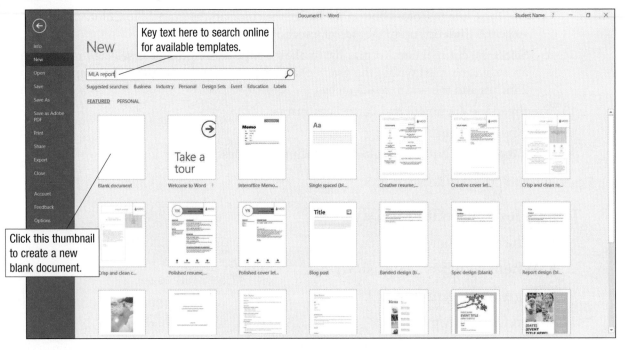

Figure 83.3 Template Search Results

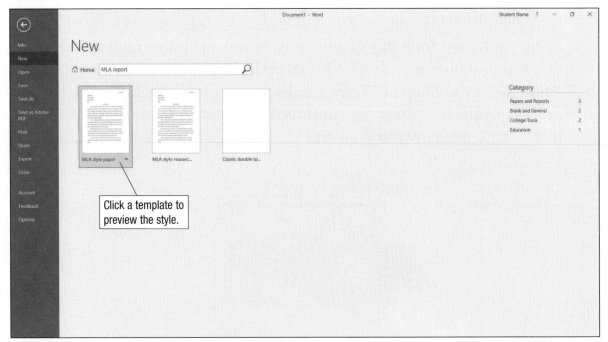

Figure 90.4 Completed Golf Play Day Flyer for Document 90.3

Join us for a Benefit Play Day!

- **Where:** Aldeen Golf Course
- **When:** Monday, August 31, 2020
- **Sign In:** Beginning at 9:15 a.m.
- **Tee Off:** 10 a.m.
- **Meal:** Steak, baked potato, salad, dessert
- **Cost:** $60 per player or $200 per foursome
- **Benefit:** Area schools' golf teams

Bring your clubs for a day of golf and fun and an opportunity to support golf teams at our area schools!

Sign up by August 17 either by calling Andy in the Pro Shop at 555-6916 or by sending an email including the names of your team members to aldeengolfclub@ppi-edu.net.

Player 1

Player 2

Player 3

Player 4

And try to stay on the fairways and greens!

Ending the Session

The Online Lab automatically saved the work you completed for this session. You may continue with the next session or exit the Online Lab and continue later.

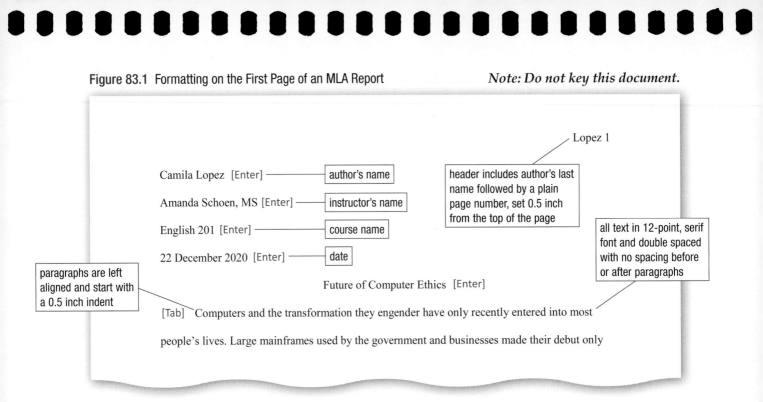

Figure 83.1 Formatting on the First Page of an MLA Report   *Note: Do not key this document.*

Using a Word Template

A template is a type of Word file that is used to create documents with consistent formatting. Template files have the extension *.dotx*. However, when you double-click a template file, it opens a new document file with the extension *.docx*. A file created from a template contains all of the formatting and text present in the original template file.

Word provides many preformatted templates. These files can be accessed by clicking the File tab and then clicking *New*. This displays the New backstage area, shown in Figure 83.2. Note the Blank document template that displays in the upper left corner.

Key *MLA report* in the search box, as shown in Figure 83.2, and then press Enter to search online for available MLA style templates. When the search results are displayed, as shown in Figure 83.3, click the *MLA style research paper* thumbnail to see a preview of the template. Note that, because these are online templates, your search results may vary from what you see in the figures.

Figure 83.4 shows the template preview window in the New backstage area. When it first opens, the template preview window displays the first page of the document. Click the Create button to open a new document based on the selected template.

Unit 19 Business Publications

Formatting in MLA Style

In this session, you will create reports according to the style and formatting guidelines in the *Modern Language Association (MLA) Handbook.* Table 83.1 lists some of the key aspects of the MLA style, and Figure 83.1 shows how they look when applied to a document.

Table 83.1 MLA Formatting Guidelines for Reports

Paper Element	Formatting Guidelines
paragraph alignment	left aligned, paragraphs begin with 0.5-inch indent
font	12-point serif font, such as Cambria, Constantia, Times New Roman, or Palatino Linotype
margins	1-inch top, bottom, left, and right margins (default)
line spacing	2.0 line spacing (with 0 points of spacing before and after paragraphs) throughout document, including Works Cited page
title page	not used; instead, the information is included on the first page of the report
first page of report	includes author's name, instructor's name, course name, and date, each on one line and flush left
report title	begins one hard return after the date, centered in plain text (no bold or italic formatting) with the first letter of each major word capitalized; followed by one hard return
header/page numbers	header set 0.5 inch from the top of the document and at the right margin and includes the writer's last name followed by one space and the page number (digits only); numbering the first page may be optional, depending on guidelines provided by the person requesting the manuscript or research paper
side headings	not required by the MLA style, but may be used to increase the document's readability; when included, important to use consistent formatting throughout the document
long quotations	quotes longer than four lines introduced with a colon and indented 0.5 inch from the left margin

Session 91

Changing Fonts in Business Publications

Session Objectives

- Change the typeface and type style
- Change the type size
- Key a letter and an agreement
- Compose a meeting notice
- Efficiently produce documents in mailable form

Getting Started

Exercise 91.1 If you are continuing immediately from Session 90, you can skip the Exercise 91.1 warm-up drill. However, if you exited the Online Lab at the end of Session 90, warm up by completing Exercise 91.1.

Exercise 91.2 Begin your session work by completing Exercise 91.2, a timed short drill, in the Online Lab.

Assessing Your Speed and Accuracy

Complete Timing 91.1 in the Online Lab using the timing text on the next page. At the end of the timing, the Online Lab will display your WPM rate and any errors. Results will be saved in your Timings Performance report. If you have been surpassing the speed and accuracy goals identified in the Online Lab, set slightly more challenging goals and strive to exceed them. *Note: With this session, the default WPM goal for 5-minute timings has been increased by 5 WPM in the Online Lab. However, your instructor may have customized this goal.*

Complete one 5-minute timing on the timing text below.

5-Minute Timing

Timing 83.3

There are many new and different materials and techniques being used for model railroad scenery. In a practical sense, the only function of a model railroad background is to provide a realistic setting for the model trains to run through. And usually, the better the background, the more believable the trains become. The drama of a streamliner rolling across the country at high speed or the fascinating deliberation of a peddler freight slowly switching onto a weed-grown branch line cannot be duplicated with scenery. An accurately detailed train running through nice scenery makes for a model of reality that is not often achieved in other kinds of modeling.

Scenery does other things for a model railroad, too. By covering the necessary wood structure work, scenery keeps the viewers from looking below track level to the underpinnings and other necessary detail. The background brings the viewer's eye to the top of the layout where the action is. Scenery also protects the rolling stock by keeping it up off the floor.

For many folks, scenery building is the part of model railroading they like best. For others, it is a hobby within the hobby that provides an outlet for their creative talents. However, background building need not be an artistic endeavor. If you can paint a boxcar, build a kit, or follow a schedule, you can build very believable scenery.

Building good scenery is the least expensive part of making a model railroad. A new system gaining wide use is one that uses water-soluble materials. Everything mixes together, cleanup is easy, and tools and brushes last for a long time. Because water is the common mixer, building goes as fast as you can work, without having to wait for one layer or texture to dry before applying the next. You can start an area before eating your evening meal and finish the scene before retiring for the night.

**Timing
91.1**

During an earlier time in history, many houses had a very unusual and unique feature that was not actually a physical portion of the house. This unique creation was known as the gazebo. The homeowners preferred to place the structure in a restful place, sometimes in an apple orchard or among the flowers in a garden. The site of the gazebo was usually one that was isolated from a disturbing view and any annoying sounds or noises. The purpose of erecting the gazebo was to provide a haven of rest for people who wished to relax and meditate.

The gazebo was a quiet and restful place. The building was very often painted a darker color to help it blend into the surrounding landscape or environment. The openings were all screened to keep out any annoying pests and insects. In addition to being screened, all window openings had some kind of window coverings, commonly sturdy draperies that could be raised or lowered to adjust lighting. Those draperies could also be used to compensate for any change in weather conditions that might arise. The beautiful summer place was normally furnished in a simple and tasteful manner. Because the gazebo was a spacious place, an ample amount of furnishings could be arranged within one area. Some comfortable chairs, a sofa, and usually a table or two would comprise the simple furnishings. The gazebo was a nice room in which a person could think quietly, have afternoon tea, read, or even take a lengthy nap. As a haven of rest, a gazebo provided a quiet, relaxing retreat from a daily routine of hectic and busy living.

As technology rapidly progressed and the pace of everyday living increased at a faster rate, the gazebo soon slipped into the past and was forgotten. For some unknown reason, many people just didn't have or want to take the time to relax.

People have begun to realize that there is obviously a lack of restful interludes in their lives. It is quite possible for an inventive person to construct a gazebo patterned after earlier models. Larger firms have even assembled some kits that contain the necessary parts and materials for constructing a gazebo. A main problem is to select a quiet and restful site on which to erect the gazebo.

Session 83

Preparing Reports in MLA Style

Session Objectives

- Format a report according to MLA style
- Use a Word template
- Insert in-text citations
- Create a Works Cited page
- Compose a manuscript
- Efficiently produce documents in mailable form

Getting Started

Exercise 83.1 If you are continuing immediately from Session 82, you may skip the Exercise 83.1 warm-up drill. However, if you exited the Online Lab at the end of Session 82, warm up by completing Exercise 83.1.

Exercise 83.2 Begin your session work by completing Exercise 83.2, a timed short drill, in the Online Lab.

Assessing Your Speed and Accuracy

Complete Timings 83.1 through 83.3 in the Online Lab. At the end of each timing, the Online Lab will display your WPM rate and any errors. Results will be saved in your Timings Performance report. If you have been surpassing the speed and accuracy goals identified in the Online Lab, set slightly more challenging personal goals and strive to exceed them.

Complete two 1-minute timings on the timing text below. If you meet or exceed both speed and accuracy goals for Timing 83.1, push for greater speed on Timing 83.2.

1-Minute Timings

Timings 83.1–83.2 An old pocket watch is an object of beauty. Many people collect quality antique watches because they contain some of the finest artistic engraving that was so common years ago. The better watches were made of gold or silver and had ornate and intricate symbols, scenes, or an initial or two engraved on the exterior. A watch fob was also common. It was attached to the watch chain and represented companies, groups, and other popular renderings of that time. Many watches, chains, and fobs are priceless family possessions today.

Understanding Fonts

A font consists of three parts: typeface, type style, and type size. A typeface (sometimes referred to as a *font face*) is a set of characters with a common design and shape. Typefaces may be decorative, blocked, or plain. Typefaces are either *monospaced* or *proportional*. A monospaced typeface allots the same amount of horizontal space for each character. Courier and Consolas are examples of monospaced typefaces. A proportional typeface allots a varying amount of space for each character, based on the width of the character. For example, a lowercase *i* would be allotted less space than an uppercase *M*. Calibri and Times New Roman are examples of proportional typefaces.

Typefaces are also divided into two other categories: *serif* and *sans serif*. A serif is a small line at the end of a character stroke. Traditionally, a serif typeface is used with documents that contain a lot of text because the serifs help move the reader's eyes across the page. A sans serif typeface does not have serifs (*sans* is French for *without*). Sans serif typefaces are commonly used for headlines and other shorter pieces of text. The text you are reading now is in a serif typeface, whereas the "Understanding Fonts" heading above is in a sans serif typeface. Table 91.1 lists some common serif and sans serif typefaces.

Table 91.1 Examples of Serif and Sans Serif Typefaces at 10.5 Points

Serif Typefaces	Sans Serif Typefaces
Bookman Old Style	Arial
Cambria	Calibri
Constantia	Candara
Courier New	Consolas
Garamond	Corbel
Palatino Linotype	Helvetica
Times New Roman	Tahoma

Figure 82.3 Sources Content for Document 82.2—continued

Authors: Martin Ishmael

Web Page Title: Value RAM for 2020

Name of Website: My Peripherals Are Just Fine

Accessed Date: May 26, 2020

Address: http://ppi-edu.net/MyInternalWorks/ValueRAM

Reinforcing Writing Skills

An outline is a valuable tool when preparing documents such as manuscripts. In the last session, you were given an example of how to format an outline. The next step is to apply what you have learned regarding outline content and formatting. For the Document 82.3 activity, you will prepare an outline for the information collected as part of the Document 81.4 activity. Keep in mind that you will eventually prepare a manuscript from this outline.

In the "Reinforcing Writing Skills" section of Session 81, eight steps were presented for preparing a manuscript. The first three steps were used to complete the Document 81.4 activity, which included identifying a topic, researching the topic, and taking notes. Step 4 in the process is to prepare an outline to be used in composing a manuscript. You will complete this step in the following document activity.

Document
82.3

Preparing an Outline

Read all instructions below before starting this document activity.

1 Navigate to the Document 82.3 launch page in the Online Lab and then click the Launch Activity button to open **Doc082.03** in the activity window.

2 Turn off the automatic numbered lists feature.

3 Change the default paragraph formatting for this document to single spacing with no spacing after paragraphs.

4 Set a right tab at 0.5 inch and set left tabs as needed (0.75 inch, 1.0 inch, and 1.25 inches).

5 Key the outline for your manuscript. Include the title and at least three levels of headings.

6 Proofread the document and correct any errors.

7 Save the document.

8 Click the Submit button to upload the document for instructor review.

Ending the Session

The Online Lab automatically saved the work you completed for this session. You may continue with the next session or exit the Online Lab and continue later.

Changing the Typeface and Type Style

In most instances so far in this book, the text in the document activities has been set in the default typeface of Calibri and the default type size of 11 points. Changing the typeface is a quick and easy task that can greatly improve the appearance and/or readability of a document.

To change the typeface, select the text and then click the *Font* option box arrow in the Font group on the Home tab, shown in Figure 91.1. Clicking the *Font* option box arrow will display a drop-down gallery of font options. Click a font name in this gallery to apply the typeface. If you change the typeface prior to keying any text in the document, the default font for the current document will change to the selected typeface.

You already have experience applying bold, italic, and underline formatting to text. These formatting options are examples of type styles. The buttons for applying these type styles are located in the bottom row of the Font group on the Home tab (see Figure 91.1). The standard style of a typeface is referred to as *regular*. (In other words, regular type is not bold, italic, or underlined.)

Changing the Type Size

Type size is measured vertically in units called *points*. A point is approximately $\frac{1}{72}$ of an inch, so a capital letter that is set in 72-point font is 1 inch tall. The greater the point size, the larger the characters. Figure 91.2 shows examples of different sizes of the same typeface (Calibri).

To change the font size, click the *Font Size* option box arrow and then click a point size in the drop-down gallery. Alternatively, click the Increase Font Size button or the Decrease Font Size button (see Figure 91.1). Clear formatting from selected text by clicking the Clear All Formatting button.

In the following document activities, you will practice keying and formatting fonts in a letter, a financial agreement, and a meeting notice. In each activity, you will begin by changing both the typeface and type size of the font used in the document.

Figure 91.1 Font Group on the Home Tab

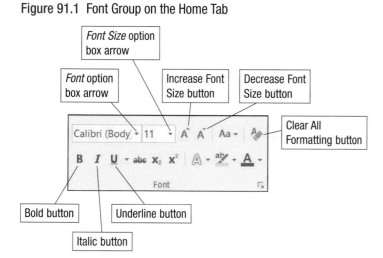

Font Size option box arrow

Font option box arrow

Increase Font Size button

Decrease Font Size button

Clear All Formatting button

Bold button

Underline button

Italic button

Figure 91.2 Font Size Examples

8-point Calibri

12-point Calibri

18-point Calibri

Enter twice between the entries. *Note: Do not apply italic formatting to the punctuation or space following an italic title. Also, do not format the web addresses as hyperlinks.*

5 Proofread the document and correct any errors.

6 Save the document.

7 Click the Check button to upload the document for checking.

8 If errors are reported by the Online Lab, view the results document, correct the errors in the submitted document, save the document, and then click the Check Again button.

Figure 82.3 Source Content for Document 82.2

Books

Authors: Jon Gordon, Karen Lankisch, Nancy Muir, Denise Seguin, Anita Verno

Title: Our Digital World: Introduction to Computing, 4th ed.

City of Publication: St. Paul

Publisher: Paradigm Publishing, Inc.

Year: 2017

Author: Sare Petee

Title: The Wonder of a Computer

City of Publication: St. Paul

Publisher: Paradigm Publishing, Inc.

Year: 2020

Author: Anne-Luise S. Pedersen

Title: My Computer Can Take Your Computer

City of Publication: New York

Publisher: Vorgod Press

Year: 2019

Web Pages

Authors: Margit Skov

Web Page Title: Build for the Future

Name of Website: Make It Look Easy

Published Date: May 2, 2020

Address: http://ppi-edu.net/MakeItLookEasy/2020/05/02/

---

continues

Document **Business Letter with Custom Font**
91.1
Read all instructions below before starting this document activity.

1 Navigate to the Document 91.1 launch page in the Online Lab and then click the Launch Activity button to open **Doc091.01** in the activity window.

2 Change the font to 12-point Bookman Old Style by completing the following steps:

   a Click the *Font* option box arrow in the Font group on the Home tab, scroll down the drop-down gallery, and then click *Cambria*.

   b Click the *Font Size* option box arrow in the Font group on the Home tab and then click *12* at the drop-down gallery.

3 Key the letter shown in Figure 91.3 in the block-style format. The document contains a letterhead. If necessary, reference the format for a block-style business letter presented in Figure 67.1.

   a Key July 22, 2020 as the letter's date.

   b Key the reference initials tvp and the file name below the title line. Also include a reference to the enclosure that will be sent with the letter.

4 Proofread the document and correct any errors.

5 Save the document.

6 Click the Check button to upload the document for checking.

7 If errors are reported by the Online Lab, view the results document, correct the errors in the submitted document, save the document, and then click the Check Again button.

Figure 91.3 Block-Style Business Letter Content for Document 91.1

Theodore Millingston, MD ¶ Oregon View Medical Clinic ¶ 1227 South Hamilton ¶ St. Paul, MN 55108 ¶ Dear Dr. Millingston: ¶ Randolph M. Raye has retained the law firm of Moyer & Associates for injuries received in an automobile accident on March 3, 2020. ¶ Please provide us with medical information that you have on this patient regarding the accident. We would like copies of any doctors' or nurses' notes, lab reports, and x-ray results. Please include only records concerning injuries incurred at the time of the accident. ¶ We would also like an itemized statement for all medical charges to date for this injury. ¶ A signed release form from our client is enclosed. Thank you for your cooperation. ¶ Sincerely yours, ¶ Danielle A. Kentfield ¶ Paralegal

- List bibliography entries alphabetically, according to the author's last name.
- End each entry with a period and press Enter twice before beginning the next entry.

Table 82.4 Bibliography Citations according to Chicago Style

Books

Author Last Name, Author First Name. *Book Title.* City of Publication: Publisher, Year.

Example of single-author book (author's name is reversed, beginning with surname followed by a comma):

> Veyette, Patricia J. *Life with Me.* Watseka: Forrest Press, 2019.

Example of multiple-author book (only first author's name is reversed):

> Veyette, Patricia J. and James P. Forrest. *The Wonderful Life of Daisies.* Watseka: Forrest Press, 2019.

Articles from Periodicals (journals, magazines, newspapers, etc.)

Author Last Name, Author First Name. "Article Title." *Name of Publication.* Issue Date.

Example of single-author article:

> Jensen, Jon. "How to Paint a Room." *The Handy Homeowner.* July 2020.

Web Pages

Author Last Name, Author First Name. "Web Page Title." *Name of Website.* Published, Last modified, and/or Accessed Date. http://www.address.

Example:

> Greene, Jill. "Glass Half Full." *The Processing of Attitude.* Published December 19, 2019. http://ppi-edu.net/TheProcessingofAttitude.

 Success Tip

Not all interpretations of the style manuals are the same. Remember to follow the specific directions from your workplace or instructor carefully.

Document 82.2 Bibliography in Chicago Style

Read all instructions below before starting this document activity.

1. Navigate to the Document 82.2 launch page in the Online Lab, and then click the Launch Activity button to open **Doc082.02** in the activity window.

2. Change the default formatting for the document by completing the following steps:

    a. Change the font to 12-point Bookman Old Style, and set it as the default for this document only.

    b. Change the default paragraph spacing for this document to single spacing with no spacing after paragraphs and a hanging indent at 0.5 inch.

3. Key the title of the document by completing the following steps:

    a. Change the paragraph alignment to center alignment, turn on bold formatting, key BIBLIOGRAPHY, and then turn off bold formatting.

    b. Press Enter twice and then change the paragraph alignment to left aligned.

4. Key the bibliography using the content shown in Figure 82.3. Format the references according to the style shown in Table 82.4 and present the sources in the correct order. Press

steps continue

Document Financial Agreement with Custom Font and Formatting

91.2 Read all instructions below before starting this document activity.

1 Navigate to the Document 91.2 launch page in the Online Lab and then click the Launch Activity button to open **Doc091.02** in the activity window.

2 Change the font to 12-point Garamond.

3 Key the title of the document by completing the following steps:

   a Press Ctrl + E to change the paragraph alignment to center alignment, press Ctrl + B to turn on bold formatting, and then key FINANCIAL AGREEMENT.

   b Press Ctrl + B to turn off bold formatting, press Enter, press Ctrl + L to change the paragraph alignment back to left alignment, and then press Enter again.

4 Key the text shown in Figure 91.4. Allow Word to automatically format the numbered list and lettered sublist. *Note: The lists in Figure 91.4 are not formatted correctly. If Word does not automatically format the numbered list, turn on the automatic numbered list feature by displaying the AutoCorrect dialog box and inserting a check mark in the* **Automatic numbered lists** *check box.*

   a Key the text for the first three numbered items and then press Enter.

   b To begin the lettered sublist list, click the Increase Indent button in the Paragraph group. Key the three items in the lettered sublist, pressing Enter after each item.

   c Click the Decrease Indent button in the Paragraph group and then key the last numbered item.

   d Press Enter twice to end the numbered list.

   e Key the last paragraph of the agreement and then press Enter twice.

5 Key SIGNATURE, press the spacebar, key 25 underscores, press the spacebar, key DATE, press the spacebar, and then key 25 underscores. *Hint: To key an underscore, press and hold down the Shift key and then press the Hyphen key.*

6 Change the format of the lettered sublist in the document from letters followed by periods to letters followed by close parentheses by completing the following steps:

   a Position the insertion point in the lettered sublist.

   b Click the Numbering button arrow in the Paragraph group on the Home tab.

   c In the *Numbering Library* section, click the option that shows *a)*, *b)*, and *c)* formatting.

7 Proofread the document and correct any errors.

8 Save the document.

9 Click the Check button to upload the document for checking.

10 If errors are reported by the Online Lab, view the results document, correct the errors in the submitted document, save the document, and then click the Check Again button.

Figure 82.1 Manuscript Content for Document 82.1—continued

alternating current (AC) provided from your wall outlet to lower voltages in the form of direct current (DC). A laptop computer also contains a battery that is charged when you plug the cable into your wall outlet.

Your operating system is capable of sending a signal to the power supply to instruct it to sleep or hibernate. This action puts your computer into a lower power mode or no-power mode without losing your current, unsaved work. To take some computers out of sleep or hibernation mode, you can move the mouse or press any key. For most systems, however, you have to briefly press the power button.

Insert Footnote 3

Figure 82.2 Footnotes Content for Document 82.1

Footnote 1: Jon Gordon et al., *Our Digital World: Introduction to Computing*, 4th ed. (St. Paul: Paradigm Publishing, Inc., 2017), 66-68.

Footnote 2: Reprinted with permission of the publisher. Sare Petee, *The Wonder of a Computer* (St. Paul: Paradigm Publishing, Inc., 2018), 4.

Footnote 3: Margit Skov, "I Make It Look Easy," *Tower of Power*, November 14, 2019, http://ppi-edu.net/IMakeItLookEasy/2019/11/14/.

Preparing a Bibliography

A bibliography page is a formal listing of the sources you used to create your research paper. This list includes sources from which you quoted or paraphrased material as well as other sources you simply consulted for more information. The bibliography is placed on a separate page at the end of the research paper and may be titled *BIBLIOGRAPHY*, *REFERENCES*, or *WORKS CITED*.

The format for entries in a bibliography may vary slightly from one style manual to another. Organizations, educational institutions, or instructors may require a specific format. Always consult your employer or instructor for the preferred style to follow. Table 82.4 provides examples of bibliography references formatted according to *The Chicago Manual of Style*.

When setting up a bibliography page for documents in this unit, use the following guidelines:

- Use the default margins in Word.
- Use the same font as the body of the research paper.
- Use single spacing within entries, one blank line between entries, and no spacing before or after paragraphs.
- Set a 0.5-inch hanging indent so that the second and subsequent lines of each bibliography entry will be indented from the left margin.
- Center and key the title *BIBLIOGRAPHY* in bold formatting at the top of the page.
- Begin each entry at the left margin.
- Use one space after punctuation marks.
- Make sure URLs break before a punctuation mark (except http://) so that the reader does not interpret the URL as ending before it should. If necessary, press Shift + Enter before typing the URL to ensure the entire URL displays on one line.

Figure 91.4 Agreement Content for Document 91.2

We are committed to providing you with the best possible care. If you have medical insurance, we are anxious to help you receive your maximum allowable benefits. In order to achieve these goals, we need your assistance and your understanding of our payment policy.

1. Payment for services is due at the time of your visit unless payment arrangements have been made in advance with our staff. We accept cash, check, or credit cards.

2. Returned checks and balances older than 30 days may be subject to additional collection fees and interest charges of 2 percent per month.

3. We will gladly discuss your proposed treatment and answer any questions relating to your insurance. You must realize, however, the following:

   a. Your insurance is a contract between you, your employer, and the insurance company. We are not a party to that contract.

   b. Our fees are generally considered to fall within the acceptable range by most companies, and therefore they are covered up to the maximum allowance determined by each carrier.

   c. Not all services are covered benefits in all contracts. Some insurance companies arbitrarily select certain services they will not cover.

4. Our relationship is with you, not your insurance company. While filing of insurance claims is a courtesy that we extend to our patients, all charges are your responsibility from the date the services are rendered.

If you have any questions about the above information or any uncertainty regarding insurance coverage, please contact us.

Document 91.3 Meeting Notice with Custom Font and Formatting

Read all instructions below before starting this document activity.

1 Navigate to the Document 91.3 launch page in the Online Lab and then click the Launch Activity button to open **Doc091.03** in the activity window.

2 Change the font to 14-point Arial Black.

3 Key the text shown in Figure 91.5. In the fourth line, make sure to set the word *to* in lowercase letters. *Note: Press Enter once at the end of each line except for the last line.*

steps continue

Figure 82.1 Research Paper Content for Document 82.1—continued

a container where the various working pieces of your computer slot into one compact package. Circuits on the motherboard connect the various components contained on it.

Central Processing Unit (CPU). The central processing unit (CPU), which is a microprocessor (also called by the shorter terms *processor* or *core*), sits on the motherboard. The CPU processes a user's requests, such as opening documents or formatting text. A CPU is a thin wafer or "chip" made up of a semiconducting material, such as silicon. It contains an integrated circuit made up of a combination of miniaturized components and drives the system's computing capabilities. (Note that the term *central processing unit* is sometimes, albeit incorrectly, used to refer to the case that contains the processor and everything else within this case.) *Insert Footnote 2*

Memory. The motherboard also holds different types of memory. Read-only memory (ROM) is the permanent, or nonvolatile, memory of a computer hardwired into a chip. In a PC, the read-only memory stores the BIOS, which stands for *basic input/output system*. During the boot-up sequence, the BIOS checks devices such as your memory, monitor, keyboard, and disc drives to ensure they are working properly and to start them up. It also directs the hard drive to boot up and load the operating system (OS) to memory.

Random access memory (RAM) chips are slotted into the motherboard and are used to store programs and data while the computer is in use. This memory is temporary, or volatile. Each memory location in RAM can be accessed in any order, which speeds up processing. (This differs from storage devices, which store and retrieve data one file at a time.)

Expansion Cards. While some computers have built-in sound or graphics cards, others include them as expansion cards. These cards enable input and output of sound or images. Your laptop computer can also accommodate PC cards that slot into a built-in card reader to provide other kinds of functionality such as additional memory or wireless networking capabilities.

Power Supply

All computing devices require power to work, whether that power comes by plugging a cord into a wall outlet, operating off a charged battery, or using power from solar cells. A power supply in a desktop or laptop computer is located where the power cord is inserted into the system unit. This metal box housed in the CPU contains the connection for the power cord and a cooling fan to keep the connection from overheating. The power supply switches

continues

Figure 91.5 Notice Content for Document 91.3

BEEBE ELEMENTARY SCHOOL
PARENTS MEETING
THURSDAY, NOVEMBER 19, 2020
7:00 to 8:30 P.M.
REFRESHMENTS WILL BE SERVED!

4   Select all of the text in the document and then change the paragraph alignment to center alignment.

5   Vertically center the text on the page. *Hint: Change the setting at the Page Setup dialog box with the Layout tab selected. If necessary, review the instructions for vertically centering text in Session 66.*

6   Proofread the document and correct any errors.

7   Save the document.

8   Click the Check button to upload the document for checking.

9   If errors are reported by the Online Lab, view the results document, correct the errors in the submitted document, save the document, and then click the Check Again button.

Reinforcing Writing Skills

Meeting notices need to be complete, accurate, and easily readable to be useful and effective. Typically, meeting notices are prepared using a sans serif typeface and a type size large enough to be read from a distance. As in the Document 91.3 activity, text in a meeting notice is typically centered both horizontally and vertically on the page.

In the following document activity, practice developing and producing a meeting notice for an upcoming event you are promoting or planning to attend.

Document 91.4

Composing a Meeting Notice

Read all instructions below before starting this document activity.

1   Navigate to the Document 91.4 launch page in the Online Lab and then click the Launch Activity button to open **Doc091.04** in the activity window.

2   Select an appropriate typeface, type style, and type size for the meeting notice and apply that font to the document.

3   Key the content of the meeting notice.

4   Align the text so that it is centered horizontally and vertically on the page.

5   Proofread and correct any errors.

6   Save the document.

7   Click the Submit button to upload the document for instructor review.

Ending the Session

The Online Lab automatically saved the work you completed for this session. You may continue with the next session or exit the Online Lab and continue later.

c When keying paragraph headings, turn on bold formatting *after* pressing the Tab key. Format the period at the end of the indented headings in bold, but do not format the space following the period in bold.

d When keying an italic term, do not format the space following the term in italic. If the italic term consists of multiple words, format the space between the words in italic. Do not insert the footnote reference numbers as you key the text. You will do that in the next step.

5 Key the footnotes shown in Figure 82.2, placing the reference numbers in the document as noted in Figure 82.1 and considering the following as you key:

a When inserting a footnote in the document, position the insertion point directly after the end-of-sentence punctuation, before the space following the sentence.

b After keying the footnote content, do not press Enter.

c If a footnote contains a web address, do not allow Word to format it as a hyperlink.

d Within a footnote reference, do not format the punctuation or space after a publication title in italic.

6 Format the page numbers in the document by completing the following steps:

a Double-click in the bottom margin of the first page to display the footer pane.

b Click the *Different First Page* check box in the Options group on the Header & Footer Tools Design tab to insert a check mark.

c Click the Page Number button in the Header & Footer group, point to *Bottom of Page*, and then click *Plain Number 2*.

d Move the insertion point to the header pane on the second page.

e Click the Page Number button in the Header & Footer group, point to *Top of Page*, and then click *Plain Number 3*.

f Double-click in the body of the document to make it active.

7 Format the *Power Supply* heading so that it stays with the following paragraph by inserting a check mark in the *Keep with next* option at the Paragraph dialog box with the Line and Page Breaks tab selected.

8 Proofread the document and correct any errors.

9 Save the document.

10 Click the Check button to upload the document for checking.

11 If errors are reported by the Online Lab, view the results document, correct the errors in the submitted document, save the document, and then click the Check Again button.

Figure 82.1 Research Paper Content for Document 82.1

Compare a typical desktop and laptop computer and you'll find that, although they may be packaged differently, they each contain similar hardware that processes data, provides battery power, offers ports for making connections with peripheral devices and networks, and stores data.

What's Contained on the Motherboard?

Insert Footnote 1

If you were to open up a PC tower, you'd see that the motherboard is the primary circuit board on the computer. It holds the central processing unit, BIOS, memory, and other components. The motherboard is really just

continues

Creating Newsletter Columns

Session Objectives

- Insert a section break
- Format text into multiple columns
- Add vertical lines between columns
- Modify fonts
- Balance columns
- Efficiently produce documents in mailable form

Getting Started

Exercise 92.1 If you are continuing immediately from Session 91, you can skip the Exercise 92.1 warm-up drill. However, if you exited the Online Lab at the end of Session 91, warm up by completing Exercise 92.1.

Exercise 92.2 Begin your session work by completing Exercise 92.2, a timed short drill, in the Online Lab.

Assessing Your Speed and Accuracy

Complete Timing 92.1 in the Online Lab using the timing text on the next page. At the end of the timing, the Online Lab will display your WPM rate and any errors. Results will be saved in your Timings Performance report. If you have been surpassing the speed and accuracy goals identified in the Online Lab, set slightly more challenging goals and strive to exceed them.

⧓ Reinforcing Word Skills

The following document activity will require you to apply some previously learned Word skills. This section will review some of those skills.

One way to control where text ends on a page is with the Widow/Orphan control feature, which prevents the first or last line of a paragraph from being left on a page by itself. Word treats headings as single-line paragraphs; therefore, they are not affected by Widow/Orphan control. The most logical placement of a heading is on the same page as the paragraph that follows it. Sometimes, however, Word will end a page immediately after a heading. To prevent a heading from being separated from the paragraph that follows it, the heading can be formatted to force Word to keep it with the following text. Most often, this will move the heading to the following page.

To format a heading so it stays with the paragraph that follows it, complete the following steps:

1 Click anywhere within the heading.

2 Click the Paragraph group dialog box launcher on the Home tab.

3 Click the Line and Page Breaks tab.

4 Click the *Keep with next* check box in the *Pagination* section to insert a check mark.

5 Click OK to apply the setting and close the dialog box.

Practice controlling the pagination of a document in the following document activity.

Document 82.1 **Research Paper with Footnotes**

Read all instructions below before starting this document activity.

1 Navigate to the Document 82.1 launch page in the Online Lab and then click the Launch Activity button to open **Doc082.01** in the activity window.

2 Format the document as follows:

a At the Paragraph dialog box with the Indents and Spacing tab selected, change the line spacing to double spacing with no spacing after each paragraph. Make this setting the default setting for this document only.

b At the Paragraph dialog box with the Line and Page Breaks tab selected, confirm that the Widow/Orphan control feature is active. ***Hint: A check mark should display in the*** **Widow/Orphan control** ***check box.***

c At the Font dialog box, change the font to 12-point Bookman Old Style and then set it as the default for this document only.

3 Key the main heading of the document by completing the following steps:

a Change the paragraph alignment to center alignment, turn on bold formatting, key THE PARTS THAT MAKE UP YOUR COMPUTER, and then turn off bold formatting.

b Press Enter and then change the paragraph alignment to left alignment.

4 Key the text in Figure 82.1. Consider the following as you key the document:

a Press Tab at the start of each paragraph.

b Turn off bold formatting *before* pressing Enter after keying the side headings.

steps continue

Timing 92.1

What a wonderful day when a bicyclist can approach the challenge of riding uphill with a smile instead of a grimace. To help you get there, you need to focus on two components of climbing: agility and sustainable power at lactate threshold.

Lactate threshold (LT) is the intensity at which lactate levels in the blood start to rise quickly. You can improve your stamina by climbing at or just below your current lactate threshold. For example, you might do four 12-minute hill repeats--you're going hard, but could speed up if you had to--separated by six minutes of easy spinning. Bicyclists have been doing workouts like this for several decades.

The negative side to focusing solely on this type of training, however, is that you will develop fitness that only partially matches the real-world challenges of climbing. You also have to develop what some cycling experts call agility--the ability to handle changes in pace and power output.

Part of successful climbing is learning when to use your power and when to recover. When you are headed uphill, anything from changes in pitch to the distractions of other riders can cause your power and cadence to fluctuate more than they would during a structured workout. You may need to accelerate and push harder to keep up or stand up and get out of the saddle. If you are trying to ride up a hill as quickly as possible, you need to be producing more power on steep sections and a little less on flatter sections, without any wild fluctuations.

The more time you spend climbing, the faster you will develop agility. However, if you live in a flat area or ride mostly on the trainer, then you will need to add or increase a wider variety of power and cadence levels into your threshold workouts.

Remember that the extra effort in training is well worthwhile. The truth about hills is that the scenery is worth the suffering you endure. At the end of the ride, you have beautiful memories of the landscape and a great workout.

To create a footnote in Word, complete the following steps:

1 Position the insertion point in the text at the end of the content that is to be referenced; for example, after a period at the end of paraphrased text or immediately after the quotation mark at the end of a quote.

2 Click the References tab.

3 Click the Insert Footnote button in the Footnotes group. A superscript number is inserted in the document and a separator line appears at the bottom of the page with a corresponding superscript number below it.

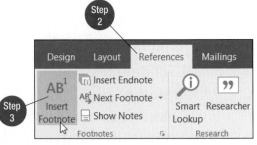

4 With the insertion point positioned at the right of the superscript number below the separator line, key the footnote entry. Do not press Enter at the end of the footnote text.

5 Click in the body of the research paper to continue keying the paper.

Formatting Research Papers Using Chicago Style

The Chicago Manual of Style formatting guidelines that are shown in Table 82.2 have been simplified for this session. In manuscripts or research papers, headings are used to highlight the important ideas and sections in the document. The heading formats used in this session are listed in Table 82.3.

Table 82.2 Formatting Guidelines for Research Papers according to Chicago Style

Paper Element	Formatting Guidelines
paragraph alignment	left aligned, paragraphs begin with 0.5-inch tab
font	12-point serif font such as Cambria, Constantia, or Times New Roman; footnotes should use the same font but in 10-pt size (Word will change automatically)
margins	1-inch top, bottom, left, and right margins (default)
line spacing	double spacing (with 0 points of spacing before and after paragraphs) except in footnotes (Word will change automatically)
report title	begins at top margin, centered, bold, all capital letters, followed by one Enter
page numbers	first page: plain number (digit only) centered in the footer
	second and subsequent pages: plain number (digits only) at the top right of the headers

Table 82.3 Heading Formatting for Research Papers according to Chicago Style

Heading Level	Formatting Style
main/first level	centered, bold, all letters capitalized, press Enter once after
side/second level	align at the left margin, bold, main words capitalized, press Enter once before and after
paragraph/third level	run in with paragraphs and begin where other paragraphs begin (for example, on a tab indent), bold, main words capitalized, end with a bold period, and follow with a space (not bold)

Ergonomic Tip

Keep your wrist straight when using your mouse or another pointing device.

Formatting Text into Columns

When preparing a document, it is important to consider readability, which refers to the ease with which a person can read and understand groups of words. The length of the lines within a document can enhance or detract from the readability of the text. If the line length is too long (the document has narrow margins), the reader may lose his or her place on the line and have a difficult time finding the start of the next line below. To improve the readability of some documents, such as newsletters or reports, you may want to set the text in columns. In columns, text flows from the bottom of one column to the top of the next.

Text can be formatted in columns using options available by clicking the Columns button in the Page Setup group on the Layout tab (see Figure 92.1). Either click a preset option at the Columns button drop-down list or define more specifications for column settings, such as inserting lines between columns, by adjusting the settings at the Columns dialog box (see Figure 92.2). Display the Columns dialog box by clicking *More Columns* at the Columns button drop-down list.

When you select text and then apply column formatting using the Columns button, Word inserts a continuous section break at the beginning and end of the selected text. A continuous section break is an invisible divider between different groups of text. Inserting a section break allows you to apply different layout and formatting options to text on either side of the break. *Note: Section breaks are visible on screen if the Show/Hide ¶ button is active.*

To insert a continuous section break in a document, click the Breaks button in the Page Setup group on the Layout tab and then click *Continuous* in the *Section Breaks* section of the drop-down list (see Figure 92.3).

Word automatically lines up columns so that they balance, except on the last page of text set in columns. To balance columns on the last page, insert a continuous section break at the end of the columned text.

Practice using these features by completing the following document activities.

Figure 92.1 Columns Button Drop-Down List

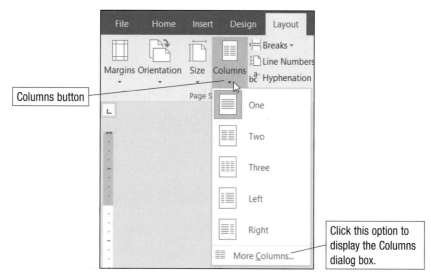

Footnotes are numbered references that appear at the foot (bottom) of the page. A footnote usually includes the author's name, publication title, place of publication, publisher, date of publication, and the page numbers of the information cited. The information cited in the body of the document is followed by a superscript (raised) number that corresponds to the source information at the bottom of the page.

Endnotes are numbered references that appear at the end of the document on a separate page before the Works Cited, References, or Bibliography page. The numbers correspond to superscript numbers found within the body of the document. Endnotes may include additional explanation of material cited in the text of a report.

The choice between footnotes and endnotes is often made by the instructor or client for whom the document is being created. Footnotes make it convenient for the reader to check a reference without losing focus on the content, whereas endnotes create a more streamlined appearance.

Applying Chicago Guidelines for Inserting Footnotes

In general, a style guide will govern the presentation format for the footnotes to be included. Table 82.1 shows formatting guidelines for footnotes when using *The Chicago Manual of Style*.

Word provides the Footnote feature to help you format footnotes in a research paper. Click the Insert Footnote button and Word automatically inserts superscript (raised) numbers after the quoted or paraphrased text, adds a horizontal line separating the text from the footnotes, and numbers the footnotes in order. If a footnote is later added or deleted, Word will automatically renumber the footnotes to accommodate the change. Each footnote entry begins at the left margin and is set in a smaller font size than the body of the text.

Table 82.1 Footnote Entries according to Chicago Style

Books

[1] Author First Name Author Last Name, *Book Title* (City of Publication: Publisher, Year), Page Number.

Example of single-author book:

[2] Patricia J. Veyette, *Life with Me* (Watseka: Forrest Press, 2019), 141.

Example of multiple-author book:

[3] Patricia J. Veyette, Alonso Smyth, and James P. Forrest, *The Wonderful Life of Daisies* (Watseka: Forrest Press, 2019), 375-388.

Example of multiple-author book with four or more authors:

[4] Patricia J. Veyette et al., *Planting Annuals in the Midwest* (Watseka: Forrest Press, 2018), 29-35.

Reprinted Publications

[5] Reprinted with permission from copyright holder name, *Publication Title* (City of Publication: Publisher, Year), Page Number.

Example:

[6] Reprinted with permission from Patricia Forrest, *The Baseball Field Next Door* (Watseka: Forrest Press, 2019), 98-100.

Web Pages

[7] Author First Name Author Last Name, "Web Page Title," *Name of Website*, published Date [or accessed date if published date unknown], http://www.address.

Example:

[8] Jill Greene, "The Processing of Attitude," *Glass Half Full*, accessed July 15, 2020, http://ppi-edu.net/TheProcessingofAttitude/GlassHalfFull.

Figure 92.2 Columns Dialog Box

Columns
Presets
One
Two
Three
Left
Right
Number of columns: 2
Line between
Width and spacing
Col #:
Width:
Spacing:
1:
3"
0.5"
2:
3"
Equal column width
Preview
Apply to:
Whole document
Start new column
OK
Cancel
Click an option in the *Presets* section or adjust the number of columns in the *Number of columns* measurement box.
Insert a check mark in this check box to insert a line between columns.
Preview the column settings here.
Specify column width and spacing options in the *Width* and *Spacing* measurement boxes.
Use this option box to apply column formatting to the selected text, the whole document, or from the insertion point to the end of the document.

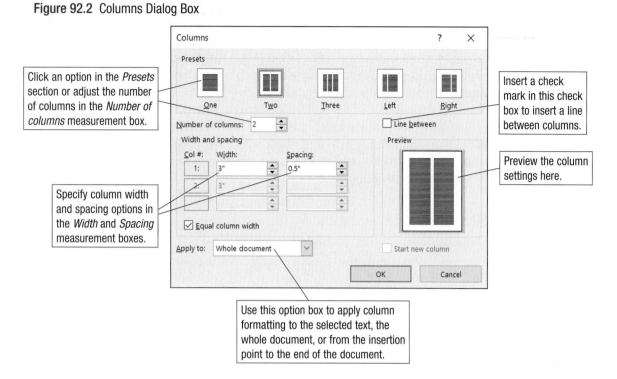

Figure 92.3 Breaks Button Drop-Down List

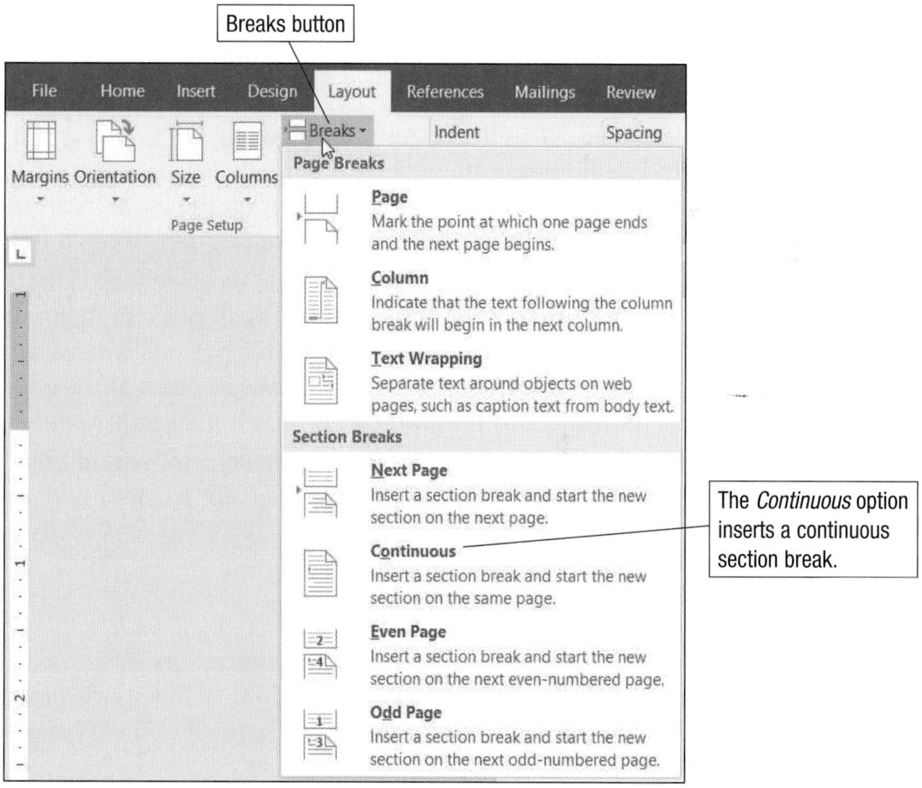

Breaks button
File
Home
Insert
Design
Layout
References
Mailings
Review
Breaks
Indent
Spacing
Margins
Orientation
Size
Columns
Page Setup
Page Breaks
Page
Mark the point at which one page ends and the next page begins.
Column
Indicate that the text following the column break will begin in the next column.
Text Wrapping
Separate text around objects on web pages, such as caption text from body text.
Section Breaks
Next Page
Insert a section break and start the new section on the next page.
Continuous
Insert a section break and start the new section on the same page.
Even Page
Insert a section break and start the new section on the next even-numbered page.
Odd Page
Insert a section break and start the new section on the next odd-numbered page.
The *Continuous* option inserts a continuous section break.

Citing Sources in Research Papers

Research papers are created in all types of business and educational institutions. Writing-style organizations such as the Modern Language Association (MLA) and the American Psychological Association (APA) provide guidelines for formatting research papers and citing the sources used in them. *The Chicago Manual of Style* (Chicago, also referred to as *CMS*) is another popular style reference. The method for citing sources may be determined by the style guidelines of your workplace, by your publisher or instructor, or by your preference, if no other guideline is provided. In the later sessions in this unit, you will work with each of the above style guides to identify sources. Research papers in this session will use a footnote and bibliography format from *The Chicago Manual of Style*, Sixteenth Edition.

When to Cite Sources

An important part of the research writing process is crediting the source of ideas or information you have used to create your document. This process recognizes the work of others, gives credibility to your ideas, and provides evidence of the research you conducted. An advantage of citing sources is that your readers can find and evaluate the quality of your references, if they choose to do so. It does not matter the type of source—whether printed matter, a website, or a conversation—to use another writer's words or ideas without giving credit is called *plagiarism*, which is in all cases unethical and, in some cases, illegal. You must give credit to another individual if you use his or her ideas within your own work.

You need to cite your source whether you directly quote or paraphrase from it. A direct quotation should be enclosed in quotation marks, indicating that the content is another person's exact words or ideas. If the quotation is longer—four lines or more—the quoted content should be indented one-half inch from both the left and right margins and the quotation marks should be omitted.

To format a longer quotation, key the paragraph, select the text, and then click the Paragraph group dialog box launcher. With the Indents and Spacing tab selected in the dialog box, change the values in the *Left* and *Right* measurement boxes in the *Indentation* section to *0.5"*. Alternatively, you can select the paragraph, drag the Left Indent marker on the horizontal ruler 0.5 inch to the right, and then drag the Right Indent marker on the horizontal ruler 0.5 inch to the left.

When directly quoting, you may wish to omit one or more words. In those instances, use an ellipsis, which is a series of three spaced periods (. . .), in place of the omitted word or phrase. Press the spacebar once *before and after* each of the three periods when an ellipsis is used within a sentence. Four periods (. . . .) are used when an ellipsis appears at the end of a statement. The first period does not receive a space in front of it when an ellipsis ends a sentence.

In formal writing, material that has been paraphrased from another source (not quoted exactly), should also be credited to the original source, but it does not need to be enclosed in quotation marks.

Formatting Citations

There are several methods for identifying the sources used to develop a research paper. When you quote directly or paraphrase from another source, identify the nonoriginal content with in-text citations, footnotes, or endnotes. The style of these citations will vary depending on the style guide being used.

In-text citations, sometimes referred to as *text notes*, use parentheses to reference the source used. This consists of the author's last name and the page number—for example, *(Veyette 159)*. If the quoted or paraphrased text indicates the name of the source, it can be acceptable to list only the page number in the in-text citation. The full source details are listed at the end of the research paper on a Works Cited, References, or Bibliography page.

Document Newsletter with Column Formatting
92.1
Read all instructions below before starting this document activity.

1   Navigate to the Document 92.1 launch page in the Online Lab and then click the Launch Activity button to open **Doc092.01** in the activity window.

2   Key the text shown in Figure 92.4. Center the title and press Enter once after the title. Allow Word to automatically format the bulleted list. *Note: The bulleted list is not formatted correctly in Figure 92.4. Make sure to fix any automatic capitalizations in the bulleted text, and do not apply italic formatting to the punctuation that displays after italicized words.*

3   Proofread the document and correct any errors. *Hint: The text* **Separate trustees may** *starts a new paragraph.*

4   Turn on the display of nonprinting characters, select all of the text in the document (press Ctrl + A), copy the text (press Ctrl + C), position the insertion point at the end of the last paragraph, insert a page break (press Ctrl + Enter), and then paste the text after the page break (press Ctrl + V).

5   Set the body of the article on the first page of the document in two columns by completing the following steps:

   a   Scroll up to the first page of the document.

   b   Select the text from *What Is a Trust?* to the last paragraph on the first page, which ends *and the duration of the agreement.* **Note: Select the nonprinting paragraph mark after the last paragraph as well. Do not select the page break.**

   c   Click the Layout tab.

   d   Click the Columns button in the Page Setup group.

   e   Click *Two* at the drop-down list.

6   On the first page of the document, format the title as 18-point Arial Black and the two main headings as 14-point Arial with bold formatting by completing the following steps:

   a   Double-click the title, *TRUSTS.* **Note: The nonprinting paragraph mark will also be selected.**

   b   Click the Home tab.

   c   Click the *Font* option box arrow and then click *Arial Black* at the drop-down gallery.

   d   Click the *Font Size* option box arrow and then click *18* at the drop-down gallery.

   e   Triple-click within the text *What Is a Trust?* to select the heading, press and hold down the Ctrl key, triple-click within the text *How Is a Trust Created?*, and then release the Ctrl key.

   f   Click the *Font* option box arrow in the Font group and then click *Arial* at the drop-down gallery.

   g   Click the *Font Size* option box arrow and then click *14* at the drop-down gallery.

   h   Click the Bold button in the Font group.

7   Set the body of the article on the second page of the document in three columns with a line between each of the columns by completing the following steps:

   a   Scroll to the second page of the document.

   b   Select the text from *What Is a Trust?* to the last paragraph, which ends *and the duration of the agreement.* **Note: Select the nonprinting paragraph mark after the last paragraph in the selection as well, but do not select the blank line following the paragraph.**

   c   Click the Layout tab.

   d   Click the Columns button in the Page Setup group.

   e   Click *More Columns* at the drop-down list.

steps continue

Complete one 5-minute timing on the timing text below.

5-Minute Timings

Timing
82.3

Throughout the years, major earthquakes have taken a costly toll in human lives and property destruction. Whole cities have been destroyed and millions of people have lost their lives because of this phenomenon of nature. Experts simply have not been equipped with better methods to use in forecasting those tremors. In the 1970s, good methods of predicting large quakes came into being. Early warnings could now be issued to enable people to leave the area before the tremors would commence. Persons all over this earth worked together to find better ways of predicting quakes. Early warning systems became a primary goal among nations. The Chinese were responsible for a massive amount of emerging data and facts about earthquakes.

Changes in ground tilt, seismic waves, and local magnetic fields are some signals of forthcoming quakes. Early warning signals can be monitored by scientists. Some laypeople have been taught to observe animal life around them. It seems that animals have the instinct for detecting some changes in the local magnetic field. They become relatively frantic in behavior. Zookeepers have long been aware of this element of nature. Some experts feel that animals can hear the high frequency noises of rock breaking below the earth's surface. Human ears cannot detect these sounds. By observing common animals, experts can foretell a big quake before it all begins. The key is a watchful citizenry and the experts' knowledge of earthquakes and their warning signs.

Seismologists now observe certain sites around the world that are quite predisposed to earthquake activity. Citizens are a great help in this innovative endeavor. Enormous areas are still not protected by a good system of detection. Setting up enough stations along known faults would give us a tremendous opportunity to save many human lives. If an effective type of early warning were given, all precautions could then be taken to prevent the high rate of casualties.

Ergonomic Tip

When seated at your computer, do not cross one leg over the other or sit on either leg. This inhibits circulation, causing fatigue.

   f   Click *Three* in the *Presets* section.

   g Click the *Line between* check box to insert a check mark.

   h Click OK.

  8 On the second page of the document, change the font of the title, *TRUSTS*, to 20-point Arial Black and the font of the two main headings to 12-point Arial Black. ***Note: Format the nonprinting paragraph mark following each heading.***

  9 Proofread the document, paying attention to the formatting you applied in this activity, and correct any errors.

 10 Save the document.

 11 Click the Check button to upload the document for checking.

 12 If errors are reported by the Online Lab, view the results document, correct the errors in the submitted document, save the document, and then click the Check Again button.

Figure 92.4 Newsletter Content for Document 92.1

TRUSTS

What Is a Trust?

A trust is an agreement under which money or other assets are held and managed by one person for the benefit of another. Different types of trusts may be created to accomplish specific goals. Each kind may vary in the degree of flexibility and control it offers.

Among the common benefits which trust arrangements offer are the following:

- providing personal and financial safeguards
- postponing or avoiding unnecessary taxes
- establishing a means of controlling or administering property
- meeting other social or commercial goals

How Is a Trust Created?

Certain elements are necessary to create a legal trust, including a trustor, trustee, beneficiary, trust property, and trust agreement.

The person who provides property and creates a trust is called a *trustor*. This person may also be referred to as the *grantor*, *donor*, or *settlor*.

The trustee is the individual, institution, or organization that holds legal title to the trust property and is responsible for managing and administering those assets. If not designated by name, a trustee will be appointed by the court. In some cases, a trustor can serve as the trustee.

continues

Formatting Footnotes, Research Papers, and Bibliographies in Chicago Style

Session Objectives

- Prepare a manuscript with footnotes in Chicago style
- Control the pagination of headings
- Prepare a bibliography
- Prepare an outline
- Efficiently produce documents in mailable form

Getting Started

Exercise 82.1 If you are continuing immediately from Session 81, you may skip the Exercise 82.1 warm-up drill. However, if you exited the Online Lab at the end of Session 81, warm up by completing Exercise 82.1.

Exercise 82.2 Begin your session work by completing Exercise 82.2, a timed short drill, in the Online Lab.

Assessing Your Speed and Accuracy

Complete Timings 82.1 through 82.3 in the Online Lab. At the end of each timing, the Online Lab will display your WPM rate and any errors. If you have been surpassing the speed and accuracy goals identified in the Online Lab, set slightly more challenging personal goals and strive to exceed them.

Complete two 1-minute timings on the timing text below. Timings 82.1 and 82.2 use the same paragraph. If you meet or exceed both speed and accuracy goals for Timing 82.1, push for greater speed on Timing 82.2.

1-Minute Timings

Timings 82.1–82.2 Before embarking on that fun driving vacation, take a few minutes to make certain that the windows on your automobile are spotless so that your view is as unobstructed as possible. Plan to get an early start, before traffic conditions are congested. An earlier start makes an extended drive seem easier. The trip will be much smoother if someone is with you to share the responsibilities of reading the map, locating road signs, or finding gas stations and good restaurants. Do not drive to the point of exhaustion. Take a break frequently for fresh air to awaken senses and sharpen driving ability. Stopping to exercise your legs every two to three hours is ideal.

Figure 92.4 Newsletter Content for Document 92.1—continued

Separate trustees may also be named to manage different parts of a trust estate.

The beneficiary is the person who is to receive the benefits or advantages of a trust. In general, any person or entity may be a beneficiary, including individuals, corporations, or associations.

To be valid, a trust must hold some property to be administered. The trust property may be any asset, such as stocks, real estate, cash, a business, or insurance. In other words, either "real" or "personal" property may comprise trust property. Trust property may also include some future interest or right to future ownership, such as the right to receive proceeds under a life insurance policy when the insured dies. Property is made subject to the trust by a transfer to the trustee commonly called a *gift in trust*.

The trust agreement is a contract that formally expresses the understanding between the trustor and the trustee. It generally contains a set of instructions to describe the manner in which the trust property is to be held and invested, the purposes for which its benefits are to be used, and the duration of the agreement.

Document 92.2 **Article with Column Formatting**

Read all instructions below before starting this document activity.

1 Navigate to the Document 92.2 launch page in the Online Lab and then click the Launch Activity button to open **Doc092.02** in the activity window.

2 Insert a continuous section break at the end of the first paragraph of text in the document by completing the following steps:

   a Position the insertion point at the end of the first paragraph of text in the document, after the words *and communication devices*.

   b Click the Layout tab.

   c Click the Breaks button in the Page Setup group.

   d Click *Continuous* in the *Section Breaks* section.

3 Select the heading *System Unit* through the end of the document and then format it in two columns. *Hint: Select the nonprinting paragraph mark at the end of the last paragraph.*

4 Balance the columns by inserting a continuous section break at the end of the last paragraph in the document.

5 Save the document.

6 Click the Check button to upload the document for checking.

7 If errors are reported by the Online Lab, view the results document, correct the errors in the submitted document, save the document, and then click the Check Again button.

Document 81.4 Planning Manuscript Preparation and Identifying Sources

Read all instructions below before starting this document activity.

1. Navigate to the Document 81.4 launch page in the Online Lab and then click the Launch Activity button to open **Doc081.04** in the activity window.

2. Select the topic for your manuscript.

3. Use the Internet, magazines, journals, newspapers, books, and interviews to research the topic you selected for background information. Use at least four different references.

4. Format the document as follows:

   a. Change the default paragraph formatting in the document to double spaced with no spacing after paragraphs.

   b. Change the default font style and size in the document to a serif font in an easy-to-read size.

   c. Place your name, date, and the page number at the top of each page (the first page and all subsequent pages).

5. On the first page of the document, key a working manuscript title and a short paragraph about the topic, stating why this topic is of interest to you. Insert a page break after the paragraph.

6. Key a list of sources you will be referencing in the manuscript. For each, include the title, author, publisher, publication date, and pages. Format the document so that each source starts a new page and then key notes about the topic you have researched from the sources.

7. Proofread the document and correct any errors.

8. Save the document.

9. Click the Submit button to upload the document for instructor review.

Ending the Session

The Online Lab automatically saved the work you completed for this session. You may continue with the next session or exit the Online Lab and continue later.

Reinforcing Writing Skills

When writing an article or newsletter, it is important to consider your audience. If the audience is not familiar with the topic, you must make sure to *contextually* explain the terms or concepts presented within the body of the article in an interesting and engaging way. For an example of an article that contextually defines terms and concepts, review the 5-minute timing at the beginning of this session or the text used in Document 92.2. In the following document activity, practice composing a document that introduces a hobby or area of interest or expertise to a reader who has little experience with or knowledge of the topic.

Document 92.3

Composing an Article on a Topic of Interest to You

Read all instructions below before starting this document activity.

1 Navigate to the Document 92.3 launch page in the Online Lab and then click the Launch Activity button to open **Doc092.03** in the activity window.

2 Compose a one-page document on a hobby in which you are interested or a topic on which you are an expert. Follow these specifications as you draft and produce this document:

- Assume that the reader knows very little about the topic and work to engage him or her in learning about it.

- Include a title and at least two major headings.

- Format the document in two columns with a vertical line between them.

- Select an appropriate typeface, type size, and type style for the body, title, and headings of the article. When selecting fonts for the document, keep readability in mind. Consider using a serif font for the body and a sans serif font for the title and headings. Also, try to enhance the tone of the document with the fonts you select.

3 Proofread and correct any errors in the document.

4 Save the document.

5 Click the Submit button to upload the document for instructor review.

Ending the Session

The Online Lab automatically saved the work you completed for this session. You may continue with the next session or exit the Online Lab and continue later.

Figure 81.4 Outline Content for Document 81.3—continued

→→→2.→Sharp turns at the Clairemont Street north and south exits¶

→→→3.→Steep grades on the east and west approaches to Fairfax Drive¶

→→→4.→Intersection of Clairemont and Fairfax does not line up¶

→→D.→Accidents¶

¶

→III.→Proposal¶

¶

→→A.→Recommendations¶

→→B.→Financing¶

→→→1.→Railroad¶

→→→2.→Department of Transportation funding¶

→→→3.→City/county funding

Reinforcing Writing Skills

The most efficient method of preparing a manuscript is to divide the process into the following steps:

1　Identify the topic.

2　Research the topic for background information.

3　Take notes on cards or in some type of electronic format, such as Microsoft OneNote. Include the sources of the information (title, author, publisher, publication date, page number).

4　Prepare an outline of the major ideas using Word. Edit and revise the outline.

5　Compose a rough draft of the manuscript in Word. Include quotations from source notes or other information obtained from your research.

6　Revise the writing and edit the document for punctuation, spelling, grammar, word choice, and capitalization.

7　Prepare an abstract of the manuscript.

8　Prepare a bibliography, works cited, or references page.

For the following document activity, you are to complete Steps 1 to 3 from the previous list for preparing a manuscript. The information you obtain will be used to complete a manuscript in later sessions. You may choose your own topic or use one of the following:

• Qualifications for an Occupation I Plan to Pursue

• Key Components of Purchasing a Tablet or Laptop Computer

• How to Dress for Success

Converting Text to Table Format and Table Content to Text

Session Objectives

- Convert text to a table
- Convert a table to text
- Format fonts within a document
- Create an informational flyer
- Efficiently produce documents in mailable form

Getting Started

Exercise 93.1   If you are continuing immediately from Session 92, you can skip the Exercise 93.1 warm-up drill. However, if you exited the Online Lab at the end of Session 92, warm up by completing Exercise 93.1.

Exercise 93.2   Begin your session work by completing Exercise 93.2, a timed short drill, in the Online Lab.

Assessing Your Speed and Accuracy

Complete Timing 93.1 in the Online Lab using the timing text on the following page. At the end of the timing, the Online Lab will display your WPM rate and any errors. Results will be saved in your Timings Performance report. If you have been surpassing the speed and accuracy goals identified in the Online Lab, set slightly more challenging goals and strive to exceed them.

Manuscript Outline

Read all instructions below before starting this document activity.

1   Navigate to the Document 81.3 launch page in the Online Lab and then click the Launch Activity button to open **Doc081.03** in the activity window.

2   Before keying any text, turn off the automatic numbered lists feature. *Hint: Click the File tab, click* **Options**, *click* **Proofing** *in the left panel, and then click the AutoCorrect Options button to display the AutoCorrect dialog box, where you can make the changes.*

3   Change the default line spacing for the document to single spacing with no spacing after paragraphs.

4   Use the horizontal ruler or the Tabs dialog box to set a right tab at 0.5 inch and left tabs at 0.75 inch, 1 inch, and 1.25 inches.

5   Press Enter as needed to move the insertion point approximately 2 inches from the top of the page. *Hint: The insertion point should be 2.1 inches from the top of the page.*

6   Key the title and subtitle of the outline by completing the following steps:

   a   Change the paragraph alignment to center alignment, turn on bold formatting, key RECOMMENDATIONS FOR THE NORTH CROSSING, turn off bold formatting, and then press Enter twice.

   b   Key Prepared by Sven Hartanovich and then press Enter. *Note: The subtitle should be centered but not bold.*

   c   Change the paragraph alignment to left alignment and then press Enter twice.

7   Key the outline shown in Figure 81.4. The pink arrow symbols reflect the nonprinting tab symbols (Tab key).

8   Proofread the document and correct any errors. Check that the roman numerals, letters, and arabic numbers are properly aligned, and compare the layout to the document shown in Figure 81.3.

9   Save the document.

10   Click the Check button to upload the document for checking.

11   If errors are reported by the Online Lab, view the results document, correct the errors in the submitted document, save the document, and then click the Check Again button.

Figure 81.4 Outline Content for Document 81.3

→I. →Purpose¶

¶

→II.→The Problem¶

¶

→→A.→Existing conditions¶

→→B.→Traffic¶

→→C.→Congestion¶

→→→1.→Railroad traffic—15 trains per day¶

continues

Timing
93.1

In the very early 1900s, President Theodore Roosevelt supposedly had an encounter with a black bear. As the old legend goes, Teddy (as the President was fondly referred to) refused to kill a bear that had been tied up to a tree during one of his trips to the far frontier country. The nation was so entranced with this deed that a new stuffed toy known as the teddy bear was invented. Since that time, teddy bears have been identified with feelings of security, kindness, and caring.

Children of all ages enjoy the security of hugging a teddy bear. In fact, many police officers carry a supply of teddy bears with them at all times. Whenever a child is injured or frightened, the police officer will give a teddy bear to the child to soothe him or her. For some reason, just hugging a cuddly teddy bear gives a child a sense of security and happiness. Teddy bears have a calming effect.

Adults are also drawn to the magic of teddy bears. Many people collect bears of all sizes and shapes. The price of a teddy bear can range from one dollar to several hundred dollars. Some well-known bears often sell for as much as $100 per inch. The most desired teddy bear collectible is one that has jointed limbs, large feet, felt paws, long curving arms, and glass or shoe-button eyes.

Whatever the reason, the magic and mystique of a teddy bear's charm will continue to attract people of all ages. If you are interested in becoming a collector of teddy bears, many good books have been written on that colorful and interesting topic. When you are looking at teddy bears to purchase, look for those that are in good condition. Sometimes you can find a good buy at garage sales, estate sales, or online.

You will also need to learn how to keep your teddy bear collection in good condition. Keeping a teddy bear clean is the key to your success or failure in collecting teddy bears.

 Ergonomic Tip

When using a mouse, hold it loosely. Click the buttons with a light touch. This will prevent your wrist and hand from becoming fatigued.

Outlines have different formats than manuscripts. Figure 81.3 shows the outline that you will key in the next document activity. As shown in Figure 81.3, outlines are typically keyed with single-spaced paragraph formatting. The title or main heading begins 2 inches from the top of the page and is centered, bolded, and keyed in all capital letters. If there is a subtitle, it appears two lines below the main heading, centered, not bolded, and with the main words capitalized. Press the Enter key three times between the heading or subheading and the first line of the outline.

Format the body of the outline with one blank line above and below major division headings, which are usually numbered with roman numerals (I., II., and III.). The next level below the major headings is lettered (A., B., and C.), and the subsequent level is numbered (1., 2., and 3.). Do not include an extra line space between second- and third-level outline entries.

The capitalization style of headings within outlines may vary. When keying an outline, make sure the automatic numbered lists feature is turned off and set the tabs with a right tab at 0.5 inch and left tabs at 0.75 inch, 1.0 inch, and 1.25 inches.

Success Tip

In a well-developed outline, all sections have at least two entries. So, for example, if you have an *A.* entry, you should also have a *B.* entry.

Figure 81.3 Outline Format Sample for Document 81.3

RECOMMENDATIONS FOR THE NORTH CROSSING

Prepared by Sven Hartanovich

I.   Purpose

II.   The Problem

    A. Existing conditions
    B. Traffic
    C. Congestion
        1. Railroad traffic—15 trains per day
        2. Sharp turns at the Clairemont Street north and south exits
        3. Steep grades on the east and west approaches to Fairfax Drive
        4. Intersection of Clairemont and Fairfax does not line up
    D. Accidents

III. Proposal

    A. Recommendations
    B. Financing
        1. Railroad
        2. Department of Transportation funding
        3. City/county funding

Converting Text to a Table

In addition to setting text in columns to improve readability, it can also be helpful to set text in a table format. In Word, you can convert an existing section of text into a table. To do so, separate the text that should appear in different cells with a separator character. A separator character can be a nonprinting paragraph mark, a nonprinting Tab character, a comma, or another character that you choose. Convert text to a table by completing the following steps:

1 Select the text to be converted to a table.

2 Click the Insert tab.

3 Click the Table button in the Tables group.

4 Click *Convert Text to Table* at the drop-down list. This displays the Convert Text to Table dialog box.

5 Key the number of columns in the *Number of columns* measurement box.

6 Select the appropriate option in the *Separate text at* section of the dialog box.

7 Click OK.

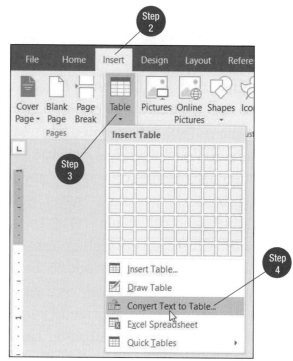

In the following document activities, you will practice producing documents that require you to convert text to tables.

Document 93.1 **Informational Flyer with Text Converted to a Table**

Read all instructions below before starting this document activity.

1 Navigate to the Document 93.1 launch page in the Online Lab and then click the Launch Activity button to open **Doc093.01** in the activity window.

2 Key the text shown in Figure 93.1. Do not accept Word's automatic formatting of the web address in the document.

steps continue

Figure 81.2 Manuscript Content for Document 81.2—continued

do not make more profit than a similar store located off the campus and often do not make as large a profit. ¶ The major purpose of any school bookstore is convenience. It allows students to purchase necessities quickly. When there is not time to walk, bike, or ride the bus downtown or to a shopping mall, it is most convenient to walk over to the campus bookstore. A campus bookstore's success is not measured solely by the dollars it produces but by the convenience it provides for student*s*, faculty, and staff. ¶ **THE CHALLENGE** ¶ Individualization. Bookstores are often managed by national companies, which then tailor the store to the needs of the individual campus. For instance, an instructor may request that an item be "packaged" so the students are all using the same materials and can purchase them at one time. They may need textbooks and software packed together. The price may seem high, but it may be a bargain in the end. ¶ T-shirts and other items with the school's logo on them often cannot be ordered in large enough quantities to give a bargain price. This is also the case for supplies the students may need. In this case, students are paying for the convenience and/or the personalization. ¶ Digitization. Our world is becoming more digitized every day. Bookstores are offering digital solutions in order to survive. They are evolving in order to meet specific needs, which change fast and come with high expectations. ¶ Changes are Evident. New services are being added to make the stores *more* relevanter—some are offering printing stations, which cater to photos or e-texts. Some are even offering drop-off and pick-up places for dry cleaning. ¶ Book rental programs are again becoming more common. Students do not necessarily want digit*al* texts; instead they want better prices. ¶ Websites. Bookstores' websites are becoming more important to their existence. Some of them are featuring "early-bird discounts" if the books are ordered before classes begin and for pickup at the store. Many sites offer price-comparison tools, which go out and check the price of online booksellers for comparison. Often the shipping may make the book more expensive th*a*n purchasing it at the bookstore, and the delivery time *might* be problematic.

Preparing Manuscript Outlines

A critical step in the preparation of an effective manuscript is to develop an outline. Creating an outline simplifies the actual writing of a manuscript. With an outline as a reference, the writer has a clear picture of what to include in the manuscript, the order in which to present the information, and the details that are relevant to the content. An outline is critical if there are multiple writers working on creating a manuscript.

3 Make the following formatting changes:

  a Select the title (including the nonprinting paragraph mark), change the paragraph alignment to center alignment, change the font to 14-point Arial Black, and change the font color to Red (second option in the *Standard Colors* section).

  b Apply 12-point Elephant font and underline formatting to the four headings in the document. ***Hint: Format the nonprinting paragraph mark following each of the headings.***

4 Proofread the document and correct any errors.

5 Select all of the text in the document, copy the text, position the insertion point at the end of the last paragraph, insert a page break, and then paste the text after the page break.

6 Convert the text on the second page of the document into a two-column table by completing the following steps:

  a Select all of the text on the second page, from the title *SAFETY TIPS FOR TRAVELERS* through the words *visit http://faa.gov/Go/PackSafe web page*. **Note: Include the nonprinting paragraph mark at the end of the last paragraph, but do not include the blank line after the paragraph.**

  b Click the Insert tab.

  c Click the Table button in the Tables group.

  d Click *Convert Text to Table* at the drop-down list.

  e At the Convert Text to Table dialog box with the number in the *Number of columns* measurement box selected, key 2.

  f If *Paragraphs* is not selected in the *Separate text at* section of the Convert Text to Table dialog box, click the option to select it.

  g Click OK.

7 In the table, merge cells A1 and B1, change the height of the first row to 0.8 inches, and align the text in cell A1 to the top center of the cell. ***Hint: If you need help with this step, review Session 72.***

8 Format the second page of the document so that the table is centered vertically on the page by completing the following steps:

  a Select all of the text on the second page of the document (the table plus the nonprinting paragraph mark below it).

  b Click the Layout tab.

  c Click the Page Setup group dialog box launcher.

  d Click the Layout tab in the Page Setup dialog box.

  e In the *Page* section, click the *Vertical alignment* option box arrow and then click *Center* at the drop-down list.

  f Click the *Apply to* option box arrow and then click *Selected text* at the drop-down list.

  g Click OK.

9 Proofread the document and confirm that the formatting has been applied correctly. Correct any errors that you find in the document.

10 Save the document.

11 Click the Check button to upload the document for checking.

12 If errors are reported by the Online Lab, view the results document, correct the errors in the submitted document, save the document, and then click the Check Again button.

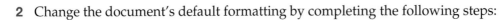

2 Change the document's default formatting by completing the following steps:

   a Change the default line spacing for the document to double spacing with no spacing after paragraphs.

   b Change the default font to 12-point Cambria.

3 Key the main title and subtitle of the manuscript by completing the following steps:

   a Press Enter three times to position the insertion point approximately 2 inches from the top of the page.

   b Change the paragraph alignment to center alignment, turn on bold formatting, key COMPETITIVE PRICING IN THE BOOKSTORE, and then press Enter.

   c Key Based on Interviews with Bookstore Managers, turn off bold formatting, and then press Enter.

   d Change the paragraph alignment to left alignment.

4 Key the manuscript content shown in Figure 81.2, implementing the changes indicated by the proofreading marks. Remember to press Tab for each paragraph start. Format the side headings and paragraph headings within the document per the formatting guidelines outlined in Table 81.2. *Hint: Some changes in capitalization will be required. When keying a side heading that is immediately followed by a paragraph heading, do not turn off the bold formatting until the paragraph heading (including the period) is keyed.*

5 Insert a Plain Number 3 page number at the top of the page of the second and subsequent pages of the document. The header of the first page of the document should be blank.

6 Proofread the document and correct any errors.

7 Save the document.

8 Click the Check button to upload the document for checking.

9 If errors are reported by the Online Lab, view the results document, correct the errors in the submitted document, save the document, and then click the Check Again button.

Figure 81.2 Manuscript Content for Document 81.2

The goal of any school bookstore is to serve students as effectively as possible. Do most school bookstores attain that function or do some of them take advantage of residents on campus who find it difficult to shop off the campus grounds? ¶ **FINDINGS** ¶ Recent Research Studies. The findings indicate that school bookstore prices for most items frequently are higher than those prices charged by stores located off campus. These same studies also reveal that although students feel it is unfair for the campus bookstore to have higher prices, they also feel it is convenient for them to purchase ~~cretin~~ certain items ~~their~~ there. ¶ Manager Interview Results. Managers of selected bookstores indicate that most items are sold at the retail prices suggest_ed_ by the manufacture_r_. Large stores located off campus ~~who~~ that buy in bulk can sell the same item for less because of the discounts they receive from the manufacturer. ¶ Most bookstores do not sell enough to get a large volume discount. The same interview revealed that most school bookstores

side heading

continues

Figure 93.1 Informational Flyer Content for Document 93.1

SAFETY TIPS FOR TRAVELERS [Enter]

[Enter]

What's in Your Baggage?

Common items used every day may seem harmless. However, when transported by air, they can become dangerous. During flight, variations in pressure and temperature can cause items to leak, generate toxic fumes, or ignite.

Items Prohibited by the FAA

The following are items that are prohibited by the Federal Aviation Administration (FAA): flammable aerosols, fireworks, burning paste, model-rocket motors, explosive primers, strike-anywhere matches, fuels, camping gas, lighter refills, paints, solvents, alcohols, self-inflating rescue backpacks, chemical kits, compressed oxygen, scuba tanks, flares, and gas-powered tools. The Transportation Security Administration (TSA) will confiscate such items and will report the traveler to the FAA.

Lithium and Lithium-Ion Batteries

These types of batteries catch fire when improperly handled and are prohibited in checked baggage. They are allowed in carry-on baggage only, not exceeding 100 watt-hours each (limit two at 160 total watt-hours). The http://faa.gov/Go/PackSafe web page provides battery-size guidance. Carry batteries in their original packaging, in separate plastic bags, or with electrical tape covering battery contacts. Do not use aircraft powerports to charge batteries when not in use.

Carrying Prohibited Items on Aircraft

Carrying prohibited items on aircraft violates US federal law. Violators are subject to imprisonment and penalties of $500,000 or more. For more information, consult an airlines agent or visit the http://faa.gov/Go/PackSafe web page.

Figure 81.1 Manuscript Content for Document 81.1—continued

A cone consists of many open scales, each with two seeds at the base. Most conifers bear both male and female cones on the same tree, although junipers and some others bear male and female cones on separate trees. The male cone is usually quite small, about one centimeter long or less. It is found where the needles meet the branches or at the ends of short branches.

The female cone (the one that everyone thinks of when picturing a pinecone) consists of outgrowths, or scales, and a central core called a bract. Young seeds, or ovules, are found near the bract.

Pollen grains are the male reproductive body and are shed by the male cone only. All conifers are normally wind-pollinated, and some of them produce huge amounts of pollen. (Think of spring allergies when the tree pollination is rampant.)

When the ovule is ready for pollination, some of the cells form a sticky "pollination drop." Pollen grains that land on the pollination drop are drawn down into the pollen chamber as the moisture evaporates and the drop dries up. A pollen tube is formed at that point that then begins to grow down slowly toward the female reproductive cell in the heart of the ovule. After a period of several weeks to a year, the pollen tube grows down to the female cell, which is then fertilized.

Cones vary in shape, weight, and how long their seeds can remain dormant and still germinate. The seed coat that protects conifer seeds is usually dry and firm and often extends into a thin wing, which helps to facilitate dispersal by the wind.

The seeds of some conifers are ready to germinate immediately after fertilization. Others require a rest period of weeks, months, or even years. The cones of jack pines, for example, remain on the tree for at least several years and open very slowly. Fire stimulates jack pine cones to open and release their seeds, so jack pines are often the first conifer to become established in recently burned areas.

**Document
81.2 Edited Unbound Manuscript**

Read all instructions below before starting this document activity.

1 Navigate to the Document 81.2 launch page in the Online Lab and then click the Launch Activity button to open **Doc081.02** in the activity window.

steps continue

Document Informational Document with Text Converted to a Table

93.2 Read all instructions below before starting this document activity.

1 Navigate to the Document 93.2 launch page in the Online Lab and then click the Launch Activity button to open **Doc093.02** in the activity window.

2 Change the font for the title *Computer Hardware*—including the nonprinting paragraph mark—to 16-point Cooper Black and remove the bold formatting.

3 Convert the text from the heading *System Unit* to the end of the document (including the nonprinting paragraph mark at the end of the last paragraph of text) into a two-column table. Allow the columns to be defined by Tab characters rather than paragraph marks.

4 Insert two rows at the bottom of the table and then key Storage Devices in cell A5 and Communication Devices in cell A6. The headings should be automatically formatted as bold.

5 Format the document so that the text and the table are centered vertically on the page.

6 Proofread the document and confirm the formatting has been applied correctly. Correct any errors that you find in the document.

7 Save the file.

8 Click the Check button to upload the document for checking.

9 If errors are reported by the Online Lab, view the results document, correct the errors in the submitted document, save the document, and then click the Check Again button.

Converting a Table to Text

Word allows you to convert a table to text by using the Convert to Text button in the Data group on the Table Tools Layout tab. When converting a table to text, you can choose how the data will be separated when it is extracted from the table. Choices include nonprinting paragraph marks or tabs, commas, or another character that you choose.

To convert a table to text, complete the following steps:

1 Click a cell in the table you wish to convert.

2 Click the Table Tools Layout tab.

3 Click the Convert to Text button in the Data group.

4 At the Convert Table To Text dialog box, click a separator option in the *Separate text with* section.

5 Click OK.

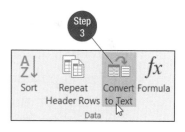

In the following activity, you will practice converting a table to text.

4   Key the manuscript content shown in Figure 81.1. Remember to press Tab at the beginning of each paragraph. Also, format the side heading and the two paragraph headings within the document per the formatting guidelines outlined in Table 81.2. *Hint: Some changes in capitalization will be required. When keying paragraph headings, turn on bold formatting after pressing Tab and turn off bold formatting before keying the space following the period at the end of the heading.*

5   Insert a Plain Number 3 page number at the top of the second and subsequent pages of the document. The header of the first page of the document should be blank.

6   Proofread the document and correct any errors.

7   Save the document.

8   Click the Check button to upload the document for checking.

9   If errors are reported by the Online Lab, view the results document, correct the errors in the submitted document, save the document, and then click the Check Again button.

Figure 81.1 Manuscript Content for Document 81.1

During our early school years, many of us collected leaves, usually as a science class project to learn how to identify trees and shrubs. But there are other ways, such as seed or fruit collecting, which are equally effective. Seeds, especially those within cones, are fascinating to find and identify.

Two classes of trees

Trees are organized into two classes: angiosperms and gymnosperms.

Angiosperms. The first of the two classes, angiosperms, includes most of the common flowering plants. This large group of about 300 families and nearly 20,000 species dominates the earth's vegetation. The seeds of angiosperms are enclosed in an ovary of fruit. Trees in this group include elm, locust, apple, and hickory.

The sepals and petals may be quite showy in order to attract pollinators (like bees), or quite aerodynamic in wind-pollinated plants. (Think of the maple tree's winged fruits, which can swirl and twirl like helicopters.)

Angiosperms are important as a major food source, both directly and indirectly (through consumption by animals). These trees are also a primary source of consumer goods, providing building materials, fibers for making textiles, fruits, spices, herbs, chemicals, and even pharmaceuticals.

Gymnosperms. This is the other class of trees, which includes the coniferous (cone-bearing) trees and other plants having seeds not enclosed in an ovary. Most familiar of the gymnosperms are pines, firs, and spruces. But included in the nearly 700 species are members of the yew, redwood, ginkgo, and cedar families, too.

continues

Document 93.3 Contact Listings with Tables Converted to Text

Read all instructions below before starting this document activity.

1 Navigate to the Document 93.3 launch page in the Online Lab and then click the Launch Activity button to open **Doc093.03** in the activity window.

2 Convert the first table in the document to text, using tabs as the separator characters.

3 Convert the second table in the document to text, using commas as the separator characters.

4 Save the document.

5 Click the Check button to upload the document for checking.

6 If errors are reported by the Online Lab, view the results document, correct the errors in the submitted document, save the document, and then click the Check Again button.

Reinforcing Editing Skills

When writing and formatting documents, it is important to apply formatting that will help the reader quickly and accurately read and understand the presented information. Also, when developing documents such as informational flyers, it is important to consider what information is critical to the reader. Practice these skills in the following document activity.

Document 93.4 Revising an Informational Flyer

1 Navigate to the Document 93.4 launch page in the Online Lab and then click the Launch Activity button to open **Doc093.04** in the activity window.

2 Rewrite and reformat the text shown in Figure 93.1. Edit the content so that the reader has to read as little as possible but will still receive all of the necessary information from the original document. The document should also be appealing to look at and easy to follow.

3 Proofread and correct any errors in the document.

4 Save the document.

5 Click the Submit button to upload the document for instructor review.

Ending the Session

The Online Lab automatically saved the work you completed for this session. You may continue with the next session or exit the Online Lab and continue later.

⋙ Reinforcing Word Skills

The following document activity will require you to apply some previously learned Word skills. This section will review some of those skills.

When a new document is opened, it contains the default settings of 11-point Calibri font with 1.08 line spacing and 8 points of spacing after paragraphs. To properly format a manuscript, you will need to change the default font and line spacing in the document.

Changing the Default Font

To change the default font style in a new document, complete the following steps:

1 Click the Font group dialog box launcher on the Home tab.
2 At the Font dialog box, click the Font tab, if it is not already selected.
3 Scroll down the *Font* list box and then click the desired font name.
4 Click the desired font size in the *Size* list box.
5 Click the Set As Default button.
6 At the message box, make sure the *This document only?* option is selected and then click OK.

Changing the Default Line Spacing

To change the default line spacing in a new document to the appropriate manuscript format, complete the following steps:

1 Click the Paragraph group dialog box launcher on the Home tab.
2 At the Paragraph dialog box, click the Indents and Spacing tab, if it is not already selected.
3 Change the value in the *After* measurement box to *0 pt* by clicking the down arrow twice.
4 Click the *Line spacing* option box arrow and then click *Double* at the drop-down list.
5 Click the Set As Default button.
6 At the message box, make sure the *This document only?* option is selected and then click OK.

Practice keying manuscripts using these formatting guidelines in the following document activities.

Document 81.1 **Unbound Manuscript**

Read all instructions below before starting this document activity.

1 Navigate to the Document 81.1 launch page in the Online Lab and then click the Launch Activity button to open **Doc081.01** in the activity window.
2 Change the default formatting of the document as follows:
   a Change the default line spacing to double spacing with no spacing after paragraphs.
   b Change the default font to 12-point Cambria.
3 Key the main title of the manuscript by completing the following steps:
   a Press Enter three times to position the insertion point approximately 2 inches from the top of the page.
   b Change the paragraph alignment to center alignment, turn on bold formatting, key IDENTIFYING TREES AND SHRUBS, turn off bold formatting, and then press Enter.
   c Change the paragraph alignment to left alignment.

steps continue

Session 94

Using Templates to Create Agendas and Newsletters

Session Objectives

- Create a newsletter using a template
- Create an agenda using a template
- Key text into a template
- Apply shape fills, shape outlines, and shape styles to shapes and text boxes
- Efficiently produce documents in mailable form

Getting Started

Exercise 94.1   If you are continuing immediately from Session 93, you can skip the Exercise 94.1 warm-up drill. However, if you exited the Online Lab at the end of Session 93, warm up by completing Exercise 94.1.

Exercise 94.2   Begin your session work by completing Exercise 94.2, a timed short drill, in the Online Lab.

Assessing Your Speed and Accuracy

Complete Timing 94.1 in the Online Lab using the timing text on the following page. At the end of the timing, the Online Lab will display your WPM rate and any errors. Results will be saved in your Timings Performance report. If you have been surpassing the speed and accuracy goals identified in the Online Lab, set slightly more challenging goals and strive to exceed them.

Preparing Manuscripts

A manuscript is a document that is prepared for publication purposes. It might be published as a magazine or journal article, a research report, a newsletter, or even a book. In an academic setting, manuscripts are often term papers that are completed for a particular course. Manuscripts are usually multiple-page documents, but they can be as short as one page.

Manuscripts can be bound or unbound, depending on their length. Unbound manuscripts are generally short—one to four pages. Bound manuscripts are usually five or more pages and typically include a title page, an abstract, the body of the document with footnotes or endnotes, and references.

Publishers may have their own rules for manuscript preparation, which must be followed if the manuscript is to be accepted. While you do not need to memorize all of the different formats, you should be able to format a manuscript according to the guidelines provided. Careful attention must be paid to the details—spacing, punctuation, sequence—if you hope to get a manuscript published.

Table 81.1 details some common formatting guidelines for unbound manuscripts. Heading formats will be different from manuscript to manuscript. Several common options are listed in Table 81.2. Headings are not a requirement, but they tend to help the writer to organize the manuscript content and the reader to follow and understand it.

Table 81.1 Formatting Guidelines for Unbound Manuscripts

Manuscript Element	Formatting Guidelines
paragraph alignment	left aligned, paragraphs begin with 0.5-inch indent
font	12-point serif font (font that contains small strokes at the ends of a character stroke), such as Cambria, Bookman Old Style, or Times New Roman
margins	1-inch top, bottom, left, and right margins (default)
line spacing	double line spacing (with 0 points of spacing before and after paragraphs)
report title	centered, bold, all capital letters, set 2 inches from the top of the page
page numbers	first page: no page number second and subsequent pages: plain number (digits only) at the top-right corner of the header

Table 81.2 Heading Formatting Styles for Manuscripts

Heading Level	Formatting Style
main/first level	centered, bold, all capital letters, press Enter once before and after
side/second level	align at the left margin, bold, capitalize first letter of each major word, press Enter once before and after
paragraph/third level	run in with paragraphs and begin where other paragraphs begin, bold, capitalize the first letter of each major word, end with a bold period, and follow with a space (not bold)

Timing 94.1

Most people are accustomed to shopping in the grocery market for vegetables and fresh produce. We choose the health-giving vegetables from rows of sterile storage bins. Many people cannot even recall or remember the great flavor of vegetables that have been freshly picked from a garden. Because of skyrocketing prices, too many people cannot afford to purchase the ideal amounts of vegetables needed for a person's good health and well-being.

A logical answer to the problem of obtaining an inexpensive, yet flavorful, supply of vegetables is to grow your own. With some seeds, a small parcel of land, a few tools, and lots of energy, you can experience the joy of gardening. You will receive many benefits from a tasty supply of fresh vegetables that have a flavor not possible with the produce in any grocery store or market.

You should select a sunny location for the garden. It should be one that has an adequate exposure to sunlight, a supply of water, and fertile soil. You might wish to locate your garden close to your residence, for convenience. You should devise a planting arrangement that blends and harmonizes with your surrounding landscape. Any plan should include your favorite kinds of vegetables in quantities that are adequate to feed all the members of your family. The best planting time will definitely depend upon the area in which you live. In warmer climates, the produce is planted and harvested much earlier in the year. In a colder climate, the growing season is much shorter and the harvest is much later in the season.

Because there are periods during the year when you won't be able to harvest vegetables directly from the garden, you should also think of ways to preserve the produce for later use. Two very popular ways of preserving produce are canning and freezing. Even if you have not had experience in preserving produce, there are many good books, easy tips, and other information available for you to follow.

 Ergonomic Tip

If your chair is adjustable, experiment to find numerous comfortable positions. Adjust the chair often throughout your workday.

Complete one 5-minute timing on the timing text below.

5-Minute Timing

Timing
81.3

Over the past decades, many of us simply threw away all items that were no longer deemed to be of any great value. Because of this wasteful viewpoint, many of our nation's landfills are filled to capacity. During the early 1990s, a new wave of awareness arose about how items could be used again in a different form. We have learned that our natural resources are not infinite. If we don't recycle our resources, we'll use them all up.

Newspapers are probably the best example of how easy it is to recycle household items. Every day 2 million trees are cut down and 56 million newspapers are thrown away. Newspapers are used to make new paper. Recycled newspapers also cut down on the number of trees that need to be harvested each year.

Other items that can be used again are aluminum items, tin cans, glass, motor oil, and many types of plastic. It is a known fact that one small recycled aluminum can saves enough energy to run a TV set for three hours or keep a 100-watt bulb burning for almost four hours. Aluminum is a durable and sustainable metal; two-thirds of the aluminum ever produced is in use today. When you recycle tin and aluminum cans, glass or plastic, all you need to do is rinse the items so that they are clean. Most communities provide a service to pick up recycled items or have a place to drop off what you want to recycle. In some communities, you can even turn in recycled items at special centers for cash.

Make recycling a habit in your daily life. Encourage others to become active in recycling efforts. Your personal effort will help reach the goal of saving energy, conserving natural resources, and extending the lives of our landfills. You will also begin to feel that you are doing something positive for your world.

✚ Ergonomic Tip

An important piece of furniture in an office is an ergonomic chair. A chair with adjustable height, seat, and back support is best.

Using Word Templates

In previous sessions, you prepared and formatted informational flyers to enhance their readability and presentation. In this session, you will work with files created from Word templates to create an agenda and a newsletter.

Selecting a Template

As explained in Session 83, a template is used to create documents with consistent formatting. Template files have the extension *.dotx*. However, when you open a new file based on a template, it has the regular document extension, *.docx*. A file created from a template contains all of the formatting and text present in the original template file.

Word provides many preformatted templates. Access these templates by clicking the File tab and then clicking *New*. This displays the New backstage area, shown in Figure 94.1. Note the Blank document template that displays in the upper left corner of the template options.

Key *agenda* in the search text box, as shown in Figure 94.1, and then press Enter to search online for available agenda templates. When the search results are displayed, as shown in Figure 94.2, click a thumbnail to see a preview of the file. *Note: Because these are online templates, your search results may vary from what you see in the figures in this book.*

When the template preview first opens, the template preview window displays a description of the template alongside the first page of the document. Click the Create button to open a new document based on the selected template.

Figure 94.1 New Backstage Area

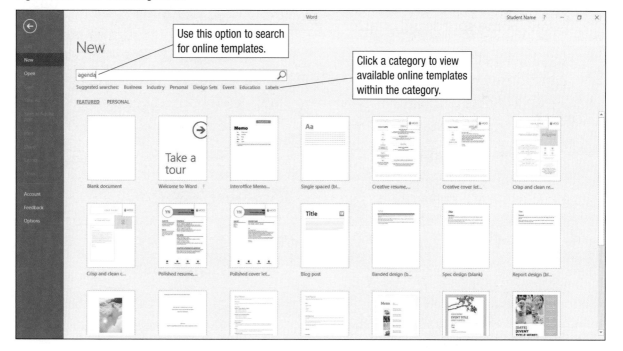

Complete two 1-minute timings on the timing text below. If you do not key at or above the WPM rate identified in the Online Lab on Timing 81.1, concentrate on speed on Timing 81.2. If you meet the Online Lab's WPM goal but make more errors than the goal set in the Online Lab on Timing 81.1, concentrate on accuracy on Timing 81.2. However, if you meet or exceed both timing goals for Timing 81.1, push for greater speed on Timing 81.2.

1-Minute Timings

**Timings
81.1–81.2**

On wagon trains and in prospecting encampments, the cook was often referred to as the "sourdough." Many of the cooks were famous for their breads, which often required a starter dough. If the starter was good enough to become famous, a cook was often rewarded with extra compensation and raises. Many believe sourdough was named after individuals who ventured into the Alaskan wilderness, but San Francisco starter for sourdough began around the era of the gold rush. To make this leavened bread starter easier to carry, the "sourdoughs" added flour to make a very firm ball. They carried the ball in a cloth flour satchel until baking time when it would be diluted with water. Because the winter evenings could get very frigid, they sometimes slept with the sourdough starter to prevent it from freezing. Families on wagon trains would often be given a bit of starter for their homestead if they hadn't brought any from home. Some sourdough starter is generations old.

Figure 94.2 Available Agenda Templates

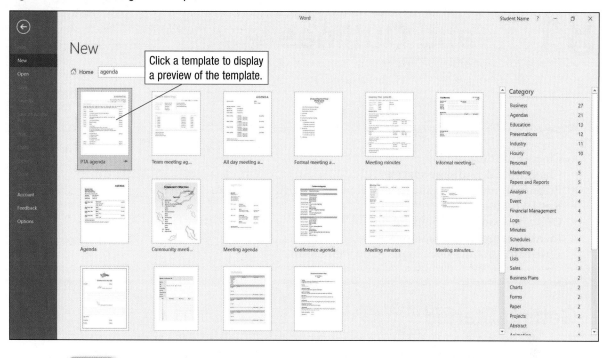

Success Tip

You can create your own template by creating a document and then selecting *Word Template (*.dotx)* from the *Save as type* option box at the Save As dialog box. When you create a template, by default, it will be stored in the Custom Office Templates folder in the Documents folder on the computer's hard drive. To display the template, click the File tab, click *New*, and then click the *PERSONAL* option.

For the first two document activities in this session, rather than using template files with .dotx extensions, you will use documents that have already been created from template files. (The file used in the Document 94.1 activity comes from an online template available in Word.) In the third document activity, you will choose a template from the New backstage area and then use it to create a document.

Success Tip

Gridlines are nonprinting cell boundaries that are helpful when editing a table. To display gridlines, click the View Gridlines button in the Table group on the Table Tools Layout tab.

Session 81

Keying Unbound Manuscripts and Outlines

Session Objectives

- **Change the default font**
- **Change the default line spacing**
- **Prepare an unbound manuscript following specific guidelines**
- **Key an outline**
- **Organize manuscript preparation**
- **Identify sources for a manuscript**
- **Efficiently produce documents in mailable form**

Getting Started

Exercise 81.1 If you are continuing immediately from Session 80, you may skip the Exercise 81.1 warm-up drill. However, if you exited the Online Lab at the end of Session 80, warm up by completing Exercise 81.1.

Exercise 81.2 Begin your session work by completing Exercise 81.2, a timed short drill, in the Online Lab.

Assessing Your Speed and Accuracy

Complete Timings 81.1 through 81.3 in the Online Lab. At the end of each timing, the Online Lab will display your WPM rate and any errors. Results will be saved in your Timings Performance report. If you have been surpassing the speed and accuracy goals identified by the Online Lab, set slightly more challenging personal goals and strive to exceed them. *Note: With this session, the default WPM goals for both 1-minute and 5-minute timings have been increased by 5 WPM in the Online Lab. However, your instructor may have customized these goals.*

Document **Agenda Document Using a Template**
94.1
Read all instructions below before starting this document activity.

1 Navigate to the Document 94.1 launch page in the Online Lab and then click the Launch Activity button to open **Doc094.01** in the activity window.

2 Edit the document to match the agenda shown in Figure 94.3. The document you start with displays the agenda in a table format. To see the cell boundaries within the table, click inside the table and then click the View Gridlines button in the Table group on the Table Tools Layout tab. Delete rows as needed using buttons on the Table Tools Layout tab. *Hint: To add the additional presenter names, press Ctrl + Tab to move the insertion point to the next tab stop within a cell. If necessary, you may need to reset the left tab at the 2.3 inch mark on the horizontal ruler for the cells containing the presenter names.*

3 Proofread the document and confirm that the formatting has been applied correctly and consistently. Correct any errors that you find in the document.

4 Save the document.

5 Click the Check button to upload the document for checking.

6 If errors are reported by the Online Lab, view the results document, correct the errors in the submitted document, save the document, and then click the Check Again button.

Figure 94.3 Agenda Content and Format for Document 94.1

AGENDA

Long-Range Planning Committee Meeting
February 17, 2020
9:00 a.m. – 12 noon

Meeting called by **Dr. Patricia Bladger**

Attendees:	Sonja Ahillen, Steve Burke, Sam Macahley, Yvette Malleres
Please read:	Minutes of January 20, 2020
Please bring:	iPad

9:00 a.m. – 10:00 a.m.	**Introduction**		
	Continental Breakfast		Rainbow Room
	Welcome	Dr. Patricia Bladger	

10:00 a.m. – 11:30 a.m.	**Business Meeting**		
	Approval of Agenda	Dr. Patricia Bladger	
	Approval of January 20 Minutes	Dr. Patricia Bladger	
	Illumination Subcommittee Report	Sam Macahley	Como Conference
	By-laws Subcommittee Report	Yvette Malleres	
	Landscaping Subcommittee Report	Steve Burke	

| **11:30 a.m. – 12 noon** | **Wrap-up** | | |
| | Q&A Panel | All Members | Como Conference |

Additional Instructions:
Please make sure you turn off all cell phones prior to entering the meeting rooms. Thanks.

Unit 17
Manuscripts and Research Papers Part II

Editing Text in a Placeholder or Text Box

Placeholders and text boxes are commonly used in templates. When you click inside a placeholder or text box, the text inside the placeholder or text box is selected, as shown in Figure 94.4. With the text selected, simply key new text in the placeholder or text box. You can also change the font of selected text by using options in the Font group on the Home tab.

Figure 94.4 shows a placeholder with selected text inside a text box. The inner gray border that displays will not print. The outer text box border can be formatted to print or not print. If you want it to print, you may format it with different line styles, widths, and colors, and you can fill the text box with color or apply shape styles by using features on the Drawing Tools Format tab.

Using the Drawing Tools Format Tab

When you click a text box in a document, the Drawing Tools Format tab will become available. Click the Drawing Tools Format tab to make it the active tab, as shown in Figure 94.5. Apply predesigned styles to the text box and change the shape fill, outline, and effects with options in the Shape Styles group. Use options in the Arrange group and Size group to size and position a text box. Customize the text within the text box with options in the WordArt Styles group and Text group.

Figure 94.4 Selected Placeholder and Text Box Text

[Grab your reader's attention with a great quote from the document or use this space to emphasize a key point. To place this text box anywhere on the page, just drag it.]

Figure 94.5 Drawing Tools Format Tab

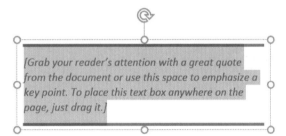

Figure 80.3 Business Report Content for Document 80.2—continued

3. The combination of steep grades and the at-grade roadway causes congestion, as normal traffic is not able to pass slow-moving traffic. This problem is compounded on East Madison Street where a steep grade is encountered.

4. Madison Street east of the intersection and Madison Street west of the intersection do not line up. A sharp right turn is also required from Dewey Street northeast going east on Madison Street. As motorists traveling east on Madison Street assume they have the right-of-way, they do not hesitate to cross over the dividing line into the rightmost eastbound lane, often creating potential accidents with Dewey Street motorists.

Proposal

Recommendation. The committee recommends that the intersection be rebuilt. The grade of Madison Street is considerable, rising 44 feet 6 inches in the relatively short distance of 417 feet, an 11 percent grade. East of the intersection the situation is somewhat improved. The rise of 30 feet is made over a distance of 808 feet, a somewhat lesser rise in twice the distance (a 6 percent grade).

Financing. The cost of the rebuilding project is estimated to be approximately $3.4 million. Federal and state funding are available. As the major expense will involve the removal of dirt so that the roadway goes under the railroad tracks, it may be possible to persuade the railroad to provide part of the money required for such a rebuilding project.

Ending the Session

The Online Lab automatically saved the work you completed for this session. You may continue with the next session or exit the Online Lab and continue later.

Document
94.2

Newsletter with Formatted Text Boxes

Read all instructions below before starting this document activity.

1 Navigate to the Document 94.2 launch page in the Online Lab and then click the Launch Activity button to open **Doc094.02** in the activity window.

2 Customize the title of the newsletter by completing the following steps:

   a Turn on the display of nonprinting characters. Select *Newsletter Title* and then key THE INSIDER. *Hint: The text will have a gray background when it is selected.*

   b With the insertion point in the title text box, press Ctrl + E or click the Center button in the Paragraph group on the Home tab.

3 Select *Newsletter Date* and then key Summer 2020. Do not replace the nonprinting new line command symbol.

4 Change the issue number to 2. (Do not change the volume number.)

5 Select *A. Datum Corporation*, key The Armstrong Development Group, and then change the font size of the text—including the nonprinting paragraph mark—to 14 points.

6 In the left panel of the newsletter, delete the text box that contains *Special Interest Articles* and three bulleted item placeholders. *Hint: Click the text box border to select the entire text box and then press the Delete key. Make sure you do not delete the entire column.*

7 Select all of the text in the *Individual Highlights* text box and then key the following, pressing Enter at the end of each line:

Armstrong Consulting
1234 Middleway Drive
Stringtown, IL 60001
618.555.5645

8 Select the text you keyed in Step 7, remove the bold and italic formatting, and then change the font size to 10 points.

9 Select the *Lead Story Headline* heading and then key Armstrong Group Breaks Ground for Retail.

10 Key the first article in the newsletter by completing the following steps:

   a Select all of the text in the first text box column under the *Armstrong Group Breaks Ground for Retail* heading and then press the Delete key. *Hint: Delete the text within the text box; do not delete the text box.*

   b Select all of the text in the next text box (which has moved to the first column position and begins with the text *contains, for example, employees*) and then press the Delete key.

   c Select all of the text in the last text box (which has moved to the first column position) and then press the Delete key.

   d With the insertion point positioned before the nonprinting paragraph mark for the first article, key the text shown in Figure 94.6. As you key, text will flow to the additional columns in the placeholder. *Hint: Allow Word to automatically insert the symbol in the word **café**.*

11 Select the *Second Story Headline* heading and then key First in United States.

12 Follow the same procedure for deleting the placeholder text in the second article that you followed for the first article and then key the text shown in Figure 94.7.

13 Change the background image of the left sidebar (the vertical green rectangle) of the newsletter by completing the following steps:

   a Click in an open area of the left sidebar (the vertical green rectangle) to select the background image.

steps continue

Figure 80.3 Business Report Content for Document 80.2—continued

roads have tended to be located in the valleys, where lesser slopes are available. Such locations, however, limit the continuity, which results in many jogs and offsets in the street system.

Train traffic, which at this point is the main double track line (mainline) of the Chicago and Eastern Railroad Line with several side tracks south of Madison Street, is a serious barrier to automobile traffic and has long been recognized as bad. A separation of grades was planned by the railroad more than 30 years ago, but the expense involved was so great that no steps have ever been taken to carry out the needed reconstruction.

Traffic. Studies have shown travel patterns in the city to be of three basic types: local traffic within the city, travel from outlying regions into the city and returning, and external traffic passing through the city. Industry located in the northern part of the city probably is responsible for the largest part of the traffic. The greatest proportion of traffic to and from these industries originates to the north and east.

There are three routes serving the northwest section of the city: Starr Avenue/Birch Street, US Highway 129/Birch Street, and CTH Q/Birch Street. Of these, because of the contraction of a major interchange viaduct not in progress, the majority of the traffic naturally travels west on Birch Street from US Highway 129. A good arterial street connection between this route and the downtown area is therefore vitally important.

Accidents. During the past 6 months, there have been 25 accidents recorded at the intersection. With three exceptions, these accidents were all attributed to the at-grade railroad crossing. In one instance, a motorist collided with a train traveling on the southbound track.

Congestion. In addition to peak-hour capacities, congestion is caused by four existing conditions:

1. A major delay is created by the at-grade level crossing of the railroad. Heavy vehicular traffic, 15 regular trains and several locals, and switching movement each day make it quite evident that the railroad represents a significant disruption to traffic flow.

2. Due to reasons previously mentioned, sharp turns at the Birch Street/Germania and Germania/East Madison intersections cause a general slowdown of traffic, which often affect traffic flow at the crossing.

continues

b Click the Drawing Tools Format tab.

c Click the Shape Fill button arrow in the Shape Styles group.

d Point to *Texture*.

e Click *Canvas* (second column, first row) at the side menu.

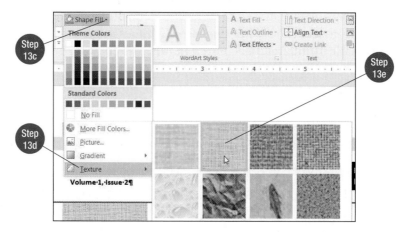

14 With the left sidebar still selected, change the outline line weight to 2¼ points by completing the following steps:

a Click the Shape Outline button arrow in the Shape Styles group on the Drawing Tools Format tab.

b Point to *Weight*.

c Click *2¼ pt* at the side menu.

15 Select the text box containing the address and phone number for Armstrong Consulting and then change the font color to Black, Text 1 (second column, first row in the *Theme Colors* section).

16 Format the banner of the newsletter by completing the following steps:

a Click twice in the newsletter banner, in the blank space between the *THE INSIDER* title and the issue number, to select the banner text box. **Hint: Do not select the text box containing the newsletter title.**

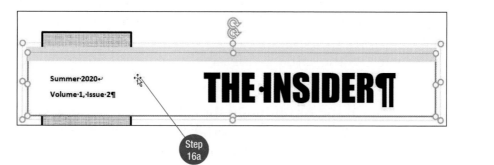

b Click the More Shape Styles button in the Shape Styles group on the Drawing Tools Format tab.

c Click *Subtle Effect - Blue, Accent 1* (second column, fourth row in the *Theme Styles* section).

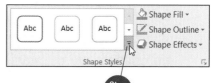

d Click the Shape Outline button arrow in the Shape Styles group.

e Click *Black, Text 1* (second column, first row in the *Theme Colors* section).

steps continue

   c When keying indented paragraph headings, turn off bold formatting after keying the period at the end of the heading. Do not format the space following the heading in bold. For indented paragraph headings that are not immediately preceded by a side heading, turn on bold formatting *after* pressing the Tab key.

   d Allow Word to automatically format the numbered list. Increase the indent of the list so the numbers align with the paragraph indent, and add an extra line space between list items. *Note: If the numbered list does not format automatically, check the* **Automatic numbered lists** *option in the AutoFormat As You Type tab in the AutoCorrect Options dialog box. Review Session 79 if necessary.*

5 Insert a plain page number (*Plain Number 3*) at the right margin of the header on the second and subsequent pages of the report. Do not include the page number on the first page.

6 Proofread the document and correct any errors.

7 Save the document.

8 Click the Check button to upload the document for checking.

9 If errors are reported by the Online Lab, view the results document, correct the errors in the submitted document, save the document, and then click the Check Again button.

Figure 80.3 Business Report Content for Document 80.2

RECOMMENDATIONS FOR THE MADISON STREET CROSSING

This report contains the basic data gathered and analyzed to make recommendations regarding the Madison Street crossing. The recommendation made by this committee strongly supports the rebuilding of the crossing as soon as possible.

Purpose

The purpose of this committee was to study possible alternatives for alleviating the traffic problem at the Madison Street crossing. This includes recommendations for an arterial street improvement, which would serve the central part of the city, provide access to the downtown area and the major industrial complex, link US Highway 129 with the east/west arterial street system across the Little Tennessee River, and eliminate the serious and chronic problem with the Chicago and Eastern Railroad traffic.

The objective of the recommendation is to relieve traffic congestion, which affects the business and industrial portions of the city, while also providing for safety and more efficient travel.

The Problem

Existing Conditions. Topography and the location of commercial business have primarily determined the character and location of the street network in the immediate area. Because of the steep grades in certain areas, several industries are located on the plateau of the river. As a result, access

continues

17 Proofread the document and confirm the formatting has been applied correctly. Correct any errors that you find in the document.

18 Save the document.

19 Click the Submit button to upload the document for instructor review.

Figure 94.6 Content for First Article in Document 94.2

Construction is under way for the 105,000-square-foot, mixed-use Village Market complex.

The 50,000-square-foot, bi-level supermarket in the Village Market complex, the first in Chicago, is being created by Groundy's Supermarkets. Groundy's is a leading Midwest grocery chain and operates over 150 retail grocery stores and 80 pharmacies in the Midwest.

Pasanos Fresh Market will emphasize fresh produce, meat, seafood, bakery, and deli as prepared foods available for breakfast, lunch, and dinner. It will also offer natural and organic products and a selection of homeopathic remedies. Other features will include a wine and spirits department, sushi bar, and an Italian-themed café featuring espresso, gelato, and panini.

Rachael Atwater, Armstrong's Director of Development, reports that Forks II has leased nearly 10,000 square feet from Pasanos. Forks II will provide a venue for dining, private parties, and special events.

Pasanos will be an enormous convenience not only to people making their home at Lakeshore West but for our residential and commercial neighbors.

Figure 94.7 Content for Second Article in Document 94.2

Atlanta-based Westwood Hotels announces plans to develop a distinctive Westwood Tru hotel in the Aqua Building at Lakeshore West.

Westwood Tru is scheduled to open in the fall of 2020 and will be a full-service, luxury facility with 334 guest rooms. Other planned features include a 12,000-square-foot ballroom, 25,000 square feet of total meeting space, and a 150-seat restaurant and bar. In addition, Westwood guests will have full access to the exceptional amenity center and fitness package of the internationally acclaimed, mixed-use Aqua Building that was recently named Skytower of the Year by Regents, the international building database.

continues

Figure 80.2 Business Memo Report Format for Document 80.1

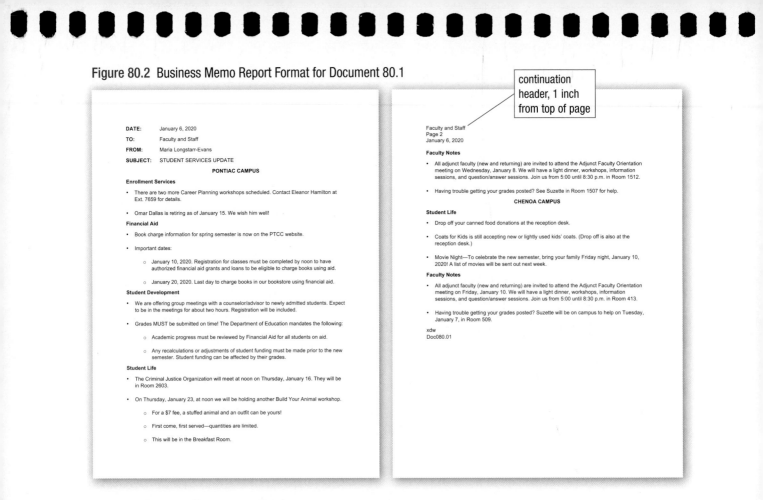

continuation header, 1 inch from top of page

Document 80.2

Formal Bound Business Report

Read all instructions below before starting this document activity.

1 Navigate to the Document 80.2 launch page in the Online Lab and then click the Launch Activity button to open **Doc080.02** in the activity window.

2 Format the document margins for a bound report.

3 Key the report title by completing the following steps:

a Press Enter three times to move the insertion point approximately 2 inches from the top of the page.

b Change the paragraph alignment to center alignment.

c Turn on bold formatting.

d Key the title shown in Figure 80.3.

e Turn off bold formatting.

f Press Enter and then change the paragraph alignment to left alignment.

4 Key the body of the report shown in Figure 80.3. Consider the following as you key the report:

a Press Tab at the start of each paragraph.

b When keying side headings that are immediately followed by an indented paragraph heading, do not turn off bold formatting until after keying the paragraph heading. In contrast, when keying side headings that are not immediately followed by an indented paragraph heading, turn off bold formatting before pressing Enter.

steps continue

Figure 94.7 Content for Second Article in Document 94.2—continued

The award is considered the world's top honor for high-rise architecture and is presented annually since 2000 to new skyscrapers that show outstanding architectural design and functionality.

In announcing its planned joint venture with Armstrong, Westwood President and Chief Executive Officer Bradley Keinman said it would mark the company's most important investment as part of Westwood's growth strategy.

"Our goal is to establish flagship hotels in major cities throughout the United States, and Westwood Tru is a major step towards realizing that dream," he announced.

Reinforcing Writing Skills

In the next document activity, you will create a personal newsletter based on an online template of your choice from those available at the New backstage area in Word.

Document 94.3

Creating a Personal Newsletter

Read all instructions below before starting this document activity.

1   Navigate to the Document 94.3 launch page and then minimize the Online Lab.

2   Open Word and, at the opening screen, search for and then select a newsletter template. When selecting a template, choose a style that will be appropriate for a newsletter about yourself that you can send to your personal contacts. Click a template thumbnail to display a preview of the template. Click the Create button to open a new document using that template. *Note: If Word is already open on your computer, you will need to click the File tab and then click the* **New** *option before searching for a template.*

3   Build the newsletter and include the following information:
   • Your personal contact details
   • Information about your work or school
   • An article that is a review of a movie, novel, or restaurant that you recommend
   • An article with updates on a hobby or volunteer organization
   • An appropriate title for each article
   • The label *Volume 1, Issue 1*

4   Customize the design of the document to make the newsletter readable and attractive.

5   Proofread and correct any errors in the newsletter.

6   Save the document with the file name **Doc094.03_Newsletter_XXX**, replacing *XXX* with your initials. Close the document and then close Word.

7   Return to the document activity launch page in the Online Lab, click the Upload Document button, and then select your completed file to upload it for instructor review.

Ending the Session

The Online Lab automatically saved the work you completed for this session. You may continue with the next session or exit the Online Lab and continue later.

Figure 80.1 Business Memo Report Content for Document 80.1

DATE: January 6, 2020 ¶ **TO:** Faculty and Staff ¶ **FROM:** Maria Longstarr-Evans ¶ **SUBJECT:** STUDENT SERVICES UPDATE ¶ **PONTIAC CAMPUS** ¶ **Enrollment Services** ¶ • There are two more Career Planning workshops scheduled. Contact Eleanor Hamilton at Ext. 7659 for details. ↵¶ • Omar Dallas is retiring as of January 15. We wish him well! ¶¶ **Financial Aid** ¶ • Book charge information for spring semester is now on the PTCC website. ↵¶ • Important dates: ↵¶ ○ January 10, 2020. Registration for classes must be completed by noon to have authorized financial aid grants and loans to be eligible to charge books using aid. ↵¶ ○ January 20, 2020. Last day to charge books in our bookstore using financial aid. ¶¶¶ **Student Development** ¶ • We are offering group meetings with a counselor/advisor to newly admitted students. Expect to be in the meetings for about two hours. Registration will be included. ↵¶ • Grades MUST be submitted on time! The Department of Education mandates the following: ↵¶ ○ Academic progress must be reviewed by Financial Aid for all students on aid. ↵¶ ○ Any recalculations or adjustments of student funding must be made prior to the new semester. Student funding can be affected by their grades. ¶¶¶ **Student Life** ¶ • The Criminal Justice Organization will meet at noon on Thursday, January 16. They will be in Room 2603. ↵¶ • On Thursday, January 23, at noon we will be holding another Build Your Animal workshop. ↵¶ ○ For a $7 fee, a stuffed animal and an outfit can be yours! ↵¶ ○ First come, first served—quantities are limited. ↵¶ ○ This will be in the Breakfast Room. ¶¶¶ **Faculty Notes** ¶ • All adjunct faculty (new and returning) are invited to attend the Adjunct Faculty Orientation meeting on Wednesday, January 8. We will have a light dinner, workshops, information sessions, and question/answer sessions. Join us from 5:00 until 8:30 p.m. in Room 1512. ↵¶ • Having trouble getting your grades posted? See Suzette in Room 1507 for help. ¶¶ **CHENOA CAMPUS** ¶ **Student Life** ¶ • Drop off your canned food donations at the reception desk. ↵¶ • Coats for Kids is still accepting new or lightly used kids' coats. (Drop off is also at the reception desk.) ↵¶ • Movie Night—To celebrate the new semester, bring your family Friday night, January 10, 2020! A list of movies will be sent out next week. ¶¶ **Faculty Notes** ¶ • All adjunct faculty (new and returning) are invited to attend the Adjunct Faculty Orientation meeting on Friday, January 10. We will have a light dinner, workshops, information sessions, and question/answer sessions. Join us from 5:00 until 8:30 p.m. in Room 413. ↵¶ • Having trouble getting your grades posted? Suzette will be on campus to help on Tuesday, January 7, in Room 509.

Session 95

Production Progress Check: Business Publications

Session Objectives

- **Apply features presented in Sessions 91–94**
- **Efficiently produce documents in mailable form**

Getting Started

Exercise 95.1   If you are continuing immediately from Session 94, you can skip the Exercise 95.1 warm-up drill. However, if you exited the Online Lab at the end of Session 94, warm up by completing Exercise 95.1.

Exercise 95.2   Begin your session work by completing Exercise 95.2, a timed short drill, in the Online Lab.

Assessing Your Speed and Accuracy

Complete Timing 95.1 in the Online Lab using the timing text on the next page. At the end of the timing, the Online Lab will display your WPM rate and any errors. Results will be saved in your Timings Performance report. If you have been surpassing the speed and accuracy goals identified in the Online Lab, set slightly more challenging goals and strive to exceed them.

To help you succeed, carefully review the instructions and content for each document before keying. To minimize formatting errors identified by the document checker, be sure to follow the directions carefully.

Success Tip

Turn on the display of nonprinting characters to help check the consistency and accuracy of your formatting.

Document 80.1 — Multiple-Page Business Memo Report

Read all instructions below before starting this document activity.

1 Navigate to the Document 80.1 launch page in the Online Lab and then click the Launch Activity button to open **Doc080.01** in the activity window.

2 Change the default font for the document to Arial. Keep the size at 11 points.

3 Key the memo report using the text shown in Figure 80.1 and use the document shown in Figure 80.2 for formatting reference. Consider the following instructions as you key the text:

a Format the guide words and the following punctuation in bold, but turn off bold formatting before pressing Tab.

b Format all of the headings in the memo in bold. The two main headings are set in all capital letters and are centered. Because the two main headings are immediately followed by a bold subheading, you do not need to turn off bold formatting until after you key the subheading. After you key the subheadings, turn off bold formatting before pressing Enter.

c Allow Word to automatically format bulleted lists. When keying the bulleted lists, keep the first-level bullets aligned at the left margin (decrease the indent) and use the solid, black, round bullet format. For the second-level bullets, use the open-circle bullet. Include an extra line space between bulleted items (Shift + Enter).

d Key the reference initials xdw and the file name at the end of the memo report.

4 Create a vertical continuation header using the *Blank* option for the second page of the memo report. The header should begin 1 inch from the top of the page.

5 Proofread the document and correct any errors.

6 Save the document.

7 Click the Check button to upload the document for checking.

8 If errors are reported by the Online Lab, view the results document, correct the errors in the submitted document, save the document, and then click the Check Again button.

Timing 95.1

Accidents happen. But if you are the parent of one of the 30 million kids younger than 14 who participate in organized youth sports, simple preventive steps can help save your child's smile and keep them off the injured list and hospital emergency rooms. A board certified pediatric dentist has indicated that dental and facial injuries represent a high percentage of total injuries in youth sports. These include soccer, football, baseball, basketball, hockey, lacrosse, cheerleading, and many other recreational sports.

The National Youth Sports Foundation for Safety reports that dental injuries are the most common type of oral facial injury sustained when kids play sports and more than five million teeth are knocked out each year during the course of games, scrimmages, and competition. Nearly 80 percent of these injuries involve the upper front teeth.

If a tooth gets knocked out, act quickly. Examine the tooth and, if clean, try to put it back in the mouth. If it is dirty, do not rinse; put it in milk as soon as possible and only touch the crown. Roots can be damaged by touch. Then take the child and the tooth immediately to the dentist, preferably within 30 minutes.

Protective gear like helmets and pads are standard gear for most sports, but we must remember the need to protect the child's smile with mouth guards. Protective gear like mouth guards worn during games and practice can help prevent injuries to the mouth, teeth, lips, cheeks, and tongue. Be aware that not all mouth guards are alike. For approximately $200, a custom-made mouth guard fitted by your dentist is probably the best protection you can buy. They even come in a variety of school and team colors and can last for years. Another type includes the "boil-and-bite" variety for kids with braces and baby teeth since they can be replaced frequently as the child grows. Also, there are those that can be bought in the store off the shelf, which kids tend to discard at the first opportunity.

Mouth guards need to be comfortable or the chance of getting kids to keep them in their mouth is fruitless. Even though mouth guards are usually used in organized sports, there are higher-risk recreational activities like skateboarding, bicycling, rollerblading, and gymnastics that should be considered for the use of protective mouth guards.

Complete one 3-minute timing on the timing text below.

3-Minute Timing

Timing 80.3

A computer network consists of two or more computing or other devices connected by a medium, such as a wireless signal or a cable. Whereas the signal is broadcast through the air, a cable is a wire that runs underground, below streets. A computer network provides a way to connect with others and share files and resources such as printers or an Internet connection. Networks are now found in all schools, towns, and large and small firms.

In business settings, networks allow you to communicate with employees, suppliers, vendors, customers, and government agencies. Many companies have their own network, called an intranet, which is a private network within the company's "walls." Some companies also offer an extension of their internal network, called an extranet, to suppliers and customers. For example, a supplier might be allowed to access information on a company's internal network to make sure the company does not run short of a vital part for its manufacturing process.

In your home, networks are useful for sharing resources among members of your family. For example, using a home network, you might share one printer or fax machine among three or four computers. With time, you can add more than one device to the home network, all for a small cost.

Ergonomic Tip
To prevent eye strain, position the copy that you are working from so that it is the same distance from your eyes to the copy as it is from your eyes to the computer monitor.

Checking Production Progress: Business Reports

Sessions 76 through 79 discussed the procedures for creating business reports in memo, formal, and specialized formats. In this session, you will be assessed on how accurately you can key these types of documents. In the following document activities, each completed document is to be useable or "mailable," which means that it contains no errors. A document that requires corrections before being distributed is not considered *mailable*.

Your goal is to key each email and memo in mailable form. If you are missing errors that should have been corrected or your instructor believes you can work more efficiently, he or she may ask you to repeat document activities.

Ergonomic Tip

There is no one "right" position in which to sit; to maximize comfort and health, frequently adjust your sitting position.

Checking Production Progress: Business Publications

Sessions 91 through 94 discussed the procedures for preparing business publications. In this session, you will be assessed on how accurately you can produce and key these types of documents. Each completed file is to be "mailable," which means that it is properly formatted and contains no errors. A document that requires corrections is not considered *mailable*.

Your goal is to key each email and memo in mailable form. If you are missing errors that should have been corrected or your instructor believes you can work more efficiently, he or she may ask you to repeat document activities. To help you succeed, carefully review the instructions and content for each document before keying it. To minimize formatting errors identified by the Online Lab, be sure to follow the directions carefully. Review the content of Sessions 91 through 94 if you are unsure of how to complete a specific task.

Document 95.1

Flyer with Custom Formatting

Read all instructions below before starting this document activity.

1 Navigate to the Document 95.1 launch page in the Online Lab and then click the Launch Activity button to open **Doc095.01** in the activity window.

2 Change the font to 16-point Garamond.

3 Key the text shown in Figure 95.1. *Note: Press Enter once at the end of each line except for the last line.*

4 Select all of the text in the document and change the paragraph alignment to center alignment.

5 Select the first line including the nonprinting paragraph mark, change the font to 24-point Arial Black, apply underline formatting, and then change the font color to Red (second option in the *Standard Colors* section).

6 Vertically center the text on the page. *Hint: You do not need to select any text in the document to do this.*

7 Proofread the document and correct any errors.

8 Save the document.

9 Click the Check button to upload the document for checking.

10 If errors are reported by the Online Lab, view the results document, correct the errors in the submitted document, save the document, and then click the Check Again button.

Figure 95.1 Flyer Content for Document 95.1

WINTER SEASON SALE

Arbor Shops on the Mall

Saturday, March 21, 2020

9:00 a.m. to 9:30 p.m.

All Items 20% to 50% off Retail Prices!

Session

80

Production Progress Check: Business Reports Part II

Session Objectives

- **Apply features presented in Sessions 76–79**
- **Efficiently produce documents in mailable form**

Getting Started

Exercise 80.1 If you are continuing immediately from Session 79, you can skip the Exercise 80.1 warm-up drill. However, if you exited the Online Lab at the end of Session 79, warm up by completing Exercise 80.1.

Exercise 80.2 Begin your session work by completing Exercise 80.2, a timed short drill, in the Online Lab.

Assessing Your Speed and Accuracy

Complete Timings 80.1 through 80.3 in the Online Lab. At the end of each timing, the Online Lab will display your WPM rate and any errors. Results will be saved in your Timings Performance report. If you have been surpassing the speed and accuracy goals identified in the Online Lab, set slightly more challenging personal goals and strive to exceed them.

Complete two 1-minute timings on the timing text below. If you meet or exceed both speed and accuracy goals for Timing 80.1, push for greater speed on Timing 80.2.

1-Minute Timings

Timings 80.1–80.2   Distinctive forms of clouds and precipitation, as well as winds, are common to storms. Precipitation is the weather bureau's name for all forms of water falling from the sky. Thunder is the first signal of an incoming storm. Signals of the hurricane, however, move in with little or no noise. An alert weather watcher is well aware of the danger signals. First, the wispy, veil-like cirrus clouds appear and dance on the horizon. Then, small, fluffy cumulus clouds speed across the sky below high decks of darkening clouds.

Document with Multiple Columns

Read all instructions below before starting this document activity.

1 Navigate to the Document 95.2 launch page in the Online Lab and then click the Launch Activity button to open **Doc095.02** in the activity window.

2 Key the text shown in Figure 95.2. *Note: When keying the headings and subheadings, be sure to turn off bold formatting before pressing Enter.*

3 Format the two section headings in bold, 14-point Arial Black font. *Note: When selecting the text, include the nonprinting paragraph mark. If you applied bold formatting to the headings as you keyed them, you do not need to turn on bold formatting in this step.*

4 In the first section of the document, select the subheadings and corresponding paragraphs from the subheading *User IDs and Passwords* to the text *install the spyware unknowingly.* and then format the selected text in two columns. *Note: When selecting the text, do not include the nonprinting paragraph mark at the end of the selection.*

5 In the second section of the document, select the subheadings and corresponding paragraphs from the subheading *Wireless Device Security* to the text *in appropriate conduct.* and then format the selected text in three columns with a line between the columns. *Note: When selecting the text, do not include the nonprinting paragraph mark at the end of the selection.*

6 Proofread the document and correct any errors.

7 Save the document.

8 Click the Check button to upload the document for checking.

9 If errors are reported by the Online Lab, view the results document, correct the errors in the submitted document, save the document, and then click the Check Again button.

Figure 95.2 Content for Document 95.2

SECTION 1: UNAUTHORIZED ACCESS

Like uncharted wilderness, the Internet lacks borders. This inherent openness is what makes the Internet so valuable and yet so vulnerable. Over its short life, the Internet has grown so quickly that the legal system has not been able to keep pace. The security risks posed by networks and the Internet include unauthorized access and information theft.

Hackers, computer experts who seek programming and security challenges, are responsible for most cases of unauthorized access. Some hackers exploit sites and programs that have poor security measures in place. For more challenging sites, hackers use sophisticated programs and strategies to gain

continues

Reinforcing Writing Skills

An abstract is a condensed version of a document. Generally speaking, an abstract highlights the important parts of a much longer version of a document. Usually the length of an abstract is kept to 150 to 200 words.

Document 79.3

Composing an Abstract for an RFP

Read all instructions below before starting this document activity.

1 Navigate to the Document 79.3 launch page in the Online Lab and then click the Launch Activity button to open **Doc079.03** in the activity window.

2 Compose an abstract for the RFP you keyed and formatted in the Document 79.1 activity. The abstract should be presented in a simple paragraph style using Word's default settings. Use the Word Count feature in the Status bar to determine the length of your abstract. *Note: To display the word count in the Status bar, right-click the Status bar and then click* **Word Count** *at the shortcut menu.*

3 Proofread the document and correct any errors.

4 Save the document.

5 Click the Submit button to upload the document for instructor review.

Ending the Session

The Online Lab automatically saved the work you completed for this session. You may continue with the next session or exit the Online Lab and continue later.

Figure 95.2 Content for Document 95.2—continued

access. Many hackers claim they hack merely because they like the challenge of trying to defeat security measures. These individuals rarely have a more malicious motive and generally do not aim to destroy or damage the sites that they invade. In fact, many hackers dislike being identified with those who seek to cause damage. They refer to hackers with malicious or criminal intent as *crackers*.

User IDs and Passwords

To gain entry over the Internet to a secure computer system, most hackers focus on finding a working user ID and password combination. User IDs are easy to come by and are generally not secure information. Sending an email, for example, displays the sender's user ID in the return address, making it very public. The only missing element is the password. Hackers know from experience which passwords are common; they have programs that generate thousands of likely passwords and they try them systematically over a period of hours or days.

System Backdoors

Programmers can sometimes inadvertently aid hackers by providing unintentional entrance to networks and information systems. One such unintentional entrance is a system "backdoor," which is a user ID and password that provides the highest level of authorization. Programmers innocently create a backdoor in the early days of system development to allow other programmers and team members to access the system to fix problems. Through negligence or by design, the user ID and password are sometimes left behind in the final version of the system. Perhaps years later, when the backdoor has been forgotten, people who know about it can then enter the system, bypassing the security.

continues

Document 79.2 Cover Page for a Response to an RFP

Read all instructions below before starting this document activity.

1 Navigate to the Document 79.2 launch page in the Online Lab and then click the Launch Activity button to open **Doc079.02** in the activity window.

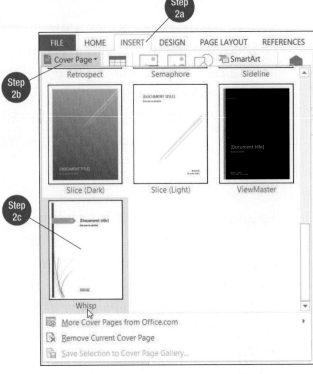

2 Insert the Whisp cover page template in the document by completing the following steps:

a Click the Insert tab.

b Click the Cover Page button in the Pages group.

c Scroll down the drop-down list and then click *Whisp* in the *Built-In* section.

3 Key the text for the cover page by completing the following steps:

a Click *Date* to select the Date placeholder; click the down arrow; and then locate and select August 14, 2020 on the calendar.

b Click *Document title* to select the Title placeholder.

c Key Proposal for Internet Marketing Services.

d Press Tab to select the Subtitle placeholder and then key Response to Request for Proposal.

e Click in the Author placeholder to select it and then key Patricia Forrest. ***Note: Select any existing text in the Author placeholder before typing the new text.***

f Press Tab to select the Company placeholder and then key checkyourhotel. ***Note: The text box is formatted for all capital letters and will convert your keystrokes automatically.***

4 Turn on the display of nonprinting characters by clicking the Show/Hide ¶ button in the Paragraph group on the Home tab.

5 At the top of the first page, delete the page break and the paragraph mark before it by pressing Ctrl + Home to move the insertion point to the beginning of the document and then pressing the Delete key twice.

6 Turn off the display of nonprinting characters by clicking the Show/Hide ¶ button.

7 Proofread the document and correct any errors. Figure 79.9 on the previous page shows the completed document.

8 Save the document.

9 Click the Check button to upload the document for checking.

10 If errors are reported by the Online Lab, view the results document, correct the errors in the submitted document, save the document, and then click the Check Again button.

Figure 95.2 Content for Document 95.2—continued

Spoofing

A sophisticated way to break into a network via the Internet involves spoofing, which is the process of fooling another computer by pretending to send information from a legitimate source. It works by altering the address that the system automatically puts on every message sent. The address is changed to one that the receiving computer is programmed to accept as a trusted source of information.

Spyware

Spyware is a type of software that allows an intruder to spy upon someone else's computer. This alarming technology takes advantage of loopholes in the computer's security systems and allows a stranger to witness and record another person's every mouse click and keystroke as it occurs. The spy can record activities and gain access to passwords and credit card information. Spyware generally requires the user to install it on the machine that is being spied upon, so it is highly unlikely that random strangers on the Internet could simply begin watching your computer. In the workplace, however, someone might be able to install the software without the victim's knowledge. Disguised as a friendly email attachment, for example, the program can operate like a virus that gets the unwary user to install the spyware unknowingly.

SECTION 2: INFORMATION THEFT

Information can be a company's most valuable possession. Stealing corporate information, a crime included in the category of industrial espionage, is unfortunately both easy to do and difficult to detect. This is due in part to the invisible nature of software and data. If a cracker breaks into a company network and manages to download the company database from the network onto a disk, there is no visible sign to the company that anything is amiss. The original database is still in place, working the same way it always has.

continues

Creating Cover Pages

Microsoft Word provides a number of predesigned cover pages. Using them is simple—you choose the cover page design and key the text the way you want it. Access the predesigned cover pages by clicking the Cover Page button in the Pages group on the Insert tab. Figure 79.9 shows a cover page created from the Whisp cover page template, which is available from the list of built-in options in Word. You will create this cover page in the next document activity.

Figure 79.9 Cover Page Created for Document 79.2

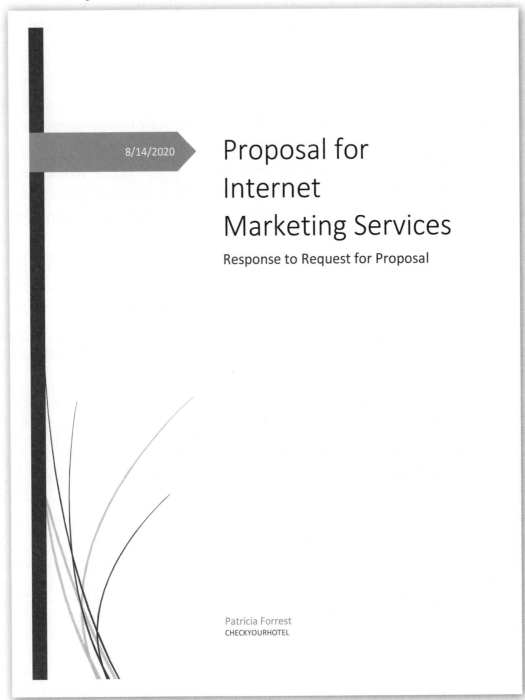

8/14/2020

Proposal for Internet Marketing Services

Response to Request for Proposal

Patricia Forrest
CHECKYOURHOTEL

Figure 95.2 Content for Document 95.2—continued

Wireless Device Security

The growing number of wireless devices has created a new opportunity for data theft. Wireless devices such as cameras, smartphones, networked computers, and input and output peripherals are inherently less secure than wired devices. Home users, in particular, tend not to bother turning on security controls on their wireless routers, such as requiring a password to search the web. A wired connection, such as a cable between a keyboard and a computer, can't be as easily intercepted as a wireless radio transmission. To intercept company emails on a wireless network, all a competitor needs to do is park a computer-laden van outside the building and use their hacking systems to listen in. In theory, a domestic Wi-Fi network comes armed with a high degree of security. The wireless router that's central to a domestic Wi-Fi network has several built-in protection features. Firewall software intercepts hackers' attempts, and encryption devices scramble data inside the network so that it isn't readable without an encryption key.

Data Browsing

Data browsing is a less damaging form of information theft that involves an invasion of privacy. Workers in many organizations have access to networked databases that contain private information about people. Accessing this information without an official reason is against the law. The IRS had a particularly large problem with data browsing in the late 1990s. Some employees were fired and the rest were given specialized training in appropriate conduct.

Document 95.3 Document Converted to a Table

Read all instructions below before starting this document activity.

1 Navigate to the Document 95.3 launch page in the Online Lab and then click the Launch Activity button to open **Doc095.03** in the activity window.

2 Key the text shown in Figure 95.3. Change the paragraph alignment of the title and subtitle to center alignment. Press Tab after the headings within the document, as indicated in the figure.

3 Set the title in 14-point Copperplate Gothic Bold and the subtitle in 12-point Copperplate Gothic Light. *Note: When selecting the text, include the nonprinting paragraph marks.*

4 Convert the text from the heading *Check-In* through the text *perform their duties.*—including the nonprinting paragraph mark at the end of the last paragraph of text—to a two-column table. Allow the columns to be defined by Tab characters.

steps continue

Figure 79.7 Table Content for Section 6 of Document 79.1

Products	Standard	Platinum	Titanium
Email List Management	X	X	X
Hotel Newsletters	X	X	X
RSS Feeds		X	X
Hotel eCards		X	X
Search Engine Optimization		X	X
Custom Hotel Ratings			X
Director of Internet Sales			X
Web Page Design			X
Wikipedia Listing Service			X
Monthly Prices	$350	$750	$1525

Figure 79.8 RFP Response Created for Document 79.1

Proposal for Internet Marketing Services   15

SECTION 3. OUR INTERNET SERVICES

Our professionals are experienced and will establish a
hotel will be provided with a plan to establish a power
requirements. We focus on creating websites that will
easy to use. This will lead to increased bookings and re
website can be found on the Internet.

3.1   EMAIL LIST MANAGEMENT & NEWSLETTERS

We realize that it is vital to be able to commu
CheckYourHotel provides services to help you

3.1.1   Email Data Capture. This is the most va
perhaps the most negative aspect of e
your guests by creating an email data
standards, and will be welcomed and s
double opt-in email data capture syste

3.1.2   Email Database. A properly managed e
way to reach your customer base as it

3.2   HOTEL ECARDS

These cards are interactive and ideal for marke
your guests advertise your hotel for you.

3.3   OPTIMIZED SEARCH ENGINE

The number one requested service is vital to th

3.3.1   Platinum Report. This is a standardized
establish your website's ranking at any
categories. Your Platinum Report estab
phrases.

3.3.2   Website Information Critique. We aud
their placement. This assists in your w
spiders (software that searches the co
to find your site and capture informati
tags need to be optimized to aid the s

3.3.3   Keyword and Phrase Identification. We
specific market. We will work with you
phrases are the most applicable to the
rank them.

CheckYour

Proposal for Internet Marketing Services   16

3.4   DIRECTOR OF INTERNET SALES AND MARKETIN

The Director of Internet Sales and Marketing p
your Internet sales and data capture strategies
General Manager with full accounting that will
makers monthly.

3.5   SOCIAL MEDIA WEB DESIGN AND WIKIPEDIA S

These two services are offered with our Titani
increase exposure for your site. Social media s
your customers and prospective customers, to
sites. Meanwhile, the Wikipedia Listing Service

SECTION 4. WEBSITE

In order to make your website functional, your websit
aesthetically pleasing website that reflects the charact
Your goal, and therefore our goal, is to have your custo
as many pages as possible way past the Home page—a

4.1   SEARCH ENGINE FRIENDLY

At CheckYourHotel we can make changes quic
regional, and national changes in business and
connecting engines.

4.2   VISION REPRESENTED

We understand it is important that your websi
manner consistent with the hotel's individual a

4.3   PROTOCOL STRUCTURE

We can guarantee that the data configuration
protocol so the website looks as appealing and

SECTION 5. HOTEL PI

Our Absolute Voice system delivers tracking reports on
services, call measurement reports, and call monitorin
with respect to calls initiated using our assigned numb

We provide updated data on call traffic generated dire
access are made available via private login numbers an
monitor calls, or evaluate traffic. This will answer ques
a direct result of the website.

CheckYou

Proposal for Internet Marketing Services   17

SECTION 6. COSTS

The following table illustrates the products and packages available. Your current needs may be met in
any of our three packages. When planning for the future, you may wish to consider either the Platinum
or Titanium packages.

Products	Standard	Platinum	Titanium
Email List Management	X	X	X
Hotel Newsletters	X	X	X
RSS Feeds		X	X
Hotel eCards		X	X
Search Engine Optimization		X	X
Custom Hotel Ratings			X
Director of Internet Sales			X
Web Page Design			X
Wikipedia Listing Service			X
Monthly Prices	$350	$750	$1525

CheckYourHotel

5   Adjust the width of the first column to 2.6 inches and then adjust the width of the second column to 4 inches. *Hint: Select each column individually and adjust the widths in the Cell Size group on the Table Tools Layout tab.*

6   Select the left column of the table and then change the font to 12-point Copperplate Gothic Bold.

7   Proofread the document and correct any errors.

8   Save the document.

9   Click the Check button to upload the document for checking.

10 If errors are reported by the Online Lab, view the results document, correct the errors in the submitted document, save the document, and then click the Check Again button.

Figure 95.3   Content for Document 95.3

AIRLINE INFORMATION

Things You Need to Know to Make Your Trip Safe and Comfortable

Check-In [Tab] Customers are advised to check in 90 minutes before their scheduled departure for domestic flights when checking bags, 60 minutes with no bags, and 2 hours for international flights. Adequate check-in time will help ensure your reservation and seat assignment. Please be on board and in your seat with your seat belt fastened 10 minutes prior to departure time.

Luggage [Tab] Passengers may carry one piece of luggage and one personal item on board. Carry-on items, including laptop computers, must be placed in the overhead bin or under the seat in front of you. To avoid additional charges, all luggage must meet size and weight requirements. Liability for loss, delay, or damage to baggage is limited, so carry valuables on board with you.

Beverage Service [Tab] Only alcohol served by a flight attendant to customers age 21 or older may be consumed on board. By FAA rule, alcohol may not be served to customers who appear intoxicated.

Smoking [Tab] Smoking is not permitted. Also, smokeless tobacco and e-cigarettes may not be used at any time while on board.

continues

Figure 79.5 Section 4 Content for Document 79.1—continued

¶

4.3 → PROTOCOL STRUCTURE↵

↵

We can guarantee that the data configuration of the website supports search engine friendly protocol so the website looks as appealing and user-friendly as it works.¶

¶

Figure 79.6 Sections 5 and 6 Content for Document 79.1

SECTION 5. HOTEL PHONE TRACKING¶

¶

Our Absolute Voice system delivers tracking reports on phone systems and includes voice response services, call measurement reports, and call monitoring through delivery of call data via the Internet with respect to calls initiated using our assigned numbers.¶

¶

We provide updated data on call traffic generated directly as a result of your website. Reporting and access are made available via private login numbers and are accessible anytime you wish to run reports, monitor calls, or evaluate traffic. This will answer questions about how much traffic is being received as a direct result of the website.¶

¶

SECTION 6. COSTS¶

¶

The following table illustrates the products and packages available. Your current needs may be met in any of our three packages. When planning for the future, you may wish to consider either the Platinum or Titanium packages.¶

¶

Remove hanging indent

Figure 95.3 Content for Document 95.3—continued

Seat Belts [Tab] Turbulence is air movement that cannot be seen and that often occurs unexpectedly. While everything possible is done to avoid turbulence, it is the most likely threat to your in-flight safety. Unless you must leave your seat, keep your seat belt fastened at all times, even when the seat-belt sign is off.

Disability Assistance [Tab] Passengers with disabilities who need assistance, including obtaining wheelchairs, should contact the airline representative. Per government regulations, service animals traveling in the cabin to assist passengers with physical or emotional needs are not required to travel in a kennel. If you are in a bulkhead seat, you may be asked to move to another seat to accommodate a service animal.

Carry-on Pets [Tab] Pets must stay in closed and/or zippered kennels and be kept under the seat in front of you at all times. The airlines assume no liability for the well-being of carry-on pets.

Powerports [Tab] On most aircraft, there is a USB outlet at each seat in First Class and Business Class and in select rows in the main cabin for powering approved electronic devices. Only one device per outlet is allowed.

Electronic Equipment/Personal Devices [Tab] Personal electronic devices may be used during boarding until the flight attendant's announcement to switch them off. After the announcement, all portable electronic devices must remain off and properly stored (electronic devices include but are not limited to ebook readers). During flight, your flight attendant will inform you when approved devices may be used. Audio and video equipment may be used only with headsets, and noise-canceling headsets may be activated. The use of still and video cameras, film or digital, is permitted only for recording of personal events. Unauthorized photography or video recording of airline personnel, other customers, aircraft equipment, or procedures is strictly prohibited. Never activate two-way pagers, radios, TV sets, remote controls, cordless computer mouses, or commercial TV cameras. All devices with transmitting capabilities must be switched off except Wi-Fi 802.11. Wi-Fi 802.11 devices may be used (when authorized) only on aircraft equipped with in-flight Internet service. If in-flight Internet service is provided, it is intended for customer access to the Internet, email, and VPN only. Any voice, audio, video,

continues

Figure 79.4 Section 3 Content for Document 79.1—continued

strategies. Reporting is issued directly to the hotel's General Manager with full accounting that will be provided to the hotel and to all hotel decision makers monthly.¶

¶

3.5 → SOCIAL MEDIA WEB DESIGN AND WIKIPEDIA SERVICES↵

↵

These two services are offered with our Titanium package to provide you with more ways to increase exposure for your site. Social media sites help your hotel business to stay in touch with your customers and prospective customers, to promote local events, and to drive traffic to their sites. Meanwhile, the Wikipedia Listing Service will get your hotel listed on Wikipedia.¶

¶

Figure 79.5 Section 4 Content for Document 79.1

SECTION 4. WEBSITE DEVELOPMENT¶

¶

Remove hanging indent —In order to make your website functional, your website design is critical. Our designers will create an aesthetically pleasing website that reflects the character of your facility and appeals to your customer. Your goal, and therefore our goal, is to have your customers contact your website and explore through as many pages as possible way past the Home page—and, as a result, contact you.¶

¶

Turn on hanging indent —4.1 → SEARCH ENGINE FRIENDLY↵

↵

At CheckYourHotel we can make changes quickly, allowing your hotel the ability to react to local, regional, and national changes in business and leisure traffic through your website and connecting engines.¶

¶

4.2 → VISION REPRESENTED↵

↵

We understand it is important that your website represent your vision and organization in a manner consistent with the hotel's individual and corporate identity.¶

continues

Figure 95.3 Content for Document 95.3—continued

or other photography (motion or still), recording, or transmission while on any aircraft is strictly prohibited, except to the extent specifically permitted by the airlines. Before landing, your flight attendant will announce when to switch off and store all electronic devices. These devices must remain off until the plane is at the gate and the seat-belt sign has been switched off.

Federal Law [Tab] Federal law prohibits passengers from threatening or intimidating the flight crew or interfering as crew members perform their duties.

Document 95.4

Agenda Document Using a Template

Read all instructions below before starting this document activity.

1 Navigate to the Document 95.4 launch page in the Online Lab and then click the Launch Activity button to open **Doc095.04** in the activity window.

2 Turn on the display of nonprinting characters. Update the agenda template so that your document matches the content shown in Figure 95.4.

3 Proofread the document and correct any errors.

4 Save the document.

5 Click the Check button to upload the document for checking.

6 If errors are reported by the Online Lab, view the results document, correct the errors in the submitted document, save the document, and then click the Check Again button.

Figure 79.4 Section 3 Content for Document 79.1—continued

↵

These cards are interactive and ideal for marketing online through email. Our eCards will help your guests advertise your hotel for you.¶

¶

3.3 → OPTIMIZED SEARCH ENGINE↵

↵

The number one requested service is vital to the success of the Internet Marketing Services.¶

¶

(Increase indent)

3.3.1→ <u>Platinum Report</u>. This is a standardized report for many different industries, which will establish your website's ranking at any given time in any of the search engine friendly categories. Your Platinum Report establishes benchmarks based on keywords and phrases.¶

¶

3.3.2→ <u>Website Information Critique</u>. We audit your current website and review meta tags and their placement. This assists in your website search engine placement. Search engine spiders (software that searches the content of the Web on a daily basis) need to be able to find your site and capture information, phrases, and keywords from your site. Meta tags need to be optimized to aid the search engine spiders in finding your pages.¶

¶

3.3.3→ <u>Keyword and Phrase Identification</u>. We direct your keywords and phrases to your specific market. We will work with you at your direction to establish which words and phrases are the most applicable to the targets as well as the order in which you would rank them.¶

¶

(Decrease indent)

3.4 → DIRECTOR OF INTERNET SALES AND MARKETING↵

↵

The Director of Internet Sales and Marketing provides the first point of contact as it relates to all your Internet sales and data capture

continues

Figure 95.4 Agenda Content and Format for Document 95.4

AGENDA

Finance Committee

September 21, 2020
1:00 p.m. – 5:00 p.m.

Meeting called by **Jonathan Tebanini, Chair**

Attendees:	Sam Carathurs, LaToya Jacobs, Tabby Willinsky
Please bring:	Laptop or tablet; minutes of August 18, 2020

Time	Item	Person	Location
1:00 p.m. – 1:15 p.m.	**Introduction** Welcome Approval of August 18, 2020, Minutes	Jonathan Tebanini	Delaware
1:15 p.m. – 1:45 p.m.	**Financial Report** August 2020	Jonathan Tebanini	Delaware
1:45 p.m. – 3:00 p.m.	**Auditor Review** Annual Audit	LaToya Jacobs	Delaware
3:00 p.m. – 3:30 p.m.	**Break with Refreshments**		Florida
3:30 p.m. – 4:30 p.m.	**Investment Policy Strategies** Discussion	Sam Carathurs	Delaware
4:30 p.m. – 5:00 p.m.	**Wrap-up** Next Meeting Date Announced	Jonathan Tebanini	Delaware

Additional Instructions:
Do not bring cell phones!

Ending the Session

The Online Lab automatically saved the work you completed for this session. You may continue with the next session or exit the Online Lab and continue later.

12 Proofread the document and correct any errors. Compare the formatting to the document shown in Figure 79.8.

13 Turn on the automatic numbered lists feature. *Hint: Do this by inserting a check mark in the* **Automatic numbered lists** *check box at the AutoCorrect dialog box with the AutoFormat As You Type tab selected.*

14 Save the document.

15 Click the Check button to upload the document for checking.

16 If errors are reported by the Online Lab, view the results document, correct the errors in the submitted document, save the document, and then click the Check Again button.

Figure 79.4 Section 3 Content for Document 79.1

SECTION 3. OUR INTERNET SERVICES¶

¶

Our professionals are experienced and will establish a marketing plan customized to your needs. Your hotel will be provided with a plan to establish a powerful Internet presence that meets your requirements. We focus on creating websites that will perform well in various search engines and are easy to use. This will lead to increased bookings and revenue for our clients. We can make sure your website can be found on the Internet.¶

¶

(Turn on hanging indent) 3.1 → EMAIL LIST MANAGEMENT & NEWSLETTERS↵

↵

We realize that it is vital to be able to communicate with your guests—current, past, and future. CheckYourHotel provides services to help you manage that communication.¶

¶

(Increase indent) 3.1.1→ Email Data Capture. This is the most valuable aspect of web-based marketing. Spam is perhaps the most negative aspect of email-based marketing. We can help you reach your guests by creating an email data capture program that is secure, meets all federal standards, and will be welcomed and seen by the audience you intended. We use a double opt-in email data capture system.¶

¶

3.1.2→ Email Database. A properly managed email database is the most cost-effective and best way to reach your customer base as it expands.¶

¶

(Decrease indent) 3.2 → HOTEL ECARDS↵

continues

Legal Documents and Legal Office Project

e Key the two paragraphs of text, pressing Enter twice after each paragraph.

f Press Ctrl + E, press Ctrl + B, key SECTION 6. COSTS, and then press Ctrl + B.

g Press Enter twice.

h Press Ctrl + L to change the paragraph alignment to left alignment.

i Key the paragraph that begins *The following table* and then press Enter twice.

j Save the document.

8 Rather than inserting a table using the Table button on the Insert tab, set tabs and key the table shown in Figure 79.7 by completing the following steps:

a Set a left tab at 0.5 inch and center tabs at 3 inch, 4.25 inch, and 5.5 inch marks on the horizontal ruler.

b Press Tab, press Ctrl + B, key Products, press Tab, key Standard, press Tab, key Platinum, press Tab, key Titanium, press Ctrl + B, and then press Enter.

c Key the rest of the table content, pressing Tab before each product name. Do not press Enter after keying the last row of the table.

d Save the document.

9 Insert a header with a bottom border on all pages of the document by completing the following steps:

a Insert a header using the *Blank* option.

b Click the text placeholder, key Proposal for Internet Marketing Services, and then press the Tab key twice.

c Click the Page Number button in the Header & Footer group, point to *Current Position*, and then click *Plain Number*.

d Click the Home tab, click the Borders button arrow in the Paragraph group, and then click *Bottom Border* at the drop-down gallery.

e Save the document.

10 Insert a footer with a top border on all pages of the document by completing the following steps:

a Click the Header & Footer Tools Design tab.

b Click the Footer button in the Header & Footer group and then click *Edit Footer*.

c Press Tab, press Ctrl + B, and then key CheckYourHotel.

d Click the Home tab, click the Borders button arrow in the Paragraph group, and then click *Top Border* at the drop-down gallery.

e Save the document.

11 Change the starting page number for the document to *15* by completing the following steps:

a Click the Header & Footer Tools Design tab.

b Click the Page Number button in the Header & Footer group.

c Click *Format Page Numbers* to display the Page Number Format dialog box.

d In the *Page numbering* section, click in the *Start at* measurement box and then key 15.

e Click OK.

f Click the Close Header and Footer button or double-click in the body of the document to make the document active.

g Save the document.

steps continue

Session 96

Caption and Summons

Session Objectives

- Create a legal terms and definitions table
- Convert text to a table
- Create and insert AutoText
- Format a summons
- Insert a file
- Apply Page X of Y page numbering
- Efficiently produce documents in mailable form

Getting Started

Exercise 96.1 If you are continuing immediately from Session 95, you may skip the Exercise 96.1 warm-up drill. However, if you exited the Online Lab at the end of Session 95, warm up by completing Exercise 96.1.

Exercise 96.2 Begin your session work by completing Exercise 96.2, a timed short drill, in the Online Lab.

Assessing Your Speed and Accuracy

Complete Timing 96.1 in the Online Lab using the timing text on the next page. At the end of the timing, the Online Lab will display your WPM rate and any errors. Results will be saved in your Timings Performance report. If you have been surpassing the speed and accuracy goals identified in the Online Lab, set slightly more challenging personal goals and strive to exceed them. *Note: With this session, the default WPM goal for 3-minute timings has been increased by 5 WPM in the Online Lab. However, your instructor may have customized this goal.*

5 Key the text shown in Figure 79.4, Section 3 of the RFP response document by completing the following steps:

   a Press Ctrl + E to change the paragraph alignment to center alignment, press Ctrl + B to turn on bold formatting, key SECTION 3. OUR INTERNET SERVICES, and then press Ctrl + B to turn off bold formatting.

   b Press Enter twice.

   c Press Ctrl + L to change the paragraph alignment to left alignment.

   d Key the paragraph that begins *Our professionals are experienced* and then press Enter twice.

   e Set the paragraph indentation to a hanging 0.5-inch indent. ***Hint: Use the Paragraph dialog box.***

   f Key 3.1, press Tab, key EMAIL LIST MANAGEMENT & NEWSLETTERS, and then press Shift + Enter twice.

   g Key the paragraph that begins *We realize that* and then, at the end of the paragraph, press Enter twice.

   h Click the Increase Indent button in the Paragraph group on the Home tab to change the indent to 0.5 inch.

   i Key subsections 3.1.1 and 3.1.2, pressing Tab after the numbers, setting the paragraph headings (but not the period following the headings) as underlined, and then pressing Enter twice after each section.

   j Press the Decrease Indent button in the Paragraph group on the Home tab to remove the indent.

   k Continue keying the rest of section 3 shown in Figure 79.4. At the end of section 3.5, press Enter twice.

   l Save the document.

6 Key the text shown in Figure 79.5, Section 4 of the RFP response document by completing the following steps:

   a Press Ctrl + E, press Ctrl + B, key SECTION 4. WEBSITE DEVELOPMENT, and then press Ctrl + B.

   b Press Enter twice.

   c Press Ctrl + L to change the paragraph alignment to left alignment.

   d Turn off the hanging indent. ***Hint: In the Paragraph dialog box, set the indentation to* (none).**

   e Key the paragraph that begins *In order to make* and then press Enter twice.

   f Set the paragraph indentation to a hanging 0.5-inch indent.

   g Key the text for subsections 4.1 through 4.3. At the end of the paragraph for subsection 4.3, press Enter twice.

   h Save the document.

7 Key the text shown in Figure 79.6, Sections 5 and 6 of the RFP response document by completing the following steps:

   a Press Ctrl + E, press Ctrl + B, key SECTION 5. HOTEL PHONE TRACKING, and then press Ctrl + B.

   b Press Enter twice.

   c Press Ctrl + L to change the paragraph alignment to left alignment.

   d Turn off the hanging indent.

steps continue

Timing 96.1

Working in a legal office can be both interesting and exciting. You will have an opportunity to learn many things about the law by working under the supervision of an attorney. Every client of the office is different, and every case is different. You, as a legal administrative assistant, will format documents, but you may also have an opportunity to observe a happy couple as they adopt a much-wanted child, assist a young couple as they purchase their first home, or work with a couple dissolving a marriage. You may be assigned to sit in on a meeting where a will is being signed or where a partnership agreement to begin a new business is being signed, or you may be asked to prepare a charter to organize a new corporation. Some legal administrative assistants go to court with their attorneys to provide support, including such responsibilities as locating and organizing items in a trial notebook.

A legal assistant in a small firm will be involved in working with many types of documents and cases; whereas in a large firm the responsibilities may be focused on specific areas of law and specific responsibilities. It is important to be aware of the confidential nature of the legal matters that you may be dealing with. Everything that occurs in the office must stay in the office--nothing should be repeated or discussed with anyone outside the firm, including your family and close friends.

Preparing Legal Documents

Every day, a vast number of legal documents are prepared. Legal documents require special formatting and considerations, and the features available in Word can expedite the process of creating them. In this unit, you will use Word features and functions with which you are already familiar, together with new features, to prepare a variety of legal documents.

The documents you will prepare represent a sampling of the different types of legal documents involved in a divorce case. These sessions are not intended to replace a regular course in legal theory and application. Rather, they are designed to give you an opportunity to apply your knowledge of word processing features and functions to the preparation of some common legal documents. You will also learn some basic legal terminology.

Each country, state, province, county, and/or city may have specific requirements for how legal documents are to be formatted. For these sessions, you will use Word's default 1-inch margins and 11-point Calibri font for all documents. Follow the instructions regarding line and paragraph spacing within each document. You will also set custom tabs as you create the documents in this unit. (See Session 79 to review setting tabs, if necessary.)

To set a tab using the Tabs dialog box, complete the following steps:

1 Click the Paragraph group dialog box launcher on the Home tab.

2 At the Paragraph dialog box, click the Tabs button in the bottom left corner.

3 At the Tabs dialog box, key the location (in inches) of the tab stop in the *Tab stop position* text box.

4 Select the type of tab in the *Alignment* section of the Tabs dialog box.

5 Click the Set button to set the tab.

6 Repeat Steps 3 through 5 for each tab that needs to be set.

7 When all of the tabs have been set, click OK to apply the new tab stops to the document.

Deleting Tabs

To delete a tab from the horizontal ruler, position the arrow pointer over the tab symbol on the horizontal ruler, click and hold down the left mouse button, drag the tab symbol downward and off the ruler, and then release the mouse button. *Note: If you set another tab by mistake, use Undo to remove it.*

To delete a tab using the Tabs dialog box, display the Tabs dialog box, select the tab to be deleted in the *Tab stop position* list box, click the Clear button (or click the Clear All button if you want to remove all of the tabs), and then click OK to close the Tabs dialog box.

Document 79.1 **Bid Response to an RFP**

Read all instructions below before starting this document activity.

1 Navigate to the Document 79.1 launch page in the Online Lab and then click the Launch Activity button to open **Doc079.01** in the activity window.

2 Before keying any text, check that the automatic numbered lists feature is turned off.

3 Change the default format of the document to single spacing with no spacing after paragraphs.

4 Show paragraph marks and other hidden formatting symbols by clicking the Show/Hide ¶ button in the Paragraph group on the Home tab.

steps continue

Document 96.1   Legal Terms for Session 96

Read all instructions below before starting this document activity.

1. Navigate to the Document 96.1 launch page in the Online Lab and then click the Launch Activity button to open **Doc096.01** in the activity window.

2. Key Legal Terminology and then press Enter.

3. Key the terms and definitions shown in Figure 96.1, pressing Tab after each term and pressing Enter after each definition except the last one. Apply italic formatting according to the text shown in the figure. *Hint: If a definition ends with an italic term, be sure to turn off italic formatting before pressing Enter. Note: The text will not wrap the same as in the figure, and the layout will be adjusted after the list terms and definitions are keyed.*

4. Convert the list to a table by completing the following steps:

   a. Select the text from the word *Term* through the last definition.

   b. Click the Insert tab, click the Table button in the Tables group, and then click *Convert Text to Table* at the drop-down list to display the Convert Text to Table dialog box.

   c. Adjust the settings at the Convert Text to Table dialog box as follows:

      i. Confirm that 2 displays in the *Number of columns* measurement box in the *Table size* section. *Hint: If a number other than 2 appears in this measurement box, there is most likely an incorrect number of tabs between one or more of the terms and definitions. Click Cancel to close the dialog box and then check the document.*

      ii. Click the *AutoFit to contents* option in the *AutoFit behavior* section.

      iii. Confirm that the *Tabs* option is selected in the *Separate text at* section.

      iv. Click OK.

5. On the Table Tools Design tab, confirm that only the *Header Row* and *First Column* options are selected in the Table Style Options group. *Hint: Remove the check mark from the* **Banded Rows** *check box.*

6. Click the Table Tools Design tab, click the More Table Styles button in the Table Styles group, and then click *List Table 3 - Accent 1* (second column, third row in the *List Tables* section).

7. With the table selected, click the Home tab and then display the Paragraph dialog box. Make sure the *Don't add space between paragraphs of the same style* check box does not contain a check mark and then change the line spacing of the table to single spacing with 8 points of spacing after paragraphs. *Hint: You may need to click the* **Don't add space between paragraphs of the same style** *check box twice to remove the check mark.*

8. Click anywhere within the *Legal Terminology* title and then click the *Title* style option in the Styles gallery on the Home tab.

9. Proofread the document and correct any errors.

10. Save the document.

11. Click the Check button to upload the document for checking.

12. If errors are reported by the Online Lab, view the results document, correct the errors in the submitted document, save the document, and then click the Check Again button.

Figure 79.2 Tab Alignment Examples

Left Tab	Center Tab	Right Tab	Decimal Tab	Bar Tab
Valencia	Washington	Olympia	22.908	
Yang	Oregon	Salem	1,655.05555	
Nicholson	California	Sacramento	623.5	

You can set tabs before keying text or you can key text using the default tab stops and then set the tabs as desired. When tabs are set before keying the text, the tab formatting is inserted in the paragraph mark at the end of the line. Each time you press the Enter key, the paragraph mark is copied down to the next line and the tab stops remain in place for the next line.

If you key the text before setting tabs, press the Tab key before keying each new column entry, including the first one. After the text is keyed, select the lines of text to be formatted with the new tabs and then set the tabs.

After a tab has been set, it can be moved to a new location. To move a tab, position the arrow pointer on the tab symbol on the horizontal ruler, click and hold down the left mouse button, drag the symbol to the new location on the ruler, and then release the mouse button.

When setting tabs, consider the following:

- If your tab does not appear exactly where you want it on the horizontal ruler, or if you did not get the tab type desired, use Undo (Ctrl + Z) and start again.
- Word will automatically remove (clear) tabs to the left of the first tab set.
- Word's default setting of placing a left tab every 0.5 inch will continue to the right of the last tab set.

Setting Tabs Using the Horizontal Ruler

If you do not see a horizontal ruler along the top of your document just below the ribbon, click the View tab and then click the *Ruler* check box in the Show group to insert a check mark, as shown in Figure 79.3. The numbers on the horizontal ruler represent inches from the left margin of the document.

Use the horizontal ruler to set a tab by completing the following steps:

1 Click the Alignment button above the vertical ruler until it displays the desired type of tab. Refer to Table 79.1 for tab icon descriptions.

2 Click the position on the horizontal ruler where you want to set the tab stop. The tab symbol will display at that location on the ruler.

Setting Tabs Using the Tabs Dialog Box

You can use the Tabs dialog box to set tabs at a precise measurement, to clear tabs, or to set character leaders to appear before the text keyed at a tab.

Figure 79.3 Show group on the View tab

Ruler check box

☑ Ruler
☐ Gridlines
☐ Navigation Pane
Show

Figure 96.1 Legal Terms and Definitions for Document 96.1

Term → Definition ¶

Allegations → Statements the plaintiff expects to prove ¶

Answer → A document in which the defendant admits or denies each allegation or claim made in the complaint and defends against those charges ¶

Circuit court → A state court that has original judicial power in several counties or a district ¶

Clerk of the court → A court official whose job includes filing documents, officially issuing summonses, and keeping records of court proceedings ¶

Divorce → Legal process of ending a marriage by a court of law in which grounds or reasons are required ¶

Garnishment → A legal claim against part of a person's earnings ¶

Judgment → A court decision ¶

Lien → A claim against property to secure a debt ¶

Litigation → Process of carrying on a lawsuit when one party sues another party in a court of law ¶

Petition → A formal written request or plea for specific court action; also known as a *complaint* or *declaration* ¶

Petitioner → The party who is suing another in a court of law; may also be known as the *plaintiff* ¶

Respondent → The party who is being sued in a court of law; may also be known as the *defendant* ¶

SBN → State Bar Number, which represents attorney membership in a state bar association ¶

State Bar Association → Licensing body that authorizes attorneys to practice law within a state ¶

Statutes → Laws enacted and passed by a legislative body ¶

Summons → A legal order to appear in court, including instructions about the length of time within which the defendant must respond

Preparing Legal Captions

Documents prepared for civil or criminal cases require a heading called a *caption* that shows the state, county, court, petitioner (or plaintiff), respondent (or defendant), case number, and the type of case. Captions in this unit will begin at the top margin. Figure 96.2 illustrates a caption in a divorce case. As the divorce case progresses, additional documents will be created using this caption with minor changes.

Setting a Hanging Indent

As shown in Figure 79.1, paragraphs in an RFP contain hanging indents. In a hanging indent, the second and subsequent lines of text are indented from the left margin and are aligned. A hanging indent is generally used in numbered and bulleted lists and is produced automatically in Word.

To manually set a hanging indent, complete the following steps:

1. Click the Paragraph group dialog box launcher on the Home tab.
2. Click the Indents and Spacing tab, if it is not already selected.
3. In the *Indentation* section, click the *Special* option box arrow and then click *Hanging* at the drop-down list.
4. Word will automatically change the number in the *By* measurement box to *0.5″*. This setting can be adjusted by clicking the up or down arrows. For the document activities in this session, use the default setting.
5. Click OK to apply the settings and to close the dialog box.

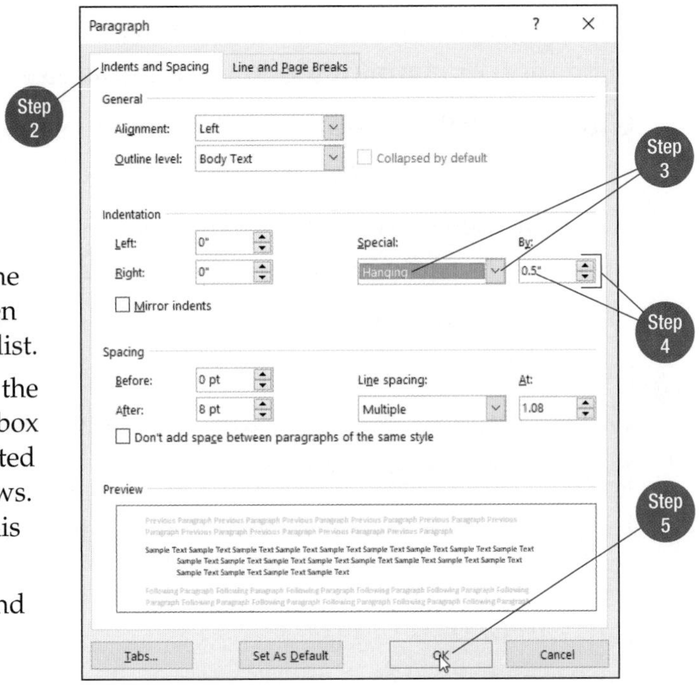

Manipulating Tabs

In a new, blank document, Word provides a tab stop every 0.5 inch beginning at the left margin, although these default tabs are *not* shown on the horizontal ruler. In some situations, these default tab stops are appropriate; in other situations, you may want to create your own tab stops. There are two methods of setting tabs: on the horizontal ruler or at the Tabs dialog box.

Word features five types of tab alignment (and two indents) that can be accessed using the Tabs dialog box or the Alignment button immediately above the vertical ruler. The five tab stops that may be set are described in Table 79.1. Figure 79.2 shows how text is aligned when each tab is used.

Table 79.1 Types of Tab Alignment

	A **left tab** stop sets the leftmost position of text that will then run to the right as you key.
	A **center tab** stop sets the position of the middle of the text. The text centers on this position as you key.
	A **right tab** stop sets the rightmost position of the text. As you key, the text moves to the left.
	A **decimal tab** stop aligns a list of numbers at their decimal points. No matter how many digits a number has, the decimal point will be in the same position. (You can only align numbers around a decimal point; you cannot use a decimal tab to align text. In addition, decimal tabs will only work with decimal points; you cannot use them to align numbers around a different character, such as a hyphen.)
	A **bar tab** stop does not position text. Rather, it inserts a vertical bar at the tab position.

Figure 96.2 Sample Caption

STATE OF WISCONSIN   CIRCUIT COURT   ROCK COUNTY

_____

In re the marriage of:

LAUREN MARISSA CARIMI
5534 NORTH ROBIN CREST DRIVE
JANESVILLE, ROCK COUNTY, WISCONSIN 53545,

                                                        SUMMONS
                    Petitioner,   Case No.: _____

                                                        DIVORCE

-and-

MARCUS CAMERON CARIMI
524 STAFFORD ROAD
JANESVILLE, ROCK COUNTY, WISCONSIN 53545,

                    Respondent.

_____

Setting Tabs and Creating Lines for a Caption

Custom tab settings were used for the various parts of the caption shown in Figure 96.2. This particular caption contains a left tab at the l.5-inch mark, a center tab at the 3.25-inch mark, a left tab at the 4-inch mark, and a right tab at the 6.5-inch mark. The following list explains which text is aligned at each tab:

CIRCUIT COURT	center tab at 3.25 inches
ROCK COUNTY	right tab at 6.5 inches
SUMMONS	left tab at 4.0 inches
Petitioner,	left tab at 1.5 inches
Case No.:	left tab at 4.0 inches
DIVORCE	left tab at 4.0 inches
Respondent.	left tab at 1.5 inches

Although there are various ways to create the horizontal lines you see in the document, in this unit you should create them in the following way: position the insertion point where the line should start, turn on underlining (Ctrl + U), and then press Tab so that the line ends at 6.5 inches (the right margin of the document). Be sure to turn off underlining before you continue to key the document. If you do not follow this procedure, the Online Lab will mark it as an error in your document.

Creating and Using AutoText

The caption shown in Figure 96.2 will be used for additional documents regarding this divorce case. Instead of having to key and proofread the caption over and over again, you can save the

Reinforcing Word Skills

The document activities in this session will require you to apply some previously learned Word skills. This section will review some of those skills.

Changing Line and Paragraph Spacing

The default line spacing in Word 2016 is 1.08 lines with 8 points of spacing after each paragraph. To change the line spacing of a document to single spacing with no spacing after paragraphs, complete the following steps immediately upon opening the new document:

1 Click the Paragraph group dialog box launcher on the Home tab.

2 Click the Indents and Spacing tab, if it is not already selected.

3 In the *Spacing* section, click the *After* measurement box down arrow until *0 pt* displays or select *8* in the measurement box and then key *0*.

4 Click the *Line spacing* option box arrow and then click *Single* at the drop-down list.

5 Click OK to close the dialog box and apply the changes to the document.

Turning Off Automatic Formatting of Numbered Lists

Word's AutoFormat feature provides options to automatically format text as you are preparing your document. For example, if you key a word immediately followed by two hyphens (--) and another word and then a space or return, the two hyphens will automatically be formatted as a type of dash called an *em dash* (—).

Word will automatically create a numbered list if you key a number followed by a period or hyphen and then press the spacebar or Tab. This option can be turned on or off at the AutoCorrect dialog box. The RFP response document created in this session uses a numbered list to organize its content, but when you key the text you want to make sure Word does not automatically format the numbered list.

Follow these steps to check the AutoFormat settings on your computer and turn off automatic formatting of numbered lists.

1 Click the File tab.

2 Click *Options* to display the Word Options dialog box.

3 In the left panel of the Word Options dialog box, click *Proofing*.

4 Click the AutoCorrect Options button to display the AutoCorrect dialog box.

5 Click the AutoFormat As You Type tab at the AutoCorrect dialog box.

6 In the *Apply as you type* section, if there is a check mark in the *Automatic numbered lists* check box, click to remove it.

7 Click OK to save the changes and close the AutoCorrect dialog box.

8 Click OK to close the Word Options dialog box and to return to the document.

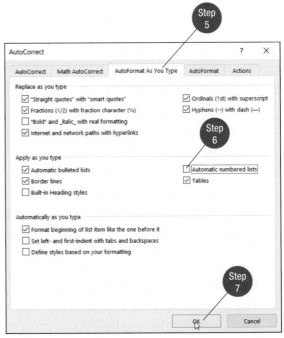

content as a building block in the AutoText gallery and then insert the text in later documents. The AutoText gallery is located at the Quick Parts button drop-down list.

To save the caption to the AutoText gallery, complete the following steps:

1 Select the text to be saved.
2 Click the Insert tab.
3 Click the Quick Parts button in the Text group.
4 Point to *AutoText* at the drop-down list.
5 Click *Save Selection to AutoText Gallery* at the side menu to display the Create New Building Block dialog box.

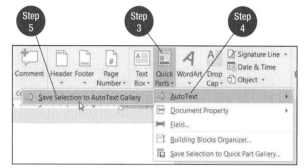

6 At the Create New Building Block dialog box, complete the following steps:

a Key a descriptive name, such as Caption, in the *Name* text box.

b Make sure *AutoText* displays in the *Gallery* option box. If not, click the *Gallery* option box arrow and then click *AutoText*.

c Click the *Category* option box arrow and then choose a category from the list. Alternatively, click *Create New Category* at the drop-down list and then key a name such as Legal in the *Name* text box in the Create New Category dialog box. Click OK to close the Create New Category dialog box.

d Key a description in the *Description* text box.

e Click the *Save in* option box arrow and then click *Normal.dotm* (or *Normal*, if file extensions are not displayed) to save the caption in the Normal template.

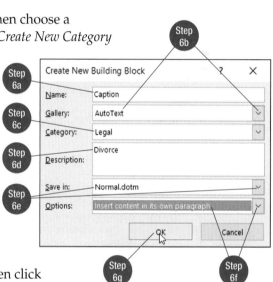

f Click the *Options* option box arrow and then click *Insert content in its own paragraph.*

g Click OK to close the Create New Building Block dialog box.

To insert the caption building block into a new document, complete the following steps:

1 Change the default line spacing for the document to single spacing with no spacing after paragraphs. *Hint: Be sure to click the Set As Default button at the Paragraph dialog box.*
2 Click the Insert tab.
3 Click the Quick Parts button in the Text group.
4 Point to *AutoText* and then click *Caption* in the *Legal* section of the side menu. *Note: The names of the AutoText entry and the section will vary depending on the names you choose when creating them.*

In the following document activities, you will create a caption, save it to the AutoText gallery, and then insert it into a document. Plan your time so that you are able to complete the Document 96.2 and 96.3 activities in one work session on the same computer. Otherwise, the AutoText entry you create in the Document 96.2 activity may not be available for placement in the Document 96.3 activity.

Preparing a Request for Proposal and Bid Response

In addition to memo business reports and formal business reports, there are a variety of specialized business report formats. While banking, law, medicine, publishing, transportation, communication, manufacturing, education, and government all have specialized report formats that are unique to their respective operations, certain other specialized business reports are commonly used in all types of businesses. One such document is the request for proposal (RFP).

An RFP is a specialized business report that requires a unique format. An organization uses an RFP to invite vendors and service providers to submit bids for something such as the creation of an electronic document filing system or an Internet-based telephone system, paving a parking lot, or cafeteria/catering services. A bid response is the vendor or service provider's reply or proposal offering products or services to address the needs stated in the RFP.

Review the excerpt of an RFP shown in Figure 79.1. Typical formatting for an RFP includes:

- 1-inch side, top, and bottom margins
- Main headings and section titles that are horizontally centered in bold font using all capital letters
- Text formatted as indented paragraphs under subheadings
- No page numbers on the first page and a plain page number aligned at the right margin of the header on the pages following the first page

In addition to including a page number, the header or footer may also contain information about the subject of the RFP or the name of the company preparing the document. The formatting of the bid response is similar to that of the RFP.

Figure 79.1 Portion of an RFP Document   *Note: Do not key this document.*

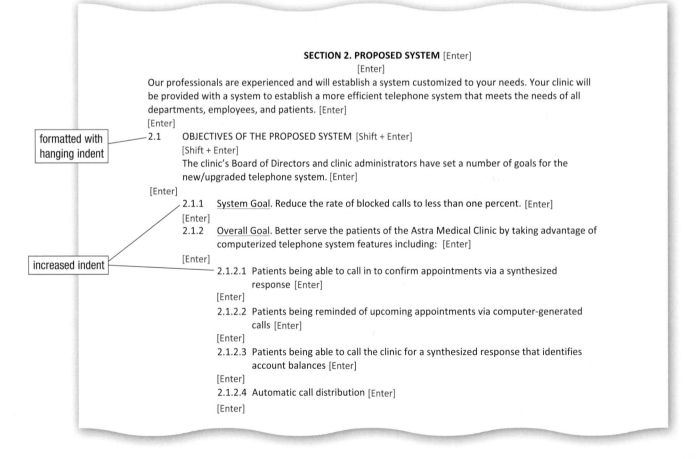

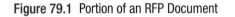

Document **Legal Caption**

96.2   Read all instructions below before starting this document activity.

1   Navigate to the Document 96.2 launch page in the Online Lab and then click the Launch Activity button to open **Doc096.02** in the activity window.

2   Change the default line spacing for the document to single spacing with no spacing after paragraphs.

3   Set the following tabs in the document:

> Left tab at 1.5 inches
> Center tab at 3.25 inches
> Left tab at 4.0 inches
> Right tab at 6.5 inches

Hint: If you do not place the tab correctly on the horizontal ruler, drag it to the correct position or drag it off of the ruler and then insert a new tab.

4   Key the document shown in Figure 96.3. The figure shows the text and the nonprinting characters to guide your formatting of the document. Consider the following as you key the document:

a   After keying ROCK COUNTY, press Enter, press Ctrl + U, press Tab four times, press Ctrl + U, and then press Enter twice.

b   After keying Case No:, press the spacebar, press Ctrl + U, press Tab, press Ctrl + U, and then press Enter twice.

c   Key a hyphen before and after the word *and*. Do not allow Word to automatically capitalize *and*.

d   After keying Respondent. at the bottom of the document, press Enter, press Ctrl + U, press Tab four times, press Ctrl + U, and then press Enter twice.

5   Proofread the document and correct any errors.

6   Select the text and save it as a caption by completing the following steps:

a   Press Ctrl + A to select the text to be saved (including the paragraph marks below the last line).

b   Click the Insert tab, click the Quick Parts button in the Text group, point to *AutoText*, and then click *Save Selection to AutoText Gallery* at the side menu.

c   Fill in the Create New Building Block dialog box as follows:

Name:	Caption
Gallery:	*AutoText*
Category:	Click *Create New Category*, key Legal, and then click OK.
Description:	Divorce
Save in:	*Normal.dotm*
Options:	*Insert content in its own paragraph*

d   Click OK. *Note: If a message appears asking if you want to redefine the building block entry, click Yes.*

7   Save the document.

8   Click the Check button to upload the document for checking.

9   If errors are reported by the Online Lab, view the results document, correct the errors in the submitted document, save the document, and then click the Check Again button.

1-Minute Timings

Timings
79.1–79.2

There are many different kinds of cheeses. People have eaten an amazing variety of cheeses for many years from the milk of many kinds of animals. Different processes of making, aging, and seasoning fine cheeses produce a myriad of textures and flavors. Stabilizing cheese is often difficult, as particular conditions can produce changes of a flavor in the same cheese made in the same region. Flavoring depends upon the type of feed given to the animal and the time of year. Only the expert cheesemaker can produce fine cheeses for all to enjoy.

Complete one 3-minute timing on the timing text below.

3-Minute Timing

Timing
79.3

Have you tried waterskiing? If you have enjoyed any type of water activities, you could certainly have considerable fun waterskiing. Some people own boats that are used entirely for pulling water-skiers. Large boats and motors are required for pulling either adults or youngsters. A boat owner normally provides an ample supply of safety equipment for water-skiers.

Learning to water-ski is not a difficult problem. Your first venture around the lake might be quite short if you lose your balance. You may, however, whiz over the lake and remain upright the entire time. Your ability to balance yourself on the skis plays a major role in your success as a water-skier.

Any expert water-skier can perform a wide variety of tricks on the water. Experts ski on only one ski, while others have learned to ski without any skis at all. Water shows, which are now quite popular, offer the viewer a variety of maneuvers on water skis. A quite unusual event is watching a skier "soar" through the air on a kite and land gracefully on skis. Waterskiing is an exciting experience for almost anyone.

⊞ Ergonomic Tip

Standing or convertible desks offer an alternative to working in a seated position. However, working in the same posture for lengthy periods is never healthy, so it's important to take breaks and change position when possible. Consult the US Occupational Safety and Health administration (http://osha.gov) for more on alternative working positions.

Figure 96.3 Caption for Document 96.2

```
STATE·OF·WISCONSIN→          →          CIRCUIT·COURT →          →          ROCK·COUNTY¶
         →              →              →              →                           ¶
¶
In·re·the·marriage·of:¶
¶
BAILEY·KATHLEEN·MATTHEWS¶
1145·NORTH·HARMONY·DRIVE¶
JANESVILLE,·ROCK·COUNTY,·WISCONSIN·53545,¶
         →              →              →    SUMMONS¶
         →    Petitioner,    →         →    Case·No.:·_____→_____¶
¶
         →              →              →    DIVORCE¶
-and-¶
¶
TIMOTHY·PAUL·MATTHEWS¶
245·GARFIELD·STREET¶
JANESVILLE,·ROCK·COUNTY,·WISCONSIN·53545,¶
¶
         →    Respondent.¶
         →              →              →                           ¶
¶
¶
```

Document 96.3 Summons with AutoText Caption

Read all instructions below before starting this document activity.

1 Navigate to the Document 96.3 launch page in the Online Lab and then click the Launch Activity button to open **Doc096.03** in the activity window.

2 Change the document's default line spacing to single spacing with no spacing after paragraphs.

3 Insert the *Caption* AutoText building block created in the Document 96.2 activity by completing the following steps:

  a Click the Insert tab.

  b Click the Quick Parts button in the Text group.

  c Point to *AutoText* and then click *Caption* in the *Legal* section of the side menu.

4 Press the Backspace key once so that the insertion point is positioned immediately before the second paragraph mark below the caption. Turn on the display of nonprinting characters, if necessary, to make sure the insertion point is positioned in the correct location.

5 Key the text shown in Figure 96.4. *Note: The tab stops within the caption do not carry over to the rest of the document. Below the caption, the tab settings revert to the default 0.5 inch.*

6 Proofread the document and correct any errors.

7 Save the document.

8 Click the Check button to upload the document for checking.

9 If errors are reported by the Online Lab, view the results document, correct the errors in the submitted document, save the document, and then click the Check Again button.

Creating a Request for Proposal with a Cover Page

Session Objectives

- **Prepare a specialized business report**
- **Change line spacing in a document**
- **Turn off automatic formatting of numbered lists**
- **Use hanging indents**
- **Manipulate tabs**
- **Create a cover page from a template**
- **Compose an abstract**
- **Efficiently produce documents in mailable form**

Getting Started

Exercise 79.1 If you are continuing immediately from Session 78, you can skip the Exercise 79.1 warm-up drill. However, if you exited the Online Lab at the end of Session 78, warm up by completing Exercise 79.1.

Exercise 79.2 Begin your session work by completing Exercise 79.2, a timed short drill, in the Online Lab.

Assessing Your Speed and Accuracy

Complete Timings 79.1 through 79.3 in the Online Lab. At the end of each timing, the Online Lab will display your WPM rate and any errors. Results will be saved in your Timings Performance report. If you have been surpassing the speed and accuracy goals identified in the Online Lab, set slightly more challenging personal goals and strive to exceed them.

Complete two 1-minute timings on the timing text on the following page. If you meet or exceed both speed and accuracy goals for Timing 79.1, push for greater speed on Timing 79.2.

Figure 96.4 Content for Document 96.3

THE STATE OF WISCONSIN ¶

¶

To the person named above as respondent: ¶

¶

→ You are hereby notified that the petitioner has filed a petition for a divorce against you. The Petition, which is attached, states the nature and basis of the legal action. ¶

¶

→ Within 20 days of receiving this Summons, you must provide a written response, as that term is used in ch. 802, Wis. Stats. to the Petition. The court may reject or disregard an answer that does not follow the requirements of the statutes. The response must be sent or delivered to this court, whose address is: ¶

¶

→ Clerk of Circuit Court ¶
→ Rock County Courthouse ¶
→ 51 South Main Street ¶
→ Janesville, Wisconsin 53545 ¶

¶

and to Theresa Flanagan Law Offices; the petitioner's attorney, whose address is: ¶

¶

→ Attorney Theresa Flanagan ¶
→ Theresa Flanagan Law Offices ¶
→ 10 Main Street, Suite 204 ¶
→ Janesville, Wisconsin 53545 ¶

¶

→ You may have an attorney help or represent you. ¶

¶

→ If you do not provide a proper response within 20 days, the court may grant a judgment against you for the award of money or other legal action requested in the petition, or you may lose your right to object to anything that is or may be incorrect in the petition. ¶

¶

→ A judgment may be enforced as provided by law. A judgment awarding money may become a lien against any real estate you own now or in the future and may also be enforced by garnishment of wages or seizure of property.

Document
78.4

Composing a Memo Report

1 Navigate to the Document 78.4 launch page in the Online Lab and then click the Launch Activity button to open **Doc078.04** in the activity window.

2 Read the scenario in Figure 78.5 and then identify what information is relevant and will help the reader understand your response. Also, identify information that will help the reader take the action you want.

3 Compose a memo report containing a proposal to improve the situation described. To help with the planning process, refer back to Session 76, Document 76.3, Planning a Response. Write the memo to the faculty council president, indicate that the memo is from you, and include an appropriate subject line. Include side headings within the document and mention photos that will be provided as enclosures with the report.

4 Proofread the document and correct any errors.

5 Save the document.

6 Click the Submit button to upload the document for instructor review.

Figure 78.5 Scenario for Document 78.4

You are the president of the student body at your school, and the student council is upset with the school's parking arrangements.

Selected administrators have reserved parking spots close to the buildings housing their offices. Faculty members and support staff have access to reserved parking lots that are close to the buildings where their classes are held.

Student parking areas are located well away from the campus buildings, and there is no protection from the elements. In addition, there is no short-term parking where students can park long enough to pick up materials from their instructors, the library, or the student union.

As president of the student body, you have been directed by the student council to prepare a memo report containing a proposal to the head administrator of your school to request that the administration improve the parking situation for students.

Ending the Session

The Online Lab automatically saved the work you completed for this session. You may continue with the next session or exit the Online Lab and continue later.

Inserting Text from a File

Another method of reusing text that you have already created and formatted is to insert the contents of one document into another. For example, a legal document might include pages from state law documents. Once the standard legislative text has been formatted and saved, that file may be inserted into future documents requiring the same language.

To insert text from another file, complete the following steps:

1 Position the insertion point where you want to insert the text.
2 Click the Insert tab.
3 Click the Object button arrow in the Text group.
4 Click *Text from File* at the drop-down list.
5 Locate and select the file in the Insert File dialog box and then click the Insert button.

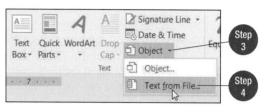

Using Page Number Options

When preparing legal documents, it is particularly important to number the pages and to identify how many pages total are in the document. This ensures that the entire document has been prepared and presented and also assures the reader that there are no missing pages. Word provides this capability in the *Page X of Y* section in the Page Number button drop-down list. The *X* represents the current page number and the *Y* represents the total number of pages in the document.

To add Page X of Y page numbers centered at the bottom of a document, complete the following steps:

1 Click the Insert tab.
2 Click the Page Number button in the Header & Footer group.
3 Point to *Bottom of Page* at the drop-down list.
4 Scroll down the side menu and then click *Bold Numbers 2* in the *Page X of Y* section.
5 Double-click in the body of the document to make the document active.

3 Set the default font for this document to 12-point Times New Roman.

4 Find all instances of *comcntr* and replace them with the words *community center*. **Hint: Use the Replace All button.**

5 Find all instances of *motel* and replace them with *hotel*.

6 Select the text from the first paragraph (begins *The city is considering*) through the end of the document and then change the paragraph alignment to justified alignment. **Hint: Use a button in the Paragraph group on the Home tab.**

7 Cut the *Conclusion* heading and the paragraph that follows it and then paste them under the title so that the text appears as the first section in the report.

8 Change *Conclusion* to *Executive Summary*.

9 Set the document to automatically hyphenate, but not to hyphenate words in all capital letters. Limit the consecutive hyphens to two hyphens.

10 Triple-click the *Executive Summary* heading, change the font to 12-point Lucida Sans, and then apply the Blue, Accent 1 font color (fifth column, first row in the *Theme Colors* section). **Note: Keep the bold formatting.**

11 Use the Format Painter to apply the same font style used for the *Executive Summary* heading to the rest of the side (second-level) headings within the report and then turn off Format Painter. **Note: Make sure you apply the formatting to the nonprinting paragraph mark at the end of each heading.**

12 Triple-click the document title, change the font to 14-point Lucida Sans, and then apply the Purple, Accent 4 font color (eighth column, first row in the *Theme Colors* section). **Note: Keep the bold formatting.**

13 Proofread the document and correct any errors, paying special attention to the formatting changes made.

14 Save the document.

15 Click the Check button to upload the document for checking.

16 If errors are reported by the Online Lab, view the results document, correct the errors in the submitted document, save the document, and then click the Check Again button.

Reinforcing Writing Skills

When preparing multiple-page documents such as reports or manuscripts, it is important to think of visual elements that can help focus the reader's attention on the content. One way to do this is to use brief headings and subheadings that identify the major parts of the topic. Headings also divide the information into parts that can be comprehended more easily.

Generally, several levels of headings are used in formal reports and manuscripts, while only first-, second-, and sometimes third-level headings (also known as *main*, *side*, and *paragraph* headings) are used in memo reports. Remember that the purpose of the headings is to direct the reader's attention to essential information.

Another means of enhancing the readability of your document is to use images. You learn how to insert and format these elements in Unit 18.

Complete Summons

Read all instructions below before starting this document activity.

1 Navigate to the Document 96.4 launch page in the Online Lab and then click the Launch Activity button to open **Doc096.04** in the activity window.

2 Move the insertion point to the end of the document (Ctrl + End) and then press Enter twice.

3 Insert the file named **Doc096.04_Summons_Legislation_InsertFile** by completing the following steps:

a Click the Insert tab.

b Click the Object button arrow in the Text group.

c Click *Text from File* at the drop-down list.

d Click the *Documents* folder in the Navigation pane of the Insert File dialog box.

e Double-click the *Paradigm* folder, double-click the *Keyboarding* folder, and then double-click the *DocumentActivityFiles* folder.

f Double-click *Doc096.04_Summons_Legislation_InsertFile.docx*. Do not reformat or edit the inserted content.

4 If necessary, move the insertion point to the end of the document (Ctrl + End), press Enter, press Tab, and then key Dated this _____ day of November, 2020. as shown in Figure 96.5. To create the blank underline, press the spacebar once after *this*, key five underscores, and then press the spacebar once before typing the rest of the text. Press Enter twice at the end of the date line. ***Hint: To key an underscore, press and hold down the Shift key and then press the Hyphen key.***

5 Set a left tab at the 3.25-inch mark on the horizontal ruler and a right tab at the 6.5-inch mark.

6 Key the remaining content shown in Figure 96.5. The figure shows the text and the nonprinting characters to help guide your formatting of the document. To create the signature line, press Ctrl + U, press Tab, press Ctrl + U, and then press Enter. Include bold formatting as shown in the figure. Do not press Enter after the last line of text.

steps continue

Figure 96.5 Content for Document 96.4

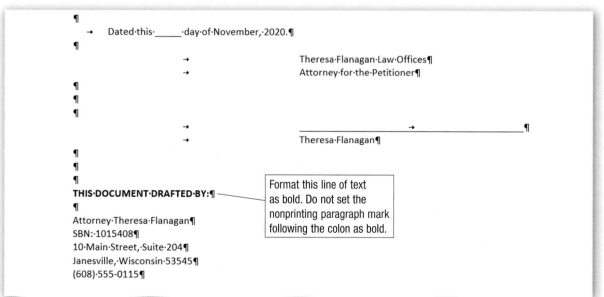

Allowing for Hyphenation

By default, text in a Word document is not hyphenated. However, when text is allowed to hyphenate in a document, longer words can break at the end of lines, which can improve the display of text. For text that is left aligned, allowing Word to hyphenate words can keep the right margin from appearing too ragged. In justified text, allowing Word to hyphenate can help even out the amount of space between words in a line.

To hyphenate words automatically in a document, except words that consist of all capital letters, and to limit the number of consecutive hyphens (the number of lines in a row that end with a hyphen), complete the following steps:

1 Click the Layout tab.

2 Click the Hyphenation button in the Page Setup group.

3 Click *Hyphenation Options* at the drop-down list to display the Hyphenation dialog box.

4 Click the *Automatically hyphenate document* check box to insert a check mark.

5 Click the *Hyphenate words in CAPS* check box to remove the check mark.

6 Click the *Limit consecutive hyphens to* measurement box up arrow until 2 displays.

7 Click OK to close the Hyphenation dialog box.

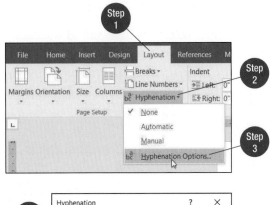

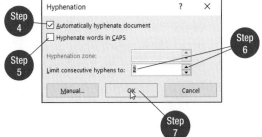

If you want to control where a hyphen appears in a word, click *Manual* from the Hyphenation button drop-down list. Word will display the Manual Hyphenation dialog box, which will show each hyphenated word in the document, one at a time. You can choose where to hyphenate a selected word or direct Word not to hyphenate a specific word by clicking the Cancel button in the Manual Hyphenation dialog box.

Success Tip

To ensure that you have searched the entire document, move the insertion point to the beginning of the document (press Ctrl + Home) before beginning a Find or a Find and Replace action. When you open a document, the insertion point is always positioned at the beginning.

Document 78.3 **Formal Business Report with Hyphenation**

Read all instructions below before starting this document activity.

1 Navigate to the Document 78.3 launch page in the Online Lab and then click the Launch Activity button to open **Doc078.03** in the activity window.

2 Format the document margins so that they are appropriate for an unbound report.

steps continue

7 Insert Page X of Y page numbers using the *Bold Numbers 2* option at the bottom of all pages of the document.

8 Review the format of your document by comparing it against Figure 96.6. Proofread the content keyed from Figure 96.5 and correct any errors. Do not change the content inserted from the inserted file.

9 Save the document.

10 Click the Check button to upload the document for checking.

11 If errors are reported by the Online Lab, view the results document, correct the errors in the submitted document, save the document, and then click the Check Again button.

Figure 96.6 Completed Document 96.4

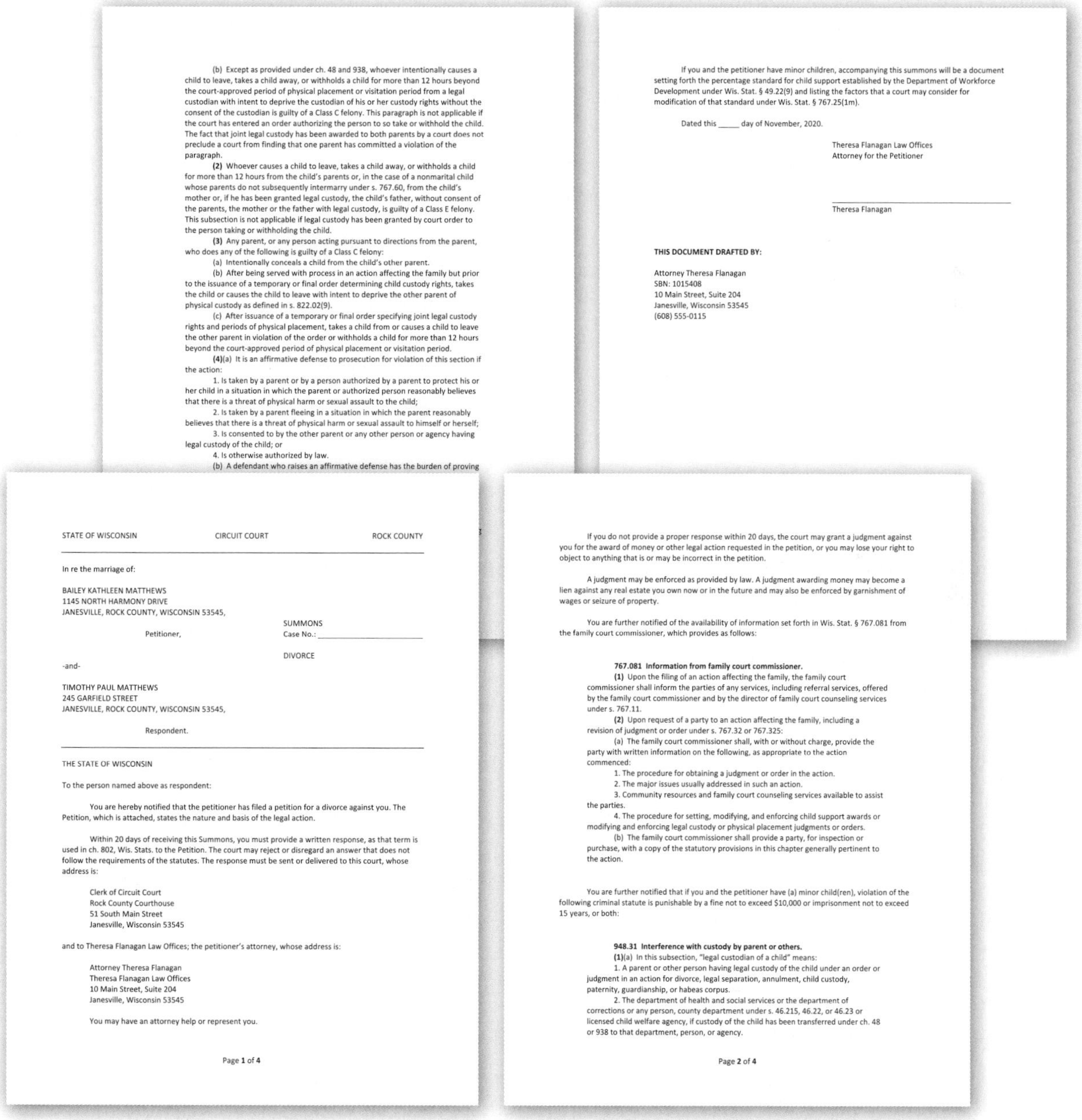

STATE OF WISCONSIN CIRCUIT COURT ROCK COUNTY

In re the marriage of:

BAILEY KATHLEEN MATTHEWS
1145 NORTH HARMONY DRIVE
JANESVILLE, ROCK COUNTY, WISCONSIN 53545,

Petitioner,

SUMMONS
Case No.: ____________

DIVORCE

-and-

TIMOTHY PAUL MATTHEWS
245 GARFIELD STREET
JANESVILLE, ROCK COUNTY, WISCONSIN 53545,

Respondent.

THE STATE OF WISCONSIN

To the person named above as respondent:

You are hereby notified that the petitioner has filed a petition for a divorce against you. The Petition, which is attached, states the nature and basis of the legal action.

Within 20 days of receiving this Summons, you must provide a written response, as that term is used in ch. 802, Wis. Stats. to the Petition. The court may reject or disregard an answer that does not follow the requirements of the statutes. The response must be sent or delivered to this court, whose address is:

Clerk of Circuit Court
Rock County Courthouse
51 South Main Street
Janesville, Wisconsin 53545

and to Theresa Flanagan Law Offices; the petitioner's attorney, whose address is:

Attorney Theresa Flanagan
Theresa Flanagan Law Offices
10 Main Street, Suite 204
Janesville, Wisconsin 53545

You may have an attorney help or represent you.

Page **1** of **4**

If you do not provide a proper response within 20 days, the court may grant a judgment against you for the award of money or other legal action requested in the petition, or you may lose your right to object to anything that is or may be incorrect in the petition.

A judgment may be enforced as provided by law. A judgment awarding money may become a lien against any real estate you own now or in the future and may also be enforced by garnishment of wages or seizure of property.

You are further notified of the availability of information set forth in Wis. Stat. § 767.081 from the family court commissioner, which provides as follows:

767.081 Information from family court commissioner.
(1) Upon the filing of an action affecting the family, the family court commissioner shall inform the parties of any services, including referral services, offered by the family court commissioner and by the director of family court counseling services under s. 767.11.
(2) Upon request of a party to an action affecting the family, including a revision of judgment or order under s. 767.32 or 767.325:
(a) The family court commissioner shall, with or without charge, provide the party with written information on the following, as appropriate to the action commenced:
1. The procedure for obtaining a judgment or order in the action.
2. The major issues usually addressed in such an action.
3. Community resources and family court counseling services available to assist the parties.
4. The procedure for setting, modifying, and enforcing child support awards or modifying and enforcing legal custody or physical placement judgments or orders.
(b) The family court commissioner shall provide a party, for inspection or purchase, with a copy of the statutory provisions in this chapter generally pertinent to the action.

You are further notified that if you and the petitioner have (a) minor child(ren), violation of the following criminal statute is punishable by a fine not to exceed $10,000 or imprisonment not to exceed 15 years, or both:

948.31 Interference with custody by parent or others.
(1)(a) In this subsection, "legal custodian of a child" means:
1. A parent or other person having legal custody of the child under an order or judgment in an action for divorce, legal separation, annulment, child custody, paternity, guardianship, or habeas corpus.
2. The department of health and social services or the department of corrections or any person, county department under s. 46.215, 46.22, or 46.23 or licensed child welfare agency, if custody of the child has been transferred under ch. 48 or 938 to that department, person, or agency.

Page **2** of **4**

(b) Except as provided under ch. 48 and 938, whoever intentionally causes a child to leave, takes a child away, or withholds a child for more than 12 hours beyond the court-approved period of physical placement or visitation period from a legal custodian with intent to deprive the custodian of his or her custody rights without the consent of the custodian is guilty of a Class C felony. This paragraph is not applicable if the court has entered an order authorizing the person to so take or withhold the child. The fact that joint legal custody has been awarded to both parents by a court does not preclude a court from finding that one parent has committed a violation of the paragraph.
(2) Whoever causes a child to leave, takes a child away, or withholds a child for more than 12 hours from the child's parents or, in the case of a nonmarital child whose parents do not subsequently intermarry under s. 767.60, from the child's mother or, if he has been granted legal custody, the child's father, without consent of the parents, the mother or the father with legal custody, is guilty of a Class E felony. This subsection is not applicable if legal custody has been granted by court order to the person taking or withholding the child.
(3) Any parent, or any person acting pursuant to directions from the parent, who does any of the following is guilty of a Class C felony:
(a) Intentionally conceals a child from the child's other parent.
(b) After being served with process in an action affecting the family but prior to the issuance of a temporary or final order determining child custody rights, takes the child or causes the child to leave with intent to deprive the other parent of physical custody as defined in s. 822.02(9).
(c) After issuance of a temporary or final order specifying joint legal custody rights and periods of physical placement, takes a child from or causes a child to leave the other parent in violation of the order or withholds a child for more than 12 hours beyond the court-approved period of physical placement or visitation period.
(4)(a) It is an affirmative defense to prosecution for violation of this section if the action:
1. Is taken by a parent or by a person authorized by a parent to protect his or her child in a situation in which the parent or authorized person reasonably believes that there is a threat of physical harm or sexual assault to the child;
2. Is taken by a parent fleeing in a situation in which the parent reasonably believes that there is a threat of physical harm or sexual assault to himself or herself;
3. Is consented to by the other parent or any other person or agency having legal custody of the child; or
4. Is otherwise authorized by law.
(b) A defendant who raises an affirmative defense has the burden of proving

If you and the petitioner have minor children, accompanying this summons will be a document setting forth the percentage standard for child support established by the Department of Workforce Development under Wis. Stat. § 49.22(9) and listing the factors that a court may consider for modification of that standard under Wis. Stat. § 767.25(1m).

Dated this _____ day of November, 2020.

Theresa Flanagan Law Offices
Attorney for the Petitioner

____
Theresa Flanagan

THIS DOCUMENT DRAFTED BY:

Attorney Theresa Flanagan
SBN: 1015408
10 Main Street, Suite 204
Janesville, Wisconsin 53545
(608) 555-0115

Table 78.1 Options at the Expanded Find and Replace Dialog Box

Choose this option...	To...
Match case	Exactly match the case of the search text. For example, search for *Book* and select the *Match case* option and Word will stop at *Book* but not *book* or *BOOK*.
Find whole words only	Find a whole word, not a part of a word. For example, search for *her* without selecting *Find whole words only* and Word will stop at *there*, *here*, *hers*, and so on.
Use wildcards	Use special characters as wildcards to search for specific text.
Sounds like (English)	Match words that sound alike but are spelled differently: *know* and *no*, for example.
Find all word forms (English)	Find all forms of the word entered in the *Find what* text box. For example, enter *hold* and Word will stop at *held* and *holding*.
Match prefix	Find only those words that begin with the letters in the *Find what* text box. For example, enter *per* and Word will stop at words such as *perform* and *perfect* but skip words such as *super* and *hyperlink*.
Match suffix	Find only those words that end with the letters in the *Find what* text box. For example, enter *ly* and Word will stop at words such as *accurately* and *quietly* but skip words such as *catalyst* and *lyre*.
Ignore punctuation characters	Ignore punctuation within characters. For example, enter *US* in the *Find what* text box and Word will stop at *U.S.*
Ignore white-space characters	Ignore spaces between letters. For example, enter *F B I* in the *Find what* text box and Word will stop at *FBI*.

Using Format Painter

Font styles, color, size, and effects are set using options in the Font group on the Home tab. Applying a series of formats to a heading or paragraph of text can be time consuming. However, if you need to apply the same format to several different pieces of text in a document, the Format Painter can be a useful tool.

Because Format Painter works like the copy and paste features, the Format Painter button is located in the Clipboard group on the Home tab (see Figure 78.4). When you click the Format Painter button, it copies the format applied to the text where the insertion point is currently located. After you click the Format Painter button, the mouse pointer displays as an I-beam pointer with a paint brush icon next to it when positioned over text. Select the text to which you want to apply the formatting and then release the mouse button. Once you release the mouse button, Format Painter is turned off and the mouse pointer returns to its normal setting. If you want to apply formatting to more than one block of text, double-click the Format Painter button to keep the feature turned on. When you are finished, click the Format Painter button to deactivate the feature.

Figure 78.4 Clipboard Group on the Home Tab

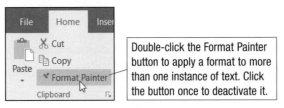

Double-click the Format Painter button to apply a format to more than one instance of text. Click the button once to deactivate it.

Creating a Divorce Summons Using an Existing Document

In the previous document activities, you built a divorce summons document. Much of the content in a summons consists of standard language, using content dictated by state law or by the attorney's office. To improve efficiency in a law office, you would use an existing file or template file to create such documents. As explained in Session 94, a template file has a .dotx extension. You can create a template file by selecting *Word Template (*.dotx)* from the *Save as type* option box in the Save As dialog box. When you double-click a template file to open it, a copy of the file with a .docx extension opens for editing.

In the next document activity, you will treat the launched document as if it were a document created from a template file. The document will be signed in November, so only the petitioner and respondent information on the first page needs changing.

Document 96.5 **Summons for Divorce Created from an Existing Document**

Read all instructions below before starting this document activity.

1 Navigate to the Document 96.5 launch page in the Online Lab and then click the Launch Activity button to open **Doc096.05** in the activity window.

2 Key the information about the petitioner:

> MARK JAMES LITTLETON
> 876 GREENWAY AVENUE
> FOOTVILLE, ROCK COUNTY, WISCONSIN 53537

3 Key the information about the respondent:

> PING XIANG LITTLETON
> N1937 UNKE ROAD
> EDGERTON, ROCK COUNTY, WISCONSIN 53533

4 Proofread the document and correct any errors. *Hint: Make sure there are commas following the ZIP codes for both the petitioner and the respondent.*

5 Save the document.

6 Click the Check button to upload the document for checking.

7 If errors are reported by the Online Lab, view the results document, correct the errors in the submitted document, save the document, and then click the Check Again button.

Ending the Session

The Online Lab automatically saved the work you completed for this session. You may continue with the next session or exit the Online Lab and continue later.

3 Key the search text in the *Find what* text box.

4 Key the replacement text in the *Replace with* text box.

5 Click the Find Next button to locate the first occurrence of the text in the *Find what* text box.

6 Click the Replace button to replace the found text with the text in the *Replace with* text box.

7 Continue clicking the Find Next button, replacing the found text as desired, until all occurrences in the document have been found, and then click OK.

8 Close the dialog box.

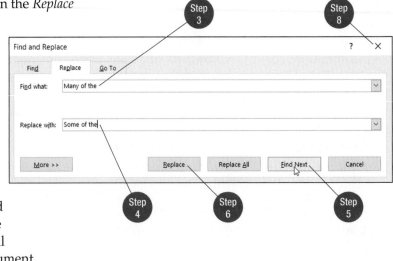

There are options within the Find and Replace dialog box that allow the user to choose specific conditions for finding text. To access these options, click the More button at the Find and Replace dialog box to expand it and reveal the *Search Options* section. (When the Find and Replace dialog box is expanded, the More button changes to the Less button. Click the Less button to hide the *Search Options* section of the dialog box.) Figure 78.3 shows the Find and Replace dialog box with the *Search Options* section displayed.

In the *Search Options* section, the options in the *Search* option box direct how the Find and Replace feature will search in the document. When *All* is selected, Word will search the entire document. When *Up* is selected, Word will search from the location of the insertion point to the beginning of the document. When *Down* is selected, Word will search from the insertion point to the end of the document. Click to insert check marks in the check boxes in the *Search Options* section to refine the search and replace actions. Each option and its function is described in Table 78.1.

Figure 78.3 Find and Replace Dialog Box with Replace Tab Selected and *Search Options* Section Displayed

Petition with Minor Children

Session Objectives

- Add to a table of legal terms and definitions and then sort the table
- Format a petition with minor children
- Format long multilevel lists
- Control pagination using the *Keep lines together* setting
- Efficiently produce documents in mailable form

Getting Started

Exercise 97.1 If you are continuing immediately from Session 96, you may skip the Exercise 97.1 warm-up drill. However, if you exited the Online Lab at the end of Session 96, warm up by completing Exercise 97.1.

Exercise 97.2 Begin your session work by completing Exercise 97.2, a timed short drill, in the Online Lab.

Assessing Your Speed and Accuracy

Complete Timing 97.1 in the Online Lab using the timing text on the next page. At the end of the timing, the Online Lab will display your WPM rate and any errors. Results will be saved in your Timings Performance report. If you have been surpassing the speed and accuracy goals identified in the Online Lab, set slightly more challenging personal goals and strive to exceed them.

Figure 78.2 Letter Content for Document 78.2—continued

proposed that the City and County of Eau Claire adopt our proposal to build a hotel, a multipurpose arena, and a parking ramp. The funds for this undertaking would come from two sources: the private sector (responsible for the hotel) and public funds generated by general revenue bonds. In addition to ensuring an economically stable downtown area, the arena would create 8,000 new jobs. Conventions, sports, and cultural events would be scheduled that otherwise would not have been possible since an arena was not available. ¶ If the City Council gives a "green light" to this proposal, it is imperative that the land necessary for this project be acquired immediately. Land values will skyrocket; so the sooner we act, the less it will cost. I will attend next Tuesday's council meeting to present this proposal and answer questions. ¶ Sincerely, ¶ Alicia Zenisek, President ¶ Eau Claire City/County Planning Board

Reinforcing Word Skills

The following document activity will require you to apply some previously learned Word skills. This section will review some of those skills.

Finding and Replacing Text

With Word's Find and Replace feature, you can look for specific characters or words and replace them with other characters or words. You can complete tasks such as the following:

- Exchange one word or expression for another throughout a document—replace instances of *motel* with *hotel*, for example.
- Use abbreviations for common phrases when keying text and then replace the abbreviations with the full text later.
- Set up standard documents with generic names and replace them with other names to create personalized documents.

To use the Find and Replace feature, complete the following steps:

1 Press Ctrl + Home to position the insertion point at the beginning of the document.

2 Click the Replace button in the Editing group on the Home tab to display the Find and Replace dialog box with the Replace tab selected.

steps continue

3-Minute Timing

Most of us do not have the knack for organizing our possessions efficiently. Crowded kitchen cabinets, overflowing bedroom closets, and tightly packed living room bookcases show that it is much easier for people to collect things than to arrange proper storage for them.

Storage helps to ease our daily living. It is a means of organizing possessions so that the things we need are at hand and the things we will need in the future are put aside, awaiting future use. Well-planned storage allows us to utilize household space to best advantage.

When planning to reorganize storage areas, you should determine how often each item will be used. How and where articles should be stored depends upon how frequently you use them. Those things you use daily should be stored in the primary living areas of your house--usually as close as possible to where you use them. "Live" storage is for articles such as books, music, cleaning tools, cooking paraphernalia, and everyday clothing. "Dead" storage items are relegated to the basement, attic, or garage, locations that are relatively inaccessible. These types of storage areas are the places to store possessions used once a month or seasonally.

Document 97.1 Legal Terms

Read all instructions below before starting this document activity.

1 Navigate to the Document 97.1 launch page in the Online Lab and then click the Launch Activity button to open **Doc097.01** in the activity window.

2 Position the insertion point at the end of the last definition and then press Tab to create a new row at the bottom of the table.

3 Key the terms and definitions shown in Figure 97.1, pressing Tab to move from cell to cell as needed. Since the table has already been formatted, you can key the terms and the definitions without turning bold on and off (with the exception of the italicized terms within the definitions). *Hint: If a definition ends with an italicized term, be sure to turn off italic formatting before pressing Tab.*

4 Proofread the newly keyed entries and correct any errors.

5 Select the rows containing the new terms. Change the spacing after paragraphs to 8 points and make sure the line spacing is set at single spacing.

6 Sort the table alphabetically by terms. *Hint: Refer to Session 74 to review sorting data in tables, if necessary.*

7 Insert Page X of Y page numbering at the bottom center of all pages of the document using the *Bold Numbers 2* option.

8 Save the document.

9 Click the Check button to upload the document for checking.

10 If errors are reported by the Online Lab, view the results document, correct the errors in the submitted document, save the document, and then click the Check Again button.

Figure 78.1 Report Content for Document 78.1—continued

made for a few months, it is recommended that we move at once. All indications are that the city will move to build a new hotel, parking ramp, and community center. Immediately upon announcement, it is estimated that land values will rise from 150 to 300 percent overnight. Therefore, we recommend that we act immediately.

Document 78.2

Transmittal Letter

Read all instructions below before starting this document activity.

1 Navigate to the Document 78.2 launch page in the Online Lab and then click the Launch Activity button to open **Doc078.02** in the activity window.

2 Set the default font for this document to 12-point Times New Roman.

3 Key a block-style letter using the content shown in Figure 78.2. The letter will accompany an unbound report.

   a Key June 9, 2020 as the date of the letter.

   b Key the reference initials mjm, the file name, and a reference to the enclosure under the signature line.

   c Indicate that copies are being sent to the following people:

> Bob Applegate, Planning Commissioner
> Keisha Eisenfein, Economic Development Committee
> Jackie Pedersen, Visitor's Bureau
> Bruce Watson, Chamber of Commerce

4 Proofread the document and correct any errors.

5 Save the document.

6 Click the Check button to upload the document for checking.

7 If errors are reported by the Online Lab, view the results document, correct the errors in the submitted document, save the document, and then click the Check Again button.

Figure 78.2 Letter Content for Document 78.2

Mr. Hamid Jensen ¶ Eau Claire City Council ¶ 720 Oxford Street ¶ Eau Claire, WI 54701-4962 ¶ Dear Hamid: ¶ The proposal from the City/County Planning Board for the Downtown Development Project is enclosed. Individuals contacted for input on this proposal came from the Eau Claire Planning Commissioner, the President of the Eau Claire Chamber of Commerce, the Chair of the Eau Claire Economic Development Committee, and the Director of the Eau Claire Visitor's Bureau. ¶ It is

continues

Figure 97.1 Legal Terms for Document 97.1

Child custody → An award of the primary care of the child, usually to one of the parents

Child support → Money paid by one parent to the other for the continuous support of a minor child

Custodial parent → Parent granted custody of a child

Maintenance → Payments to support a spouse or ex-spouse; also called *spousal support* or *alimony*

Minor child → A child who has not reached the age of majority (usually 18 years of age)

Physical custody → Identifies which parent is responsible for the primary care and maintenance of a child and where the child shall live

Visitation rights → The rights of the non-custodial parent to visit or have the child(ren) visit

Pursuant → According to a recommended technique or authority

Restraining order → A court order that can protect someone from being physically or sexually abused, threatened, stalked, or harassed; also referred to as a *temporary restraining order* or *protective order*

Creating a Petition with Minor Children

In Session 96, you created a summons for a divorce case. In this session, you will create a petition with minor children document that would accompany a summons as it is delivered to a respondent. The purpose of the summons and petition with minor children is to start an action for a divorce or legal separation by a person with minor children.

Inserting the Section Symbol

Legal documents often include the section symbol (§), which is a special character. To insert this symbol, complete the following steps:

1 Click the Insert tab.
2 Click the Symbol button in the Symbols group.
3 Click *More Symbols* to display the Symbol dialog box.

steps continue

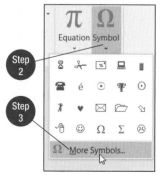

Figure 78.1 Report Content for Document 78.1—continued

Proposal

The relationship among the proposed hotel, the parking ramp, and the community center is basic. The ramp and community center are needed if the hotel is to be successful. The community center will adjoin the hotel and can be used for conventions. A new parking ramp will be needed to handle the cars of hotel guests and the city at large.

Without the hotel, the parking ramp and community center could not be paid for and might be of little use. The hotel is needed to prevent the downtown area from declining and to help pay for the new facilities. The excess tax revenues generated by the hotel would pay for the community center.

Cost Information

The tentative costs for construction of the three projects are as follows: $16.2 million for the hotel, $10.5 million for the community center, and $6.8 million for the parking ramp. The hotel would be paid for through the sale of stocks and through private investors. The parking ramp and community center would be financed through the sale of general obligations bonds. The loan on the parking ramp will be retired by the revenue it takes in over a period of 17 years. The community center would be paid for by the city over a period of 20 years.

Financing

The project will be financed by private enterprise (the hotel) and public funds. A recent study by Dana Woodinski and Associates concluded that there would need to be changes in parking-utility-rate schedules and that the total parking utility rates would generate sufficient revenue to pay for a new parking ramp. In addition, the city manager has stated that the newly generated private construction (the hotel), added to the city's assessed valuation, would generate tax revenue in excess of the amount required to pay the debt on a new community center. The city would finance the project through revenue bonds and/or through general obligation bonds.

Conclusion

It is the consensus of the City/County Planning Board that our organization purchase as much property as possible in the downtown area bordered by North Farwell Street, West Grand Avenue, North Barstow Street, and Gibson Street. Although the city's final decision will not be

continues

4 Click the Special Characters tab.

5 Double-click *Section* in the *Character* list box.

6 Click the Close button.

Step 4

Step 5

[Symbol dialog box]

Symbol

Symbols | Special Characters

Character: Shortcut key:

— Em Dash   Alt+Ctrl+Num -
– En Dash   Ctrl+Num -
‑ Nonbreaking Hyphen   Ctrl+Shift+_
¬ Optional Hyphen   Ctrl+-
  Em Space
  En Space
  1/4 Em Space
° Nonbreaking Space   Ctrl+Shift+Space
© Copyright   Alt+Ctrl+C
® Registered   Alt+Ctrl+R
™ Trademark   Alt+Ctrl+T
§ Section
¶ Paragraph
… Ellipsis   Alt+Ctrl+.
' Single Opening Quote   Ctrl+`,`
' Single Closing Quote   Ctrl+`,`
" Double Opening Quote   Ctrl+`,"

AutoCorrect...   Shortcut Key...

Insert   Cancel

 Success Tip

Another way to insert the section symbol is to press and hold down the Alt key, key 0167 on the numeric keypad, and then release the Alt key. The symbol will appear after you release the Alt key.

Formatting Multilevel Lists

The built-in number formats in Word work well for short lists, but when a list contains 10 or more items, formatting issues can appear. The periods following the numbers may no longer align and/or there may be too much or too little space after the double-digit numbers compared to the single-digit numbers. Figure 97.2 shows a portion of a multilevel list that has been aligned using the default settings in Word.

Figure 97.2 Incorrectly Formatted Multilevel List Using the Word Default Settings

8. No other action for divorce or legal separation by either of the parties has been commenced or is now pending in any other court or before any judge in this state or elsewhere.

9. The Petitioner and Respondent have not been previously married.

Periods for the one-digit numbers do not align with the periods for the two-digit numbers.

10. The parties have not entered into any marital or premarital agreement as to child legal custody, child support, placement of the child, maintenance of either party, property division, or other issues.

11. The following custody information is given in compliance with Sec. 822.09, Wis. Stats.:

Lettered sublist is indented too far to the right below the numbered list for a legal document.

a. The minor child named above presently resides with Petitioner at 1145 North Harmony Drive, Janesville, Rock County, Wisconsin 53545.

Figure 78.1 Report Content for Document 78.1

⏌DOWNTOWN DEVELOPMENT PROJECT⏌

The city is considering building a jointly sponsored downtown development project. This development would include a hotel, a community center, and a large parking ramp. The hotel would be financed by private investors; the parking ramp and community center would be financed by taxpayers. In addition, a private developer is considering the construction of a new office and bank complex directly across the street from the new hotel site.

Purpose

The Purpose of this report is to present data on the proposed projects that will allow our organization to make plans for our future in the inner city. The basic problem that must be considered is whether the projected facilities will actually be built. If we are to be in on the "ground floor" of such a development, we must make the basic decision to commit funds within the next 60 to 90 days.

Background. Since 2014, the central business district of our city has contributed fewer and fewer tax dollars to the city. Property values have decreased and likewise the tax base. As the tax contributions from this area are lost, it becomes necessary to make them up elsewhere in the city. The tax burden is placed on the community at large. It is estimated that the project currently under consideration will double the tax base of the downtown business district.

City Goals. According to the latest forecast by the state Department of Resource Development, our county, which is strategically located on the Interstate System, will absorb over 80 percent of all population growth in the west central section of the state in the next four decades. The focal point of our city's vitality is its central area. A primary goal of the City Council and Planning Commission, therefore, is to strengthen this area as the center of business life, government, administration, medical services, and cultural opportunity for the west central area of the state. An essential reason for constantly strengthening and improving the downtown area of our city is the maintenance and preservation of its existing economic assets. The central section of our city represents existing capital investments in excess of $150 million, more than 15 percent of the city's tax base, and employment for approximately 8,000 people.

continues

Word provides the option of defining or editing new multilevel lists to accommodate double-digit numbers. Adjust the settings for an existing multilevel list by completing the following steps:

1 Key the list and then position the insertion point within a first-level item in the list.

2 Click the Multilevel List button in the Paragraph group on the Home tab.

3 Click *Define New Multilevel List* at the drop-down list.

4 Modify the first-level entries in the Define new Multilevel list dialog box as follows:

   a Confirm that *1* is selected in the *Click level to modify* list box.

   b In the *Position* section, click the *Number alignment* option box arrow and then click *Right* at the drop-down list.

   c Change the number in the *Aligned at* measurement box to *0.6"*.

   d Change the number in the *Text indent at* measurement box to *0.8"*.

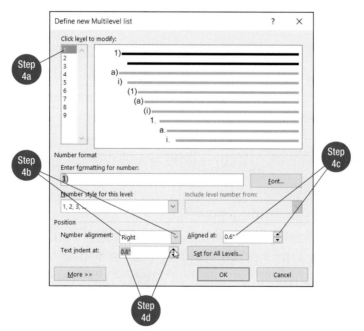

5 Modify the second-level entries in the Define new Multilevel list dialog box as follows:

   a Click *2* in the *Click level to modify* list box.

   b In the *Position* section, click the *Number alignment* option box arrow and then click *Right* at the drop-down list.

   c Change the number in the *Aligned at* measurement box to *0.95"*.

   d Change the number in the *Text indent at* measurement box to *1.1"*.

   e Click OK to apply the settings and close the dialog box.

In Document 97.2, you will apply these formatting settings to lists keyed in a petition with minor children.

Preparing a Letter of Transmittal for a Formal Business Report

Formal business reports usually include a letter of transmittal and a title page. Typically, a letter of transmittal is addressed to the person(s) who requested the report. The letter usually includes the following information:

- A brief description of what is being transmitted
- A brief background of what the report is about and the name of the person, group, or company that prepared it
- Specific examples of the most significant findings contained in the report
- Suggested actions to be taken by the recipient (or, in some instances, the subject) of the report

If the letter of transmittal is bound with the report, inside the front cover, the left margins of both the bound report and the letter of transmittal are generally 1.5 inches. However, if the binding process does not require additional space at the left margin, the default 1-inch left margin is used.

An alternative to binding the letter of transmittal with the report is to send the letter as a separate sheet with the report as an enclosure. Company policy and procedure manuals will identify the preferred method.

In the following document activities, you will key a formal business report and the corresponding letter of transmittal.

Document 78.1

Formal Business Report

Read all instructions below before starting this document activity.

1. Navigate to the Document 78.1 launch page in the Online Lab and then click the Launch Activity button to open **Doc078.01** in the activity window.

2. Change the margins so that they are appropriate for a bound report.

3. Press Enter three times to move the insertion point approximately 2 inches from the top of the document.

4. Key the report shown in Figure 78.1, implementing the proofreading marks as you key. Consider the following as you key the report:

   a. Press Tab at the start of each paragraph.

   b. Apply bold formatting to the headings. Turn off bold formatting before pressing Enter or the spacebar after a heading. For paragraph headings, turn on bold formatting after pressing Tab.

5. Insert a plain page number (*Plain Number 3*) at the right margin of the header on the second page of the report. Do not include the page number on the first page. *Hint: Insert a check mark in the **Different First Page** check box in the Options group on the Header & Footer Tools Design tab.*

6. Proofread the document and correct any errors.

7. Save the document.

8. Click the Check button to upload the document for checking.

9. If errors are reported by the Online Lab, view the results document, correct the errors in the submitted document, save the document, and then click the Check Again button.

Document
97.2

Petition with Minor Children

Read all instructions below before starting this document activity.

1. Navigate to the Document 97.2 launch page in the Online Lab and then click the Launch Activity button to open **Doc097.02** in the activity window.

2. In the caption, select the title *SUMMONS* and then key PETITION WITH MINOR CHILDREN. *Note: Do not press Enter after keying the new title.*

3. Press Ctrl + End to move the insertion point to the end of the document and then key the text shown in Figure 97.3. Consider the following as you key the content:

   a. Allow Word to automatically format the numbered list. Use the Increase Indent button and Decrease Indent button to format the list levels.

   b. Include a blank line between paragraphs and between numbered and lettered list items. *Note: Not all Shift + Enter and Enter notations are marked in the figure.*

   c. When keying any of the paragraphs of text, make sure that the text is formatted with a 0.5-inch tabbed indent rather than a line indent. *Hint: After pressing Tab following a numbered list, the AutoCorrect feature may format the following paragraph with an indented first line. Reject this formatting and start all indented paragraphs with a nonprinting Tab symbol. Confirm that the nonprinting Tab symbol is present by turning on the display of nonprinting characters.*

   d. Apply bold formatting as indicated in the figure. *Hint: Do not format the nonprinting Tab symbol at the start of the paragraph or the paragraph mark at the end of the paragraph as bold.*

4. Click in the first numbered list and format the indents by completing the following steps:

   a. Click the Multilevel List button in the Paragraph group on the Home tab.

   b. Click *Define New Multilevel List* at the drop-down list.

   c. Modify the first-level entries so that the numbers align at the right at 0.6 inch and that the text indent is set at 0.8 inch. *Hint: Do not forget to select the **Right** option in the **Number alignment** option box.*

   d. Modify the second-level entries so that the letters align at the right at 0.95 inch and the text indent is set at 1.1 inches.

   e. Click OK.

5. Click in the second numbered list and format the indents by completing the following steps:

   a. Click the Multilevel List button in the Paragraph group on the Home tab.

   b. Click *Define New Multilevel List* at the drop-down list.

   c. Modify the first-level entries so that the numbers align at the right at 0.6 inch and the text indent is set at 0.8 inch.

   d. Click OK.

6. Click in the lettered list on the third page of the document and format the indents by completing the following steps:

   a. Click the Multilevel List button in the Paragraph group on the Home tab.

   b. Click *Define New Multilevel List* at the drop-down list.

   c. Modify the first-level entries so that the numbers align at the right at 0.6 inch and the text indent is set at 0.8 inch.

   d. Click OK.

steps continue

**Timings
78.1–78.2**

If you are employed in a retail store, you may be asked to use a bar code reader. These are the devices that are utilized to scan the little series of lines, or bar codes, on most packaged merchandise. Most kinds of readers use electromagnetic light beams to scan the bars and read their widths; the black bars absorb light while the white portions between the bars reflect light. Camera-based readers actually take a picture of the bar code. The scanned code is then sent to a connected computing device to track transactions. Learning to use a bar code reader isn't difficult, and if your employer uses such a reader, it can save you and your coworkers a lot of time otherwise consumed in tracking inventory and transactions manually.

Complete one 3-minute timing on the timing text below.

3-Minute Timing

**Timing
78.3**

A plant's life cycle begins with a seed. Depending upon its kind, a seed may be very large or of dust-like smallness, but inside each seed's protective coating exists an embryo plant and, in most cases, a supply of stored food (starch, proteins, oils) to start the embryo on its way. When germination conditions are favorable, the seed's stored food supply will launch the embryo plant into growth and sustain it until it is capable of manufacturing its own food.

Seeds sprout, or germinate, when given favorable conditions. Such conditions include moisture and a certain amount of warmth. Some seeds have other special requirements: light or absence of light, a period of dormancy, very high or very low temperatures, weathering, or exposure to acids or grinding to soften and crack the seed coat. When germination occurs, the seed coat splits, a rootlet starts downward, and a sprout bearing seed leaves makes its way toward the soil surface. Most garden plants have two seed leaves. The life of a plant is amazing; nature is wonderful.

✚ Ergonomic Tip
Position your monitor so that you are not distracted by movement within your peripheral vision when you work at your computer.

7   Move the insertion point to the end of the document (Ctrl + End), press Enter, press Tab, and then key DATED this _____ day of November, 2020. For the blank underline, press the spacebar once after the word *this*, key five underscores, and then press the spacebar once. Press Enter four times after the date line.

8   Set a left tab at the 3.25-inch mark on the horizontal ruler and a right tab at the 6.5-inch mark on the ruler.

9   Key the remaining content shown in Figure 97.4. The figure shows the text and the nonprinting characters to guide your formatting of the document.

   a   For the first signature line, press Tab, press Ctrl + U, press Tab, press Ctrl + U, and then press Enter. Press Tab, key Bailey Kathleen Matthews, Petitioner, and then press Enter three times.

   b   For the blank underline for the subscribed date, key five underscores, press the spacebar once, key day of November, 2020., and then press Enter four times.

   c   For the notary signature line, press Ctrl + U, press Tab, press Ctrl + U, and then press Enter.

   d   For the commission line, key My commission:, press the spacebar once, press Ctrl + U, press Tab, press Ctrl + U, and then press Enter four times.

   e   Include bold formatting as shown in the figure. Make sure the paragraph marks following lines of bold text are not bold. Do not press Enter after the last line of text.

10   Insert Page X of Y page numbering at the bottom of all pages of the document using the *Bold Numbers 2* option.

11   Improve the page breaks in the document by completing the following steps:

   a   The second item in the second numbered list breaks across pages 2 and 3 of the document. Position the insertion point anywhere within the five lines of text in the numbered item and then click the Paragraph group dialog box launcher. Click the Line and Page Breaks tab, click the *Keep lines together* check box in the *Pagination* section to insert a check mark, and then click OK.

   b   Position the insertion point to the left of the nonprinting Tab symbol in front of the *WHEREFORE, Petitioner requests relief* paragraph and insert a page break to keep the signatures together on the last page of the document.

12   Proofread the document and correct any errors, checking it against the completed document shown in Figure 97.5.

13   Save the document.

14   Click the Check button to upload the document for checking.

15   If errors are reported by the Online Lab, view the results document, correct the errors in the submitted document, save the document, and then click the Check Again button.

Session 78

Preparing Formal Business Reports with Letters of Transmittal

Session Objectives

- **Prepare a letter of transmittal for a formal business report**
- **Use Find and Replace**
- **Use Format Painter**
- **Turn on automatic hyphenation**
- **Edit a formal business report**
- **Compose a memo report proposal**
- **Efficiently produce documents in mailable format**

Getting Started

Exercise 78.1   If you are continuing immediately from Session 77, you may skip the Exercise 78.1 warm-up drill. However, if you exited the Online Lab at the end of Session 77, warm up by completing Exercise 78.1.

Exercise 78.2   Begin your session work by completing Exercise 78.2, a timed short drill, in the Online Lab.

Assessing Your Speed and Accuracy

Complete Timings 78.1 through 78.3 in the Online Lab. At the end of each timing, the Online Lab will display your WPM rate and any errors. Results will be saved in your Timings Performance report. If you have been surpassing the speed and accuracy goals identified in the Online Lab, set slightly more challenging personal goals and strive to exceed them.

Complete two 1-minute timings on the timing text on the following page. If you meet or exceed both speed and accuracy goals for Timing 78.1, push for greater speed on Timing 78.2.

Figure 97.3 Petition with Minor Children Content for Document 97.2

[Tab] Petitioner, Bailey Kathleen Matthews, by her attorney, Theresa Flanagan, as and for her Petition states: [2 Enters]

1. Petitioner, Bailey Kathleen Matthews, is an adult individual who resides at 1145 North Harmony Drive, Janesville, Rock County, Wisconsin 53545. The Petitioner was born on September 28, 1979, and her social security number is on file herein. Petitioner is not employed outside of the home. [Shift + Enter, Enter]

2. Respondent, Timothy Paul Matthews, is an adult individual who resides at 245 Garfield Street, Janesville, Rock County, Wisconsin 53545. The Respondent was born on October 8, 1978, and his social security number is on file herein. Respondent is employed by ABC Supply. [Shift + Enter, Enter]

3. The parties were married on February 14, 2003, at Monroe, Wisconsin. [Shift + Enter, Enter]

4. One child has been born to or adopted by the parties during this marriage, namely: [Shift + Enter, Enter]

   a. Ashley Carrie Matthews, date of birth, December 22, 2014. [Shift + Enter, Enter]

   b. No other children have been born to either party during this marriage. [Shift + Enter, Enter]

   c. The Petitioner is a fit and proper person to have the legal custody of the minor child. [Shift + Enter, Enter]

5. The Petitioner is not now pregnant.

6. The parties have resided in Rock County for more than thirty (30) days next preceding the commencement of this action and the State of Wisconsin for more than six (6) months next preceding the commencement of this action.

7. The marriage is irretrievably broken.

8. No other action for divorce or legal separation by either of the parties has been commenced or is now pending in any other court or before any judge in this state or elsewhere.

9. The Petitioner and Respondent have not been previously married.

10. The parties have not entered into any marital or premarital agreement as to child legal custody, child support, placement of the child, maintenance of either party, property division, or other issues.

continues

Reinforcing Writing Skills

In Session 76, the *Reinforcing Writing Skills* section focused on the critical writing step of planning document content *before* beginning to write. In the Document 76.3 activity, you prepared a plan to write a promotional report regarding the new product line for Mama's Pizza Company. In this session, you are to write the report from the plan you developed. Before beginning the Document 77.4 activity, access the planning document you created for Document 76.3.

Document 77.4

Writing a Promotional Business Report

Read all instructions below before starting this document activity.

1 Navigate to the Document 77.4 launch page in the Online Lab and then click the Launch Activity button to open **Doc077.04** in the activity window.

2 Press Enter three times and key a title for your report.

3 Compose a promotional report to be given to the store manager regarding the new product at Mama's Pizza Company. The report should be between one and three pages long.

4 Review the content of the report, using the following questions as a guide. If necessary, revise the report after completing your review.

   a Does the report respond well to the request?

   b Does the document have a clear purpose? Is this purpose reinforced?

   c Is the information relevant? Will the reader understand the message? Will the reader take the action requested?

   d Are the sentences clear, concise, and convincing?

   e Are the document's grammar, word usage, punctuation, and capitalization correct?

   f Are headings used effectively?

5 Insert a plain page number (*Plain Number 3*) at the right margin of the header on the second and subsequent pages of the report. Do not include the page number on the first page.

6 Proofread the document and correct any errors.

7 Save the document.

8 Click the Submit button to upload the document for instructor review.

Ending the Session

The Online Lab automatically saved the work you completed for this session. You may continue with the next session or exit the Online Lab and continue later.

11. The following custody information is given in compliance with Sec. 822.09, Wis. Stats.:

    a. The minor child named above presently resides with Petitioner at 1145 North Harmony Drive, Janesville, Rock County, Wisconsin 53545.

    b. Within the last five (5) years the minor child has lived with both parents at 1145 North Harmony Drive, Janesville, Rock County, Wisconsin 53545.

    c. Neither party has previously participated as a party, witness, or in any other capacity in other litigation concerning the custody of the above-named minor child in this or any other case.

    d. The Petitioner is unaware of any other custody proceedings concerning the above-named minor child pending in a court of this or any other state.

    e. The Petitioner knows of no person not a party to this action who has physical custody of the minor child or claims to have custody or visitation rights with respect to the minor child.

    f. The Petitioner understands that as a party to this action, she has a continuing duty to inform this court of any custody proceedings brought concerning the child in this or any other state of which Petitioner obtains information during this proceeding. [4 Enters]

[Tab] YOU ARE HEREBY NOTIFIED that pursuant to § 767.117, Wis. Stats., during the pendency of this action, both parties are prohibited from and may be held in contempt of court for: [2 Enters]

1. Harassing, intimidating, physically abusing, or imposing any restraint on the personal liberty of the other party or of a minor child of either of the parties. [Shift + Enter, Enter]

2. Encumbering, concealing, damaging, destroying, transferring or otherwise disposing of property owned by either or both of the parties, without the consent of the other party or any order of the court, except in the usual course of business, and in order to secure necessities or in order to pay reasonable costs and expenses of the action, including attorney fees. [Shift + Enter, Enter]

3. Establishing a residence with a minor child of the parties outside the state of Wisconsin or more than 150 miles from the residence of the other party within the state without the consent of the other party or an order of the court or Circuit Court Commissioner. [Shift + Enter, Enter]

continues

3 Key the information shown in Figure 77.4, following the directions regarding the number of times to press Enter. As you key the text, consider the following:

   a Format the title (three lines keyed in all capital letters) in bold. Turn off bold formatting before pressing Enter at the end of the title.

   b Alphabetize the list of report authors by last name.

4 Change the vertical page alignment to center alignment. *Hint: Review Session 66, if necessary.*

5 Proofread the document and correct any errors.

6 Save the document.

7 Click the Check button to upload the document for checking.

8 If errors are reported by the Online Lab, view the results document, correct the errors in the submitted document, save the document, and then click the Check Again button.

Figure 77.4 Title Page Content for Document 77.3

AN OVERVIEW OF THE DIGITAL SERVICES PROVIDED [Enter]

BY THE PRODUCTION DEPARTMENT [Enter]

OF DIGITAL DISTINCTION, INC. [12 Enters]

Submitted to [2 Enters]

Division Presidents [Enter]

Vice Presidents [Enter]

Publishers [Enter]

Sales and Marketing Managers [12 Enters]

Prepared by [2 Enters]

Alan Holbert [Enter]

Caesar Gonzaga [Enter]

Lynn Gullickrud [Enter]

Arya Patel [Enter]

Devonte Tuffs [2 Enters]

Production Department [Enter]

Digital Distinction, Inc. [2 Enters]

April 29, 2020

4. Removing a minor child of the parties from the state of Wisconsin for more than 90 consecutive days without the consent of the other party or an order of the court or Circuit Court Commissioner. [Shift + Enter, Enter]

5. Concealing a minor child of the parties from the other party without the consent of the other party or an order of the court or Circuit Court Commissioner. [3 Enters]

[Tab] These restraining orders apply until the action is dismissed, final judgment in the action is entered, or the court orders otherwise. [2 Enters]

[Tab] **A VIOLATION OF THE ABOVE RESTRAINING ORDERS MAY RESULT IN PUNISHMENT FOR CONTEMPT, WHICH MAY INCLUDE MONETARY PENALTIES, IMPRISONMENT, AND OTHER SANCTIONS AS PROVIDED FOR IN § 785.04, WIS. STATS.** [2 Enters]

[Tab] A violation of paragraphs 3, 4, or 5 above is not a contempt of court if the court finds that the action was taken to protect a party or a minor child of the parties from physical abuse by the other party and that there was no reasonable opportunity under the circumstances for the party to obtain an order authorizing the action. [2 Enters]

[Tab] WHEREFORE, Petitioner requests relief as follows: [2 Enters]

A. For an absolute divorce. [Shift + Enter, Enter]

B. Custody of the minor child and primary physical placement.

C. Allocating periods of physical placement of the minor child between Petitioner and Respondent.

D. An award of child support for benefit of the minor child.

E. For a division of the property and debts of the parties.

F. For an award of attorney's fees for Petitioner bringing this action.

G. For such other and further relief as the court deems appropriate. [2 Enters]

Figure 77.3 Table Content for Document 77.2

Program Name	File Extension(s)
ActiveX Streaming Format	asf
Ad Lib Sample	smp
Amiga SVX	svx
Covox V8	v8
Creative Labs VOC	VOC
Dialogic VOX ADPCM	vox
Gravis Patch	pat
AIFF (Macintosh)	aif
MIDI SDS	sds
MPEG	mp3, mp4
NeXt/Sun (Java)	au, snd
QuickTime	avi
Real Audio	ra
Sample Vision	smp
Sonic Foundry	sfv
Sound Designer II	Sd2
Waveform	wav
Windows Media	wma, wmv

13 Save the document.

14 Click the Check button to upload the document for checking.

15 If errors are reported by the Online Lab, view the results document, correct the errors in the submitted document, save the document, and then click the Check Again button.

Document 77.3 **Title Page for a Bound Business Report**

Read all instructions below before starting this document activity.

1 Navigate to the Document 77.3 launch page in the Online Lab and then click the Launch Activity button to open **Doc077.03** in the activity window.

2 Before keying, change the formatting as follows:

a Change the default line spacing for this document to single spacing with no spacing after paragraphs.

b Change the left margin to 1.5 inches. (Do not set as the document's default.)

c Change the paragraph alignment to center alignment. (Do not set as the document's default.)

steps continue

Figure 97.4 Signature Lines for the Petition with Minor Children for Document 97.2

¶
¶
¶
→   _____→_____¶
→   Bailey·Kathleen·Matthews,·Petitioner¶
¶
¶
Subscribed·and·sworn·to·before·me·this¶
_____·day·of·November,·2020.¶
¶
¶
¶
_____→_____¶
Notary·Public,·State·of·Wisconsin¶
My·commission:·_____→_____¶
¶
¶
¶
THIS·DOCUMENT·DRAFTED·BY:¶
¶
Attorney·Theresa·Flanagan¶
SBN:·1015408¶
10·Main·Street,·Suite·204¶
Janesville,·Wisconsin·53545¶
(608)·555-0115¶

> Format this line of text as bold. Do not set the nonprinting paragraph mark following the colon as bold.

Figure 97.5 Completed Petition with Minor Children for Document 97.2

STATE OF WISCONSIN   CIRCUIT COURT   ROCK COUNTY

In re the marriage of:

BAILEY KATHLEEN MATTHEWS
1145 NORTH HARMONY DRIVE
JANESVILLE, ROCK COUNTY, WISCONSIN 53545,

     Petitioner,

PETITION WITH MINOR CHILDREN
Case No.: _____

DIVORCE

-and-

TIMOTHY PAUL MATTHEWS
245 GARFIELD STREET
JANESVILLE, ROCK COUNTY, WISCONSIN 53545,

     Respondent.

Petitioner, Bailey Kathleen Matthews, by her attorney, Theresa Flanagan, as and for her Petition states:

1. Petitioner, Bailey Kathleen Matthews, is an adult individual who resides at 1145 North Harmony Drive, Janesville, Rock County, Wisconsin 53545. The Petitioner was born on September 28, 1979, and her social security number is on file herein. Petitioner is not employed outside of the home.

2. Respondent, Timothy Paul Matthews, is an adult individual who resides at 245 Garfield Street, Janesville, Rock County, Wisconsin 53545. The Respondent was born on October 8, 1978, and his social security number is on file herein. Respondent is employed by ABC Supply.

3. The parties were married on February 14, 2003, at Monroe, Wisconsin.

4. One child has been born to or adopted by the parties during this marriage, namely:

   a. Ashley Carrie Matthews, date of birth, December 22, 2014.

   b. No other children have been born to either party during this marriage.

   c. The Petitioner is a fit and proper person to have the legal custody of the minor child.

5. The Petitioner is not now pregnant.

Page 1 of 4

6. The parties have resided in Rock County for more than thirty (30) days next preceding the commencement of this action and the State of Wisconsin for more than six (6) months next preceding the commencement of this action.

7. The marriage is irretrievably broken.

8. No other action for divorce or legal separation by either of the parties has been commenced or is now pending in any other court or before any judge in this state or elsewhere.

9. The Petitioner and Respondent have not been previously married.

10. The parties have not entered into any marital or premarital agreement as to child legal custody, child support, placement of the child, maintenance of either party, property division, or other issues.

11. The following custody information is given in compliance with Sec. 822.09, Wis. Stats.:

   a. The minor child named above presently resides with Petitioner at 1145 North Harmony Drive, Janesville, Rock County, Wisconsin 53545.

   b. Within the last five (5) years the minor child has lived with both parents at 1145 North Harmony Drive, Janesville, Rock County, Wisconsin 53545.

   c. Neither party has previously participated as a party, witness, or in any other capacity in other litigation concerning the custody of the above-named minor child in this or any other case.

   d. The Petitioner is unaware of any other custody proceedings concerning the above-named minor child pending in a court of this or any other state.

   e. The Petitioner knows of no person not a party to this action who has physical custody of the minor child or claims to have custody or visitation rights with respect to the minor child.

   f. The Petitioner understands that as a party to this action, she has a continuing duty to inform this court of any custody proceedings brought concerning the child in this or any other state of which Petitioner obtains information during this proceeding.

YOU ARE HEREBY NOTIFIED that pursuant to § 767.117, Wis. Stats., during the pendency of this action, both parties are prohibited from and may be held in contempt of court for:

1. Harassing, intimidating, physically abusing, or imposing any restraint on the personal liberty of the other party or of a minor child of either of the parties.

Page 2 of 4

continues

Figure 77.2 Business Report Content for Document 77.1—continued

projected services required are available when they are needed, and this in turn will ensure the continued growth of all DDI publishing divisions.

Beginning January 1, the Production Department will become a profit center for DDI, as described in Directive 1057. While our first responsibility will be to the DDI publishing divisions, our services will be available to nonpublishing corporations with high volumes of internal publications (annual expenditures of $85,000 and up). This includes newsletter production, training materials, and company publications such as a prospectus or an annual report.

Document 77.2

Formal Unbound Business Report Containing a Table

Read all instructions below before starting this document activity.

1 Navigate to the Document 77.2 launch page in the Online Lab and then click the Launch Activity button to open **Doc077.02** in the activity window.

2 Turn on the display of nonprinting characters. *Hint: Click the Show/Hide ¶ button in the Paragraph group on the Home tab.*

3 Delete the last sentence of the second paragraph. The sentence begins *With this information* and ends *with potential clients*. *Note: Make sure to delete the space before the sentence as well.*

4 Reverse the order of the last two paragraphs in the report so that the paragraph that begins *Beginning February 1* appears before the paragraph that begins *You, as publishers*.

5 Move the *Summary* heading and the three paragraphs that follow it to the top of the document, immediately below the title. Make sure there are tabs at the beginning of each paragraph but no tab before the heading.

6 Edit the *Summary* heading to read *Executive Summary*.

7 Position the insertion point at the end of the paragraph following the *Audio Conversion for Computer Files.* heading, press the spacebar, key Formats available are as follows:, and then press Enter.

8 Insert a table with 2 columns and 19 rows and then key the text shown in Figure 77.3. *Note: Do not allow Word to automatically capitalize the first letter of the entries in the second column.*

9 Format the table as follows:

   a Select the first row and then apply bold formatting.

   b AutoFit the contents of the cells.

   c Select the table and then click the Increase Indent button in the Paragraph group on the Home tab once so that the content of the first column of the table aligns with the 0.5-inch paragraph indents.

   d Confirm that there is only one paragraph mark under the table.

10 Format the *Video Production* heading so that it stays with the following paragraph.

11 Proofread the document and correct any errors, paying special attention to the spacing between paragraphs. Make sure there are no extra hard returns at the end of the document.

12 Turn off the display of nonprinting characters.

steps continue

2. Encumbering, concealing, damaging, destroying, transferring or otherwise disposing of property owned by either or both of the parties, without the consent of the other party or any order of the court, except in the usual course of business, and in order to secure necessities or in order to pay reasonable costs and expenses of the action, including attorney fees.

3. Establishing a residence with a minor child of the parties outside the state of Wisconsin or more than 150 miles from the residence of the other party within the state without the consent of the other party or an order of the court or Circuit Court Commissioner.

4. Removing a minor child of the parties from the state of Wisconsin for more than 90 consecutive days without the consent of the other party or an order of the court or Circuit Court Commissioner.

5. Concealing a minor child of the parties from the other party without the consent of the other party or an order of the court or Circuit Court Commissioner.

These restraining orders apply until the action is dismissed, final judgment in the action is entered, or the court orders otherwise.

A VIOLATION OF THE ABOVE RESTRAINING ORDERS MAY RESULT IN PUNISHMENT FOR CONTEMPT, WHICH MAY INCLUDE MONETARY PENALTIES, IMPRISONMENT, AND OTHER SANCTIONS AS PROVIDED FOR IN § 785.04, WIS. STATS.

A violation of paragraphs 3, 4, or 5 above is not a contempt of court if the court finds that the action was taken to protect a party or a minor child of the parties from physical abuse by the other party and that there was no reasonable opportunity under the circumstances for the party to obtain an order authorizing the action.

Page **3** of **4**

WHEREFORE, Petitioner requests relief as follows:

A. For an absolute divorce.

B. Custody of the minor child and primary physical placement.

C. Allocating periods of physical placement of the minor child between Petitioner and Respondent.

D. An award of child support for benefit of the minor child.

E. For a division of the property and debts of the parties.

F. For an award of attorney's fees for Petitioner bringing this action.

G. For such other and further relief as the court deems appropriate.

DATED this _____ day of November, 2020.

_____
Bailey Kathleen Matthews, Petitioner

Subscribed and sworn to before me this
_____ day of November, 2020.

_____
Notary Public, State of Wisconsin
My commission: _____

THIS DOCUMENT DRAFTED BY:

Attorney Theresa Flanagan
SBN: 1015408
10 Main Street, Suite 204
Janesville, Wisconsin 53545
(608) 555-0115

Page **4** of **4**

Ending the Session

The Online Lab automatically saved the work you completed for this session. You may continue with the next session or exit the Online Lab and continue later.

Figure 77.2 Business Report Content for Document 77.1—continued

Music and sound effects can be introduced into your program via our Roland V-STUDIO 700 digital audio workstation. The Roland system offers full synchronization with your video master, along with DVD-quality digital sound.

Cinelerra Video Editor. Our most recent acquisition, the Cinelerra system, gives us state-of-the-art digital video editing capabilities. Some of the many features of this system include:

- Supports video of any size or speed
- Works in both RGBA and YUVA
- Includes a compositing engine
- Uses four screens
  - Timeline
  - Viewer
  - Resource window
  - Compositor

Contact Us

The material presented here is an overview of the services we offer. If you have questions about any of the services listed or would like an evaluation of your current publications, call the Production Department (Ext. 7780), and we'll schedule a meeting with you. It helps if you bring samples of the publications you want to upgrade or reformat.

The services provided by the Production Department are not limited to what is contained in this report. We can provide additional services if the need arises. Let us know your needs, and we'll take it from there.

Summary

The educational publishing industry is changing. If we are to continue to grow and prosper, we must change with it. The computer, the Internet, and new devices emerging every day have changed the way we access and receive information. Educational media has become an interactive process, allowing the end user to not only retrieve information but also receive instant feedback while learning.

You, as publishers, are in a unique position to view where things are heading. Keep the Production Department informed on the types of services you will be requiring in the future. By doing this, you will ensure that the

continues

Marital Settlement Agreement and Final Divorce Documents

Session Objectives

- Format a Marital Settlement Agreement document
- Format a Findings of Fact, Conclusions of Law, and Judgment of Divorce document
- Use the Find feature to locate and change variable information
- Insert text from files containing standard language
- Efficiently produce documents in mailable form

Getting Started

Exercise 98.1 If you are continuing immediately from Session 97, you may skip the Exercise 98.1 warm-up drill. However, if you exited the Online Lab at the end of Session 97, warm up by completing Exercise 98.1.

Exercise 98.2 Begin your session work by completing Exercise 98.2, a timed short drill, in the Online Lab.

Assessing Your Speed and Accuracy

Complete Timing 98.1 in the Online Lab using the timing text on the next page. At the end of the timing, the Online Lab will display your WPM rate and any errors. Results will be saved in your Timings Performance report. If you have been surpassing the speed and accuracy goals identified in the Online Lab, set slightly more challenging personal goals and strive to exceed them.

Figure 77.2 Business Report Content for Document 77.1—continued

soundproof and are large enough to accommodate large-group recordings. They can also be utilized for video shoots. Their 20-foot ceilings allow plenty of room for additional lighting.

Digital Editing. Our sonic solutions DSP-Quattro 5 and Roland V-STUDIO 700 digital audio workstations offer seamless, precise editing of recorded audio tracks. These systems offer DVD-quality sound, and, since they are digital, do not suffer from generation loss. Your audio program can be copied, edited, and changed as many times as you desire without ever losing the slightest bit of quality.

Music and Sound Effects. We have a number of music libraries possessing a broad range of music to create just the right mood for your program. If you desire an original score, that's also possible through our MIDI studio.

Our sound effects library is a work in progress, having been started back in the 1950s. It contains many one-of-a-kind, vintage sound effects that would be difficult to find anywhere else. If a sound effect doesn't exist in our library, we'll create it in our sound studios.

DVD Mastering. We create the duplication masters in the manufacturing of your audio DVDs. It is our responsibility to ensure that quality is maintained throughout the process. After all, the DVD can only be as good as the source from which it was originally generated.

Audio DVD or Recordable DVD (DVD-R). We can take your audio program and convert it to an audio DVD. Digital Distinction also has the equipment to manufacture small runs of DVDs (100 or fewer).

Video Production

Audio for Video. The Production Department can take your English-narrated video and change it to Chinese, French, German, Japanese, Spanish, or whatever language you desire. This all happens in our sound studios where professional voice talents synchronize their narration with your video. The voice talent monitors the video and matches voice patterns to the lip movements of the people on the screen. This technique results in video that appears to have been originally produced in that language.

continues

Timing 98.1

Divorce is a procedure for terminating a marriage. Divorce is a matter that affects not only the parties who are ending a marriage but also the lives of children and other concerned family members. It is likely that you can name friends or family members who have had to deal with the stress of going through a divorce.

The reasons a divorce is granted are called grounds. Each state has passed laws stating the grounds on which divorces can be granted, and those laws vary significantly from one state to another. There are fault grounds and no-fault grounds for divorce.

Some typical grounds for divorce in states where fault divorces are granted are cruel and inhuman treatment (also known as inappropriate marital conduct), abandonment and nonsupport, desertion, habitual drunkenness, living apart from each other for a period of time, being convicted of certain crimes, and adultery.

The basis on which a no-fault divorce is granted is known as irreconcilable differences or irretrievable breakdown. It allows two people to agree to terminate a marriage with neither party being charged with wrongdoing.

In states where fault divorces are granted, the party initiating the divorce action is a plaintiff or complainant, and the opposing party is the defendant. The termination of the marriage is a divorce, and the documents filed are a complaint and an answer.

In states that allow for no-fault divorces, the party initiating the action is the petitioner, and the answering party is the respondent. The termination of the marriage is a dissolution, and the documents filed are a petition and a response.

Creating a Marital Settlement Agreement Document

The Marital Settlement Agreement (MSA) is the contractual agreement between a divorcing couple that resolves issues that are part of the divorce proceedings. A comprehensive MSA will address custody and child placement, child support and maintenance, and property division. An MSA includes an agreement as to the division of the parties' assets and liabilities, including their real estate, personal property, cash assets, retirement plans, deferred income accounts, 401K accounts, individual retirement accounts, and pension plans.

Because most of the language in the MSA is standard, in the following document activity you will create the MSA by inserting text from another file and then updating the information as it relates to the details of the settlement.

   c When keying the paragraph headings, turn off bold formatting after keying the period at the end of the heading. Do not format the space following the heading in bold. For paragraph headings that are not immediately preceded by a side heading, turn on bold formatting *after* pressing the Tab key.

   d Allow Word to automatically format the bulleted list with solid, black, round bullets for the first-level entries and open, round bullets for the second-level entries. Increase the indent of the first-level entries to align with the paragraph indent.

  5 Format the *Video Production* heading so it stays with the paragraph that follows it (located on the next page). *Hint: At the Paragraph dialog box with the Line and Page Breaks tab selected, click the **Keep with next** check box to insert a check mark. Do not insert a hard page break.*

  6 Insert a plain page number (*Plain Number 3*) at the right margin of the header on the second and subsequent pages of the report. Do not include the page number on the first page. *Hint: Insert a check mark in the **Different First Page** check box in the Options group on the Header & Footer Tools Design tab.*

  7 Proofread the document and correct any errors.

  8 Save the document.

  9 Click the Check button to upload the document for checking.

 10 If errors are reported by the Online Lab, view the results document, correct the errors in the submitted document, save the document, and then click the Check Again button.

Figure 77.2 Business Report Content for Document 77.1

AN OVERVIEW OF THE DIGITAL SERVICES PROVIDED BY THE PRODUCTION DEPARTMENT OF DIGITAL DISTINCTION, INC.

Digital Distinction's Production Department is a recording/postproduction facility offering a variety of services. The Production Department offers on-site recording studios, digital recording, editing and mixing, and a state-of-the-art digital video editing suite.

The purpose of this report is to make sure that management of not only our division but also those in all other divisions of DDI are aware of the many production services that Digital Distinction has to offer. The services provided along with a brief description of how they can best be utilized follows. With this information, managers and executives will be in a better position to take advantage of our services when the need arises and enable us to expand our customer base by sharing this information with potential clients.

Audio Production

    Audio Recording Studios. We have two on-site sound studios for recording your audio projects on DVDs or CDs. The studios are completely

continues

Document **Marital Settlement Agreement**
98.1

Read all instructions below before starting this document activity.

1 Navigate to the Document 98.1 launch page in the Online Lab and then click the Launch Activity button to open **Doc098.01** in the activity window.

2 In the caption, select the title *SUMMONS* and then key MARITAL SETTLEMENT AGREEMENT. *Note: Do not press Enter after keying the new title.*

3 Select the horizontal line next to *Case No.*, press Ctrl + U to turn off the underline formatting, and then key 14FA1029. Confirm that there is one space (and no nonprinting Tab character) between the colon and the keyed number and that the case number is not underlined.

4 Press Ctrl + End to move the insertion point to the end of the document and then key the text shown in Figure 98.1. Do not press Tab at the beginning of the text. Press Enter twice following the paragraph as indicated in the figure.

5 Display the Insert File dialog box (click *Text from File* from the Object button drop-down list) and then insert the **Doc098.01_MSA_InsertFile** document by completing the following steps:

a Click the *Documents* folder.

b Double-click the *Paradigm* folder, double-click the *Keyboarding* folder, and then double-click the *DocumentActivityFiles* folder.

c Double-click *Doc098.01_MSA_InsertFile.docx*.

6 Use the Find feature to make the following changes in the document:

a Find the one instance of *INSERT NAME* and key Ashley Carrie Matthews.

b Find the one instance of *INSERT BIRTH DATE* and key December 22, 2014.

c Find the one instance of *INSERT DETAILS* and key every other weekend and on Wednesdays from 4 p.m. to 8 p.m. The parties have agreed upon a holiday schedule. *Hint: After making the replacement, make sure there is only one period at the end of the paragraph.*

d Find the one instance of *INSERT AMOUNT* and key Seven Hundred Dollars ($700).

e Find the one instance of *INSERT ADDRESS* and key 1145 North Harmony Drive, Janesville, Wisconsin 53545.

f Find the one instance of *INSERT FIRST AND MIDDLE NAME* and key Ashley Carrie.

7 Move the insertion point to the end of the document (press Ctrl + End) and then set right tabs at the 3.0-inch and 6.5-inch marks on the horizontal ruler and a left tab at the 3.5-inch mark.

8 Key the remaining content shown in Figure 98.2. The figure shows the text and the nonprinting characters to guide your formatting of the document.

a For the first blank underline for the date, key Dated this, press the spacebar once, key five underscores, press the spacebar once, and then key day of April, 2020.

steps continue

To format a heading so it stays with the next paragraph, complete the following steps:

1 Click anywhere within the heading.

2 Click the Paragraph group dialog box launcher on the Home tab.

3 At the Paragraph dialog box, click the Line and Page Breaks tab, if it is not already selected.

4 Click the *Keep with next* check box in the *Pagination* section to insert a check mark.

5 Click OK or press the Enter key to close the dialog box.

Document **Formal Bound Business Report with Headings, a Bulleted List,**
77.1 **and Numbered Pages**

Read all instructions below before starting this document activity.

1 Navigate to the Document 77.1 launch page in the Online Lab and then click the Launch Activity button to open **Doc077.01** in the activity window.

2 Because this will be a bound report, change the left margin to 1.5 inches.

3 Key the report title by completing the following steps:

a Press Enter three times to move the insertion point approximately 2 inches from the top of the page.

b Press Ctrl + E to change the paragraph alignment to center alignment.

c Press Ctrl + B to turn on bold formatting.

d Key the two-line title shown in Figure 77.2, pressing Shift + Enter at the end of the first line of the title.

e Press Ctrl + B to turn off bold formatting.

f Press Enter and then press Ctrl + L to change the paragraph alignment back to left alignment.

4 Key the body of the report shown in Figure 77.2. Consider the following as you key the report:

a Press Tab at the start of each paragraph.

b When keying side headings that are immediately followed by an indented paragraph heading, do not turn off bold formatting until after keying the paragraph heading. In contrast, when keying side headings that are not immediately followed by a paragraph heading, turn off bold formatting before pressing Enter.

steps continue

b   Press Enter three times.

c   To create the first signature line, press Ctrl + U, press Tab, and then press Ctrl + U.

d   Press Enter and then key Bailey Kathleen Matthews.

e   Press Enter three times.

f   Key the second and third date lines, following the instructions in Step 8a. Press Tab twice between the two date lines, as shown in Figure 98.2.

g   Press Enter three times.

h   Create the second and third signature lines, following the instructions in Step 8c.

i   Key the names Timothy Paul Matthews and Dale Bensten, Attorney for the Respondent as shown in Figure 98.2. *Note: Do not press Enter following the attorney's title at the bottom of the document.*

9   Check to make sure that each page ends appropriately, without one line being left alone on either the top or bottom of a page. (Although the Widow/Orphan control feature is active, it will not control the paragraph breaks between pages because the paragraphs end with Shift + Enter instead of Enter.) If any lines have been left alone at the top or bottom of a page, use the *Keep lines together* check box at the Paragraph dialog box with the Line and Page Breaks tab selected to fix this issue.

10   Insert page numbers using the Page X of Y format and *Bold Numbers 2* option at the bottom of all pages of the document.

11   Proofread the document for the parts that you keyed and formatted, checking the document against the completed document shown in Figure 98.3.

12   Save the document.

13   Click the Check button to upload the document for checking.

14   If errors are reported by the Online Lab, view the results document, correct the errors in the submitted document, save the document, and then click the Check Again button.

Figure 98.1 Content for Document 98.1

> This Agreement is between BAILEY KATHLEEN MATTHEWS, Petitioner, and TIMOTHY PAUL MATTHEWS, Respondent. In consideration of the mutual terms and provisions as hereinafter stated, both parties agree that the terms and provisions of this Agreement may be incorporated by the court in the pending divorce action between the parties in the Conclusions of Law and Judgment to be entered therein; however, this Agreement shall independently survive any such Judgment; and in that respect the parties agree as follows: [2 Enters]

Inserting Page Numbers

To insert a plain page number at the right margin of the header, complete the following steps:

1 Click the Insert tab.

2 Click the Page Number button in the Header & Footer group.

3 Point to *Top of Page* at the drop-down list.

4 Click *Plain Number 3* at the side menu.

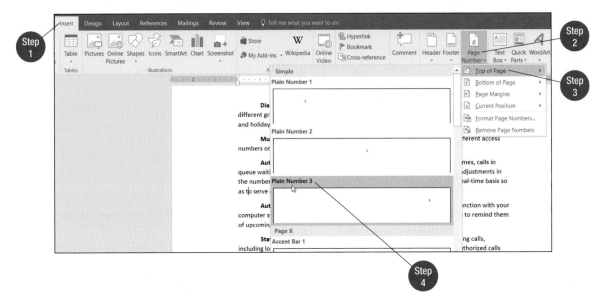

When inserting a header or footer on pages following the first page of a document, it is easier to key the first page and at least part of the second page of the document before inserting the header and footer information. Remember that if you do not want the page number to appear on the first page of the document, you must click to insert a check mark in the *Different First Page* check box in the Options group on the Header & Footer Tools Design tab.

Controlling Pagination of Headings

When you are keying a document and you reach the end of page, Word automatically starts a new page. When the Widow/Orphan control feature is turned on, Word prevents the first line of a paragraph from being left at the bottom of one page and the last line of a paragraph from beginning a new page.

Word treats headings as single-line paragraphs, which means they are not affected by Widow/Orphan control. The most logical placement of a heading is on the same page as the paragraph that follows it. Sometimes, however, Word will end a page immediately after a heading. To prevent a heading from being separated from the paragraph that follows it, the heading can be formatted to force Word to keep the two pieces together (usually by moving the heading to the next page).

Figure 98.2 Signature Lines for the Marital Settlement Agreement for Document 98.1

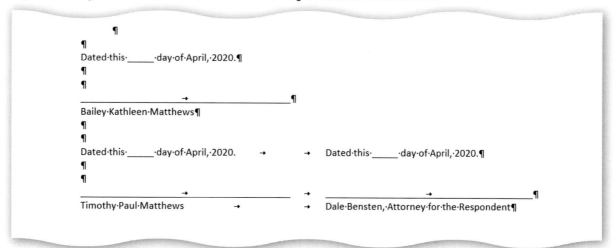

¶
¶
Dated·this·_____·day·of·April,·2020.¶
¶
¶
_____→_____¶
Bailey·Kathleen·Matthews¶
¶
¶
Dated·this·_____·day·of·April,·2020.   →   →   Dated·this·_____·day·of·April,·2020.¶
¶
¶
_____→_____ → _____→_____¶
Timothy·Paul·Matthews   →   →   Dale·Bensten,·Attorney·for·the·Respondent¶

Figure 98.3 Completed Marital Settlement Agreement for Document 98.1

STATE OF WISCONSIN   CIRCUIT COURT   ROCK COUNTY

In re the marriage of:

BAILEY KATHLEEN MATTHEWS
1145 NORTH HARMONY DRIVE
JANESVILLE, ROCK COUNTY, WISCONSIN 53545,

                                    MARITAL SETTLEMENT AGREEMENT
        Petitioner,   Case No.: 14FA1029

                                    DIVORCE
-and-

TIMOTHY PAUL MATTHEWS
245 GARFIELD STREET
JANESVILLE, ROCK COUNTY, WISCONSIN 53545,

        Respondent.

This Agreement is between BAILEY KATHLEEN MATTHEWS, Petitioner, and TIMOTHY PAUL MATTHEWS, Respondent. In consideration of the mutual terms and provisions as hereinafter stated, both parties agree that the terms and provisions of this Agreement may be incorporated by the court in the pending divorce action between the parties in the Conclusions of Law and Judgment to be entered therein; however, this Agreement shall independently survive any such Judgment; and in that respect the parties agree as follows:

1. CUSTODY AND PHYSICAL PLACEMENT

    a. Both parents are fit and proper persons to have joint legal custody of the minor child. It is in the present best interest of the minor child that both parents be granted joint legal custody of the minor child, namely, Ashley Carrie Matthews, born December 22, 2014.

    b. Petitioner shall be designated the primary caretaker and shall have primary physical placement of the minor child at all times and hours except the Respondent shall have physical placement of the minor child every other weekend and on Wednesdays from 4 p.m. to 8 p.m. The parties have agreed upon a holiday schedule.

    c. In that both parents are to be granted joint legal custody of the minor child, said persons shall jointly have the right to make all major decisions concerning the child.

    d. In the event any disputes arise as to custody or physical placement, either party may request the family court commissioner to refer the matter to the director of family court counseling services for mediation (and a legal custody and physical placement study). Both parties shall cooperate with the mediator and counseling service.

Page **1** of 6

    e. Both parties shall have access to the child's medical, dental, and school records, as well as to the child's court or treatment records and the child's records relating to protective services.

    f. Neither party shall remove the minor child from the State of Wisconsin for a period of time exceeding ninety (90) consecutive days nor establish legal residence for any minor child outside the State of Wisconsin or within the State at a distance of 150 miles or more from the other parent without first giving at least sixty (60) days' notice to the other parent to allow for objection. Further, neither party shall interfere with the custody of the child or the parental rights of the other parent as prohibited in Sec. 948.31, Stats.

2. CHILD SUPPORT

    a. The Respondent shall pay an amount equal to 25 percent of his gross income, commencing on the first pay period after the divorce, as and for support of the minor child.

    b. Child support shall continue until the child reaches eighteen (18) or is earlier emancipated or until the child reaches age nineteen (19), if that child is pursuing an accredited course of instruction leading to the acquisition of a high school diploma or its equivalent.

    c. All child support payments shall be by income assignment. The Respondent's employer shall be ordered to withhold 25 percent of the Respondent's gross income from the money due on a per week basis and send the payment to:

        Wisconsin Support Collections Trust Fund
        PO Box 7440
        Milwaukee, Wisconsin 53274

    d. In the event payor becomes unemployed, the child support payments shall be made in cash or by money order or certified check, and made payable to the Wisconsin Support Collections Trust Fund. If the payments are made by personal check, they shall be paid fourteen (14) days in advance.

    e. Both parties shall notify the Wisconsin Support Collections Trust Fund and the other party in writing of any change of address within ten (10) days of such change pursuant to Section 767.263, Stats. Further, the Respondent shall notify the Wisconsin Support Collections Trust Fund and the other party within ten (10) days of any change of employer and of any substantial change in the amount of his income such that his ability to pay child support is affected.

    f. The Respondent shall pay simple interest at the rate of 1.5 percent per month on any amount unpaid, commencing the first day of the second month after the month in which the amount was due.

3. MEDICAL HEALTH CARE EXPENSES

    a. Both parties shall maintain the minor child on their comprehensive medical and hospitalization insurance policy provided through their employment, or obtain such a policy, and shall maintain the same until the child reaches the age of majority or until said child has

Page **2** of 6

continues

Formatting the Title Page of a Formal Business Report

When beginning a title page, leave approximately 2 inches of space between the top and middle groups of text and between the middle and bottom groups of text. After you have keyed the required information for the title page, vertically center the text on the page by selecting *Center* in the *Vertical alignment* option box in the Page Setup dialog box with the Layout tab selected. If necessary, adjust the space between the groups of text for better balance on the page. Table 77.3 lists guidelines for formatting a business report title page. For the Document 77.3 activity, specific placement directions for the title page will be provided in order to ensure accurate document checking in the Online Lab.

Reinforcing Word Skills

The document activities in this session will require you to apply some previously learned Word skills. This section will review those skills. One of the document activities will require inserting a table. If necessary, refer to the sessions in Unit 15 to review table skills.

Centering Information Horizontally

Headings within reports need to be centered on the page. To center text, click the Center button in the Paragraph group on the Home tab or press Ctrl + E. If a title is to be set on two lines, press Shift + Enter before keying the second line. After keying the line or paragraph that is to be centered, press Enter and then click the Align Left button in the Paragraph group or press Ctrl + L to return the paragraph alignment to left alignment.

Table 77.3 Formatting Guidelines for a Formal Business Report Title Page

Title Page Element	Formatting Guidelines
line spacing	single with 0 points spacing after paragraphs
margins	same as the body of the report: 1-inch left margin if unbound and 1.5-inch left margin if bound; all other margins 1 inch
alignment	vertically and horizontally centered
top third of page	name or title of the report keyed in bold and all capital letters
middle third of page	recipient(s) of the report, including name(s), title(s), and location(s)
bottom third of page	preparer(s) of the report, including name(s), company affiliation, and report date; usually listed in alphabetical order

reached the age of nineteen (19) so long as the child is pursuing an accredited course of instruction leading to the acquisition of a high school diploma or its equivalent. Both parties shall promptly make all necessary premium payments.

b. The parties shall split equally the liability of all hospital, medical, dental, orthodontia and related expenses not covered by insurance for the minor child.

c. Petitioner shall be entitled to all applicable rights of conversion or continuation of the health insurance policy currently in force, and Respondent shall cooperate in such conversion or continuation; however, Petitioner shall be solely liable for the expense and maintenance of any such health coverage for and on her own behalf.

4. **LIFE INSURANCE**

a. Both parties shall maintain in full force and pay the premiums on the life insurance which is presently carried through their employment or obtain comparable insurance with the minor child of the parties named as sole and irrevocable primary beneficiary until the youngest minor child reaches the age of majority or until said child has reached the age of nineteen (19) so long as the child is pursuing an accredited course of instruction leading to the acquisition of a high school diploma or its equivalent. Both parties shall furnish each other with copies of such policies or evidence of there being such insurance in force during the term of the obligation, and with proof of beneficiary designation, if requested.

b. Neither party shall borrow against any such policy or use any such policy as collateral or impair its value in any manner without the express written consent of the other party or order of the court.

c. This obligation may be satisfied by provision in a Will or Trust.

5. **MAINTENANCE**

a. The Respondent shall pay the amount of Seven Hundred Dollars ($700) per month as maintenance payments.

b. The maintenance shall terminate in five years.

c. Pursuant to Internal Revenue Code Section 71, the maintenance payments shall be included as income on Petitioner's income tax returns beginning in calendar year 2020. In addition, such payments shall be a deduction on Respondent's income tax returns pursuant to Internal Revenue Code Section 215, beginning in the same calendar year.

d. All maintenance payments shall be by income assignment. The Respondent's employer shall be ordered to withhold funds sufficient from money due on a weekly basis and send such payment to the Clerk of the Circuit Court of Rock County.

e. Both parties shall notify the Wisconsin Support Collections Trust Fund and the other party in writing of any change of address within ten (10) days of such change pursuant to Section 767.263, Stats. Further, the Respondent shall notify the Wisconsin Support Collections Trust

Page **3** of **6**

Fund and the other party within ten (10) days of any change of employer and of any substantial change in the amount of his income such that his ability to pay maintenance is affected.

6. **PROPERTY DIVISION**

As a full, fair, final, and complete property division but in addition to maintenance as agreed above, the property of the parties shall be divided as follows:

a. Petitioner is awarded:

i. Household furniture, fixtures, furnishings, appliances, and household effects in her possession at the time of the trial;

ii. All pension and retirement benefits, including profit sharing plans;

iii. Life Policies in her name, subject to the provision of Section IV of this Agreement, and cash surrender values, if any;

iv. Cash and deposit accounts in her name;

v. Personal belongings, including clothing and jewelry, in her possession at the time of trial.

b. Respondent is awarded:

i. Household furniture, fixtures, furnishings, appliances, and household effects in his possession at the time of the trial;

ii. All pension and retirement benefits, including his profit sharing plan;

iii. Life Policies in his name, subject to the provision of Section IV of this Agreement, and cash surrender values, if any;

iv. Cash and deposit accounts in his name;

v. Personal belongings, including clothing and jewelry, in his possession at the time of trial.

c. Residence: The Petitioner shall be awarded all right, title, and interest in the residence of the parties located at 1145 North Harmony Drive, Janesville, Wisconsin 53545 and the Respondent shall be divested of all right, title and interest therein, and saved harmless from any and all liability thereon. The Respondent shall execute a quit claim deed terminating his interest in said property.

Page **4** of **6**

7. **DEBTS**

The parties shall be responsible for all debts and obligations of the parties incurred after the commencement of this action.

8. **TAXES**

a. The parties acknowledge that under Wisconsin's community property law each party shall be taxed on one-half of the total marital income from January 1, to the date of the granting of the divorce judgment. Furthermore, the parties acknowledge that under the community property law each party shall be credited with one-half of the total withholding payments made during the aforesaid period of time. The parties further acknowledge that the itemized deductions accrued and/or paid from January 1, to the date of divorce shall be divided equally between the parties.

b. The Petitioner shall have the right to claim the child, namely Ashley Carrie, as a dependent for federal and state income tax purposed provided that one or both parents fulfill the tax code requirements for claiming the dependency exemption. The Respondent will sign IRS Form 8332, Release of Claim to Exemption for Child of Divorced or Separated Parents for the child for each tax year, provided all payments on behalf of the child are current as of the end of the tax year.

c. The parties agree to file joint federal and combined income tax returns for the year 2019.

d. The parties shall share any tax refunds, both federal and state, for the year 2019.

e. Each party shall hold the other harmless from any and all liability resulting from the other party's joining in the execution of the 2019 tax returns.

f. Each of the parties shall be responsible for his/her own capital gains taxes, including interest, deficiencies, and penalties, should any be incurred in the transfer of property pursuant to this Agreement.

9. **ATTORNEY FEES**

Each of the parties shall be responsible for his or her own attorney fees, no contribution being required by either party.

10. **EXECUTION OF DOCUMENTS**

Now or in the future, upon demand, the parties agree to execute and deliver any and all documents which may be necessary to carry out the terms and conditions of this Agreement.

Page **5** of **6**

11. **VOLUNTARY EXECUTION**

Each party acknowledges that this Marital Settlement has been entered into of his or her own volition with full knowledge and information, including tax consequences. Each believes the terms and conditions to be fair and reasonable. No coercion or undue influence has been used by or against either party in making this agreement.

12. **DIVESTING OF PROPERTY RIGHTS**

Except as otherwise provided for in this agreement, each party shall be divested of and each party waives, renounces, and gives up pursuant to § 767.255, Stats., all right, title, and interest in and to the property awarded to the other. All property and money received and retained by the parties shall be the separate property of the respective parties, free and clear of any right, title, interest, or claim of the other party, and each party shall have the right to deal with and dispose of his or her separate property as fully and effectively as if the parties had never been married.

13. **MUTUAL RELEASES**

Neither party may, at any time hereafter, sue the other, or his or her heirs, personal representative, and assigns, for the purpose of enforcing any or all of the rights relinquished and/or waived under this agreement. Both parties also agree that in the event any suit shall be commenced, this release, when pleaded, shall constitute a complete defense to any such claim or suit so instituted by either party.

14. **FULL DISCLOSURE AND RELIANCE**

Pursuant to § 767.27, Stats., each party warrants to the other that there has been an accurate, complete, and current disclosure of all income, assets, debts, and liabilities. Both parties understand and agree that deliberate failure to provide complete disclosure constitutes perjury. The property referred to in this agreement represents all the property that either party has any interest in or right to, whether legal or equitable, owned in full or in part by either party, separately or by the parties jointly. This agreement is founded on a financial disclosure statement of each part an exhibit at trial, which documents are incorporated by reference herein. Both parties relied on these financial representations when entering into this agreement.

Dated this _____ day of April, 2020.

_____
Bailey Kathleen Matthews

Dated this _____ day of April, 2020.   Dated this _____ day of April, 2020.

_____   _____
Timothy Paul Matthews   Dale Bensten, Attorney for the Respondent

Page **6** of **6**

Formatting Headings in Formal Business Reports

The main purpose of headings in a formal business report is to call the reader's attention to the important ideas and sections in the document. Table 77.2 lists the formatting styles for the headings to be used in document activities for this session. Figure 77.1 shows examples of the three heading levels formatted in a formal business report.

Table 77.2 Heading Formatting Styles

Heading Level	Formatting Style
main/first level	centered, bold, all capital letters, press Enter once before and after
side/second level	aligned at the left margin, bold, main words capitalized, press Enter once before and after
paragraph/third level	run in with paragraphs and begin where other paragraphs begin (for example, on a tab indent), bold, main words capitalized, end with a bold period, and follow with a space (not bold)

Figure 77.1 Heading Levels for a Formal Business Report

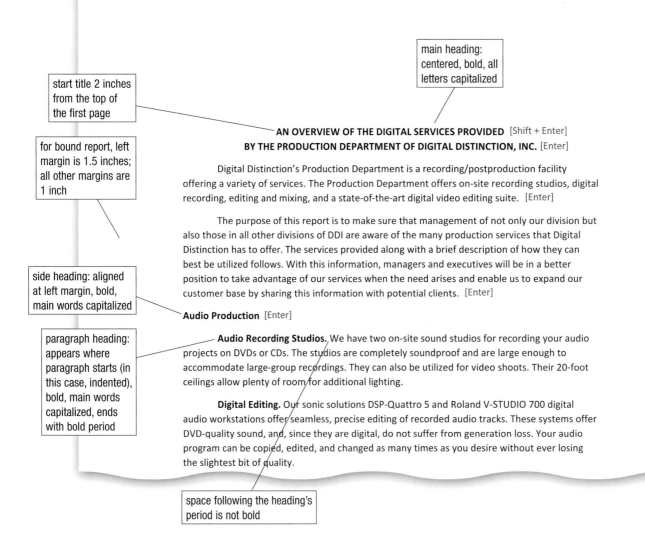

start title 2 inches from the top of the first page

main heading: centered, bold, all letters capitalized

for bound report, left margin is 1.5 inches; all other margins are 1 inch

side heading: aligned at left margin, bold, main words capitalized

paragraph heading: appears where paragraph starts (in this case, indented), bold, main words capitalized, ends with bold period

AN OVERVIEW OF THE DIGITAL SERVICES PROVIDED [Shift + Enter]
BY THE PRODUCTION DEPARTMENT OF DIGITAL DISTINCTION, INC. [Enter]

Digital Distinction's Production Department is a recording/postproduction facility offering a variety of services. The Production Department offers on-site recording studios, digital recording, editing and mixing, and a state-of-the-art digital video editing suite. [Enter]

The purpose of this report is to make sure that management of not only our division but also those in all other divisions of DDI are aware of the many production services that Digital Distinction has to offer. The services provided along with a brief description of how they can best be utilized follows. With this information, managers and executives will be in a better position to take advantage of our services when the need arises and enable us to expand our customer base by sharing this information with potential clients. [Enter]

Audio Production [Enter]

Audio Recording Studios. We have two on-site sound studios for recording your audio projects on DVDs or CDs. The studios are completely soundproof and are large enough to accommodate large-group recordings. They can also be utilized for video shoots. Their 20-foot ceilings allow plenty of room for additional lighting.

Digital Editing. Our sonic solutions DSP-Quattro 5 and Roland V-STUDIO 700 digital audio workstations offer seamless, precise editing of recorded audio tracks. These systems offer DVD-quality sound, and, since they are digital, do not suffer from generation loss. Your audio program can be copied, edited, and changed as many times as you desire without ever losing the slightest bit of quality.

space following the heading's period is not bold

Creating a Findings of Fact, Conclusions of Law, and Judgment of Divorce Document

After the service of the summons and petition, or the filing of a joint petition, there is a minimum waiting period before a final judgment of divorce or legal separation can be granted. During this waiting period, there are some automatic restrictions on what parties can do. Once the judge has granted the divorce, the petitioner must submit a Findings of Fact, Conclusions of Law, and Judgment of Divorce document for the judge to sign.

You will create a Findings of Fact, Conclusions of Law, and Judgment of Divorce document in the next document activity. Much of the language in this document is standard or is from a statute, so you will insert two files into a caption document and then update the content for the specific case.

Document 98.2 Findings of Fact, Conclusions of Law, and Judgment of Divorce

Read all instructions below before starting this document activity.

1 Navigate to the Document 98.2 launch page in the Online Lab and then click the Launch Activity button to open **Doc098.02** in the activity window.

2 Edit the caption as follows:

   a Delete the word *SUMMONS* and the three nonprinting tab characters preceding the word in the document. Keep the blank line space in the document.

   b Select the line to the right of *Case No.*, press Ctrl + U to turn off the underline formatting, and then key 14FA1029. Confirm that there is one space (and no nonprinting Tab character) between the colon and the keyed number and that the case number is not underlined.

   c Select the word *DIVORCE* and then key FINDINGS OF FACT, CONCLUSIONS OF. Press Enter, press Tab three times, and then key LAW, AND JUDGMENT OF DIVORCE.

3 Move the insertion point to the end of the document (Ctrl + End), change the paragraph alignment to center alignment (Ctrl + E), turn on bold formatting (Ctrl + B), key TRIAL, turn off bold formatting (Ctrl + B), press Enter, change the paragraph alignment to left alignment (Ctrl + L), and then press Enter.

4 Set left tabs at the 1.0-inch, 1.5-inch, and 2-inch marks on the horizontal ruler and a right tab at the 6.5-inch mark.

5 Key the text shown in Figure 98.4. Consider the following as you key the content:

   a Allow Word to automatically format the numbered lists.

   b Key the bold and centered heading according to the instructions in Step 3.

   c Use Shift + Enter to create an extra line between items within the numbered list. Follow the formatting instructions indicated by the nonprinting characters in Figure 98.4. The line breaks in the figure will not match the line breaks in your document. *Hint: The ↵ symbol indicates the New Line Command, which means to press Shift + Enter.*

   d To key the write-on lines, press Ctrl + U, press Tab, press Ctrl + U, press Shift + Enter, and then press Enter.

steps continue

Parts of a Formal Business Report

Formal business reports usually begin with an executive summary and make substantial use of graphic elements, including tables, pictures, graphs, and schematics. In addition, a formal report may include the following:

- Letter of Transmittal
- Table of Contents
- List of Exhibits
- Source Notes
- Bibliography

Depending on the length of the report, as well as company policies and procedures, formal business reports are commonly placed in some type of booklet with an eye-catching cover and tabbed sections throughout to help the reader quickly find particular areas of interest.

Readability of Formal Business Reports

Formal business reports are important information sources in the workplace. Managers and other executives use them regularly to make key decisions regarding sales, marketing, advertising, investments, and future growth plans for the company. Correct formatting, accurate content, and a high level of readability help ensure that the vital content of the report is communicated clearly. Contributors to readability include:

- Words that convey a clear meaning—generally simple, commonly used words
- Sentences of 25 words or fewer, so that the reader does not get lost in the content of long sentences
- Paragraphs of fewer than 10 lines, so that the reader is more likely to read rather than scan the content
- Side headings to help readers focus their attention on what is being presented

Formatting Formal Business Reports

Table 77.1 identifies the formatting guidelines to be used when keying a formal business report.

Table 77.1 Formatting Guidelines for a Formal Business Report

Report Element	Formatting Guidelines
paragraph alignment	left aligned, paragraphs can be flush left or indented, bulleted and numbered lists align on the paragraph start position
margins	if an unbound report, use default margins: 1-inch top, bottom, left, and right; if a bound report, use 1-inch top, bottom, and right margins, and a 1.5-inch left margin (see Figure 77.1)
line spacing	default (1.08-line spacing with 8 points of spacing after paragraphs); press Enter once after paragraphs, including headings
report title	begins approximately 2 inches from the top of the page (press Enter three times before keying the title), center, bold, and key in all capital letters (see Figure 77.1)
page numbers	first page: no page number second and subsequent pages: plain number (digits only) in the right margin of the header

Presiding: → Judge Randall Werner¶

Place: → Rock County Courthouse¶

→ 51 South Main Street, Janesville, Wisconsin 53545¶

Date: → April 10, 2020¶

¶

Date of granting of judgment of divorce: April 10, 2020¶

¶

Appearances: Petitioner Bailey Kathleen Matthews in person and with her attorney; Respondent Timothy Paul Matthews in person and with his attorney ¶

¶

FINDINGS OF FACT ¶

¶

1. For at least six months before the commencement of this action, both parties were continuous residents of the state of Wisconsin, and of this county for at least 30 days prior to the commencement, further, all necessary parties have been duly served and ordered to appear, 120 days have lapsed since the date of service of the summons and petition upon the Respondent. ↵

   ¶

2. The Petitioner in this action is Bailey Kathleen Matthews. ↵

   ↵

   Residence: → 1145 North Harmony Drive, Janesville, Wisconsin 53545 ↵
   Birthdate: → September 28, 1979 ↵
   Occupation: → None ↵
   ↵

   Income: ↵
   → Current monthly earnings: ↵
   → → Gross: → $0.00 ↵
   → → Net: → $0.00 ↵
   ↵

   → Other income: → _____ ↵
   ¶

3. The Respondent in this action is Timothy Paul Matthews. ↵
   ↵

continues

Complete one 3-minute timing on the timing text below.

3-Minute Timing

Timing 77.3

Many people have never had the opportunity to see a trade dollar coin. In fact, many folks have heard of silver dollars but don't know about the trade dollar.

During the late 1860s and early 1870s, a great international trade developed between the United States and China. Chinese merchants did not want the US paper currency; they preferred "hard money" and their favorite was silver. The US silver dollar weighed 412.5 grains and was slightly lighter than other crown-size silver coins of the world, so it was not so readily accepted. Accordingly, beginning in 1873, a special silver dollar called the trade dollar was minted. The weight of the coin was prominently stated on the reverse of the coin.

The trade dollar served its purpose fairly well, and from 1873 through 1878 approximately 35 million were made. At first trade dollars could be used in the United States itself, but this caused confusion about the two types of dollars--which was worth more? By not being legal tender in the United States, trade dollars actually sold for less than face value for many years--no one wanted them.

Ergonomic Tip

Minimize eye strain by positioning your monitor screen so that there is no glare from the sun or from overhead lighting. If your workstation is located near windows, position your desk so that the windows are on the left or right side.

Creating Formal Business Reports

Formal business reports are similar in many ways to memo business reports. Both are part of an organizational loop, which consists of moving information upward in an organization and then moving instructions downward based on the findings of the report. In addition, both use default line spacing, side headings, and formatted lists to aid in readability.

Several differences exist between the two types of reports. Memo business reports are typically five or fewer pages, whereas formal business reports are longer, generally six or more pages. Some formal business reports are hundreds of pages long. In a memo business report, the report date, the recipient(s), the sender(s), and the subject are identified at the top of the first page. In contrast, a formal business report has a separate title page containing similar information.

Residence: → 245 Garfield Street, Janesville, Wisconsin 53545 ↵

Birthdate: → October 8, 1978 ↵

Occupation: → Materials Buyer at ABC Supply ↵

↵

Income: ↵

→ Current monthly earnings: ↵

→ → Gross: → $8,000↵

→ → Net: → $5,000 (after deducting federal and state income taxes, social security) ↵

↵

→ Other income: → _____ ↵

¶

4. The parties were married on February 14, 2003, at Monroe, Wisconsin. ↵

¶

5. The following minor child has been born to or adopted by the parties: ↵

↵

Minor's Name: → Ashley Carrie Matthews↵

Date of Birth: → December 22, 2014↵

Soc. Sec. No.: → On file↵

¶

a. Specific responsibility for payment of medical and dental expenses has been made in the Marital Settlement Agreement. ↵

¶

b. There are no emancipated children of this marriage. ↵

¶

c. No other minor children were born to the parties during this marriage. ↵

¶

d. The wife is not pregnant. ↵

¶

6. Neither party has begun any other action for divorce, legal separation, or annulment anywhere. ↵

¶

7. Neither party has been previously divorced. ↵

¶

continues

Session
77
Producing Formal Business Reports

Session Objectives

- **Format a formal business report**
- **Center text horizontally**
- **Insert page numbers**
- **Control pagination of headings**
- **Insert a table in a document**
- **Format a title page for a formal business report**
- **Compose a report from planning notes**
- **Efficiently produce documents in mailable format**

Getting Started

Exercise 77.1 If you are continuing immediately from Session 76, you may skip the Exercise 77.1 warm-up drill. However, if you exited the Online Lab at the end of Session 76, warm up by completing Exercise 77.1.

Exercise 77.2 Begin your session work by completing Exercise 77.2, a timed short drill, in the Online Lab.

Assessing Your Speed and Accuracy

Complete Timings 77.1 through 77.3 in the Online Lab. At the end of each timing, the Online Lab will display your WPM rate and any errors. Results will be saved in your Timings Performance report. If you have been surpassing the speed and accuracy goals identified in the Online Lab, set slightly more challenging personal goals and strive to exceed them.

Complete two 1-minute timings on the timing text below. If you meet or exceed both speed and accuracy goals for Timing 77.1, push for greater speed on Timing 77.2.

1-Minute Timings

Timings 77.1–77.2

A visit to a town in a quiet valley gives energy, vitality, and stamina to a tired person. Nothing rivals a pleasant trip to revive the spirits. Heavy problems seem to disappear, and frustrating troubles fade. Vivid images of a different way of life conjure impressive vistas of peace. Save those agitated nerves and prevent hostile reactions. Attempt to take advantage of happenings that raise the spirits; you deserve the very best.

8. The marriage is irretrievably broken. ↵

¶

9. The parties' assets, their interests therein, the values thereof, and their encumbrances and debts are found to be as set forth in the financial disclosure form, which was updated as required by the statute on the record and marked as an exhibit at the time of trial, and is on file herein. ↵

¶

10. There is no arrearage of record for child support as of the date of trial. ↵

¶

11. The parties' Marital Settlement Agreement is found to be fair and reasonable, is approved in its entirety, and is incorporated by reference as the judgment of this court.

6 Save and proofread the document.

7 After keying the last item in Figure 98.4, complete the following steps:

a Press Shift + Enter and then press Enter.

b After the number *12* appears, click the Numbering button in the Paragraph group on the Home tab to turn off numbering.

c Click the Decrease Indent button to move the insertion point to the far left margin (the 0-inch mark on the horizontal ruler).

8 Key the text shown in Figure 98.5. Consider the following as you key the content:

a Change the paragraph alignment to center alignment (Ctrl + E), turn on bold formatting (Ctrl + B), key CONCLUSIONS OF LAW AND JUDGMENT, turn off bold formatting, press Enter, change the paragraph alignment to left alignment (Ctrl + L), and then press Enter.

b Key 12. and allow Word to automatically format the numbered list. Use the Increase Indent button to format the sublist.

c Format text in bold according to the figure. Turn off bold formatting before pressing the spacebar after keying the periods following the run-in headings. For item 15, turn off bold formatting before pressing Shift + Enter following the heading.

d Use Shift + Enter to create an extra line space between items within the numbered list. Follow the formatting instructions indicated by the nonprinting characters in Figure 98.5. The line breaks in the figure will not match the line breaks in your document.

steps continue

4 **Select your information.**

What information is relevant? What will help the reader understand your document? What will help the reader react positively and/or take the desired action?

5 **Plan the organization of your information.**

What should be said first? In what order should you present your points? What should be said in closing?

The following document activity offers an opportunity to practice planning a document.

Document
76.3 **Planning a Response**

Read all instructions below before starting this document activity.

1 Navigate to the Document 76.3 launch page in the Online Lab and then click the Launch Activity button to open **Doc076.03** in the activity window.

2 In the document, key the following words, each on a separate line: Purpose, Reader, Ideas, Information, and Organization. These words correspond with the steps of the planning process.

3 Read the description of the scenario in Figure 76.3 and then plan an effective response to the situation.

4 In the document, list the information related to each of the words you keyed in Step 2. You will use these notes to prepare a response letter in a later activity. Feel free to enhance the information in your planning notes.

5 Proofread the document and correct any errors.

6 Save the document.

7 Click the Submit button to upload the document for instructor review.

Figure 76.3 Scenario for Document 76.3

You work as a sales assistant for Mama's Pizza Company. Mama's has begun making all of its pizzas with low-cholesterol, low-fat cheeses and meats, which has decreased the number of calories by half. A report in a recent issue of *Waist Watcher's Magazine* calls Mama's Pizza "the healthiest in the Midwest." Your boss thinks this testimonial will help Mama's high sales figures rise even higher, and she asks you to write a promotional report that can be distributed to all Mama's store managers for their input.

Ending the Session

The Online Lab automatically saved the work you completed for this session. You may continue with the next session or exit the Online Lab and continue later.

CONCLUSIONS OF LAW AND JUDGMENT¶

¶

12. **Divorce.** The marriage between the Petitioner, Bailey Kathleen Matthews, who resides at 1145 North Harmony Drive, Janesville, Wisconsin 53545 and is by occupation unemployed, and the Respondent, Timothy Paul Matthews, who resides at 245 Garfield Street, Janesville, Wisconsin 53545 and is by occupation a materials buyer at ABC Supply, is dissolved, and the parties are divorced effective immediately on the 10th day of April, 2020, except as the parties are informed by the court that under Sec. 765.03(2), Stats.: ↵

↵

It is unlawful for any person, who is or has been a party to an action for divorce in any court in this state, or elsewhere, to marry again until six months after judgment of divorce is granted, and the marriage of any such person solemnized before the expiration of six months from the date of the granting of judgment of divorce shall be void. ↵

¶

13. **Child/Family Support.** Commencing the first pay period after the hearing, the Respondent shall pay to the Petitioner as child support the sum equal to 25 percent of his gross income per month. ↵

¶

14. **Maintenance.** Commencing the day of the month following the hearing, the Respondent shall pay to the Petitioner as maintenance Seven Hundred Dollars ($700) per month for a period of five (5) years. ↵

¶

15. **Custody and Physical Placement.** ↵

¶

a. Both parties are awarded the joint legal custody of the following child: Ashley Carrie Matthews. ↵

↵

Primary physical placement of the child is awarded to the Petitioner with periods of physical placement allocated as indicated in the Marital Settlement Agreement. ↵

¶

continues

Dragging and Dropping Text

When you drag and drop text, you cut the text from the original spot and paste it into the new spot. To drag and drop text, follow these steps:

1 Select the text to be moved.

2 Click and hold the left mouse button down and then drag the insertion point to the location where you want to place the text.

3 Release the mouse button.

If the block of text is not in the right place, click the Undo button (or press Ctrl + Z) and then repeat the process. When dragging and dropping text, it is important to make certain that there are no extra or missing spaces before or after the block of text.

Practice using these methods to edit an existing document in the following document activity.

Document 76.2 **Revised Memo Report**

Read all instructions below before starting this document activity.

1 Navigate to the Document 76.2 launch page in the Online Lab and then click the Launch Activity button to open **Doc076.02** in the activity window.

2 Delete the first bulleted item and then key Attach the commands you use the most to the ribbon. as a new first bullet.

3 Delete the paragraph that precedes the numbered list (begins with *According to* Device Magazine) and then key *Device Magazine* has developed the following list showing the basics of what can be done with ribbon customization:. **Note: Make sure the space following the magazine title is not formatted as italic.**

4 Switch the order of the numbered items 3 and 4 so that the item beginning with *Choose to show only icons* appears before the item beginning *Rename any tab, group, or command*. Make sure to check the spacing around the items after you rearrange them.

5 Edit the header on the second page to match the information on the first page.

6 Proofread the changes made to the document.

7 Save the document.

8 Click the Check button to upload the document for checking.

9 If errors are reported by the Online Lab, view the results document, correct the errors in the submitted document, save the document, and then click the Check Again button.

Reinforcing Writing Skills

Planning the content of a document may be the most important step in the writing process. The more carefully you plan the information and the order in which to present it, the clearer and more effective your communication will be.

The following are some steps to consider when planning a writing project:

1 **Define your purpose.**

What is your goal? What are you trying to accomplish through your writing?

2 **Identify your reader.**

Who will read your material? What do you know about the reader that will help in developing your document?

3 **Determine the ideas you may want to include.**

What are the possibilities? Depending on the report, even the most far-fetched ideas belong here!

b. A person who is awarded periods of physical placement, a child of such a person, a person with visitation rights, or a person with physical custody of a child may notify the family court commissioner of any problem he or she has relating to any of these matters. Upon notification, the family court commissioner may refer any person involved in the matter to the director of family court counseling services for mediation to assist in resolving the problem. ↵
¶

c. Each party who is granted joint legal custody or, in a sole custody arrangement, the parent not granted sole custody shall file a medical history form with the court in compliance with Sec. 767.24(7m), Stats. ↵
¶

d.

9　Format the numbered list and lettered sublists in the document as follows:

  a　Modify the first-level entries so that the numbers align at the right at 0.2 inch and that the text indent is set at 0.45 inch. *Hint: Do not forget to select the* **Right** *option in the* **Number alignment** *option box.*

  b　Modify the second-level entries so that the letters align at the right at 0.55 inch and that the text indent is set at 0.7 inch. *Hint: Do not forget to select the* **Right** *option in the* **Number alignment** *option box.*

10　Save the document.

11　Insert the Change of Residence of Child content from another file by completing the following steps:

  a　Move the insertion point to the end of the document.

  b　Click the Object button arrow in the Text group on the Insert tab and then click *Text from File* at the drop-down list.

  c　Click the *Documents* folder in the Insert File dialog box, double-click the *Paradigm* folder, double-click the *Keyboarding* folder, double-click the *DocumentActivityFiles* folder, and then double-click ***Doc098.02_ChangeofResidenceofChild_InsertFile.docx***. Do not reformat or edit the inserted content.

  d　Move the insertion point immediately to the left of *Change of Residence of Child* at the bottom of the third page of the document, press the Backspace key once, and then press Enter. The inserted text will now start after the letter *d*.

  e　Confirm the insertion by checking the document against the image shown in Figure 98.6.

steps continue

Selecting Text

There are many ways to select text. The following are some of the most common methods:

- Position the mouse pointer on the first character of the text to be selected, click and hold down the left mouse button, drag the mouse to the last character of the text to be selected, and then release the mouse button.
- Move the insertion point to the left of the first character of the text to be selected, press and hold down the Shift key, and then move the insertion point to the end of the text to be selected. You can move the insertion point by using the arrow keys, by using various keyboard short-cuts, or by clicking the mouse.
- To select a single word, double-click the word.
- To select a paragraph, triple-click a character within the paragraph. Alternatively, double-click in the selection bar in the left margin next to the paragraph.

Moving Text

To move a block of text from one place to another, follow these steps:

1 Select the text to be moved.
2 Click the Cut button in the Clipboard group on the Home tab. You can also use the keyboard shortcut Ctrl + X. (To help you remember this shortcut, picture the letter *X* as a pair of scissors.)
3 Move the insertion point to the location where the cut text is to be placed.
4 Click the Paste button in the Clipboard group on the Home tab. You may also use the keyboard shortcut Ctrl + V. (Think of the letter *V* as a proofreader's insert mark.)

Whenever you move text, make sure to check the spacing before and after the words in the areas where you cut and pasted the text. Click the Show/Hide ¶ button in the Paragraph group on the Home tab to display all of the paragraph breaks and spaces in the text.

> **Success Tip**
>
> If you cut the wrong text or paste it in the wrong place, press Ctrl + Z to undo the action.

Copying Text

To copy a block of text from one place to another, follow these steps:

1 Select the text to be copied.
2 Click the Copy button in the Clipboard group on the Home tab. You can also use the keyboard shortcut Ctrl + C.
3 Move the insertion point to the location where the copied text is to be placed.
4 Click the Paste button in the Clipboard group on the Home tab or press Ctrl + V.

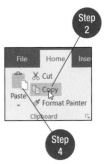

Deleting Text

To delete text, select it and then press the Delete key, press the Backspace key, click the Cut button, or press Ctrl + X. Note that if you use the Delete key or the Backspace key to delete the text, the text will not be available for pasting.

Figure 98.6 Portion of Document 98.2 After Completing Step 11

the·director·of·family·court·counseling·services·for·mediation·to·assist·in·resolving·the·
problem.↵
¶
c. → Each·party·who·is·granted·joint·legal·custody·or,·in·a·sole·custody·arrangement,·the·parent·
not·granted·sole·custody·shall·file·a·medical·history·form·with·the·court·in·compliance·with·
Sec.·767.24(7m),·Stats.↵
¶
d. → **Change·of·Residence·of·Child.**·Notice·is·hereby·given·of·the·provisions·of·Sec.·767.327,·Stats.:↵
↵
767.327 ° **Moving·the·child's·residence·within·or·outside·the·state.**↵
(1)°NOTICE·TO·OTHER·PARENT.↵
(a)·If·the·court·grants·periods·of·physical·placement·to·more·than·one·parent,·it·shall·order·a·

12 Move the insertion point to the end of the document and then press the Decrease Indent button to change *e.* to *16*.

13 Insert the *16. Arrearage* through *22. Entry of Judgment* content from another file by completing the following steps:

   a With the insertion point positioned at the end of the document (to the right of the *16.*), click the Object button arrow in the Text group on the Insert tab and then click *Text from File*.

   b Click the *Documents* folder in the Insert File dialog box, double-click the *Paradigm* folder, double-click the *Keyboarding* folder, double-click the *DocumentActivityFiles* folder, and then double-click **Doc098.02_Arrearage_InsertFile.docx**. Do not reformat or edit the inserted content.

14 With the insertion point at the end of the document, press the Backspace key once to delete the *16.* and then click the Decrease Indent button twice to move the insertion point to the left margin of the document.

15 Key Dated this 10th day of April, 2020. and then press Enter twice. **Note: Allow Word to automatically format the superscript letters.**

16 Adjust the tab settings on the horizontal ruler so that there is only a left tab at the 3.25-inch mark and a right tab at the 6.5-inch mark. **Hint: To remove a tab, drag it down and off the horizontal ruler.**

17 Press Tab, type BY THE COURT:, and then press Enter four times.

18 Key the remaining content shown in Figure 98.7. The figure shows the text and the nonprinting characters to guide the formatting of the content. Consider the following as you key:

   a For each of the signature lines, press Ctrl + U, press Tab, press Ctrl + U, and then press Enter.

   b For the blank underline for the date, key five underscores.

   c Do not press Enter after the last line of text.

steps continue

Figure 76.2 Memo Business Report Content for Document 76.1—continued

custom group. ¶ 5. The most amazing feature is that you can export your customized tabs into a file that can be imported for use on other computers. ¶ 6. You can also implement administrative policies as part of organizational policies to control roaming of customizations. For example, you might allow user customizations to be available on any network computer upon login, or allow distribution of customizations to multiple users through the use of operating scripts. ¶ You can rename and change the order of the default tabs and groups that are built into Word 2016. However, you cannot rename the default commands, change the icons associated with these default commands, or change the order of these commands. ¶ To begin the customization process, click the File tab, click *Options*, and then click *Customize Ribbon* in the left panel of the Word Options dialog box. (Another way to open the Word Options dialog box is to right-click any tab on the ribbon and then click *Customize the Ribbon*.) By default, the Word Options dialog box will display *Popular Commands* in the *Choose commands from* option box and *Main Tabs* in the *Customize the Ribbon* option box. To create a new tab on the ribbon, click the New Tab button. Name the new tab by right-clicking it in the *Main Tabs* list box, clicking *Rename*, and then keying the new tab's name in the Rename dialog box. ¶ Let's discuss this further at next week's team meeting. I have talked with Karen Lubeck in IT, and she assigned Jerry to work with us regarding the administrative requirements.

Reinforcing Word Skills

The document activities in this session will require you to apply some previously learned Word skills. This section will review some of those skills. You will, at times, create a new report by changing or rearranging the content of an old one. Rather than rekeying the document in the revised content order, Word allows you to cut, copy, and paste text, which saves time and helps you work more efficiently.

Cutting, Copying, and Pasting Text

When a document needs extensive revisions, such as deleting, copying, or moving blocks of text, these edits can be done by cutting and pasting. *Cutting and pasting* text means that text is deleted (cut) from its present location and then inserted (pasted) at a new location. *Copying and pasting* means almost the same thing, except that the text is copied from its original location rather than deleted, resulting in two instances of the same text existing in the document.

When cutting and pasting, you work with blocks of text. A block of text is a portion of text that you have selected; it can be as small as one character or as large as an entire page or document.

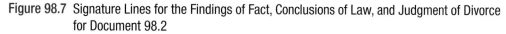

Figure 98.7 Signature Lines for the Findings of Fact, Conclusions of Law, and Judgment of Divorce for Document 98.2

¶
→   BY·THE·COURT:¶
¶
¶
¶
→
→   _____ →   ¶
Circuit·Court·Judge¶
¶
Approved·this·_____·day·of·April,·2020.¶
¶
¶
¶
By·_____ → _____ ¶
Attorney·Dale·Bensten¶
Bensten·Law·Office¶
Attorney·for·the·Respondent¶
¶
¶
¶
By·_____ → _____ ¶
Attorney·Theresa·Flanagan¶
Flanagan·Law·Offices¶
Attorney·for·the·Petitioner¶

19 Insert Page X of Y page numbering at the bottom of all pages of the document using the *Bold Numbers 2* option.

20 Improve the page breaks in the document by completing the following steps:

a At the bottom of page 1, position the insertion point immediately to the left of *Income* and then press Shift + Enter.

b At the bottom of page 3, position the insertion point immediately to the left of *767.327* and then press Shift + Enter.

c Format item 22 so that it appears at the top of page 9 by applying the *Keep with next* setting at the Paragraph dialog box with the Line and Page Breaks tab selected.

21 Proofread the document and correct any errors, checking the document against the selected pages of the completed document shown in Figure 98.8.

22 Save the document.

23 Click the Check button to upload the document for checking.

24 If errors are reported by the Online Lab, view the results document, correct the errors in the submitted document, save the document, and then click the Check Again button.

4   Create a vertical continuation header using the *Blank* option. The header should begin 1 inch from the top margin on the second page of the report. The header should include the recipient's name, the page number (key Page, press the spacebar, and then insert an automatic page number field), and the date of the memo. ***Hint: Format the document to have a different first page header.***

5   At the bottom of the document, key the reference initials gmk and the file name.

6   Proofread the document and correct any errors.

7   Save the document.

8   Click the Check button to upload the document for checking.

9   If errors are reported by the Online Lab, view the results document, correct the errors in the submitted document, save the document, and then click the Check Again button.

Figure 76.2 Memo Business Report Content for Document 76.1

DATE: April 15, 2020 ¶ **TO:** Marketing Team ¶ **FROM:** Hans Melrose ¶ **SUBJECT:** CUSTOMIZING THE RIBBON IN WORD 2016 ¶ I found some interesting material regarding adding new tabs to Word's ribbon for my frequently used tasks and would like to share what I've learned. ¶ In Microsoft Office 2016, you may: ¶ • Customize the ribbon to group commands that you most frequently use. ¶ • Organize tabs on the ribbon to display the commands most relevant for each of the task areas in the application, thereby increasing the ease of access. ¶ • Create separate custom ribbons within each application, keeping features you need right where you need them. ¶ • Share a customized ribbon with another computer by using import and export. ¶ According to *Device Magazine*, the following is a basic list of what ribbon customization can offer you: ¶ 1. You can create your own custom tabs and custom groups based on the types of document design and the activities you undertake with Office. ¶ 2. You can add custom and built-in groups to both custom and built-in tabs. Drag and drop in the Word Options dialog box with *Customize Ribbon* selected in the left panel to add and rearrange tabs and groups, as well as reorganize commands to quickly create custom groups. ¶ 3. You can rename any tab, group, or command, as well as change the icon used for any command. You can hide a tab without actually deleting it (so that it can be reused later), and you can remove built-in groups from built-in tabs. ¶ 4. If you hate too much clutter on your tabs, you can choose to show only icons (no labels) for commands in a custom group. This allows you to fit many commands into a single

continues

Figure 98.8 Completed Findings of Fact, Conclusions of Law, and Judgment of Divorce for Document 98.2—Pages 1, 2, 3, and 9

STATE OF WISCONSIN   CIRCUIT COURT   ROCK COUNTY

In re the marriage of:

BAILEY KATHLEEN MATTHEWS
1145 NORTH HARMONY DRIVE
JANESVILLE, ROCK COUNTY, WISCONSIN 53545,

        Petitioner,   Case No.: 14FA1029

        FINDINGS OF FACT, CONCLUSIONS OF
        LAW, AND JUDGMENT OF DIVORCE

-and-

TIMOTHY PAUL MATTHEWS
245 GARFIELD STREET
JANESVILLE, ROCK COUNTY, WISCONSIN 53545,

        Respondent.

TRIAL

Presiding: Judge Randall Werner
Place: Rock County Courthouse
    51 South Main Street, Janesville, Wisconsin 53545
Date: April 10, 2020

Date of granting of judgment of divorce: April 10, 2020

Appearances: Petitioner Bailey Kathleen Matthews in person and with her attorney; Respondent Timothy Paul Matthews in person and with his attorney

FINDINGS OF FACT

1. For at least six months before the commencement of this action, both parties were continuous residents of the state of Wisconsin, and of this county for at least 30 days prior to the commencement, further, all necessary parties have been duly served and ordered to appear, 120 days have lapsed since the date of service of the summons and petition upon the Respondent.

2. The Petitioner in this action is Bailey Kathleen Matthews.

    Residence: 1145 North Harmony Drive, Janesville, Wisconsin 53545
    Birthdate: September 28, 1979
    Occupation: None

Page 1 of 9

Income:
    Current monthly earnings:
        Gross: $0.00
        Net: $0.00

    Other income: _____

3. The Respondent in this action is Timothy Paul Matthews.

    Residence: 245 Garfield Street, Janesville, Wisconsin 53545
    Birthdate: October 8, 1978
    Occupation: Materials Buyer at ABC Supply

Income:
    Current monthly earnings:
        Gross: $8,000
        Net: $5,000 (after deducting federal and state income taxes, social security)

    Other income: _____

4. The parties were married on February 14, 2003, at Monroe, Wisconsin.

5. The following minor child has been born to or adopted by the parties:

    Minor's Name: Ashley Carrie Matthews
    Date of Birth: December 22, 2014
    Soc. Sec. No.:   On file

    a. Specific responsibility for payment of medical and dental expenses has been made in the Marital Settlement Agreement.

    b. There are no emancipated children of this marriage.

    c. No other minor children were born to the parties during this marriage.

    d. The wife is not pregnant.

6. Neither party has begun any other action for divorce, legal separation, or annulment anywhere.

7. Neither party has been previously divorced.

8. The marriage is irretrievably broken.

9. The parties' assets, their interests therein, the values thereof, and their encumbrances and debts are found to be as set forth in the financial disclosure form, which was updated as required by the statute on the record and marked as an exhibit at the time of trial, and is on file herein.

Page 2 of 9

---

10. There is no arrearage of record for child support as of the date of trial.

11. The parties' Marital Settlement Agreement is found to be fair and reasonable, is approved in its entirety, and is incorporated by reference as the judgment of this court.

CONCLUSIONS OF LAW AND JUDGMENT

12. **Divorce.** The marriage between the Petitioner, Bailey Kathleen Matthews, who resides at 1145 North Harmony Drive, Janesville, Wisconsin 53545 and is by occupation unemployed, and the Respondent, Timothy Paul Matthews, who resides at 245 Garfield Street, Janesville, Wisconsin 53545 and is by occupation a materials buyer at ABC Supply, is dissolved, and the parties are divorced effective immediately on the 10th day of April, 2020, except as the parties are informed by the court that under Sec. 765.03(2), Stats.:

    It is unlawful for any person, who is or has been a party to an action for divorce in any court in this state, or elsewhere, to marry again until six months after judgment of divorce is granted, and the marriage of any such person solemnized before the expiration of six months from the date of the granting of judgment of divorce shall be void.

13. **Child/Family Support.** Commencing the first pay period after the hearing, the Respondent shall pay to the Petitioner as child support the sum equal to 25 percent of his gross income per month.

14. **Maintenance.** Commencing the day of the month following the hearing, the Respondent shall pay to the Petitioner as maintenance Seven Hundred Dollars ($700) per month for a period of five (5) years.

15. **Custody and Physical Placement.**

    a. Both parties are awarded the joint legal custody of the following child: Ashley Carrie Matthews.

    Primary physical placement of the child is awarded to the Petitioner with periods of physical placement allocated as indicated in the Marital Settlement Agreement.

    b. A person who is awarded periods of physical placement, a child of such a person, a person with visitation rights, or a person with physical custody of a child may notify the family court commissioner of any problem he or she has relating to any of these matters. Upon notification, the family court commissioner may refer any person involved in the matter to the director of family court counseling services for mediation to assist in resolving the problem.

    c. Each party who is granted joint legal custody or, in a sole custody arrangement, the parent not granted sole custody shall file a medical history form with the court in compliance with Sec. 767.24(7m), Stats.

    d. **Change of Residence of Child.** Notice is hereby given of the provisions of Sec. 767.327, Stats.:

Page 3 of 9

---

22. **Entry of Judgment.** The clerk of courts per Sec. 806.06(1), (2), Stats., shall enter this judgment forthwith by affixing a file stamp that is dated.

Dated this 10th day of April, 2020.

    BY THE COURT:

    _____
    Circuit Court Judge

Approved this _____ day of April, 2020.

By _____
Attorney Dale Bensten
Bensten Law Office
Attorney for the Respondent

By _____
Attorney Theresa Flanagan
Flanagan Law Offices
Attorney for the Petitioner

Page 9 of 9

Ending the Session

The Online Lab automatically saved the work you completed for this session. You may continue with the next session or exit the Online Lab and continue later.

Figure 76.1 Sample Memo Business Report—continued

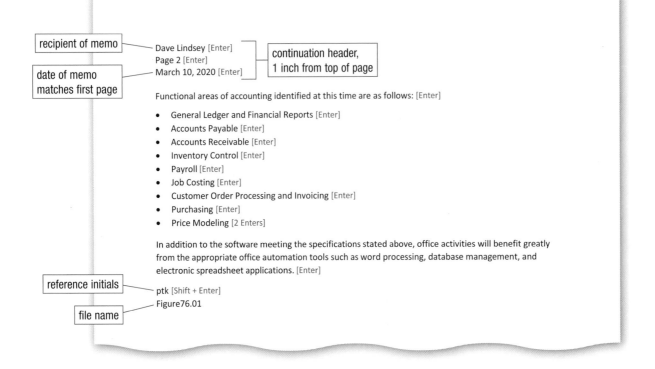

recipient of memo — Dave Lindsey [Enter]
Page 2 [Enter]
date of memo matches first page — March 10, 2020 [Enter]

continuation header, 1 inch from top of page

Functional areas of accounting identified at this time are as follows: [Enter]

- General Ledger and Financial Reports [Enter]
- Accounts Payable [Enter]
- Accounts Receivable [Enter]
- Inventory Control [Enter]
- Payroll [Enter]
- Job Costing [Enter]
- Customer Order Processing and Invoicing [Enter]
- Purchasing [Enter]
- Price Modeling [2 Enters]

In addition to the software meeting the specifications stated above, office activities will benefit greatly from the appropriate office automation tools such as word processing, database management, and electronic spreadsheet applications. [Enter]

reference initials — ptk [Shift + Enter]
file name — Figure76.01

Document 76.1

Multiple-Page Memo Business Report with Numbered and Bulleted Lists

Read all instructions below before starting this document activity.

1 Navigate to the Document 76.1 launch page in the Online Lab and then click the Launch Activity button to open **Doc076.01** in the activity window.

2 Change the default font for this document to 12-point Times New Roman. ***Note: Set the default font for this document only.***

3 Key the memo report using the text shown in Figure 76.2 and the format illustrated in Figure 76.1. Consider the following instructions as you key the text:

a Because the font is larger than the font used in the report shown in Figure 76.1, you will need to press Tab twice after keying *TO:* but only once after typing the other guide words. Be sure to turn off the bold formatting prior to pressing Tab.

b Allow Word to automatically format the bulleted list and the numbered list, but remember to add an extra line space between the bulleted and numbered items. For the bulleted list, use the standard solid, black, round bullets. Because the paragraphs begin flush left in this document, decrease the indent of the lists so that the bullets and numbers are flush to the left margin. ***Hint: Click the Decrease Indent button in the Paragraph group on the Home tab.***

c Within the body of the memo, do not format the space or punctuation following bold or italic text as bold or italic.

steps continue

Last Will and Testament, and Living Will

Session Objectives

- Add to a table of legal terms and definitions and then sort the table
- Format a table header row to repeat on subsequent pages
- Fill in fields in a protected document
- Unprotect a document
- Apply line numbering to a document
- Complete a document containing check boxes
- Prepare a Last Will and Testament
- Prepare a Living Will
- Efficiently produce documents in mailable form

Getting Started

Exercise 99.1 If you are continuing immediately from Session 98, you may skip the Exercise 99.1 warm-up drill. However, if you exited the Online Lab at the end of Session 98, warm up by completing Exercise 99.1.

Exercise 99.2 Begin your session work by completing Exercise 99.2, a timed short drill, in the Online Lab.

Assessing Your Speed and Accuracy

Complete Timing 99.1 in the Online Lab using the timing text on the next page. At the end of the timing, the Online Lab will display your WPM rate and any errors. Results will be saved in your Timings Performance report. If you have been surpassing the speed and accuracy goals identified in the Online Lab, set slightly more challenging personal goals and strive to exceed them. *Note: With this session, the default WPM goal for 5-minute timings has been increased by 5 WPM in the Online Lab. However, your instructor may have customized this goal.*

for memo reports. Memo reports typically use the default 1-inch margins for all pages, are more than one page long, set the guide words in bold formatting followed by one or two tabs, frequently have side headings, and often require numbered or bulleted paragraphs.

For the memo reports created in this unit, the subject lines will be keyed in all caps. The body of the report is formatted using the default line spacing of 1.08, with 8 points of spacing after paragraphs. Figure 76.1 shows an example of a memo report. Review this sample before completing the Document 76.1 activity.

Figure 76.1 Sample Memo Business Report *Note: Do not key this document.*

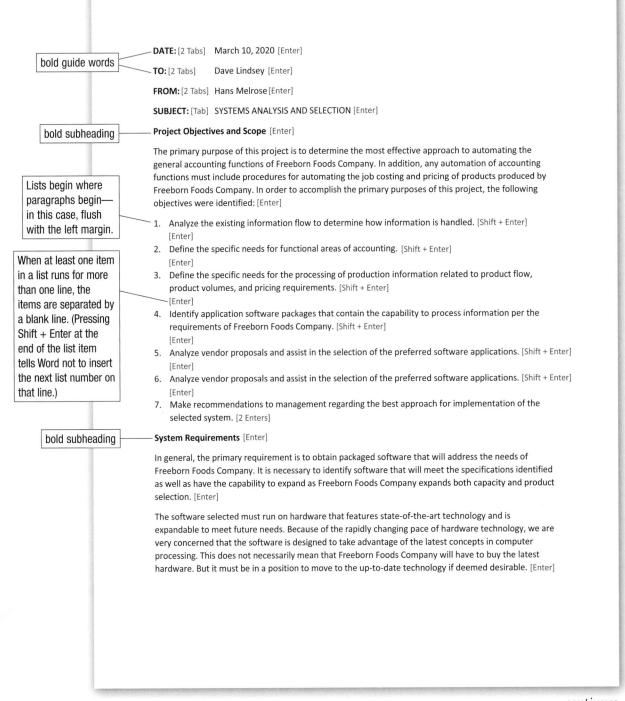

Timing 99.1

Becoming a good writer doesn't just happen; it involves a great deal of hard labor. Effective writing involves more than placing on paper your spoken words and thoughts. To be a successful writer, any beginner must know how to structure ideas or thoughts. You must also be aware of the basics required for written communication. Remember that good writing is a skill that must be developed most carefully.

The first step in preparing any article or other type of writing is to plan carefully. You must first choose which objectives or goals are to be attained in the document. In addition, you must labor to define the scope within which to present your ideas. Too often, writers select sound objectives but do not limit the scope of the writing and usually end up with a myriad of ideas that are not needed or connected to any major goals. It is a good habit to always keep in mind the purpose and potential outcome of your article.

After you have selected your objectives, you must then begin the process of careful research. The minimum amount of research needed for the article will depend upon the project itself. While you are doing that research, you should begin early to organize your thoughts about the material that you have gathered. You must select the best method of presenting the material in the final copy to best meet the needs of readers. A complete outline will be of continuous help when identifying the prime points and keeping them in the proper order. A good outline forces you to structure your thinking early in the complete process of writing your own report.

From an outline, you will be able to structure the actual report so that the ideas develop naturally. In a first draft, you will only be concerned with putting the thoughts into paragraphs. At this very crucial time, write quickly. Concentrate on the conversion of all the outline points into sentences and paragraphs. Keep your mind and thoughts on ideas; don't attempt revision at this stage. Don't allow a deep concern about grammar or spelling to invade your major goal of writing your thoughts in a logical order.

Using Specialized Word Skills to Prepare Legal Documents

Preparing documents in a legal office will most likely involve the use of a variety of specialized Word skills. For example, you may work with password-protected documents. These documents are restricted and cannot be edited, or can only be edited in limited ways.

Complete one 3-minute timing on the timing text below. *Note: With this session, the default WPM goal for 3-minute timings has been increased by 5 WPM in the Online Lab. However, your instructor may have customized this goal.*

3-Minute Timing

Timing 76.3

Does anyone really know why people enjoy gardening? Over 587 surveys show that most people who garden specify they want that special homegrown flavor; others grow their own food to be more economical; and still other people garden just to have an enjoyable hobby that provides pleasure, pride, and satisfaction.

The pleasures of gardening are many: getting outdoors, exercising, putting your hands in the soil, growing things, and the special pride that comes with the harvest. Many folks want to have the feeling of being self-sufficient, or at least partly so, and to have some control over what they eat. Most people like to have garden-fresh food without any preservatives. All of these are good reasons for gardening. It is truly one of America's most popular leisure activities.

Of course, for homesteaders and other people who garden on a large scale, it is a way of life and a means of subsistence. In order to satisfy your gardening desires and goals, whatever they may be, it is important to be persistent in what you are doing. For after all, the final harvest is the true objective of gardening.

Ergonomic Tip
To help reduce repetitive stress injuries, do not bend your wrists while keying.

Preparing Memo Business Reports

Business reports serve as a vehicle for collecting information used to make decisions. Reports move upward in an organization, and directives prepared from the findings presented in reports move downward. Thus, reports and directives form an organizational loop.

There are three categories of business reports: memo business reports, formal business reports, and specialized business reports. This session focuses on the memo business report (commonly referred to as a *memo report*). A memo report is usually a brief document that is direct and informal in tone. This type of report is typically one to five pages in length and does not contain a title page, table of contents, or bibliography.

The format of a memo report is similar to that of a memorandum (or *memo*), with a four-part heading that includes the guide words *DATE, TO, FROM,* and *SUBJECT,* although the order and style of these guide words may vary. Unlike standard memos, which are formatted with approximately 2 inches of space at the top of the page and do not apply any text formatting (such as bold or italics) to the date, recipient, sender, and subject headings, there is no uniform format

Before studying new, specialized Word skills, complete the following document activity in which you will key terms and definitions that are used in formal wills and living wills.

Document 99.1

Legal Terms

Read all instructions below before starting this document activity.

1 Navigate to the Document 99.1 launch page in the Online Lab and then click the Launch Activity button to open **Doc099.01** in the activity window.

2 Position the insertion point at the end of the last definition and then press Tab to create a new row at the bottom of the table.

3 Key the terms and definitions shown in Figure 99.1, pressing Tab to move from cell to cell as needed. Since the table has already been formatted, you can key the terms and definitions without turning bold on and off. Apply italic formatting to alternative terms as indicated in Figure 99.1. *Hint: If a definition ends with an italic term, be sure to turn off italic formatting before pressing Tab.*

4 Proofread the newly keyed entries and correct any errors.

5 Select the rows containing the new terms. Change the spacing after paragraphs to 8 points and make sure the line spacing is set at single spacing.

6 Sort the table alphabetically by terms.

7 Format the first row, the row with the *Term* and *Definition* headings, so that the row repeats at the top of the first and subsequent pages of the table by completing the following steps:

   a Select the row containing the *Term* and *Definition* headings.

   b Click the Repeat Header Rows button in the Data group on the Table Tools Layout tab.

   c Deselect the row. Scroll to pages 2 and 3 and confirm that the *Term* and *Definition* row appears at the top of each page.

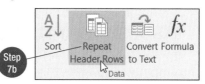

8 Save the document.

9 Click the Check button to upload the document for checking.

10 If errors are reported by the Online Lab, view the results document, correct the errors in the submitted document, save the document, and then click the Check Again button.

Figure 99.1 Legal Terms for Document 99.1

Domicile → The place of a person's official or legal residence

Living Will → An instrument that instructs the physician in advance how to proceed when a patient has a terminal condition with no hope of recovery; also referred to as a *Healthcare Directive*

Formal Will → A will that has been prepared following all the formalities of law

Testator → A male who makes a will

Testatrix → A female who makes a will

continues

Session
76

Preparing Memo Business Reports

Session Objectives

- Key a memo business report with bulleted and numbered paragraphs
- Cut, copy, and paste text
- Drag and drop text
- Plan a writing project
- Efficiently produce documents in mailable format

Getting Started

Exercise 76.1 If you are continuing immediately from Session 75, you may skip the Exercise 76.1 warm-up drill. However, if you exited the Online Lab at the end of Session 75, warm up by completing Exercise 76.1.

Exercise 76.2 Begin your session work by completing Exercise 76.2, a timed short drill, in the Online Lab.

Assessing Your Speed and Accuracy

Complete Timings 76.1 through 76.3 in the Online Lab. At the end of each timing, the Online Lab will display your WPM rate and any errors. Results will be saved in your Timings Performance report. If you have been surpassing the speed and accuracy goals identified in the Online Lab, set slightly more challenging personal goals and strive to exceed them.

Complete two 1-minute timings on the timing text below. If you do not key at or above the WPM rate identified in the Online Lab on Timing 76.1, concentrate on speed on Timing 76.2. If you meet the Online Lab's WPM goal but make more errors than the goal set in the Online Lab on Timing 76.1, concentrate on accuracy on Timing 76.2. However, if you meet or exceed both goals for Timing 76.1, push for greater speed on Timing 76.2.

1-Minute Timings

Timings 76.1–76.2

Most people enjoy taking an annual vacation. Along with not having to go to work during that time, a vacation provides people with a fine opportunity to visit some locations that they may have dreamed of seeing for a long time. Some individuals, however, like to return to the same location each year. The mountains, oceans, lakes, and other sites offer both exciting and relaxing prospects to the vacationer. To other people, staying at home for a "staycation" is the ideal solution. Having enough time to do some of the needed duties at home can be utopian and the height of luxury.

Figure 99.1 Legal Terms for Document 99.1—continued

Last Will and Testament → An instrument in which a person states how his or her property is to be distributed after his or her death; also referred to as a *will*

Legally binding → Obligated by law; can be enforced in a court of law

Personal Representative → An individual named in a will to administer the provisions of the will; also referred to as *executor* (male) or *executrix* (female)

Beneficiary → An individual named to receive income or inheritance from a will

Codicil → An addition or amendment to a will to add provisions, revoke articles, and/or update the will

Guardian → An individual named to oversee and manage the affairs of a minor child

Provision → A clause or agreement requiring some specific action

Predecease → To die before someone else or some event

Descendant → An offspring of a certain ancestor, family, or group

Execute → To complete or make valid by signing, sealing, and delivering

Working in a Document with Restricted Formatting and Editing

Word allows you to protect a document or form from changes made by other users. For example, a document can be protected so that no changes can be made to that document, or so that text can only be keyed in specific fields. A password is assigned by the person who protects the document, and the document can be unprotected only with that password. Passwords used to protect Word documents are case-sensitive, and Word cannot recover information if the password is lost or forgotten. To protect a document, click the Review tab, click the Restrict Editing button in the Protect group, determine the desired formatting and editing restrictions at the Restrict Editing task pane, and then click the Yes, Start Enforcing Protection button in the task pane. At the Start Enforcing Protection dialog box, type a password, confirm the password, and then close the dialog box. A password is not required to protect a form. To unprotect a locked document, click the Restrict Editing button in the Protect group; click the Stop Protection button at the bottom of the Restrict Editing task pane; and then, if necessary, key the password in the Unprotect Document dialog box.

Legal documents usually contain standard legal language as well as information specific to each document, such as the name of the person signing the document. In the Document 99.2 activity, you will work with a document (a will) that has been restricted to only allow you to fill in fields. When the document opens in Word, the first field will be active. Key the necessary text in that field and then press the Tab key to move to the next field in the document. After filling in the fields in the Document 99.2 activity, you will unprotect the document for practice.

Unit 16

Business Reports Part II

Success Tip

In a protected document with fields, press Tab to move to the next field and Shift + Tab to move to the previous field.

Completing a Document with Check Boxes

In addition to text fields, documents may be created with other form elements, such as check box fields. Check boxes are useful for indicating *Yes* and *No* and for lists of options that the respondent can select by inserting check marks. To create an entry in a check box field, simply click the check box and an *X* will be inserted automatically. If you click a check box in error, click it again to remove the *X*.

Applying Line Numbering to a Document

Word provides the option to include automatic line numbering in a document, which generates continuous line numbers that appear along the left side of the page. Numbering lines can be helpful in many different types of legal documents. In an employment contract, for example, rather than referring to a page number, section number, paragraph number, and subparagraph number (such as "page 33, Section 25.3, third paragraph, fourth line"), the reviewer can simply identify the line number in question. Wills are typically sent to the maker (the testator or testatrix) for review before a signing date is determined. Numbering the lines makes it much easier to communicate corrections or changes.

To apply line numbers to a document, complete the following steps:

1 Click the Layout tab.
2 Click the Line Numbers button in the Page Setup group.
3 Click *Continuous* at the drop-down list to generate the automatic numbering.

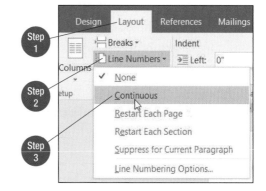

To omit line numbering in specific paragraphs, select the text, click the Line Numbers button, and then click *Suppress for Current Paragraph* at the drop-down list.

Line numbering may be used with any type of line spacing. In the Document 99.3 activity, you will be provided with a will that is already formatted, and you will change the line spacing and apply line numbering.

Creating a Last Will and Testament

A Last Will and Testament is a document in which a person describes in writing how his or her property is to be distributed and who is to handle his or her affairs after death. In order to make a will, the maker must be of sound mind and legal age. *Sound mind* means the person understands that he or she is creating a will that will be legally binding. Furthermore, the person understands how much property he or she owns and who should receive the property after his or her death. For a will to be legally binding, it must be executed (signed and witnessed) according to the required formalities of law.

Document **Sorting Table Contents**
75.4
Read all instructions below before starting this document activity.

1   Navigate to the Document 75.4 launch page in the Online Lab and then click the Launch Activity button to open **Doc075.04** in the activity window.

2   Create the table shown in Figure 75.4. (You will format the column widths in a later step.)

3   Format the table so that all of the table borders are ½-point, double lines set in the Black, Text 1 color (second column, first row in the *Theme Colors* section).

4   Change the height of the six rows to 0.5 inch. Change the width of the first column to 2.5 inches and width of the second column to 2 inches.

5   Insert a new first row in the table, merge the two cells in the new row, and key LAWN SPORTS PLAYED IN 2020 IN THE UNITED STATES in cell A1.

6   Select the table and then change the cell alignment of the cells in the table to center text horizontally and vertically within the cells.

7   Apply Orange shading (in the *Standard Colors* section) to cell A1.

8   Sort the contents of the table so that the games are listed in descending order by the indicated percentage. *Hint: Select rows 2 through 7 before clicking the Sort button and make sure the* **No header row** *option is selected.*

9   Split cell A4 into three columns and then move *Softball* and *Wiffle Ball* into the new cells. Delete the two slashes.

10 Select the entire table and then press Ctrl + E to center it horizontally on the page.

11 Proofread the table and correct any errors.

12 Save the document.

13 Click the Check button to upload the document for checking.

14 If errors are reported by the Online Lab, view the results document, correct the errors in the submitted document, save the document, and then click the Check Again button.

Figure 75.4 Table Content for Document 75.4

Baseball/Softball/Wiffle Ball	34%
Football	27%
Frisbee	43%
Horseshoes	21%
Tossing Games	37%
Volleyball	22%

Ending the Session

The Online Lab automatically saved the work you completed for this session. You may continue with the next session or exit the Online Lab and continue later.

Document **Last Will and Testament with Fields**
99.2
Read all instructions below before starting this document activity.

1 Navigate to the Document 99.2 launch page in the Online Lab and then click the Launch Activity button to open **Doc099.02** in the activity window.

2 With the first field (*NAME*, in the document tite) active, key BAILEY KATHLEEN MATTHEWS. The text keyed in this field will be automatically formatted as bold.

3 Press Tab to navigate to the next field (*Name*) and then key Bailey Kathleen Matthews.

4 Continue keying text into the active fields using the following field data. Press Tab or Shift + Tab to navigate between active fields. *Note: Some of the fields will appear more than once in the document. Key the same data in each of the fields, as indicated.*

City	Janesville
Child's Name	Ashley Carrie Matthews
Pers Rep Name	Brooke Neumaier
Alt Pers Rep Name	Olivia Schoepp
Guardian Name	Jennifer Larsen
Guardian City	Milton
Guardian State	Wisconsin
Alt Guardian Name	Christina Ulrich
Alt Guardian City	Palatine
Alt Guardian State	Illinois
Name	Bailey Kathleen Matthews

5 Proofread the information in the fields. *Hint: Word's spelling and grammar checker will not mark words that are incorrectly spelled within fields.*

6 Unprotect the document by completing the following steps:

a Click the Review tab.

b Click the Restrict Editing button in the Protect group.

c Click the Stop Protection button at the bottom of the Restrict Editing task pane.

d Key WillForm in the *Password* text box at the Unprotect Document dialog box.

e Click OK or press Enter.

f Click the Close button in the Restrict Editing task pane.

7 Proofread the document and correct any errors.

8 Save the document.

9 Click the Submit button to upload the document for instructor review.

Document **Modifying Table Contents and Drawing a Border**

75.3 Read all instructions below before starting this document activity.

1 Navigate to the Document 75.3 launch page in the Online Lab and then click the Launch Activity button to open **Doc075.03** in the activity window.

2 Create the table shown in Figure 75.3.

3 Insert a row below the *Dr. Frederick Molcher* row and then key Rehabilitation in the *SPECIALTY* column of the new row.

4 Copy the contents of cell C6 and paste it into cell C4.

5 Merge cell A3 with cell A4.

6 Merge cell B3 with cell B4.

7 Apply the List Table 3 - Accent 1 table style (second column, third row in the *List Tables* section) to the table.

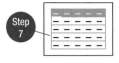

8 Draw a ¾-point, double wavy line (19th option under *No Border*) with the Orange pen color (in the *Standard Colors* section) below the column headings.

9 Proofread the table and correct any errors.

10 Save the document.

11 Click the Check button to upload the document for checking.

12 If errors are reported by the Online Lab, view the results document, correct the errors in the submitted document, save the document, and then click the Check Again button.

Figure 75.3 Table Content for Document 75.3

DOCTOR	SPECIALTY	LOCATION
Dr. Michel Williams	Orthopedic Surgery	St. Luke's Hospital
Dr. Frederick Molcher	Physical Medicine	Fox Valley Surgical Center
Dr. Alicia Schneider	Spinal Surgery	Alexian Brothers Hospital
Dr. Craig Oryhon	Sports Medicine	Aurora Urgent Care Center
Dr. Lori Tan	Joint Replacement Surgery	Orthopedic Surgeons LLC

Document **Last Will and Testament with Numbered Lines**
99.3

Read all instructions below before starting this document activity.

1   Navigate to the Document 99.3 launch page in the Online Lab and then click the Launch Activity button. The Online Lab will open **Doc099.03** in the activity window.

2   Select all of the text in the document (Ctrl + A) and then change the line spacing to double spacing. Do not change the spacing before or after paragraphs.

3   Move the *Article VI* heading to the top of page 3 by selecting the *Keep with next* option.

4   Apply line numbers to the document by completing the following steps:

   a   Click the Layout tab.

   b   Click the Line Numbers button in the Page Setup group.

   c   Click *Continuous* at the drop-down list.

5   Suppress line numbers for select paragraphs by completing the following steps.

   a   Select the two-line title at the top of the document, click the Line Numbers button, and then click *Suppress for Current Paragraph* at the drop-down list.

   b   Use similar steps to suppress line numbering from the signature area (from *I sign this Will on the* through the end of the document).

6   Confirm that the line that begins *laws of the State of Wisconsin authorize* is marked with line number 69.

7   Save the document.

8   Click the Check button to upload the document for checking.

9   If errors are reported by the Online Lab, view the results document, correct the errors in the submitted document, save the document, and then click the Check Again button.

Creating a Living Will

A Living Will is different from a Last Will and Testament. A Living Will (or Healthcare Directive) allows the maker, or declarant, to instruct physicians and other healthcare personnel in advance about the conditions under which to provide or withdraw medical treatment when there is no reasonable expectation of recovery. A Living Will may instruct a physician not to allow a person to be kept alive by life-support equipment or instruct the physician not to *withdraw* life-support equipment. A Living Will is signed, witnessed, and notarized, as is a Last Will and Testament. In Document 99.4, you complete a standard Living Will.

Document **Living Will**
99.4

Read all instructions below before starting this document activity.

1   Navigate to the Document 99.4 launch page in the Online Lab and then click the Launch Activity button to open **Doc099.04** in the activity window.

2   Select the maker's name line in the first paragraph of the document and then key Bailey Kathleen Matthews as underlined text. *Hint: The commas should not be underlined.*

3   Click the *NO* check boxes to answer no to each of the three questions in the form.

4   Position the insertion point in the line space directly below *Signed* at the top of the second page of the document, set a left tab at the 1-inch mark on the horizontal ruler, press Tab, and then key Bailey Kathleen Matthews.

5   Position the insertion point immediately to the left of the line following the *Address* heading, turn on underline formatting, and then key 1145 North Harmony Drive, Janesville, WI 53545.

steps continue

Document
75.2

Formatting a Table

Read all instructions below before starting this document activity.

1 Navigate to the Document 75.2 launch page in the Online Lab and then click the Launch Activity button to open **Doc075.02** in the activity window.

2 Insert a table containing four columns and four rows.

3 Key the text into the table as shown in Figure 75.2.

4 Change the width of columns 2 and 4 to 0.5 inch.

5 Change the width of columns 1 and 3 to 1.8 inches.

6 Align the text in columns 2 and 4 to the bottom right corners of the cells.

7 Insert three rows at the top of the table.

8 Merge the cells in each of the three rows, so each row contains only one cell.

9 Key the following in the first three rows:

Cell A1: LONG GROVE LIFE AND LEISURE

Cell B1: July/August 2020

Cell C1: Table of Contents

10 Format cells A1, B1, and C1 so that the text is aligned to the top center of the cells.

11 Change the height of cell A1 to be 0.4 inch.

12 Proofread the table and correct any errors.

13 Save the document.

14 Click the Check button to upload the document for checking.

15 If errors are reported by the Online Lab, view the results document, correct the errors in the submitted document, save the document, and then click the Check Again button.

Figure 75.2 Table Content for Document 75.2

What's Cooking	79	Style Book	86
The Arts	82	Quintessential People	93
Teaching	83	Quintessential Travelers	124
Business	84	Fitness	128

6 Position the insertion point immediately to the left of the line following the *Date of Birth* heading, turn on underline formatting, and then key September 28, 1979.

7 At the bottom of the second page of the document, key St. Mary's Hospital on the first line, key Dr. Robert Heins on the second line, Attorney Theresa Flanagan on the third line, and Brooke Neumaier on the last line. ***Note: You do not need to turn on underline formatting.***

8 Proofread the document and correct any errors, comparing it to the document shown in Figure 99.2.

9 Save the document.

10 Click the Check button to upload the document for checking.

11 If errors are reported by the Online Lab, view the results document, correct the errors in the submitted document, save the document, and then click the Check Again button.

Figure 99.2 Completed Living Will for Document 99.4

Ending the Session

The Online Lab automatically saved the work you completed for this session. You may continue with the next session or exit the Online Lab and continue later.

Checking Production Progress: Tables

Sessions 71 through 74 discussed the procedures for preparing and formatting tables. In this session, you will be assessed on how quickly and accurately you can key this type of document. In the following document activities, each completed file is to be "mailable," which means that it contains no errors. A document that requires corrections is not considered *mailable*.

Your goal is to key each email and memo in mailable form. If you are missing errors that should have been corrected or your instructor believes you can work more efficiently, he or she may ask you to repeat document activities. To help you succeed, carefully review the document instructions and the document before launching the document activity. *Note: Review the content of Sessions 71 through 74 if you are unsure how to complete a specific task.*

Document 75.1 Inserting and Formatting a Table

Read all instructions below before starting this document activity.

1   Navigate to the Document 75.1 launch page in the Online Lab and then click the Launch Activity button to open **Doc075.01** in the activity window.

2   Insert a table containing four columns and six rows.

3   Key the information into the table as shown in Figure 75.1.

4   Format the data in column 2 to be aligned to the top center of the cells.

5   Format the data in column 4 to be aligned to the top right corners of the cells.

6   Insert a row at the top of the table and make the following changes to the new row:

   a   Merge the cells.

   b   Key Contents in the cell.

   c   Format the text in the cell to be aligned to the top center of the cell.

7   Apply the List Table 3 - Accent 6 table style (seventh column, third row in the *List Tables* section) to the table.

8   Set the titles in cells C2 through C7 in bold formatting.

9   Proofread the table and correct any errors.

10   Save the document.

11   Click the Check button to upload the document for checking.

12   If errors are reported by the Online Lab, view the results document, correct the errors in the submitted document, save the document, and then click the Check Again button.

Figure 75.1 Table Content for Document 75.1

Letter from the Editor	28	Style Book	86
Guest Essay	32	Open Spaces	88
Interview	38	People	93
About Town	47	Travelers	124
Community	70	Fitness	128
At Home	78	Snapshots	132

Session 100

Using Mail Merge to Create Legal Documents

Session Objectives

- Use the Mail Merge feature to create letters
- Use the Mail Merge feature to create envelopes
- Use the Mail Merge feature to create memos
- Efficiently produce documents in mailable form

Getting Started

Exercise 100.1 If you are continuing immediately from Session 99, you may skip the Exercise 100.1 warm-up drill. However, if you exited the Online Lab at the end of Session 99, warm up by completing Exercise 100.1.

Exercise 100.2 Begin your session work by completing Exercise 100.2, a timed short drill, in the Online Lab.

Assessing Your Speed and Accuracy

Complete Timing 100.1 in the Online Lab using the timing text on the next page. At the end of the timing, the Online Lab will display your WPM rate and any errors. Results will be saved in your Timings Performance report. If you have been surpassing the speed and accuracy goals identified in the Online Lab, set slightly more challenging personal goals and strive to exceed them.

Complete one 5-minute timing on the timing text below.

5-Minute Timing

Timing 75.3

Repetitive-stress injuries are more common for many workers and employers all over the nation. Injuries of this type affect muscles and joints of people who do one particular motion over and over repetitively during the course of a typical work day.

Of special interest to users of computers is one such injury known as the carpal tunnel syndrome. This injury results from a repeated "squeezing" of the important nerves in your wrists over a period of time. Sometimes the injury will produce chronic pain and weakened finger dexterity. In some cases, surgery may even be necessary.

You can certainly prevent this injury even if you use the computer keyboard on a daily basis for long periods of time. One of the first things you need to practice is keeping your wrists straight. Resting the palms of your hands on the keyboard itself or on the desk places your wrists in an unnatural position and causes strain on the nerves in your wrists. Many beginners like to rest their hands as they work at the computer keyboard. While it may seem easier at the time, placing your wrists in a bent position also places strain on finger movement. You will never acquire speed or accuracy if you let yourself get into the bad habit of resting the palms of your hands on the desk or keyboard.

Another method of preventing wrist injury is using the ergonomic products that are on the market. These products are made especially for use with the keyboard or the mouse. The design of the products varies from a simple wrist splint to a cushioned wrist rest. The prices of the products also vary; some are below $25. However, even the top prices may not be too high if the product will help you prevent a serious impairment that could endanger your health for the rest of your life.

Perhaps the best way to prevent wrist injury is to develop the habit of using the keyboard correctly from the beginning. If you pay attention to your keying habits, the results will be a more productive life.

Ergonomic Tip

When you are under stress, take a moment to close your eyes and breathe deeply.

**Timing
100.1**

Acquiring a desire for good literature is largely up to an individual. Each person must make an effort to explore many new types of reading material and to decide which type fits his or her own desires and experiences. There are major guidelines that can be helpful in your quest to select good reading material.

Good literature, regardless of the type, usually reflects a past experience or helps to interpret life for a reader. Any idea must be presented clearly to the reader. The major idea or thought should be woven throughout a well-developed plot or story line. When beginning a reading improvement program, you must be certain that you possess a desire to gain more knowledge about good reading materials. The next step is to supply yourself with excellent books. Just reading a book will not suffice; you must allow adequate time to meditate, digest, and ponder the material you have read.

Excellent literature can give you a rewarding experience. Experts have said that the ultimate test of any excellent piece of reading material comes when reading it again. If you enjoy the literature the second time and discover some new aspect, then the book, poem, or composition is good literature.

Fiction is the most widely read type of literature. Any plot or story that isn't based on pure, factual information would formally be classified as fiction. This type of literature is a vehicle for many to experience all sorts of adventure and action without ever stirring from a favorite, quiet comfortable chair.

Using Mail Merge

The Mail Merge feature in Word is used to create personalized versions of a single, main document, such as a form letter that is to be sent to multiple clients. For the most part, the versions contain the same information, yet some of the content is unique to each document. For example, in letters to your clients, you can address each recipient by name and include the date of his or her specific appointment. The unique information in each letter is retrieved from entries in a data source file that you create.

Conduct a Mail Merge by completing the following steps:

1   Format the main document. The main document contains the text and graphics that will be the same in every version of the merged document—for example, the body text in a form letter.

2   Create a data source file. A data source file is a file that contains the information to be merged into a document, such as the names and addresses of the recipients of a letter.

steps continue

Session
75
Production Progress Check: Tables Part II

Session Objectives

- **Apply features presented in Sessions 71–74**
- **Efficiently produce documents in mailable form**

Getting Started

Exercise 75.1 If you are continuing immediately from Session 74, you may skip the Exercise 75.1 warm-up drill. However, if you exited the Online Lab at the end of Session 74, warm up by completing Exercise 75.1.

Exercise 75.2 Begin your session work by completing Exercise 75.2, a timed short drill, in the Online Lab.

Assessing Your Speed and Accuracy

Complete Timings 75.1 through 75.3 in the Online Lab. At the end of each timing, the Online Lab will display your WPM rate and any errors. Results will be saved in your Timings Performance report. If you have been surpassing the speed and accuracy goals identified in the Online Lab, set slightly more challenging personal goals and strive to exceed them.

Complete two 1-minute timings on the timing text below. If you meet or exceed both speed and accuracy goals for Timing 75.1, push for greater speed on Timing 75.2.

1-Minute Timings

Timings 75.1–75.2
Hundreds of years ago, wood was the prime source of most energy needs. Later on, wood was replaced by coal. Presently, oil and gas are major sources of energy. These resources provide heat, electricity, and the energy to run automobiles. In the near future, most people will quite likely have to rely upon a number of combined energy sources. Solar power from the sun and wind power are likely prospects for providing energy. Americans can no longer rely on a single energy source for the bulk of their energy.

3 Refine the list of recipients, if necessary. Word creates a copy of the main document for each recipient in your data source file. If you want to create copies for only certain recipients in your data source file, you can indicate that only those recipients should receive the letter.

4 Add Mail Merge fields (placeholders) to the main document. These fields will be replaced by the variable information in your data source file.

5 Preview and complete the merge. You can preview each copy of the document before you print the whole set.

Mail Merge may be used for creating letters, emails, envelopes, labels, and directories. In this session, you will create letters and envelopes for a client mailing, as well as key memos to other attorneys. Mail Merge commands are located on the Mailings tab. The Mail Merge wizard is a tool that takes you through the six steps of a mail merge. You will practice using the Mail Merge wizard in the following document activity.

Document 100.1

Letters Created with the Mail Merge Wizard

Read all instructions below before starting this document activity.

1 Navigate to the Document 100.1 launch page and then minimize the Online Lab. Start Word 2016 and then complete the following steps:

  a Click the File tab; click *Open* in the left panel, if necessary; and then click the *Browse* option to display the Open dialog box.

  b Click the *Documents* folder in the Navigation pane at the left side of the Open dialog box.

  c Double-click the *Paradigm* folder, double-click the *Keyboarding* folder, and then double-click the *DocumentActivityFiles* folder.

  d Double-click **Doc100.01_TFLetterhead.docx**.

2 After the document opens, start the Mail Merge wizard by completing the following steps:

  a Click the Mailings tab.

  b Click the Start Mail Merge button in the Start Mail Merge group.

  c Click *Step-by-Step Mail Merge Wizard* at the drop-down list.

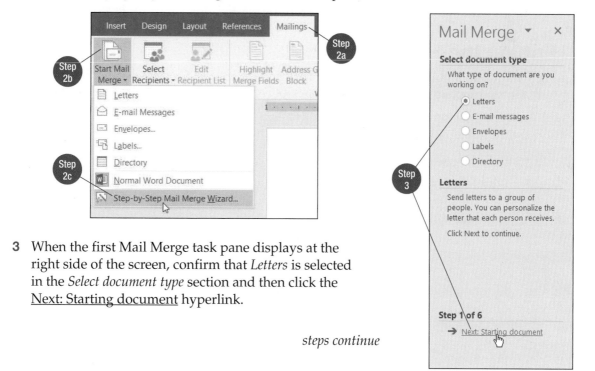

3 When the first Mail Merge task pane displays at the right side of the screen, confirm that *Letters* is selected in the *Select document type* section and then click the Next: Starting document hyperlink.

steps continue

Reinforcing Writing Skills

Letters that present data or statistics sometimes include tables. However, tabular data (data presented in a table) generally are accompanied by an explanation, analysis, or summary that provides more information. In this writing activity, you will discuss survey results that reveal attitudes about how people accumulate wealth. In the letter, indicate how your attitudes are similar or are different from the results.

Document 74.4

Summarizing Tabular Data

Read all instructions below before starting this document activity.

1 Navigate to the Document 74.4 launch page in the Online Lab and then click the Launch Activity button to open **Doc074.04** in the activity window.

2 Write a personal business letter to your instructor that presents the results of a survey that asked 50 respondents, "What is the primary factor that contributes to a person's wealth?" The results are shown in Figure 74.6. In your letter, introduce the question and the number of respondents, then include a table that lists responses, and finally conclude with a paragraph that identifies how your attitudes align or diverge from the reported results.

3 Proofread and correct any errors in the letter.

4 Save the document.

5 Click the Submit button to upload the document for instructor review.

Figure 74.6 Table Content for Document 74.4

Intellect	50%
Personal values	45%
Luck	35%
Passion about my work	30%
Overwhelming desire not to be poor	14%

Ending the Session

The Online Lab automatically saved the work you completed for this session. You may continue with the next session or exit the Online Lab and continue later.

4 At the second Mail Merge task pane, confirm that *Use the current document* is selected in the *Select starting document* section and then click the <u>Next: Select recipients</u> hyperlink.

5 At the third Mail Merge task pane, click *Type a new list* in the *Select recipients* section and then click the <u>Create</u> hyperlink in the *Type a new list* section of the task pane.

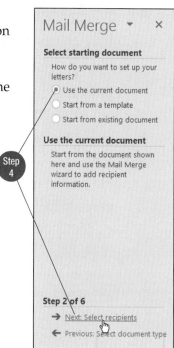

6 Create a new address list by completing the following steps:

a Click the Customize Columns button in the New Address List dialog box.

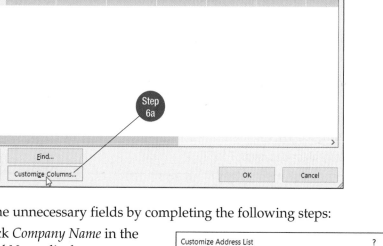

b Remove the unnecessary fields by completing the following steps:

 i. Click *Company Name* in the *Field Names* list box.

 ii. Click the Delete button.

 iii. At the message box, click Yes.

 iv. Click *Address Line 2* in the *Field Names* list box, click the Delete button, and then click Yes.

 v. Click *Country or Region* in the *Field Names* list box, click the Delete button, and then click Yes.

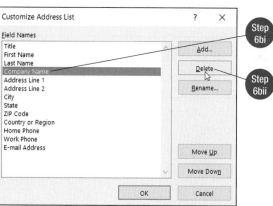

steps continue

Figure 74.4 Block-Style Business Letter Content for Document 74.3

Ms. Shira Palenti
89921 S. Maple Court
Gatlinburg, TN 37737

Dear Ms. Palenti:

The world doesn't need another reality show, celebrity scandal, or "as seen on TV" product. It does need another good success story. If you are ready to embark on a new profession or take your career to a higher level, **Infinity Career College** will prepare you to succeed.

Infinity is more than a place to take a class or earn your degree. It is a community of workforce development experts, dedicated professors, and knowledgeable advisors all working toward one goal—*your success*. Whether it is helping you define your strengths and interests, advising you about viable career options, or supporting you while you earn the credentials you need, you can start or continue your success story here.

Learn more about **Infinity Career College** by attending one of our general information sessions listed in the following table.

Sincerely,

Figure 74.5 Table Content for Document 74.3

DATE	TIME	LOCATION
Wednesday, August 12	6-7 p.m.	Student Center Building A Room A532
Saturday, August 15	9-10 a.m.	Student Center Building C Room C233

    vi.   Click *Home Phone* in the *Field Names* list box, click the Delete button, and then click Yes.

    vii.   Click *Work Phone* in the *Field Names* list box, click the Delete button, and then click Yes.

    viii.   Click *E-mail Address* in the *Field Names* list box, click the Delete button, and then click Yes.

c Rename a field in the address list by completing the following steps:

    i.   Click *Address Line 1* in the *Field Names* list box.

    ii.   Click the Rename button.

    iii.   In the Rename Field dialog box with the text selected in the *To* text box, key Address.

    iv.   Click OK.

d Add a field to the address list by completing the following steps:

    i.   Click the *ZIP Code* field name in the *Field Names* list box.

    ii.   Click the Add button.

    iii.   Key Doc in the *Type a name for your field* text box in the Add Field dialog box and then click OK.

    iv.   Click OK to close the Customize Address List dialog box.

e Key the content for the fields in the New Address List dialog box as shown in Figure 100.1. Press Tab to move to the next field or row in the table. ***Hint: Be careful not to add any spaces at the end of the entries.***

f Proofread the contents of the entries in the New Address List dialog box and then click OK to close the dialog box.

g At the Save Address List dialog box, key Doc100.01_data_source in the *File name* text box and then click Save.

steps continue

Figure 100.1 New Address List Content for Document 100.1

Title	First Name	Last Name	Address	City	State	ZIP Code	Doc
Mr.	Byron	Eckert	5309 Russell Blvd., #7	Milton	WI	53563-4413	Last Will and Testament
Ms.	Kerri	Liebenstein	432 N. Hwy 51	Janesville	WI	53545-4346	Living Will
Dr. and Mrs.	Miguel	Perez	10834 Dallman Road	Edgerton	WI	53534-1951	Wills
Mrs.	Sally	Petrakis	138 Pioneer Drive	Beloit	WI	53511-9923	updated Last Will and Testament

Document
74.2

Merging and Splitting Cells

Read all instructions below before starting this document activity.

1 Navigate to the Document 74.2 launch page in the Online Lab and then click the Launch Activity button to open **Doc074.02** in the activity window.

2 Insert two new rows above the first row of the table by completing the following steps:

   a With the insertion point positioned in cell A1, click the Table Tools Layout tab.

   b Click the Insert Above button in the Rows & Columns group twice.

3 Merge the cells in the first row of the table.

4 Key Downtown Store Hours and Locations in cell A1, apply bold formatting to the text, and align the text to the top center of the cell.

5 Split cell B2 into three columns by completing the following steps:

   a Click in cell B2.

   b Click the Split Cells button in the Merge group on the Table Tools Layout tab.

   c Key 3 in the *Number of columns* measurement box and then click OK.

6 Key Open in cell B2, key Close in cell B3, and key Location in cell B4.

7 Split cell C2 into three columns, key 7 p.m. in cell C3, and delete */7 p.m.* from cell C2.

8 Follow the procedure outlined in Step 7 for the remaining cells containing time data.

9 Save the document.

10 Click the Check button to upload the document for checking.

11 If errors are reported by the Online Lab, view the results document, correct the errors in the submitted document, save the document, and then click the Check Again button.

Document
74.3

Inserting a Table in a Block-Style Business Letter

Read all instructions below before starting this document activity.

1 Navigate to the Document 74.3 launch page in the Online Lab and then click the Launch Activity button to open **Doc074.03** in the activity window.

2 Create a block-style business letter using the text shown in Figure 74.4. The document contains a letterhead that automatically positions the insertion point near the 2-inch mark on the page. You do not need to press the Enter key before keying the date.

   a Key July 15, 2020 as the current date.

   b Apply bold and italic formatting as shown in the figure. *Note: In the second paragraph, the text* your success *is bold and italic.*

   c Indicate that the letter is from Robert C. Milligan, Admissions Director, and key the reference initials mtb followed by the file name.

3 Position the insertion point at the end of the last paragraph in the body of the letter (after *in the following table.*), press Enter, and then insert a table containing three columns and three rows.

4 Key the table content shown in Figure 74.5. *Note: For the contents of the cells in the* **LOCATION** *column, press Enter after keying each line except the last line in each cell.*

5 Proofread the document and correct any errors.

6 Save the document.

7 Click the Check button to upload the document for checking.

8 If errors are reported by the Online Lab, view the results document, correct the errors in the submitted document, save the document, and then click the Check Again button.

h Click OK to close the Mail Merge Recipients dialog box.

i Click the Next: Write your letter hyperlink in the Mail Merge task pane.

7 Key the contents of the letter by completing the following steps:

a Click in the document, key November 6, 2020, and then press Enter twice.

b Click the Address block hyperlink located in the *Write your letter* section of the task pane.

c Click OK at the Insert Address Block dialog box.

d Press Enter.

e Click the Greeting line hyperlink located in the *Write your letter* section of the task pane.

f Click the punctuation (third) option box arrow in the *Greeting line format* section of the Insert Greeting Line dialog box, click : (colon), and then click OK.

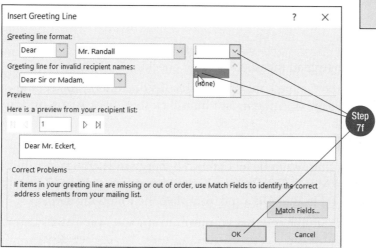

g Press Enter.

h Key the contents of the letter shown in Figure 100.2. The *«Doc»* field will need to be entered in several places. When you get to that field in the letter, click the More items hyperlink in the Mail Merge task pane, click *Doc* in the *Fields* list box at the Insert Merge Field dialog box, click the Insert button, and then click the Close button.

i At the bottom of the letter, include the reference initials for Virginia R. Cowan and the file name *Doc100.01*, along with a notation for an enclosure.

8 In the *Step 4 of 6* section of the Mail Merge task pane, click the Next: Preview your letters hyperlink.

9 Select the name and street address lines (do not select the city and state line), click the Home tab, click the Line and Paragraph Spacing button in the Paragraph group, and then click *Remove Space After Paragraph* at the drop-down list.

10 In the *Step 5 of 6* section of the task pane, click the Next: Complete the merge hyperlink.

steps continue

7 Sort the content in the second table in the document in descending order using the data in the second column by completing the following steps:

a Click in a cell in the second table.

b Click the Sort button in the Data group on the Table Tools Layout tab.

c In the Sort dialog box, click the *Header row* option in the *My list has* section.

d Click the *Sort by* option box arrow and then click *Close*.

e Click the *Descending* option.

f Click OK.

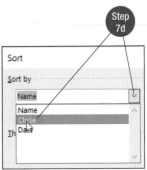

8 Sort the content in the third table in the document in ascending order using the data in the third column by completing the following steps:

a Click in a cell in the third table.

b Click the Sort button in the Data group.

c In the Sort dialog box, click the *Header row* option in the *My list has* section.

d Click the *Sort by* option box arrow and then click *Date*.

e Click the *Ascending* option.

f Click OK.

9 Save the document.

10 Click the Check button to upload the document for checking.

11 If errors are reported by the Online Lab, view the results document, correct the errors in the submitted document, save the document, and then click the Check Again button.

Splitting Cells in a Table

In Session 72, you practiced merging two cells in a table. To merge cells, you select the cells you want to merge and then click the Merge Cells button in the Merge group on the Table Tools Layout tab. You can also split a cell in a table. To split a cell, complete the following steps:

1 Position the insertion point in the cell that you want to split.

2 Click the Split Cells button in the Merge group on the Table Tools Layout tab to display the Split Cells dialog box.

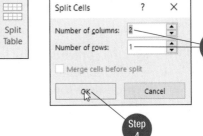

3 Indicate the number of rows or columns into which you want to split the cell.

4 Click OK.

Figure 100.2 Letter Content for Document 100.1

Thank you for allowing me to assist in drafting your «Doc». Our follow-up file indicates that it has been about four weeks since I last spoke with you.

Because the «Doc» is not legally valid until it is signed and witnessed, it is important that we finalize this as soon as possible. A draft copy is enclosed for your convenience. If there are corrections or changes that need to be made, please call me as soon as possible. When you call, you may also schedule an appointment at a time that is convenient for you to stop in to approve and sign the finalized document.

I look forward to hearing from you within the next week. Please let me know if you have any questions or concerns about the «Doc» or if I can assist you in any other way.

Sincerely,

Theresa Flanagan
Attorney at Law

11 Click the Close button to close the Mail Merge task pane.

12 Position the insertion point immediately to the right of the date and then press Enter twice to better position the body of the letter on the page.

13 Save the document with the name **Doc100.01**, close the document, and then close Word.

14 Return to the document activity launch page in the Online Lab, click the Upload Document button, and then select your completed Doc100.01 file to upload it for instructor review.

You can also use Mail Merge to prepare envelopes for a series of letters. You will practice using this Word feature in the following document activity. For this activity, we will assume that Theresa Flanagan's law office uses letterhead envelopes with a preprinted return address.

Document 100.2 **Envelopes Created with the Mail Merge Wizard**

Read all instructions below before starting this document activity.

1 Navigate to the Document 100.2 launch page and then minimize the Online Lab. Start Word 2016 and click the *Blank document* template.

2 At the blank document that appears, start the Mail Merge wizard by completing the following steps:

a Click the Mailings tab.

b Click the Start Mail Merge button.

c Click *Step-by-Step Mail Merge Wizard* at the drop-down list.

3 At the first Mail Merge task pane, click *Envelopes* in the *Select document type* section of the Mail Merge task pane and then click the <u>Next: Starting document</u> hyperlink.

steps continue

Sorting Content in Table Columns

Read all instructions below before starting this document activity.

1 Navigate to the Document 74.1 launch page in the Online Lab and then click the Launch Activity button to open **Doc074.01** in the activity window.

2 Create the table shown in Figure 74.3.

3 Proofread the table and correct any errors.

4 Select the entire table, press Ctrl + C to copy it, position the insertion point below the table, press Enter, and then press Ctrl + V to paste a copy of the table. The document will now contain two identical tables.

5 With the insertion point positioned below the second table, press Enter, and then press Ctrl + V to paste a second copy of the table. The document will now contain three identical tables. *Hint: If necessary, turn on the display of nonprinting characters. Make sure that there is only one paragraph mark after the third table.*

6 Sort the contents of the first table in ascending order using the data in the first column by completing the following steps:

a Click in a cell in the first table.

b Click the Table Tools Layout tab.

c Click the Sort button in the Data group.

d At the Sort dialog box, click the *Header row* option in the *My list has* section.

e Confirm that *Name* appears in the *Sort by* option box and that the *Ascending* option is selected.

f Click OK.

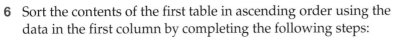

steps continue

Figure 74.3 Table Content for Document 74.1

Name	Close	Date
Stock C	$39.43	7-8-2020
Stock E	$43.43	6-24-2020
Stock A	$30.30	7-1-2020
Stock B	$19.56	4-1-2020
Stock D	$7.28	5-20-2020

4 At the second Mail Merge task pane, confirm that *Change document layout* is selected and then click the <u>Envelope options</u> hyperlink.

5 At the Envelope Options dialog box, confirm that *Size 10* is selected in the *Envelope size* list box on the Envelope Options tab. If it is not, click the *Envelope size* option box arrow and then click *Size 10* at the drop-down list. Click OK to close the dialog box.

6 In the *Step 2 of 6* section of the task pane, click the <u>Next: Select recipients</u> hyperlink.

7 At the third Mail Merge task pane, confirm that *Use an existing list* is selected in the *Select recipients* section and then complete the following steps:

a Click the <u>Browse</u> hyperlink in the *Use an existing list* section.

b In the Select Data Source dialog box, click the *Documents* folder, double-click the *Paradigm* folder, double-click the *Keyboarding* folder, double-click the *DocumentActivityFiles* folder, and then double-click **Doc100.02_data_source.mdb**.

c Click OK at the Mail Merge Recipients dialog box.

8 In the *Step 3 of 6* section of the task pane, click the <u>Next: Arrange your envelope</u> hyperlink and then complete the following steps:

a Turn on the display of nonprinting characters.

b Position the insertion point in the delivery address text box in the bottom center of the envelope and then click the <u>Address block</u> hyperlink in the *Arrange your envelope* section of the task pane.

c Click OK to close the Insert Address Block dialog box.

9 In the *Step 4 of 6* section of the task pane, click the <u>Next: Preview your envelopes</u> hyperlink.

10 In the *Step 5 of 6* section of the task pane, click the <u>Next: Complete the merge</u> hyperlink.

11 Click the Close button in the upper right corner of the Mail Merge task pane.

12 Save the document with the name **Doc100.02**, close the document, and then close Word.

13 Return to the document activity launch page in the Online Lab, click the Upload Document button, and then select your completed Doc100.02 file to upload it for instructor review.

Ergonomic Tip

Just as glare on a computer monitor can cause eye fatigue, so too can trying to read reference documents without proper lighting. To illuminate reference documents, use a desk lamp or a task light. Remember to position this light source so that it does not cause glare on the computer monitor.

Sorting Table Data and Splitting Cells

After you create a table in a Word document, you may need to change the presentation of the table contents. The Table Tools Layout tab provides tools to help you do this. In this session, you will learn how to sort cell contents as well as how to split cells.

Sorting Data in a Table

Tables provide a logical structure for presenting information. When you create a table, you organize data in columns and rows, but sometimes you may need to change the order of the data. Word contains a feature that makes it easy for you to sort table contents in ascending or descending order. This sorting feature allows you to change the layout of your table without having to rekey the information. Begin by selecting the data you want sorted, and, with the Table Tools Layout tab selected, click the Sort button in the Data group (see Figure 74.1).

Clicking the Sort button will display the Sort dialog box (see Figure 74.2). In the Sort dialog box, use options in the *Sort by* section to indicate how to sort the selected data. Click an option box arrow to display options for each setting. You can sort by more than one column by selecting options in the *Then by* sections. To make the table's column headings appear in the *Sort by/Then by* drop-down lists, select the *Header row* option in the *My list has* section of the Sort dialog box.

Figure 74.1 Data Group on the Table Tools Layout Tab

Figure 74.2 Sort Dialog Box

Document 100.3

Memos Created with the Mail Merge Wizard

Read all instructions below before starting this document activity.

1. Navigate to the Document 100.3 launch page and then minimize the Online Lab. Start Word 2016 and then complete the following steps:

   a. Click the File tab; click *Open* in the left panel, if necessary; and then click the *Browse* option to display the Open dialog box.

   b. Click *Documents* in the Navigation pane at the left side of the Open dialog box.

   c. Double-click the *Paradigm* folder, double-click the *Keyboarding* folder, and then double-click the *DocumentActivityFiles* folder.

   d. Double-click *Doc100.03_TFMemo.docx*.

2. After the document opens, start the Mail Merge wizard.

3. At the first Mail Merge task pane, confirm that *Letters* is selected in the *Select document type* section of the task pane and then click the <u>Next: Starting document</u> hyperlink.

4. At the second Mail Merge task pane, confirm that *Use the current document* is selected and then click the <u>Next: Select recipients</u> hyperlink.

5. At the third Mail Merge task pane, click *Type a new list* and then click the <u>Create</u> hyperlink.

6. Create a new address list using the information shown in Figure 100.3. Remove, rename, and/or add fields to the address list and then key the content shown in the figure.

7. Proofread the contents of the entries in the New Address List dialog box and then click OK to close the dialog box.

8. At the Save Address List dialog box, key Doc100.03_data_source in the *File name* text box and then click Save.

9. Click OK to close the Mail Merge Recipients dialog box.

10. Click the <u>Next: Write your letter</u> hyperlink in the Mail Merge task pane.

11. Key the contents of the memo shown in Figure 100.4. Insert the fields as indicated in the figure.

12. At the bottom of the memo, include the reference initials for Brenda A. Rogers and the file name *Doc100.03*. Also include a reference to an attachment. *Note: Key* Attachment *rather than* Enclosure.

13. Proofread the document and correct any errors.

14. In the *Step 4 of 6* section of the task pane, click the <u>Next: Preview your letters</u> hyperlink.

15. In the *Step 5 of 6* section of the task pane, click the <u>Next: Complete the merge</u> hyperlink.

16. Close the Mail Merge task pane.

17. Save the document with the name **Doc100.03**, close the document, and then close Word.

18. Return to the document activity launch page in the Online Lab, click the Upload Document button, and then select your completed Doc100.03 file to upload it for instructor review.

Figure 100.3 New Address List Content for Document 100.3—Mail Merge Wizard Step 3

Attorney	Student	Day	Date	Time
Mary Goldmann	Sayid Shammas	Friday	May 8	10:00 a.m.
Dayna Gibeaut	Matt Coyer	Monday	May 11	2:30 p.m.
Javier Moreno	Brianne Elliott	Monday	May 11	10:15 a.m.
Nick Hutchinson	Crystal Darwin	Tuesday	May 12	3:45 p.m.

Complete one 5-minute timing on the timing text below.

5-Minute Timing

Timing 74.3

Words are fascinating to think about. When you are first learning to read, words are strange marks on a piece of paper that mean nothing to you. As you begin to translate those strange marks on the paper to words that mean something to you, words begin to make sense. You can read a book, write a letter, and begin to understand the wonderful world around you.

Certain words produce a strong emotion. Consider how you feel when you hear the words hate, love, weak, strong, courage, and honesty. Each one of those words will bring a special feeling to you. Perhaps the word will help you recall a pleasant event or a special person in your life.

Other words produce a tingling sensation in our taste buds. When you hear the words bitter and sour, your taste buds begin to tingle with a zest. Often you will think of a food that produces this sensation. Or if you hear words such as sweet, creamy, and delicious, you will probably start to think of some very special foods you always enjoy.

Words of action produce different feelings in people. Quick means something quite different from the word slow. Or, if you look at the word lazy, you certainly don't think of someone who is active and concerned with getting the job done. Finished or unfinished are examples of two directly opposed ideas.

How and when we use words will mark our success in dealing with other people. Harsh, unkind words will provoke defensive feelings ranging from anger to discomfort. Courteous words and kind words of encouragement will go a long way in creating a good relationship with another person. How you react to words spoken by another person also is a good indication of character. Reacting to angry words with more angry words will not solve any problems. But, trying to find out why the other person is using angry words will go a long way in the solving of any conflict that arises. Reacting to kind words with more kind words will usually produce a very wonderful situation.

Figure 100.4 Memo Content for Document 100.3

To: «Attorney»

From: Theresa Flanagan

Date: April 29, 2020

Re: Student Mock Interviews

Thank you for agreeing to provide a practice interview for a South High School student. According to their instructor, Jason Crawford, four students will be coming to our offices this year.

Conference Room B has been reserved for these interviews, which should each take approximately 20 minutes.

You are scheduled to interview «Student» at «Time» on «Day», «Date».

Attached is the rating form provided by Mr. Crawford. Please take a few minutes to review it before conducting the interview.

If you have any questions, please let me know. I know the students will benefit from the experience.

Ending the Session

The Online Lab automatically saved the work you completed for this session. You may continue with the next session or exit the Online Lab and continue later.

Session 74 — Sorting Content and Splitting Cells in Tables

Session Objectives

- **Sort data in a table**
- **Split cells**
- **Insert a table into a business letter**
- **Summarize tabular data**
- **Efficiently produce documents in mailable form**

Getting Started

Exercise 74.1

If you are continuing immediately from Session 73, you may skip the Exercise 74.1 warm-up drill. However, if you exited the Online Lab at the end of Session 73, warm up by completing Exercise 74.1.

Exercise 74.2

Begin your session work by completing Exercise 74.2, a timed short drill, in the Online Lab.

Assessing Your Speed and Accuracy

Complete Timings 74.1 through 74.3 in the Online Lab. At the end of each timing, the Online Lab will display your WPM rate and any errors. Results will be saved in your Timings Performance report. If you have been surpassing the speed and accuracy goals identified in the Online Lab, set slightly more challenging personal goals and strive to exceed them.

Complete two 1-minute timings on the timing text below. If you meet or exceed both speed and accuracy goals for Timing 74.1, push for greater speed on Timing 74.2.

1-Minute Timings

Timings 74.1–74.2

Balloon rides have recently become one of the most exciting adventures for many intrepid people. If you have never taken a balloon ride, an adventure awaits you. Floating over the scenic hills and plains is the best way to escape crowds. In these days of hurried car and jet plane travel, imagine floating over the beautiful valleys and hills in gentle winds. You will be able to thoroughly relax and enjoy the breathtaking views. The next time you really want to unwind, consider a balloon ride.

Session 101 · Legal Office Project: Overview and Background

Getting Started

Beginning with this session, you will develop your own warm-up drills. Before keying document activities, spend at least two or three minutes warming up in the Online Lab.

The following are some examples of exercises to key as warm-up drills. Use one or more of them as a warm-up drill for each of the remaining sessions in this text.

Exercise 101.1 — Alphabetic Keys and Numeric Keys Locations Drill

Repeat the following drill lines two or more times.

1   aa bb cc dd ee ff gg hh ii jj kk ll mm nn oo pp qq rr ss tt uu vv ww xx yy zz

2   11 22 33 44 55 66 77 88 99 00

Alphabetic Thinking Drill

Key the alphabet backward, keying each letter twice and keying a space between each letter pair. Do not look at the previous drill line above or your fingers when keying.

Numeric Thinking Drill

Key numbers backward from 100 by 3s—for example, 100 97 94 91 88, and so on. Key one space between numbers.

Two-Letter Combination Thinking Drill

Key as many words as you can using the same two-letter combination at the beginning of each word—for example, for the letters *bu*, key bug, buddy, buggy, buck, but, butter, bullet, bum, bun, bus, buffalo, bulb, and so on.

Alphabetic Keys Location Drill

Key the following sentence, changing the number of lazy dogs each time you key in order to include numeric key practice.

The quick brown fox jumped over the 16 lazy dogs.

Balanced-Hand Words Drill

Key this drill line to build speed. Balanced-hand words can be keyed faster than words keyed with one hand.

The pale maid paid for the vivid title and the wig she fit to the girl.

Accuracy Drill

Key this drill line to help develop accuracy and to help coordinate eye and finger movements.

Establish minimum standards plus exhibit a rational imagination whenever possible.

6 With the table still selected, change the size of the cells by completing the following steps:

   a   Click the Table Tools Layout tab.

   b   Key 0.5 in the *Table Row Height* measurement box and then press Enter.

   c   Key 1 in the *Table Column Width* measurement box and then press Enter.

7 Center the table horizontally by completing the following steps:

   a   Select the table, if it is not already selected.

   b   Press Ctrl + E.

8 Change the cell alignment of all cells in the table to center text horizontally and vertically within the cells.

9 Proofread the table and correct any errors.

10 Save the document.

11 Click the Check button to upload the document for checking.

12 If errors are reported by the Online Lab, view the results document, correct the errors in the submitted document, save the document, and then click the Check Again button.

Reinforcing Writing Skills

Organizing your personal information and keeping track of your schedule are important tasks in today's busy world. One way to do this is to keep a daily, weekly, or monthly calendar of your activities and appointments and any related information.

You can use Word's table feature to develop a weekly schedule of your activities. It can be updated daily, saved, revised for next week, carried with you, and passed on to family members and friends. Create this calendar in the following document activity.

Document 73.5

Creating a Weekly Schedule of Activities and Appointments

Read all instructions below before starting this document activity.

1 Navigate to the Document 73.5 launch page in the Online Lab and then click the Launch Activity button to open **Doc073.05** in the activity window.

2 Using the techniques you have learned for creating tables, prepare a weekly calendar of your class schedule, work schedule, personal schedule, and any other appointments or commitments you might have. Indicate the days of the week in rows and the time slots in columns. Include a title for the schedule as well as a subtitle describing the period of time.

3 Proofread and correct any errors in the document.

4 Save the document.

5 Click the Submit button to upload the document for instructor review.

Ending the Session

The Online Lab automatically saved the work you completed for this session. You may continue with the next session or exit the Online Lab and continue later.

Speed Drill

Key this drill line to help develop speed.

Now is the time for all good people to come to the aid of their country.

Legal Office Project Overview

To further refine your professional keyboarding and word processing proficiency, it is critical that you develop decision-making skills. The following project will help you reach this goal. When assigned a project such as this one, you must be able to do the following things:

- Understand the purpose of the project.
- Set completion dates and times for all items and activities.
- Understand exactly what needs to be done for each activity.
- Be aware of any special requirements related to the activities to be completed.
- Plan and organize your work so that you can complete the project as quickly and accurately as possible.
- Carefully check that your work is correct in terms of format, content, and adherence to instructions.

For this project, you are employed in a legal office where you are responsible for producing a variety of business-related documents for which you must identify and assign priorities to the related tasks and actions. As is expected in an office, you are to work quickly and accurately and use your time wisely. Most of the document activities in this project will not be automatically graded.

It is important that you understand the context and scope of work to be completed before you dive into completing specific project tasks. To achieve this, read the entire contents of this session as well as the contents of Sessions 102, 103, 104, and 105 before you begin document preparation.

The Legal Office project is divided into the following activities:

- **Session 101:** Digest the overview and background information for the project and then create and print a calendar document for tracking events.
- **Session 102:** Design and prepare the documentation of a file naming system.
- **Sessions 103 to 105:** Complete the document activities in the order that you have specified, not in the order presented in the sessions.

Legal Office Project Scenario

As mentioned above, for this project, you are working in a legal office. Table 101.1 provides contact information related to the office where you work. The current date is January 6, 2020.

Situation

You are the legal administrative assistant to attorneys Charles L. Beem and Kayla B. Southworth. You are also a notary public (a person who is authorized to perform legal formalities). Beem and Southworth, LLC, specializes in family law. The majority of their work involves wills and estate planning, custodial issues, divorces, and separations.

Because the attorneys are often unavailable—they are either in court or meeting with clients—you function without direct supervision. In addition to preparing and receiving documents, sending and receiving email messages, and responding to telephone calls and voicemail messages, you have the responsibility of greeting walk-in visitors and clients. You are also the direct supervisor

b With the arrow pointer displaying as a pencil icon, position the pencil icon at the right of the insertion point, click and hold down the left mouse button, drag over to the 5-inch mark on the horizontal ruler and down to the 7-inch mark on the vertical ruler, and then release the mouse button. *Hint: If the horizontal and vertical rulers are not visible, click the View tab and then click the **Ruler** check box in the Show group to insert a check mark.*

c Draw four vertical lines inside the table, approximately 1 inch apart.

d With the pencil icon active, draw six horizontal lines inside the table, approximately 1 inch apart.

3 Click in cell A1 and then key in the data as shown in Figure 73.9.

4 Erase the last inside horizontal line (the line below the *80 and older* row) by completing the following steps:

a Click the Table Tools Layout tab, if it is not already selected.

b Click the Eraser button in the Draw group.

c With the eraser icon active, drag over the last inside horizontal line in the table. *Note: Make sure you do not delete any column borders.*

d If necessary, click the Eraser button to turn off the eraser.

5 Change the style of the borders in the table by completing the following steps:

a Select the table.

b Click the Table Tools Design tab, if it is not already selected.

c Click the *Line Style* option box arrow in the Borders group and then click the solid, single line style option at the drop-down list (first option under *No Border*).

d Click the *Line Weight* option box arrow and then click *1 ½ pt* at the drop-down list.

e Click the Pen Color button arrow and then click *Black, Text 1* (second column, first row in the *Theme Colors* section).

f Click the Borders button arrow and then click *All Borders* at the drop-down gallery.

Figure 73.9 Table Data for Document 73.4

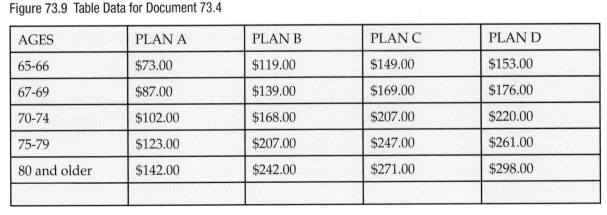

AGES	PLAN A	PLAN B	PLAN C	PLAN D
65-66	$73.00	$119.00	$149.00	$153.00
67-69	$87.00	$139.00	$169.00	$176.00
70-74	$102.00	$168.00	$207.00	$220.00
75-79	$123.00	$207.00	$247.00	$261.00
80 and older	$142.00	$242.00	$271.00	$298.00

steps continue

Table 101.1 Contact Information for Legal Office Project

Company Name:	Beem and Southworth, LLC Attorneys-at-Law
Address:	PO Box 6919 7736 Elm Street Janesville, WI 53545-6919
Office Telephone:	(608) 555-1300
Office Fax:	(608) 555-1301
Website:	http://ppi-edu.net/BeemAndSouthworth
Attorney Charles L. Beem's email address:	cbeem@ppi-edu.net
Attorney Kayla B. Southworth's email address:	ksouthworth@ppi-edu.net
Intern Gabrielle Lee's email address:	glee@ppi-edu.net

of a part-time intern, Gabrielle Lee from Blackhawk Technical College, who works on Mondays, Wednesdays, and Fridays from noon to 5:00 p.m. You also maintain calendars for both attorneys and make travel arrangements as needed. You are expected to make many decisions on your own.

Special Instructions and Explanations

You have been on vacation since the end of the previous year and are returning to work on Monday, January 6, at 8:00 a.m. Neither attorney will be in the office until later in the day, but both have been in the office over the holidays, checked their email, or called in to retrieve voicemail. You find a pile of "to-do" tasks on your desk.

The attorneys use the same document formats that have been used in the previous sessions. The documents prepared for their signatures are to be error-free in both content and format.

For some of the document activities in Session 104, you are instructed to make reservations of various kinds. For these activities, use the Internet to research available options, use hypothetical information in your composed reports, or follow directions provided by your instructor.

Document 101.1 January 2020 Calendar

Read all instructions below before starting this document activity.

1 Navigate to the Document 101.1 launch page in the Online Lab and then click the Launch Activity button to open **Doc101.01** in the activity window.

2 Create a January 2020 calendar using a Word table. Reference Figure 101.1 to determine the corresponding day for each date. Leave enough space so that you can document actions and due dates within the cells of the table, and use landscape orientation. Make the weekday cells wider than the weekend cells since they will need to accommodate more text.

3 Copy and paste the table twice in the same document, and label each calendar: one for you and your intern to share, and one for each of the two attorneys.

4 As you read through the rest of the sessions in this unit, key details of when project-related activities happen or will happen into your copy of the calendar. Also include attorney-specific schedule information in the appropriate attorney's calendar.

5 Proofread the document and correct any errors.

6 Save the document.

7 Print the document for reference as you work through the project.

8 Click the Submit button to upload the document for instructor review.

Figure 73.8 Table Data for Document 73.3

COMMUNICATION	WORD PROCESSING	SOFTWARE	DESKTOP PUBLISHING	GRAPHICS
Email	Alignment	Explorer	Camera Ready	Bitmapped
Facebook	Copy	Excel	Online Image	Grid
Internet	Cut	PowerPoint	Em Dash	Palette
Messaging	Document	Safari	Font	Pixel
Twitter	Move	Word	Justification	Resolution

8   Center the two lines of text above the table.

9   Select the column headings (row 1) and then change the cell alignment to align text to the bottom left corners of the cells.

10   Proofread the table and correct any errors.

11   Save the document.

12   Click the Check button to upload the document for checking.

13   If errors are reported by the Online Lab, view the results document, correct the errors in the submitted document, save the document, and then click the Check Again button.

Drawing Table Borders

Another method for creating a table is to draw it. To draw a table, click the Table Tools Layout tab and then click the Draw Table button in the Draw group. You can also draw a table by clicking the Insert tab, clicking the Table button in the Tables group, and then clicking *Draw Table* at the drop-down list. The arrow pointer will display as a pencil icon. With this pencil icon active, click and drag in the document to draw the outside border of the new table and then continue to build the table by drawing the rows and columns within the outside border. The pencil will draw using the line style, weight, and color indicated by the settings in the Borders group on the Table Tools Design tab. After drawing the desired row and column borders within the table, click in the table, key the table data, and then adjust the cell sizes.

If you draw a line in a table in error, you can erase it. To access the erase function, click the Table Tools Layout tab and then click the Eraser button in the Draw group. Clicking this button will turn the insertion point into an eraser icon. Click or drag over a table border to erase it. Clicking the Undo button will also erase the previously drawn line.

In the following document activity, you will draw a new table and use tools found on both the Table Tools Design and Table Tools Layout tabs.

Document 73.4

Drawing a Table

Read all instructions below before starting this document activity.

1   Navigate to the Document 73.4 launch page in the Online Lab and then click the Launch Activity button to open **Doc073.04** in the activity window.

2   Draw a table in the document by completing the following steps:

a   Click the Insert tab, click the Table button in the Tables group, and then click *Draw Table* at the drop-down list.

steps continue

Figure 101.1 January 2020 Calendar Example for Document 101.1

January 2020

S	M	T	W	T	F	S
			1	2	3	4
5	6	7	8	9	10	11
12	13	14	15	16	17	18
19	20	21	22	23	24	25
26	27	28	29	30	31	

Creating and Documenting a File Naming System

All of the work completed in the Online Lab has been saved automatically and the files are organized by session. All document activity file names were predetermined and numbered in order. Although this file management system works well for a course like this, such a system would not work within a business environment.

It is important to develop a file naming system and an electronic folder structure for saving documents. These systems should be organized to allow for easy retrieval of files and should include file names that identify the type of document, the attorney responsible for the file, and the date the file was created. Such a system is critical to productivity.

Document names created in Word are limited to a maximum of 255 characters in length, including the drive letter and any folder names as well as any spaces. File names cannot include any of the characters listed in Table 101.2.

Table 101.2 Characters Not Allowed in Word Document File Names

Character Name	Character
asterisk	*
backslash	\
colon	:
forward slash	/
greater than sign	>
less than sign	<
pipe symbol	|
question mark	?
quotation mark	"

Document **Formatting Borders in a Table**
73.3 Read all instructions below before starting this document activity.

1 Navigate to the Document 73.3 launch page in the Online Lab and then click the Launch Activity button to open **Doc073.03** in the activity window.

2 Key ELECTRONIC AGE TERMS, press Enter, key By Category, and then press Enter.

3 Create the table shown in Figure 73.8.

4 Apply the triple line style to the outside borders of the first row of the table by completing the following steps:

a Select the first row of the table.

b Click the Table Tools Design tab, if it is not already selected.

c Click the *Line Style* option box arrow in the Borders group.

d At the drop-down list, click the first double line style option (two lines of equal weight).

e Click the Borders button arrow in the Borders group.

f Click *Outside Borders* at the drop-down gallery.

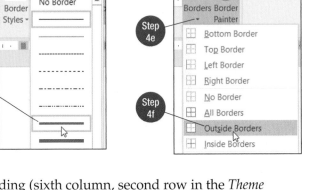

5 Apply Orange, Accent 2, Lighter 80% shading (sixth column, second row in the *Theme Colors* section) to the first row of the table.

6 Apply the single, 2¼-point line in Orange, Accent 2, Darker 50% (sixth column, last row in the *Theme Colors* section) to the inside vertical borders of rows 2 through 6 by completing the following steps:

a Select rows 2 through 6.

b Click the Table Tools Design tab, if it is not already selected.

c Click the *Line Style* option box arrow in the Borders group and then click the solid, single line style option at the drop-down list (first option under *No Border*).

d Click the *Line Weight* option box arrow and then click *2¼ pt* at the drop-down list.

e Click the Pen Color button arrow and then click *Orange, Accent 2, Darker 50%* (sixth column, last row in the *Theme Colors* section).

f Click the Borders button arrow and then click *Inside Vertical Border* at the drop-down gallery.

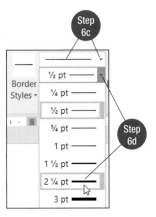

7 Apply a double wavy line in Dark Blue to the bottom border of row 6 by completing the following steps:

a Select row 6.

b Click the *Line Style* option box arrow in the Borders group and then click the double wavy line option (19th option under *No Border*).

c Click the Pen Color button arrow and then click *Dark Blue* in the *Standard Colors* section.

d Click the Borders button arrow and then click *Bottom Border* at the drop-down gallery.

steps continue

When planning a file and folder naming system, consider the following guidelines to ensure availability, "findability," and accessibility of files:

- Avoid long names. Err on the side of brevity, but still make sure files are easily identifiable.

- Use underscores instead of spaces. In the Web environment, a space is sometimes translated to be read as %20, which can cause confusion. A hyphen (-) may also be used to separate words, or the first letter of each word may be capitalized. (As examples, a document that contains Mr. Smith's original will could have as part of its name *Smith_will_original*, *Smith-will-original*, or *SmithWillOriginal*.)

- When file names require dates, format them consistently. It is helpful to base them on a recognized standard such as *YYYYMMDD* or *YYYY_MM_DD*.

- If you utilize versions of documents, specify the version of the file using the letter *v* and a two-digit number (v01, v02, etc.).

- Most importantly, be consistent! Choose a style for each of the elements mentioned above and stick with it. This will make file and folder management much easier for everyone involved.

In the next activity, you will develop a proposal for a file naming system and folder structure. All files are stored on the firm's local area network. Currently, folders for each of the attorneys, for you, and for the intern are saved on the hard drive of the firm's server. However, there is no current standard for storing files within these folders. Your mission is to create a folder structure and determine a system for naming these folders and the files they contain.

Before designing your folder structure and file naming system, be sure to review the company background, incoming documents (such as email attachments), and documents you will be creating. (Document activities are described in Sessions 103, 104, and 105.) Once you have designed your system, complete the following document activity.

You will create a proposal for your system in a memo business report to everyone in the office. Because you will be using the Online Lab to complete the document activities for this project, the Online Lab will still name the files. If your instructor provides different instructions for managing the files created for this project, follow those instructions rather than those in the textbook.

Document 101.2

File Names and Folder Structure

Read all instructions below before starting this document activity.

1 Navigate to the Document 101.2 launch page in the Online Lab and then click the Launch Activity button to open **Doc101.02** in the activity window.

2 Address the memo business report to Gabrielle Lee, use your name as the person sending the memo report, and key January 6, 2020 as the current date.

3 In the body of the memo report, document the details of the file naming system and folder structure you developed. The memo report should be clearly written so that anyone reviewing your report will know how and where to name and save any documents they create.

   a In the first paragraph, explain why you have developed the system.

   b In the middle paragraphs, include the details of your system.

   c In the concluding paragraph, request feedback by Wednesday, January 15. *Note: Enter that due date in the calendar created in the Document 101.1 activity.*

   d At the bottom of the memo, key the file name you would have used for the document if you had saved it using the file naming system described in the memo. *Note: The actual file name will remain **Doc101.02** so that the Online Lab recognizes the file.*

4 Proofread the document and correct any errors.

5 Save the document.

6 Click the Submit button to upload the document for instructor review.

Formatting Table Borders

Word also provides tools that allow you to change the way the borders of cells in a table display. Select the cells in the table to which you want to apply a border design and then click the *Line Style* option box arrow in the Borders group on the Table Tools Design tab. Select the line style from the drop-down list (see Figure 73.6) to apply it. Similarly, choose the line weight by clicking an option from the *Line Weight* option drop-down list, and choose the color of the line by clicking the Pen Color button arrow and clicking a color at the drop-down list.

To apply the selected line style, weight, and color, choose a border option. Click the Borders button arrow in the Borders group to display a gallery of border format options (see Figure 73.7) to apply to the selected cells in a table. Select the border style from the drop-down gallery to apply it to the selected cells.

Figure 73.6 *Line Style* Option Drop-Down List

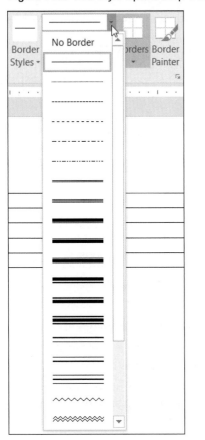

Figure 73.7 Borders Button Drop-Down Gallery

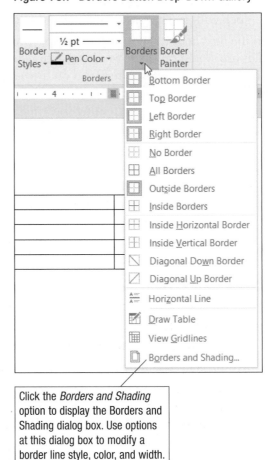

Click the *Borders and Shading* option to display the Borders and Shading dialog box. Use options at this dialog box to modify a border line style, color, and width.

Session 102 — Legal Office Project: Determining Priorities and Planning Work

Getting Started

Exercise 102.1
Unless you are continuing immediately after completing Session 101, spend at least two to three minutes warming up before completing the document activities in this session. See Session 101 for suggested warm-up text.

Working in the Legal Office

In this session of the project, you will review all of the required items for the project (see Sessions 103 through 105) to assess what needs to be done and in what time frame. You will determine what is involved with each task and assign priority levels. In order to complete tasks by their deadlines, you will need to estimate the amount of time needed for each activity and decide whether you or Gabrielle, your part-time intern, will complete the task. *Note: Although you have an assistant in this scenario and may hypothetically assign work to her, you will be the one to complete all of the tasks.*

Document 102.1
To-Do List

Read all instructions below before starting this document activity.

1. Navigate to the Document 102.1 launch page in the Online Lab and then click the Launch Activity button to open **Doc102.01** in the activity window.

2. Review the tasks to complete this project (Sessions 103 through 105) and then key the tasks into the table provided in **Doc102.01** so that each task appears on a separate line.

3. Assign a priority level to each task according to the following guidelines:
   - Priority 1: activities to be completed by the end of the day today, January 6
   - Priority 2: activities to be completed by the end of the day tomorrow, Tuesday, January 7
   - Priority 3: activities that can wait until the end of the week or later

4. After all document activities have been added to the table, sort the table by priority number so that the first-priority items appear at the top of the table. If the table displays on two or more pages, repeat the header row of the table.

5. In the footer, key the file name you would assign to the document based on the file naming system you developed. *Note: The actual file name will be **Doc102.01** so that the Online Lab recognizes the file.*

6. Proofread the document and correct any errors.

7. Save the document.

8. Print a copy for your reference as you work through the activities.

9. Click the Submit button to upload the document for instructor review.

Document
73.2

Applying Shading to a Table

Read all instructions below before starting this document activity.

1 Navigate to the Document 73.2 launch page in the Online Lab and then click the Launch Activity button to open **Doc073.02** in the activity window.

2 Key THE BIG FIVE AFRICAN WILD ANIMALS and then press Enter.

3 Create the table shown in Figure 73.5.

4 Apply orange shading to the first row of the table by completing the following steps:

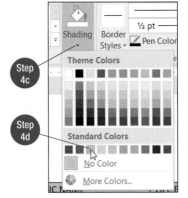

a Position the mouse pointer over the left edge of any cell in the first row until the mouse pointer displays as a black arrow pointing up and to the right and then double-click the left mouse button to select the row.

b Click the Table Tools Design tab, if it is not already selected.

c Click the Shading button arrow in the Table Styles group.

d Click *Orange* in the *Standard Colors* section.

5 Select cells A2 through A6, click the Shading button arrow, and then click the *Blue, Accent 1, Lighter 80%* shading option (fifth column, second row in the *Theme Colors* section).

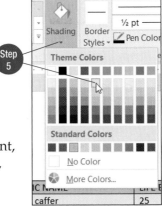

6 Center the heading above the table.

7 Proofread the table and correct any errors.

8 Save the document.

9 Click the Check button to upload the document for checking.

10 If errors are reported by the Online Lab, view the results document, correct the errors in the submitted document, save the document, and then click the Check Again button.

Figure 73.5 Table Data for Document 73.2

COMMON NAME	SCIENTIFIC NAME	LIFE EXPECTANCY (IN YEARS)
African Buffalo	Syncerus caffer	25
African Elephant	Loxodonta africana	60
Leopard	Panthera pardus	20
Lion	Panthera leo	20
White Rhinoceros	Ceratotherium simum	45

Success Tip

While table style names stay consistent, the location of a particular style within the Table Styles drop-down gallery may change depending on the monitor's resolution setting.

Document Email
102.2
Read all instructions below before starting this document activity.

1 Navigate to the Document 102.2 launch page in the Online Lab and then click the Launch Activity button to open **Doc102.02** in the activity window.

2 Compose an email to your part-time intern, Gabrielle Lee, as a cover note for the to-do list you created in the previous document activity, which would be sent as an attachment to the email. In the email, ask Gabrielle to review the attachment and to begin the activities assigned to her. Ask her to inform you at the end of the day what she has accomplished. Remember to use professional language and proper spelling, capitalization, and grammar in your message. *Note: In this activity, and the remaining email activities in this unit, make sure to press the Enter key twice to begin a new paragraph and do not press the Tab key while typing the message body.*

3 Proofread the document and correct any errors.

4 Save the document.

5 Click the Submit button to upload the document for instructor review.

Figure 73.2 Table Data for Document 73.1

ENTREES	CHOICE NO. 1	CHOICE NO. 2	CHOICE NO. 3	PAGES
PASTA	Quick Pasta Salad	Macaroni Salad	Spaghetti Salad	1-4
VEGETARIAN	Sweet Potato Casserole	Spinach Casserole	Carrot Salad	5-7
SEAFOOD	Oven Fried Fish	Crab Gumbo	Seafood Chowder	8-11
OUTDOOR GRILLING	Potatoes on the Grill	Teriyaki Steak	Maple Glazed Ham	12-15
CROCKPOT	Round Steak	Apple Butter	Cider Beef Stew	16-20

Applying Shading

In addition to applying styles, you can create your own shading for use in a table. To apply shading, select the cells in the table you want to shade and then click the Shading button arrow in the Table Styles group on the Table Tools Design tab to display a palette of available color options (see Figure 73.3). The color options are separated into a *Theme Colors* section and a *Standard Colors* section. Hover the mouse pointer over a color to see its name and a live preview of the color applied to the cells. Click a color to apply it to the currently selected cells in the table.

If you find that the choices in the color palette are too limited, click the *More Colors* option at the Shading button drop-down gallery to display the Colors dialog box (see Figure 73.4). The Colors dialog box contains a Standard tab and a Custom tab. With the Standard tab selected, click a color and then click OK to apply it. With the Custom tab selected, click an area of the *Colors* square and then adjust the color by dragging the slider button on the vertical slider bar or by changing the number values in the *Red*, *Green*, and *Blue* measurement boxes. Click OK to apply the color, or click Cancel to close the dialog box. Once you apply a color from the Colors dialog box, the color option will appear in the *Recent Colors* section of the Shading button drop-down gallery.

Once you apply a shade to a table, the paint bucket image on the Shading button will indicate that color choice. Click the (paint bucket section of the) Shading button to apply the same color to other selected cells in the table. To change the color of the paint bucket, click the Shading button arrow to display the drop-down gallery and then click a different color option.

Figure 73.3 Shading Button Color Palette

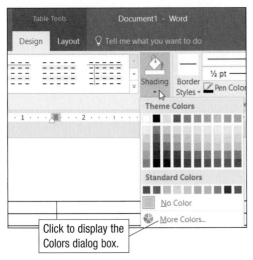

Click to display the Colors dialog box.

Figure 73.4 Colors Dialog Box

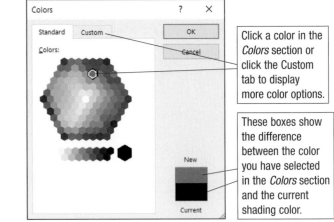

Click a color in the *Colors* section or click the Custom tab to display more color options.

These boxes show the difference between the color you have selected in the *Colors* section and the current shading color.

Session

103

Legal Office Project: Production Documents Part I

Getting Started

Exercise 103.1 Unless you are continuing immediately after completing Session 102, spend at least two to three minutes warming up before completing the document activities in this session. See Session 101 for suggested warm-up text.

Working in the Legal Office

Now that you have completed Sessions 101 and 102, you are ready to complete the activities for the project. These activities should be completed in the order specified in the to-do list you created in Session 102, regardless of the order in which they appear in this session. Although speed is important, accuracy and proper formatting are equally, if not more, critical.

Document 103.1 Terms Table

Read all instructions below before starting this document activity.

1 Navigate to the Document 103.1 launch page in the Online Lab and then click the Launch Activity button to open **Doc103.01** in the activity window.

2 Consider the following scenario and instructions:

> Attorney Beem has forwarded to you a copy of the email message shown in Figure 103.1 and has asked you to respond to the request. He notes that he would also be willing to speak to the class sometime in February, if they are interested.

3 The table shown in **Doc103.01** contains the terms and definitions you keyed in Sessions 96, 97, and 99. Select the 20 terms and definitions that you think will be most helpful to students preparing to work in a legal office. Edit the file so that only these 20 terms are included.

4 Proofread the document, paying special attention to the format, and correct any errors.

5 Save the document.

6 Click the Submit button to upload the document for instructor review.

Figure 73.1 Table Tools Design Tab

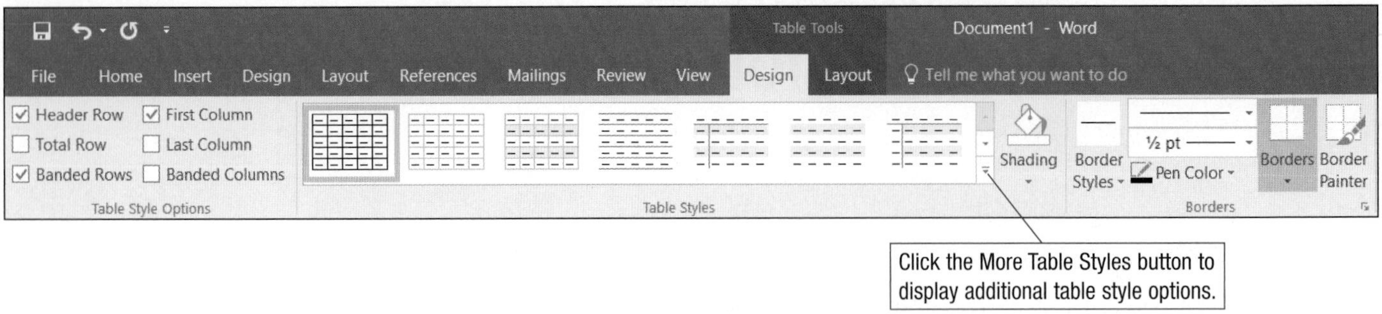

Click the More Table Styles button to display additional table style options.

Using the Table Tools Design Tab

Whereas Session 72 focused on features available on the Table Tools Layout tab, this session will focus on what you can do with the tools on the Table Tools Design tab. This tab, shown in Figure 73.1, contains three groups: the Table Style Options group, the Table Styles group, and the Borders group. In this session, you will work with the tools in the Table Styles and Borders groups.

Using Table Styles

The Table Styles group provides 105 table style options. Click the More Table Styles button to display the Table Styles drop-down gallery. When you hover the mouse pointer over a style option, a ScreenTip with the style name will appear and the active table in your document will display with that style. The ability to preview how the table will look when a particular style is applied to it (called *live preview*) will help you choose the style that is most suitable for your table. Click a style to apply it to the table.

Document 73.1

Applying a Table Style

Read all instructions below before starting this document activity.

1 Navigate to the Document 73.1 launch page in the Online Lab and then click the Launch Activity button to open **Doc073.01** in the activity window.

2 Key GREAT RECIPES COOKBOOK and then press Enter.

3 Create a table that contains five columns and six rows and then key the text in the cells as shown in Figure 73.2.

4 Apply an orange grid table style to the table by completing the following steps:

   a Click the Table Tools Design tab.

   b Click the More Table Styles button in the Table Styles group.

   c Click the *Grid Table 4 - Accent 2* option (third column, fourth row in the *Grid Tables* section).

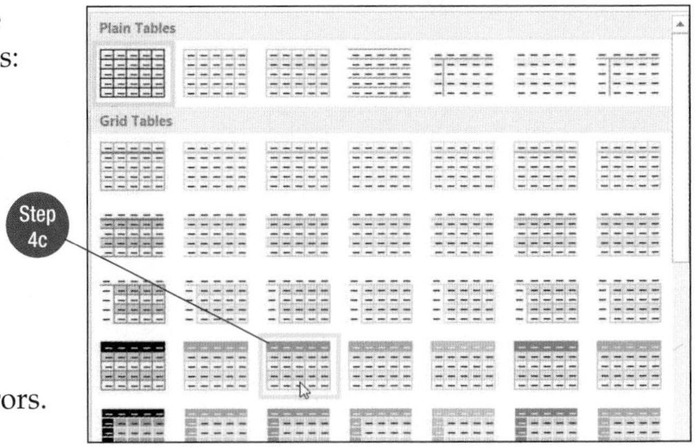

Step 4c

5 Center the heading above the table.

6 Proofread the table and correct any errors.

7 Save the document.

8 Click the Check button to upload the document for checking.

9 If errors are reported by the Online Lab, view the results document, correct the errors in the submitted document, save the document, and then click the Check Again button.

Figure 103.1 Email Message for Document 103.1

| To... | cbeem@ppi-edu.net |
| Subject: | Request for Legal Terminology |

Attorney Beem,

Would you please send me a list of 20 legal terms and definitions that you most often use in your everyday legal activities?

I teach legal transcription at Blackhawk Technical College, and I would like to use these legal words in the students' transcription exercises. Keying these words and definitions would help prepare my students for work in a legal office. Your list will be combined with terms I receive from other attorneys. Hopefully, I can compile approximately 200 of the most frequently used legal terms and their definitions.

Your support is really appreciated, and the students will certainly benefit from learning current legal terminology.

Please send the terms and definitions to me at the address below by Friday, January 10.

Jasmine Raymond, Instructor
Legal Transcription Program
Blackhawk Technical College
PO Box 6004
Janesville, WI 53547-6004
jraymond@ppi-edu.net

Document **Email Response**

103.2 Read all instructions below before starting this document activity.

1 Navigate to the Document 103.2 launch page in the Online Lab and then click the Launch Activity button to open **Doc103.02** in the activity window.

2 Using the email template provided, compose a message to Ms. Raymond. Indicate that Attorney Beem asked you to respond to her request, express your appreciation for being able to help the instructor and her students, and reference the table, which you will be attaching. Encourage further communication and remember to include Attorney Beem's offer to address the class.

steps continue

Complete one 5-minute timing on the timing text below.

5-Minute Timing

Timing
73.3

Apples are one of the most interesting and complex foods that are available to our diet. A crunchy apple can taste very tart, or it can taste sweet and smooth. The colors of apples can vary from bright red to yellow to green. The odor of a sweet-smelling apple will entice even the most finicky of eaters to try this sweet fruit.

Apples are used in many ways. After an apple has been washed thoroughly, you can then simply eat it. Eating an apple provides you with a quick and easy snack. An apple has a minimum fat content and contains a small amount of calories. As a healthy food in your diet, an apple will provide fiber for digestion.

You can cook apples in a variety of ways. Perhaps the most basic way of cooking an apple is to bake it. Baked apples can be topped with brown sugar, raisins, nuts, cream topping, or even exotic sauces. You can eat a baked apple warm from the oven or cold from the refrigerator. For those who want a more complicated dessert, apple tarts and crunchy apple casseroles can be prepared. You can use a tasty variety to make a jam or jelly to spread on bread. Other methods of using apples range from simple apple juice to applesauce.

Apples can be fun. At Halloween, children of all ages play the age-old game of bobbing for apples. The apples are placed in a very large container of water. The object of the game is to see who can grab an apple just using the mouth, no hands allowed. The pioneer children used to play with dolls made out of dried apples. A few seeds for the facial features and some corn husks for the clothes made the lowly apple into a very charming play toy.

Apples are a very healthy food. In comparison to other foods, the food content of an apple makes it an inexpensive dietary addition. All of us should make an effort to include apples in our everyday diet.

⚕ Ergonomic Tip

Boost your energy and lower stress by walking or exercising during your lunch break.

3 At the bottom of the email, for this and all future external email correspondence, include the following (see Table 101.1 on page 407):

    your name

    your title (Legal Administrative Assistant)

    company name

    company phone number

4 Proofread the document and correct any errors.

5 Save the document.

6 Click the Submit button to upload the document for instructor review.

Document 103.3 **Living Will for Dalal A. Kamdar**

Read all instructions below before starting this document activity.

1 Navigate to the Document 103.3 launch page in the Online Lab and then click the Launch Activity button to open **Doc103.03** in the activity window.

2 **Doc103.03** contains the standard Living Will instrument (legal document). If necessary, review Session 99 for details about preparing a Living Will. Use the information in the phone message from Attorney Southworth shown in Figure 103.2 to complete a Living Will for Mrs. Kamdar. (You will create a Living Will for her husband in the next document activity.) Remember to enter this appointment on Attorney Southworth's calendar (created in Session 101). *Note: For the signature line on page 2, insert a left tab at the 1-inch mark on the horizontal ruler before keying Dalal A. Kamdar's name underneath the signature line.*

3 Proofread the document and correct any errors.

4 Save the document.

5 Click the Check button to upload the document for checking.

6 If errors are reported by the Online Lab, view the results document, correct the errors in the submitted document, save the document, and then click the Check Again button.

Figure 103.2 Voicemail Message for Document 103.3, Document 103.4, and Document 103.5

Monday, January 6, 9:00 a.m.

This is Kayla Southworth. My client, Mrs. Dalal Kamdar called this morning requesting that Living Wills be created. Neither she nor her husband wish to have feeding tubes or life-sustaining measures. She would like to have the documents ready for signing when they meet with me and confirmed their tentative appointment for Wednesday at 9 a.m. to have their Last Will and Testaments executed.

Dalal A. Kamdar's date of birth is June 17, 1993; her husband (Brent M. Kamdar) was born on August 23, 1989. Their home address is 483 N. Second Street, Fort Atkinson, WI 53583-6471. They each will be providing a copy to Fort Memorial Hospital and to me.

Session 73 — Formatting the Design of Tables

Session Objectives

- Apply table styles
- Apply shading to tables
- Format table borders
- Draw a table
- Create a calendar
- Efficiently produce documents in mailable form

Getting Started

Exercise 73.1 If you are continuing immediately from Session 72, you may skip the Exercise 73.1 warm-up drill. However, if you exited the Online Lab at the end of Session 72, warm up by completing Exercise 73.1.

Exercise 73.2 Begin your session work by completing Exercise 73.2, a timed short drill, in the Online Lab.

Assessing Your Speed and Accuracy

Complete Timings 73.1 through 73.3 in the Online Lab. At the end of each timing, the Online Lab will display your WPM rate and any errors. Results will be saved in your Timings Performance report. If you have been surpassing the speed and accuracy goals identified in the Online Lab, set slightly more challenging personal goals and strive to exceed them.

Complete two 1-minute timings on the timing text below. If you meet or exceed both speed and accuracy goals for Timing 73.1, push for greater speed on Timing 73.2.

1-Minute Timings

Timings 73.1–73.2 Many fine artists and illustrators played a key role in recording the history and growth of our country. Many of the early illustrations and drawings were very good, while others were distorted. Quite like the writers, some artists viewed the land through different eyes, and thus the final products were varied. Some efforts of those very fine and skilled writers and artists have become a quite important and treasured part of our history. Indeed, we owe a debt of gratitude and respect to this unheralded and forgotten group of early settlers.

Document
103.4

Living Will for Brent M. Kamdar

Read all instructions below before starting this document activity.

1 Navigate to the Document 103.4 launch page in the Online Lab and then click the Launch Activity button to open **Doc103.04** in the activity window.

2 **Doc103.04** contains the standard Living Will instrument. Use the information from the voicemail message shown in Figure 103.2 to complete a Living Will for Mr. Kamdar. *Note: For the signature line on page 2, insert a left tab at the 1-inch mark on the horizontal ruler before keying Brent M. Kamdar's name.*

3 Proofread the document and correct any errors.

4 Save the document.

5 Click the Check button to upload the document for checking.

6 If errors are reported by the Online Lab, view the results document, correct the errors in the submitted document, save the document, and then click the Check Again button.

Document
103.5

Email Message Confirming Kamdar Appointment

Read all instructions below before starting this document activity.

1 Navigate to the Document 103.5 launch page in the Online Lab and then click the Launch Activity button to open **Doc103.05** in the activity window.

2 Compose an email message to Attorney Southworth about the Kamdars' appointment to sign their Wills. Tell her that you have also prepared Living Wills based on the information in the voicemail message you received from her.

3 Proofread the document and correct any errors.

4 Save the document.

5 Click the Submit button to upload the document for instructor review.

3   Change the alignment of the text in the second column of the table so that the text is centered vertically and horizontally in the cells by completing the following steps:

   a   Select the *State* column of the table.

   b   Click the Align Center button in the Alignment group.

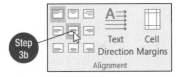

4   Change the alignment of the text in the third and fourth columns of the table so that the text is centered vertically and aligned to the right side of the cells by completing the following steps:

   a   Select the third and fourth columns of the table. *Hint: Select the third column, press and hold down the Shift key, select the fourth column, and then release the Shift key.*

   b   Click the Align Center Right button in the Alignment group.

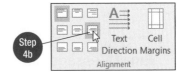

5   Save the document.

6   Click the Check button to upload the document for checking.

7   If errors are reported by the Online Lab, view the results document, correct the errors in the submitted document, save the document, and then click the Check Again button.

Reinforcing Writing Skills

At work, your supervisor may ask you to create a table to display a collection of information. While he or she may not specify exactly how to do this, you will most likely be expected to create and format the table quickly. You will need to know how to make efficient and effective layout and formatting decisions. Practice designing a table by completing the following document activity.

Document 72.7   **Designing a Golf Club Data Table**

Read all instructions below before starting this document activity.

1   Navigate to the Document 72.7 launch page in the Online Lab and then click the Launch Activity button to open **Doc072.07** in the activity window.

2   Create a table clearly listing the number and percentage of golf-club brands used by participants in the Senior PGA golf tour. Include the brand names, corresponding number of clubs, and percentages for each brand. The data to use is as follows: Titleist, 61 and 38.1%; Callaway, 47 and 29.3%; TaylorMade, 33 and 20.8%; Odyssey, 15 and 9.3%; and Cleveland, 4 and 2.5%.

3   Format the table using skills learned in this or previous sessions.

4   Proofread and correct any errors in the table.

5   Save the document.

6   Click the Submit button to upload the document for instructor review.

Ending the Session

The Online Lab automatically saved the work you completed for this session. You may continue with the next session or exit the Online Lab and continue later.

Session 104

Legal Office Project: Production Documents Part II

Getting Started

Exercise 104.1 Unless you are continuing immediately after completing Session 103, spend at least two to three minutes warming up before completing the document activities in this session. See Session 101 for suggested warm-up text.

Working in the Legal Office

These are additional activities for the project. Remember, they are to be completed in the order specified in the to-do list you created in Session 102, regardless of the order they appear in this session.

Document 104.1 **Email Message Regarding Travel Arrangements**

Read all instructions below before starting this document activity.

1   Use the Internet to research the travel arrangements requested in the email message shown in Figure 104.1.

2   Navigate to the Document 104.1 launch page in the Online Lab and then click the Launch Activity button to open **Doc104.01** in the activity window.

3   Compose an email to Attorney Beem with the requested information: two options for roundtrip flights and costs, hotel amenities and costs, and car rental costs. Present the information in an easy-to-read format.

4   Proofread the email and correct any errors.

5   Save the document.

6   Click the Submit button to upload the document for instructor review.

Figure 104.1 Email for Document 104.1

To...	legaladmin@ppi-edu.net
Subject:	Travel plans

I have decided to attend that legal technology conference in Phoenix, Arizona, on January 25 and 26. My wife, Alison, will accompany me, and we are planning to extend the trip to enjoy a few days' vacation in the sun. We would like to leave from Chicago (O'Hare Airport) on January 22, after 6 p.m. and return anytime on January 31. We prefer to fly Delta Airlines and want the most economical airfare available, although I would like two options from which to choose.

continues

Document **Adjusting and Distributing Column Widths in a Table**

72.5 Read all instructions below before starting this document activity.

1 Navigate to the Document 72.5 launch page in the Online Lab and then click the Launch Activity button to open **Doc072.05** in the activity window.

2 AutoFit the last column of the table by positioning the mouse pointer over the last column's right border, until it displays as a left-and-right-pointing arrow with a double vertical line in the middle, and then double-clicking the left mouse button.

3 Distribute the widths of the *Last Name* and *First Name* columns evenly by completing the following steps:

a Select the *Last Name* and *First Name* columns. ***Hint: Select the*** **Last Name** ***column, press and hold down the Shift key, select the*** **First Name** ***column, and then release the Shift key.***

b Click the Table Tools Layout tab.

c Click the Distribute Columns button in the Cell Size group.

4 Save the document.

5 Click the Check button to upload the document for checking.

6 If errors are reported by the Online Lab, view the results document, correct the errors in the submitted document, save the document, and then click the Check Again button.

Changing Cell Alignment

By default, text in a table cell aligns to the top left corner of the cell. The default alignment can be changed by selecting the cell or cells and then clicking the appropriate alignment button in the Alignment group on the Table Tools Layout tab (see Figure 72.4). The nine alignment button options include Align Top Left, Align Top Center, Align Top Right, Align Center Left, Align Center, Align Center Right, Align Bottom Left, Align Bottom Center, and Align Bottom Right. When you hover the mouse pointer over the buttons in the Alignment group, a ScreenTip with the button name and a description of the alignment style that button will apply displays.

Figure 72.4 Alignment Group on the Table Tools Layout Tab

To change the alignment of data in a cell, position the insertion point in the cell and click the desired alignment button in the Alignment group on the Table Tools Layout tab. To change the alignment of data in a column or in a row, select the column or row and then click the alignment button.

Document **Creating a Table and Changing Data Alignment**

72.6 Read all instructions below before starting this document activity.

1 Navigate to the Document 72.6 launch page in the Online Lab and then click the Launch Activity button to open **Doc072.06** in the activity window.

2 Change the alignment of the text in the first column of the table so that the text is centered vertically and aligned to the left side of the cells by completing the following steps:

a Select the *City* column of the table.

b Click the Table Tools Layout tab.

c Click the Align Center Left button in the Alignment group.

steps continue

Figure 104.1 Email for Document 104.1—continued

> The conference will be held at the Phoenix Airport Marriott. Please research hotel amenities and room rates for me.
>
> We want to rent a car for the entire duration of our stay. I prefer Hertz and would like a midsize car. Of course, I'd like the best rates available. Please check to see if airline miles are awarded for the hotel and car rental.
>
> I'd appreciate having this information by late afternoon on Tuesday. Thanks!
>
> C. Beem

Document 104.2

Summons

Read all instructions below before starting this document activity.

1 Navigate to the Document 104.2 launch page in the Online Lab and then click the Launch Activity button to open **Doc104.02** in the activity window. *Note: Plan your time so that you are able to complete the Document 104.2 and 104.3 activities in one work session on the same computer. Otherwise, the AutoText entry you create in the Document 104.2 activity may not be available for placement in the Document 104.3 activity.*

2 Using the standard document provided, complete the Summons requested in the voicemail message shown in Figure 104.2 using the details provided in the handwritten message in Figure 104.3. Replace the placeholder information with the details related to this case. If necessary, review Session 96 for information on preparing a summons and saving a caption as a building block in the AutoText gallery.

3 Replace the two instances of *A-Name* in the document with *Charles L. Beem*. Also, key a space followed by his SBN number, 1029758, under his signature line on the last page.

4 Proofread the document and correct any errors.

5 Save the document.

6 Because you will need this caption (with minor edits) for the Petition with Minor Children to be created in Document 104.3, select the caption, including the first nonprinting paragraph mark below the bottom line, and save it to the AutoText gallery. *Hint: Click the Insert tab, click the Quick Parts button, point to AutoText, and then click Save Selection to AutoText Gallery.* Use the following settings for the caption:

> *Name:* Caption   *Category: Legal*
>
> *Gallery: AutoText*   *Save in: Normal*
>
> *Options: Insert content in its own paragraph*

Note: Leave the **Description** *field blank. If the computer you are using already has a building block named* **Caption** *saved, you will be asked if you want to redefine the building block entry. If so, click Yes.*

7 Click the Check button to upload the document for checking.

8 If errors are reported by the Online Lab, view the results document, correct the errors in the submitted document, save the document, and then click the Check Again button.

Changing Column Width and Row Height

When you create a table using the Table button in the Tables group on the Insert tab, all columns are of equal width and all rows are of equal height. The Cell Size group on the Table Tools Layout tab provides several tools for adjusting the height or width of a row or column in a table (see Figure 72.3).

After keying text into a table, position the insertion point in one of the cells in the table, click the AutoFit button in the Cell Size group, and then click *AutoFit Contents* at the drop-down list. This action will automatically adjust the column widths based on the size of the contents of each column. You can also use AutoFit to adjust the width of an individual column by moving the mouse pointer over the right border of a column until it turns into a left-and-right-pointing arrow with a double vertical line in the middle (◄╫►) and then double-clicking the left mouse button.

Figure 72.3 Cell Size Group on the Table Tools Layout Tab

To size the table to fill the space or window available on the page, click the AutoFit button and then click *AutoFit Window* at the drop-down list. If you want to distribute space evenly between more than one row or one column, select the rows or columns and then click either the Distribute Rows button or the Distribute Columns button in the Cell Size group.

To set a specific row height or column width, use the *Table Row Height* and *Table Column Width* measurement boxes in the Cell Size group on the Table Tools Layout tab. With the insertion point in the desired row or column, adjust the number in the measurement box by clicking the up or down arrows or by selecting the number and then keying the measurement.

Practice using these features by following the steps outlined for Documents 72.4 and 72.5.

Document 72.4 Using AutoFit and Setting Row Height in a Table

Read all instructions below before starting this document activity.

1. Navigate to the Document 72.4 launch page in the Online Lab and then click the Launch Activity button to open **Doc072.04** in the activity window.

2. AutoFit the table by completing the following steps:
   a. With the insertion point positioned in the table, click the Table Tools Layout tab.
   b. Click the AutoFit button in the Cell Size group.
   c. Click *AutoFit Contents* at the drop-down list.

3. Change the height of the first row in the table to 0.4 inch using the *Table Row Height* measurement box in the Cell Size group.

4. Save the document.

5. Click the Check button to upload the document for checking.

6. If errors are reported by the Online Lab, view the results document, correct the errors in the submitted document, save the document, and then click the Check Again button.

Figure 104.2 Voicemail Message for Document 104.2 and Document 104.3

Monday, December 30, 3:00 p.m.

    Hi. This is Chuck. I just met with Megan Gatten to begin divorce proceedings against her husband, Luke. I told Mrs. Gatten that the documents would be ready by 4 p.m. Monday afternoon. She plans to stop in after work to sign them. My handwritten notes include the necessary information for you to generate a Summons and a Petition for Divorce using your standard documents. I left the notes in your in-basket.

Figure 104.3 Handwritten Message for Document 104.2 and Document 104.3

FROM THE DESK OF ATTORNEY CHARLES L. BEEM

DATE _12/30/19_   TIME _2:30 p.m._

Petitioner:
MEGAN R. GATTEN
6471 SCHUMACHER ROAD
BELOIT, ROCK COUNTY, WISCONSIN 53511
Date of Birth: January 13, 1979
Employer: Hormel Foods

Respondent:
LUKE J. GATTEN
5334 EASY STREET, #14
BELOIT, ROCK COUNTY, WISCONSIN 53511
Date of Birth: June 26, 1981
Employer: Kerry, Inc.

Date and Place of Marriage: March 1, 2009, Sauk City, Wisconsin
Minor Child: Andrew Mark Gatten, born January 29, 2013

Document 104.3   Petition with Minor Children

Read all instructions below before starting this document activity.

1 Navigate to the Document 104.3 launch page in the Online Lab and then click the Launch Activity button to open **Doc104.03** in the activity window.

2 Using the standard document provided, complete the Petition with Minor Children requested. Review Session 97, if necessary, for information on formatting a petition with minor children. Assuming you have access to the AutoText entry created and saved during the Document 104.2 activity, delete the existing caption and then insert the AutoText caption you created. *Hint: Update the **SUMMONS** title in the inserted AutoText caption.* Check that there are no extra hard returns before the caption. After the bottom line of the caption,

steps continue

Cutting, Copying, and Pasting Row, Column, and Cell Contents

After selecting a row or column, it is possible to cut or copy and then paste selected content using keyboard shortcuts. For example, you can move or copy a row to another position in a table by selecting it, cutting it using the keyboard shortcut Ctrl + X (or copying it using the keyboard shortcut Ctrl + C), selecting the row directly below where you want the row to be pasted, and then pressing Ctrl + V. The row you paste will appear above the selected row. Similarly, after selecting and cutting or copying a column in a table, select the column directly to the right of where you want the column to be pasted and then press Ctrl + V. The cut or copied column will appear to the left of the selected column.

Selecting a cell in a table will select the cell contents, not the cell itself. You can select and cut the contents of one cell and then paste them into another cell. When you cut the contents of a cell and then paste them into another cell, the source cell will be empty and the pasted contents will display in the destination cell.

Document 72.3

Cutting and Pasting in a Table

Read all instructions below before starting this document activity.

1 Navigate to the Document 72.3 launch page in the Online Lab and then click the Launch Activity button to open **Doc072.03** in the activity window.

2 Cut the *Insert Below* row and then paste it between the *Insert Above* row and the *Insert Left* row by completing the following steps:

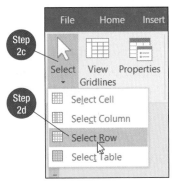

   a Click in a cell in the *Insert Below* row.

   b Click the Table Tools Layout tab.

   c Click the Select button in the Table group.

   d Click *Select Row* at the drop-down list.

   e Press Ctrl + X.

   f Click in a cell in the *Insert Left* row.

   g Click the Select button in the Table group.

   h Click *Select Row* at the drop-down list.

   i Press Ctrl + V.

3 Cut the *Group* column and paste it to the left of the *Button* column by completing the following steps:

   a Select the *Group* column.

   b Press Ctrl + X.

   c Select the *Button* column.

   d Press Ctrl + V.

4 Select the contents of the *Distribute Rows* row's *Action* cell (cell C16), press Ctrl + C to copy the contents, and then paste them into the *Action* cell in the *Distribute Columns* row (cell C17).

5 Edit the contents of the *Distribute Rows* row's *Action* cell (cell C16) so that it reads *Distribute height equally between selected rows*. (Do not key a period at the end of the phrase.)

6 Save the document.

7 Click the Check button to upload the document for checking.

8 If errors are reported by the Online Lab, view the results document, correct the errors in the submitted document, save the document, and then click the Check Again button.

there should be one nonprinting paragraph mark before the text continues. *Note: If you do not have access to the AutoText entry created in Activity 104.2, you will need to open Doc104.02 and complete Step 6 in Activity 104.2 to create the AutoText entry again.*

3   Replace the two instances of *A-Name* in the document with Charles L. Beem. Also, key 1029758 in place of *A-SBN* in the *THIS DOCUMENT DRAFTED BY* section on the last page.

4   Update all placeholder text with the appropriate information provided in Figure 104.3. The following is a list of placeholder text items:

P-Name

P-Address

P-DOB

P-Employer

R-Name

R-Address

R-DOB

R-Employer

Date of Marriage

Marriage City and State

Child Name

Child DOB

A-SBN

Hint: Using the Find feature will help you quickly locate these notations.

5   Proofread the document and correct any errors.

6   Save the document.

7   Click the Check button to upload the document for checking.

8   If errors are reported by the Online Lab, view the results document, correct the errors in the submitted document, save the document, and then click the Check Again button.

Document
104.4

Email Response

Read all instructions below before starting this document activity.

1   Navigate to the Document 104.4 launch page in the Online Lab and then click the Launch Activity button to open **Doc104.4** in the activity window.

2   Consider the following scenario:

Your employer requested that you become a notary public. To do this, you submitted an application to the state and took an oath to faithfully perform the duties of the office. You purchased a notary seal and your commission is currently valid. On Monday, January 6, you receive the email shown in Figure 104.4 from your friend Anne Marie Squire.

3   Compose and key a response using the email document open in the Online Lab. In your response, let Anne Marie know a time that would be good based on your schedule and her deadline.

4   Proofread the document and correct any errors.

5   Save the document.

6   Click the Submit button to upload the document for instructor review.

Selecting Cells, Columns, and Rows

To select a cell, a column, a row, or an entire table, use the Select button in the Table group on the Table Tools Layout tab. If you want to select a row, position the insertion point in any cell in that row, click the Select button in the Table group, and then click *Select Row* at the drop-down list. If you want to select a column in the table, position the insertion point in any cell in that column, click the Select button, and then click *Select Column*. The selections are cumulative, so if you click *Select Column* with a table row already selected, you will end up selecting the entire table.

You can also use the mouse pointer to select columns, cells, and rows in a table. To select a column, position the mouse pointer at the top of the column you want to select until the pointer displays as a black down arrow and then click the left mouse button. Select adjacent columns by pointing to the top of the first column, clicking and holding down the left mouse button, dragging the mouse pointer to the last column, and then releasing the mouse button. To select nonadjacent columns, press and hold down the Ctrl key while selecting the columns.

To select a cell (not just the text in a cell), position the mouse pointer along the left edge of the cell until the mouse pointer displays as a black arrow pointing up and to the right and then click the left mouse button. To select nonadjacent cells, press and hold down the Ctrl key while selecting the cells. Select adjacent cells by positioning the mouse pointer in the first cell to be selected, clicking and holding down the left mouse button, dragging the mouse pointer to the last cell to be selected, and then releasing the mouse button.

To select a row using the mouse pointer, position the mouse pointer along the left edge of any cell in the row until the mouse pointer displays as a black arrow pointing up and to the right and then double-click the left mouse button. Alternatively, position the mouse pointer just outside the left edge of the table (in the selection bar) near the row you want to select. When the mouse pointer displays as a white arrow pointing up and to the right, click the left mouse button once.

Document 72.2

Deleting a Table and Rows and Columns in a Table

Read all instructions below before starting this document activity.

1   Navigate to the Document 72.2 launch page in the Online Lab and then click the Launch Activity button to open **Doc072.02** in the activity window.

2   Delete the bottom table in the document by completing the following steps:

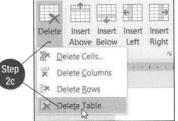

   a   Click in any cell in the bottom table.

   b   Click the Table Tools Layout tab.

   c   Click the Delete button in the Rows & Columns group and then click *Delete Table* at the drop-down list.

3   In the remaining table, delete the rows related to year 2022 by completing the following steps:

   a   Select the last four rows of the table.

   b   Click the Delete button in the Rows & Columns group and then click *Delete Rows* at the drop-down list.

4   Delete the last column of the table by completing the following steps:

   a   Click in any cell in the last column of the table.

   b   Click the Delete button in the Rows & Columns group and then click *Delete Columns* at the drop-down list.

5   Save the document.

6   Click the Check button to upload the document for checking.

7   If errors are reported by the Online Lab, view the results document, correct the errors in the submitted document, save the document, and then click the Check Again button.

Figure 104.4 Email Message for Document 104.4

To... legaladmin@ppi-edu.net

Subject: Need Documents Notarized

Hi!

Jerry and I have some documents for the property we're buying in Arkansas. They need to be notarized and returned to Hot Springs by the end of this week.

Would you be able to notarize our signatures if we stop in after 4:30 this afternoon? If not, when might be a good time?

Thanks in advance.

Anne Marie
anniesquire@ppi-edu.net

Document **Program Announcement**
104.5
Read all instructions below before starting this document activity.

1 Navigate to the Document 104.5 launch page in the Online Lab and then click the Launch Activity button to open **Doc104.05** in the activity window.

2 Consider the following scenario:

You are the program chair of the local chapter of the International Association of Administrative Professionals, and you have arranged a speaker for the next meeting on January 29. The meeting details are outlined in Figure 104.5, but they are not listed in any particular order.

The event should be promoted using an attractive, informative flyer that can be emailed to all members and posted at their places of employment as well as on the chapter's website. The announcement needs to be done this week, and the earlier, the better!

3 Using the file open in the Online Lab, create a one-page announcement for this event. Include some related graphics or imagery. Be sure to answer all the important questions—who, what, where, and when.

4 Proofread the document and correct any errors.

5 Save the document.

6 Click the Submit button to upload the document for instructor review.

4 Insert one column at the right side of the table by completing the following steps:

  a Click in a cell in the second column.

  b Click the Insert Right button in the Rows & Columns group on the Table Tools Layout tab.

  c Key the following in the cells in the new third column: C1: Total; C5: $26,931; C9: $17,938; C13: $13,721.

5 Insert a new column between the second and third columns by completing the following steps:

  a Position the mouse pointer immediately above the border between the second and third columns until the insert column icon displays.

  b Click the insert column icon.

  c Key the following in the cells in the new third column: C1: Sales; C2: $7,396; C3: $7,218; C4: $6,841; C5: $5,476; C6: $5,216; C7: $4,491; C8: $4,538; C9: $3,693; C10: $3,512; C11: $3,275; C12: $3,145; C13: $3,789.

6 Insert a new row at the top of the table and merge the cells by completing the following steps:

  a Click in a cell in the first row.

  b Click the Insert Above button in the Rows & Columns group on the Table Tools Layout tab.

  c With the new row selected, click the Merge Cells button in the Merge group.

  d Key QUARTERLY SALES FOR THREE YEARS in cell A1.

7 Proofread the document by checking it against Figure 72.2.

8 Save the document.

9 Click the Check button to upload the document for checking.

10 If errors are reported by the Online Lab, view the results document, correct the errors in the submitted document, save the document, and then click the Check Again button.

Figure 72.2 Completed Table for Document 72.1

QUARTERLY SALES FOR THREE YEARS			
Year	Quarter	Sales	Total
2018	1	$7,396	
	2	$7,218	
	3	$6,841	
	4	$5,476	$26,931
2019	1	$5,216	
	2	$4,491	
	3	$4,538	
	4	$3,693	$17,938
2020	1	$3,512	
	2	$3,275	
	3	$3,145	
	4	$3,789	$13,721

Figure 104.5 Details for Program Announcement for Document 104.5

Tuesday, January 28
5:30 Networking and Dinner
6:30 Program
7:30 Business Meeting
8:00 Adjournment

Location: Pontiac Convention Center, 2809 Pontiac Drive, Janesville
Program topic: Advancing Your Career through Social Networking: What
LinkedIn, Twitter, Blogs, and Facebook Can Do for You
Presenter: Jamela Rich, IT Specialist, UW-Rock County
Menu:
Vegetarian Lasagna served with Italian Green Beans and Cherry Tomatoes
New York Cheesecake with Fresh Berries
Coffee, tea, or soda

Registration:
$20 Members or $25 Guests

RSVP by 4 p.m. Friday, 1/25
Contact: Billie Westbrook, bwestbrook@ppi-edu.net, 608-555-4346

Figure 72.1 Table Tools Layout Tab

[Screenshot of the Table Tools Layout Tab ribbon in Microsoft Word]

Using the Table Tools Layout Tab

When the insertion point is positioned in a table, the Table Tools Design and Table Tools Layout tabs are available. These contextual tabs include additional formatting features that help you modify your tables. In this session, you will learn to use features in the Table, Rows & Columns, Merge, and Cell Size groups on the Table Tools Layout tab (see Figure 72.1).

Changing the Layout of a Table

Insert rows or columns in a table by clicking the Table Tools Layout tab and then clicking the appropriate button in the Rows & Columns group. Before clicking one of these buttons, make sure that the insertion point is in the correct position in the table.

Another method for inserting a new row is to position the mouse pointer on the left border of the table at the approximate location of the desired new row until the insert row icon displays and then click the icon. A new row is inserted below the insert row icon. To insert a column using this technique, position the mouse pointer above the column border at the approximate location of the new column and then click the insert column icon that displays. (See the image illustrating Step 5a on the next page.) This inserts a new column immediately left of the insert column icon. Click the Delete button in the Rows & Columns group to display options to delete a cell, a column, or a row in a table, or to delete the entire table.

To merge two or more adjacent cells, select the cells and then click the Merge Cells button in the Merge group. To split a cell, position the insertion point in the cell that you want to split and then click the Split Cells button in the Merge group to display the Split Cells dialog box. At this dialog box, indicate how many columns or rows you want the cell to be split into and then click OK.

Document 72.1

Inserting Rows and Columns and Merging Cells in a Table

Read all instructions below before starting this document activity.

1. Navigate to the Document 72.1 launch page in the Online Lab and then click the Launch Activity button to open **Doc072.01** in the activity window.

2. Insert four rows above the second row by completing the following steps:
   a. Click in cell A2, which contains *2019*.
   b. Click the Table Tools Layout tab.
   c. Click the Insert Above button in the Rows & Columns group four times.
   d. In the new cell A2, key *2018* and then key 1, 2, 3, and 4 in cells B2 through B5.
      Hint: Press the Down Arrow key to move down through the cells in column B.

3. Insert four rows at the bottom of the table by completing the following steps:
   a. Click in the last row of the table.
   b. Click the Insert Below button in the Rows & Columns group on the Table Tools Layout tab four times.
   c. In the new cell A10, key *2020* and then key 1, 2, 3, and 4 in cells B10 through B13.

steps continue

Session
105

Legal Office Project:
Production Documents Part III

Getting Started

Exercise 105.1 Unless you are continuing immediately after completing Session 104, spend at least two to three minutes warming up before completing the document activities in this session. See Session 101 for suggested warm-up text.

Working in the Legal Office

This session contains the remaining documents for the project. Remember that they are to be completed in the order specified in the to-do list you created in Session 102, regardless of the order in which they appear in this session. Although speed is important, accuracy and proper formatting are equally, if not more, critical.

Document 105.1 Last Will and Testament with Fields

Read all instructions below before starting this document activity.

1 Navigate to the Document 105.1 launch page in the Online Lab and then click the Launch Activity button. The Online Lab will open **Doc105.01** in the activity window.

2 Key the information from the attorney's email message shown in Figure 105.1 in the appropriate text placeholders. *Note: This document allows keying only in placeholders. If necessary, review Session 99 for information about creating a Last Will and Testament.*

3 Proofread the document keyed into the fields.

4 Unprotect the document by keying the password BeemSouthworth. *Note: The Online Lab will not check a password protected file.*

5 Proofread the document and correct any errors.

6 Save the document.

7 Click the Check button to upload the document for checking.

8 If errors are reported by the Online Lab, view the results document, correct the errors in the submitted document, save the document, and then click the Check Again button.

Figure 105.1 Email Message for Document 105.1

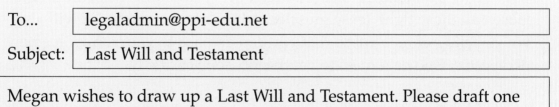

To...	legaladmin@ppi-edu.net
Subject:	Last Will and Testament

Megan wishes to draw up a Last Will and Testament. Please draft one using our standard document. I would like Megan to be able to take it home with her Monday afternoon when she comes in to sign her Summons and Petition documents.

continues

Complete one 5-minute timing on the timing text below.

5-Minute Timing

Timing 72.3

Healthy work habits are easy to acquire when you use a computer. You just need to concentrate on what you are doing and how you are doing it. Habits are built through a constant focus on practicing correctly each time you sit in front of that computer screen; concentration is very important.

Your eyes are one of your most precious gifts. Computer screens can cause eyestrain if you aren't careful. Consult with your doctor often and take his/her advice about how you can cut down on the wear and tear of your eyes. You should always adjust the screen to eye level, about 20 inches from your eyes.

The screen should slant backward at an approximate five-degree angle. If you wear glasses, you may need another prescription to work with computer screens. Poorly fitted glasses will result in eye problems. If you have to tilt your head backwards to look through your glasses, you will also have neck and shoulder cramps. Avoid staring at the screen for long periods of time. Get into the habit of glancing away from your screen frequently. Each hour, take a short break. Get up and move away from the computer; remember, concentrate on relaxing.

Muscle fatigue is also a serious hazard of computer users. When you remain in the same position for a long time, you may experience a backache, sore neck, or tense shoulders. If your elbows rest comfortably at your sides and you don't have to lean forward, your desk is the right height. You should also sit up straight and not slouch, slump, or cross your legs. The important thing to keep in mind is body balance.

Whenever you have to keep adjusting your body and moving around, you are not sitting properly. You can also do mini-stretching exercises at your workstation to ease any muscles that are beginning to feel the strain. You can also remember to take a break every hour and walk around to loosen all those tight, tense muscles. A break from your work will also give you a feeling of renewal so that you can go back to your job with a new perspective and eagerness to get the job done correctly.

 Ergonomic Tip

Well-padded, rounded arm, wrist, and palm rests are excellent supplementary supports to use as you key.

Figure 105.1 Email Message for Document 105.1—continued

Name	Megan Renee Gatten
City	Beloit
Child's Name	Andrew Mark Gatten
Pers Rep Name	Barbara Rittenhouse
Alt Pers Rep Name	Karen King
Guardian Name	Joni Tonelli
Guardian City	South Beloit
Guardian State	Illinois
Alt Guardian Name	Krista Schmitt
Alt Guardian City	Evansville
Alt Guardian State	Wisconsin
C. Beem	

Document 105.2

Follow-up Letters Created Using Mail Merge

Read all instructions below before starting this document activity.

1 Review the content of the email message shown in Figure 105.2.

2 Navigate to the Document 105.2 launch page and then minimize the Online Lab. Start Word 2016 and then complete the following steps:

   a Click the File tab; click *Open* in the left panel, if necessary; and then click the *Browse* option to display the Open dialog box.

   b Click the *Documents* folder in the Navigation pane at the left side of the Open dialog box.

   c Double-click the *Paradigm* folder, double-click the *Keyboarding* folder, and then double-click the *DocumentActivityFiles* folder.

   d Double-click **Doc105.02_BeemLetterhead.docx**.

3 After the document opens, start the step-by-step Mail Merge wizard.

4 At the first Mail Merge task pane, confirm that *Letters* is selected and then click the <u>Next: Starting document</u> hyperlink.

5 At the second Mail Merge task pane, confirm that *Use the current document* is selected and then click the <u>Next: Select recipients</u> hyperlink.

6 At the third Mail Merge task pane, click *Type a new list* and then click the <u>Create</u> hyperlink.

7 Create a new address list using the information shown in Figure 105.3 by completing the following steps:

   a Remove unnecessary fields, rename fields, and/or add fields to the address list, and then key the content shown in Figure 105.3.

   b Proofread the contents of the entries at the New Address List dialog box and then click OK to close the dialog box.

steps continue

Session
72

Modifying the Layout of Tables

Session Objectives

- Insert and delete table rows and columns
- Delete a table
- Merge and split cells
- Select cells, rows, columns, and tables
- Cut, copy, and paste rows, columns, and cell contents
- Change column width and row height
- Align text in cells
- Design a table to show specific data
- Efficiently produce documents in mailable form

Getting Started

Exercise 72.1 If you are continuing immediately from Session 71, you may skip the Exercise 72.1 warm-up drill. However, if you exited the Online Lab at the end of Session 71, warm up by completing Exercise 72.1.

Exercise 72.2 Begin your session work by completing Exercise 72.2, a timed short drill, in the Online Lab.

Assessing Your Speed and Accuracy

Complete Timings 72.1 through 72.3 in the Online Lab. At the end of each timing, the Online Lab will display your WPM rate and any errors. Results will be saved in your Timings Performance report. If you have been surpassing the speed and accuracy goals identified in the Online Lab, set slightly more challenging personal goals and strive to exceed them.

Complete two 1-minute timings on the timing text below. If you meet or exceed both speed and accuracy goals for Timing 72.1, push for greater speed on Timing 72.2.

1-Minute Timings

Timings 72.1–72.2   A road atlas and a travel guide are necessities for today's traveler. The atlas provides detailed state maps and always includes a city and town finder index. Also included may be Canadian province maps, US city maps, and special interest maps. The travel guide may contain lists of special events, theme parks, state hunting and fishing license fees, tourist information, hotel/motel rating charts, and toll road information. These maps usually also show small towns with small symbols and large cities with larger symbols.

   c At the Save Address List dialog box, key Doc105.02_data_source in the *File name* text box and then click Save.

   d Click OK to close the Mail Merge Recipients dialog box.

8 Click the <u>Next: Write your letter</u> hyperlink in the Mail Merge task pane.

9 Key the contents of the letter shown in Figure 105.4. Consider the following as you key the letter:

   a Key January 8, 2020 and then press Enter twice. *Note: You may choose to prepare this document on a different date according to the priorities you set in Session 101.*

   b Insert the fields as indicated in Figure 105.4.

   c Make sure that the greeting-line field is followed by a colon.

   d After pressing Enter twice following *Sincerely,* set a left tab at the 3.25-inch mark on the horizontal ruler, key Charles L. Beem, and then press Tab to key the signature line for Kayla B. Southworth. Press Shift + Enter and then key the title lines for both attorneys.

   e Key the reference initials for the person you assigned to complete this task (either yourself or Gabrielle Lee) followed by the appropriate file name according to the file naming system you developed in Session 101. Include a reference to the enclosure.

10 In the *Step 4 of 6* section of the task pane, click the <u>Next: Preview your letters</u> hyperlink.

11 Fix the spacing of the address block in the letter.

12 Proofread the document and correct any errors.

13 In the *Step 5 of 6* section of the task pane, click the <u>Next: Complete the merge</u> hyperlink.

14 Close the Mail Merge task pane.

15 Position the insertion point immediately to the right of the date and then press Enter twice to better position the body of the letter on the page.

16 Save the document with the name **Doc105.02**, close the document, and then close Word.

17 Return to the document activity launch page in the Online Lab, click the Upload Document button, and then select your completed Doc105.02 file to upload it for instructor review.

Figure 105.2 Email Message for Document 105.2

To...	legaladmin@ppi-edu.net
Subject:	Follow-up Letters

As you know, Attorney Southworth and I presented a session at the Senior Fair held on December 29. We had so many attendees that there were not enough brochures for everyone. We promised to send copies to those who indicated an interest by providing their names and addresses.

Can you follow up and send out the materials to Mr. and Mrs. Yarborough, Ms. Comfrey, Dr. and Mrs. Beauregaard, and Dr. Buttone?

C. Beem

Figure 71.6 Calendar Content for Document 71.3

MAY

M	T	W	T	F	S	S
				1	2	3
4	5	6	7	8	9	10
11	12	13	14	15	16	17
18	19	20	21	22	23	24
25	26	27	28	29	30	31

Reinforcing Writing Skills

Tables have a number of common uses in business communication. For example, tables are ideal for summarizing and comparing information. Tables can present greater amounts of detailed information than can be presented in a paragraph. For example, a table can effectively show the start date, employee identification number, and telephone number of each employee, as well as how much each employee gets paid and his or her sales history. Practice creating a document that presents and analyzes data in the following document activity.

Document 71.4 **Presenting and Analyzing Data**

Read all instructions below before starting this document activity.

1 Navigate to the Document 71.4 launch page in the Online Lab and then click the Launch Activity button to open **Doc071.04** in the activity window.

2 In the document, create a table showing your name plus the names of four friends who are currently in school. For each person, include his or her first and last names, the name of the school he or she attends, the number of years completed in school, and his or her phone number.

3 In the document, above the table, add a heading and a paragraph introduction telling what the data is about. Below the table, add a short paragraph that explains what can be concluded about the data shown in the table.

4 Proofread and correct any errors in the document.

5 Save the document.

6 Click the Submit button to upload the document for instructor review.

Ending the Session

The Online Lab automatically saved the work you completed for this session. You may continue with the next session or exit the Online Lab and continue later.

Figure 105.3 New Address List Content for Document 105.2 Mail Merge Wizard Step 3

Title	First Name	Last Name	Address	City	State	ZIP Code
Mr. and Mrs.	Theodore	Yarborough	118 Bungalow Place	Beloit	WI	53511-9657
Ms.	Suzann	Comfrey	101 Heighbult	Orfordville	WI	53576-7169
Dr. and Mrs.	Hector	Beauregaard	401 North Polk Street	Brodhead	WI	53520-2140
Dr.	Madeline	Buttone	2329 Humiston Road	Monroe	WI	53566-4809

Figure 105.4 Letter Content for Document 105.2

«AddressBlock»

«GreetingLine»

Thank you for attending our presentation about creating a Living Will and Power of Attorney for Health Care during the Senior Fair last week.

Enclosed is a copy of the brochure that you requested. We were overwhelmed with the number of people in attendance and attribute that to the increasing awareness of the importance of healthcare planning before a trauma occurs.

We are pleased to offer you a 20 percent discount should you wish to create or update a Living Will or Power of Attorney for Health Care. This special offer will be available through the end of next month.

Please call our office to schedule an appointment at your convenience. We look forward to serving you.

Sincerely,

Charles L. Beem Kayla B. Southworth
Attorney at Law Attorney at Law

Figure 71.5 Table Content for Document 71.2

Filet Mignon	6 oz	$12.95
Top Sirloin	8 oz	$6.49
Boneless Pork Chop	10 oz	$4.75
Boneless Chicken Breast	4 oz	$2.39
Angus Burger	8 oz	$4.98
Filet of Sole	7 oz	$5.25

5   Position the insertion point below the table, press Enter, and then key These prices are subject to change.

6   Proofread and correct any errors in the document.

7   Save the document.

8   Click the Check button to upload the document for checking.

9   If errors are reported by the Online Lab, view the results document, correct the errors in the submitted document, save the document, and then click the Check Again button.

Document 71.3   Creating a Table Using a Quick Tables Template

Read all instructions below before starting this document activity.

1   Navigate to the Document 71.3 launch page in the Online Lab and then click the Launch Activity button to open **Doc071.03** in the activity window.

2   Insert a calendar-style table using the *Quick Tables* option from the Table button drop-down list by completing the following steps:

a   Click the Insert tab.

b   Click the Table button in the Tables group.

c   Point to *Quick Tables* to display the side menu and then click *Calendar 2*.

3   Edit the dates of the calendar to match the dates shown in Figure 71.6. ***Hint: Select the cells containing the dates and then press Delete to clear their contents.***

4   Proofread and correct any errors in the document.

5   Save the document.

6   Click the Check button to upload the document for checking.

7   If errors are reported by the Online Lab, view the results document, correct the errors in the submitted document, save the document, and then click the Check Again button.

Document 105.3

Envelopes Created with the Mail Merge Wizard

Read all instructions below before starting this document activity.

1 Navigate to the Document 105.3 launch page and then minimize the Online Lab. Start Word 2016 and click the *Blank document* template.

2 At the blank document, start the step-by-step Mail Merge wizard.

3 At the first Mail Merge task pane, click *Envelopes* and then click the <u>Next: Starting document</u> hyperlink.

4 At the second Mail Merge task pane, confirm that *Change document layout* is selected and then click the <u>Envelope options</u> hyperlink.

5 At the Envelope Options dialog box, confirm that *Size 10* is selected in the *Envelope size* list box and then click OK.

6 In the *Step 2 of 6* section of the task pane, click the <u>Next: Select recipients</u> hyperlink.

7 At the third Mail Merge task pane, confirm that *Use an existing list* is selected in the *Select recipients* section and then complete the following steps:

   a Click the <u>Browse</u> hyperlink in the *Use an existing list* section.

   b In the Select Data Source dialog box, click the *Documents* folder, double-click the *Paradigm* folder, double-click the *Keyboarding* folder, double-click the *DocumentActivityFiles* folder, and then double-click **Doc105.03_data_source.mdb**.

   c At the Mail Merge Recipients dialog box, click the OK button.

8 In the *Step 3 of 6* section of the task pane, click the <u>Next: Arrange your envelope</u> hyperlink, turn on the display of nonprinting characters, and then insert the address block field in the delivery address block area of the envelope.

9 In the *Step 4 of 6* section of the task pane, click the <u>Next: Preview your envelopes</u> hyperlink.

10 In the *Step 5 of 6* section of the task pane, click the <u>Next: Complete the merge</u> hyperlink.

11 Click the Close button to close the Mail Merge task pane.

12 Save the document with the name **Doc105.03**, close the document, and then close Word.

13 Return to the document activity launch page in the Online Lab, click the Upload Document button, and then select your completed Doc105.03 file to upload it for instructor review.

Document 105.4

Prenuptial Agreement Draft

Read all instructions below before starting this document activity.

1 Read the email message shown in Figure 105.5. The text of the prenuptial agreement document referenced by the attorney is shown in Figure 105.6.

2 Navigate to the Document 105.4 launch page in the Online Lab and then click the Launch Activity button to open **Doc105.04** in the activity window.

3 Key the document shown in Figure 105.6. Use Word's default margins, line spacing, and font and consider the following instructions as you key the document:

   a Change the paragraph alignment to center alignment, turn on bold formatting, and then key PRENUPTIAL AGREEMENT. Turn off bold formatting before pressing Enter at the end of the title.

   b For the first set of blank underlines, use 5 underscores after *this*, 10 underscores after *of*, and 30 underscores for each of the two name lines in the first paragraph. Do not underline *and*. One space should precede and follow each of the lines created, except there should not be a space after the last line before the period.

steps continue

3 Insert a table that contains three columns and six rows by completing the following steps:

   a Click the Insert tab.

   b Click the Table button in the Tables group.

   c Move the mouse pointer down and to the right until the text above the grid displays as *3×6 Table* and then click the left mouse button.

4 Key the text shown in Figure 71.4 in the cells of the table. Apply bold formatting to the text in the first row. ***Hint: Press Tab to move quickly from cell to cell.***

5 Position the insertion point below the table, press Enter, and then key These are the predicted high and low temperatures for the upcoming trip.

6 Proofread and correct any errors in the document.

7 Save the document.

8 Click the Check button to upload the document for checking.

9 If errors are reported by the Online Lab, view the results document, correct the errors in the submitted document, save the document, and then click the Check Again button.

Figure 71.4 Table Content for Document 71.1

City	State	High/Low
Des Moines	Iowa	92/63
Austin	Texas	98/69
Spokane	Washington	78/64
Myrtle Beach	South Carolina	88/71
Madison	Wisconsin	90/60

Document
71.2

Creating a Table Using the Insert Table Dialog Box

Read all instructions below before starting this document activity.

1 Navigate to the Document 71.2 launch page in the Online Lab and then click the Launch Activity button to open **Doc071.02** in the activity window.

2 Key Specials and then press Enter.

3 Insert a table that is made up of three columns and six rows by completing the following steps:

   a Click the Insert tab.

   b Click the Table button in the Tables group.

   c Click *Insert Table* at the drop-down list.

   d At the Insert Table dialog box, with the number in the *Number of columns* measurement box selected, key 3.

   e Press Tab to select the number in the *Number of rows* measurement box and then key 6.

   f Click OK.

4 Key the text shown in Figure 71.5 in the cells of the table. Do not make any formatting changes to the table's cells.

steps continue

c Key Wisconsin for the state in the second paragraph and the ninth numbered item. Do not format the state's name as underlined text.

d Allow Word to automatically format the numbered list, but use the settings in the Define new Multilevel list dialog box to modify entries as follows:

    i. Use the *1)* and *a)* for the style of the numbered list entries.

    ii. Modify the first-level entries so that the numbers align at the right at 0.15 inch and the text indent is set at 0.35 inch.

    iii. Modify the second-level entries so that the letters align at the left at 0.35 inch and the text indent is set at 0.6 inch. *Note: The second-level alignment is different than the first-level alignment.*

e When keying the numbered list, remember to press Shift + Enter and then Enter at the end of each numbered item, including the last item.

f For the blank underline for the date at the end of the document, use 5 underscores after *this* and 10 underscores after *of*. Press Enter after the date line.

g To create the signature lines, with the insertion point positioned two lines below the date line, set a right tab at the 3-inch mark on the horizontal ruler. Press Enter and then use underline formatting and the Tab key to create the signature lines. Press Shift + Enter after each signature line and then key the words under the signature lines. Press Enter twice between each signature line.

4 Insert a watermark that identifies this document as being in draft form by completing the following steps:

a Click the Design tab.

b Click the Watermark button in the Page Background group.

c Click *DRAFT 1* in the *Disclaimers* section of the drop-down list.

5 Insert Page X of Y page numbering at the bottom of all pages of the document using the *Bold Numbers 2* option.

6 Format the fourth item in the numbered list, which begins *The parties agree that neither,* so that the entire paragraph displays on the same page by completing the following steps:

a Position the insertion point within the fourth item's paragraph.

b Click the Paragraph group dialog box launcher.

c If necessary, click the Line and Page Breaks tab.

d Click the *Keep lines together* check box in the *Pagination* section to insert a check mark.

e Click OK.

7 Proofread the document and correct any errors. Compare the formatting of the document against the image shown in Figure 105.7.

8 Save the document.

9 Click the Check button to upload the document for checking.

10 If errors are reported by the Online Lab, view the results document, correct the errors in the submitted document, save the document, and then click the Check Again button.

Figure 71.2 Table Button Drop-Down List

Figure 71.3 Insert Table Dialog Box

Use this grid to select the number of columns and rows.

Click here to display the Insert Table dialog box.

Click here to display a list of preformatted table templates.

Enter values into these measurement boxes to select the number of columns and rows.

Entering Text in a Table Cell

To enter text or numbers into a cell, position the insertion point in that cell and then key the data. When you create a table, the insertion point displays in cell A1. Move the insertion point to other cells by clicking in the desired cell or by using the arrow keys to move from cell to cell. You can also press Tab to move to the next cell or press Shift + Tab to move to the previous cell.

If the text you key in a cell does not fit on one line, the text will wrap to the next line within that cell. If you press Enter within a cell, the insertion point will move to the next line within the same cell. The height of the cell will increase to accommodate the new line of text, as will the height of all of the cells in that row.

To edit text within a cell, double-click to select a single word or triple-click to select the entire contents of the cell. Once all information has been entered into the table cells, move the insertion point below the table by clicking the blank line below the table or by pressing the Down Arrow key until the insertion point appears below the table.

Adding a Row to an Existing Table

Once a table has been created, you can adjust the number of columns or rows in that table. If you position the insertion point in the last cell of the table and press Enter, a new row will be inserted at the end of the table. You can undo this action by pressing Ctrl + Z or by clicking the Undo button on the Quick Access Toolbar. You will investigate other ways to change the number of columns or rows in a table in Session 72.

Document 71.1 Creating a Table Using the Table Button Grid

Read all instructions below before starting this document activity.

1 Navigate to the Document 71.1 launch page in the Online Lab and then click the Launch Activity button to open **Doc071.01** in the activity window.

2 Turn on bold formatting, key CURRENT FORECAST, turn off bold formatting, and then press Enter.

steps continue

Figure 105.5 Email Message for Document 105.4

To...	legaladmin@ppi-edu.net
Subject:	Sample Prenuptial Agreement

I have found a sample prenuptial agreement and would like you to prepare a clean copy for a meeting I have next Monday. Because it is a draft, please add a background watermark to the document.

K. Southworth

Figure 105.6 Agreement Content for Document 105.4

PRENUPTIAL AGREEMENT

This premarital agreement is made on this _____ day of _____, 20XX, between _____ and _____.

Whereas the parties intend to marry under the laws of the State of _____, and wish to set forth in advance of their marriage the rights and privileges that each will have in the property of the other in the event of death, divorce, or other circumstance which results in the termination of their marriage;

Whereas the parties have made to each other a full and complete disclosure of their assets, as set forth in Exhibits 1 and 2 to this agreement;

Whereas both parties have been represented by independent counsel of their own choosing, and whereas both parties have received a full and complete explanation of their legal rights, the consequences of entering into this premarital agreement, and the rights they would possess were it not for their voluntary entry into this agreement; and

Whereas both parties acknowledge that they have read and understand this agreement, have not been subjected to any form of coercion, duress, or pressure,

continues

Creating Tables

Tables are commonly used in business documents that contain large amounts of numerical data. Manuscripts and business reports are two examples of these types of documents. Numerical information can be difficult and impractical to present in sentence and paragraph form, but when it is presented in a table, the reader has an opportunity to visualize and comprehend the total picture. Tables can also be used to present non-numerical information or a combination of numerical and non-numerical information, depending on the circumstance.

Before creating a table, you should analyze the content you want to display to determine which information will be listed in columns and which information will be listed in rows. Columns are vertical and rows are horizontal. It is helpful to have an idea of how many columns and rows you will need before you create the table, but you can easily add or delete columns and rows later if you decide that your original choices need to be adjusted.

Figure 71.1 shows a 3 × 5 table (three columns and five rows). Columns in a table are identified with letters from left to right, beginning with A, and rows are numbered from the top down, beginning with 1. (Letter and number identifiers are for reference purposes only—they do not display in a Word table.) The places where columns and rows intersect are called *cells*. Cells in a table have a cell designation that is a combination of the column letter and the row number. The cell in the upper left corner of the table is cell A1. The cell to the right of A1 is B1, the cell to the right of B1 is C1, and so on. The cells below A1 are A2, A3, A4, and so on. The lines that form the cells of the table are called *borders*.

Inserting a Table

Insert a table in a document by clicking the Insert tab and then clicking the Table button in the Tables group, which displays the drop-down grid shown in Figure 71.2. Use the Table button drop-down grid to create a table by selecting cells in the grid or by clicking the *Insert Table* option and then selecting the number of columns and rows in the *Table size* section of the Insert Table dialog box (see Figure 71.3). Alternatively, you can point to the *Quick Tables* option at the Table button drop-down list and then click a table style from the list of preformatted templates.

Figure 71.1 Table with Three Columns and Five Rows

cell A1		
Fairmont	Dallas	(630) 555-7676
Hilton	Seattle	(847) 555-2188
Holiday Inn	Chicago	(312) 555-3000
Hyatt	New York	(360) 555-4500
Sheraton	Los Angeles	(206) 555-9900

cell borders   column B   row 3

Figure 105.6 Agreement Content for Document 105.4—continued

and believe this agreement to be fair and to represent their intentions with regard to their assets and to any estate that shall result from their marriage;

The parties hereby agree as follows:

1) Each party shall separately retain all of his or her rights in his or her separate property, as enumerated in Exhibits 1 and 2 to this agreement, free and clear of any claim of the other party, without regard to any time or effort invested during the course of the marriage in the maintenance, management, or improvement of that separate property.

2) At all times, the parties shall enjoy the full right and authority with regard to their separate property as each would have had if not married, including but not limited to the right and authority to use, sell, enjoy, manage, gift, and convey the separate property. Both parties agree to execute any documentation necessary to permit the other to exercise these rights, provided the act of executing the documentation does not impose upon them any legal or financial responsibility for the separate property of the other.

3) The parties agree that each shall be responsible for any tax obligations associated with their separate property.

4) The parties agree that neither shall contest the validity or provisions of any will, account, trust agreement, or other instrument executed by the other which disposes of either individual's separate property or which creates any interest therein in another. To the extent that such an action would create any right or interest in the separate property of the other, both parties hereby waive any right in the property of the other, whether created by statute or common law, including but not limited to any right to elect against the will of the other, or to take an intestate share of the other's property. The wife hereby waives any dower interest in the husband's separate property, and the husband hereby waives any courtesy interest in the wife's separate property.

5) In the event of separation or divorce, the parties shall have no right against each other for division of property existing of this date.

continues

Complete one 5-minute timing on the timing text below.

5-Minute Timing

In our modern world of hurry, hurry, and hurry some more, many of us experience a common malady that is shared by many people. That malady is widely known as stress. Stress causes feelings of tension that may result in not being able to accomplish everyday tasks effectively. Sometimes stress can result in a loss of sleep or appetite. Most people who have had stressful episodes report that they feel there is just never enough time in the day to finish all the tasks.

Exercise is one important way to relieve tension. When you find that a task seems to be too difficult to finish, just take a long walk. You will be amazed at how much better you feel. As an added benefit, you will also find out that after a long, refreshing walk, you will probably be able to complete that task quickly and efficiently.

Setting goals and priorities is also another method to relieve that stressful feeling you might have. You need to decide which tasks are the most important tasks to finish. If there are any jobs that you can eliminate, you will feel less hurried. You need to set up a list of things you need to do, a list of things you would like to do, and a list of things that you could do some other time.

Eating properly is also another means toward relieving stress. If you do not eat the proper foods, your body will surely revolt and cause you many problems. Certain foods are good for quick energy; other foods are good for long-range energy needs. Taking time to eat slowly is another good food tip. If you gulp your food quickly, you will not be able to digest that food properly. You could end up with a headache, a stomachache, or even an illness from poor eating habits; illness is a terrible condition.

A good idea for relieving stress is to take a few moments each day to enjoy the simple things around you. Smell the flowers, notice the birds in the trees, listen to music, or visit with a companion. Surely you will begin to feel the tensions ease.

Ergonomic Tip

Reduce sources of environmental stress such as noise, heat, and glare in your workspace.

Figure 105.6 Agreement Content for Document 105.4—continued

6) Both parties acknowledge that they possess sufficient education and job skills to adequately provide for their own support, and hereby waive any claim to spousal support (alimony) except in the event that:

a) One of the parties suffers medical disability and the other remains both employed and physically able, in which case the disabled party may receive reasonable spousal support consistent with state law until such time as the disability is resolved, or the other spouse retires or becomes disabled from working, either by agreement or by judicial determination;

b) The parties mutually agree that one of the parties shall reduce the spouse's work hours, or shall refrain from working, in order to care for any children born during the course of the marriage, in which case, if the parent's employability is affected by this full or partial withdrawal from employment, that parent may receive reasonable remedial spousal support consistent with the state law for a period of not more than two years, either by agreement or judicial determination.

7) In the event of separation or divorce, marital property acquired after marriage shall remain subject to division, either by agreement or by judicial determination.

8) This agreement shall be binding and inure to the benefit of the parties, their successors, assigns, and legal representatives.

9) Without regard to the location of any property affected by this agreement, this agreement shall be interpreted and enforced under the laws of the State of _____. In the event that any portion of this agreement shall be held invalid or unenforceable, it is the intent of the parties that all provisions of this agreement be regarded as separable, and that all remaining provisions remain in full force and effect. It is further the desire of the parties that all provisions of this agreement be considered as evidence of their intentions by any court, arbitrator,

continues

Session

71

Creating Tables

Session Objectives

- **Create a table**
- **Enter data in a table**
- **Design a table to compare data**
- **Efficiently produce documents in mailable form**

Getting Started

Exercise 71.1 If you are continuing immediately from Session 70, you may skip the Exercise 71.1 warm-up drill. However, if you exited the Online Lab at the end of Session 71, warm up by completing Exercise 71.1.

Exercise 71.2 Begin your session work by completing Exercise 71.2, a timed short drill, in the Online Lab.

Assessing Your Speed and Accuracy

Complete Timings 71.1 through 71.3 in the Online Lab. At the end of each timing, the Online Lab will display your WPM rate and any errors. Results will be saved in your Timings Performance report. If you have been surpassing the speed and accuracy goals identified in the Online Lab, set slightly more challenging personal goals and strive to exceed them. *Note: With this session, the default WPM goal for 3-minute timings has been increased by 5 WPM in the Online Lab. However, your instructor may have customized this goal.*

Complete two 1-minute timings on the timing text below. If you do not key at or above the WPM rate identified in the Online Lab on Timing 71.1, concentrate on speed on Timing 71.2. If you meet the Online Lab's WPM goal but make more errors than the goal set in the Online Lab on Timing 71.1, concentrate on accuracy on Timing 71.2. However, if you meet or exceed both goals for Timing 71.1, push for greater speed on Timing 71.2.

1-Minute Timings

Timings 71.1–71.2

> When traveling, it is better to be "safe than sorry." Use debit cards or credit cards rather than carrying large amounts of cash. The cash you carry should be in small denominations. Be aware of your surroundings and never discuss the amount of money you are carrying. Leave unessential nontravel papers, such as local checkbooks, at home. Keep track of your plane, train, or bus tickets; they can be converted to cash. It is an excellent idea to photocopy all documents and store the copies in the hotel safe. In addition to being safe, one other advantage of credit cards is that many of them have very reasonable transaction rates.

Figure 105.6 Agreement Content for Document 105.4—continued

mediator, or other authority which seeks to divide their estate, and that their intentions be respected whatever the legal status of this agreement or any of its terms.

10) This agreement and the exhibits attached hereto contain the entire agreement of the parties. This agreement may only be amended by a written document duly executed by both parties.

Signed this _____ day of _____, 20XX.

_____
Fiancé

_____
Fiancée

Signed in the presence of:

_____
Witness

_____
Witness

Tables Part II

Figure 105.7 Formatted Final Agreement for Document 105.4

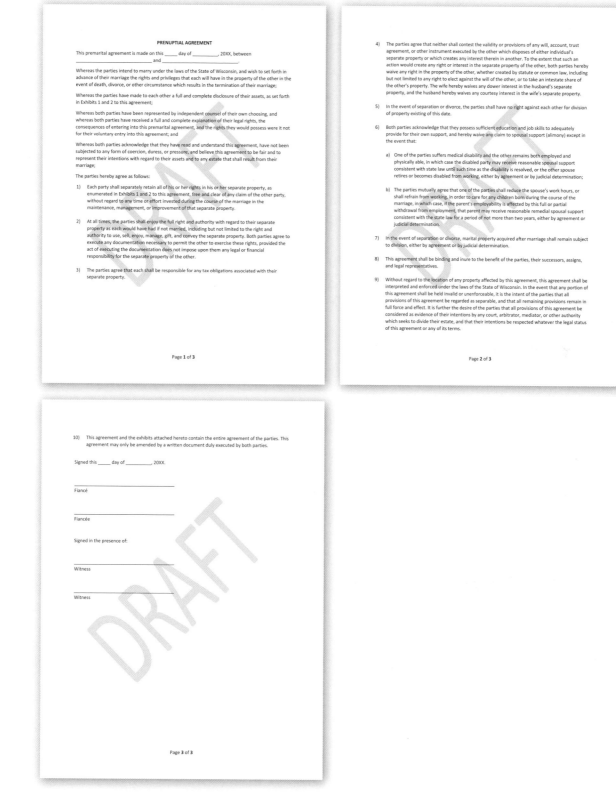

Ending the Session

The Online Lab automatically saved the work you completed for this project. You may continue with the next session or exit the Online Lab and continue later.

Figure 70.4 Letter Content for Document 70.4—continued

If you wish to pay additional amounts to your escrow account, please contact our Customer Services department. If you wish to pay an additional amount to your principal balance, please advise us in writing stating the amount you wish to be applied to the principal balance each month. This amount my by changed yearly.

We are always glad to answer any question you may have concerning your mortgage load. If you should need assistance, please contact us Monday through Friday, 8:30 a.m. to 5:00 p.m. EST at (888) 555-1093. You may also chat with a live agent at http://bank1mortgage.ppi-edu.net.

Please contact us immediately if you change banks, change accounts within the same bank, or if your wish to stop the PAID service.

Ending the Session

The Online Lab automatically saved the work you completed for this session. You may continue with the next session or exit the Online Lab and continue later.

Unit 21

Medical Documents and Medical Center Project

Figure 70.4 Multiple-Page Business Letter Content for Document 70.4

Ms. Kimberly Thornblade
4256 Maple Lane
Minneapolis, MN 55407

Dear Ms. Thornblade:

It is a pleasure to welcome you as one of our <u>Pre-Authorized Instant Deduction</u> mortgage loan customers. The June 1 payment will be first to be automatically deducted from your designated bank account. The deduction from your checking account will occur on the due date of your loan payment or the next 10 business days thereafter.

If you have already mailed your June 1 payment and it is applied to your account on or before the due date, the PAID service will begin with the July 1 payment. If your payment has not been posted to the account before the schedule debit, a payment will be automatically deducted from your account. Of your account becomes delinquent, the delinquent payments will be automatically deducted from you account.

Each year you will receive the following statements:

- Year-End Statement: In January of each year, we will mail a statement of information on your mortgage for the previous year. This will include interest paid, taxes and insurance paid, as well as the principle paid on your balance. This statement is to be used in conjunction with income tax preparation.
- Escrow Analysis: This analysis is performed each year to determine that the amount necessary to collect each month is sufficient to pay your taxes and insurance. This analysis also ensures that you not paying too much, which could happen if taxes were to be lowered or the insurance rates were reduced.

continues

Session
106

History and Physical Reports

Session Objectives

- **Create a table containing medical terms and definitions**
- **Create a history and physical report template and document**
- **Efficiently produce documents in mailable form**

Getting Started

Exercise 106.1 Unless you are continuing immediately after completing Session 105, spend at least two to three minutes warming up before completing the document activities in this session. See Session 101 for suggested warm-up text.

Preparing Medical Reports

Medical documents are prepared every day with word processing programs in doctors' offices, clinics, and hospitals. As you move from one field of business—for example, medicine, law, banking, or manufacturing—to another, you will find specialized reports that are formatted in distinct and specific ways. The medical documents you will prepare in this unit represent a sampling of the kinds of documents that exist. The information presented is not intended to replace a course in medical terminology, medical transcription, or electronic health records. Rather, the purpose of the document activities in this unit is to provide you with the opportunity to apply word processing features and functions in the preparation of some common medical documents.

Before proceeding with the first document activity in this session, note that in this unit, you are working with a variety of specialized reports for the medical field. Recall that in Unit 16, you keyed three types of business reports: memo reports, formal reports, and specialized reports. Whereas there are similarities in memo and formal business reports, specialized reports, such as the medical reports discussed in this unit, are different in some ways from the other types of business reports.

One example of how specialized medical reports differ from memo business reports and formal business reports is the use of paragraphs. For medical reports, information is not separated into distinct paragraphs. Rather, medical documents are commonly keyed using standard templates. The use of consistent headings in different reports provides a guide for organizing information consistently across documents. Consistency in the order and phrasing of headings is important because it allows quick access to information and assists in maintaining electronic medical records. Templates that contain these standard headings are useful tools when transcribing dictated content and can decrease the production time and increase efficiency when keying medical reports.

Each office, clinic, or hospital will have specific requirements for formatting medical documents. When you first key documents for an organization, you should check the company procedure manual to learn what types of reports are generated and how they are formatted.

In this session and the following four sessions, you will prepare a template file and key a sample report for several report types. Following the sessions on the basic report types, a Production Progress Check on medical reports is presented in Session 111.

Your bank must be a member of the *National Automated Clearinghouse Associations (NACHA)* in order for the deduction to take place. Once your authorization from is received, we will enter the necessary data into our computer system and verify with your bank that the information is accurate. This processing will take approximately 30 days.

Please continue to make your payments until you receive written notification that the Pre-Authorized Instant Deduction will begin. This notice will be mailed at least 10 calendar days prior to the ~~do~~ due date of the payment.

If you have any questions concerning the PAID system, please contact me at (888) 555-1021.

Sincerely,

Heather B. Richards, Customer Service Representative

Document 70.4 Multiple-Page Business Letter with Bulleted Paragraphs and Underlined Text

Read all instructions below before starting this document activity.

1 Navigate to the Document 70.4 launch page in the Online Lab and then click the Launch Activity button to open **Doc070.04** in the activity window.

2 Review the contents of the letter shown in Figure 70.4. Note that there are no additional errors to be corrected.

3 Key the letter, formatting it as a block-style business letter.

    a Key May 11, 2020 as the date.

    b Add an additional line space between the two items in the bulleted list.

    c Use *Sincerely,* as the closing and indicate that the letter is from Heather B. Richards, Customer Service Representative.

    d Key the reference initials trf and the file name.

    e Add a vertical-style continuation header to the second page.

4 Proofread the document and correct any errors.

5 Save the document.

6 Click the Check button to upload the document for checking.

7 If errors are reported by the Online Lab, view the results document, correct the errors in the submitted document, save the document, and then click the Check Again button.

Sessions 112 through 115 contain a project for a medical center. The project will simulate the working environment of a medical office. In addition to keying the medical documents, you will assign priorities for work to be completed and identify what must be done.

This session features a history and physical (H&P) report. A history and physical report is a comprehensive document that is used as the foundation for the patient's medical record. This report will document the immediate problem that prompted the patient to seek medical help, a social and family history, and the findings of a complete physical exam. The primary purpose of the history and physical report is to help the medical provider diagnose the medical condition, which is the basis for the patient's care and treatment.

You will begin your session work by keying a medical terminology list. Becoming familiar with medical terminology will help improve your keying speed and accuracy. Also, this activity will allow you to apply some table formatting skills learned in previous sessions.

Document 106.1

Medical Terminology List

Read all instructions below before starting this document activity.

1 Navigate to the Document 106.1 launch page in the Online Lab and then click the Launch Activity button to open **Doc106.01** in the activity window.

2 Insert a table that contains 2 columns and 16 rows using the Insert Table dialog box.

3 Set the width of the first column to 2 inches and the width of the second column to 4.64 inches.

4 Merge cells A1 and B1, format the contents of the merged cell so it is centered and aligns to the top center of the cell, key MEDICAL TERMINOLOGY, and then apply bold formatting to the row.

5 Select row 2 and then apply bold formatting.

6 Key Term in cell A2 and then key Definition in cell B2.

7 Key the terms and definitions shown in Figure 106.1. *Note: The text will wrap differently than shown in the figure.*

8 Sort the terms in alphabetic order.

9 Proofread the document and correct any errors.

10 Save the document.

11 Click the Check button to upload the document for checking.

12 If errors are reported by the Online Lab, view the results document, correct the errors in the submitted document, save the document, and then click the Check Again button.

Figure 106.1 Terms and Definitions for Document 106.1

Edema	A condition in which the body tissues contain excessive fluid
Rheumatic fever	A systemic, inflammatory disease that varies in severity and duration
Tachycardia	Abnormally rapid heart rate, over 100 beats per minute
Scarlet fever	An acute contagious disease characterized by sore throat, strawberry tongue, fever, red rash, and rapid pulse

continues

Figure 70.2 Letter Content for Document 70.2—continued

system. We are excited about the possibility of installing one of these systems at Sierra University in San Francisco. ¶ I have one comment regarding our expenses. In order to get home in time for a specially-called division meeting, we left Newark on an earlier flight and had to upgrade our tickets to first class. That was the only seating available. Please let me know if this is a problem. ¶ Sincerely, ¶ Marlis Overgard, PhD ¶ Associate Dean ¶ Enclosures

Document 70.3

Business Letter with Indented, Justified, Italic, and Underlined Text

Read all instructions below before starting this document activity.

1. Navigate to the Document 70.3 launch page in the Online Lab and then click the Launch Activity button to open **Doc070.03** in the activity window.

2. Review the contents of the letter shown in Figure 70.3. Note that there are no additional errors to be corrected.

3. Key the letter, formatting it as a block-style business letter.

   a. Key August 14, 2020 as the date.

   b. Key the reference initials mno and the file name and include a notation for an enclosure.

   c. Select the third paragraph in the body of the letter, indent it 0.5 inch from the left and right margins, and then change the paragraph alignment to justified alignment.

4. Proofread the document and correct any errors.

5. Save the document.

6. Click the Check button to upload the document for checking.

7. If errors are reported by the Online Lab, view the results document, correct the errors in the submitted document, save the document, and then click the Check Again button.

Figure 70.3 Business Letter Content for Document 70.3

Mr. and Mrs. Daniel Nguyen
17431 Foxfire Lane
San Rafael, CA 94903

Dear Mr. and Mrs. Nguyen:

Thank you for your interest in the <u>Pre-Authorized Instant Deduction (PAID)</u> method of making your monthly mortgage payment. Please read this letter and the enclosed agreement carefully. Sign the agreement and return it with a voided check or a checking deposit slip to Bank One Mortgage Corporation, 406 Park Club Lane, Buffalo, NY 14232-4590.

continues

Figure 106.1 Terms and Definitions for Document 106.1—continued

Yellow fever	An acute infectious disease characterized by jaundice, throat tenderness, vomiting, and hemorrhages
Hepatosplenomegaly	Enlargement of the liver and spleen
Ultrasound	Inaudible sound in the frequency range of about 20,000 to 10,000,000,000 cycles per second; an imaging process to outline the shape of various tissues and organs in the body
Pneumonia	Infection of one or both of the lungs caused by bacteria, viruses, or chemical irritant
Thrombophlebitis	Inflammation of a vein along with the formation of a blood clot
Palpitation	Rapid, violent, or throbbing pulsing or fluttering of the heart
Jugular	Referring to the throat or neck
Venous	Referring to the veins or blood passing through them
Coagulation	The clotting process
Thrombosis	The formation, development, or existence of a blood clot within the circulatory system

Document 106.2 **History and Physical Report Template**

Read all instructions below before starting this document activity.

1 Navigate to the Document 106.2 launch page in the Online Lab and then click the Launch Activity button to open **Doc106.02** in the activity window.

2 Change the line spacing to single spacing with no spacing after paragraphs.

3 Turn on the display of nonprinting characters.

4 Set a left tab at the 2-inch mark on the horizontal ruler.

5 Key the following:

PATIENT NAME:[Tab][Enter]

MR #:[Tab][Enter]

PHYSICIAN:[Tab][Enter]

DATE:[Tab][Enter]

6 Remove the left tab from the horizontal ruler and then press Enter. *Note: The insertion point should be two lines below the* **DATE** *heading.*

7 Key the headings, signature line, and reference information for the History and Physical report using the information provided in Figure 106.2. Do not key spaces after the

steps continue

Figure 70.1 Personal Business Letter Content for Document 70.1—continued

are not aware of. Could you check to see what pricing is available for each of the following options? ¶ 1. No prehotel, no air, and Cabin D level ¶ 2. No prehotel, no air, and Cabin C level ¶ 3. Prehotel, air, and Cabin D level ¶ 4. Prehotel, air, and Cabin C level ¶ If we do a post-stay for two days in Stockholm and get our own hotel, will the cruise line pay our *transfer fees* from the ship to the hotel? Will it also pay the *transfer fees* from the hotel to the airport? ¶ The cruise line has a referral program giving us a $200 shipboard credit if we refer someone. Can we refer Pedro and Alicia? If so, will they get a credit also? ¶ A lot of questions, right? No hurry is needed for the answers, but I would like a response within the next few weeks. As always, we appreciate your attentive service. ¶ Sincerely, ¶ Jamal T. Buchanon ¶ 2182 N. Adams Boulevard ¶ Olney, IL 62450

Document 70.2 **Business Letter with Underlined Text**

Read all instructions below before starting this document activity.

1 Navigate to the Document 70.2 launch page in the Online Lab and then click the Launch Activity button to open **Doc070.02** in the activity window.

2 Review the contents of the letter shown in Figure 70.2. Note that there are no errors in the figure to be corrected.

3 Key the letter, formatting it as a block-style business letter.

 a Key July 15, 2020 as the date.

 b Key the reference initials cyl and the file name and include a notation for four enclosures.

 c Position the insertion point immediately to the left of the date and then press Enter twice. Since this letter is rather short, adding extra hard returns will better "frame" the content on the page.

4 Proofread the document and correct any errors.

5 Save the document.

6 Click the Check button to upload the document for checking.

7 If errors are reported by the Online Lab, view the results document, correct the errors in the submitted document, save the document, and then click the Check Again button.

Figure 70.2 Business Letter Content for Document 70.2

Ms. Martha Headrick ¶ Distant Learning Systems, Inc. ¶ 4309 Wisconsin Avenue ¶ Washington, DC 20008-6280 ¶ Dear Ms. Headrick: ¶ Enclosed with this letter are the expense statements for Tom Landwehr and me for our trip to Franklin Lakes, New Jersey, to evaluate the <u>Dynamic Distant Learning System</u> your firm has designed. ¶ We certainly enjoyed meeting with you and the members of your staff. They did a great job in demonstrating all facets of the

continues

colons. For the signature line, key 30 underscores (Shift + Hyphen), and do not let Word automatically format the line as a horizontal line running the width of the document. *Hint: Press Ctrl + Z to undo the change.*

8 Key the header and footer information by completing the following steps:

a Insert a header using the *Blank* option and then format the document so that it contains a different first page header and footer.

b Format the header and footer so they appear 1 inch from the top of the page and 1 inch from the bottom of the page, respectively.

c On the first page, key (continued) at the left margin of the footer.

d On the second page, insert a header using the *Blank* header option and then key the following as a vertical continuation header.

HISTORY AND PHYSICAL
PATIENT NAME:
MR #:
DATE:
Page

e Insert a plain number following the word *Page*. **Note: Do not set the word Page in italics.**

f Confirm that there is one blank line (one nonprinting paragraph mark) below the page number in the header.

9 Turn off the display of nonprinting characters.

10 Proofread the document and correct any errors.

11 Save the document.

12 Click the Check button to upload the document for checking.

13 If errors are reported by the Online Lab, view the results document, correct the errors in the submitted document, save the document, and then click the Check Again button.

Figure 106.2 Headings for the History and Physical Report for Document 106.2

CHIEF COMPLAINT [3 Enters]

HISTORY OF PRESENT ILLNESS [3 Enters]

PAST MEDICAL HISTORY [3 Enters]

SURGICAL HISTORY [3 Enters]

SOCIAL HISTORY [3 Enters]

FAMILY HISTORY [3 Enters]

ALLERGIES [3 Enters]

CURRENT MEDICATIONS [3 Enters]

REVIEW OF SYSTEMS [Enter]

GENERAL: [Enter]

SKIN: [Enter]

HEAD: [Enter]

continues

Checking Production Progress: Business Correspondence

Sessions 66 through 69 discussed the procedures for preparing and formatting personal and business correspondence. In this session, you will be assessed on how accurately you can key these types of documents. In the following document activities, each completed letter is to be "mailable," which means that it contains no errors. A document that requires corrections is not considered *mailable*.

Your goal is to key each document in mailable form. If you are missing errors that should have been corrected or your instructor believes you can work more efficiently, he or she may ask you to repeat document activities. To help you succeed, carefully review the document instructions and the document before keying. The figures may be missing required items such as the file name and enclosure notations. In addition, there may be errors in punctuation, capitalization, and word use that have not been corrected.

Document 70.1

Personal Business Letter with Bold and Italic Text and a Numbered List

Read all instructions below before starting this document activity.

1 Navigate to the Document 70.1 launch page in the Online Lab and then click the Launch Activity button to open **Doc070.01** in the activity window.

2 Review the contents of the letter shown in Figure 70.1. Note that there are no errors in the figure to be corrected.

3 Key the text shown in Figure 70.1 as a personal business letter.

   a Key November 16, 2020 as the date.

   b Apply bold and italic formatting as indicated in the figure and allow Word to automatically format the numbered list. Do not add a blank line space between the items in the numbered list.

   c Vertically center the text on the page.

4 Proofread the document and correct any errors.

5 Save the document.

6 Click the Check button to upload the document for checking.

7 If errors are reported by the Online Lab, view the results document, correct the errors in the submitted document, save the document, and then click the Check Again button.

Figure 70.1 Personal Business Letter Content for Document 70.1

Mr. Sam Hopkins ¶ Worldwide Cruise Travel Agency ¶ 3487 S. Maple Way ¶ Chicago, IL 60601 ¶ Dear Mr. Hopkins: ¶ Firstly, let me thank you for planning such a wonderful trip to South Africa—it was fantastic. ¶ Secondly, my wife and I are considering the Baltic Cruise that Pedro and Alicia introduced to us. We have a few questions when you have some time to research and answer them. ¶ We are **International Society Gold** members and our membership number is 3285900102. Therefore, I believe there are some discounts available to us as repeat clients and possibly others that we

continues

EYES: [Enter]

EARS: [Enter]

NOSE, SINUSES: [Enter]

MOUTH AND THROAT: [Enter]

NECK: [Enter]

BREASTS: [Enter]

RESPIRATORY: [Enter]

CARDIAC: [Enter]

GASTROINTESTINAL: [Enter]

GENITOURINARY: [Enter]

GYNECOLOGIC: [Enter]

MUSCULOSKELETAL: [Enter]

PERIPHERAL VASCULAR: [Enter]

NEUROLOGIC: [Enter]

HEMATOLOGIC: [Enter]

ENDOCRINE: [Enter]

PSYCHIATRIC: [2 Enters]

PHYSICAL EXAMINATION[Enter]

GENERAL: [Enter]

VITAL SIGNS: [Enter]

SKIN: [Enter]

HEENT: [Enter]

NECK: [Enter]

LYMPH NODES: [Enter]

THORAX AND LUNGS: [Enter]

CARDIOVASCULAR: [Enter]

BREASTS: [Enter]

ABDOMEN: [Enter]

PELVIS: [Enter]

ANORECTAL: [Enter]

PERIPHERAL VASCULAR: [Enter]

continues

Complete one 3-minute timing on the timing text below.

3-Minute Timing

**Timing
70.3**

Ethics are the rules we use to determine the right and wrong things to do in our lives. Most ethical beliefs are learned during childhood and are derived from our family, society, and religious tradition. For example, many people in our society hold to the belief that telling a lie, stealing, and driving under the influence of alcohol are ethically wrong behaviors. If we have internalized a code of ethical principles, we grow up instinctively knowing the right thing to do without consciously reflecting on the ethical basis for our decision.

Occasionally, however, situations arise that force us to consciously recall our ethical principles to choose the right thing to do. This often occurs when we are faced with novel or unfamiliar situations. If examining our own ethical guidelines fails to assist us in new situations, we may have to adopt other ethical guidelines or modify our own guidelines to arrive at a correct decision.

Realizing that ethics is not the same as laws or regulations is important. Ethics differ from laws in that they are internalized principles that influence the decisions we make. A law is an external rule that, if violated, is punishable by society. Laws usually stem from ethical beliefs, but because people differ in what they consider to be ethical behavior, there will always be groups or individuals who find some laws unethical.

People make ethical decisions every day. From the moment we wake up until we fall asleep at night, we make choices regarding such matters as how to use resources prudently to protect the environment, how to treat others who are different than we are, how to spend our money wisely, and so on.

 Ergonomic Tip

To relieve muscle stress, do the following exercise. With your fingers interlaced in front of you, push your palms away from your body and then raise your straightened arms above your head with your palms to the ceiling. Lower your linked hands behind your head. Move your elbows and shoulders back until you feel the stretch of muscles in your arms and upper back. Then stretch your palms up to the ceiling again.

MUSCULOSKELETAL: [Enter]

EXTREMITIES: [Enter]

NEUROLOGIC: [Enter]

MENTAL STATUS: [2 Enters]

DIAGNOSTIC STUDIES [3 Enters]

LABORATORY DATA [3 Enters]

IMPRESSION [3 Enters]

PLAN [5 Enters]

_____ [Enter]

, MD [2 Enters]

xxx/xxx [Enter]

D: [Enter]

T:

Document 106.3 **History and Physical Report**

Read all instructions below before starting this document activity.

1 Navigate to the Document 106.3 launch page in the Online Lab and then click the Launch Activity button to open **Doc106.03** in the activity window.

2 Turn on the display of nonprinting characters.

3 Key the report shown in Figure 106.3. If a heading is not used in the final report, delete it from the document. Make sure there is only one blank line (two Enters) between sections of the report. Do not allow Word to automatically format the numbered list. Key a space, not a tab, after the numbers in the numbered list. Decrease the indent so that the numbered text begins at the left margin. *Note: There should be one space between the first and middle initials of the physician's name.*

4 Key the signature line and the reference information at the bottom of the report. There should be three blank lines (four Enters) between the last section and the signature line.

a The physician signing the report is the same physician listed at the top of the report.

b Key the reference initials ckw for the dictator's initials and tlm for the transcriptionist's initials.

c Key the dictation date (at the right of *D:*) and transcription date (at the right of *T:*) to match the date of the report. There should be one space between the colon and the date.

5 Key the information needed for the second page header.

6 Turn off the display of nonprinting characters.

7 Proofread the document and correct any errors.

8 Save the document.

9 Click the Check button to upload the document for checking.

10 If errors are reported by the Online Lab, view the results document, correct the errors in the submitted document, save the document, and then click the Check Again button.

Session 70

Production Progress Check: Business Correspondence Part II

Session Objectives

- Apply Word features and skills presented in Sessions 66–69
- Efficiently produce documents in mailable form

Getting Started

Exercise 70.1 If you are continuing immediately from Session 69, you may skip the Exercise 70.1 warm-up drill. However, if you exited the Online Lab at the end of Session 69, warm up by completing Exercise 70.1.

Exercise 70.2 Begin your session work by completing Exercise 70.2, a timed short drill, in the Online Lab.

Assessing Your Speed and Accuracy

Complete Timings 70.1 through 70.3 in the Online Lab. At the end of the timing, the Online Lab will display your WPM rate and any errors. Results will be saved in your Timings Performance report. If you have been surpassing the speed and accuracy goals identified in the Online Lab, set slightly more challenging personal goals and strive to exceed them.

Complete two 1-minute timings on the timing text below. If you meet or exceed both speed and accuracy goals for Timing 70.1, push for greater speed on Timing 70.2.

1-Minute Timings

Timings 70.1–70.2

If you are thinking about purchasing vacation property, your choice of a real estate broker is as important as a safari leader on a trek through the jungle. Make sure your broker is well established, reputable, and easy to relate to. It is also excellent if the broker works for a company that has been in business for a fairly long time and has a good reputation. Finally, it's very important that your broker be licensed by the appropriate local and state agencies. For your protection, select the right real estate broker.

Figure 106.3 History and Physical Report Content for Document 106.3

PATIENT NAME:	Jacob D. Carr
MR #:	21345
PHYSICIAN:	C. K. Winston, MD
DATE:	03/09/2020

HISTORY OF PRESENT ILLNESS

Patient is a 40-year-old male admitted for treatment of deep vein thrombophlebitis in his left lower extremity. Patient has always been healthy, has never been hospitalized, and has had no medical problems until recently. About 6 weeks ago, he developed a superficial thrombophlebitis of the left lower extremity. He was treated for this without incident and seemed to improve. About 1 week ago, he was trying to get back into shape and started working out on a treadmill. He noted some discomfort in his left calf, which he attributed to muscle pain and continued his exercise. Over the past 24 hours, the left lower extremity has become more painful and swollen. He has been seen by Dr. Winston at the Riverside Medical Center and a Doppler ultrasound was performed, demonstrating clear evidence of deep venous thrombosis. He was not admitted for treatment of the condition. He has not had any undue shortness of breath nor has he had any palpitations, cough, or chest pain. He notes that he usually runs a rapid pulse in the range of 80 or 90.

PAST MEDICAL HISTORY

Patient has had the usual childhood diseases without rheumatic or scarlet fever, yellow jaundice, pneumonia, or kidney infection.

SURGICAL HISTORY

No previous surgeries.

SOCIAL HISTORY

He does not smoke and drinks alcohol only rarely.

FAMILY HISTORY

Patient's mother and father are still living, as well as one brother and one sister. There is no family history of cancer or coagulation disorders.

continues

Figure 69.5 Job Posting for Document 69.3

Wanted: Part-time office assistant. Hours flexible. Post-secondary education
and work experience preferred. Pay commensurate with background.
Must be proficient in Microsoft Word, Excel, and Access. Must be able
to communicate effectively with clients over the phone and face-to-face.
Apply to Jose Schumacher, Box 82, Your Town/City, State ZIP.

3   Compose a personal business letter that will get you an interview. Remember to vertically
    center the letter on the page.

4   Proofread and correct errors in word use, sentence construction, punctuation, capitalization,
    and spelling.

5   Save the document.

6   Click the Submit button to upload the document for instructor review.

Ending the Session

The Online Lab automatically saved the work you completed for this session. You may continue
with the next session or exit the Online Lab and continue later.

ALLERGIES

No known allergies.

CURRENT MEDICATIONS

He is currently taking ibuprofen for pain but no other medications.

PHYSICAL EXAMINATION

GENERAL: Patient is a well-developed male who appears somewhat older than his stated age.

VITAL SIGNS: Blood pressure 140/80. Pulse 100.

HEENT: Normal.

NECK: Supple. Jugular venous pressure was normal.

THORAX AND LUNGS: Clear.

CARDIOVASCULAR: Not enlarged. First sound single, second sound normally split.

ABDOMEN: Obese, without hepatosplenomegaly. Bowel sounds normal.

EXTREMITIES: Edema in left lower extremity below the mid-thigh. Peripheral pulses were normal. There was calf tenderness and a positive Homans.

NEUROLOGIC: Normal.

IMPRESSION

1. Deep vein thrombophlebitis, left lower extremity.
2. Tachycardia.

_____

C. K. Winston, MD

ckw/tlm

Ending the Session

The Online Lab automatically saved the work you completed for this session. You may continue with the next session or exit the Online Lab and continue later.

Figure 69.4 Multiple-Page Letter Content for Document 69.2—continued

You'll find your new membership credentials—including your *GlobalPerks Platinum* membership card, personalized luggage tags, and Benefits Guide—inside this package. For complete details on your Platinum benefits, as well as program terms and conditions, please refer to your Benefits Guide. Your new *GlobalPerks Platinum* membership card will be activated on **March 1, 2020,** is and valid through February 28, 2021.

no bold

Linking more than 500 cities in over 90 countries on six continents, the global alliance of Southeast and ITW Airlines puts that world within your reach. Add *the* the privileges of your *GlobalPerks Platinum* membership, and you'll discover an infinite number of possibilities for relaxed travel and convenience.

Congratulations on your achievement of *GlobalPerks Platinum.* We look *membership* forward to seeing you on board a Southeast or ITW flight soon and to serving you often in the coming year.

Reinforcing Writing Skills

Many of the documents created in the workplace or for personal use are responses to prior documents. For example, you may receive a memo from your supervisor or from a coworker that asks for your analysis of a situation or for your reaction to an idea. Because the purpose of your action and the identity of your reader have already been identified, the next important step in creating your response is to determine what information you must include. Ask yourself the following questions:

1   What information is relevant to the situation?
2   What information will help the reader understand my message?
3   What information will prompt the reader to act in a positive manner and take the action I want?

With the information you want to communicate defined, the next step is to plan the organization of your response:

1   How can you arrange the information to make it clear and to achieve your purpose?
2   What should you say first?
3   What should be the final statement?

Consider these questions as you complete the following document activity.

Document 69.3   **Responding to a Job Advertisement with a Personal Business Letter**

Read all instructions below before starting this document activity.

1   Navigate to the Document 69.3 launch page in the Online Lab and then click the Launch Activity button to open **Doc069.03** in the activity window.
2   Review the job posting shown in Figure 69.5. Assume that you decide to pursue this job opening. Read the advertisement carefully and mentally plan your response using the six questions stated previously.

steps continue

■■■■■■■■■■■■■■■■■■■■■■■■■■■■■■■■■■■■■

Consultation Reports

Session Objectives

- **Create a table containing medical terms and definitions**
- **Create a consultation report template and document**
- **Increase productivity by using Find and Replace**
- **Efficiently produce documents in mailable form**

Getting Started

Exercise 107.1 Unless you are continuing immediately after completing Session 106, spend at least two to three minutes warming up before completing the document activities in this session. See Session 101 for suggested warm-up text.

Preparing Consultation Reports

In a hospital, medical center, or clinic, the admitting physician may request a consultation by a surgeon or specialist. The surgeon or specialist examines the patient and then dictates a report of the examination, a plan for treatment or surgery, and a prognosis for the patient. The documentation of this examination and evaluation is called a *consultation report*.

As noted in Session 106, document templates help to organize information and to increase productivity and efficiency among the medical office staff. Another Word tool that can help to improve productivity and efficiency is the Find and Replace feature. In the third document activity in this session, you will key a consultation report with two-letter abbreviations, which you will later replace with full words using Find and Replace.

Document 107.1 Medical Terminology List

Read all instructions below before starting this document activity.

1 Navigate to the Document 107.1 launch page in the Online Lab and then click the Launch Activity button to open **Doc107.01** in the activity window.

2 Use the Insert Table dialog box to insert a table that contains 2 columns and 21 rows.

3 Change the width of the first column to 2 inches and the width of the second column to 4.64 inches.

4 Merge cells A1 and B1, format the contents of the merged cell so it is centered and aligns to the top center of the cell, and then key MEDICAL TERMINOLOGY.

5 Key Term in cell A2 and then key Definition in cell B2.

6 Key the terms and definitions shown in Figure 107.1.

steps continue

5 Save the document.

6 Click the Check button to upload the document for checking.

7 If errors are reported by the Online Lab, view the results document, correct the errors in the submitted document, save the document, and then click the Check Again button.

Figure 69.4 Multiple-Page Letter Content for Document 69.2

Dr. Katja Rupnik
3128 Pineview Drive
Columbia, SC 29203-1578

Dear Dr. Rupnik:

Because you are one of Southeast and International TransWorld (ITW) Airlines' most distinguished customers, ~~I am~~ delighted to welcome you to *GlobalPerks Platinum* membership for 2020. In edition to loggin 73,200 miles in 2019, you also have a lifetime credit of over one million air miles on Southeast Airlines. That's an incredible record.

Your *GlobalPerks Platinum* membership entitles you to a host of exclusive benefits and privileges including:

- **Access to Southeast's Global Clubs** located in 16 cities with 4 more opening in 2020. In addition to a quiet place to relax, the club rooms provide magazines, refreshments, restrooms, ~~and~~ free Internet access, and flight check-in
- **Unlimited First Class Upgrades** on any available Southeast flight within the and seat assignment services 48 contiguous United States, as well as flights to Alaska, Canada, Mexico, and the Caribbean.
- **A 50% Mileage Bonus** on credited flight mileage.
- **PlatinumLine Priority Reservations**, an exclusive number dedicated to serving Platinum members' needs. For reservations and information, call (888) 555-6043 any time—this line is available 24 hours a day, 7 days a week.
- **Guaranteed Confirmed Reservations** on any sold-out Southeast-operated flight to any city we serve when you purchase a full Coach fare at least 24 hours before departure.
- **First or Global Business Class Check-in** on Southeast and ITW flights, and pre-boarding privileges on Southeast even when you're traveling in Coach Class. *em dash*
- **Global Perks Packs**, an exclusive selection of Bonus Mile offers, discounts for car rental, motels and hotels, weekend air travel, and more.

continues

7 Apply the List Table 3 - Accent 5 table style (sixth column, third row in the *List Tables* section) to the table.

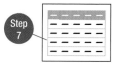

8 Select row 2 and then apply bold formatting. ***Hint: You may need to click the Bold button twice.***

9 Proofread the document and correct any errors.

10 Save the document.

11 Click the Check button to upload the document for checking.

12 If errors are reported by the Online Lab, view the results document, correct the errors in the submitted document, save the document, and then click the Check Again button.

Figure 107.1 Terms and Definitions for Document 107.1

Abdominal	Referring to the abdomen and its function and disorders
Adhesion	Fibrous bands of scar tissue attached to organs
Bowel	The large intestine
Cardiac	Referring to the heart
Comminuted fracture	A bone broken into pieces
Compression	State of being squeezed together
Diabetes mellitus	A metabolic disorder characterized by hyperglycemia and glycosuria resulting from inadequate production or use of insulin
Ecchymosis	Bruising of the skin
Fragmentation	Breaking up into pieces or fragments
Hematochezia	Passage of blood per rectum, usually in stool
Hypercholesterolemia	High levels of cholesterol in the blood
Hysterectomy	Operation that removes the uterus
Intertrochanteric	Located between the greater and lesser trochanter of the femur
Lateral	Referring to the side
Melena	Black tarry feces resulting from intestinal hemorrhage
Neurovascular	Involving both the nervous and vascular systems
Obstruction	Blocking of a structure that prevents normal functioning
Trochanter	Either of the two bony projections at the upper end of the femur
Vital signs	Breathing rate, pulse, blood pressure, and temperature

Figure 69.3 Multiple-Page Letter Content for Document 69.1—continued

speeds two and four times. Voice and speech recognition systems are available that provide an alternative to keyboarding input; however, keyboarding remains the most efficient and cost-effective way to do most data entry and document composition.

~~Joan,~~ I suggest that you offer a counterproposal to your chancellor and academic deans that will enhance the marketability of your graduates. Make it mandatory that a keyboarding pretest be given to all incoming students. Individuals who do not reach a minimum proficiency level ~~are~~ *would be* required to complete a keyboarding course or courses depending on the keyboarding activities related to the career being pursued by the student. The test ~~is to~~ *would* address the ability of the students to think and key without looking at their fingers and key at least two times faster than they can write. The average individual writes at 12 WPM.

If I can be of help to you in constructing this test ~~and/~~or establishing performance outcomes, please contact me at (888) 555-6711 or email a message to me at jbouchard@ppi-edu.net.

Document 69.2

Multiple-Page Letter with Bulleted Paragraphs and Bold and Italic Text

Read all instructions below before starting this document activity.

1. Navigate to the Document 69.2 launch page in the Online Lab and then click the Launch Activity button to open **Doc069.02** in the activity window.

2. Key the business letter shown in Figure 69.4, implementing the proofreading marks as you key.

   a. Key February 3, 2020 as the date.

   b. Apply bold and italic formatting as shown in the figure. *Hint: Do not format the spaces or punctuation following the formatted text.*

   c. Format the bulleted list using solid, black, round bullets.

   d. Add an extra line space between the bulleted paragraphs (including the last one). *Note: Make sure there is no space between the period at the end of each bulleted paragraph and the Shift + Enter line break.*

   e. Use the closing *Sincerely,* and indicate that the letter is being sent by John T. Williams, Vice President, Marketing. *Hint: Key the sender's name on one line and the title and department on the next.*

   f. After the title line, key the reference initials ebo and the file name and include a notation for two enclosures.

3. Create a vertical header for the second page of the letter. Use the *Blank* header option. *Note: Refer to Figure 69.2 to see the type of information to be keyed in the header.*

4. Proofread and correct any errors in the letter.

steps continue

Document 107.2 **Consultation Report Template**

Read all instructions below before starting this document activity.

1 Navigate to the Document 107.2 launch page in the Online Lab and then click the Launch Activity button to open **Doc107.02** in the activity window.

2 Change the line spacing to single spacing with no spacing after paragraphs.

3 Turn on the display of nonprinting characters.

4 Set a left tab at the 2-inch mark on the horizontal ruler.

5 Key the following:

PATIENT NAME:[Tab][Enter]

MR #:[Tab][Enter]

DOB:[Tab][Enter]

PHYSICIAN:[Tab][Enter]

CONSULTANT:[Tab][Enter]

DATE OF CONSULT:[Tab][Enter]

6 Remove the left tab from the horizontal ruler and then press Enter. *Note: The insertion point should be two lines below the* **DATE OF CONSULT** *heading.*

7 Key the headings, signature line, and reference information for the Consultation report using the information provided in Figure 107.2. For the signature line, key 30 underscores, and do not let Word automatically format the signature line. (Press Ctrl + Z to undo the change.) Do not key spaces after the colons at the bottom of the document.

8 Turn off the display of nonprinting characters.

9 Proofread the document and correct any errors.

10 Save the document.

11 Click the Check button to upload the document for checking.

12 If errors are reported by the Online Lab, view the results document, correct the errors in the submitted document, save the document, and then click the Check Again button.

Figure 107.2 Headings for the Consultation Report for Document 107.2

REASON FOR CONSULTATION [3 Enters]

PHYSICAL EXAMINATION [3 Enters]

DIAGNOSTIC STUDIES [3 Enters]

IMPRESSION [3 Enters]

RECOMMENDATIONS [5 Enters]

_____ [Enter]

, MD [2 Enters]

xxx/xxx [Enter]

D: [Enter]

T:

Figure 69.3 Multiple-Page Letter Content for Document 69.1

Dr. Joan Gallagher
Quincy Community College
805 Lafayette Boulevard
Bridgeport, CT 06603-4459

Dear Dr. Gallagher: *g*

Please share the following with your chancellor and academic deans. If keyboarding is to be eliminated in your community college, I assume that English will be dropped from your school as well. Your administrators must be made aware that keyboarding is a tool of *literacy*. According to the US Department of Labor, ~~currently~~ at least 90 percent of all jobs ~~will~~ involve some form of keyboarding as part of the daily work activities.

Here is some ~~fruit~~ for thought: *food*

1. Remember that we are in the *Information Age - a* world where computers have become essential.   *1/M*

2. Think of managers and professionals trying to compose email messages ~~using their two index fingers~~ and entering information into databases and spreadsheets, developing presentations using computer software packages designed to do this, or *surfing the net* for information related to their profession *using their two index fingers.*

3. Think of the nurses and doctors who must use the computer to look up information on patients and have to look at their keyboards and watch their fingers as they enter a patient's record number.

4. ~~Have you~~ noticed the overnight delivery service drivers and the keypad they must use to track packages and delivery times. The input is similar to using a numeric keypad to enter information and unless they can touch key, *their* ~~there~~ time is wasted.

5. *watch* Wait in line sometime at an airline counter or hotel registration desk to check in and the agent or desk clerk uses two fingers to enter required information.

The individual who cannot think and key by touch will be at a distinct disadvantage in the world of work. The ability to think and key without looking at the keyboard increases writing and ~~two-finger~~ keyboarding

continues

Document
107.3

Consultation Report

Read all instructions below before starting this document activity.

1 Navigate to the Document 107.3 launch page in the Online Lab and then click the Launch Activity button to open **Doc107.03** in the activity window.

2 Turn on the display of nonprinting characters.

3 Key the report shown in Figure 107.3. If a heading is required and is not available in the base file, key the heading. Make sure there is only one blank line between sections of the report. Do not allow Word to automatically format the numbered list. Key a space, not a tab, after the numbers in the numbered list.

4 Key the signature line and the reference information at the bottom of the report. There should be three blank lines between the last section and the signature line.

   a The physician signing the report is the consulting physician listed at the top of the report.

   b Key the reference initials alb for the dictator's initials and tlm for the transcriptionist's initials.

   c Key the dictation and transcription dates to match the date of the consultation. There should be one space between the colon and the date.

5 Use Find and Replace to search the document and replace the following letter pair placeholders with the corresponding medical terms. *Hint: Do not replace the letter pairs when they appear within words.*

   a Find instances of *ic* and replace them with *intertrochanteric*.

   b Find instances of *hy* and replace them with *hypercholesterolemia*.

   c Find instances of *nr* and replace them with *neurovascular*.

6 Turn off the display of nonprinting characters.

7 Proofread the document and correct any errors.

8 Save the document.

9 Click the Check button to upload the document for checking.

10 If errors are reported by the Online Lab, view the results document, correct the errors in the submitted document, save the document, and then click the Check Again button.

Figure 107.3 Consultation Report Content for Document 107.3

PATIENT NAME:	Haku A. Osaki
MR #:	5534
DOB:	01/11/1945
PHYSICIAN:	S. J. North, MD
CONSULTANT:	E. L. Berman, MD
DATE OF CONSULT:	05/13/2020

REASON FOR CONSULTATION

Patient is a 75-year-old male who slipped and fell at his home. He landed on his right hip and sustained a displaced comminuted ic hip fracture

continues

7 Key the date portion of the header by following these steps:

   a Confirm that your insertion point is in the correct position. If you are keying a vertical style header, press Enter so that the insertion point appears one line below the page number. If you are using the horizontal style header, click the right placeholder.

   b Key the date as it appears on the first page of the letter. *Note: The date in a header must always match the date on the first page of the letter. If a letter is edited on a different date than it was keyed, be sure to change both the date on the first page and the date in the header.*

8 Click the Close Header and Footer button in the Close group or double-click in the body of the document.

If you need to make changes to the contents of a header later, double-click in the header to make it active, make your changes, and then click the Close Header and Footer button or double-click in the body of the document to make the document active.

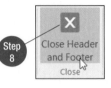

Document 69.1 **Multiple-Page Letter with Numbered Paragraphs and Italic Text**

Read all instructions below before starting this document activity.

1 Navigate to the Document 69.1 launch page in the Online Lab and then click the Launch Activity button to open **Doc069.01** in the activity window.

2 Key the letter shown in Figure 69.3, formatting it as a business letter.

   a Key March 13, 2020 as the date.

   b Implement the proofreading marks and set text in italics as shown in the figure. *Hint: Do not format the spaces or punctuation following the italic phrases.*

   c Allow Word to automatically format the numbered list. Add one extra line space between the numbered items by pressing Shift + Enter.

   d Remove the hyperlink for the email address.

   e Use the closing *Sincerely*, and indicate that the letter is being sent by Jaana Bouchard, Marketing Manager.

3 Create a horizontal continuation header on the second page of the letter. Use the *Blank (Three Columns)* header option and remember to click in each text placeholder to key or insert the appropriate information. *Note: Refer to Figure 69.2 to see the type of information to be entered in the three text placeholders of the header. A check mark has already been inserted in the **Different First Page** check box since the document already contains a header on the first page.*

4 After the title line, key the reference initials cuv and the file name.

5 Proofread and correct any errors in the letter.

6 Save the document.

7 Click the Check button to upload the document for checking.

8 If errors are reported by the Online Lab, view the results document, correct the errors in the submitted document, save the document, and then click the Check Again button.

Figure 107.3 Consultation Report Content for Document 107.3—continued

with fragmentation of the lesser trochanter areas as well. He is presently comfortable on bed rest in the emergency room. Pertinent medical problems include noninsulin-dependent diabetes mellitus, hy, and history of unknown lower extremity surgery. The remainder of his social history and family history is noted in Dr. North's admission record. A review of systems is unremarkable.

PHYSICAL EXAMINATION

On physical examination, the patient is alert, oriented, and comfortable on bed rest, with stable vital signs. The upper extremities have full range of motion without tenderness and nr status is intact, as well as the left lower extremity. No tenderness on lateral pelvic compression. Thoracic and lumbar spine nontender to palpation, and he has full range of motion to his cervical spine. The remainder of the HEENT, lungs, cardiac, and abdominal exam is noted in Dr. North's pre-anesthetic medical evaluation. The right lower extremity rests in a foreshortened and externally rotated position with no swelling and no ecchymosis. His nr status is intact.

X-RAYS

Review of x-rays demonstrates a comminuted right ic hip fracture with comminution of the greater trochanter, as well as the lesser trochanter.

IMPRESSION

1. Right comminuted ic hip fracture.
2. Noninsulin-dependent diabetes mellitus.
3. Hy.

RECOMMENDATIONS

The patient is being admitted and taken to surgery this evening for open reduction and internal fixation of high right ic hip fracture. The need for surgery was discussed with the family and patient. The risks, potential complications, and treatment alternatives were discussed. The plan is to proceed with surgery tonight. Consent was obtained with the patient's understanding.

Ending the Session

The Online Lab automatically saved the work you completed for this session. You may continue with the next session or exit the Online Lab and continue later.

4 Click the *Different First Page* check box to insert a check mark. This option is located in the Options group on the Header & Footer Tools Design tab, a contextual tab that is available when the header or footer is active. Selecting the *Different First Page* option means that the second and subsequent pages of a document will have a different header than the first page. In a letter, the first page includes the recipient's name and the date in the body of the letter, so this information is not needed in the first page header.

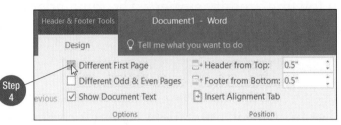

5 Click the first *[Type here]* placeholder and then key the recipient's name. If you are keying a vertical header using the *Blank* header option, there will be one text placeholder. If you are keying a horizontal header using the *Blank (Three Columns)* option, there will be three text placeholders. In either header format, you do not need to delete the placeholder(s); just click in it and key the text.

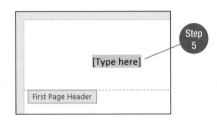

6 Key the page number portion of the header by following these steps:

a Confirm that your insertion point is in the correct position. If keying a vertical style header, press Enter so that the insertion point appears one line below the recipient's name, key *Page*, and then press the spacebar. (Headers contain single line spacing by default.) If you are using the horizontal style header, click the middle placeholder but do not key *Page*.

b Click the Page Number button in the Header & Footer group on the Header & Footer Tools Design tab.

c At the drop-down list, point to *Current Position* and then click *Plain Number* at the side menu.

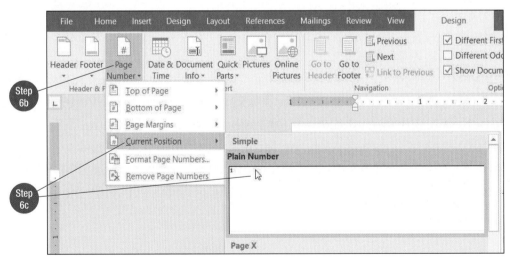

steps continue

Session
108

Operative Reports

Session Objectives

- Create a table containing medical terms and definitions
- Create an operative report template and document
- Increase productivity by using Find and Replace
- Efficiently produce documents in mailable form

Getting Started

Exercise 108.1 Unless you are continuing immediately after completing Session 107, spend at least two to three minutes warming up before completing the document activities in this session. See Session 101 for suggested warm-up text.

Preparing Operative Reports

When surgery is performed on a patient, a report of the surgery is dictated by the surgeon. This report, called an *operative report*, is transcribed and placed in the patient's record. Generally, the report contains a preoperative and postoperative diagnosis and describes the condition of the patient after surgery.

Document 108.1 Medical Terminology List

Read all instructions below before starting this document activity.

1 Navigate to the Document 108.1 launch page in the Online Lab and then click the Launch Activity button to open **Doc108.01** in the activity window.

2 Use the Insert Table dialog box to insert a table that contains 2 columns and 16 rows.

3 Change the width of the first column to 2 inches and the width of the second column to 4.64 inches.

4 Merge cells A1 and B1, format the contents of the merged cell so it is centered and aligns to the top center of the cell, key MEDICAL TERMINOLOGY, and then apply bold formatting.

5 Select row 2 and then apply bold formatting

6 Key Term in cell A2 and then key Definition in cell B2.

7 Key the terms and definitions shown in Figure 108.1.

8 Apply Green, Accent 6, Lighter 80% shading (last column, second row in the *Theme Colors* section) to rows 1 and 2 of the table.

9 Remove the inside vertical border for all rows (except row 1, which has no inside borders) in the table.

steps continue

Figure 69.2 Continuation Header Options

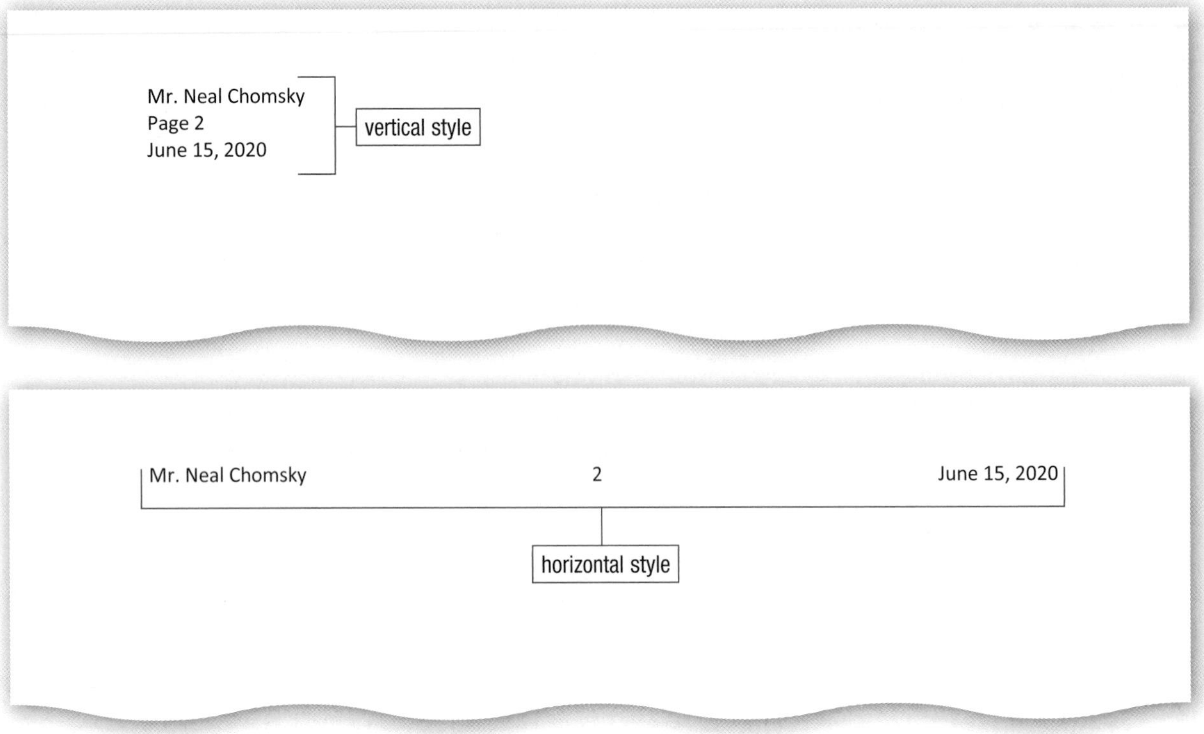

Mr. Neal Chomsky
Page 2
June 15, 2020
— vertical style

Mr. Neal Chomsky   2   June 15, 2020

horizontal style

Word has automated the process of inserting headers. Headers may be inserted at any time; however, it is simpler to insert a header after the document has been keyed—or at least after you begin to key the second page.

After keying a letter that is more than one page long, position the insertion point in a location on the second page and then follow these steps to insert a header:

1 Click the Insert tab.

2 Click the Header button in the Header & Footer group.

3 Click the appropriate header format option from the drop-down list. The *Blank* option is used for the vertical (three-line) header and the *Blank* (*Three Columns*) option is used for the horizontal style (one-line) header.

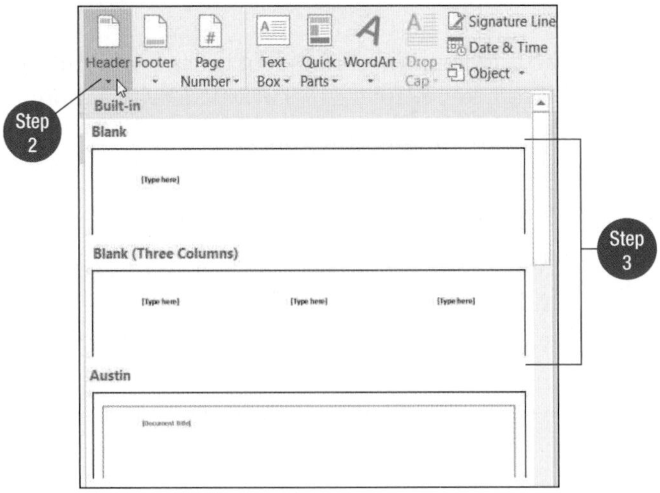

steps continue

10 Proofread the document and correct any errors.

11 Save the document.

12 Click the Check button to upload the document for checking.

13 If errors are reported by the Online Lab, view the results document, correct the errors in the submitted document, save the document, and then click the Check Again button.

Figure 108.1 Terms and Definitions for Document 108.1

Abductor	Muscle that contracts to pull a limb away from the body
Carpal tunnel syndrome	Condition in which pressure is placed on the median nerve where it goes through the carpal tunnel of the wrist; causes soreness and weakness of the muscles of the thumb and fingers
Cortex	Outer layer of an organ
Fascia	A fibrous membrane that covers and separates muscles
Femoral	Referring to the thigh bone or femur
Hemostasis	Stopping the flow or circulation of blood
Irrigate	To wash out with a stream of liquid
Latency	Condition of being hidden or inactive
Lumbosacral	Referring to the vertebrae in the lower back
Parietal	Referring to, or forming, the wall of a cavity
Peritoneum	Membrane that lines the abdominal cavity
Radiculopathy	Spinal nerve root disorder
Transverse	Lying crosswise
Viscera	Internal organs enclosed within the abdomen

Document 108.2 **Operative Report Template**

Read all instructions below before starting this document activity.

1 Navigate to the Document 108.2 launch page in the Online Lab and then click the Launch Activity button to open **Doc108.02** in the activity window.

2 Change the line spacing to single space with no spacing after paragraphs.

3 Turn on the display of nonprinting characters.

4 Set a left tab at the 2-inch mark on the horizontal ruler.

continues

Make sure Widow/Orphan control is turned on by following these steps:

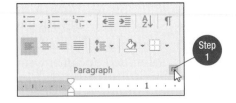

1 On the Home tab, click the Paragraph group dialog box launcher.

2 Click the Line and Page Breaks tab, if it is not already selected.

3 If there is no check mark next to *Widow/Orphan control*, click the check box to insert a check mark and make the option active.

4 Click OK to apply the changes and close the dialog box.

Even with Widow/Orphan control turned on, it may be necessary to force a page break within a document. Forcing a page break is discussed in the next section, and will be used beginning with Business Reports in Unit 16.

Inserting a Hard Page Break

To insert a page break in a document, position the insertion point where you want the break to occur, click the Insert tab, and then click the Page Break button in the Pages group (see Figure 69.1) or press the keyboard shortcut Ctrl + Enter. A page break that is created using the Page Break button or the keyboard shortcut is called a *hard page break*.

Inserting Headers

A letter that is longer than one page should include a continuation header on the second page and on any subsequent pages. The header of a business letter contains three pieces of information: the name of the addressee (the recipient of the letter), the page number, and the date. The two most common formats for continuation headers are the vertical style and the horizontal style. As shown in Figure 69.2, the vertical style uses three separate lines, whereas the horizontal style puts all of the information on one line.

Figure 69.1 Page Break Button in the Pages Group

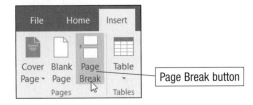

5 Key the following:

    PATIENT NAME:[Tab][Enter]

    MR #:[Tab][Enter]

    SURGEON:[Tab][Enter]

    ASSISTANT:[Tab][Enter]

    DATE OF SURGERY:[Tab][Enter]

6 Remove the left tab from the horizontal ruler and then press Enter. *Note: The insertion point should be two lines below the* **DATE OF SURGERY** *heading.*

7 Key the headings, signature line, and reference information for the Operative report using the information provided in Figure 108.2. Do not key spaces after the colons. For the signature line, key 30 underscores, and do not let Word automatically format the signature line. *Hint: Press Ctrl + Z to undo the change.*

8 Turn off the display of nonprinting characters.

9 Proofread the document and correct any errors.

10 Save the document.

11 Click the Check button to upload the document for checking.

12 If errors are reported by the Online Lab, view the results document, correct the errors in the submitted document, save the document, and then click the Check Again button.

Figure 108.2 Headings for the Operative Report for Document 108.2

PREOPERATIVE DIAGNOSIS [3 Enters]

POSTOPERATIVE DIAGNOSIS [3 Enters]

NAME OF OPERATION [3 Enters]

ANESTHESIA [3 Enters]

INDICATIONS [3 Enters]

INFORMED CONSENT [3 Enters]

PROCEDURE [3 Enters]

ESTIMATED BLOOD LOSS [3 Enters]

COMPLICATIONS [3 Enters]

SPECIMENS [5 Enters]

_____ [Enter]

, MD [2 Enters]

xxx/xxx [Enter]

D: [Enter]

T:

Complete one 3-minute timing on the timing text below.

**Timing
69.3**

When purchasing dry beans, inspect the package and look for firm, clean, whole beans of uniform size and color. Some varieties, such as large limas, are more susceptible to being broken or having broken seed coats than are other varieties. However, broken or wrinkled beans will seldom affect the taste of the finished bean dish. For consistent quality, locate a brand you like and stick with it.

Canned beans are acceptable for at least 150 kinds of bean recipes, and their best attribute is their timesaving qualities. Some beans, such as dark, red kidneys, are difficult to find, except in cans.

If you have a problem finding your favorite bean in dry or canned form, it might be because of the lack of demand for it in some stores. If you add your request to those already received by the store manager, you will probably soon find the store carrying that particular type of bean. The supermarket management is not going to know you are missing it if you do not mention it to them. Remember, all types of beans are an excellent choice to maintain your health.

Ergonomic Tip

To relieve pressure in your neck and shoulders, tilt your head back toward the ceiling and then down toward your chest. Repeat this a number of times to stretch your muscles.

Preparing Multiple-Page Letters

Most business letters fit on one page. However, some letters are more complex or detailed and may require additional pages. There are a few guidelines to consider when formatting multiple-page letters. For example, do not leave the complimentary closing, signature, etc., alone on its own page. If this content flows to a new page, you will have to modify the document so that other content flows to that page as well. You will learn how to do this in the following sections.

Word's default settings cause content to stop approximately 1 inch from the bottom of each page. This automatic page break is called a *soft page break*. Word's default settings also prevent undesirable breaks between pages, such as leaving one line of a paragraph on a page by itself. This feature is called *Widow/Orphan control*.

Operative Report

Read all instructions below before starting this document activity.

1 Navigate to the Document 108.3 launch page in the Online Lab and then click the Launch Activity button to open **Doc108.03** in the activity window.

2 Turn on the display of nonprinting characters.

3 Key the report shown in Figure 108.3. If a heading is not used in the final report, delete it from the document. Make sure that there is only one blank line between sections of the report.

4 Key the signature line and the reference information at the bottom of the report. There should be three blank lines between the last section and the signature line.

   a The physician signing the report is the surgeon listed at the top of the report.

   b Key the reference initials das for the dictator's initials and pbv for the transcriptionist's initials.

   c Key the dictation and transcription dates to match the date of the surgery. There should be one space between the colon and the date.

5 Search the document and replace the following letter pair placeholders with the corresponding medical terms. *Hint: Do not replace the letter pairs when they appear within words.*

   a Find instances of *ic* and replace them with *intertrochanteric*.

   b Find instances of *im* and replace them with *intermedullary*.

   c Find instances of *tr* and replace them with *trochanter*.

6 Turn off the display of nonprinting characters.

7 Proofread the document and correct any errors.

8 Save the document.

9 Click the Check button to upload the document for checking.

10 If errors are reported by the Online Lab, view the results document, correct the errors in the submitted document, save the document, and then click the Check Again button.

Figure 108.3 Operative Report Content for Document 108.3

PATIENT NAME:	Oscar Hernandez
MR #:	1109
SURGEON:	D. A. Strauss, MD
ASSISTANT:	A. V. Zjac, MD
DATE OF SURGERY:	03/23/2020

PREOPERATIVE DIAGNOSIS
Comminuted ic right hip fracture.

POSTOPERATIVE DIAGNOSIS
Comminuted ic right hip fracture.

continues

Session
69

Preparing Multiple-Page Business Letters

Session Objectives

- **Identify the difference between soft and hard page breaks**
- **Activate Widow/Orphan control**
- **Create continuation headers in multiple-page letters**
- **Create a personal business letter in response to a job advertisement**
- **Efficiently produce documents in mailable form**

Getting Started

Exercise 69.1

If you are continuing immediately from Session 68, you may skip the Exercise 69.1 warm-up drill. However, if you exited the Online Lab at the end of Session 68, warm up by completing Exercise 69.1.

Begin your session work by completing Exercise 69.2, a timed short drill, in the Online Lab.

Assessing Your Speed and Accuracy

Exercise 69.2

Complete Timings 69.1 through 69.3 in the Online Lab. At the end of the timing, the Online Lab will display your WPM rate and any errors. Results will be saved in your Timings Performance report. If you have been surpassing the speed and accuracy goals identified in the Online Lab, set slightly more challenging personal goals and strive to exceed them.

Complete two 1-minute timings on the timing text below. If you meet or exceed both speed and accuracy goals for Timing 69.1, push for greater speed on Timing 69.2.

1-Minute Timings

Timings 69.1–69.2

Stock markets in the United States, which opened before the central banks announced their move, finished lower for the day. The statement came out in the middle of the trading day, an hour and a half before the markets closed. Borrowing costs for banks across the United States fell, which is an encouraging sign. These lower costs showed investors were willing to take money out of assets considered safe and invest in riskier assets like stocks.

Figure 108.3 Operative Report Content for Document 108.3—continued

NAME OF OPERATION

Open reduction internal fixation, right ic hip fracture. Richards im hip compression screw system, 14 mm im rod, 95 mm lag screw, one set screw, sleeve, and two 36 mm distal cortical interlocking screws.

ANESTHESIA

Spinal anesthesia.

PROCEDURE

The patient was brought to the operating room and underwent spinal anesthesia followed by sterile prep and drape of the right lower extremity in a routine fashion. The patient was on the fracture table with the right lower extremity secured in a traction boot and the left lower extremity comfortably padded with Gelfoam and in a padded stirrup. An x-ray was utilized to demonstrate desired reduction of fracture fragments. An incision was made proximal to the greater tr, identifying the greater tr. A pin and drill allowed entrance into the im canal by lateral visualization. Serial reaming was done down the canal to judge the size of the 4-inch medullary rod. The rod went to 15 mm and was accepted at 14 mm. The canal was reamed to 18 mm proximally, and the rod was placed down the canal. The rod sounded without difficulty and the 14 mm rod was placed. Step reaming was accomplished and a lag screw was then placed that measured 95 mm. A sleeve was tapped across the outer cortex and through the channel of the bone. Upon placement of the screw and sleeve, the set screw was placed with a torque wrench from proximal to distal. After it was secured, the two distal cortical interlocking screws were placed across jig and sleeve. The wounds were all irrigated with normal saline and polymyxin bacitracin solution. The band and the abductor fascia were closed with a #1 Vicryl simple running suture. A drain deep to the abductor fascia was inserted and then closed with 2-0 Vicryl running stitch. The patient tolerated the procedure well and returned to the recovery room in stable condition.

Ending the Session

The Online Lab automatically saved the work you completed for this session. You may continue with the next session or exit the Online Lab and continue later.

Reinforcing Writing Skills

The inductive method of developing a paragraph places the topic sentence at the end of the paragraph rather than at the beginning. A writer uses the inductive method to lead the reader to a desired conclusion. The inductive method is often used to communicate bad news. Rather than present unpleasant facts right away, the writer provides a buffer of information first. A good example of the inductive method is illustrated in the letter created for Document 68.3. Take a moment to re-read the letter shown in Figure 68.4.

Letters that advertise products or services may also be written using the inductive method. The paragraph that follows is an example of one such letter. In this case, the writer is seeking an interview for a job that has not been advertised. Thus, she needs to explain her situation before getting to the purpose of her letter.

My name is Jacki Splitek, and I have been working as a commercial travel agent for 10 years. I'm interested in relocating to the Atlanta area. One of my clients who travels a great deal indicated that your agency was opening a branch in DeKalb County, Georgia. I will be in Atlanta May 19 to May 24. May I meet with you on May 20, sometime between 9 a.m. and noon, to discuss a job with your agency?

Practice composing a letter that includes an inductive paragraph in the following document activity.

Document 68.4

Composing a Personal Business Letter with an Inductive Paragraph

Read all instructions below before starting this document activity.

1. Navigate to the Document 68.4 launch page in the Online Lab and then click the Launch Activity button to open **Doc068.04** in the activity window.

2. Prepare a rough draft of a personal business letter to your instructor. Use your instructor's name and school address and the format you learned in Session 66.

3. In the body of the letter, write at least two paragraphs. In the first paragraph, describe to your instructor the type of job you would like to have in the future. In the second paragraph, use the inductive method to compose a paragraph of four to six sentences asking your instructor for a letter of recommendation.

4. After completing the draft, analyze the content on screen. Does the topic sentence of your inductive paragraph clearly state the main idea or topic? Do the sentences that precede the topic sentence reinforce and expand on the content? If needed, make changes in the inductive paragraph.

5. Add formatting to enhance your letter.

6. Proofread and correct any errors in the letter.

7. Save the document.

8. Click the Submit button to upload the document for instructor review.

Ending the Session

The Online Lab automatically saved the work you completed for this session. You may continue with the next session or exit the Online Lab and continue later.

Session 109

Radiology Reports

Session Objectives

- Create a table containing medical terms and definitions
- Create a radiology report template and document
- Increase productivity by using Find and Replace
- Efficiently produce documents in mailable form

Getting Started

Exercise 109.1 Unless you are continuing immediately after completing Session 108, spend at least two to three minutes warming up before completing the document activities in this session. See Session 101 for suggested warm-up text.

Preparing Radiology Reports

Radiology is a medical specialty that uses various types of imaging techniques in the diagnosis and treatment of disease. Ultrasound, x-rays, CAT (or CT) scans, and MRI imaging are common types of radiological techniques. During the course of treating a patient, a medical provider may prescribe an x-ray or ultrasound procedure. Upon completion of the procedure, the radiologist dictates a report. This audio report is then either transcribed automatically via a voice recognition system or keyed by a transcriptionist. This report then becomes part of the patient's record.

Document 109.1 Medical Terminology List

Read all instructions below before starting this document activity.

1. Navigate to the Document 109.1 launch page in the Online Lab and then click the Launch Activity button to open **Doc109.01** in the activity window.
2. Use the Insert Table dialog box to insert a table that contains 2 columns and 11 rows.
3. Change the width of the first column to 2 inches and the width of the second column to 4.64 inches.
4. Select row 1 and then merge the cells.
5. Key MEDICAL TERMINOLOGY in cell A1 and then format the contents of the cell so it is centered and aligns to the top center of the cell.
6. Key the terms and definitions shown in Figure 109.1. *Note: A row containing the column headings will be inserted after the table content has been keyed.*
7. Apply the Grid Table 5 Dark - Accent 2 table style (third column, fifth row in *Grid Tables* section) to the table.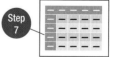
8. Sort the table so the terms appear alphabetically. *Hint: Ensure that you select only the terms and definitions, not the title of the table, before sorting.*

steps continue

4   Proofread the document and correct any errors.

5   Save the document.

6   Click the Check button to upload the document for checking.

7   If errors are reported by the Online Lab, view the results document, correct the errors in the submitted document, save the document, and then click the Check Again button.

Figure 68.4 Business Letter Content for Document 68.3

Mr. John MacLennan
24809 Spanish Trace Drive
Maryland Heights, MO 63042-3385

Dear John:

As a valued customer of ~~the~~ Ozark Travel and Cruise Center, Ltd., we want you to be aware of what is happening in the airline industry. Changes are being made that adversely affect travel agencies and their clientele. Here is a sampling of what has taken place so far this year:

1. World Airlines lowered the base commission paid to travel agencies from **10%** *percent* to **8%**. Within a week of the announcement, all other major airlines matched this policy.

2. TransAmerican Airlines capped the maximum commission they would pay travel agencies on round-trip tickets at **$50** and **$25** on a one-way ticket. Again, all major airlines followed suit.

3. Unlike last year's changes, the changes this year affects **any and all** tickets we issue; our compensation for these tickets has been reduced by **20%**. *percent*

Unfortunately, this action initiated by the major airlines requires action on our part. Effective immediately for all new reservations, we will charge a transaction fee of $15 per ticket. This will help us recover only a portion of the lost revenue.

I believe a travel agency is still the most cost-effective way of wading through the thousands of constantly changing schedules and prices. We want to continue serving your travel needs. Please call me at (800) 555-1025 should you have questions.

Sincerely,

Carl C. Higgins, CTC
President

Figure 109.1 Terms and Definitions for Document 109.1

Endotracheal tube	Tube used to make an airway through the trachea
Jejunum	The second part of the small intestine, from the duodenum to the ileum
Sternotomy	The procedure of cutting through the breastbone
Ileum	Lower three-fifths of the small intestine
Enteroclysis	Imaging test using contrast dye to see how liquid moves through the small intestine
Dilation	Expansion of an opening, organ, or vessel
Mediastinal drain	Drain in the septum or chest cavity
Barium	A soft metallic element used with x-rays
Fluoroscope	A device consisting of a fluorescent screen and roentgen tube; makes visible the shadows of objects placed between the tube and the screen
Pneumothorax	A collection of air or gas in the chest cavity resulting from a cut through the chest wall

9 Position the insertion point in cell A1 and then insert a new row below the first row.

10 Split the new row into two columns.

11 Format the column widths so that they align with the columns in the body of the table.

12 Key Term in cell A2 and Definition in cell B2.

13 Apply bold formatting to the text in the second row and make sure second-row text aligns to the top center of the cells.

14 Proofread the document and correct any errors.

15 Save the document.

16 Click the Check button to upload the document for checking.

17 If errors are reported by the Online Lab, view the results document, correct the errors in the submitted document, save the document, and then click the Check Again button.

Document 109.2

Radiology Report Template

Read all instructions below before starting this document activity.

1 Navigate to the Document 109.2 launch page in the Online Lab and then click the Launch Activity button to open **Doc109.02** in the activity window.

2 Change the line spacing to single spacing with no spacing after paragraphs.

3 Turn on the display of nonprinting characters.

4 Set a left tab at the 2-inch mark on the horizontal ruler.

steps continue

Figure 68.3 Business Letter Content for Document 68.2

Ms. Brienna Sanchez ¶ National Consultant ¶ PPI Publishing Company ¶ 2732 South Kenneth ¶ Chicago, IL 60642-2488 ¶ Dear Brienna: ¶ I reviewed your PowerPoint presentation, *Keyboarding Today and in the Future*. The presentation is really well done; you did a super job covering all facets of the topic. There are several things, although not critical, that you might add to the presentation. ¶ 1. Following the workstation ergonomics display, add a slide that includes a picture of a personal computer and printer with labeled components. ¶ 2. Right after this slide, add two more: one featuring a close-up of the alphanumeric keyboard and another containing the full keyboard (all 101 keys). See the enclosed sketch that includes labels that call attention to critical components. ¶ 3. One other slide to consider adding is a close-up of the toolbar and a description of the function of each icon. This slide would follow the slide with the image of the blank document scream. ¶ Again, you have a great program that will be enjoyed by those who see it. It certainly is comprehensive and easy to digest. ¶ Sincerely, ¶ Barun Abdullah ¶ Marketing Manager

4 Proofread the document and correct any errors.

5 Save the document.

6 Click the Check button to upload the document for checking.

7 If errors are reported by the Online Lab, view the results document, correct the errors in the submitted document, save the document, and then click the Check Again button.

Document 68.3 **Business Letter with Custom Left and Right Margins, Bold Text, and Numbered Paragraphs**

Read all instructions below before starting this document activity.

1 Navigate to the Document 68.3 launch page in the Online Lab and then click the Launch Activity button to open **Doc068.03** in the activity window.

2 Key the text shown in Figure 68.4, implementing the proofreading marks as you key and formatting the letter as a business letter.

a Key April 24, 2020 as the current date of the letter.

b Make sure to apply bold formatting as indicated in the figure. *Hint: Refer to Appendix B, Proofreading Marks, if necessary.*

c Allow Word to automatically format the numbered list. Do not add an extra line space between the items in the list.

d Key the reference initials adt and the file name under the title line.

3 Change the left and right margins of the letter to 1.5 inches.

steps continue

5 Key the following:
    PATIENT NAME:[Tab][Enter]
    MR #:[Tab][Enter]
    REQUESTING PHYSICIAN:[Tab][Enter]
    DATE:[Tab][Enter]

6 Remove the left tab from the horizontal ruler and then press Enter. *Note: The insertion point should be two lines below the* **DATE** *heading.*

7 Key the headings, signature line, and reference information for the Radiology report using the information provided in Figure 109.2. Do not key spaces after the colons. For the signature line, key 30 underscores, and do not let Word automatically format the signature line. *Hint: Press Ctrl + Z to undo the change.*

8 Turn off the display of nonprinting characters.

9 Proofread the document and correct any errors.

10 Save the document.

11 Click the Check button to upload the document for checking.

12 If errors are reported by the Online Lab, view the results document, correct the errors in the submitted document, save the document, and then click the Check Again button.

Figure 109.2 Headings for the Radiology Report for Document 109.2

NAME OF TEST [3 Enters]

IMPRESSION [5 Enters]

_____ [Enter]

, MD [2 Enters]

xxx/xxx [Enter]

D: [Enter]

T:

Document
109.3

Radiology Report

Read all instructions below before starting this document activity.

1 Navigate to the Document 109.3 launch page in the Online Lab and then click the Launch Activity button to open **Doc109.03** in the activity window.

2 Turn on the display of nonprinting characters.

3 Key the report shown in Figure 109.3. Select the heading *NAME OF TEST* and then key BARIUM EN. After keying the report, make sure that there is only one blank line between sections of the report.

4 Key the signature line and the reference information at the bottom of the report. There should be three blank lines between the last section and the signature line.

   a The physician signing the report is K. E. Kassane.

   b Key the reference initials kek for the dictator's initials and elt for the transcriptionist's initials.

   c Key the dictation and transcription dates to match the date of the report. There should be one space between the colon and the date.

steps continue

Figure 68.2 Business Letter Content for Document 68.1—continued

1. Members are assigned to a section of the village close to their homes. A badge, an orange vest with reflector tape, and a pair of work gloves are issued to each member.

2. We gather each Saturday morning at our assigned section, pick up our tools, and start to work.

3. Work activities include raking, trimming trees and bushes, sweeping, and picking up debris.

4. We work for 1-1/2 hours each week. Summer hours are 6:30 to 8:00 a.m., and winter hours are 7:30 to 9:00 a.m.

5. We meet once a month following our work schedule on the third Saturday at the Community Services Center for a meeting, coffee, and donuts.

There are other activities scheduled at various times to include an annual picnic in April or May and a holiday luncheon in December. If you would like to be a member of the Denham Springs Prides, please fill out and return the enclosed membership card. We will send you a badge, vest, and gloves and inform you of your work area. It is gratifying to belong to an organization that improves the appearance of our community.

Sincerely,

Donna J. Horton
Membership Chair

Document 68.2

Business Letter with Numbered Paragraphs and Italic Text

Read all instructions below before starting this document activity.

1. Navigate to the Document 68.2 launch page in the Online Lab and then click the Launch Activity button to open **Doc068.02** in the activity window.

2. Read the text shown in Figure 68.3 and use proofreading marks to note any necessary corrections before keying the letter.

3. Key the text shown in Figure 68.3. Follow the formatting guidelines for a business letter introduced in Session 67.

   a. Key March 13, 2020 as the current date of the letter.

   b. In the first paragraph of the letter, set the presentation title in italic as shown in the figure. *Note: Do not format the period in italic that follows the presentation name.*

   c. Allow Word to automatically format the numbered list as you key. Add an extra line space between items in the numbered list.

   d. Key the reference initials btm and the file name and include a notation for an enclosure.

steps continue

Figure 109.3 Radiology Report Content for Document 109.3

PATIENT NAME: Tabitha Rosemond

MR #:   4113

REQUESTING PHYSICIAN: Y. A. Yakamura, MD

DATE: 05/22/2020

BARIUM EN

A barium en through an Anderson tube was completed. Scout film was used, which shows small-bowel loops. The long intestinal tube is noted to be coiled upon itself with its tip in the area of the pj. A diluted barium en contrast material was administered via syringe and followed under fl control. The pj loops appeared normal. The fl reveals that loops begin to dilate within the area of gaseous dilation showing the slowest passage of barium. Closer to the mid-ileum area there appears to be a narrowing in the pelvis after which the small bowel resumes normal caliber. The exact location of this is difficult to ascertain with certainty, but the finding is consistent with an adhesive band.

IMPRESSION

Partial small-bowel obstruction in the mid-ileum.

5   Search the document and replace the following letter pair placeholders with the corresponding medical terms. *Hint: Do not replace the letter pairs when they appear within words.*

   a   Find instances of *en* and replace them with *enteroclysis*.

   b   Find instances of *pj* and replace them with *proximal jejunum*.

   c   Find instances of *fl* and replace them with *fluoroscope*.

6   Turn off the display of nonprinting characters.

7   Proofread the document and correct any errors.

8   Save the document.

9   Click the Check button to upload the document for checking.

10   If errors are reported by the Online Lab, view the results document, correct the errors in the submitted document, save the document, and then click the Check Again button.

Ending the Session

The Online Lab automatically saved the work you completed for this session. You may continue with the next session or exit the Online Lab and continue later.

Figure 68.1 Paragraph Group on the Home tab

Numbering button

If bulleted or numbered paragraphs are lengthy, improve the readability of the list by creating an extra line space between each paragraph. To create this extra line space, press Shift + Enter and then Enter, rather than just Enter, after each line.

Practice keying business letters with numbered lists in the following document activities.

Document 68.1

Business Letter with Numbered Paragraphs and Underlined Text

Read all instructions below before starting this document activity.

1 Navigate to the Document 68.1 launch page in the Online Lab and then click the Launch Activity button to open **Doc068.01** in the activity window.

2 Read the text shown in Figure 68.2 and use proofreading marks for any necessary corrections before keying the letter.

3 Key the text shown in Figure 68.2. Follow the style for a business letter introduced in Session 67.

   a Key June 19, 2020 as the current date of the letter.

   b Underline *Denham Springs Prides* as shown in the figure. *Hint: Do not underline the period following the name.*

   c Allow Word to automatically format the numbered list as you key. Add an extra line space between items in the numbered list by pressing Shift + Enter. *Note: If Word does not automatically format the numbered list, make sure automatic numbering is turned on by clicking the File tab, clicking* **Options**, *clicking* **Proofing** *in the left panel, clicking the AutoCorrect Options button, clicking the AutoFormat As You Type tab, and then inserting a check mark in the* **Automatic numbered lists** *check box.*

   d Key the reference initials lcc and the file name and include a notation for an enclosure.

4 Proofread the document and correct any errors.

5 Save the document.

6 Click the Check button to upload the document for checking.

7 If errors are reported by the Online Lab, view the results document, correct the errors in the submitted document, save the document, and then click the Check Again button.

Figure 68.2 Business Letter Content for Document 68.1

Ms. Maureen Landeau
30588 West Knight Drive
Denham Springs, LA 70726-1023

Dear Ms. Landeau:

Thank you for your telephone call requesting information about the <u>Denham Springs Prides</u>. We were established in March 2007 and how have over 300 members. Here is a schedule of our activities:

continues

Session 110 Discharge Summary Reports

Session Objectives

- Create a table containing medical terms and definitions
- Create a discharge summary report template and document
- Increase productivity by using Find and Replace
- Efficiently produce documents in mailable form

Getting Started

Exercise 110.1 Unless you are continuing immediately after completing Session 109, spend at least two to three minutes warming up before completing the document activities in this session. See Session 101 for suggested warm-up text.

Preparing Discharge Summary Reports

A discharge summary report is prepared each time a patient is discharged from a hospital or medical center. The discharge summary report (also called a discharge order) contains much of the same information as the history and physical report but also includes a record of any surgical procedures, radiology reports, consultation information, and the condition of the patient upon discharge. The discharge summary report also includes instructions for follow-up care.

Document 110.1 Medical Terminology List

Read all instructions below before starting this document activity.

1. Navigate to the Document 110.1 launch page in the Online Lab and then click the Launch Activity button to open **Doc110.01** in the activity window.
2. Use the Insert Table dialog box to insert a table that contains 2 columns and 9 rows.
3. Change the width of the first column to 2 inches and the width of the second column to 4.64 inches.
4. Key Term in cell A1 and then key Definition in cell B1.
5. Key the terms and definitions shown in Figure 110.1.
6. Format the first row of the table as follows:
   a. Apply Green, Accent 6, Darker 25% shading (last column, fifth row in the *Theme Colors* section).
   b. Apply the White, Background 1 font color (first column, first row in the *Theme Colors* section).
   c. Apply bold formatting.

steps continue

Complete one 3-minute timing on the timing text below.

3-Minute Timing

Timing 68.3

If your animal is to be professionally shown at dog shows, then it will probably be necessary that you keep the dog's coat fairly long. Dedicated breeders of particular breeds feel that a dog's long coat is part of the heritage and beauty of the breed. However, for the ordinary dog that is not going to be shown professionally, a dog with long hair that is dirty and matted is just not nice to have around. A dog that is clean and neat will find itself much more welcome than one whose long coat has been neglected.

A professional groomer can make a dog look wonderful. However, you must be prepared. Some groomers will be reluctant to clip your longhaired dog. Rest assured that a short haircut is not going to injure your animal in any way. If you don't have the time to keep a long coat brushed, your dog will be much more comfortable with a short haircut. A short coat will also make it easier to treat any skin problems or to battle fleas. Some people simply prefer the appearance of a short puppy cut. If the groomer absolutely refuses to groom your dog any way except what is called for in the breed standard, find a groomer who is more concerned with your animal's comfort.

 Ergonomic Tip
Breathe deeply and rhythmically to calm down when under stress.

Using Numbered Paragraphs in Business Letters

Word allows you to create numbered paragraphs and lists in the same way you create bulleted lists. By default, when you start a paragraph with *1.* followed by a space or tab, Word will begin a numbered list. This means that Word indents the number and replaces the space with a nonprinting Tab character. If the numbered paragraph continues to a second line, the Word Wrap feature begins the second line with a hanging indent. In other words, the runover line will align with the text that follows the nonprinting Tab character, not with the number. To stop the numbering of paragraphs, press Enter twice.

Once a numbered list has been formatted, you can remove the formatting by selecting the list and clicking the Numbering button in the Paragraph group on the Home tab (see Figure 68.1). Or, if you wish to change the formatting of a numbered list (to a lettered list, for example), click the Numbering button arrow and then click the desired formatting option at the drop-down gallery.

7 Format rows 2 through 9 as follows:

   a Apply Green, Accent 6, Lighter 80% shading (last column, second row in the *Theme Colors* section).

   b Change the font to 12-point Cambria.

8 Sort the table so that the terms appear alphabetically.

9 Position the insertion point at the top of the document by pressing Ctrl + Home, press Enter, and then key MEDICAL TERMINOLOGY. Triple-click the heading and then format it in 11-point Arial Black and change the paragraph alignment for the heading to center alignment.

10 Proofread the document and correct any errors.

11 Save the document.

12 Click the Check button to upload the document for checking.

13 If errors are reported by the Online Lab, view the results document, correct the errors in the submitted document, save the document, and then click the Check Again button.

Figure 110.1 Terms and Definitions for Document 110.1

Cholecystectomy	Removal of the gallbladder
Amniocentesis	Puncture of the amniotic sac with a needle and syringe in order to remove amniotic fluid
Pancreatitis	Inflammation of the pancreas
Cholecystitis	Inflammation of the gallbladder
Cholelithiasis	Formation or presence of bile stones in the gallbladder
Ambulatory	Able to move or walk
Para	A woman who has produced an infant weighing 500 g or more or over 20 weeks gestation, regardless of whether or not the infant was alive at birth
Gravida	A pregnant woman

Session 68

Numbering Paragraphs in Business Letters

Session Objectives

- **Number paragraphs in business letters**
- **Build better paragraphs using the inductive method**
- **Efficiently produce documents in mailable form**

Getting Started

Exercise 68.1 If you are continuing immediately from Session 67, you may skip the Exercise 68.1 warm-up drill. However, if you exited the Online Lab at the end of Session 67, warm up by completing Exercise 68.1.

Exercise 68.2 Begin your session work by completing Exercise 68.2, a timed short drill, in the Online Lab.

Assessing Your Speed and Accuracy

Complete Timings 68.1 through 68.3 in the Online Lab. At the end of the timing, the Online Lab will display your WPM rate and any errors. Results will be saved in your Timings Performance report. If you have been surpassing the speed and accuracy goals identified in the Online Lab, set slightly more challenging personal goals and strive to exceed them.

Complete two 1-minute timings on the timing text below. If you meet or exceed both speed and accuracy goals for Timing 68.1, push for greater speed on Timing 68.2.

1-Minute Timings

Timings 68.1–68.2
The circus parades of the 1800s succumbed to change and have been lured into the realm of oblivion. The last echoes of the circus calliope are muted in yesteryear's golden sunset. Also gone are the thud of horses' hooves and the rumble of the splendid wagons that once moved over the roads. The circus brought relief from daily tasks when our nation was young. It introduced glitter, skill and daring, and wild animals to the nation's hardworking pioneers.

Document 110.2 Discharge Summary Report Template

Read all instructions below before starting this document activity.

1 Navigate to the Document 110.2 launch page in the Online Lab and then click the Launch Activity button to open **Doc110.02** in the activity window.

2 Change the line spacing to single spacing with no spacing after paragraphs.

3 Turn on the display of nonprinting characters.

4 Set a left tab at the 2-inch mark on the horizontal ruler.

5 Key the following:

    PATIENT NAME:[Tab][Enter]
    MR #:[Tab][Enter]
    PHYSICIAN:[Tab][Enter]
    ADMISSION DATE:[Tab][Enter]
    DISCHARGE DATE:[Tab][Enter]

6 Remove the left tab from the horizontal ruler and then press Enter. *Note: The insertion point should be two lines below the* **DISCHARGE DATE** *heading.*

7 Key the headings, signature line, and reference information for the Discharge Summary report using the information provided in Figure 110.2. Do not key spaces after the colons. For the signature line, key 30 underscores, and do not let Word automatically format the signature line. *Hint: Press Ctrl + Z to undo the change.*

8 Turn off the display of nonprinting characters.

9 Proofread the document and correct any errors.

10 Save the document.

11 Click the Check button to upload the document for checking.

12 If errors are reported by the Online Lab, view the results document, correct the errors in the submitted document, save the document, and then click the Check Again button.

Figure 110.2 Headings for the Discharge Summary Report for Document 110.2

ADMITTING DIAGNOSIS [3 Enters]

DISCHARGE DIAGNOSIS [3 Enters]

HOSPITAL COURSE [3 Enters]

DISCHARGE INSTRUCTIONS [3 Enters]

DISCHARGE MEDICATIONS [5 Enters]

_____ [Enter]

, MD [2 Enters]

xxx/xxx [Enter]

D: [Enter]

T:

Reinforcing Writing Skills

In the deductive method of developing a paragraph, the main idea or topic is presented in the opening sentence, which is known as the *topic sentence*. The sentences that follow reinforce and expand on the content of the topic sentence. Notice how the topic sentence in the following paragraph provides a focal point for understanding the rest of the sentences.

> The lack of uniform telecommunication standards among computers of different makes and models has hurt computer manufacturers and end users. Mobile computers function on proprietary operating systems. Thus, communication between systems of different makes and models is not possible without some type of conversion taking place. Although manufacturers have worked toward standardizing protocols (a set of agreed-on rules and guidelines for establishing formats and procedures used in telecommunications), the problem persists.

Practice composing a letter that includes a deductive paragraph in the following document activity.

Document 67.4

Composing a Personal Business Letter with a Deductive Paragraph

Read all instructions below before starting this document activity.

1   Navigate to the Document 67.4 launch page in the Online Lab and then click the Launch Activity button to open **Doc067.04** in the activity window.

2   In the document, key a rough draft of a personal business letter to your instructor. Use your instructor's name and school address and follow the format you learned in Session 66.

3   In the body of the letter, write at least two paragraphs. In the first paragraph of your letter, tell your instructor how you will be using the skills learned in this course. In the second paragraph, use the deductive method to compose a paragraph of four to six sentences on a topic related to the first paragraph.

4   After completing the draft, analyze the content on screen. Does the first sentence of your deductive paragraph clearly state the main idea or topic? Do the sentences that follow reinforce and expand on the content of the topic sentence? If needed, make changes in the deductive paragraph.

5   Add formatting to enhance your letter.

6   Proofread and correct any errors in the letter.

7   Save the document.

8   Click the Submit button to upload the document for instructor review.

Ending the Session

The Online Lab automatically saved the work you completed for this session. You may continue with the next session or exit the Online Lab and continue later.

Discharge Summary Report

Read all instructions below before starting this document activity.

1 Navigate to the Document 110.3 launch page in the Online Lab and then click the Launch Activity button to open **Doc110.03** in the activity window.

2 Turn on the display of nonprinting characters.

3 Key the report shown in Figure 110.3. If a heading is not used in the final report, delete it from the document. If a heading is required and is not available in the base file, key the heading. Do not allow Word to automatically format the numbered list. Key a space rather than a tab after the numbers in the numbered list. Make sure there is only one blank line between sections of the report.

4 Key the signature line and the reference information at the bottom of the report. There should be three blank lines between the last section and the signature line.

a The physician signing the report is the physician listed at the top of the report.

b Key the reference initials trw for the dictator's initials and wmn for the transcriptionist's initials.

c Key the dictation and transcription dates to match the discharge date. There should be one space between the colon and the date.

5 Search the document and replace the following letter pair placeholders with the corresponding medical terms. *Hint: Do not replace the letter pairs when they appear within words.*

a Find instances of *pn* and replace them with *pancreatitis*.

b Find instances of *ch* and replace them with *cholecystectomy*.

c Find instances of *cl* and replace them with *cholelithiasis*.

6 Turn off the display of nonprinting characters.

7 Proofread the document and correct any errors.

8 Save the document.

9 Click the Check button to upload the document for checking.

10 If errors are reported by the Online Lab, view the results document, correct the errors in the submitted document, save the document, and then click the Check Again button.

Figure 110.3 Discharge Summary Report Content for Document 110.3

PATIENT NAME:	Eldon Leonard
MR #:	603-44
PHYSICIAN:	T. R. Wolmack, MD
ADMISSION DATE:	06/23/2020
DISCHARGE DATE:	06/24/2020

DISCHARGE DIAGNOSIS
Chronic cholecystitis with cl.

continues

Figure 67.4 Business Letter Content for Document 67.3

Ms. Tanja Kuehnemund
3007 Lakeside Drive, Apt. 699
Arlington, TX 76012

Dear Tanja:

As the newest member of our field force, I want you to ~~no~~ *Know* that there is help available. Once you are settled in, contact our National Healthcare Consultant, **Lynn Graver,** at (206) 555-9044. Arrange for Lynn to spend a week with you calling on the clinics in your territory. Lynn has spent over 10 years managing a healthcare facility in Washington.

The value of Lynn's visits to the field cannot by *re* overstated. Proper planning, research and scheduled appointment *s* is, *are* of course, a must. Here are some appointment-setting guidelines:

• *Bullets*

Do your homework! Check with Lynn to see ~~of~~ *if* she has identified any of the clinics in your area as model ~~sights~~. *sites*

Be flexible, but make sure you have firm appointments with clinic administrators; a group setting with key decision makers present is the desirable goal.

Reconfirm all appointments by phone, email message, or even a reminder card.

Remember, **the importance of Lynn's presence must be stressed** to the administrators. She has a wealth of knowledge on healthcare administration. She is happy to offer advice on problems faced by healthcare administrators. She knows how and which modules of our software can assist clinics in enhancing ~~clinical~~ services to their patients.

Sincerely,

Bruce Graybill
National Sales Manager

OPERATION

Laparoscopic ch with operative cholangiogram, 06/23/2020.

HOSPITAL COURSE

The patient was in the hospital with severe gallstone pn in May of 2020. At that time the patient had an ultrasound, which showed cl. Once the pn subsided and his CAT scan findings had reverted to normal, he was admitted; a ch was performed on June 23, 2020. The procedure went well but was quite difficult because of a severely scarred, contracted gallbladder packed with stones. The ductal system was slightly dilated and the pancreatic duct filled easily. Postoperatively, the patient has done well. The morning after surgery, he was ambulatory, eating a general diet, and comfortable with oral pain medication. He is being discharged at this time. He had a Jackson-Pratt drain placed at surgery, and this was removed on the morning of discharge.

DISCHARGE INSTRUCTIONS

Patient has no restrictions on his diet or activity.

DISCHARGE MEDICATIONS

1. Continue on preadmission colchicine 0.6 mg.
2. Vicodin 5 mg 1-2 by mouth every four to six hours as needed for pain.

PLAN

I will see him in my office in about two weeks.

Ending the Session

The Online Lab automatically saved the work you completed for this session. You may continue with the next session or exit the Online Lab and continue later.

Figure 67.3 Block-Style Business Letter Content for Document 67.2

Ms. Kathleen Williams ¶ 37 Walnut Street, Apt. 918 ¶ Foxborough, MA 02037-1109 ¶ Dear Mr. Williams: ¶ Please let me introduce myself and my company to you. Recently **GlobalCom** took over the telecommunication responsibilities for Intergroup Financial Investors. I am your point of contract for any questions or concerns you may have regarding this relationship. Your communications will be the same with one minor change. ¶ All Intergroup representatives are now using **GlobalCom** on a secondary carrier status. When you make a business-related long distance phone call, you must first dial our PIC code 10888. These calls will be registered on the master bill copy that Mary Hamm will receive at corporate headquarters. ¶ This program separates personal and business calls and eliminates the need for the corporation to reimburse you for business-related calls. Enclosed is my business card and a brief company overview. Please call me if you have questions. ¶ Sincerely, ¶ Brent O'Hara ¶ Account Executive

Document 67.3

Business Letter with Bullets and Bold Text

Read all instructions below before starting this document activity.

1 Navigate to the Document 67.3 launch page in the Online Lab and then click the Launch Activity button to open **Doc067.03** in the activity window.

2 Read the text shown in Figure 67.4 and use proofreading marks to note any additional corrections before keying the letter.

3 Key the text shown in Figure 67.4, implementing the proofreading marks as you key and formatting the letter as a block-style business letter. The document contains a letterhead that automatically positions the insertion point at the 2-inch mark on the page. You do not need to press Enter before keying the date.

   a Key June 15, 2020 as the current date.

   b When formatting the bulleted list, use solid black round bullets.

   c Apply bold formatting as indicated in Figure 67.4. *Note: Be careful not to set in bold spaces or punctuation before or after the text that is to appear in bold. When two or more formatted words appear in a row, format the space between the words.*

   d Key the reference initials rtn and the file name.

4 Proofread the document and correct any errors.

5 Save the document.

6 Click the Check button to upload the document for checking.

7 If errors are reported by the Online Lab, view the results document, correct the errors in the submitted document, save the document, and then click the Check Again button.

Session 111 Production Progress Check: Medical Documents

Session Objectives

- **Demonstrate proficiency in preparing medical documents**
- **Efficiently produce documents in mailable form**

Getting Started

Exercise 111.1 Unless you are continuing immediately after completing Session 110, spend at least two to three minutes warming up before completing the document activities in this session. See Session 101 for suggested warm-up text.

Preparing Medical Documents

Before completing an exercise that simulates the work environment at the Riverside Medical Center, you will key four of the medical reports introduced in this unit. Your goal is to efficiently key these documents with all errors (format and content) corrected.

Document 111.1 Consultation Report

Read all instructions below before starting this document activity.

1 Navigate to the Document 111.1 launch page in the Online Lab and then click the Launch Activity button to open **Doc111.01** in the activity window.

2 Turn on the display of nonprinting characters.

3 Key the report shown in Figure 111.1. If a heading is not used in the final report, delete it from the document. Make sure there is only one blank line between sections of the report.

4 Key the signature line and the reference information at the bottom of the report. There should be three blank lines between the last section and the signature line.

   a The physician signing the report is the consulting physician listed at the top of the report.

   b Key the reference initials dvc for the dictator's initials and rpp for the transcriptionist's initials.

   c Key the dictation and transcription dates to match the date of the consultation. There should be one space between the colon and the date.

5 Search the document and replace the following letter pair placeholders with the corresponding medical terms. *Hint: Do not replace the letter pairs when they appear within words.*

   a Find instances of *n-o* and replace them with *neuro-ophthalmic*.

   b Find instances of *em* and replace them with *extraocular motility*.

   c Find instances of *ap* and replace them with *appendicular musculature*.

   d Find instances of *sp* and replace them with *supranuclear palsy*.

steps continue

A review of research findings that impact keyboarding and applications methodology.

I look forward to working with you and your faculty, administrators, and staff. From past experiences, I know you have an extremely enthusiastic group, and their enthusiasm is contagious. If there is anything I need to know before August 14, please call me at (888) 555-8486 or send me an email message at jmitchell@ppi-edu.net.

Sincerely,

Javier Mitchell, EdD
National Consultant

Document 67.2 Business Letter with Bold, Justified, and Indented Text

Read all instructions below before starting this document activity.

1. Navigate to the Document 67.2 launch page in the Online Lab and then click the Launch Activity button to open **Doc067.02** in the activity window.

2. Read the text shown in Figure 67.3 and use proofreading marks to note any necessary corrections before keying the letter.

3. Key the text shown in Figure 67.3, starting with the date line. Follow the style presented in Figure 67.1. The document contains a letterhead that automatically positions the insertion point at the 2-inch mark on the page. You do not need to press Enter before keying the date. Follow these guidelines:

   a. Key September 8, 2020 as the current date of the letter.

   b. Key the reference initials mdt and the file name, include a notation for three enclosures, and indicate that a copy of the letter is being sent to Mary Hamm.

   c. Set the company name *GlobalCom* in bold wherever it appears in the body of the letter. *Hint: Do not format the space following the company name in bold.*

4. Adjust the formatting of the letter as follows:

   a. Change the paragraph alignment of the three paragraphs in the body of the letter to justified alignment.

   b. Format the second paragraph in the body of the letter so that it is indented 0.5 inch from both the left and right margins.

5. Proofread the document and correct any errors.

6. Save the document.

7. Click the Check button to upload the document for checking.

8. If errors are reported by the Online Lab, view the results document, correct the errors in the submitted document, save the document, and then click the Check Again button.

6 Turn off the display of nonprinting characters.

7 Proofread the document and correct any errors.

8 Save the document.

9 Click the Check button to upload the document for checking.

10 If errors are reported by the Online Lab, view the results document, correct the errors in the submitted document, save the document, and then click the Check Again button.

Figure 111.1 Consultation Report Content for Document 111.1

PATIENT NAME:	Alfred J. Marchant
MR #:	9035
DOB:	10/12/1965
PHYSICIAN:	L. V. Gibbons, MD
CONSULTANT:	D. V. Crosby, MD
DATE OF CONSULT:	09/14/2020

PHYSICAL EXAMINATION

Upon n-o examination, the patient's pupils are symmetrically reactive without evidence of ptosis. He now has complete absence of volitional vertical eye movements with very slowed horizontal saccade. Doll's-head-eye maneuver shows full em reflexes. The general neurologic examination showed an increased tone involving the ap.

IMPRESSION

Progressive sp (Steele-Richardson-Olszewski syndrome).

RECOMMENDATIONS

In the near future, the patient will likely require a feeding tube placement because of problems with aspiration. I have discussed with the patient and his son the aggressiveness of future medical care with regard to treatment of aspiration pneumonia and the complications of being totally immobilized. We plan on helping out on a regular basis at this point.

2   Read the text shown in Figure 67.2 and use proofreading marks to note any necessary corrections before keying the letter. *Note: If using the ebook, print this page and mark the printout.*

3   Key the text shown in Figure 67.2. The file does not contain a letterhead since you are preparing this letter for preprinted letterhead stationery, so you will need to move the insertion point 1.9 inches from the top of the document. Follow the style presented in Figure 67.1 and include the following formatting guidelines:

   a   Press Enter three times and then key July 15, 2020 as the current date of the letter.

   b   Format the list of four topics (starts with *An introduction* and ends with *applications methodology*) as a bulleted list with check mark bullets.

   c   Remove the hyperlink from the email address.

   d   Key the reference initials tlk and the file name and then indicate that a copy of the letter is being sent to Roger Galvin. *Hint: Because only one person is receiving a copy, use one space instead of a Tab after the copy notation.*

4   Proofread the document and correct any errors.

5   Save the document.

6   Click the Check button to upload the document for checking.

7   If errors are reported by the Online Lab, view the results document, correct the errors in the submitted document, save the document, and then click the Check Again button.

Figure 67.2 Business Letter Content for Document 67.1

Dr. DeeAnn Killian
Academic Dean
Taylor Business Institute
120 West 35th Street
New York, NY 10002-6793

Dear Dr. Killian:

Here are the topics that I plan to cover at the Taylor Business Institute in-service workshop for faculty, administrators, and staff on August 14 from 1 to 3 a.m.:

An introduction to the psychological princeiples of psychomotor skill building with examples of how they can be applied in teaching students to master keyboarding and applications skills using computers.

An overview of the historical development of instructional materials used in teaching keyboarding and applications.

A call to challenge traditional methodologies based on conditions that no longer exist.

continues

Operative Report

Read all instructions below before starting this document activity.

1 Navigate to the Document 111.2 launch page in the Online Lab and then click the Launch Activity button to open **Doc111.02** in the activity window.

2 Turn on the display of nonprinting characters.

3 Key the report shown in Figure 111.2. If a heading is not used in the final report, delete it from the document. If a heading is required but is not available in the base file, key the heading. Make sure there is only one blank line between sections of the report.

4 Key the signature line and the reference information at the bottom of the report. There should be three blank lines between the last section and the signature line.

   a The physician signing the report is the surgeon listed at the top of the report.

   b Key the reference initials fjs for the dictator's initials and adt for the transcriptionist's initials.

   c Key the dictation and transcription dates to match the date of the surgery.

5 Search the document and replace the following letter pair placeholders with the corresponding medical terms. *Hint: Do not replace the letter pairs when they appear within words.*

   a Find instances of *Pt* and replace them with *Percutaneous transluminal.*

   b Find instances of *ay* and replace them with *angioplasty.*

   c Find instances of *ag* and replace them with *angiographic.*

6 Turn off the display of nonprinting characters.

7 Proofread the document and correct any errors.

8 Save the document.

9 Click the Check button to upload the document for checking.

10 If errors are reported by the Online Lab, view the results document, correct the errors in the submitted document, save the document, and then click the Check Again button.

Figure 111.2 Operative Report Content for Document 111.2

PATIENT NAME:	Sean J. O'Connell
MR #:	5773
SURGEON:	F. J. Schillar, MD
ASSISTANT:	G. A. Hasart, ORT
ANESTHESIOLOGIST:	K. E. Lundigen, MD
DATE OF SURGERY:	03/16/2020

PREOPERATIVE DIAGNOSIS

This is a 65-year-old white male with coronary artery disease with recently unstable symptoms who underwent coronary arteriography last Friday, revealing a high-grade stenosis and circumflex coronary artery with some

continues

Common Letter Notations

In addition to the major sections of a business letter, several notations are used if they are appropriate to a particular letter. Some of these are shown in Figure 67.1.

- **Enclosure:** This indicates that a document or another item is included with the letter. If multiple enclosures are included, use *Enclosures* and then include the number of enclosed pages.
- **Attachment:** An attachment is similar to an enclosure, but the item is actually attached (by tape or staple, for example) to the document rather than simply being enclosed. This notation is typically used for items included with memos.
- **Copy:** This notation lists, in alphabetical order by last name, any additional people who will receive copies of the letter. Use *cc* followed by a colon. (Use Ctrl + Z to undo the AutoCorrect change that changes the first *c* from a lowercase to a capital C.) If only one person is receiving a copy, insert one space between the colon and the name. If multiple people are receiving copies, press Tab after the colon so that the other names will align correctly below the first name.

Using Bullets to Highlight Items

Some letters include a list of items (words, phrases, or sentences) that are to be set apart from the body of the letter for clarity or special emphasis. These items can appear in a numbered list, which will be discussed in Session 68, or they can be preceded by a bullet, producing a bulleted list. A wide variety of shapes are available for bullets. Some common shapes include a circle, a square, a diamond, or an arrow.

When creating a bulleted list, by default Word will include a nonprinting Tab character between the bullet symbol and the text that follows it. If the bulleted item is more than one line long, Word will begin the second line with a hanging indent. In other words, the start of the second line of the bulleted item will align with the first word of the bulleted paragraph rather than with the bullet.

Follow these steps to create a bulleted list:

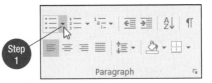

1 In the Paragraph group on the Home tab, click the Bullets button arrow.

2 Click the bullet style from the options provided in the drop-down gallery. This will insert a bullet followed by a nonprinting Tab character.

3 Key the text of the first bulleted item.

4 Press Enter and then key the next bulleted item.

5 To turn off bulleting, press Enter twice. This will position the insertion point at the start of the first paragraph following the bulleted list.

To create a bulleted list from text that has already been keyed, select the paragraphs or lines of text that you wish to include in the list, click the Bullets button arrow, and then click a bullet style from the drop-down gallery. Word will insert a bullet at the beginning of each line that follows a hard return.

To remove bullet formatting, select the bulleted text and then click the Bullets button.

Document 67.1 **Business Letter with Bullets**

Read all instructions below before starting this document activity.

1 Navigate to the Document 67.1 launch page in the Online Lab and then click the Launch Activity button to open **Doc067.01** in the activity window.

steps continue

Figure 111.2 Operative Report Content for Document 111.2—continued

associated thrombus. He was continued on medications over the weekend and was stable. He was brought back at this time for ay of the lesion.

POSTOPERATIVE DIAGNOSIS

Coronary artery disease.

NAME OF OPERATION

Pt ay, circumflex coronary artery.

ANESTHESIA

Lidocaine 2% anesthesia.

INFORMED CONSENT

Informed consent was obtained.

PROCEDURE

In the postabsorptive state and following 2 mg of Versed given in the laboratory, the patient was prepped and draped in the usual fashion. Lidocaine 2% anesthesia was administered to the right femoral region. An 8-French introducer sheath was placed into the right femoral artery and 15,000 units of heparin was given intravenously and a heparin drip begun. A #3 8-French left guide catheter was used. The lesion crossed with an ACS 0.014 high-torque floppy guidewire and dilated with a Mansfield slider ST balloon catheter. There was a good ag result. After ensuring ag and hemodynamic stability, all guidewires and guiding catheters were withdrawn from the body. The sheath was sutured in place and the patient returned to his room in good condition.

Document 111.3 **Radiology Report**

Read all instructions below before starting this document activity.

1 Navigate to the Document 111.3 launch page in the Online Lab and then click the Launch Activity button to open **Doc111.03** in the activity window.

2 Turn on the display of nonprinting characters.

3 Key the report shown in Figure 111.3. Make sure there is only one blank line between sections of the report. *Note: In the base document, the heading* **NAME OF TEST** *is to be replaced with the actual test name—in this case,* **PORTABLE CHEST X-RAY.**

steps continue

MULL-SMITH REALTORS
1344 Peachtree Lane
Richmond, VA 16054-2379
(800) 555-1049
FAX (800) 555-1050
http://mull-smith.ppi-edu.net

| letterhead |

September 26, 2020 [Enter] ——— | date line (begins approximately 2 inches from the top of the document) |

[Enter]

Mr. Doug Fitterer [Shift + Enter]
General Manager [Shift + Enter]
Normandale Hills Estates [Shift + Enter] — | inside address |
1860 West Lee Parkway [Shift + Enter]
Hilldale, VA 16060-2134 [Enter]

Dear Mr. Fitterer: [Enter] ——— | salutation |

Enclosed are the resumes for three of the candidates to be interviewed at the downtown Marriot next
Wednesday. Please review these resumes plus the other three that were delivered by courier last
Wednesday. [Enter]

The interviews will be scheduled on an hourly basis beginning at 9 a.m. and will continue until 3 p.m.
with an hour break at noon. Please let me know if this schedule is not acceptable. I can be reached at
(800) 555-1049. [Enter]

| body |

Sincerely, [Enter] ——— | closing |

[Enter]

John Pelligrini [Shift + Enter] ——— | signature line |
Branch Manager [Enter] ——————————— | title line |

dm   [Shift + Enter] ——— | reference initials |
Doc067.02   [Shift + Enter] ——————— | file name |
Enclosures 2 [Shift + Enter] ——— | enclosure notation |
cc: [Tab] Lorn Hayes [Shift + Enter]
    [Tab] Arlene Rintz | copy notation |

4 Key the signature line and the reference information at the bottom of the report. There should be three blank lines between the last section and the signature line.

   a The physician signing the report is S. E. King.

   b Key the reference initials sek for the dictator's initials and blo for the transcriptionist's initials.

   c Key the dictation and transcription dates to match the date of the report.

5 Search the document and replace the following letter pair placeholders with the corresponding medical terms. *Hint: Do not replace the letter pairs when they appear within words.*

   a Find instances of *en* and replace them with *endotracheal*.

   b Find instances of *pv* and replace them with *perihilar vascular*.

   c Find instances of *po* and replace them with *pneumothorax*.

6 Turn of the display of nonprinting characters.

7 Proofread the document and correct any errors.

8 Save the document.

9 Click the Check button to upload the document for checking.

10 If errors are reported by the Online Lab, view the results document, correct the errors in the submitted document, save the document, and then click the Check Again button.

Figure 111.3 Radiology Report Content for Document 111.3

PATIENT NAME:	Sofia A. York
MR #:	2743
REQUESTING PHYSICIAN:	B. T. Houston, MD
DATE:	05/12/2020

PORTABLE CHEST X-RAY

A single portable view of the chest was taken after open-heart surgery. A comparison was made with an earlier study of the same date. The en tube is now in place, as is a Swan-Ganz catheter. Mediastinal drain and right chest tubes are in place. The heart appears to be generous in size and the right border is somewhat indistinct of pv structure. There is no sign of po.

IMPRESSION

Satisfactory postmedian sternotomy chest.

As in Session 66, push to prepare error-free correspondence at a job-ready efficiency level as you create each document in this session. Review instructions carefully and read and edit each letter before starting to key.

Parts of a Business Letter

Figure 67.1 shows the formatting used in a block-style business letter. This letter was produced using Word's default settings, which are 11-point Calibri font, 1.08 line spacing, and 8 points of spacing after paragraphs (following hard returns). Figure 67.1 includes examples of the nine major parts of a business letter, which are as follows:

- **Letterhead:** A letterhead usually includes the company logo, name, address, phone and fax numbers, and website URL. The letterhead may appear on preprinted stationery (information may be located at the top and/or bottom of the paper) or it may be part of the file used to create the letter and be printed when the letter is printed.

- **Date line:** The date line contains the current month (spelled out) followed by the day, a comma, and the year (for example, March 10, 2020).

- **Inside address:** This includes the recipient's courtesy title, name, job title, department, company name, and address.

- **Salutation:** A salutation greets the recipient and includes his or her courtesy title, followed by a colon.

- **Body:** The body contains the message of the letter and consists of one or more paragraphs with one hard return (Enter) at the end of each paragraph.

- **Closing:** A closing consists of a respectful farewell followed by a comma. If it contains more than one word, e.g. *Sincerely yours*, only the first letter of the first word is capitalized.

- **Signature line:** The signature line includes the sender's first and last names. Avoid using initials for the first name, to more clearly identify the sender.

- **Title line:** The title line includes the sender's business or professional title.

- **Reference initials and file name:** These consist of the initials of the person who keyed the document (included only if this person is not the author of the document) and the name of the saved file on the next line of the document. The reference initials should be set in lowercase letters. The AutoCorrect feature may change the first lowercase initial to an uppercase letter. To change it back to lowercase, press Ctrl + Z (the keyboard shortcut for the Undo command). The file name should not include the file extension (such as *.docx*).

When keying a letter to be printed on letterhead stationery, press Enter to move the insertion point approximately 2 inches from the top of the document. This will create enough space at the top of the page to accommodate the letterhead. If the letterhead is longer than 2 inches, the text should start approximately 0.5 inch below it. When keying a document from a letterhead template, the insertion point will likely be positioned in the correct location. The goal is always to produce a visually pleasing letter. If the letter is short, consider adding additional hard returns (created by pressing Enter) after the date line to better "frame" the body of the letter on the page.

Discharge Summary Report

Read all instructions below before starting this document activity.

1 Navigate to the Document 111.4 launch page in the Online Lab and then click the Launch Activity button to open **Doc111.04** in the activity window.

2 Turn on the display of nonprinting characters.

3 Key the report shown in Figure 111.4. Change the heading *DISCHARGE MEDICATIONS* to *PLAN* as indicated in Figure 111.4. Make sure there is only one blank line between sections of the report.

4 Key the signature line and the reference information at the bottom of the report. There should be three blank lines between the last section and the signature line.

   a The physician signing the report is the physician listed at the top of the report.

   b Key the reference initials gpm for the dictator's initials and ptc for the transcriptionist's initials.

   c Key the dictation and transcription dates to match the discharge date.

5 Turn off the display of nonprinting characters.

6 Proofread the document and correct any errors.

7 Save the document.

8 Click the Check button to upload the document for checking.

9 If errors are reported by the Online Lab, view the results document, correct the errors in the submitted document, save the document, and then click the Check Again button.

Figure 111.4 Discharge Summary Report Content for Document 111.4

PATIENT NAME: Lucille Cheng

MR #:   19323

PHYSICIAN: G. P. Munez, MD

ADMISSION DATE: 08/08/2020

DISCHARGE DATE: 08/12/2020

ADMITTING DIAGNOSIS

The 64-year-old female was brought to the center with a small-bowel obstruction. She had surgery once in the past for adhesions of her pelvis.

DISCHARGE DIAGNOSIS

Small-bowel obstruction, intermittent.

continues

Complete one 3-minute timing on the timing text below.

3-Minute Timing

Timing
67.3

Many American pioneer families lived in sod houses. If there were no trees or not enough timber to construct a log house, then sod was the only answer for many families.

In order to save time, many homesteaders would locate a ravine (or draw, as they were then called), where a hole could be dug into the bank, a crudely framed board door and window inserted, and presto, an instant, functional homesteader's house appeared.

Many homesteaders, however, wanted a more permanent, aboveground house. In order to cut the sod, a breaking plow was used to turn over furrows on about half an acre of ground, using care to make the furrows of even width and thickness so that the walls would rise evenly. A spade was used to cut the furrow into sod bricks about three feet long.

A float made of planks or the forks of a tree was used to transport the sod bricks to the building place. The first layer in the walls was made by placing three foot-wide bricks side by side around the foundation, except where the door would be located. After the first row was placed, the cracks were filled with fine dirt and two more layers were placed on top. Every third layer was placed crosswise to bind them together. This process was followed until the walls were high enough for the addition of a special roof.

⊕ Ergonomic Tip

Warm up your eyes before starting work by doing an eye roll. Stare straight ahead without moving your head. Slowly move your eyes in a circular pattern first clockwise and then counterclockwise. Repeat three times.

Preparing Business Letters

A variety of styles can be used for both personal and business letters. The letter format presented in this book is the *block style*. All parts of a block-style letter begin at the left margin. The block-style letter is popular because it is easy to learn and is the fastest letter style to set up. Once you have mastered the block-style letter, you will have little difficulty adjusting to other letter formats.

Business letters provide a means of communication between and among businesses and their clients and customers, while memos are used for internal communication. Because business letters are sent outside an organization, they must convey a favorable image. Adhering to proper formatting guidelines and preparing correspondence that is free from errors in spelling, punctuation, and word use all contribute to conveying a positive and professional image.

HOSPITAL COURSE

A long weighted Anderson tube was placed and the patient continued to pass gas. She had a bowel movement the second day, with decreased pain and tenderness. Most of the pain was in the lower left quadrant. She continues to improve. X-rays were repeated every day, and there is still some air in the small bowel, but this is slowly improving. Tenderness switched over to the right side of the abdomen. Bowel movements were present every day. The patient was passing fluids. On the second, third, and fourth days, there was an increase in the size of the loop of one of the small bowels. Still there was gas in the colon. After discussion with the patient, she decided that she wanted to go home. She does not have medical insurance. She was taking fluids. She was not having any tenderness or abdominal pain.

DISCHARGE INSTRUCTIONS

Patient will stay on a clear liquid diet.

PLAN

Patient will be followed as an outpatient.

Ending the Session

The Online Lab automatically saved the work you completed for this session. You may continue with the next session or exit the Online Lab and continue later.

Session 67 Building Paragraphs in Business Letters

Session Objectives

- **Review the parts of a business letter**
- **Use bullets in correspondence**
- **Build better paragraphs using the deductive method**
- **Efficiently produce documents in mailable form**

Getting Started

Exercise 67.1

If you are continuing immediately from Session 66, you may skip the Exercise 67.1 warm-up drill. However, if you exited the Online Lab at the end of Session 66, warm up by completing Exercise 67.1.

Exercise 67.2

Begin your session work by completing Exercise 67.2, a timed short drill, in the Online Lab.

Assessing Your Speed and Accuracy

Complete Timings 67.1 through 67.3 in the Online Lab. At the end of the timing, the Online Lab will display your WPM rate and any errors. Results will be saved in your Timings Performance report. If you have been surpassing the speed and accuracy goals identified in the Online Lab, set slightly more challenging personal goals and strive to exceed them.

Complete two 1-minute timings on the timing text below. If you meet or exceed both speed and accuracy goals for Timing 67.1, push for greater speed on Timing 67.2.

1-Minute Timings

Timings 67.1–67.2

Within our own galaxy, you can observe many beautiful sights. The satiny stars make a lovely domain to admire. It is easy to see all sorts of patterns in the heavens if you simply relax and turn your imagination loose. You can obtain diagrams with which to study, observe, and chart the various star patterns. If you have the equipment to look beyond our own galaxy, you will be able to observe stars and galaxies far out into space. An observatory is a marvelous place to view the heavens. The starry displays and changing seasons are not to be missed by an astronomer.

Session
112 Medical Center Project: Overview and Background

Getting Started

Exercise 112.1 Unless you are continuing immediately after completing Session 111, spend at least two to three minutes warming up before completing the document activities in this session. See Session 101 for suggested warm-up text.

Medical Center Project Overview

As a further refinement of your professional keyboarding and word processing proficiency, it is critical that you develop decision-making skills. This project is a means of helping you to develop these skills. In this project, you are placed in a simulated medical office environment where you not only have responsibilities to produce a variety of business-related documents, but you are also faced with assigning priorities to the tasks to be done and identifying the actions to be taken.

When assigned a project such as this one, you must be able to do the following things:

- Understand the purpose of the project.
- Set completion dates and times for all items and activities.
- Determine exactly what needs to be done for each activity.
- Note any special requirements related to the activities to be completed.
- Plan and organize your work so that you complete the project in the shortest possible time.
- Carefully check that your work is correct in terms of format, content, and adherence to directions.

The purpose of this project is to provide a setting as close as possible to an actual medical office. It is assumed that you have already reached competent keyboarding production skills. As is expected in an office, you are to work quickly and accurately and use your time wisely. Most of the document activities in this project will not be automatically graded.

It is important that you understand the context and scope of work to be completed before you dive into completing specific project tasks. To achieve this, read the entire contents of this session as well as the contents of Sessions 113, 114, and 115 (including the activity steps) before you begin document preparation.

The Medical Center project is divided into the following activities:

- **Session 112** Digest the overview and background information for the project and then create a calendar document for tracking events.
- **Session 113** Design and prepare the documentation of a file naming system.
- **Session 114** Prepare a report that includes document activity numbers and names, figure number references, priorities, priority justification, and actions to be taken, along with time estimates for completion and goal completion dates.
- **Session 115** Complete the document activities in the order that you have specified, not in the order presented in the session.

Document 66.4

Building Coherent Paragraphs in a Personal Business Letter

Read all instructions below before starting this document activity.

1. Navigate to the Document 66.4 launch page in the Online Lab and then click the Launch Activity button to open **Doc066.04** in the activity window.

2. Prepare a rough draft of a personal business letter to your instructor. Use the instructor's name and school address. Use your name and home address in the closing of the letter.

3. In the body of the letter, write a two- or three-paragraph response to one of the following questions:

   - What is your favorite television show, and why?
   - What is your favorite kind of music, and why?
   - Do you believe government censorship of the Internet is appropriate or not appropriate, and why?

4. After completing the draft, analyze the content on screen. Review each paragraph for coherency, using the techniques presented to improve the quality of the material. Rephrase and repeat ideas, use pronouns, and insert transitional expressions to aid in developing coherency. In addition, you are encouraged to use any of the word processing features previously presented in this course to enhance the quality of your document.

5. Proofread and correct any errors in the letter.

6. Save the document.

7. Click the Submit button to upload the document for instructor review.

Ending the Session

The Online Lab automatically saved the work you completed for this session. You may continue with the next session or exit the Online Lab and continue later.

Medical Center Project Scenario

You will be working in a medical center for this project. Table 112.1 provides contact information related to the office where you work. The current date is September 4, 2020.

Situation

You are the administrative assistant to Dr. Terrance Borman, who is the Chief Administrator of Riverside Medical Center in Portland, Oregon. Dr. Borman is in the process of coordinating the upgrade of Riverside Medical Center into a state-of-the-art facility. A new medical center building is being constructed adjacent to the current facility, which will be converted into a medical clinic to complement the work being done at the medical center. The new medical center facility is to open January 1, of next year. Prior to his appointment as the Chief Administrator, Dr. Borman had been a practicing physician at the medical center, so he has seen the organization function from the inside.

Because Dr. Borman has to spend a considerable amount of time out of the office, you must function without his direct supervision. In addition to receiving and preparing documents, sending and receiving email messages, and responding to telephone calls and voice mail messages, you have the responsibility of greeting visitors as well as Riverside Medical staff members who want to meet with Dr. Borman. You are responsible for maintaining Dr. Borman's calendar and arranging for his airline travel, hotel reservations, and car rentals. Dr. Borman commonly asks for your opinion on proposed innovations to the new medical center.

One of Dr. Borman's policies is to have all staff members serve in a backup role in some other function within the medical center. Because of your keyboarding skills, you provide backup support to the medical transcription department whenever time permits.

Special Instructions and Explanations

You have been on vacation since August 26, 2020. You have just returned to work today (Friday, September 4) at 8 a.m. Dr. Borman will not be in the office until 11 a.m. today, and he will only be there until about 1 p.m. because he plans to fly to Las Vegas to attend the North American Technology and Telecommunications Trade Show. He will leave Portland on Delta Airlines Flight 1864 today at 3:45 p.m. and arrive in Las Vegas at 5:50 p.m. He has reservations at Bally's, the site of the show, and a car has been rented for him. The show and exhibits open at 6 p.m. today and end at noon on Monday, September 7. Dr. Borman will be back in the office at 8 a.m. on Tuesday, September 8. Monday, September 7, is Labor Day, and the office is closed.

Several products that are being installed in the new Riverside Medical Center will be displayed at the show. Included in the exhibits are examples of the state-of-the-art electronic medical record system, the speech recognition system, and the scheduling system that will be used by the facility.

Table 112.1 Contact Information for Medical Office Project

Company Name:	Riverside Medical Center
Office Name:	Chief Administrator's Office
Address:	17431 N. Willamette Drive Portland, OR 97218-1230
Office Telephone:	(503) 555-6111
Office Fax:	(888) 555-2897
Dr. Terrance Borman's Email Address:	drtborman@ppi-edu.net

Figure 66.4 Personal Business Letter Content for Document 66.3—continued

excellent broker in Montgomery, we would like to have a person from this area over see our investments. It is important to us to by able to meet face to face with our investment broker.

Currently our funds are divided among the following categories: cash and short-term CDS, money market mutual funds, Treasury bonds, mutual funds, and fixed and variable annuities. *US*

Would it be possible to meet with you sometime next week to ~~review~~ *go over* our investment portfolio and review the possibility of having you <u>manage our investments</u> ~~to your brokerage firm~~? Please call me at (952) 555-1049 to set up a meeting. *any afternoon next week*

Sincerely, _____ (#)

Jonathan and Mary Greco
10789 Bren Road West
Eden Prairie, MN 55342

Reinforcing Writing Skills

A paragraph consists of a group of sentences related to a controlling idea or topic. The topic is usually stated in the first sentence, and the sentences that follow either reinforce what the writer wants the reader to grasp or provide additional information about the idea stated in the topic sentence. The material in the paragraph must be coherent—it must "hang together"—so that the reader senses the relationship of the supporting sentences to the topic sentence.

One way to build coherency is to repeat key ideas or words from a preceding sentence to help keep the reader focused on the topic. Pronouns such as *these, those, this, that*, and *they* can be used to connect thoughts from one sentence to the next. For example:

Systems Plus has a six-point program to assist the sales associates in meeting the needs of their clients. This program includes a step-by-step process beginning with the initial contact.

However, you should take care when using the previously listed pronouns. A common symptom of poor writing is unclear pronoun reference. Always reread sentences containing pronouns to make sure the pronouns that refer to something previously mentioned are clear.

Another technique for building coherency in paragraphs is to use transitional expressions. These expressions provide a link to the content that comes next. Examples of transitional expressions include words and phrases such as *consequently, therefore, however, in addition, for this reason, for example*, and *on the other hand*.

Practice composing coherent paragraphs in the following document activity.

Dr. Borman uses the same memo, email, business letter, and memo and formal business report formats that have been used in this courseware. He expects documents prepared for his signature to be without error both in content and format. You are to use any Word features available to enhance the communication process and document appearance. Dr. Borman takes his iPad with him when he is away from the office and makes it a point to check his email daily.

Document 112.1 September 2020 Calendar

Read all instructions below before starting this document activity.

1. Navigate to the Document 112.1 launch page in the Online Lab and then click the Launch Activity button to open **Doc112.01** in the activity window.

2. Create a customized September 2020 calendar using a Word table. Reference Figure 112.1 to see when each date falls in the week. Create a calendar table that will allow you to document actions and due dates within the cells of the table.

3. As you read through the rest of the sessions in this unit, key details of when project-related activities happen or will happen into the calendar table.

4. Proofread the document and correct any errors.

5. Save the document.

6. Print the document for reference as you work through the project.

7. Click the Submit button to upload the document for instructor review.

Figure 112.1 September 2020 Calendar Example for Document 112.1

September 2020

S	M	T	W	T	F	S
		1	2	3	4	5
6	7	8	9	10	11	12
13	14	15	16	17	18	19
20	21	22	23	24	25	26
27	28	29	30	31		

Personal Business Letter with Indented and Underlined Text

Read all instructions below before starting this document activity.

1 Navigate to the Document 66.3 launch page in the Online Lab and then click the Launch Activity button to open **Doc066.03** in the activity window.

2 Change the left and right margins of the document to 1.25 inches.

3 Read the text shown in Figure 66.4, reviewing the proofreading marks and checking for additional corrections before keying the letter.

4 Key the letter shown in Figure 66.4, formatting it as a personal business letter and implementing the proofreading marks as you key.

   a Key August 12, 2020 as the date of the letter.

   b Underline words as indicated in Figure 66.4.

   c Vertically center the text on the page.

5 Indent the second paragraph of the letter (begins *Currently our funds are*) 0.5 inch from the left and right margins by completing the following steps:

   a Select the paragraph.

   b Click the Paragraph group dialog box launcher on the Home tab.

   c Click the Indents and Spacing tab, if it is not already selected.

   d Click the *Left* measurement box up arrow in the *Indentation* section until *0.5"* displays.

   e Click the *Right* measurement box up arrow in the *Indentation* section until *0.5"* displays.

   f Click OK.

6 Proofread the document and correct any errors.

7 Save the document.

8 Click the Check button to upload the document for checking.

9 If errors are reported by the Online Lab, view the results document, correct the errors in the submitted document, save the document, and then click the Check Again button.

Figure 66.4 Personal Business Letter Content for Document 66.3

Mr. Keith Clarkson
Account Executive
First Brokerage Company
4525 Felte Road
Hopkins, MN 55343-9714

Dear Mr. Clarkson:

My wife and I recently moved too the Twin Cities area from Montgomery, Alabama. A mutual friend, Barbara Chamberlin, suggested that we get in touch with you to discuss our investment portfolio. While we have an
meet

continues

Session 113 Medical Center Project: Creating and Documenting a File Naming System

Getting Started

Exercise 113.1 Unless you are continuing immediately after completing Session 112, spend at least two to three minutes warming up before completing the document activities in this session. See Session 101 for suggested warm-up text.

Working in the Medical Center

As mentioned in Session 101, all of the work completed in the Online Lab has been saved automatically, and the files were organized by session. All document activity file names were predetermined and numbered in order. Although this file management system works well for a course like this, such a system would not work within a business environment.

It is important to develop a file naming and electronic folder system for saving documents. The system should be organized to allow for easy retrieval of files, both scanned images and Word documents, and include file names that identify the type of document and the date the file was created. Such a system is critical to productivity. As discussed in Unit 20, while planning a file and folder naming system, consider avoiding long names, using underscores instead of spaces, formatting dates consistently, specifying versions of files using the letter *v* and a two-digit number (*v01*, *v02*, etc.), and make sure to be consistent.

In the following activity, you will develop a proposal for a file naming system and folder structure to be used in the office of the Chief Administrator and will document your proposal in a memo. Because you will be using the Online Lab to complete the document activities for this project, the Online Lab will continue to name the files in the activities. If your instructor provides different instructions on how to manage the files created for this project, follow those instructions rather than the ones in the textbook.

Document names created in Word can be a maximum of 255 characters in length, including the drive letter and any folder names, and may include spaces. File names cannot include any of the characters listed in Table 113.1.

Table 113.1 Characters Not Allowed in Word Document File Names

Character Name	Character
asterisk	*
backslash	\
colon	:
forward slash	/
greater than sign	>
less than sign	<
pipe symbol	|
question mark	?
quotation mark	"

Document 66.2

Personal Business Letter with Custom Margins and Italic and Underlined Text

Read all instructions below before starting this document activity.

1 Navigate to the Document 66.2 launch page in the Online Lab and then click the Launch Activity button to open **Doc066.02** in the activity window.

2 Read the text shown in Figure 66.3 and mark any necessary corrections before keying the letter. *Note: If using the ebook, print this page and mark the printout.*

3 Key the text shown in Figure 66.3 according to the following guidelines:

  a Key July 14, 2020 as the date of the letter.

  b Follow the style shown in Figure 66.1 for formatting the letter. Press Enter to create paragraph breaks and Shift + Enter to create line breaks.

  c Apply italic and underline formatting as indicated in Figure 66.3.

  d Vertically center the text on the page.

4 To practice setting custom margins, change the left and right margins to 1.5 inches.

5 Proofread the document and correct any errors.

6 Save the document.

7 Click the Check button to upload the document for checking.

8 If errors are reported by the Online Lab, view the results document, correct the errors in the submitted document, save the document, and then click the Check Again button.

Figure 66.3 Personal Business Letter Content for Document 66.2

Mr. Kent Waverly, Principal ¶ LW Publications Group ¶ 505 West Broadway Avenue ¶ Denver, CO 80205 ¶ Dear Mr. Waverly: ¶ Thank you for your time on Friday and for sharing such helpful information about the opportunity with *LW Design* magazine. I was particularly impressed with the depth of your commitment to quality training and your investment in you employees. In addition, I believe that the <u>superior</u> company goals and objectives that we discussed will ensure that LW Publications Group will remain a premier Denver publisher for decades to come. ¶ One key facet of my experience that we did not discuss on Friday is my role as <u>event coordinator</u> for the annual AIS Art Fair for the last three years. I have been responsible for advertising and publicity, contracting with art vendors, manging volunteer workers, and scheduling music and entertainment during the event. The art fair has been increasingly successful and attendance has more than doubled under my leadership. ¶ I would appreciate the opportunity to meet with you again to further explore the needs of *LW Design* and the contributions I could offer to the organization. Thank you again for your consideration. ¶ Sincerely, ¶ Calista Marie Kingston ¶ 130 N. Gable Hill Drive ¶ Denver, CO 80205

Before designing your file naming system, be sure to review the company background (see Session 112), the incoming documents (see the figures in Session 115), and the documents you will be creating (see the production document activities in Session 115). Once you have designed your system, complete the following document activity.

Document 113.1

Memo Documenting Proposed File Naming System

Read all instructions below before starting this document activity.

1 Navigate to the Document 113.1 launch page in the Online Lab and then click the Launch Activity button to open **Doc113.01** in the activity window.

2 Address the memo to Terrance Borman, MD, Chief Administrator; use your name as the person sending the memo; and use September 4, 2020 as the current date. You determine the text for the subject line.

3 In the body of the memo, document the details of the file naming system and folder structure you developed. The memo should be written so that anyone reviewing your memo can locate specific documents you have prepared and know how and where to name and save documents they create related to the Chief Administrator's office.

4 At the bottom of the memo, key the file name you would assign to the document based on the file naming system you developed. *Note: The file name will remain **Doc113.01** so that the Online Lab recognizes the file.*

5 Proofread the document and correct any errors.

6 Save the document.

7 Click the Submit button to upload the document for instructor review.

Figure 66.2 Personal Business Letter Content for Document 66.1—continued

My application for admission to East Central University has already been sent to the Registrar. I indicated that I plan to pursue a **BBA** degree in **Telecommunications**. Again, thank you for taking your valuable time to share the details of your program. It help me decide where I wanted to attend college.

Sincerely yours,

Wandella Meggison
12910 White Horse Drive
Oklahoma City, OK 73142-2324

Changing Document Margins

Word's top, bottom, left, and right margins are set by default at 1 inch. These defaults work well for most correspondence. However, there are times when you will need to change the left and right margins to visually balance the letter on the page. For example, a very short letter (10 or fewer lines) often looks better with wider margins. The larger areas of white space on either side of the text more closely match the white space above and below the text, thus creating a visually balanced appearance.

To change the left and right margins in a Word document, complete the following steps:

1 Click the Layout tab.

2 Click the Page Setup group dialog box launcher.

3 Click the Margins tab at the Page Setup dialog box.

4 Click the *Left* measurement box up arrow in the *Margins* section to increase the size of the margin or click the down arrow to reduce the size of the margin.

5 Click the *Right* measurement box up arrow in the *Margins* section to increase the size of the margin or click the down arrow to reduce the size of the margin.

6 Click OK to apply the settings and close the Page Setup dialog box.

Session
114
Medical Center Project: Determining Priorities and Planning Work

Getting Started

Exercise 114.1 Unless you are continuing immediately after completing Session 113, spend at least two to three minutes warming up before completing the document activities in this session. See Session 101 for suggested warm-up text.

Working in the Medical Center

In this session of the project, you will review all the required items for the project (introduced in Session 115) and decide which ones must be completed by 11 a.m., which ones can wait until this afternoon, and which ones will be completed on Tuesday, September 8 (the day after the Labor Day holiday). The activities will include keying documents and making phone calls, sending emails, making notes on calendars, and so on. Each action will have a document activity number reference. Record your priorities and action plan in the following document activity.

Document 114.1 Memo that Documents Priorities and Actions

Read all instructions below before starting this document activity.

1. Navigate to the Document 114.1 launch page in the Online Lab and then click the Launch Activity button to open **Doc114.01** in the activity window.

2. Address the memo to your instructor, use your name as the person sending the memo, and use September 4, 2020 as the current date. You determine the text for the subject line.

3. In the body of the memo, indicate that you have reviewed the tasks and determined your priorities, and that you will communicate this information through a table. Next, create a table in the body of the memo using the headings shown in Figure 114.1. In the table, list the order in which you will complete the document activities in Session 115 and the priority level for each as follows:

   • Priority 1: activities that must be completed by 11 a.m., September 4 (today)

   • Priority 2: activities that must be completed by this afternoon, September 4

   • Priority 3: activities that can wait to be completed until Tuesday, September 8

4. Also in the body of the memo, explain that you have identified documents to be scanned and assigned file names to them. Reference the second table you will create (use the headings shown in Figure 114.2) listing the documents that are not available in electronic form (handwritten notes or other printed documents). Use the file naming system developed in Session 113. Conclude the memo with a statement saying your instructor should contact you if he/she has any questions about the priorities or file names.

5. At the bottom of the memo, key the file name you would assign to the document based on the file naming system you developed. *Note: The file name will remain **Doc114.01** so that the Online Lab recognizes the file.*

6. Proofread the document and correct any errors.

7. Save the document.

8. Click the Submit button to upload the document for instructor review.

Personal Business Letter with Bold and Italic Text

Read all instructions below before starting this document activity.

1 Navigate to the Document 66.1 launch page in the Online Lab and then click the Launch Activity button to open **Doc066.01** in the activity window.

2 Read the text shown in Figure 66.2 and mark any necessary corrections before keying the letter. *Note: If using the ebook, print these pages and mark the printout.*

3 Key the text shown in Figure 66.2 according to the following guidelines:

   a Use Word's default formatting settings and follow the style shown in Figure 66.1. Press Enter to create paragraph breaks and Shift + Enter to create line breaks.

   b Apply bold and italic formatting as indicated in Figure 66.2.

   c Vertically center the text on the page.

4 Proofread the document and correct any errors.

5 Save the document.

6 Click the Check button to upload the document for checking.

7 If errors are reported by the Online Lab, view the results document, correct the errors in the submitted document, save the document, and then click the Check Again button.

Figure 66.2 Personal Business Letter Content for Document 66.1

July 7, 2020

Dr. Leonard Strang, Chair
Department of Technology
East Central University
1100 East Alder Street
Ada, OK 74820-9974

Dear Dr. Strang:

Thank you for reviewing with me the programs and courses you offer in business and office information systems and telecommunications at East Central University. One of the points you made about the goals of your program really interests me. You said, "By the time a student completes our program, she or he has a *basket of solutions* to business and offce information and telecommunications problems encountered on the job."

Armed with this *basket* of knowledge, graduates of your program will feel much more confidant in the jobs they pursue. They will be definite assets to the organization that employs them as they have the expertise to solve problems in information systems and telecommunications.

continues

Figure 114.1 Table Headings for Priorities and Action Items

Priorities & Actions Items				
Document Activity Number	Priority Level	Estimated Time Needed for Completion	Action(s) to Be Taken	Completion Date

Figure 114.2 Table Headings for Scanned Documents

Scanned Documents			
Figure Number	Type of Document	File Name	Description

While Figure 66.1 shows one way to format a personal business letter, many alternative formats exist for this type of letter. For example, word processing software packages usually contain a variety of templates that can be used for personal business letters. In many of these templates, the return address appears in a block in the top left corner of the page, and the letter is automatically vertically centered between the top and bottom margins. In this session's document activities, the return address will be placed after the name of the person sending the letter.

When preparing the documents in this session, your goals are to efficiently key and create final documents in mailable form. This means that the documents contain no errors in either format or content. As you create each document in this session, push for these goals. Be sure to review instructions carefully and to read the letter before starting to key the document. Remember that you are responsible for correcting any errors in the documents you key. The figures may include errors that you will need to correct for your final document. Finding and correcting errors in these activities helps you become a *thinking* keyboarder and will improve your proofreading skills.

Vertically Centering Text on the Page

As explained in Session 38, personal business letters are typically centered vertically on the page to make them more visually pleasing. Rather than adding extra hard returns above the date, use a setting in the Page Setup dialog box to vertically center the letter text on the page. The following steps illustrate the process for vertically centering text on a page in an active document:

1 Click the Layout tab.

2 Click the Page Setup group dialog box launcher.

3 Click the Layout tab at the Page Setup dialog box.

4 Click the *Vertical alignment* option box arrow and then click *Center* at the drop-down list.

5 Click OK to close the Page Setup dialog box.

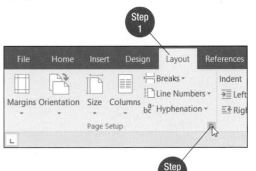

Session

115

Medical Center Project: Production Documents

Getting Started

Exercise 115.1 Unless you are continuing immediately after completing Session 114, spend at least two to three minutes warming up before completing the document activities in this session. See Session 101 for suggested warm-up text.

Working in the Medical Center

You are now ready to complete the documents activities for the project. They are to be completed in the order specified in the memo report to Dr. Borman that you completed in Session 114, regardless of the order in which they are listed in this session. Although speed is important, accuracy of the content and proper formatting are equally critical.

Document 115.1 **Email Message or Phone Call**

Read all instructions below before starting this document activity.

1 Consider the following scenario and instructions:

Originally, the flight Dr. Borman was scheduled to take was to arrive in Las Vegas at 5:50 p.m. today (Friday, September 4); however, the flight has been cancelled. The action for this document activity depends upon what you do in the Document 115.4 document activity.

Dr. Borman has forwarded you a copy of the email from Suri Weiss (see Figure 115.1). At this point, neither Dr. Borman nor Ms. Weiss knows about the change in Dr. Borman's travel schedule. You can contact Suri Weiss with the information by email or by phone. Use either the email message section or the phone record section of **Doc115.01** to represent the action taken.

If you email Suri Weiss, copy Dr. Borman. If you make the phone call, be sure to share the information with Dr. Borman when he arrives in the office at 11 a.m.

2 Navigate to the Document 115.1 launch page in the Online Lab and then click the Launch Activity button to open **Doc115.01** in the activity window.

3 Compose and key an appropriate message using the document open in the Online Lab. Include the information you will communicate to Dr. Borman at the bottom of the document. *Note: If using the email option in this activity and any of the remaining email activities in this unit, make sure to press Enter twice to begin a new paragraph and do not press Tab while typing the message body.*

4 Proofread the document and correct any errors.

5 Save the document.

6 Click the Submit button to upload the document for instructor review.

Figure 66.1 Personal Business Letter   *Note: Do not key this document.*

July 17, 2020 [Enter] ————————————————— date line

[Enter]

Ms. Teresa Zwiefelhofer, Manager [Shift + Enter]
New Jersey Heat Pump Services, Inc. [Shift + Enter]   inside address   body
1100 New Trenton Road [Shift + Enter]
Trenton, NJ 08690-4544 [Shift + Enter]

Dear Ms. Zwiefelhofer: [Enter] ————————— salutation

We have an Ultimate Plan Service Contract with you (#21209) for a home we own at 13223 Old Prospect
Road, Trenton. The current contract period is December 1, 2019, through November 30, 2020. [Enter]

We have sold the home on Old Prospect Road to Mr. and Mrs. Robert Delis of Cleveland. The closing
date for the sale of the home is July 31, 2020. Assuming the sale is completed as scheduled, please
transfer the remaining time on the Ultimate Plan Service Contract to Mr. and Mrs. Delis. They plan to
move in right away. [Enter]

By copy of this letter, I suggest that Mr. or Mrs. Delis contact you at (609) 555-1049 regarding the
continuation of this Service Contract after November 30, 2020. We definitely recommend your services. [Enter]

Sincerely, [Enter] ————————————————— closing

[Enter]

Michael Varicka [Shift + Enter]
17431 N. Butterfield Road [Shift + Enter]   The signature line includes
Trenton, NJ 08690-2388 [Enter]   the sender's mailing address.

cc: Mr. and Mrs. Robert Delis

A copy of this letter is being sent
to Mr. and Mrs. Robert Delis.

Figure 115.1 Email Message for Document 115.1

To...	drtborman@ppi-edu.net
Subject:	Dinner at the NAT&T

Terry,

I am also planning on attending the North American Technology and Telecommunications Trade Show. Can you meet me for a late dinner on Friday evening after the exhibits close?

I'm staying at Bally's and will arrive in Las Vegas at noon on Friday, September 4. I have some exciting news to share about the opening of our new medical center in Cleveland. Email me a response about dinner tonight; I'll have my tablet with me.

Suri
sweiss@ppi-edu.net

Document 115.2 **Email Message**

Read all instructions below before starting this document activity.

1 Consider the following scenario and instructions:

You have received a copy of the email shown in Figure 115.2. Dr. Borman has asked you to respond to the request.

One possible response is to prepare an email message to Deion Prado to let him know that Dr. Borman will be in Las Vegas attending the North American Technology and Telecommunications Trade Show. Note that the Trade Show ends on Monday, September 7, and that Dr. Borman will not be back in the office until Tuesday morning, September 8. The doctor's schedule will not allow time for him to give Mr. Prado a tour.

Depending on your schedule, you may consider offering to give the tour yourself. If you make the offer, be sure to give Deion Prado some idea of when and how to contact you to make arrangements for the tour.

Include the office fax number as requested.

2 Navigate to the Document 115.2 launch page in the Online Lab and then click the Launch Activity button to open **Doc115.02** in the activity window.

3 Compose and key an appropriate message using the document open in the Online Lab.

4 Proofread the document and correct any errors.

5 Save the document.

6 Click the Submit button to upload the document for instructor review.

Complete one 3-minute timing on the timing text below.

3-Minute Timing

Timing 66.3

The warm, red sun creeps up into a narrow slit separating distant mountains. Meanwhile, dark, uneven, colorful clouds send streaks of pink and purple across the sky and water.

In the harbor, white-colored fishing boats gleam in the flattering light. Sunrise seems to set fire to the corrugated red buildings, with their rippling reflections in the lake enhancing the effect. An odd-looking bird swims by with its body under water, then flips and dives out of sight. On the dock, a scowling, black-bearded fisherman strides rapidly toward one of the boats. He stops and looks directly out to sea. Directly to his right, a broad river empties into the harbor.

The harbor is where river and ocean meet. To the north, steep rocky headlands, towering cliffs, and crashing waves provide a dramatic landscape. At the point above the cliffs, a lighthouse overlooks the harbor. The majestic white column of the lighthouse is girded with broad black stripes. The sea cliffs form a concave wall behind a rugged beach strewn with driftwood, then jut out again to the ocean's edge. North of the lighthouse, the cliffs suddenly give way quickly to open beach and dunes, and miles and miles of uninterrupted sand and swaying grasses. Inland, there are cranberry bogs and, to the northeast, a quaint, fishing village.

 Ergonomic Tip

Perform stretching and breathing exercises at your desk frequently throughout the day to relieve stress and prevent physical discomfort.

Preparing Personal Business Letters

A personal business letter is a letter written by an individual to be sent to a business. Examples of personal business letters may include letters that individuals write to companies to request information or complain about a product.

Figure 66.1 shows an example of a personal business letter. Note that the return address appears at the end of the letter, below the sender's name. Reference initials and the file name are generally not used in personal business letters since the author of the letter typically keys the document. A *cc:* is placed after the sender's name and address to indicate that a copy is being sent to someone else. The letter is printed on plain paper, not on company letterhead. Because Word automatically adds extra spacing between paragraphs, press Shift + Enter at the end of the lines that do not require this extra spacing, such as in the address blocks.

Figure 115.2 Email Message for Document 115.2

To...   drtborman@ppi-edu.net

Subject: Visit to Portland

Dr. Borman,

I'll be in Portland over the Labor Day weekend to visit my parents. I'm scheduled to leave San Diego at 6:15 and will arrive at 8:30 p.m., Friday, September 4. I'm scheduled to depart at 5 p.m. on Monday, September 7. Even though it is not finished, is there any chance of touring your medical center? I realize it is a holiday weekend, and you may have other plans.

In case we don't get together, please send me your fax number. I found an article that may be of special interest to you concerning an intranet. If you haven't already done so, it appears to be something you should consider for your new medical center.

Deion Prado
dprado23@ppi-edu.net

**Document
115.3**

Email Message

Read all instructions below before starting this document activity.

1 Consider the following scenario and instructions:

> You have received the letter shown in Figure 115.3. Based on past experience, you know that Dr. Borman tries to accommodate requests to give presentations to students at Portland State University.

> Based on the other information available for this project, determine which of the two requested dates would work with Dr. Borman's schedule.

> When Dr. Borman arrives at 11 a.m., you can share this information with him. You have to decide whether to send an email message to Len George this afternoon or wait until Tuesday morning.

> Another alternative would be to assume that Dr. Borman is not able to accept the invitation. In that case, you would prepare an email message to Len George to let him know.

2 Navigate to the Document 115.3 launch page in the Online Lab and then click the Launch Activity button to open **Doc115.03** in the activity window.

3 Compose and key an appropriate message using the document open in the Online Lab. Copy Dr. Borman on the email message.

4 Proofread the document and correct any errors.

5 Save the document.

6 Click the Submit button to upload the document for instructor review.

Session 66
Vertical Centering and Adjusting Margins in Personal Business Letters

Session Objectives

- **Prepare personal business letters**
- **Vertically center text on a page**
- **Change the margins of a document**
- **Improve writing skills by constructing better paragraphs**
- **Efficiently produce documents in mailable form**

Getting Started

Exercise 66.1 If you are continuing immediately from Session 65, you may skip the Exercise 66.1 warm-up drill. However, if you exited the Online Lab at the end of Session 65, warm up by completing Exercise 66.1.

Exercise 66.2 Begin your session work by completing Exercise 66.2, a timed short drill, in the Online Lab.

Assessing Your Speed and Accuracy

Complete Timings 66.1 through 66.3 in the Online Lab. At the end of the timing, the Online Lab will display your WPM rate and any errors. Results will be saved in your Timings Performance report. If you have been surpassing the speed and accuracy goals identified in the Online Lab, set slightly more challenging personal goals and strive to exceed them.

Complete two 1-minute timings on the timing text below. If you do not key at or above the WPM rate identified in the Online Lab on Timing 66.1, concentrate on speed on Timing 66.2. If you meet the Online Lab's WPM goal but make more errors than the goal identified in the Online Lab on Timing 66.1, concentrate on accuracy on Timing 66.2. However, if you meet or exceed both goals for Timing 66.1, push for greater speed on Timing 66.2.

1-Minute Timings

Timings 66.1–66.2
Recreation is becoming increasingly popular among people of all ages. One particular sport that is growing rapidly is cross-country skiing. If a person makes an effort to get out of the house and puts on a pair of skis, cross-country skiing can be a great enjoyment. No specialized skills are needed to learn cross-country skiing. The few basic beginning instructions are simple to master. The excitement of gliding over that snowy countryside, through the magnificent forests, and over the hills is a thrill that no one should miss.

Figure 115.3 Incoming Letter for Document 115.3

Portland State University

PO Box 1700
Portland, OR 97218-0881

(503) 555-6111
School of Business

August 28, 2020

Dr. Terrance Borman
Chief Administrator
Riverside Medical Center
17431 N. Willamette Drive
Portland, OR 97218-1230

Dr. Borman:

This fall I am teaching a class called Business & Office Information Systems. The class meets on Tuesdays and Thursdays from 2:00 to 3:30 p.m. There are 34 student enrolled in this course; most of them are seniors majoring in Management Information Systems or Business Education. Our primary project for the fall semester is to develop a strategic plan to upgrade the day-to-day functions of a medical center located in Klamath Falls, Oregon.

Are you available on Tuesday, September 22, or Thursday, September 24, to share with this class your experiences in designing and administering a state-of-the-art medical center? What are the most important areas to address in developing a strategic plan? Are there new technologies available that can be used to enhance the daily activities of a medical center? Are there particular obstacles or problems that must be addressed in upgrading systems?

The class meets in room 204 of Brewer Hall, the School of Business building. If you can make it, we will reserve a visitor's parking spot for you behind Brewer Hall, at Stark and 6th Avenue. There is an entry to the security office for parking permits next to the visitor's parking area.

Classes begin on Wednesday, September 9. You can reach me via email any time before that to let me know if you are available. My email address is lgeorge@ppi-edu.net.

Sincerely yours,

Len George, Chair
MIS Department

mbr
Figure115.03

Business Correspondence Part II

Session 66
Vertical Centering and Adjusting Margins in Personal Business Letters

Session 67
Building Paragraphs in Business Letters

Session 68
Numbering Paragraphs in Business Letters

Session 69
Preparing Multiple-Page Business Letters

Session 70
Production Progress Check: Business Correspondence Part II

D]ocument Phone Message

115.4 Read all instructions below before starting this document activity.

1 Consider the following scenario and instructions:

> You have received a handwritten phone message (see Figure 115.4). You will have to take action by making one or more telephone calls.

> You might check online for flights from Portland to Las Vegas to see if Dr. Borman could catch an earlier flight. Southwest Airlines, southwest.com, has 14 flights a day, and Alaska Airlines, alaskaair.com, has 6 flights a day.

> The fact that the original flight has been delayed as well as the flight options available to Dr. Borman should be the first things to share with him when he arrives at the office at 11 a.m. Provide him with a couple of options for flights on Southwest and/or Alaska Airlines to Las Vegas that would arrive about the same time as his original flight.

> This is a sticky situation. Will Delta refund the price of the ticket if Dr. Borman cancels the trip with Delta? It seems that they should because the next Delta flight is so late. Whatever is decided, call Mona Cavendish at Delta to let her know what Dr. Borman has decided to do.

2 Navigate to the Document 115.4 launch page in the Online Lab and then click the Launch Activity button to open **Doc115.04** in the activity window.

3 Key the content of the phone conversation(s) in the document open in the Online Lab. Include the information you will communicate to Dr. Borman at the bottom of the document. Modify the document as necessary to accommodate your information.

4 Proofread the document and correct any errors.

5 Save the document.

6 Click the Submit button to upload the document for instructor review.

Figure 115.4 Phone Message for Document 115.4

IMPORTANT MESSAGE

TO _Dr. Borman_

DATE _9/4_   TIME _____ (A.M.) P.M.

M s. _Mona Cavendish_

OF _Delta Airlines_

AC/PHONE # _(888) 555-6389_

TELEPHONED ☑   PLEASE CALL ☑

CALLED TO SEE YOU ☐   WILL CALL AGAIN ☐

WANTS TO SEE YOU ☐   URGENT ☐

RETURNED CALL ☐

Message _Today's Delta flight 1864 has been canceled. You are now booked on their flight 1874, departing Portland at 8:10 p.m. and arriving in Las Vegas at 10:20 p.m. Please confirm this booking._

Operator _Blanche_

Document 65.4 — **Memo with Small Caps and Bold Formatting**

Read all instructions below before starting this document activity.

1 Navigate to the Document 65.4 launch page in the Online Lab and then click the Launch Activity button to open **Doc065.04** in the activity window.

2 Use the content in Figure 65.4 to key the memo, being careful to set *Sure Foods* in bold in the second and last paragraphs of the memo.

3 Select the one-line paragraph that reads *Sure Foods Sure Taste Good!*, apply small caps formatting, and then change the paragraph alignment to center alignment. ***Hint: The nonprinting paragraph mark at the end of the paragraph should be formatted in small caps.***

4 Key the reference initials ltl and the file name at the bottom of the memo.

5 Proofread the memo and correct any errors.

6 Save the document.

7 Click the Check button to upload the document for checking.

8 If errors are reported by the Online Lab, view the results document, correct the errors in the submitted document, save the document, and then click the Check Again button.

Figure 65.4 Memo Content for Document 65.4

TO: Store Managers and Assistant Managers ¶ FROM: Kathleen Johnson ¶ DATE: October 12, 2020 ¶ SUBJECT: Cereal Display ¶ The increased promotional activity in the cereal category offers an additional opportunity to increase milk sales. Your promotional display support of cereal items is to be located at aisle ends that are close to your milk displays. ¶ Our own **Sure Foods** products are a major contributor to operating profits. We need to do everything we can to increase the operating efficiency of not only the milk unit but also the ice cream, beverage, and bread units. To this end, we will be adding to aisle ends large signs that read: ¶ Sure Foods Sure Taste Good! ¶ With a well-planned merchandising program that offers good tie-ins and themes, I am confident that we will see increased sales and gross revenue. We should all strive to promote **Sure Foods** products. Please give this area the attention it deserves.

Ending the Session

The Online Lab automatically saved the work you completed for this session. You may continue with the next session or exit the Online Lab and continue later.

Document
115.5

Phone Message

Read all instructions below before starting this document activity.

1 Consider the following scenario and instructions:

> You have received a handwritten phone message (see Figure 115.5). You will have to take action by making a telephone call.

> You can wait until Dr. Borman arrives this morning to see what he wants to do and then call Carmela at Dr. Briceland's office to let them know if Dr. Borman will take the 1:40 appointment on September 8.

> Another alternative would be to call Dr. Briceland's office right away, accept the 1:40 appointment for Dr. Borman on Tuesday, September 8, and let Dr. Borman know what you did when he arrives at 11 a.m.

2 Navigate to the Document 115.5 launch page in the Online Lab and then click the Launch Activity button to open **Doc115.05** in the activity window.

3 Key the content of the phone conversation in the document open in the Online Lab. Include the information you will communicate to Dr. Borman at the bottom of the document.

4 Proofread the document and correct any errors.

5 Save the document.

6 Click the Submit button to upload the document for instructor review.

Figure 115.5 Phone Message for Document 115.5

IMPORTANT MESSAGE

TO _Dr. Borman_

DATE _9/3_   TIME _4:45_   A.M. (P.M)

M _s. Carmela_

OF _Dr. Briceland's office_

AC/PHONE # _555-6214_

TELEPHONED	☑	PLEASE CALL	☑
CALLED TO SEE YOU	☐	WILL CALL AGAIN	☐
WANTS TO SEE YOU	☐	URGENT	☐
	RETURNED CALL	☐	

Message _Dr. Briceland had a cancellation for Tuesday, September 8, at 1:40 p.m. If you are available, he can do your eye exam. His next opening isn't until November._

Operator _Blanche_

Document 65.3

Email with Proofreading Marks

Read all instructions below before starting this document activity.

1 Navigate to the Document 65.3 launch page in the Online Lab and then click the Launch Activity button to open **Doc065.03** in the activity window.

2 Key gharper@ppi-edu.net in the *To* text box, klarson@ppi-edu.net in the *CC* text box, and then key Sun City West (SCW) PRIDES in the *Subject* text box.

3 Key the content of the email message using the text in Figure 65.3. Make the changes indicated by the proofreading marks.

4 Proofread the document and correct any errors.

5 Save the document.

6 Click the Check button to upload the document for checking.

7 If errors are reported by the Online Lab, view the results document, correct the errors in the submitted document, save the document, and then click the Check Again button.

Figure 65.3 Email Content for Document 65.3

George, ¶ Thank you for asking about the SCW PRIDES. The word PRIDES *(italic)* is an acronym for Particular Residents Involved Doing Environmental Services. Currently we have 326 members who are either full time or winter residents of SCW. Our primary objective is to keep SCW a pristine place to live, work and enjoy life. ¶ We have 17 landscaping teams (10 to 20 members per team). The teams work on Saturday morning for two hours trimming bushes and small trees, raking the rocks, picking up trash, and sweeping the sidewalks and curbs. safety vests and gloves are provided, and we do not take attendance. ¶ We have a Tuesday morning maintenance team that repairs and sharpens tools and services our pickup truck and the 24 converted golf carts that carry our equipment. ¶ There is a safety team that makes sure our members are safe while at work. ¶ There is a refreshment team that serves coffee and donuts at our monthly meetings and our 10-man/person irrigation team takes care of our watering system. ¶ Our office team takes care of our computerized accounting system, our roster, and other communication duties. ¶ I'm sending you by surface mail a PRIDES brochure and an enrollment card. I've copied our President, Ken Larson, on this email. Please contact either of us if you have questions. We certainly welcome you as a new member of the SCW PRIDES.

Phone Message

Read all instructions below before starting this document activity.

1 Consider the following scenario and instructions:

> You have received a handwritten phone message (see Figure 115.6). You will have to take action by making a telephone call.

> One possible response in this situation would be to call Josh Gonlag right away to let him know that Dr. Borman will not be in until 11 a.m. and that he will be leaving in the afternoon for a meeting in Las Vegas. Ask Josh if he can give you some idea of the problem so that when Dr. Borman calls back, he may have a solution.

2 Navigate to the Document 115.6 launch page in the Online Lab and then click the Launch Activity button to open **Doc115.06** in the activity window.

3 Key the content of the phone conversation in the document open in the Online Lab. Include the information you will communicate to Dr. Borman at the bottom of the document.

4 Proofread the document and correct any errors.

5 Save the document.

6 Click the Submit button to upload the document for instructor review.

Figure 115.6 Phone Message for Document 115.6

IMPORTANT MESSAGE

TO _Dr. Borman_

DATE _9/4_　　　TIME _7:15_　　(A.M.) P.M.

M _Josh Gonlag_

OF _PEC Electrical Contractors_

AC/PHONE # _555-1617_

TELEPHONED	☑	PLEASE CALL	☑
CALLED TO SEE YOU	☐	WILL CALL AGAIN	☐
WANTS TO SEE YOU	☐	URGENT	☐

RETURNED CALL ☐

Message _There's a problem in the electrical service wiring requirements for the x-ray and CAT scan units at Riverside Medical Center that has to be resolved before they can continue work._

Operator _Blanche_

7 Click the Check button to upload the document for checking.

8 If errors are reported by the Online Lab, view the results document, correct the errors in the submitted document, save the document, and then click the Check Again button.

Figure 65.2 Email Content for Document 65.2

Shakil, ¶ Thanks for your question about the electronic devices that function on wireless technology and their capabilities. I assume you are referring to the devices known as *tablets*. ¶ One thing that is common in these devices is that they are all touchscreen activated. Most of the current models have all the functions of a laptop computer and include webcams, hard drives, processors, and, in some cases, detachable keyboards. ¶ Tablets gained popularity in April 2010, when Apple released its **iPad** tablet. Each year this type of device is gaining more and more users, and tablet manufacturers keep adding new features and increasing capacities. Tablets have the ability to access the Internet, play music and movies, and open documents. In addition, they are much lighter and more portable than laptops. ¶ Tablets can connect to the Internet via a Wi-Fi connection, or you can buy a data plan from your cell phone company that allows you to access the Internet wherever you are. ¶ Tablets range in price, depending on hard drive capacity and other special features. ¶ If you have other questions, please email me at **jerry.samuels@ppi-edu.net**. I've copied **Gene Brock** as he too had questions about tablets.

Document 115.7 Memo

Read all instructions below before starting this document activity.

1 Read the transcript of a phone message from Dr. Borman that was left for you Wednesday, September 2, at 1:30 p.m. (see Figure 115.7).

2 Navigate to the Document 115.7 launch page in the Online Lab and then click the Launch Activity button to open **Doc115.07** in the activity window.

3 Compose and key the requested memo in the open document.

4 Proofread the document and correct any errors.

5 Save the document.

6 Click the Submit button to upload the document for instructor review.

Figure 115.7 Voice Mail Message for Document 115.7

Wednesday, September 2, 1:30 p.m.

Hi! This is Terry Borman. Welcome back from vacation. I won't be in until 11 a.m. Friday and will be leaving at 1 p.m. When you get a chance, would you please compose a memo from me to the Riverside Medical Center Department Heads. The subject is "Demonstration of Using the Digital Disk System for Creating, Maintaining, and Updating Medical Records."

Tell the Department Heads that a demonstration has been set for September 23, 2020, from 1 to 4:30 p.m. in Room 109 of the Records Center of our new facility. Even though the contractors are still working on our new facility, this area has been completed. Representatives of the firm that has sold us this system will be on hand to demonstrate its use. Ample time will be provided to ask questions and make recommendations for adjusting the system to meet our needs. It is imperative that all department heads are in attendance. Please indicate that if a department head cannot attend, that person should email me and let me know who from the department will take the person's place. Be sure to include my email address in the memo.

Document 115.8 Certificate

Read all instructions below before starting this document activity.

1 Read the transcript of a phone message from Dr. Borman that was left for you Wednesday, September 2, at 3:05 p.m. (see Figure 115.8).

2 Navigate to the Document 115.8 launch page in the Online Lab and then click the Launch Activity button to open **Doc115.08** in the activity window.

3 Create a draft of the requested certificate in the open document.

4 Proofread the document and correct any errors.

5 Save the document.

6 Click the Submit button to upload the document for instructor review.

Figure 65.1 Memo Content for Document 65.1

TO: Dr. Ramona Ott, Dean ¶ FROM: Jolene Malona, Department Chair ¶ ⓒₐₚ/lc
DATE: Febuary 14, 2020 ¶ SUBJECT: BUSINESS SEMINAR ¶ The business
seminar I attended, Technology Applications for School Administrators,
was absolutely outstanding. ¶ When I return to Sacramento next ~~month~~ *week*,
I will have a tremendous amount of ⓢₜₑₜ ~~material~~ to share with you regarding
this program. I was able to get an extra seminar booklet that contains
the information presented, *and* ~~that~~ I will give *it* to you. It includes examples of
technology applications that can be used in our programs. ¶ Before we
attend the forthcoming program in New York City, would you please be
sure to share with me the material you developed on cloud computing ⓑf
and tablet computers. These ~~topics~~ *subjects* will be covered, but having ~~some~~ *a basic*
~~background in~~ *understanding of* these ~~areas~~ *topics* would be helpful *to me*. ¶ By the way, the person who
conducted the Technology Applications for School Administrators seminar
was Jim Casey ⓘₜₐₗᵢc of Casey, Adams, Lopez, and Associates. He will also be
giving a presentation in New York City. I ~~no~~ *know* it will be a presentation that I
lc don't want to miss. ¶ Xcj ¶ Doc065.01

Success Tip

To see whether formatting has been applied to a space or punctuation symbol, select it and then check the buttons in the Font group on the Home tab to see if any of them are active. If a button is active, click it to remove the formatting from the selected character.

Document 65.2 **Email with Bold, Italic, and Color Text**

Read all instructions below before starting this document activity.

1. Navigate to the Document 65.2 launch page in the Online Lab and then click the Launch Activity button to open **Doc065.02** in the activity window.

2. Key smansoor@ppi-edu.net in the *To* text box, gbrock@ppi-edu.net in the *CC* text box, and then key Wireless Technology in the *Subject* text box.

3. Key the content of the email message using the text in Figure 65.2. Format words, phrases, and names in bold or italics as shown. Do not allow Word to format the email address within the body of the message as a hyperlink. *Hint: Make sure to press Enter twice to begin a new paragraph and do not press Tab while keying the message body.*

4. Change the text color of the second paragraph in the email (begins *One thing that is common*) to the Red color option in the *Standard Colors* section of the Font Color palette.

5. Proofread the document and correct any errors.

6. Save the document.

steps continue

Figure 115.8 Voice Mail Message for Document 115.8

Wednesday, September 2, 3:05 p.m.

Hi! It's me, Terry, again. As you may recall, at our last Board of Directors meeting, it was recommended and approved that we institute an "Employee of the Month" program commencing with the opening of the Riverside Medical Center on January 4. Employees of both the Riverside Medical Center and the Clinic are eligible for this award. Using your creative talents, would you please design a certificate to be used in conjunction with this program? At the bottom of the certificate, provide two signature lines, one for the Chief Administrator and one for the Chief Surgeon.

Document 115.9 Invitation

Read all instructions below before starting this document activity.

1 Read the transcript of a phone message from Dr. Borman that was left for you Wednesday, September 2, at 4:36 p.m. (see Figure 115.9).

2 Navigate to the Document 115.9 launch page in the Online Lab and then click the Launch Activity button to open **Doc115.09** in the activity window.

3 Create a draft of the requested invitation in the open document.

4 Proofread the document and correct any errors.

5 Save the document.

6 Click the Submit button to upload the document for instructor review.

Figure 115.9 Voice Mail Message for Document 115.9

Wednesday, September 2, 4:36 p.m.

Hello again, it's Terry. I promise no more messages today after this one. Before the new medical center facility opens, I want to invite the Board of Directors and a number of individuals from the Portland area who have made significant contributions to our new medical center to a reception and tour of the facility.

Again, I want to take advantage of your creative talents. Would you please design an invitation for this event? The reception for the new Riverside Medical Center is to be held on Tuesday, December 29, 2020. The reception will be held in the main lobby of the new facility (17431 N. Willamette Drive) from 4 to 8 p.m. Refreshments will be served. RSVP regrets only. The parking lot in front of the main lobby will be open for our guests. I've started a guest list and will go over it with you next week to make sure we haven't missed anyone.

Ergonomic Tip

When keying from a hard-copy document, use task lighting to illuminate the document. Make sure the light does not reflect on your computer screen, and make adjustments if it does.

Checking Production Progress: Email and Memos

Sessions 61 through 64 reviewed basic word processing and document preparation and discussed the procedures for creating and formatting emails and memos. In this session, you will be assessed on how quickly and accurately you can key these types of documents. In the following document activities, each completed document is to be "mailable," which means that it contains no errors. A document that requires corrections is not considered *mailable*.

Your goal is to key each document in mailable form. If you are missing errors that should have been corrected or your instructor believes you can work more efficiently, he or she may ask you to repeat document activities. To help you succeed, carefully review the content and instructions for each document before keying. *Note: Before you begin these documents, review the content of Sessions 61 through 64 if you are unsure how to complete a specific formatting or software task.*

Document 65.1

Memo with Justified Paragraph Alignment, Indented Text, Bold and Italic Text, and Proofreading Marks

Read all instructions below before starting this document activity.

1 Navigate to the Document 65.1 launch page in the Online Lab and then click the Launch Activity button to open **Doc065.01** in the activity window.

2 Use the content in Figure 65.1 to key the memo. Make changes indicated by the proofreading marks, and set the text in bold and italics as indicated. *Note: Be careful not to set in bold or italic spaces, or punctuation before or after the text that is to appear in bold or italic, otherwise the Online Lab will indicate an error. When two or more formatted words appear next to each other, format the space between the words.*

3 Change the paragraph alignment of the four paragraphs within the body of the memo to justified alignment. Keep the paragraph alignment of the reference line containing the initials and file name as left aligned.

4 Indent the third paragraph (begins *Before we attend*) 0.5 inch from the left and right margins.

5 Proofread the document and correct any errors. *Hint: Display the nonprinting characters in the document by clicking the Show/Hide ¶ button in the Paragraph group on the Home tab. This will help you check the formatting of spaces.*

6 Save the document.

7 Click the Check button to upload the document for checking.

8 If errors are reported by the Online Lab, view the results document, correct the errors in the submitted document, save the document, and then click the Check Again button.

Business Letter

Read all instructions below before starting this document activity.

1 Navigate to the Document 115.10 launch page in the Online Lab and then click the Launch Activity button to open **Doc115.10** in the activity window.

2 Dr. Borman drafted a letter for you to key and prepare for his signature, and one of your coworkers proofread the letter while you were on vacation. The letter is shown in Figure 115.10. Key the letter, implementing the proofreading marks as you key and formatting the letter as a business letter.

   a The letter will be printed on preprinted letterhead, so the date line will need to start below the letterhead. Press Enter three times to position the insertion point approximately 2 inches from the top of the document.

   b Regardless of the day you decide to key this letter, key September 8, 2020 as the current date of the letter.

   c Key Terrance Borman, MD, followed by his title, Chief Administrator, as the signature line.

   d Key the initials bmn and the file name, Doc115.10, below Dr. Borman's title. *Note: Because the Online Lab will be checking this document, do not use the file name you developed in Session 113.*

   e Include a notation for an enclosure.

3 Proofread the document and correct any errors.

4 Save the document.

5 Click the Check button to upload the document for checking.

6 If errors are reported by the Online Lab, view the results document, correct the errors in the submitted document, save the document, and then click the Check Again button.

Figure 115.10 Block-Style Business Letter Content for Document 115.10

Martha Stitt-Gohdes, MD/ 220 River's Crossing/ Athens, GA 30601-4707 (Riverside) Dear Dr. Stitt-Gohdes: We are scheduled to open our new/ medical center on January 4, 2021. A ⑤ year strategic plan for operating this facility has been prepared by a consulting firm headquartered in Seattle, (WA.) A considerable (spell out) amount of time and energy has gone into the development of this plan. Our primary goal is to provide a state-of-the-art facility in order to better serve our patients. Often times, individuals who are close to the project as we are overlook procedures and/or technology that we should be have incorporated into the plan. I've been in touch with several Medical Center (lc/2x) Chief Administrators in the East and Midwest who have been through the process of building a new facility. I've asked them for suggestions on anything we might do to make sure that "no stone has been left unturned" to complete this project. One suggestion that has been made numerous times is

continues

Session 65 Production Progress Check: Email and Memos Part II

Session Objectives

- Apply Word features and skills presented in Sessions 61–64
- Efficiently produce documents in mailable form

Getting Started

Exercise 65.1 If you are continuing immediately from Session 64, you may skip the Exercise 65.1 warm-up drill. However, if you exited the Online Lab at the end of Session 64, warm up by completing Exercise 65.1.

Exercise 65.2 Begin your session work by completing Exercise 65.2, a timed short drill, in the Online Lab.

Assessing Your Speed and Accuracy

Complete Timings 65.1 and 65.2 in the Online Lab. At the end of each timing, the Online Lab will display your WPM rate and any errors. Results will be saved in your Timings Performance report. If you have been surpassing the speed and accuracy goals identified in the Online Lab, set slightly more challenging personal goals and strive to exceed them.

Complete two 1-minute timings on the timing text below. If you meet or exceed both speed and accuracy goals for Timing 65.1, push for greater speed on Timing 65.2.

1-Minute Timings

Timings 65.1–65.2   Relive our country's aviation past. Visit our national aerospace museum. Let your mind fly from the earth to the moon and beyond. Among many interesting and exciting exhibits, you will be able to glimpse the dawn of powered flight at Kitty Hawk and see the Golden Age of Barnstorming and the first airmail planes. You will be able to recapture the days of aerial combat of World War I. The planes of World War II are also on display with 150 space displays and other artifacts.

that we bring a third-party consultant to review our strategic plan and the systems to be incorporated. Your name has been mentioned on more than one occasion to contact for such an endeavor. Are you available to analyze our plan? If you are available, how soon could you begin reviewing what has been proposed? How long would it take to review? Would you be able to tour our facility? What would your service cost? A brochure describing our new medical center is enclosed to give you an idea of the size and scope of our operation. Sincerely yours,

One of your roles as administrative assistant is to serve as a backup to the Medical Transcription Department. The documents created in the following activities simulate documents transcribed using speech recognition software. For each report, you will begin with a document that contains standard report headings, and you will rekey the content of the report into the appropriate format. You will have to add the punctuation (commas, periods, apostrophes, etc.) to the text as you key. If a heading is not used in the transcribed content, be sure to remove the heading from the document. Similarly, if a heading or section is added, include that additional heading in the final document.

Refer to your priorities table to determine when these documents are to be completed: before 11 a.m. today, after 11 a.m. today, or on Tuesday. Key these documents in the order in which you prioritized them.

**Document
115.11**

Consultation Report

Read all instructions below before starting this document activity.

1 Navigate to the Document 115.11 launch page in the Online Lab and then click the Launch Activity button to open **Doc115.11** in the activity window.

2 Key the dictated report shown in Figure 115.11. Add the missing punctuation, and key the contents of the report according to the report's template. Add and delete headings as appropriate. Key all dictated numbers as arabic numerals, not as words.

3 Key the signature line and the reference information at the bottom of the report.

  a The physician signing the report is the consulting physician listed at the top of the report. There should be three blank lines between the last section and the signature line.

  b Key cgk for the dictator's initials and clh for the transcriptionist's initials. *Note: Use the indicated transcriptionist's initials, not your own initials, to facilitate accurate checking by the Online Lab.*

  c Key the dictation date to be the day after the consultation.

  d Key 09/08/2020 as the transcription date. *Note: This transcription date may not match the completion date you identified in Session 114. Use the indicated date to facilitate accurate checking by the Online Lab.*

4 Proofread the document and correct any errors.

5 Save the document.

6 Click the Check button to upload the document for checking.

7 If errors are reported by the Online Lab, view the results document, correct the errors in the submitted document, save the document, and then click the Check Again button.

Document 64.5

Composing a Memo that Provides Directions to Your Residence

Read all instructions below before starting this document activity.

1 Navigate to the Document 64.5 launch page in the Online Lab and then click the Launch Activity button to open **Doc064.05** in the activity window.

2 Compose a memo to your instructor that contains the directions on how to get from school to your place of residence. Be sure that the instructions are clear; for example, instead of writing "When leaving school, turn north on Main Street…," it is clearer to say "When leaving school, turn left on Main Street…," Use correct memo formatting, as shown in Figure 63.1.

3 Proofread and correct any errors in the memo.

4 Save the document.

5 Click the Submit button to upload the document for instructor review.

Ending the Session

The Online Lab automatically saved the work you completed for this session. You may continue with the next session or exit the Online Lab and continue later.

Figure 115.11 Dictated Consultation Report for Document 115.11

This is consulting doctor C G Kelly   I have a medical consultants report for August thirty first twenty twenty for Clara J Wambaugh medical record number seven eight three three   The patient was born May twenty nine nineteen fifty two Her physician is doctor M T Flores

Reason for consultation   The patient is a 68-year-old female who developed abdominal pain over the past two days   The pain is getting worse   She seems to have a full feeling   The patient says she has had an increasing abdominal girth and nausea and vomiting   The patients stool seems to be normal   She has had some loose stools with no melena or hematochezia

Past medical history   The patient has had abdominal adhesions and surgery was performed on these in two thousand thirteen   The adhesions were the result of a hysterectomy and pelvic surgery

Physical examination   The patient was seen in the emergency room where she was determined to have a small-bowel obstruction

Diagnostic studies   Laboratory data shows a WBC of seven hundred without shift   Abdominal x-rays show some air fluid levels

Impression   Small-bowel obstruction

Recommendations   The patient has been admitted to the hospital A conservative management will be tried with a long weighted Anderson tube   The patient had a difficult surgery in two thousand thirteen for adhesions   It would be better if the bowel obstruction can be resolved without surgery   She is grossly overweight and is not a good surgical candidate

Document 115.12 **Operative Report**

Read all instructions below before starting this document activity.

1 Navigate to the Document 115.12 launch page in the Online Lab and then click the Launch Activity button to open **Doc115.12** in the activity window.

2 Key the dictated report shown in Figure 115.12. Add the missing punctuation, and key the contents of the report according to the report template. Key all dictated numbers as arabic numerals, not as words, and when the word *number* is transcribed, key the symbol # rather than the word. Do not press the spacebar between the number symbol and the number.

steps continue

Figure 64.5 Memo Content for Document 64.4

TO: Rebecca Farmer, Speaker Facilitator, Jefferson Residence Halls ¶ FROM: Dr. Mercy Coeur, Director, Health Services ¶ DATE: December 4, 2020 ¶ SUBJECT: Heart Disease Symposium ¶ The Heart Disease Symposium, to be held on Friday, will cover the following topics: ¶ Angina ¶ Angina refers to severe chest discomfort, including heaviness and tightness in the chest, sweating, and shortness of breath. Angina is caused by an imbalance of oxygen supply and oxygen demand in the chest. The most common drugs prescribed for angina are beta blockers, calcium channel blockers, and nitrates. ¶ Congestive Heart Failure ¶ Symptoms of congestive heart failure include fatigue, irregular heartbeat, and swelling in the legs. Congestive heart failure is caused by an inability of the heart to pump sufficient blood to meet the metabolic needs of the tissues of the body. Drugs prescribed for congestive heart failure depend on the specific conditions, but the most common drugs include vasodilators, ACE inhibitors, and antiarrhythmic drugs such as digoxin. ¶ Myocardial Infarction ¶ Myocardial infarction is commonly known as a heart attack. Symptoms of a heart attack include chest discomfort, fatigue, sweating, indigestion-like sensations, and intense pain in the neck, throat, shoulders, and one or both arms. Heart attacks are caused by reduced blood supply to the muscles of the heart. Beta blockers and aspirin are the chief drugs used for myocardial infarction.

Reinforcing Writing Skills

When you write memos, emails, or other short documents, you are often in a hurry. You may need to quickly relay a brief piece of information or communicate about an upcoming meeting to other staff members. In your haste, you may assume your audience knows what you are thinking, rather than writing out all the necessary details. For example, assume that you are writing to a business associate to set up a meeting from 1 to 3 p.m. on Wednesday, June 17. In your memo to this person, suppose that you state the following:

> Let's meet at 1 p.m. on Wednesday. If you have questions about the proposal, we can discuss them at that time.

Analyze the message above. Did you tell the recipient which Wednesday or how long the meeting should last? Did you specify a meeting place? Will your reader know which proposal you plan to discuss? Make sure you review your document from your reader's perspective to ensure that you have included the essential information. It is better to restate information your reader may already know than to leave out important details. You will practice this in the following document activity.

3 Key the signature line and the reference information at the bottom of the report.

    a The physician signing the report is the operating physician listed at the top of the report. Dr. Orr prefers to dictate punctuation such as commas and hyphens, so these words will appear as directions in the transcript. There should be three blank lines between the last section and the signature line.

    b Key lro for the dictator's initials and clh for the transcriptionist's initials. *Note: Use the indicated transcriptionist's initials, not your own initials, to facilitate accurate checking by the Online Lab.*

    c Key the dictation date to be the day after the surgery.

    d Key 09/08/2020 as the transcription date. *Note: This transcription date may not match the completion date you identified in Session 114. Use the indicated date to facilitate accurate checking by the Online Lab.*

4 Proofread the document and correct any errors.

5 Save the document.

6 Click the Check button to upload the document for checking.

7 If errors are reported by the Online Lab, view the results document, correct the errors in the submitted document, save the document, and then click the Check Again button.

Figure 115.12 Dictated Operative Report for Document 115.12

> This is surgeon L R Orr   I have a report for September first twenty twenty for Jeanine A Kvinsland medical record number three nine nine zero   C H Pridaux, R N assisted and the anesthesiologist was doctor F A Bresch
>
> Preoperative diagnosis   Attempted vaginal birth after previous cesarean section   Failure to progress   Premature rupture of membranes
>
> Postoperative diagnosis   Please duplicate the preoperative diagnosis in the report
>
> Name of operation   Repeat low transverse cesarean section
>
> Anesthesia   Spinal anesthesia
>
> Informed consent   Obtained
>
> Procedure   After the induction of satisfactory spinal anesthesia with the patient in the lateral supine position comma she was prepped and draped in the usual manner for abdominal procedure   A Foley catheter had been inserted into the bladder comma and the abdomen was entered through a previous low transverse incision without difficulty   Upon approaching the fascia comma there was an approximate two to three cm central defect   The parietal peritoneum was then incised and entered   Then the visceral peritoneum was incised and the bladder was pushed downward   The lower uterine segment was entered transversely   The infant was delivered as noted above   The placenta was extracted manually and the uterine defect was closed in two layers

continues

Figure 64.4 Font Dialog Box

Font   ?   ×

Font   Advanced

Font: Font style: Size:
+Body   Regular   11

+Body   Regular   8
+Headings   Italic   9
Adobe Devanagari   Bold   10
Agency FB   Bold Italic   11
Algerian   12

Font color: Underline style: Underline color:
Automatic   (none)   Automatic

Effects

☐ Strikethrough   ☑ Small caps
☐ Double strikethrough   ☐ All caps
☐ Superscript   ☐ Hidden
☐ Subscript

Preview

—————————————   +BODY   —————————————

This is the body theme font. The current document theme defines which font will be used.

Set As Default   Text Effects...   OK   Cancel

> Insert a check mark in the *Small caps* check box to apply this format to the selected text or where the insertion point is located.

Document **Memo with Small Caps Headings**
64.4 Read all instructions below before starting this document activity.

1 Navigate to the Document 64.4 launch page in the Online Lab and then click the Launch Activity button to open **Doc064.04** in the activity window.

2 Use the text in Figure 64.5 to key the memo.

3 Set the headings in the body of the memo in small caps by completing the following steps:

a Double-click the heading *Angina* to select the word. *Note: Double-clicking the word also selects the nonprinting paragraph mark that follows it. Click the Show/Hide ¶ button in the Paragraph group to see this.*

b Click the Font group dialog box launcher on the Home tab.

c At the Font dialog box with the Font tab selected, click the *Small caps* check box to insert a check mark.

d Click OK.

e Repeat Steps 3a through 3d to apply small caps formatting to the remaining two headings, *Congestive Heart Failure* and *Myocardial Infarction*. *Hint: Make sure to format the nonprinting paragraph mark that follows each heading in small caps formatting.*

4 Key the initials trf and the file name at the bottom of the memo.

5 Proofread the memo and correct any errors.

6 Save the document.

7 Click the Check button to upload the document for checking.

8 If errors are reported by the Online Lab, view the results document, correct the errors in the submitted document, save the document, and then click the Check Again button.

Figure 115.12 Dictated Operative Report for Document 115.12—continued

comma the first being a running interlocking suture of number one chromic followed by an imbricating Lambert suture   Hemostasis was adequate and the visceral peritoneum was closed with number two hyphen zero chromic   The pelvis was evacuated of a blood clot and the anterior peritoneum closed with number zero chromic   Sponge pad and needle counts were correct   The fascia was dissected off comma giving a free edge comma and then this was closed with number one Maxon   The subcutaneous tissue was closed with two hyphen zero plain   The skin was closed with steel clips   The patient seemed to tolerate the procedure well and was taken to the recovery room in satisfactory condition

Document 115.13

Email Message

Read all instructions below before starting this document activity.

1 Read the note that Dr. Borman left for you Wednesday, September 2 (see Figure 115.13).

2 Navigate to the Document 115.13 launch page in the Online Lab and then click the Launch Activity button to open **Doc115.13** in the activity window.

3 Compose and key an email in the open document according to the directions in the note.

4 Proofread the document and correct any errors.

5 Save the document.

6 Click the Submit button to upload the document for instructor review.

Figure 115.13 Handwritten Message for Document 115.13

FROM THE DESK OF TERRY BORMAN

DATE _9/2_   TIME _4:30 p.m._

Hi. I keep thinking of things for you to do. Before I forget, my cell phone is in for repairs. I'll pick it up tomorrow morning on my way to the office. Please send an email message to the Medical Dept Heads' distribution list (mdhlist@ppi-edu.net) and copy me. Ask them to email me a list of how their departments might use the synthesized voice feature of our new telephone system. So far, two applications are up and running—patients can call in to get account balances and a patient-reminder system for appointments. Let them know where I'll be this weekend. This info will be used in talking with exhibitors about the feasibility of incorporating these new features to improve patient care. Ask them to respond by email before they leave for the weekend, if possible. Thanks!

Terry

Figure 64.3 Memo Content for Document 64.3

TO: Ayana Potter, Attorney ¶ FROM: David Drysdale, Accounting Services ¶ DATE: October 10, 2020 ¶ SUBJECT: Chemicals Used at Bragg Corporation, Ypsilanti, Michigan ¶ Jason Vance completed his report on the most important chemical constituents used at the Bragg Corporation frozen foods manufacturing plant in Ypsilanti, Michigan. The important chemical groups are sugars, amino acids, and organic acids. ¶ The sugars include fructose ($C_6H_{12}O_6$) and lactose ($C_{12}H_{22}O_{12}$). The sugars are purchased from the Sweet Chemical Group in Shreveport, Louisiana. ¶ The chief amino acids used at Bragg are alanine ($C_3H_7NO_2$), glycine ($C_2H_5NO_2$), and leucine ($C_6H_{13}NO_2$). The amino acids are purchased from the Peptide Foundry in Murfreesboro, Tennessee. ¶ The Bragg Corporation uses many organic acids. Chief among these are acetic acid ($C_2H_4O_2$) and citric acid ($C_6H_8O_7$). The organic acids are purchased from the Formic Company in Lubbock, Texas.

3   At the bottom of the memo, include the initials eit and the file name and indicate that a copy of the memo is being sent to Jason Vance.

4   Proofread the memo and correct any errors.

5   Save the document.

6   Click the Check button to upload the document for checking.

7   If errors are reported by the Online Lab, view the results document, correct the errors in the submitted document, save the document, and then click the Check Again button.

Applying Small Caps Formatting to Text

When small caps formatting is applied to text, letters that are ordinarily lowercase are displayed as capital letters but in a slightly smaller point size than the letters that are actually capitalized. In such text, the capital letters remain full size. For example, the sentence

When Dr. Einstein published his theory of special relativity, King Edward VII was on the throne of England.

appears in small caps format as

WHEN DR. EINSTEIN PUBLISHED HIS THEORY OF SPECIAL RELATIVITY, KING EDWARD VII WAS ON THE THRONE OF ENGLAND.

Notice the difference in letter heights between the ordinarily capitalized letters and the ordinarily lowercase letters, such as the first and second E in *Einstein*. Unlike superscript and subscript formatting, small caps formatting is a stylistic option, chosen for appearance rather than function.

To set existing text in small caps, select the text and then click the *Small caps* check box in the *Effects* section of the Font dialog box, as shown in Figure 64.4. To turn on small caps formatting before you the key the text, position the insertion point where you want the text to start and then click the *Small caps* check box in the *Effects* section of the Font dialog box.

Document 115.14 **Email Message**

Read all instructions below before starting this document activity.

1 Read the handwritten transcription of the voice mail message for Dr. Borman shown in Figure 115.14.

2 Navigate to the Document 115.14 launch page in the Online Lab and then click the Launch Activity button to open **Doc115.14** in the activity window.

3 Compose and key an email to Dr. Kohorski on behalf of Dr. Borman. When composing the response, consider the document created in Document 115.4. If you made the assumption that Dr. Borman would take the later flight, he could meet with Dr. Kohorski this afternoon. If you assumed that Dr. Borman would catch an earlier flight, you would give Dr. Kohorski alternatives for a meeting on Tuesday. Copy Dr. Borman on the response.

4 Proofread the document and correct any errors.

5 Save the document.

6 Click the Submit button to upload the document for instructor review.

Figure 115.14 Phone Message for Document 115.14

```
           IMPORTANT MESSAGE

TO  Dr. Borman
DATE  9/4          TIME  7:50      (A.M.)
                                    P.M.
M  Mel Kohorski
OF  Chief of Surgery, RSMC
AC/PHONE #  mkohorski@ppi-edu.net

TELEPHONED        ☑    PLEASE CALL      ☐
CALLED TO SEE YOU ☐    WILL CALL AGAIN  ☐
WANTS TO SEE YOU  ☑    URGENT           ☐
          RETURNED CALL   ☐

Message  Wants to meet with you sometime
after 3 p.m. today. He has a possible
replacement for the head of the Pediatrics
Department and wants to discuss this with
you. Email him a response. If you are not
available, give him other meeting times.
Operator    Blanche
```

Figure 64.2 Memo Content for Document 64.2—continued

the concentrations of Pb^{2+}, Zn^{2+}, and V^{5+} increasing with proximity to the Deer Hills Mine. ¶ For anions, we analyzed fluoride, chloride, bromide, and sulfide. Our results show that F^{1-}, Cl^{1-}, and Br^{1-} occur at normal levels in all water samples. In contrast, concentrations of S^{2-} are elevated, with concentrations at higher levels for wells closest to the mine. ¶ In conclusion, the abandoned mine waste at the Deer Hills Mine is contributing to contamination of water wells in southern Smithfield County. Furthermore, regression analysis of the concentrations of ions of lead, zinc, ferric iron (Fe^{3+}), vanadium, and sulfur and the distance of wells to the Deer Hills Mine shows a clear inverse correlation.

Applying Subscript Formatting to Text

As with superscript, in some scientific and mathematical scenarios, characters must be set in subscript. Text with subscript formatting is set lower on the line than normal text. Word automatically reduces the point size of subscripted text.

In chemistry, the number of atoms in a formula unit is indicated by subscripted numbers. For example, one molecule of sucrose (common table sugar) contains 12 atoms of carbon, 22 atoms of hydrogen, and 11 atoms of oxygen. The chemical formula is written as $C_{12}H_{22}O_{11}$. Another common molecule is water, or H_2O.

In mathematics, the base of a number is written as a subscript. The base refers to the total number of digits used in a numerical system. The decimal system that we use in everyday life is base 10, so we usually do not bother to indicate the base. But we could—if we want to be precise—write the number 47 as 47_{10}.

To set text in subscript as you key, complete the following steps:

1 Click the Subscript button in the Font group on the Home tab.

2 Key the character(s) you want to appear in subscript.

3 Click the Subscript button to turn off the formatting.

To set previously keyed text in subscript, select the character(s) and then click the Subscript button. Alternatively, you can select the character(s), click the Font group dialog box launcher, and then click the *Subscript* check box in the *Effects* section of the dialog box to insert a check mark.

Memo with Subscript Text

Read all instructions below before starting this document activity.

Document
64.3

1 Navigate to the Document 64.3 launch page in the Online Lab and then click the Launch Activity button to open **Doc064.03** in the activity window.

2 Use the contents of Figure 64.3 to key the memo, applying subscript formatting as indicated in the text.

steps continue

Document
115.15
Memo Report

Read all instructions below before starting this document activity.

1 Read the transcript of a phone message from your vacation replacement, Barb Martinelli. The message was left for you Thursday, September 3, at 5:00 p.m. (see Figure 115.15).

2 Navigate to the Document 115.15 launch page in the Online Lab and then click the Launch Activity button to open **Doc115.15** in the activity window.

3 Based on the request in the voice mail message, complete an Internet search and prepare the memo report. You will need to identify when the search and report would be done: before 11 a.m. today, after 11 a.m. today, or on Tuesday.

4 Key a description of your action plan or the results of your Internet search using the memo template provided.

5 Proofread the document and correct any errors.

6 Save the document.

7 Click the Submit button to upload the document for instructor review.

Figure 115.15 Voice Mail Message for Document 115.15.

Thursday, September 3, 5:00 p.m.

Hi and welcome back. This is Barb Martinelli. I enjoyed filling in for you while you were on vacation. Even though it was extremely busy, I enjoyed the day-to-day activities. I had to return to the Medical Records Department on Wednesday, so Dr. Borman was without help on September 2.

One thing that I wasn't able to finish, let alone start, was a memo report to Dr. Borman about websites that provide background information on voice processing (primarily speech recognition systems and synthesized voice systems and applications). He wants this report by Friday, September 11. In addition to identifying the sites, he wants a brief summary of what is available at each site and how this information would be helpful in terms of the Riverside Medical Center operations.

Ending the Session

The Online Lab automatically saved the work you completed for this project. You may continue with the next session or exit the Online Lab and continue later.

Success Tip

To precisely select one or more characters in order to apply formatting, position the insertion point to the left of the first character you want to select, press and hold down the Shift key, press the Right Arrow key until all of the desired characters have been selected, and then release the Shift key.

Document 64.2 **Memo with Superscript Text**

Read all instructions below before starting this document activity.

1 Navigate to the Document 64.2 launch page in the Online Lab and then click the Launch Activity button to open **Doc064.02** in the activity window.

2 Use the contents of Figure 64.2 to key the memo. Use a hyphen for each of the minus symbols found in the body of the memo.

3 Apply superscript formatting as indicated in Figure 64.2. *Note: Be careful not to set in superscript the spaces, characters, or punctuation before or after the text that is to appear in superscript, otherwise the Online Lab will indicate an error.*

4 At the bottom of the memo, key the initials hvb and the file name and indicate that copies of the memo are being sent to Humberto B. Alvarez, Beatrice Mandelman, Violet Martin, and Louis Ribak.

5 Proofread the memo and correct any errors.

6 Save the document.

7 Click the Check button to upload the document for checking.

8 If errors are reported by the Online Lab, view the results document, correct the errors in the submitted document, save the document, and then click the Check Again button.

Figure 64.2 Memo Content for Document 64.2

TO: Jennifer Langley, Supervisor, Smithfield County ¶ FROM: Dr. Danielle McSpadden, Chief Investigator, Groundwater Testing ¶ DATE: August 26, 2020 ¶ SUBJECT: Southern Smithfield County Well Water Analysis ¶ We concluded our analysis of the well water in southern Smithfield County. This study was done in an effort to ascertain if the abandoned Deer Hills lead-zinc deposit is a contributor to contamination of groundwater in this area. The analysis included with the report is grouped into those for cations and anions. ¶ For cations, we analyzed for sodium, potassium, magnesium, calcium, lead, zinc, iron, phosphorous, and vanadium. Our results show that Na^{1+}, K^{1+}, Mg^{2+}, Ca^{2+}, Fe^{2+}, and P^{3+} occur at normal levels in all water samples. In contrast, concentrations of Pb^{2+}, Zn^{2+}, Fe^{3+}, and V^{5+} were measured at values greater than normal levels in most wells, with

continues

Productivity Measurement Part II

Figure 64.1 Memo Content for Document 64.1—continued

And as far as trees, you'll see the tallest trees in the world: the redwoods. But if you look down, in the damp ground, you'll probably see abundant ferns. ¶ When we travel north to Oregon, the Cascade Mountains consist of a string of volcanoes, some of which have been active in the last few hundred years. I was told that the most common type of rock is andesite— named for the Andes Mountains. In addition to black bears and mule deer, you will no doubt see many squirrels and Clark's jays—named after the famous explorer, William Clark. The most impressive trees in Oregon are the Douglas-fir. I am told the name is hyphenated to indicate that the tree is not a true fir tree. ¶ In the mountains of coastal Washington, in the Olympic Mountains, there are spectacular stands of old-growth forest. Some of the trees in that area are the largest examples of those species known anywhere in the world. Most impressive are the Sitka spruce and Western hemlock— some of the individual trees are nearly 20 feet in diameter. The mountains of the Olympic Range consist of brown and beige shale and sandstone and black basalt. ¶ I hope you are looking forward to the trip.

Applying Superscript Formatting to Text

In a variety of scientific, mathematical, and business applications, characters are set in superscript format, which means they are set higher on the line than normal text. Word automatically reduces the point size of superscripted text.

In mathematics, raising a number to a power is indicated with a superscripted number. For example, raising the number five to the second power (known as *squaring* the number) is written as 5^2, as in $5^2 = 5 \times 5 = 25$. Likewise, multiplying the number 4 by itself three times (known as *cubing* the number) can be written as 4^3, as in $4^3 = 4 \times 4 \times 4 = 64$.

In chemistry, the names of electrically charged atoms (called *ions*) are written with superscripted values immediately after a chemical symbol. For example, common table salt consists of sodium (symbol Na) and chlorine (symbol Cl) ions. The ionic forms are written, respectively, as Na^{1+} and Cl^{1-}.

To set text in superscript as you key, complete the following steps:

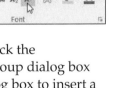

Step 1

1   Click the Superscript button in the Font group on the Home tab.
2   Key the character(s) you want to appear in superscript.
3   Click the Superscript button to turn off the formatting.

To set previously keyed text in superscript, select the character(s) and then click the Superscript button. Alternatively, you can select the character(s), click the Font group dialog box launcher, and then click the *Superscript* check box in the *Effects* section of the dialog box to insert a check mark.

Session 116

Document Productivity Check: Email, Memos, and Business Correspondence

Session Objectives

- Demonstrate the ability to format an email
- Demonstrate the ability to format a memo
- Demonstrate the ability to format a personal business letter
- Demonstrate the ability to format a block-style business letter
- Demonstrate the ability to format a two-page business letter
- Efficiently produce documents in mailable form

Getting Started

Exercise 116.1 Unless you are continuing immediately after completing Session 115, spend at least two to three minutes warming up using Exercise 116.1 before completing the document activities in this session. See Session 101 for suggested warm-up text.

Preparing Documents

This session is an assessment of the types of documents created in Unit 13, "Email and Memos Part II," and Unit 14, "Business Correspondence Part II." In the document activities in this session, you will be assessed on how accurately you can format, key, proofread, and correct emails, memos, personal business letters, business letters, and two-page letters. In the following document activities, each completed document is to be "mailable," which means that it contains no errors. A document that requires corrections is not considered *mailable*.

Your goal is to key each document in mailable form. If you are missing errors that should have been corrected or your instructor believes you can work more efficiently, he or she may ask you to repeat document activities. Be sure to check each document to make sure all parts of the document are included, such as dates, file names, and copy notations.

To help you succeed, carefully review the instructions and content of the documents before keying. Make sure you know the formatting elements and guidelines for each document to be keyed. If necessary, review the content of Units 13 and 14 if you are unsure how to complete a specific task.

By default, when you open a new Word document, clicking the Font Color button will apply the Red color from the *Standard Colors* section. Once you apply a different color using the Font Color button arrow, the color displayed on the Font Color button will change to that color.

To apply color formatting as you key, click the Font Color button arrow, click a color in the palette, key the text to be set in color, click the Font Color button arrow, and then click the *Automatic* color option or select another color.

Document
64.1

Memo with Black, Green, and Blue Text

Read all instructions below before starting this document activity.

1 Navigate to the Document 64.1 launch page in the Online Lab and then click the Launch Activity button to open **Doc064.01** in the activity window.

2 Use the contents of Figure 64.1 to key the memo. Do not apply the color formatting as you type; you will apply it in a later step. *Hint: Apply the correct formatting for a memo as shown in Session 63, Figure 63.1 (page 26).*

3 Key the initials ptm and the file name at the end of the memo.

4 Apply color as indicated in Figure 64.1, using the Green and Blue colors from the *Standard Colors* section of the palette. *Note: Be careful not to set in color the spaces, characters, or punctuation before or after the text that is to appear in color, otherwise the Online Lab will indicate an error. When two or more colored words appear next to each other, format the space or punctuation between the words in color.*

5 Proofread the memo and correct any errors. *Hint: Display nonprinting characters in the document by clicking the Show/Hide ¶ button in the Paragraph group. This will help you check that the spaces following text set in color are not set in color.*

6 Save the document.

7 Click the Check button to upload the document for checking.

8 If errors are reported by the Online Lab, view the results document, correct the errors in the submitted document, save the document, and then click the Check Again button.

Figure 64.1 Memo Content for Document 64.1

TO: Patrick Denver, PacNW August Tour Group Representative ¶ FROM: Helen York, Coordinator, Wonderful Tours ¶ DATE: July 15, 2020 ¶ SUBJECT: August Tour: Animals, Plants, and Rocks ¶ On your August tour to northern California, Oregon, and Washington, you will see a wide variety of animals, trees and other plants, and rock types. Let me give you a brief preview of what you can expect to see in each state you'll visit. ¶ In eastern California, you can expect to see bristle cone pines, giant sequoias, black bears, and white-tailed deer. The Sierra Nevada Mountains consist mostly of white-to-gray-colored granite. In the northwest part of California near the Pacific Ocean, the hills are built of brown sandstone and green serpentinite—the state rock of California. You might see herds of elk right on the beach. If you look down, you might see the bright yellow banana slugs.

continues

Document 116.1

Email Message with Proofreading Marks and Bold, Italic, and Indented Text

Read all instructions below before starting this document activity.

1 Navigate to the Document 116.1 launch page in the Online Lab and then click the Launch Activity button to open **Doc116.01** in the activity window.

2 Key jhodowanic@ppi-edu.net in the *To* line, bhedin@ppi-edu.net in the *CC* line, and Southeastern Business Education Conference in the *Subject* line.

3 Key the content of the email message using the information in Figure 116.1, implementing the proofreading marks as you key. Format the words in bold and italic as shown in Figure 116.1. Do not allow Word to format the *th* and *st* in *37th* and *21st* in superscript or to format the email address at the end of the message as a hyperlink.

4 Proofread the document and correct any errors.

5 Save the document.

6 Click the Check button to upload the document for checking.

7 If errors are reported by the Online Lab, view the results document, correct the errors in the submitted document, save the document, and then click the Check Again button.

Figure 116.1 Email Message Content for Document 116.1

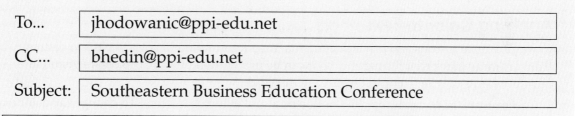

To... | jhodowanic@ppi-edu.net

CC... | bhedin@ppi-edu.net

Subject: | Southeastern Business Education Conference

Jim, ¶ Many thanks for agreeing to serve as our ^keynote speaker for our 37th Conference. The Conference will be held February 20-22, 2020, at the Georgia Center. The conference center is located on the campus of the University of Georgia in Athens. ¶ Your keynote address is scheduled for **Saturday, February 22, 8:30 a.m. to 9:45 a.m.** The title is *The Impact of Telecommunications Technology on Society in the 21st Century.* A laptop and a connected projector will be available for your ^presentation. Please bring handouts for **200 participants**. ¶ Your conference registration and Saturday luncheon are complimentary. Please email me by **January 15** what nights you will need a room at the Georgia Center. ¶ I understand that you will be flying into atlanta and then will rent a car. The fastest way to get to Athens from the Atlanta airport is to take *Interstate 20* east to Madison and then go north on *Highway 29* to Athens. It takes a little less than ~~four~~ two hours. ¶ Thanks, ¶ Lee, lgohdes@ppi-edu.net

Document 116.2

Memo with Proofreading Marks, Superscript Text, and Justified Alignment

Read all instructions below before starting this document activity.

1 Navigate to the Document 116.2 launch page in the Online Lab and then click the Launch Activity button to open **Doc116.02** in the activity window.

steps continue

Ergonomic Tip

If you wear bifocals, your screen should be set slightly below your visual resting point as you work. Make sure the screen is not angled downward. This way, you can read it as you would a book.

Applying Alternative Font Formats

In certain cases, you may want or need to apply font formatting other than roman, bold, italics, or underlining. This session will demonstrate how to apply specialized formatting such as color, superscript, subscript, and small caps to text. The document activities will use text in the body of memos to demonstrate the formats, but these formats can be used in any type of document.

Success Tip

Prepare all memos in this session according to the format presented in Session 63.

Applying Color to Text

Colors enhance memos and other documents. A font formatted in color is easy to distinguish from ordinary black font formatting, so it can be used for emphasis or to create visual interest. Furthermore, applying color to text is easy in Word.

Color formatting can be applied before or after keying characters. To change the color of previously keyed text, complete the following steps:

1   Select the text you want to format.

2   Click the Font Color button arrow in the Font group on the Home tab.

3   Click the desired color at the color palette.

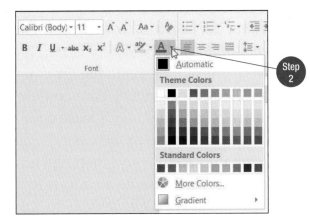

Colors on the color palette are grouped into two sections: *Theme Colors* and *Standard Colors*. Each color option has a name that displays when the arrow pointer is resting on the option on the palette. In the following document activity, you will apply colors from the *Standard Colors* section of the palette to text in a memo.

2 Key a memo using the content in Figure 116.2, implementing the proofreading marks as you key.

3 Apply superscript formatting as indicated in Figure 116.2. *Note: Be careful to apply formatting only to the numbers that are to be superscript, otherwise the Online Lab will indicate an error.*

4 Apply the colors as indicated in Figure 116.2. Use the Blue and Green colors from the *Standard Colors* section of the Font Color button drop-down gallery. *Note: The space between the blue and green text should be blue.*

5 Change the paragraph alignment of the four paragraphs within the body of the memo to justified alignment. *Note: The text in Figure 116.2 is not correctly justified.*

6 At the bottom of the memo, key the initials jsb and the file name. *Hint: Make sure the paragraph alignment for this line is set to left alignment, not justified alignment.*

7 Proofread the memo and correct any errors.

8 Save the document.

9 Click the Check button to upload the document for checking.

10 If errors are reported by the Online Lab, view the results document, correct the errors in the submitted document, save the document, and then click the Check Again button.

Figure 116.2 Memo Content for Document 116.2

TO: All Staff ¶ FROM: Rona Rodrigues, Health and Safety Officer ¶ DATE: August 31, 2020 ¶ SUBJECT: Smoking on Campus ¶ The Health and Safety Department continues to receive complaints of cigarette smoking near the building entrances and exits. Students and staff are subjected to walking though clouds of smoke, and the smell often wafts into the building. Polonium-210 (^{210}Po) is one of the many harmful substances in tobacco and cigarettes. The potential health effects of ^{210}Po in tobacco are drawing attention and awareness. ¶ The area of significant concern is just outside the Commons at the rear of the administration office. Cigarette odors are being drawn into the air intake system, which is negatively affecting the learning and work environment. In an effort to resolve this concern immediately, smoking will no longer be permitted on the patio/sidewalk area outside the Commons. A designated smoking area has been established just slightly west of the patio. This area is accessible from the door nearest Room 1913 and is located at the end of the sidewalk near the service drive. ¶ The solution proposed is intended to meet the needs of all students and staff. Effective resolution required voluntary compliance. If the resolution is deemed later ineffective, administration may consider the merits of a tobacco-free campus. ¶ If anyone has questions regarding this communication, please contact me or another member of the President's Council.

Session
64

Enhancing Memos

Session Objectives

- Use color to enhance memos
- Apply superscript and subscript formatting in a document
- Format headings in small caps
- Write clear directions in a memo
- Efficiently produce documents in mailable form

Getting Started

Exercise 64.1 If you are continuing immediately from Session 63, you may skip the Exercise 64.1 warm-up drill. However, if you exited the Online Lab at the end of Session 63, warm up by completing Exercise 64.1.

Exercise 64.2 Begin your session work by completing Exercise 64.2, a timed short drill, in the Online Lab.

Assessing Your Speed and Accuracy

Complete Timings 64.1 and 64.2 in the Online Lab. At the end of each timing, the Online Lab will display your WPM rate and any errors. Results will be saved in your Timings Performance report. If you have been surpassing the speed and accuracy goals identified in the Online Lab, set slightly more challenging personal goals and strive to exceed them.

Complete two 1-minute timings on the timing text below. If you meet or exceed both speed and accuracy goals for Timing 64.1, push for greater speed on Timing 64.2.

1-Minute Timings

Timings 64.1–64.2 To use your spare time effectively, you must have a plan. Every successful person knows how to utilize spare hours. Plans with goals are a must for enjoying leisure time. Many folks waste precious hours trying to decide what to do for recreation. By the time they decide, the leisure time has vanished. You must plan ahead for activities or relaxing times. Forget your own problems while you focus on enjoying those games, books, and vacations.

Document 116.3 Personal Business Letter with Custom Margins, Underlined Text, and Vertical Centering

Read all instructions below before starting this document activity.

1 Navigate to the Document 116.3 launch page in the Online Lab and then click the Launch Activity button to open **Doc116.03** in the activity window.

2 Key a personal business letter using the text shown in Figure 116.3.

   a Key March 2, 2020 as the date of the letter. *Note: Do not press Enter to move the date down the page. You will vertically center the text in a later step.*

   b Apply underline formatting as indicated in Figure 116.3.

   c Indent the second paragraph of the letter body (begins *One thing we did*) 0.5 inch from the left and right margins.

   d Add a notation for six enclosures.

3 Vertically center the text on the page.

4 Change the left and right margins to 1.7 inches.

5 Proofread the document and correct any errors.

6 Save the document.

7 Click the Check button to upload the document for checking.

8 If errors are reported by the Online Lab, view the results document, correct the errors in the submitted document, save the document, and then click the Check Again button.

Figure 116.3 Personal Business Letter Content for Document 116.3

Mr. Dennis Deleary, CPA ¶ Deleary, Ross, and McHardy ¶ 54 Parkway Lane ¶ Janesville, WI 53548 ¶ Dear Mr. Deleary: ¶ Enclosed are the documents supporting the completion of our tax planning packet for our <u>2019 income tax</u>. Even though we hear that Wisconsin is having unseasonably warm weather, we are not planning to be back in Wisconsin prior to April 15. Hopefully, we can complete the tax process with the documents enclosed. ¶ One thing we did differently in 2019 was pay Wisconsin property taxes for <u>both 2018 and 2019</u>. While I don't have the 2018 receipt here, I did find verification of payment online and have enclosed that printout. I hope that will be sufficient documentation. Please contact us at (758) 555-1023 if you have any questions. ¶ We hope everything is going well for you during this busy season! ¶ Sincerely, ¶ Rosa and Richard King ¶ 5253 Centennial Court ¶ Mesa, AZ 85216 ¶ Enclosures 6

Reinforcing Writing Skills

Redundancy refers to using multiple words that mean essentially the same thing. Redundancy is one form of wordiness, which means "using more language than necessary to express a thought." Wordiness makes sentences harder to read, and can sometimes even confuse their meaning.

One form of redundancy that is especially troublesome is called *tautology*, which is the needless repetition of an idea using different words. For example, in the phrase *very unique*, the word *very* is unnecessary and incorrect. The word *unique* means "one of a kind," and thus stands on its own. Something cannot be "very" or "a little" one of a kind—it either is or is not. Another common tautology occurs in the expression *Give me the reason why*. The word *why* is not needed, because *reason* already implies *why*. Other examples of commonly used tautologies are as follows, with the unnecessary words set in italics:

absolutely necessary	repeat *again*
basic fundamentals	*exact* same
past history	*true* facts
each *and every*	

When you eliminate unnecessary words, your writing will appear cleaner and your meaning will be clearer. This will help make your written communication easier for your audience to read, comprehend, and remember.

In the following activity, you will prepare a memo in which you identify at least five tautologies other than those used as examples in this session. For each example, provide the tautology on one line, a sentence or two explaining it on the second line, and then a sentence using the corrected expression on a third line. Use the following example as a model:

true facts
The word *true* is unnecessary because *facts* already implies truth.
Correct use: Please explain the facts of this case.

Document 63.6 **Composing a Memo that Discusses the Pitfalls of Tautologies**

Read all instructions below before starting this document activity.

1 Navigate to the Document 63.6 launch page in the Online Lab and then click the Launch Activity button to open **Doc063.06** in the activity window.

2 Prepare a memo to be sent to an English teacher discussing five tautologies (as described previously). Send a copy of the memo to your keyboarding instructor and key your first and last names as the sender. Use correct memo formatting, as shown in Figure 63.1.

3 Key an introductory paragraph so that the English teacher knows why you have prepared this memo.

4 Within each of the five tautology groupings, press Shift + Enter after keying the first two pieces of information so that three parts stay together in the same paragraph. Indent the left and right margins 0.5 inch. Use italics where appropriate.

5 Proofread and correct any errors in the memo.

6 Save the document.

7 Click the Submit button to upload the document for instructor review.

Ending the Session

The Online Lab automatically saved the work you completed for this session. You may continue with the next session or exit the Online Lab and continue later.

Document 116.4 **Block-Style Business Letter with Bulleted Text**

Read all instructions below before starting this document activity.

1. Navigate to the Document 116.4 launch page in the Online Lab and then click the Launch Activity button to open **Doc116.04** in the activity window.

2. Key a block-style business letter using the text shown in Figure 116.4. The letterhead is contained within the document header, so you will not need to press Enter before typing the date. Follow these guidelines as you prepare the letter:

   a. Key July 21, 2020 as the date of the letter.

   b. Format the bulleted list with the check-mark bullet in the Bullets button drop-down gallery. Add an extra blank line between the bulleted items. Decrease the indent so that the bullets begin at the left margin.

   c. At the bottom of the letter, key the initials sba and the file name. Indicate that an enclosure is included and that copies of the letter are being sent to Valerie Monet and Jarrod Rutherford.

3. Proofread the business letter and correct any errors.

4. Save the document.

5. Click the Check button to upload the document for checking.

6. If errors are reported by the Online Lab, view the results document, correct the errors in the submitted document, save the document, and then click the Check Again button.

Figure 116.4 Block-Style Business Letter Content for Document 116.4

Mr. Juan Garcia
355 Arlington Drive, Apt. 23
New York, NY 10023

Dear Mr. Garcia:

The enclosed questionnaire is from PriorityCare Research Company. We are asking for your cooperation and prompt response in completing the questionnaire. This information will assist PriorityCare in determining if an accidental injury occurred for which you or your eligible dependent filed a medical claim. PriorityCare is specifically interested in claims that were (or will be) paid by a third party, such as automobile insurance and homeowners policies, or from awards, judgments, or settlements in connection with automobile or other accidents.

PriorityCare is an independent national company specializing in third-party recovery. PriorityCare has been retained to perform recovery services on behalf of Unified Health Insurance.

continues

Document
63.5

Memo with Text Indented from the Left and Right Margins

Read all instructions below before starting this document activity.

1 Navigate to the Document 63.5 launch page in the Online Lab and then click the Launch Activity button to open **Doc063.05** in the activity window.

2 Use the content in Figure 63.8 to key the memo. Be sure to apply correct formatting, as shown in Figure 63.1. Watch for words set in bold or italics. *Hint: When two adjacent words are formatted in bold or italics, format the space between the words as well. Do not format the punctuation or the space following the last formatted word.*

3 Select the second paragraph in the body of the memo (begins *We have a contractual agreement*) and then indent it 0.5 inch from both the right and left margins by dragging the indent markers on the horizontal ruler. *Hint: Make sure that you are dragging the Left and Right Indent markers, and not the First Line or Hanging Indent markers (see Figure 63.7).*

4 Proofread the memo and correct any errors.

5 Save the document.

6 Click the Check button to upload the document for checking.

7 If errors are reported by the Online Lab, view the results document, correct the errors in the submitted document, save the document, and then click the Check Again button.

Figure 63.8 Memo Content for Document 63.5

TO: District Managers and Store Managers ¶ FROM: Carolyn Riley, Regional Manager ¶ DATE: April 24, 2020 ¶ SUBJECT: Extreme Event Power Bar Displays at Check Stands ¶ As a result of our recent conversion to 9680 terminals and turntable check stands, many of the Extreme Event Power Bar displays have been *lost in the shuffle.* ¶ We have a contractual agreement with the Extreme Event distributor that these displays will be located at every check stand. If you do not currently have these displays located at every check stand, please set them up. If you need additional displays, contact me at the Regional Office. ¶ We have until **June 1, 2020, to comply with the contract**. ¶ Thank you for your attention and follow-through on this matter. ¶ anq ¶ Doc063.05

Based on your responses to the questionnaire, PriorityCare will:

- Determine if another party is responsible for payment of your medical expenses if you (or your eligible dependent) were injured as a result of an accident where another party was at fault.

- Pursue reimbursement of these expenses from the other party.

PriorityCare is working on our behalf, and we have given them permission to contact you. Please cooperate in this effort and respond promptly. If you have any questions, please contact PriorityCare at 1-800-555-5689.

Sincerely,

Marsala Levine
Customer Service

Document 116.5

Multiple-Page Business Letter with Numbered Text

Read all instructions below before starting this document activity.

1 Navigate to the Document 116.5 launch page in the Online Lab and then click the Launch Activity button to open **Doc116.05** in the activity window.

2 Key a multiple-page business letter using the text shown in Figure 116.5. The letterhead is contained within the document header, so you will not need to press Enter before typing the date. Follow these guidelines as you prepare the letter:

   a Key February 24, 2020 as the date of the letter.

   b Format the bulleted list using the default solid, black, round bullets. Do not add an extra line space between the items in the bulleted list, and make sure Word does not automatically capitalize the first word after each bullet.

   c Allow Word to automatically format the numbered list as you key. Do not add an extra line space between the items in the numbered list.

   d Remove the hyperlink for the website address.

3 Key the closing Sincerely, and indicate that the letter is being sent by Sharon L. Buswell, Marketing Director.

4 Key the reference initials bjs and the file name.

5 Create a vertical header for the second page of the letter using the *Blank* header option.

6 Proofread the letter and correct any errors.

7 Save the document.

8 Click the Check button to upload the document for checking.

9 If errors are reported by the Online Lab, view the results document, correct the errors in the submitted document, save the document, and then click the Check Again button.

Using the Horizontal Ruler

When you open a blank Word document, the horizontal ruler may appear just below the ribbon and just above the document, as shown in Figure 63.7. The horizontal ruler can be hidden or displayed by clicking the *Ruler* check box in the Show group on the View tab.

The numbers on the horizontal ruler represent the inches from the left margin. The inches are divided into halves (larger tick marks) and eighths (smaller tick marks).

The widths of the left and right margins of a document are indicated by the portions of the horizontal ruler shown in gray. There are several ways to change these margins, but a simple way is to click the Left Indent marker or the Right Indent marker and drag it along the horizontal ruler to the desired location. You will use this approach when you prepare Document 63.5.

Indenting Text Using the Horizontal Ruler

Text in a paragraph may be indented from the right or left margin (or both), either as you key or after text has been keyed. To indent the left margin of text as you key, drag the Left Indent marker to the right to the desired location on the horizontal ruler and then key text. If, at a position later in the document, you want to return the margin to the original position, drag the Left Indent marker to the original position and then continue keying. To indent the right margin of the text as you key, drag the Right Indent marker to the left to the desired location on the horizontal ruler and then key the text.

To change the left or right indent of previously keyed text, select the text and then drag the Left Indent marker or the Right Indent marker to the desired location on the horizontal ruler. Click anywhere in the document to deselect the text.

Figure 63.7 Horizontal Ruler and Indent Markers

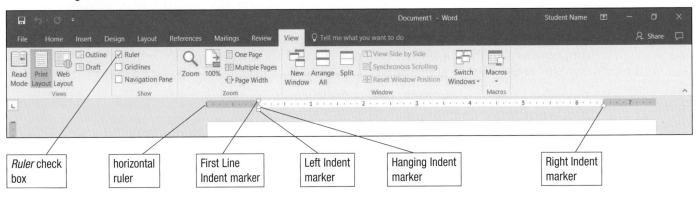

Figure 116.5 Multiple-Page Business Letter Content for Document 116.5

Ms. Vikki W. Sutcliffe
Computer Instruction Specialist
The Learning Center
PO Box 7199
Redondo, WA 98044-3252

Dear Ms. Sutcliffe:

As a computer training provider, you are faced with a situation where technology is continually reinventing itself—moving from one revolution to the next. Are you prepared to keep up? Will you master new technology to stay on top? Is your company ready to lead in this decade, or will it become a follower? With so much at stake, how will you ensure that your trainees gain the skills and knowledge to compete? We can help!

Computer Consultants of Colorado (CCC) specializes in providing state-of-the-art distance-learning and individualized computer-learning technologies, customizable training products, consulting services, and instructor-led courseware training packages.

Our online programs include a powerful assessment system to help you manage every aspect of skills assessment, allowing you to create and deliver a highly customized, just-in-time training program. The system includes tools to

- author test questions,
- map learning objectives to job requirements,
- deploy self-analyzing adaptive tests,
- identify skill gaps, and
- create and manage custom curricula.

The CCC Online team offers comprehensive services and support for all aspects of your online training and assessment solutions. Here is an overview of the support program:

1. Change Management (1 day). Presented by industry experts, this seminar will help you develop a custom action plan to implement your new systems successfully.

continues

Memo with Center Alignment

Read all instructions below before starting this document activity.

1 Navigate to the Document 63.4 launch page in the Online Lab and then click the Launch Activity button to open **Doc063.04** in the activity window.

2 Use the content in Figure 63.6 to key the memo. Be sure to apply correct formatting, as shown in Figure 63.1.

3 Change the paragraph alignment to center alignment for the paragraphs beginning *The Southern Section* and *Presentations will be*.

4 Proofread the memo and correct any errors.

5 Save the document.

6 Click the Check button to upload the document for checking.

7 If errors are reported by the Online Lab, view the results document, correct the errors in the submitted document, save the document, and then click the Check Again button.

Figure 63.6 Memo Content for Document 63.4

TO: Dr. Donna Gatling, Chair, Occupational Management Department ¶ FROM: Amaal Kulane, OMNA ¶ DATE: February 24, 2020 ¶ SUBJECT: Abstracts for Southern Section OMNA Conference ¶ The following announcement was published in an OMNA flyer: ¶ The Southern Section of the Occupational Management National Association (OMNA) is calling for abstracts of research studies that were completed on occupational management topics during the past calendar year. ¶ Presentations will be made at the annual meeting of the Southern Section of OMNA, to be held at the University of Mississippi, Oxford, July 13 and 14. ¶ Abstracts should be submitted to the attention of Dr. Gloria DeRoche, Executive Director of OMNA. All abstracts must reach OMNA headquarters in Oxford, Mississippi, by April 20, 2020. The specific topic area should be noted on the attached abstract form. ¶ ptr ¶ Doc063.04 ¶ Attachment

2. Start-Up Service (3 days). This program includes system installation and hands-on training for key staff.

3. Content Migration (2 days). This hands-on workshop includes management and other issues for conversion projects.

4. Train-the-Online-Trainer (4 days). Move your adjunct instructors into the online classroom. Program includes using online tools, such as chat sessions and conferencing, to amplify content, provide remedial direction, and schedule expert sessions.

5. Assessment and Testing Fundamentals (2 days). This session includes test construction, validation, item analysis and creation, and adaptive technology.

All programs are tailored to the needs of your organization. Prices start at $1,200. For more information, visit our website at http://ComputerConsultants.ppi-edu.net or call us toll free at (888) 555-1243.

Ending the Session

The Online Lab automatically saved the work you completed for this session. You may continue with the next session or exit the Online Lab and continue later.

Document 63.3 **Memo with Text Aligned at the Left and Right Margins**

Read all instructions below before starting this document activity.

1 Navigate to the Document 63.3 launch page in the Online Lab and then click the Launch Activity button to open **Doc063.03** in the activity window.

2 Use the content in Figure 63.5 to key the memo. Be sure to apply correct formatting, as shown in Figure 63.1 (on page 26). *Hint: Remember to press Tab the correct number of times after the guide words. Also remember that when two adjacent words are formatted in bold or italics, you should format the space between the words, but you should not format the punctuation or the space following the last formatted word.*

3 Change the paragraph alignment of the three paragraphs in the body of the memo to justified alignment. *Note: The body of the memo in Figure 63.1 does not have this formatting applied to it.*

4 Key the reference initials ksa (remember to undo any automatic capitalization) and the file name, Doc063.03, at the end of the memo. Make sure that the reference initials and file name are formatted to align at the left margin (not justified). There are no attachments or copies being sent.

5 Proofread the memo and correct any errors.

6 Save the document.

7 Click the Check button to upload the document for checking.

8 If errors are reported by the Online Lab, view the results document, correct the errors in the submitted document, save the document, and then click the Check Again button.

Figure 63.5 Memo Content for Document 63.3

TO: Store Employees ¶ FROM: Carolyn Riley ¶ DATE: March 4, 2020 ¶ SUBJECT: "Above and Beyond" Makes the Difference ¶ Thank you all for your *extra effort* last week in the many challenges we faced due to the windstorm. From the help desk, distribution center, division staff, multitude of vendors, to all the employees in the stores—the collective efforts of everyone were outstanding and genuinely appreciated. I know that many of you worked long hours and came in on your day off, going *above and beyond* in an effort to provide service to our valued customers. ¶ These types of efforts are what build credibility and a reputation for exceeding our customers' expectations. I know that we responded much faster than our competitors and made every effort to keep our stores open. We could not have done any of these things without your help. ¶ As a reward for outstanding effort, all employees will be granted a day off (with pay), redeemable any time before Thanksgiving. However, check with your supervisor before scheduling your day off.

Document Productivity Check: Tables

Session Objectives

- Demonstrate proficiency with tables
- Efficiently produce documents in mailable form

Getting Started

Exercise 117.1 Unless you are continuing immediately after completing Session 116, spend at least two to three minutes warming up using Exercise 117.1 before completing the document activities in this session. See Session 101 for suggested warm-up text.

Preparing Documents

This session is an assessment of the types of documents created in Unit 15, Tables Part II. Now that you have completed the instructional activities for creating tables, you will be assessed on how accurately you can format, key, proofread, and correct these documents. In the following document activities, each completed document is to be "mailable," which means that it contains no errors. A document that requires corrections is not considered *mailable*.

Your goal is to key each document in mailable form. If you are missing errors that should have been corrected or your instructor believes you can work more efficiently, he or she may ask you to repeat document activities. Be sure to check each document to make sure all parts of the document are included.

To help you succeed, carefully review the instructions and content of each document before keying. Make sure you know the formatting elements and guidelines for each document to be keyed. If necessary, review the content of Unit 15 if you are unsure how to complete a specific task.

Document 117.1 Adjusting Column Widths and Shading Rows in a Table

Read all instructions below before starting this document activity.

1 Navigate to the Document 117.1 launch page in the Online Lab and then click the Launch Activity button to open **Doc117.01** in the activity window.

2 Change the paragraph alignment to center alignment, turn on bold formatting, key INTERNATIONAL ASSOCIATION OF ADMINISTRATIVE PROFESSIONALS and then press Enter. Key Local Chapter Treasurer's Report and then press Enter. Key As of October 31, 2020, turn off bold formatting, and then press Enter. Change the paragraph alignment back to left alignment.

3 Insert a table with 4 columns and 23 rows and then key the text shown in Figure 117.1.

4 Format the table as follows:

a Change the width of the first column to 3 inches. Change the widths of the three remaining columns to 1.2 inches.

steps continue

Several additional methods for selecting text that you may find useful are as follows:

- Position the mouse pointer on the first character of the text to be selected, click and hold down the left mouse button, drag the mouse to the last character of the text to be selected, and then release the mouse button.
- To select more than one word, position the mouse pointer on the first word, click and hold down the left mouse button, drag over the additional words to be included in the selection, and then release the mouse button.
- Press and hold down the Shift key; use the Up, Down, Left, or Right arrow keys on the keyboard to select text; and then release the Shift key.

To deselect text with the mouse, click anywhere in the document outside the selected text.

Changing Paragraph Alignment

In Word, the default setting for text in paragraphs is aligned at the left margin and ragged at the right margin (referred to as *left aligned* or *left justified*). Text alignment can also be set to have a ragged left margin and an aligned right margin (*right aligned* or *right justified*), to have both left and right margins aligned (*justified* or *fully justified*), or to have both left and right margins ragged (*centered*). Note that when text is fully justified, Word adds extra spaces to lengthen the shorter lines. The location of the paragraph alignment buttons in the Paragraph group on the Home tab is shown in Figure 63.4. The function of each of these buttons is summarized in Table 63.2. Text can be aligned as you key, or alignment can be adjusted after the text has been keyed. If you want to return paragraph alignment to the default setting (left aligned), click the Align Left button.

To change the alignment of existing text in a paragraph, position the insertion point anywhere within the paragraph and then click the button for the desired alignment in the Paragraph group on the Home tab. If you want to align multiple paragraphs, select all of the paragraphs to be aligned and then click the alignment button.

Figure 63.4 Paragraph Group on the Home Tab with the Align Left Button Active

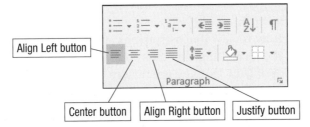

Align Left button

Center button | Align Right button | Justify button

Table 63.2 Paragraph Alignment Buttons and Functions

Paragraph Alignment	Button Name	Button	Keyboard Shortcut
at the left margin	Align Left		Ctrl + L
between margins	Center		Ctrl + E
at the right margin	Align Right		Ctrl + R
at the left and right margins	Justify		Ctrl + J

    b Select the contents of the cells containing *Receipts* and *Disbursements* and apply bold formatting. *Note: The nonprinting character following the words in the cells should also be set in bold.*

    c Format the second, third, and fourth columns to align the text to the top right corners of the cells.

    d Apply Yellow shading from the *Standard Colors* section of the Shading button drop-down gallery to the first row of the table. Apply Light Green shading from the *Standard Colors* section to the last row of the table.

5 Position the insertion point in the line immediately below the table, press Enter, and then key Submitted by Tricia Jacobs, Chapter Treasurer.

6 Proofread the document and correct any errors.

7 Save the document.

8 Click the Check button to upload the document for checking.

9 If errors are reported by the Online Lab, view the results document, correct the errors in the submitted document, save the document, and then click the Check Again button.

Figure 117.1 Table Content for Document 117.1

Balance on Hand: October 1, 2020			$3,544.03
Receipts			
Monthly Meeting Fees	$155.00		
Fundraising 50/50 Raffle	25.00		
Gift Wrap Donations	35.00		
Magazine Orders	202.20		
Chapter Dues	58.90		
Bank Interest	3.89		
Total Receipts		$479.99	
Disbursements			
Magazine Orders	$189.99		
Guest Speakers	150.00		
Meeting Food and Beverage	88.50		
Mailing Costs	12.00		
Supplies	14.68		
Fundraiser Purchases	12.56		
Miscellaneous	3.58		
Bank Fees	5.50		
Total Disbursements		$476.81	
Balance on Hand: October 31, 2020			$3,547.21

Figure 63.3 Memo Content for Document 63.2

> TO: Bryan Heller, Coordinator, Hotline Support ¶ FROM: Anita Josephson, Senior Editor ¶ DATE: December 8, 2020 ¶ SUBJECT: Citing DVDs and Online Database References ¶ Attached is a document listing some examples for citing DVDs and online database references in a bibliography. Tom Slater got these examples from Irene Rodriguez, our Business Communications Editor. ¶ This information can be used by the hotline troubleshooters responding to users of our products who have questions relating to these types of bibliographic references. If I can help you with other questions, please let me know. ¶ By the way, thanks for the summary of the most frequently asked questions from our users and how you and your staff respond to them. I'll share this information with the authors and the account managers. I know they will appreciate being aware of what users are asking about our products. ¶ mcb ¶ Doc063.02 ¶ Attachment ¶ cc: Irene Rodriguez

3 Proofread the document and correct any errors.

4 Save the document.

5 Click the Check button to upload the document for checking.

6 If errors are reported by the Online Lab, view the results document, correct the errors in the submitted document, save the document, and then click the Check Again button.

Selecting Text

Word provides a variety of methods for selecting text with either the mouse or the keyboard. Methods for selecting a word, a sentence, a paragraph, or one or more lines or paragraphs are listed in Table 63.1. Note that the selection bar is the space at the left side of the document between the edge of the page and the text. When the mouse pointer is positioned in the selection bar, the pointer turns into an arrow pointing up and to the right. The text you select will appear with a gray background.

Table 63.1 Selecting Words, Lines, Sentences, and Paragraphs

To select...	Complete these steps with the mouse or touchpad
a word	Double-click the word.
a line of text	Click in the selection bar to the left of the line.
multiple lines of text	Click and drag in the selection bar to the left of the lines.
a sentence	Press and hold down the Ctrl key, click anywhere in the sentence, and then release the Ctrl key.
a paragraph	Double-click in the selection bar next to the paragraph or triple-click anywhere in the paragraph.
multiple paragraphs	Click and drag in the selection bar to the left of the paragraphs.

Document 117.2 Editing a Table by Splitting and Distributing Columns, Sorting, and Using a Table Style

Read all instructions below before starting this document activity.

1 Navigate to the Document 117.2 launch page in the Online Lab and then click the Launch Activity button to open **Doc117.02** in the activity window.

2 Create the table shown in Figure 117.2.

3 Make the following changes to the table:

    a Split column C (*Telephone*) into two columns. (Remove the check mark from the *Merge cells before split* check box in the Split Cells dialog box.) In the new column, key the column heading Mail Code, and then key the following in the cells: D2: 5588; D3: 6344; D4: 6524; D5: 5943; D6: 5153; D7: 5436; D8: 6887; D9: 6149.

    b Insert a new column between the *Last Name* and *Telephone* columns. In the new column, key the column heading Fax and then key the following in the cells: C2: (619) 555-9898; C3: (619) 555-8701; C4: (619) 555-6322; C5: (619) 555-5214; C6: (619) 555-1593; C7: (619) 555-4268; C8: (619) 555-8252; C9: (619) 555-4404.

    c Distribute the widths of all columns in the table evenly.

    d Select the first row of the table and then apply bold formatting.

    e Sort the table in ascending order by last name.

    f Insert one new row above the first row of the table and then merge the cells in the new first row. Key RYERSON INTERIOR DESIGN, EMPLOYEE LIST in cell A1, align the text to the top center of the cell, and then change the height of the row to 0.4 inches.

    g Delete the row containing the information for Ron Geis.

    h Apply the Grid Table 4 - Accent 1 table style (second column, fourth row in the *Grid Tables* section). In the Table Style Options group on the Table Tools Design tab, ensure that check marks only display in the *Header Row* and *Banded Rows* check boxes in the Table Style Options group.

4 Proofread the document and correct any errors.

5 Save the document.

6 Click the Check button to upload the document for checking.

7 If errors are reported by the Online Lab, view the results document, correct the errors in the submitted document, save the document, and then click the Check Again button.

Figure 117.2 Table Content for Document 117.2

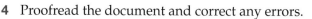

First Name	Last Name	Telephone
Beverly	Beem	(619) 555-1335
Sung-min	Bing	(619) 555-3456
William	Erzen	(619) 555-4576
Joanne	Fitzgerald	(619) 555-0003
Diego	Herrera	(619) 555-2111
Jack	Kerwin	(619) 555-8923
Ron	Geis	(619) 555-1533
Jeannie	Elliman	(619) 555-3467

3 Key the body of the memo as shown in Figure 63.2, pressing Enter after each paragraph (including the last paragraph).

4 Indicate that the person keying the memo has the initials *dgz* and that copies of the memo will be distributed to Heather Learlock, Ginger Nakamura, and Tony Palaccio by completing the following steps:

   a Key dgz and then press Shift + Enter to move to the next line. *Note: Do not allow the AutoCorrect feature to capitalize the first initial. (Press Ctrl + Z or click the Undo button on the Quick Access Toolbar to reverse this change.) Do not key your actual initials or the Online Lab will show this as an error.*

   b Key Doc063.01 and then press Shift + Enter. *Note: Do not include the extension of the file name (e.g., .docx).*

   c Key Attachment and then press Shift + Enter.

   d Key cc:, press Tab, key Heather Learlock, and then press Shift + Enter.

   e Press Tab, key Ginger Nakamura, and then press Shift + Enter.

   f Press Tab and then key Tony Palaccio. *Note: Do not press Enter or Shift + Enter at the end of the memo.*

5 Proofread the memo and correct any errors.

6 Save the document by clicking the Save button on the Quick Access Toolbar or use the keyboard shortcut Ctrl + S.

7 Click the Check button to upload the document for checking.

8 If errors are reported by the Online Lab, view the results document, correct the errors in the submitted document, save the document, and then click the Check Again button.

Figure 63.2 Memo Content for Document 63.1

Attached is the revised itinerary for the camping trip to Shenandoah National Park. ¶

Heather Learlock, Ginger Nakamura, Tony Palaccio, and I revised the schedule for the camping trip. Please note that we changed the time of departure so that we won't have to contend with the morning rush hour traffic. We believe that the new schedule will be more convenient for everyone in the group. ¶

Please let us know if you see any problems with the new schedule. ¶

Document 63.2 Memo with Basic Formatting that Discusses Online Database References

Read all instructions below before starting this document activity.

1 Navigate to the Document 63.2 launch page in the Online Lab and then click the Launch Activity button to open **Doc063.02** in the activity window.

2 Use the content in Figure 63.3 to key the memo. Be sure to apply correct formatting, as shown in Figure 63.1. *Hint: Press Shift + Enter after keying the reference initials, file name, and* Attachment. *Press the spacebar rather than Tab after keying* cc: *because there is only one person in the distribution list.*

steps continue

Document 117.3

Drawing a Table, Changing Borders, and Centering a Table Horizontally

Read all instructions below before starting this document activity.

1 Navigate to the Document 117.3 launch page in the Online Lab and then click the Launch Activity button to open **Doc117.03** in the activity window.

2 Create a table that contains 3 columns and 13 rows.

3 Key the data shown in Figure 117.3.

4 Apply a 1½-point double black line (seventh option in the *Style* option drop-down list) to the outside borders of the table. *Note: The inside border will remain ½-point single black lines.*

5 Select the table and then change the row height to 0.5 inch and the column width to 2 inches.

6 Merge the cells in the first row of the table, apply bold formatting to the text, and then align the text to the top center of the cell. Make the same changes to the row containing the text *Tuesday, February 25*.

7 Center the table horizontally on the page. *Hint: Use the Paragraph group on the Home tab.*

8 Center the table vertically on the page. *Hint: Use options at the Page Setup dialog box.*

9 Proofread the document and correct any errors.

10 Save the document.

11 Click the Check button to upload the document for checking.

12 If errors are reported by the Online Lab, view the results document, correct the errors in the submitted document, save the document, and then click the Check Again button.

Figure 117.3 Table Content for Document 117.3

Monday, February 24		
8:30 a.m.	Registration	
9:00 a.m.	Welcome	Carol O'Connor
9:15 a.m.	Keynote Speaker	Trinity Washburn
Noon	Lunch	Located in the Grand Room
1:15 p.m.	Breakout Sessions	TBA
4:00 p.m.	Adjourn	
Tuesday, February 25		
9:00 a.m.	Continental Breakfast	Located in the Main Lounge
10:00 a.m.	Keynote Speaker	Mark Vasquez
12:15 p.m.	Lunch	Located in the Grand Room
2:00 p.m.	Round-Table Discussions	Lead by Francis McTavish
4:00 p.m.	Wrap-Up and Prizes	

Figure 63.1 Sample Memo Format

Note: Do not key this document.

Memorandum, Interoffice Memorandum, and *Memo* are all acceptable titles for a memo document.

Memo

TO: [2 Tabs]   Recipient's Name [Enter]

FROM: [2 Tabs]   Sender's Name [Enter]

first and last names; department name or job title optional

DATE: [2 Tabs]   Current Date [Enter]

SUBJECT: [Tab]   Topic of Memo [Enter]

This is the first line of the message, or body, of the memo. Typically, memos are short forms of communication, perhaps one or two paragraphs. The message should be written in clear, direct sentences using correct grammar, capitalization, and punctuation. Press Enter at the end of each paragraph. [Enter]

If copies of the memo are to be sent to other individuals, arrange the names in alphabetical order at the end of the memo. Enter the "cc:" notation at the left margin to indicate "copies," press the Tab key, and then key the name of the first person who is to receive a copy. Press Shift + Enter after typing each name in the list and then press the Tab key before typing the next name. Do not press Shift + Enter or Tab after keying the last name in the list. [Enter]

xyz [Shift + Enter]
file name [Shift + Enter]
cc: [Tab] Person 1 [Shift + Enter]
    [Tab] Person 2 [Shift + Enter]
    [Tab] Person 3

reference initials (if person keying the memo is not the author of the document)

file name (without file extension)

List individuals alphabetically by last name. Press the spacebar (not the Tab key) after *cc:* if only one person is to receive a copy.

Document 63.1

Memo with Basic Formatting

Read all instructions below before starting this document activity.

1. Navigate to the Document 63.1 launch page in the Online Lab and then click the Launch Activity button to open **Doc063.01** in the activity window.

2. Key the guide words for the memo by completing the following steps:

   a. Position the insertion point to the right of *TO:*, press Tab twice, key Steve Conway, Recreation Department, and then press Enter once to move to the next line.

   b. Key FROM:, press Tab twice, key Beth Walton, and then press Enter once to move to the next line.

   c. Key DATE:, press Tab twice, key June 26, 2020, and then press Enter once to move to the next line. *Note: Do not key the actual current date or the Online Lab will show this as an error.*

   d. Key SUBJECT:, press Tab once, key Camping Trip Itinerary, and then press Enter once to move to the next line.

steps continue

Preparing a Calendar Using Quick Tables

Read all instructions below before starting this document activity.

1 Navigate to the Document 117.4 launch page in the Online Lab and then click the Launch Activity button to open **Doc117.04** in the activity window.

2 Insert the Calendar 3 table using the *Quick Tables* option at the Table button drop-down list.

3 Select the month and then key November 2020.

4 Edit the dates of the inserted calendar to match the dates shown in Figure 117.4. Delete the two extra rows at the end of the month. *Hint: You may need to turn on the display of table gridlines to view which two rows at the bottom of the calendar to delete.*

5 Center the table horizontally on the page.

6 Proofread the document and correct any errors.

7 Save the document.

8 Click the Check button to upload the document for checking.

9 If errors are reported by the Online Lab, view the results document, correct the errors in the submitted document, save the document, and then click the Check Again button.

Figure 117.4 Table Content and Formatting for Document 117.4

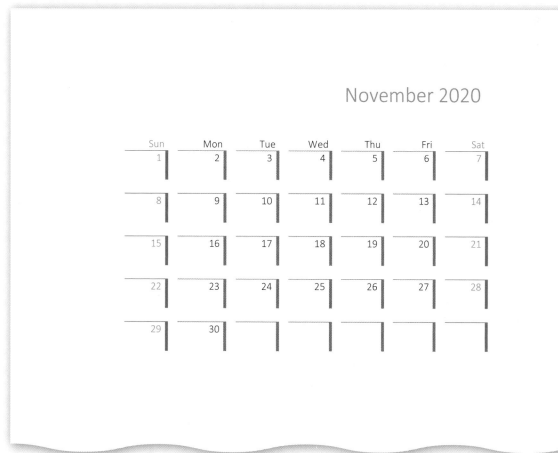

Ending the Session

The Online Lab automatically saved the work you completed for this session. You may continue with the next session or exit the Online Lab and continue later.

Ergonomic Tip

A dirty monitor is hard on your eyes. Clean your monitor regularly with an antistatic screen cleaner recommended by the screen's manufacturer.

Preparing Memos

As discussed in Session 62, email is a commonly used method of written communication. Other common types of written communication in business environments include memorandums, letters, reports, and manuscripts. This session will discuss memorandums (commonly shortened to *memos*). Memos are generally used to communicate within an organization. Memos can vary in length, but most are short.

Throughout this text, the term *memo* refers to documents that are keyed, printed, and delivered via the internal mail system of an organization. In contrast, email messages are transmitted electronically. A document that contains a memo may, however, be distributed via email as an attached file.

Formatting a Memo

Memos may be prepared on preprinted memo forms, letterhead, plain paper, or memo templates that are available in some word processing software packages. The standard format for a memo is block style, with guide words (*DATE, TO, FROM, SUBJECT*) and the message starting at the left margin. The first page of the memo begins two inches from the top of the page, while text on any following pages begins one inch from the top of the page. The order and placement of the guide words may vary from one organization to another and among the templates included with word processing software packages.

The traditional memo will be featured in this session. The order of the guide words for these memos is *TO, FROM, DATE, SUBJECT*.

The sample memo in Figure 63.1 shows common formatting for a memo prepared on plain paper. Use the guidelines shown in this example when preparing the memos in this book.

Document Productivity Check: Business Reports and Manuscripts

Session Objectives

- Demonstrate the ability to prepare a formal business report with a title page
- Demonstrate the ability to format a manuscript according to MLA style with in-text citations and a Works Cited page
- Efficiently produce documents in mailable form

Getting Started

Exercise 118.1 Unless you are continuing immediately after completing Session 117, spend at least two to three minutes warming up using Exercise 118.1 before completing the document activities in this session. See Session 101 for suggested warm-up text.

Preparing Documents

This session is an assessment of the types of documents created in Unit 16, Business Reports II, and Unit 17, Manuscripts and Research Papers II. Now that you have completed the instructional activities for creating business reports and manuscripts, you will be assessed on how accurately you can format, key, proofread, and correct these documents. In the following document activities, each completed document is to be "mailable," which means that it contains no errors. A document that requires corrections is not considered *mailable*.

Your goal is to key each document in mailable form. If you are missing errors that should have been corrected or your instructor believes you can work more efficiently, he or she may ask you to repeat document activities. Be sure to check each document to make sure all parts of the document are included.

To help you succeed, carefully review the instructions and content of each document before keying. Make sure you know the formatting elements and guidelines for each document to be keyed. If necessary, review the content of Session 77, Producing Formal Business Reports, and Session 83, Preparing Manuscripts in MLA Style, if you are unsure how to complete a specific task.

Document 118.1 **Formal Bound Business Report with Headings, Bulleted Lists, a Table, and Numbered Pages**

Read all instructions below before starting this document activity.

1 Navigate to the Document 118.1 launch page in the Online Lab and then click the Launch Activity button to open **Doc118.01** in the activity window.

steps continue

Session
63

Preparing Memos

Session Objectives

- Prepare and format memos
- Change paragraph alignment
- Select text
- Indent text using the horizontal ruler
- Compose a memo in which you present examples of tautologies
- Efficiently produce documents in mailable form

Getting Started

Exercise 63.1 If you are continuing immediately from Session 62, you may skip the Exercise 63.1 warm-up drill. However, if you exited the Online Lab at the end of Session 62, warm up by completing Exercise 63.1.

Exercise 63.2 Begin your session work by completing Exercise 63.2, a timed short drill, in the Online Lab.

Assessing Your Speed and Accuracy

Complete Timings 63.1 and 63.2 in the Online Lab. At the end of each timing, the Online Lab will display your WPM rate and any errors. Results will be saved in your Timings Performance report. If you have been surpassing the speed and accuracy goals identified in the Online Lab, set slightly more challenging personal goals and strive to exceed them.

Complete two 1-minute timings on the timing text below. If you meet or exceed both speed and accuracy goals for Timing 63.1, push for greater speed on Timing 63.2.

1-Minute Timings

Timings 63.1–63.2   Tornadoes seem to happen throughout the United States on a regular basis. They are associated with severe weather. Tornadoes are also called twisters. They can move very slowly or as fast as 70 miles an hour. The average speed is about 35 miles an hour. When the tornado hits the earth, it may travel for a few yards or more than 200 miles. The average path is about two miles before the tornado lifts from the ground and returns to the sky. Tornadoes may last as long as one hour and have winds greater than 200 miles per hour. Experts tell us to respect tornadoes.

2   Format the document margins for a bound report.

3   Press Enter until the insertion point is 1.9 inches from the top of the document to allow for a letterhead, change the paragraph alignment to center alignment, turn on bold formatting, and then key the two-line title shown in Figure 118.1. Press Shift + Enter at the end of the first line of the title.

4   Key the body of the report shown in Figure 118.1. Consider the following as you key the report:

     a   Turn off bold formatting before pressing Enter or the spacebar after a heading. *Hint: The nonprinting paragraph mark following a side heading should not be formatted as bold.*

     b   Press Tab at the start of each paragraph and confirm that a nonprinting Tab character appears at the start of each indented paragraph.

     c   Allow Word to automatically format the bulleted list with the default solid, black, round bullets for the first-level entries and hollow circle bullets for the second-level entries. Increase the indent of the first-level entries to align with the paragraph indent.

     d   Allow Word to automatically format the numbered list. Increase the indent to align with the paragraph indent.

5   Move the *Summary* heading and the paragraph that follows it to the top of the document, immediately below the title.

6   Edit the *Summary* heading to read *Executive Summary*.

7   Position the insertion point at the end of the paragraph following the *Recommendations* heading, press the spacebar, key Recommended changes for 2020/2021 are as follows:, and then press Enter.

8   With the insertion point positioned below the *Recommendations* paragraph, insert a table with three columns and seven rows and then key the text shown in Figure 118.2.

9   Format the table as follows:

     a   Select the first row, apply bold formatting, and align the text to the top center of the cells.

     b   Format the numbers (not the headings) in the second and third columns to align to the top right corners of the cells.

     c   AutoFit the contents of the cells.

     d   Select the table and then click the Increase Indent button in the Paragraph group on the Home tab.

     e   Confirm that there is one blank line below the table.

10   Insert a Plain Number 3 page number at the top right of the second and subsequent pages of the report. Do not include the page number on the first page.

11   Proofread the document and correct any errors.

12   Save the document.

13   Click the Check button to upload the document for checking.

14   If errors are reported by the Online Lab, view the results document, correct the errors in the submitted document, save the document, and then click the Check Again button.

example, the phrase *Ms. Brown insisted* is more meaningful than the phrase *Ms. Brown said*. Use a thesaurus (or the Thesaurus feature in Word) to select terms that help you create distinct images in the reader's mind.

Document 62.5 **Composing an Email Message with an Emphasis on Effective Sentences**

Read all instructions below before starting this document activity.

1   Navigate to the Document 62.5 launch page in the Online Lab and then click the Launch Activity button to open **Doc062.05** in the activity window.

2   Using the downloaded document, compose an email message to your instructor. For the email, assume that the Business department at your school is hosting a Technology Fair and that you are responsible for selling exhibit space. In the email, be sure to provide details such as dates, time, location, costs, benefits, how to contact you, and so on. The point of the email is to inform your instructor of the details of the fair and your responsibility in hosting the fair. Take special care to compose effective sentences; that is, sentences that are generally short but somewhat varied in length, and that are are constructed with words that convey a specific meaning. *Note: Make sure to press Enter twice to begin a new paragraph and do not press Tab while keying the message body.*

3   Apply bold, italics, or underlining at least three times in the email. *Note: Make sure the space or punctuation after a bold, italic, or underlined word do not have the formatting applied as well.*

4   Proofread and correct any errors in the email.

5   Save the document.

6   Click the Submit button to upload the document for instructor review.

Ending the Session

The Online Lab automatically saved the work you completed for this session. You may continue with the next session or exit the Online Lab and continue later.

Figure 118.1 Report Content for Document 118.1

TRISTATE UNIVERSITY
PROPOSED CHANGES TO PARKING AND TRANSPORTATION

The opportunity for members of the campus community to provide input on the 2020/2021 fee proposals began with individual meetings with focus groups across campus. The public was encouraged to review and provide input on the proposals and an email correspondence was sent to all active parking permit holders. Based on input received, a revised proposal was developed and released to permit holders, with an opportunity to review and provide comments. Comments were received via email, at three public meetings, and at the various campus constituent group meetings where the fee proposal was presented.

Introduction

In 2018 the Transportation Advisory Group (TAG) was formed and the process to update the Transportation Management Plan (TMP) began. The assumptions surrounding the long-range financial plans were part of the TAG's review. It is with that critical group's support, and in keeping with the direction of the TMP, that we present the 2020/2021 permit fee recommendations.

Current permit prices remain insufficient to sustain a safe and effective parking and transportation system and do not generate revenues necessary to meet future parking and transportation needs. The recommended rate increases address revenues for 2020/2021 required to meet the basic level of maintenance and operation to the Eastland campus parking and transportation system. Though we seek approval for the 2020/2021 fees only, we have provided a detailed long-range parking fee schedule. The schedule reflects adequate revenues generated to fund maintenance and operations for the system.

Challenges

PTS faces a number of challenges that must be met to ensure that Tristate University's parking and transportation system is not only maintained, but improved to ensure a safe and effective system. Taking into consideration what we believe must be done to achieve our goals, as well as the input we received from the campus community, the following changes to the permit fee structure are recommended. In addition to the recommended fee increases, other changes recommended at this time include removing the overnight parking allowance.

continues

Figure 62.5 Email Message Content for Document 62.4

Zach, ¶ I have prepared my recommendations for placement of the workstations at our new building. A layout of the propposed plan is being sent to you by courier. Note that the names of the staff who are to occupy the various workstations *is* included on the layout. ¶ The customer service information counter needs to be at the entry of the bank. The counter is to be in the shape of a half moon and stands four foot high. A six foot high partition is to be placed at the back of the half-moon with openings on either side for entry and exit of the staff. The top of partition is an excellent location to place the bank name and emblem. ¶ The personal bankers include Denise Wiley and Hope Flores need to be positioned close to the customer service counter along the west wall. Their workstations need to include space for two chairs for customers. The workstations are not to have partitions. ¶ The Loan Officers are to be located along the east wall with the glass enclosed cubicles for hearing privacy. Ann Mauer is to occupy the first cubicle. ¶ The investment counselors are to occupy the cubicles on the south wall. I recommend, Zach, that you take the office in the southeast corner. Judy Soucinek needs to be in the office next to yours. ¶ The move to the new facility is to take place beginning at noon on Saturday, June 4. We plan to be open for business "as usual" at 8:30 am, Monday, June 6. Please let me know by noon on Tuesday, May 10, whether you want to change this layout. This will give me enough time to set up the move and make sure everyone knows where they will be located.

7 If errors are reported in the Online Lab, view the results document, correct the errors in the submitted document, save the document, and then click the Check Again button.

Reinforcing Writing Skills

Strong, clear sentences use specific words and only contain those phrases necessary to convey the intended meaning. A sentence of no more than 15 to 25 words is an appropriate length, although varying sentence length within a paragraph makes the writing flow better and keeps the reader interested. Sentences consistently shorter than 10 words tend to make the content seem disjointed or "choppy;" in contrast, long sentences of 30 or more words can easily confuse readers.

Whenever possible, write with vivid words that generate a clear image or an emotion. For

Figure 118.1 Report Content for Document 118.1—continued

- Annual permit pricing change
  - Increase in Red Permit (3%)
  - Increase in Residential Permit (3%)
  - Increase in Blue Permit (12%)
- Remove overnight parking

The goals, objectives, issues, and proposals are identified annually and presented to the campus community in the form of proposed changes, and a standardized proposal process begins. This public review process is done via email, public presentations, and documents available on our website. A review of the issues presented this year, a summary of input received, and the final recommendations for approval of parking fees for 2020/2021 are outlined in this report.

Background

PTS at Tristate University is responsible for the administration, funding, operation, and maintenance of all parking facilities and components of the transportation system infrastructure on the Eastland campus.

The mission of PTS is to provide safe, convenient, and cost-effective services for Tristate University. As a self-sustaining organization, we are committed to supporting the teaching, research, operational, and public-service goals of Tristate University. We manage the University's parking and transportation resources to meet current and projected needs of the campus community while providing outstanding customer service.

As a unit within Auxiliary Services, PTS is expected to be self-sustaining and work actively toward improving financial stability. PTS continues to operate in a revenue-neutral capacity, generating revenues that are roughly equal to expenses.

Financial and Planning Assumptions

Current revenues generated are not sufficient to fund necessary transportation infrastructure capital improvements. Scheduled lot maintenance, fleet replacement, and capital reserve have been incorporated into the 10-year plan, in support of goals listed above.

continues

Applying Underline Formatting

Underlining is often used in the headings of a report or manuscript or to emphasize a word or phrase.

To underline text as you key, complete the following steps:

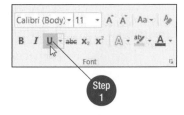

1 Click the Underline button in the Font group on the Home tab (or press Ctrl + U).

2 Key the word or words you want to be underlined.

3 Click the Underline button to turn underlining off (or press Ctrl + U).

To underline previously keyed text, complete the following steps:

1 Select the text to be underlined by pointing to where you want to begin the selection, clicking and holding down the left mouse button, dragging the pointer over the text to be underlined, and then releasing the left mouse button. *Hint: Be careful not to select and apply bold formatting to the space or punctuation after the text to be formatted; it will be marked as an error in the Online Lab.*

2 Click the Underline button in the Font group on the Home tab (or press Ctrl + U).

3 Click outside of the selected text to deselect the text.

The Underline button will appear selected (displays with a darkened background) when the insertion point is on a character that has underline formatting applied to it. A space between two underlined words should be underlined, but a space between an underlined word and a regular word should not be underlined. Punctuation following a single underlined word or phrase should also be regular.

Document 62.4

Email with Underlined Text and Proofreading Corrections

Read all instructions below before starting this document activity.

1 Navigate to the Document 62.4 launch page in the Online Lab and then click the Launch Activity button to open **Doc062.04** in the activity window.

2 Key zsanders@ppi-edu.net in the *To* line, key dness@ppi-edu.net in the *CC* line, and then key Staff Relocation in the *Subject* line.

3 Key the content of the email message shown in Figure 62.5, applying underline formatting as indicated and making the changes indicated by the proofreading marks. *Hint: Refer to Appendix B, Proofreading Marks, if necessary.*

4 Proofread the document and correct any errors.

5 Save the document.

6 Click the Check button to upload the document for checking.

Figure 118.1 Report Content for Document 118.1—continued

Permits. Unit costs for permits and overall expenses are expected to remain static relative to our campus population. Failure to continue with, or a delay in, the long-range permit pricing plan can result in budget deficits and significant delays in funding for important maintenance and operations. Continue to address compression issue of prices and determine/reach appropriate range and value of permit rates. Residential and Red permits are of equal value and should be priced accordingly.

Raising Fees. Long-range plans outline raising fees as follows: $200 (Red and Residential) by year 2024, Blue to $150 by 2022, and then level off with no increases or increases that will match inflationary rate of 3% to 6%.

Recommendations

The present operational mode does not allow funds to be secured for future parking- and transportation-related expenditures. Recommended changes are for the 2020/2021 revenue structure.

Discontinue Overnight Parking. Remove overnight parking from Blue Lot 60. The need to discontinue overnight parking in Lot 60 and convert to a daily commuter lot is recommended for the following reasons:

1. The Intermodal Transit Center (ITC) will be located on the corner of Waterford Avenue and Station Street, construction to begin summer 2020.

2. Some parking spaces in Lot 60 will be taken by the ITC construction and future functions.

3. The ITC will be a hub where people will catch public transit that serves Eastland—creating the need, beginning summer of 2020, for daily turnover and transient use of the lot.

4. Effective snow removal is essential for the Transit Center and can best be achieved with no overnight parking.

5. The ITC will bring with it more activity—ITC-customer parking, transportation-related meetings, organization use, PTS customers, etc.

Summary

Tristate University's parking and transportation plans, based upon goals established in 2016, continue to evolve. In 2017, Parking and Transportation Services (PTS) developed and formalized a long-range financial plan including permit fee increases. The timeframe to realize those goals has been extended based on input. Some deviations from the original funding

continues

Document
62.3

Email Message with Bold and Italic Items

Read all instructions below before starting this document activity.

1   Navigate to the Document 62.3 launch page in the Online Lab and then click the Launch Activity button to open **Doc062.03** in the activity window.

2   Key pfrench@ppi-edu.net in the *To* line, key ddefalco@ppi-edu.net, cnimitz@ppi-edu.net in the *CC* line, and then key Video Communications Technology Demonstration in the *Subject* line.

3   Key the content of the email message using the text in Figure 62.4. Remember to press Enter twice after each paragraph. Do not press Enter after the sender's name. Apply bold and italic formatting to the text as shown in the figure. Do not format the spaces or punctuation following the bold or italic words.

4   Proofread the document and correct any errors.

5   Save the document by clicking the Save button on the Quick Access Toolbar or by using the keyboard shortcut Ctrl + S.

6   Click the Check button to upload the document for checking.

7   If errors are reported by the Online Lab, view the results document, correct the errors in the submitted document, save the document, and then click the Check Again button.

Figure 62.4 Email Message Content for Document 62.3

Paul, ¶ We met at the Louisiana Technology Show in New Orleans last year. We were the ones who spotlighted the **video communications product technology**. ¶ Well, our technology has progressed at light speed since then. Here's where we are at this time. ¶ The *Video Packer Pro* family of Advanced Visual Communication Systems is now the leader of videoconferencing technology in PC-based video communications products. ¶ The **video communications product technology** and device design rely on a combination of high-speed fiber optic digital networks and Internet connectivity to deliver two-way, full-duplex, simultaneous video, voice, and data. The result is displayed on a flat screen television monitor and/or computer monitor at each end of the connection. ¶ Contact me via email if you would like to have an on-site demonstration. Note that I copied *Dewey DeFalco* and *Chester Nimitz* of the School of Business. They are also interested in this technology. ¶ Jake Rodgers

Figure 118.1 Report Content for Document 118.1—continued

plans include delays for reaching original target dates set for 2022. New target dates have been changed to 2026, resulting in a longer time to achieve funding. While we have not strictly followed the 6-year plan developed in 2017—for example, last year, only Gold permits increased—the fundamentals behind the plans and the goals remain the same.

Figure 118.2 Table Content for Document 118.1

	2018/2019 Fees	2020/2021 Fees
Gold	230.50	230.50
Red	175.00	180.25
Residential	175.00	180.25
Blue	125.00	140.00
Purple	100.00	100.00
Visitor	10.00	10.00

Document 118.2 **Bound Business Report Title Page**

Read all instructions below before starting this document activity.

1 Navigate to the Document 118.2 launch page in the Online Lab and then click the Launch Activity button to open **Doc118.02** in the activity window.

2 Before keying, make the following formatting changes:

a Change the line spacing to single spacing with no spacing after paragraphs. *Hint: Do not change the default setting for the document.*

b Change the left margin to 1.5 inches.

c Change the paragraph alignment to center alignment.

3 Key the title page using the information shown in Figure 118.3, pressing Enter as indicated throughout the figure. Format the title (the two lines keyed in all capital letters) in bold. Turn off bold formatting before pressing Enter at the end of the title.

4 Vertically center the text on the page.

5 Proofread the document and correct any errors.

6 Save the document.

7 Click the Check button to upload the document for checking.

8 If errors are reported by the Online Lab, view the results document, correct the errors in the submitted document, save the document, and then click the Check Again button.

Figure 62.3 Email Message Content for Document 62.2

Bashir, ¶ I just returned from the San Luis Obispo Film Festival. It was fantastic! This year they featured movies of the 1940s and 1950s. These movies described America's mood in the decade after World War II. The majority of the flicks were war movies, though musicals and silly comedies were also popular. There were also a few dramas. I think I watched a dozen movies in three days! It was tiring, but fun. ¶ What I most remember are the movie stars. **John Wayne, Robert Mitchum, and Audie Murphy** were the stars of the war movies. Audie Murphy was an actual war hero! **Bob Hope, Bing Crosby, and Cary Grant** were featured in the comedies I watched. They also showed one post-war **Marx Brothers** movie, but I didn't see it. I don't remember much about the musicals, but **Ethel Merman, Howard Keel, and Gene Kelly** were in several movies each. Finally, the dramas I liked the most had **Humphrey Bogart** in a starring role. Some of those movies really are classics. ¶ Wish you could have joined me. ¶ Best regards, ¶ Valerie

Applying Italic Formatting

Italics can also be used to make certain words stand out in a document. Italics are frequently used for book, newspaper, and magazine titles, as well as for keywords such as names and headings.

To set text in italics as you key, complete the following steps:

1 Click the Italic button in the Font group on the Home tab (or press Ctrl + I).

2 Key the word or words you want to appear in italics.

3 Click the Italic button to turn off italics (or press Ctrl + I).

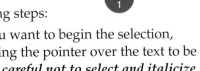

To set previously keyed text in italics, complete the following steps:

1 Select the text to be set in italics by pointing to where you want to begin the selection, clicking and holding down the left mouse button, dragging the pointer over the text to be italicized, and then releasing the mouse button. *Hint: Be careful not to select and italicize the space or punctuation after the text to be formatted; it will be marked as an error in the Online Lab.*

2 Click the Italic button in the Font group on the Home tab (or press Ctrl + I).

3 Click outside of the selected text to deselect the text.

The Italic button will appear selected (displays with a darkened background) when the insertion point is positioned on a character that has italic formatting applied to it. As with bold, spaces and punctuation between two italic words should be italic, but a space between an italic word and a regular word should be regular, without italic formatting applied to it. Punctuation following a single italic word or phrase should also be regular.

Figure 118.3 Title Page Content for Document 118.2

TRISTATE UNIVERSITY [Enter]

PROPOSED CHANGES TO PARKING AND TRANSPORTATION [12 Enters]

Submitted to [2 Enters]

Administration [Enter]

Campus Community Representatives [Enter]

Students [Enter]

Faculty and Support Staff [12 Enters]

Prepared by [2 Enters]

Robert Battum [Enter]

Julie Jacobs [Enter]

Maria Peterson [Enter]

Angela Richards [Enter]

Norman Trossack [2 Enters]

Parking and Transportation Services [Enter]

Tristate University [2 Enters]

January 21, 2020

Document 118.3 Manuscript with Citations and Works Cited Page in MLA Style

Read all instructions below before starting this document activity.

1 Navigate to the Document 118.3 launch page in the Online Lab and then click the Launch Activity button to open **Doc118.03** in the activity window.

2 Format the manuscript document as follows:

   a Change the document's default line spacing to double spacing with no spacing after paragraphs.

   b Change the document's default font to 12-point Palatino Linotype.

3 Set the document's reference style to MLA.

4 Insert a Plain Number 3 page number at the top right of all pages of the document, following the last name of the manuscript author, *Vanderhorst*.

5 Key the information about the manuscript at the top of the document. The manuscript is being prepared by Helene Vanderhorst for her instructor Kenya Kahl for the course Introductory Computer Concepts. The paper's date is 15 December 2020 and the title is *The Value of Fiber Optics*. **Hint: Refer to Figure 83.1 in Session 83 for the correct formatting of the first page of an MLA report.**

6 Key the text in Figure 118.4, implementing the proofreading marks as indicated. Press Tab at the start of each paragraph and confirm that a nonprinting Tab character appears at the start of each indented paragraph. **Hint: Key the entire figure before inserting the citations in the next step.**

steps continue

Applying Bold Formatting

One way to emphasize words or lines of text is to apply bold formatting. For example, bold is often used in report headings to help set them apart from the text. Text can be set in bold as you key, or you can apply bold formatting to previously keyed material.

To set text in bold as you key, complete the following steps:

1 Click the Bold button in the Font group on the Home tab (or press Ctrl + B).

2 Key the word or words you want to appear in bold.

3 Click the Bold button to turn off bold (or press Ctrl + B).

To set previously keyed text in bold, complete the following steps:

1 Select the text to be set in bold by pointing to where you want to begin the selection, clicking and holding down the left mouse button, dragging the pointer over the text to be bolded, and then releasing the mouse button. *Hint: Be careful not to select and apply bold formatting to the space or punctuation after the text to be formatted; it will be marked as an error in the Online Lab.*

2 Click the Bold button in the Font group on the Home tab (or press Ctrl + B).

3 Click outside of the selected text to deselect the text.

The Bold button will appear selected (displays with a darkened background) when the insertion point is on a character that has bold formatting applied to it. A space between two bold words should be bold, but a space between a bold word and a regular word (with no formatting applied) should be regular. Punctuation following a single bold word or phrase should also be regular.

⬚ocument 62.2

Email Message with Bold Text

Read all instructions below before starting this document activity.

1 Navigate to the Document 62.2 launch page in the Online Lab and then click the Launch Activity button to open **Doc062.02** in the activity window.

2 Key bsmith@ppi-edu.net in the *To* line and then key Great Old Movies! in the *Subject* line.

3 Key the content of the email message using the information in Figure 62.3. Do not press Tab at the start of each paragraph. If you accidentally press Tab, immediately press Ctrl + Z to undo the addition of the new row in the table. Press Enter twice after each paragraph. Do not press Enter after the sender's name. Apply bold formatting as shown in the figure. Format the spaces and punctuation between the bold words in bold, but do not format the punctuation or spaces following the bold names in bold. *Hint: Check whether formatting has been applied to a space or punctuation symbol by selecting it and then seeing if the Bold button in the Font group appears as active. If it is active but should not be, click the button to remove bold formatting from the selected text.*

4 Proofread the document and correct any errors.

5 Save the document by clicking the Save button on the Quick Access Toolbar or by using the keyboard shortcut Ctrl + S.

6 Click the Check button to upload the document for checking.

7 If errors are reported by the Online Lab, view the results document, correct the errors in the submitted document, save the document, and then click the Check Again button.

7 Key the source information shown in Figure 118.5, inserting the citation references in the document according to the proofreading marks in Figure 118.4. Include page references for the in-text citations when indicated.

8 Insert a Works Cited page at the end of the document by completing the following:

   a Position the insertion point at the end of the document and then insert a hard page break.

   b Change the paragraph alignment to center alignment, key Works Cited, then press Enter. *Note: Do not key the title in bold.*

   c Change the paragraph alignment to left alignment.

   d Click the Bibliography button in the Citations & Bibliography group on the References tab and then click *Insert Bibliography* at the drop-down list.

9 Proofread the document and correct any errors.

10 Save the document.

11 Click the Check button to upload the document for checking.

12 If errors are reported by the Online Lab, view the results document, correct the errors in the submitted document, save the document, and then click the Check Again button.

Figure 118.4 Manuscript Content for Document 118.3

¶ There are ~~four~~ *five* alternatives for transmitting telecommunications signals: twisted pair copper wire, copper cable, optical fiber, microwave, and satellite. When compared, each alternative has distinct advantages and disadvantages. This manuscript focuses on the value of fiber optics for "communicating information to make it knowledge." ¶ Speed of Transmission ¶ The limits of the bandwidth of fiber optic cable have not been established. Single mode fiber transmits at speed*s* above 100 GHz (100 billion cycles per second). An example of how fast that is follows: Fiber optic cable can carry *three* ~~3~~ episodes of a 30-minute TV show in one second. When compared to copper cable, fib*re* optic cable is much smaller and lighter. ~~Fiber optic cable has a diameter~~ *(insert Hendricks citation, page 91.)* of 125 microns (thinner than a human hair). ¶ Security ¶ ~~Fiber optic cable is~~ immune to electrical noises, while copper cable is adversely affected by these noises. Since electromagnetic signals are not used in transmission*s* over fiber optic cable, as opposed to copper cable, *there is* no chance of radiation ~~leaks. In addition, the optical~~ (light) *(insert Mitchell citation, page 126)* signals sent over fiber optic cable ~~cannot be tapped without detection.~~ This makes fiber cable more secure. ¶ Costs ¶ Less equipment is needed in transmitting optical signals over fiber as opposed to electromagnetic signals sent *over* copper. Optical signals sent over fiber optic cable can travel 50 miles, as opposed to 4 to 6 miles for electromagnetic signals over copper, before needing equipment to repeat/boost the signals. Great strides ~~were~~ *have*

continues

6   Save the document by pressing the Save button on the Quick Access Toolbar or use the keyboard shortcut Ctrl + S.

7   Click the Check button to upload the document for checking.

8   If errors are reported by the Online Lab, view the results document, correct the errors in the submitted document, save the document, and then click the Check Again button.

Figure 62.2 Email Message Content for Document 62.1

Allan, ¶ I think your idea of vacationing in Wyoming is outstanding. There are so many things to see and do in that state. Activities in Wyoming include great sightseeing, camping, hiking, golfing, hunting and fishing, and, in the winter, skiing. There are warm springs, glacial peaks, and museums. ¶ The most famous places to visit have to be Yellowstone and Grand Teton National Parks. These parks are located in the northwestern part of the state. The main focus of Grand Teton National Park is the dramatic Teton Range of mountains. These mountains rise more than 6,000 feet abruptly above Jackson Hole and scenic Lake MacDonald. Most of the land for Grand Teton National Park was donated by the Rockefeller family in the 1930s. ¶ Yellowstone National Park is the oldest park in the United States. It was signed into law in 1872 by President Ulysses S. Grant. Yellowstone contains geysers, enormous mountain lakes, exciting waterfalls, petrified forests, and a variety of lava flows, with jet-black obsidian! The wildlife at Yellowstone is awesome. Many visitors see bison, moose, elk, deer, both grizzly bears and black bears, wolves, coyotes, and beavers. ¶ Other parts of Wyoming have many other attractions. For example, the town of Cody—in the northern part of the state—is home to the Buffalo Bill Historical Center. It is an outstanding museum for learning about the Old West. In the town of Dubois—in west-central Wyoming—you can visit the National Bighorn Sheep Center. And in the northeastern part of the state is famous Devil's Tower. This flat-topped butte is a grooved igneous body that stands nearly 1,300 feet above the surrounding rolling plains. ¶ We look forward to seeing you soon in Wyoming! ¶ Frank Butler

 Success Tip

Do not press the spacebar after a period at the end of a paragraph.
The Online Lab will mark this as an error.

Figure 118.4 Manuscript Content for Document 118.3—continued

been made in transmitting optical signals. In 1970, a fiber optic signal transmitted ~~just over half of a mile~~ before a noticeable loss of strength. *(insert Hawkes. citation)* Today, fiber optic signals in laboratory tests have traveled 7,400 miles before losing ~~too much~~ strength. Once installed, fiber optic cable is inexpensive to maintain since it is not hampered by underground environmental conditions, as is the case with copper cable. The state of Rhode Island leads the nation with more than 97% *(percent)* of its population having access to fiber optic networks. ¶ Market Penetration ¶ Fiber optic cable is already being used extensively, and its use continues to escalate.

(insert Farooq citation)

Figure 118.5 Source Content for Document 118.3

First Citation

Type of Source: Book

Author: Hendricks, Jonathan; Larson, Ted; Roulton, Nancy

Title: Information Technology Marketplace

Year: 2016

City: Phoenix

Publisher: Blackside Publishing, Inc.

Medium: Print

Second Citation

Type of Source: Article in a Periodical

Author: Mitchell, Kennedy

Title: Wired!

Periodical Title: IT Today

Year: 2020

Month: November

Day: 10

Pages: 122-138

Medium: Print

continues

Different email software programs provide different editing and formatting features. For example, Outlook includes buttons that apply bold, italic, and underline formatting to text in an email message. As shown in Figure 62.1, these buttons appear in the Basic Text group on the Message tab. Word processing programs generally provide more formatting and editing features than email software. To take advantage of this, some people create email messages with their word processor and then copy and paste the text into their email software for transmission. Outlook and other email programs (such as Yahoo! and Gmail) do not use the same line and paragraph spacing defaults as Microsoft Word. If you copy and paste text from Word into your email software, make sure to check the line and paragraph spacing before sending the email.

Creating an Email Message

Students use a wide variety of email programs at home, school, and work. In the following document activities, you will create email messages and then perform several basic editing functions. Rather than using an email program, you will key the document activities in Word. This will make it possible for your work to be checked by the Online Lab. The documents in Session 62 have been formatted with no extra line and paragraph spacing since Outlook and other email programs generally do not have the same default spacing as Word.

Both Outlook and Word have features that allow you to bold, italicize, and underline message text. While the Bold, Italic, and Underline buttons are found in the Basic Text group on the Message tab in Outlook (as shown in Figure 62.1), these buttons are found in the Font group on the Home tab in Word. Both programs allow you to apply formatting as you key or to key text and apply formatting afterward. To apply formatting while keying text, click the appropriate button to turn the formatting on, key the text, and then click the button again to turn it off. To apply formatting after keying text, select the text and then click the appropriate formatting button. To select text, position the insertion point at the first word, click and hold down the left mouse button, drag the mouse pointer to the end of the text to be selected, and then release the mouse button. Additional methods for selecting text will be described in Session 63.

Document
62.1

Email Message

Read all instructions below before starting this document activity.

1 Navigate to the Document 62.1 launch page in the Online Lab and then click the Launch Activity button to open **Doc062.01** in the activity window.

2 The recipient's address has already been keyed in the email document. Click in the text box that contains the content placeholder text *Click or tap here to enter text* to the right of *CC* and then key aoakley@ppi-edu.net. Do not press the spacebar after keying the address.

3 Click in the text box to the right of *Subject* and then key Vacationing in Wyoming!

4 Click in the text box below the subject line and then key the content of the email message using the information in Figure 62.2. In the figure, the pink paragraph symbol (¶) is used to indicate a new paragraph. Do not press Tab to create an indent at the start of each paragraph; keep the paragraphs aligned at the left margin. If you accidentally press Tab, a new row will be added to the document table. Press Ctrl + Z to undo the addition of the new row. The document will not format the text with extra space between paragraphs, so press Enter twice at the end of each paragraph except the last paragraph. Do not press Enter after the sender's name. In the fourth paragraph of the email, key two hyphens and allow Word to replace them with an em dash. Do not press the spacebar before, between, or after keying the hyphens.

5 Proofread the document and correct any errors.

steps continue

Figure 118.5 Source Content for Document 118.3—continued

Third Citation

Type of Source: Web site

Author: Hawkes, Nathan

Name of Web Page: Today's Telecommunications

Year: 2019

Month: July

Day: 27

Year Accessed: 2020

Month Accessed: September

Day Accessed: 22

URL: http://ppi-edu.net/TodaysTelecommunications

Medium: Electronic

Fourth Citation

Type of Source: Journal Article

Author: Farooq, Sabah

Title: Fiber Optics in Telecommunications

Journal Name: Telecommunication Connections

Year: 2019

Pages: 14-23

Medium: Print

Ending the Session

The Online Lab automatically saved the work you completed for this session. You may continue with the next session or exit the Online Lab and continue later.

Ergonomic Tip

If you wear glasses, you may need to invest in an extra pair prescribed specifically for your screen-to-eye distance.

Preparing Email Messages

The term *email* is a condensed form of the original term, *electronic mail*. Email messages are prepared in much greater numbers than other business documents such as memos, letters, reports, and manuscripts. Most email messages are short, and most are never printed. The recipient of an email message has the option of deleting the message or leaving it stored on the email server or computer.

The appearance and format of email messages vary according to the specific email program. An example of an outgoing email message produced with Microsoft Outlook 2016 is shown in Figure 62.1. Typically, the header of an email message contains the sender's name and email address, the date and time the email was sent, the subject of the email, the body text, and the name and email address of the recipient. If there is more than one recipient, the names and email addresses of all recipients are generally included at the top of the email. The ellipses (three periods) following *To* and *Cc* in Figure 62.1 indicate that you can click those buttons to select an email address from a personal or business directory or contact list. Emails may also contain one or more attached documents, images, or videos.

Figure 62.1 Email Message Produced with Microsoft Outlook

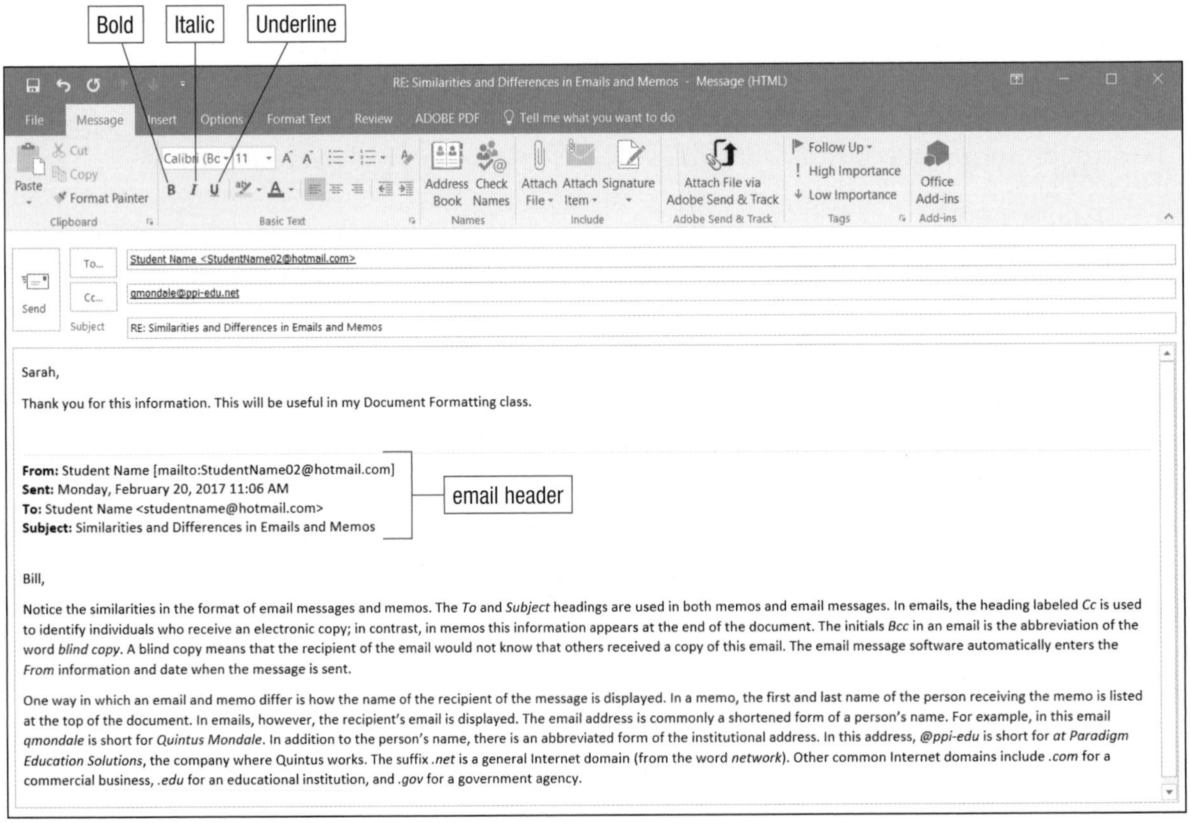

Session 119

Document Productivity Check: Graphics and Imagery

Session Objectives

- **Demonstrate proficiency with graphic elements**
- **Produce documents in mailable form**

Getting Started

Exercise 119.1 Unless you are continuing immediately after completing Session 118, spend at least two to three minutes warming up using Exercise 119.1 before completing the document activities in this session. See Session 101 for suggested warm-up text.

Preparing Documents

This session is an assessment of the types of documents created in Unit 18, Graphics and Imagery. Now that you have completed the instructional activities for inserting graphics into documents, you will be assessed on how accurately you can format, key, proofread, and correct these documents. In the following document activities, each completed document is to be "mailable," which means that it contains no errors. A document that requires corrections is not considered *mailable*.

Your goal is to key each document in mailable form. If you are missing errors that should have been corrected or your instructor believes you can work more efficiently, he or she may ask you to repeat document activities. Be sure to check each document to make sure all parts of the document are included.

To help you succeed, carefully review the instructions and content of each document before keying. Make sure you know the formatting elements and guidelines for each document to be keyed. If necessary, review the content of Unit 18 if you are unsure how to complete a specific task.

Document 119.1 Letterhead with Image, WordArt, and a Shape

Read all instructions below before starting this document activity.

1   Navigate to the Document 119.1 launch page in the Online Lab and then click the Launch Activity button to open **Doc119.01** in the activity window.

2   Insert and format an image in the document using the following information:

   a   Display the Insert Picture dialog box, click the *Documents* folder in the Navigation pane, double-click the *Paradigm* folder, double-click the *Keyboarding* folder, and then double-click the *DocumentActivityFiles* folder.

   b   Double-click **Doc119.01_Paradise.jpg**.

   c   Change the height of the image to 0.8 inch.

   d   Apply the Reflected Rounded Rectangle picture style (fifth column, first row in the Picture Styles gallery on the Picture Tools Format tab) to the image.

   e   Click the Picture Effects button in the Picture Styles group, point to *Bevel*, and then click the *Round* option (first option in the *Bevel* section).

steps continue

Session 62 Preparing Email Messages

Session Objectives

- Review basic features of emails
- Use bold, italic, and underline formatting when creating emails
- Compose an email that emphasizes the use of effective sentences
- Efficiently produce documents in mailable form

Getting Started

Exercise 62.1 If you are continuing immediately from Session 61, you may skip the Exercise 62.1 warm-up drill. However, if you exited the Online Lab at the end of Session 61, warm up by completing Exercise 62.1.

Exercise 62.2 Begin your session work by completing Exercise 62.2, a timed short drill, in the Online Lab.

Assessing Your Speed and Accuracy

Complete Timings 62.1 and 62.2 in the Online Lab. At the end of each timing, the Online Lab will display your WPM rate and any errors. Results will be saved in your Timings Performance report. If you surpassed the speed and accuracy goals identified in the Online Lab for the previous session, set slightly more challenging personal goals and strive to exceed them.

Complete two 1-minute timings on the timing text below. If you meet or exceed both speed and accuracy goals for Timing 62.1, push for greater speed on Timing 62.2.

1-Minute Timings

Timings 62.1–62.2 Imagine yourself navigating a raft hurtling through the white-water rapids of a tremendous river. The adrenaline in your body is pumping. Your knuckles are gripping the oar so tightly that they are bone-white. You call out instructions to the other 11 people in the raft, whose fates rest completely in your hands. They paddle to the extreme right, and you successfully steer your way past the jutting rocks. The invigorating water splashes your face, and all you can think of is how alive you feel.

Figure 119.1 Letterhead Design for Document 119.1

f   Change the position of the image to *Position in Top Right with Square Text Wrapping* (third column, first row in the *With Text Wrapping* section).

g   Deselect the image by clicking in the document.

3   Insert WordArt into the document using the blue WordArt style in the third column, third row of the WordArt Styles drop-down gallery and then key Paradise Pool & Spa in the text box. Format the WordArt as follows:

a   Change the position to Position in Top Left with Square Text Wrapping (first column, first row in the *With Text Wrapping* section).

b   Apply the Wave: Down text effect (first column, fifth row in the *Warp* section of the *Transform* side menu).

c   Deselect the WordArt by clicking in the document and then press Enter three times.

4   Starting at the left margin of the document, immediately to the left of the insertion point, draw a straight line shape that is 6.5 inches wide. ***Hint: Check and adjust the length of the line in the Size group on the Drawing Tools Format tab.***

5   Apply the Intense Line - Accent 5 shape style (sixth column, third row in the *Theme Styles* section) to the line.

6   Compare the letterhead to the image shown in Figure 119.1. Make any necessary adjustments or corrections.

7   Save the document.

8   Click the Submit button to upload the document for instructor review.

Document 119.2   **Business Letter with a Table and Symbols**

Read all instructions below before starting this document activity.

1   Navigate to the Document 119.2 launch page in the Online Lab and then click the Launch Activity button to open **Doc119.02** in the activity window.

2   Key a business letter using the content provided in Figure 119.2.

a   With the insertion point positioned 2.2 inches from the top of the document, key March 11, 2020 as the date of the letter.

b   Remove the hyperlink for the email address in the last paragraph.

c   Key the reference initials jsb and the file name after the title line. Include a reference to two enclosures and indicate that a copy is being sent to Gerry Quando.

3   Replace the words in the last paragraph of the letter with symbols by completing the following steps. See Table 119.1 for reference.

a   Select the word *phone* and replace it with the phone symbol. ***Hint: Do not select the space before or after the word* phone**.

steps continue

2 Click *Reports* in the Navigation pane.

3 Click *Document Performance* to open the report. The report displays in a table that shows the error results of the first check you did on each of the timed document activities.

4 Click *Attempts* to view your submitted documents and the corresponding results documents for all attempts you make on the document activities.

Reinforcing Writing Skills

Sexist words are offensive and inappropriate in professional settings. However, in many situations, writers may not be aware that they are using such prejudicial words. Note the following examples:

1 If a doctor is needed, *he* can be paged. (All doctors are not male.)

2 Call a nurse if you need help; *she* can be reached by pressing the button. (All nurses are not female.)

3 The administrative assistant should prepare *her* progress report. (Both males and females work as administrative assistants.)

One way to avoid sexist labels and stereotyping is to use plural pronouns such as *they* and *their*. When you need to use a singular pronoun, refer to both sexes at once with a pronoun phrase such as *he or she*. Or use words that do not imply a specific gender, such as *student*, *person*, or *individual*. The examples above can be transformed into gender-neutral sentences as follows:

1 If a doctor is needed, he or she can be paged.
Page a doctor if you need help.
Doctors are available by paging.

2 Call a nurse if you need help; a nurse can be reached by pressing the button.
You can call a nurse for help by pressing the button.

3 The administrative assistant should prepare a progress report.

Document 61.5

Composing a Document that Discusses Sexist Words

Read all instructions below before starting this document activity.

1 Navigate to the Document 61.5 launch page in the Online Lab and then click the Launch Activity button to open **Doc061.05** in the activity window.

2 Think of five job titles that are commonly or traditionally associated with males and five job titles frequently associated with females. Then compose and key a short document, to be sent to a school administrator or counselor, in which you describe the kinds of sexual stereotyping that occur in written communications about these positions. Give examples of how the sexist words affect attitudes and behavior in the workplace.

3 Proofread the document and correct any errors.

4 Save the document.

5 Click the Submit button to upload the document for instructor review.

Ending the Session

The Online Lab automatically saved the work you completed for this session. You may continue with the next session or exit the Online Lab and continue later.

    b Select the word *cell* and replace it with the cell phone symbol. Change the size of the symbol to 14 points.

    c Select the word *email* and replace it with the symbol of a computer.

    d Select the word *mail* and replace it with the symbol of an envelope.

4 Position the insertion point at the end of the first paragraph, press Enter, and then insert a table containing two columns and five rows. Key Session Name in A1; Getting Your Point Across Graphically with Visio in B1; Date and Time in A2; April 9, 8:30 a.m. to 11:30 a.m. in B2; Presenter in A3; Monique Moore in B3; Coordinator in A4; Margret Hubor in B4; Assistant in A5; and Judy Smithson in B5.

5 Apply the Grid Table 1 Light table style (first column, first row in the *Grid Tables* section) to the table. AutoFit the contents of the table and then center the table horizontally on the page.

6 Adjust the spacing after the table by selecting the nonprinting paragraph mark between the table and the second paragraph, clicking the Line and Paragraph Spacing button in the Paragraph group on the Home tab, and then clicking the *Remove Space After Paragraph* option at the drop-down list.

7 Proofread the document and correct any errors.

8 Save the document.

9 Click the Check button to upload the document for checking.

10 If errors are reported by the Online Lab, view the results document, correct the errors in the submitted document, save the document, and then click the Check Again button.

Figure 119.2 Letter Content for Document 119.2

Ms. Margret Hubor, Instructor ¶ Janesville Technical College ¶ 58 Gainsborough Road ¶ Janesville, WI 53101-1029 ¶ Dear Ms. Hubor: ¶ Thank you for agreeing to be a coordinator for the hands-on computer workshop during the 2020 Innovative Technology Convention at the Marriott Hotel in Chicago. The computer workshop will be held in the Avenue Ballroom on the fourth floor of the hotel. We will also have the State Room as a little office for the break-out computer workshops. Here are the other details for your session: ¶ Enclosed are copies of the workshop coordinator's guidelines and the workshop assistant's guidelines for you to use as you carry out your responsibilities. You may share the duties between the coordinator and assistant as you wish. I will also be available during the session to help facilitate the performance of your duties or help in the event of software or hardware problems. Gerry Quando, our computer technician, will also be available in the State Room most of the time. ¶ If you have any questions or if you find that you will not be able to serve as a computer workshop coordinator or assistant, please contact me immediately by phone at (563) 555-9171, cell at (563) 555-1159, email at mtrill@ppi-edu.net, or mail at 75 Grassland Avenue, Dubuque, IA 52001-4235. ¶ Sincerely, ¶ Marilyn Trill ¶ ITC Workshops Director

Document 61.4

Keying from Technical Text with Proofreading Marks

Read all instructions below before starting this document activity.

1. Navigate to the Document 61.4 launch page in the Online Lab and then click the Launch Activity button to open **Doc061.04** in the activity window.

2. Key the text shown in Figure 61.7. Press Tab to start each paragraph and implement the changes indicated by the proofreading marks.

3. Proofread the document and correct any errors.

4. Save the document.

5. Click the Check button to upload the document for checking.

6. If errors are reported by the Online Lab, view the results document, correct the errors in the submitted document, save the document, and then click the Check Again button.

Figure 61.7 Proofreading Corrections for Document 61.4

The human body contains a *wide* variety of joints. The ~~structure~~ *anatomy* of a typical joint is shown in Figure 13.1. In addition to the components shown in Figure 13.1, ligaments (non-contractile connective tissue that ties one bone to another bone) are essential to maintaining the bones in correct alignment and forming the capsule/fibrous that encloses the moving parts. Joints can be classified in a number of ways. One method of classification is joint structure. Joints can be classified by their structure into the following types: cartilaginous, articulating bone surfaces *are* covered with cartilage; fibrous, articulating bone surfaces *are* attached by fibrous connective tissue; and synovial, articulating surfaces is *are* covered by a fluid filled fibrous sack. Furthermore, joints can be classified based on whether they permit no movement, a slight degree of movement, or a variety of types of movement. Muscles are connected to bones by tough cordlike tissues called tendons. A muscle is an organ that produces movement by contracting (shortening itself). *Figure 13.2 presents a variety of joint types.*

Viewing the Document Performance Report for Completed Document Activities

The Online Lab provides a report showing the results of all of the document activities completed in the Online Lab. To view your Document Performance report, showing the document activity work you completed for Session 61, complete the following steps:

1. Click the Course Menu button to open the Online Lab Course Menu page and navigation pane, if necessary.

steps continue

Table 119.1 Symbols Used in Document 119.2

Word Replaced	Symbol Image	Font List	Character Code
phone	☎	Wingdings	40
cell	▯	Webdings	203
email	💻	Wingdings	58
mail	✉	Wingdings	43

Document 119.3

Flyer with SmartArt, Image, Borders, and Symbols

Read all instructions below before starting this document activity.

1 Navigate to the Document 119.3 launch page in the Online Lab and then click the Launch Activity button to open **Doc119.03** in the activity window.

2 Change the font size to 14 points.

3 Key the text shown in Figure 119.3.

4 Select the title (both the text and the nonprinting paragraph mark that follows it) and then change the font to 24-point Arial Black. Apply the Green, Accent 6, Darker 25% font color (last column, fifth row in the *Theme Colors* section) and change the paragraph alignment to center alignment.

5 With the insertion point positioned in the title, add a bottom paragraph border according to the following specifications:

   a Select the candy-cane style border (located immediately below the double wavy line).

   b Apply the Green, Accent 6, Darker 25% border color (last column, fifth row in the *Theme Colors* section) and change the weight of the border to 3 points.

   c Make sure the border is applied only to the bottom of the paragraph. *Hint: The* **Preview** *section of the Borders and Shading dialog box should only display a bottom border. Click any other borders to remove them. Confirm that* **Paragraph** *is selected in the* **Apply to** *option box.*

steps continue

Figure 119.3 Flyer Content for Document 119.3

Administrative Professionals Day

- Do you want to improve professionalism in your office?
- Do you need to get in touch with the current job market?
- Do you know how to dress for success?

Join us as career coach and strategist Samantha Ericson helps "improve the value, effectiveness, and professionalism that you bring to your position."

Please complete the registration form below and return it to Jessica Amandi in Room 52 by April 15. There is no cost for this professional development opportunity; however, space is limited.

Developing Proofreading Techniques

Developing effective proofreading techniques is essential whether you are writing your own documents or preparing documents for others. Proofreading involves reviewing the document you created to verify that it accurately reflects what you were supposed to key. The finished product represents you, or in a business environment, you and your employer.

When proofreading, place a ruler, an index card, or another guide below the line you are proofreading on the original or source document to help you keep your place. If you have printed your keyed version of the document, use a pen to move along the same place on your printed or hard copy as you are reading from the original. When you find differences, make proofreading marks on the printed copy to indicate changes to be made.

If you are proofreading from a printed source document against a file displayed on the computer screen, place a ruler, an index card, or another guide below the line you are proofreading on the original or source document and place your cursor at the same location on the screen. When you find a difference, immediately make the change to the electronic document.

Once changes have been made and saved, review the changes on the screen. Check them again after printing the document to make sure you made all the changes and did not make any new errors. Table 61.3 lists some common types of errors to look for while proofreading.

Table 61.3 Common Types of Errors to Look for While Proofreading

Errors	Examples and Explanations
wrong word	now/not, you/your, form/from, than/that, than/then
word endings	criterion/criteria, formed/former, keys/keyed, salary/salaries/salaried
words or names that sound alike	Aaron/Erin, conscience/conscious/conscientious, affect/effect, ensure/insure, hear/here, knew/new, principal/principle, their/there/they're, your/you're
added words	may result from losing one's place in the text while keying, causing repetition of words
omitted words	may result when a word appears in the same place in two consecutive lines and the eye skips from one line to the next when keying
transpositions	characters or words that are reversed to form a new word not detected by the spelling checker, such as *sad/ads*
numbers	correctness of dates, times, addresses, and phone numbers; missing items listed in a sequence, such as *1, 2, 4, 5* or *a, b, d, e*
punctuation errors	missing or incorrectly placed punctuation, such as a beginning quotation mark (") but no ending mark (")
capitalization errors	inconsistent or incorrect capitalization
top, bottom, and sides of document	readers' eyes tend to focus on the middle of a document, skipping over material at the top, bottom, and sides

6 Position the insertion point immediately following the period after the text *space is limited* and then press Enter twice. Insert a Vertical Arrow List SmartArt graphic (located in the *List* section). Key the information shown in the SmartArt graphic in Figure 119.4. Format the SmartArt graphic as follows:

   a Set the overall height of the graphic to 2 inches and the width to 5 inches.

   b Change the colors used in the SmartArt graphic to Colored Fill - Accent 6 (second option in the *Accent 6* section).

   c Apply the Inset SmartArt style (second column, first row in the *3-D* section).

7 Position the insertion point at the end of the document (Ctrl + End) and then press Enter twice.

8 Insert the hourglass symbol shown in Figure 119.4 (character code 54 in the Wingdings font). Press the spacebar, key Reply early to reserve your spot!, and then press Enter.

9 Insert the scissors symbol shown in Figure 119.4 (character code 35 in the Wingdings font) and then press Enter three times. ***Hint: Wingdings contains more than one scissors symbol—make sure the one you insert matches the image in Figure 119.4.***

10 Insert a right tab at the 3.5-inch mark on the horizontal ruler.

11 Key Name:, press the spacebar, press Ctrl + U, press Tab, press Ctrl + U, and then press Enter. Key Department:, press the spacebar, press Ctrl + U, press Tab, press Ctrl + U, and then press Enter. Key Phone Number:, press the spacebar, press Ctrl + U, press Tab, and then press Ctrl + U.

12 Triple-click in the *Reply early* line of text to select the paragraph and then change the font to Arial Black and apply the Green, Accent 6, Darker 25% font color (last column, fifth row in the *Theme Colors* section). Select the hourglass symbol and then change the font size to 36 points.

13 Position the insertion point immediately to the left of the scissors symbol and then add a bottom paragraph border. Click the dashed line style (the fourth option from the top). Apply the Green, Accent 6, Darker 25% border color (last column, fifth row in the *Theme Colors* section) and change the width to 2¼ points.

14 At the Insert Picture dialog box, navigate to the *DocumentActivityFiles* folder and then insert the **Doc119.03_PaperPen.jpg** image file. Format the image as follows:

   a Change the height of the image to 1.2 inches.

   b Change the position of the image to *Position in Bottom Right with Square Text Wrapping* (last column, bottom row in the *With Text Wrapping* section).

15 Save the document.

16 Click the Submit button to upload the document for instructor review.

Table 61.2 Common Proofreading Marks

Proofreading Mark	Intended Action	Proofreading Mark in Use	Corrected Copy
∧ ∨	insert	The grass grows on plains. *tall the*	The grass grows tall on the plains.
℘ ℓ	delete	The watching keeps excellent timed	The watch keeps excellent time.
◡	combine or close up	Her shoe string budget could not afford a cruise.	Her shoestring budget could not afford a cruise.
⟳	move text	The located housing development was along the river.	The housing development was located along the river.

Document 61.3

Keying from Text with Proofreading Marks

Read all instructions below before starting this document activity.

1 Navigate to the Document 61.3 launch page in the Online Lab and then click the Launch Activity button to open **Doc061.03** in the activity window.

2 Scan the marked-up text in Figure 61.6 and make sure you understand the intent of the proofreading marks. This will save you keying time and improve your efficiency. When you are finished, key the text shown in Figure 61.6. Press Tab to start each paragraph and implement the changes indicated by the proofreading marks.

3 Proofread the document and correct any errors.

4 Save the document.

5 Click the Check button to upload the document for checking.

6 If errors are reported by the Online Lab, view the results document, correct the errors in the submitted document, save the document, and then click the Check Again button.

Figure 61.6 Proofreading Corrections for Document 61.3

You might wish to send follow-up *correspondence* ~~communication~~ after an interview to solve an employer's problem, present a proposal or an idea, or reinforce the case for hiring you. Remember to stay in contact with the people who might be able to hire you in the future even if they cannot now. A good way to keep the connection going on is to present a proposal or idea that will be of interest to the person you meet. Then you can follow up again to discuss your idea of how to solve a problem for them. When you have interviewed for a specific job, your follow-up letter is a prime opportunity to reinforce that you are the right person for that job. *position*

What have you done in the past that makes it likely you will succeed in the new position? These are the items you should ~~highlight~~ *emphasize* in your follow-up letter. Also share ideas for helping too meet the specific challenges that you discussed during the interview.

Figure 119.4 Flyer Design for Document 119.3

Administrative Professionals Day

- Do you want to improve professionalism in your office?
- Do you need to get in touch with the current job market?
- Do you know how to dress for success?

Join us as career coach and strategist Samantha Ericson helps "improve the value, effectiveness, and professionalism that you bring to your position."

Please complete the registration form below and return it to Jessica Amandi in Room 52 by April 15. There is no cost for this professional development opportunity; however, space is limited.

When
- April 28, 2020
- 9 a.m. to 4 p.m.

Where
- Room 15A
- North Building

Reply early to reserve your spot!

✂ -

Name: _____

Department: _____

Phone Number: _____

Ending the Session

The Online Lab automatically saved the work you completed for this session. You may continue with the next session or exit the Online Lab and continue later.

(Displaying nonprinting characters will help you position the insertion point correctly.) When you join the two paragraphs, the line lengths of the new paragraph are automatically adjusted by the Word Wrap feature.

Document 61.2

Moving the Insertion Point and Using the Show/Hide ¶ Button

Read all instructions below before starting this document activity.

1 Navigate to the Document 61.2 launch page in the Online Lab and then click the Launch Activity button to open **Doc061.02** in the activity window.

2 If it is not already on, turn on the display of nonprinting characters by clicking the Show/Hide ¶ button in the Paragraph group on the Home tab.

3 In the first paragraph, delete the sentence *Do not be shy*.

4 Delete the last sentence in the first paragraph, which begins *Do not be afraid*.

5 In the second paragraph, delete the sentence *Tooting your own horn is a good example*.

6 Join the last paragraph (begins *This should include*) with the second-to-last paragraph (begins *When you have identified*).

7 Delete the last sentence in the document, which begins *These sentences should all start with*.

8 Proofread the document and correct any errors, paying special attention to the number of spaces between sentences and making sure there are no spaces at the end of paragraphs.

9 Turn off the display of nonprinting characters by clicking the Show/Hide ¶ button.

10 Save the document.

11 Click the Check button to upload the document for checking.

12 If errors are reported by the Online Lab, view your results document and correct the errors in the submitted document by completing the following steps:

a Click the Results button to view a document that shows your errors.

b Click the Submitted button to view the submitted document. *Hint: Click the Show Both button to view the submitted and results documents on the same screen.*

c Edit the submitted document to correct any errors, save the document (press Ctrl + S), and then click the Check Again button.

d If the Online Lab still reports errors, repeat Steps 12a–12c.

Proofreading Documents and Correcting Errors

Proofreading involves checking a document for errors. In some instances, this entails checking a newly produced document against an original document. The following section provides several tools and suggestions for proofreading.

Using Proofreading Marks

Proofreading marks are an efficient way to indicate changes or edits that need to be made to an existing document. Table 61.2 shows examples of how these marks are used to indicate inserting, deleting, combining, and moving text. Appendix B provides a more complete list of commonly used proofreading marks.

Session
120

Document Productivity Check: Business Publications

Session Objectives

- **Format a newsletter with multiple columns**
- **Convert text to a table format**
- **Use an agenda template**
- **Efficiently produce documents in mailable form**

Getting Started

Exercise 120.1 Unless you are continuing immediately after completing Session 119, spend at least two to three minutes warming up using Exercise 120.1 before completing the document activities in this session. See Session 101 for suggested warm-up text.

Preparing Documents

This session is an assessment of the types of documents created in Unit 19, Business Publications. Now that you have completed the instructional activities for creating business publications, you will be assessed on how accurately you can format, key, proofread, and correct these documents. In the following document activities, each completed document is to be "mailable," which means that it contains no errors. A document that requires corrections is not considered *mailable*.

Your goal is to key each document in mailable form. If you are missing errors that should have been corrected or your instructor believes you can work more efficiently, he or she may ask you to repeat document activities. Be sure to check each document to make sure all parts of the document are included.

To help you succeed, carefully review the instructions and content of each document before keying. Make sure you know the formatting elements and guidelines for each document to be keyed. If necessary, review the content of Unit 19 if you are unsure how to complete a specific task.

Document 120.1 Newsletter with Columns

Read all instructions below before starting this document activity.

1 Navigate to the Document 120.1 launch page in the Online Lab and then click the Launch Activity button to open **Doc120.01** in the activity window.

2 Click in the *Newsletter Title* placeholder and then key Communication Today.

3 Click in the *Type the company name* placeholder and then key ABC Enterprises.

4 Click in the *Pick the date* placeholder and then click the down arrow. Use the right arrow to scroll to June 2020 and then click the June 17 date.

steps continue

Table 61.1 Insertion Point–Movement Keyboard Shortcuts

Pressing this key or key combination...	moves the insertion point...
Ctrl + ←	one word to the left
Ctrl + →	one word to the right
End	to the end of a line
Home	to the beginning of a line
Page Down	one screen down
Page Up	one screen up
Ctrl + Home	to the beginning of a document
Ctrl + End	to the end of a document

Note that the Left and Right Arrow keys are typically located on the right side of the keyboard. However, on some keyboards they are integrated into the numeric keyboard. If this is the case on your keyboard, make sure to use the numeric lock feature (activated and deactivated by pressing the Num Lock key) before you use those keys.

Inserting Text

By default, when you open a document in Word, the program is in Insert mode and the insertion point, or cursor, is at the top of the document. In Insert mode, newly keyed content is added at the insertion point location and does not replace existing text. If you want to add text, simply click to position the insertion point—the active location on the screen—where you want to insert new text and then key the new text.

Deleting Text

In Word, you can delete text in several ways. For example, press the Backspace key to delete characters to the left of the insertion point or press the Delete key to delete characters to the right of the insertion point. For more information on using the Backspace and Delete keys to delete text, see Session 6 in *Paradigm Keyboarding & Applications I*.

Splitting and Joining Paragraphs

Word 2016 has a default line spacing of 1.08 lines, with 8 points of spacing after a paragraph. This means that the default line spacing is slightly greater than single spacing (which is 1.0 lines). With this default spacing setting, you only need to press Enter *once* to create the extra distance between paragraphs. (In later sessions, you will learn how to change line spacing to accommodate specific formats.)

To split a paragraph into two smaller paragraphs, position the insertion point immediately to the left of the letter that will be the first letter of the new paragraph and then press Enter. When you press Enter, the text is moved to the next line and additional white space is added above it. If necessary, press Tab at the beginning of the new paragraph to create an indent.

To join two paragraphs, delete the white space between them. There are two ways to do this. One method is to position the insertion point immediately before the first character of the second paragraph and then press the Backspace key until the paragraphs combine into one. The second method is to position the insertion point one space *past* the period (or other punctuation mark) at the end of the first paragraph and then press the Delete key until the paragraphs join.

5   Click in the *Edition 1, Volume I* placeholder and then key Volume 2, Issue 6.

6   Key the first article by completing the following steps:

   a   Turn on the display of nonprinting characters.

   b   Click in the *Story Title* placeholder in the first column on page 1 and then key Designing a Newsletter.

   c   Click in the *Story Subtitle or summary* placeholder and then key Applying Guidelines.

   d   Click in the placeholder text beginning *You can easily change the formatting* and then press Delete. Do not delete the section breaks.

   e   Key the article text shown in Figure 120.1.

   f   On the second page of the newsletter, select and copy the text beginning with *Size graphics, images, or* and ending with *balance to the total document.*

   g   Click in the placeholder text in the pull quote text box on page 1 to select the text and then paste the copied sentences.

7   Key the second article by completing the following steps:

   a   Click in the *Story Title* placeholder on page 2 and then key Creating a Newsletter Layout.

   b   Click in the *Story Subtitle or summary* placeholder on page 2 and then key Choosing the Right Paper.

   c   Click in the placeholder text that begins *You can easily change the formatting* and then press Delete. Do not delete the section breaks.

   d   Key the article text shown in Figure 120.2.

8   Key the third article by completing the following steps:

   a   Click in the *Story Title* placeholder in the third column of page 1 and then key Setting Margins.

   b   Click in the placeholder text immediately below the title and then press Delete.

   c   Key the article text shown in Figure 120.3.

9   Proofread the document and correct any errors.

10   Save the document.

11   Click the Check button to upload the document for checking.

12   If errors are reported by the Online Lab, view the results document, correct the errors in the submitted document, save the document, and then click the Check Again button.

Figure 61.4 Content for Document 61.1

When writing a cover letter to accompany a job application, it is best to sell yourself as a specialist as opposed to a generalist. This is important because in today's job market, companies hire specialists to solve specific problems. Keep this in mind as you write your cover letter.

When you write your cover letter, think of the letter as a marketing piece. What you are selling is yourself! Your challenge is to write a marketing communication document that is powerful and pushes the reader to action. You are trying to make the hiring manager contact you to set up an interview.

Making Changes to Keyed Documents

The Online Lab will compare your completed document to a model document, so it is important that your documents are keyed and edited carefully and accurately. Extra spaces between words or at the end of sentences as well as formatting mistakes will be marked as errors.

Using the Show or Hide Nonprinting Characters Feature

By default, when you work in Word, you are working with documents in Print Layout view, so what you see on screen is what will print. However, it can be helpful to see nonprinting characters as you are keying or editing a document. Nonprinting characters include spaces, tabs, and paragraph marks. The show or hide nonprinting characters feature in Word will either show or hide these nonprinting characters. If nonprinting characters are hidden, click the Show/Hide ¶ button in the Paragraph group on the Home tab (see Figure 61.5). When the nonprinting characters are shown, a space appears as a dot between words, a tab appears as a right-pointing arrow, and a paragraph mark (created by pressing Enter) appears as a ¶.

Moving the Insertion Point

The insertion point moves as you key text, as well as when you press the Backspace key or the Delete key. You can also move the insertion point to other locations within the document using the mouse or by using keys or key combinations. Table 61.1 lists some commonly used keyboard shortcuts for moving the insertion point. The plus (+) symbol means that you use two keys at the same time. For example, to move the insertion point to the beginning of a document, press and hold down the left Ctrl key (located to the left of the spacebar), press the Home key, and then release the Ctrl key. You will want to practice using these keyboard shortcuts as you work with documents. For more keyboard shortcuts, see Appendix A.

Figure 61.5 Paragraph Group on the Home Tab

Show/Hide ¶ button

Paragraph

Figure 120.1 Newsletter Article 1 for Document 120.1

One of the biggest challenges in creating a newsletter is balancing change with consistency. A newsletter is a document that is typically reproduced regularly, whether monthly, bimonthly, or quarterly. Each issue features new content—new ideas, new text, and new graphics or photos. However, for your newsletter to be effective, each issue must also maintain a consistent appearance. Consistency contributes to your publication's identity and gives your readers a feeling of familiarity.

As you design your newsletter, think about the elements that should remain consistent from issue to issue. Consistent newsletter features and elements may include: margin size, column layout, nameplate (the artwork and/or text that includes the name of the publication and is usually located at the top of the first page), logo, color, ruled lines, and formatting of headlines, subheads, and body text.

Focus and balance can be achieved in a newsletter through the design and size of the nameplate, the arrangement of text on the page, the use of graphics, images, or scanned photographs, and the careful use of lines, borders, and backgrounds. When you choose graphics, images, or photos, use restraint and consider the appropriateness of the images. A single, large illustration is usually more effective than several small images scattered throughout the document. Size graphics, images, or photos according to their relative importance to the content. Headlines and subheads can serve as secondary focal points as well as provide balance to the total document.

White space around a headline creates contrast and attracts the reader's eyes to the headline. Surround text with white space if you want the text to stand out. If you want to draw attention to the nameplate or headline of the newsletter, you may want to choose a bold type style and a larger type size.

Good directional flow can be achieved by using ruled lines that lead the reader's eyes through the document. Graphic elements, placed strategically throughout a newsletter, can provide a pattern for the reader's eyes to follow.

If you decide to use color in a newsletter, use it sparingly. Establish focus and directional flow by using color to highlight key information or elements in your publication.

Success Tip

When completing each document activity, your goal is to create a mailable document, which is a document that does not contain any errors.

Document 61.1

Keying a Word Document

Read all instructions below before starting this document activity.

1 Navigate to the Document 61.1 launch page in the Online Lab and then click the Launch Activity button to open Word and **Doc061.01** in the activity window.

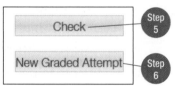

2 Key the two paragraphs of text shown in Figure 61.4. Remember to press Tab at the start of each paragraph and press Enter once at the end of the first paragraph. Your text will wrap differently since you are using a different font. As you key the text, press the Backspace key immediately to correct errors that you "feel," but do not take time to check your screen as you key. *Hint: Remember to press the spacebar once (not twice) at the end of a sentence.*

3 Read your document on the screen to look for any errors you may have missed. If you see any red or double blue lines under words, the Word spelling and grammar checker has flagged them for you to review. If you see an error, correct it.

4 Save the document by clicking the Save button on the Quick Access Toolbar or use the keyboard shortcut Ctrl + S.

5 Click the Check button to upload **Doc061.01** for checking. A progress bar on the Results button shows that the document is being checked by the Online Lab. When the evaluation is complete, the Online Lab will display a Submitted button and a Results button below the Check button. Your WPM rate and the number of errors made will display at the lower-right corner of the Online Lab screen.

6 If your instructor allows you more than one chance to get a grade for your document, click the New Graded Attempt button. This will give you a new base document that you can use to try the activity again.

7 If errors are reported by the Online Lab after your scored attempt, view your results document and correct the errors in the submitted document by completing the following steps:

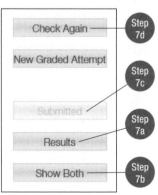

   a Click the Results button to view a document showing errors in keying and formatting. You can print this document, if necessary (press Ctrl + P).

   b Click the Show Both button to view both the submitted and results documents within the same window.

   c Click the Submitted button to return to the submitted document. (The button for the active view is grayed out.)

   d Edit the submitted document to correct any errors, save the document (press Ctrl + S), and then click the Check Again button.

   e If the Online Lab still reports errors, repeat Steps 7a–7d. When you are finished, click the Next button.

Figure 120.2 Newsletter Article 2 for Document 120.1

Paper size and type are among the first considerations when designing the layout of a newsletter. These decisions may be affected by the number of copies needed and the equipment available for creating, printing, and distributing the newsletters. Although some newsletters may be created on larger paper, most are created on standard letter-sized paper, which measures 8.5 by 11 inches. Standard, letter-sized paper is the most economical choice for printing and is easier to hold and read. In addition, letter-sized paper is cheaper to mail and fits easily in standard file folders.

When choosing the weight of the paper for a newsletter, consider the graphics or photographs to be included, the quality desired, and the cost. The heavier the stock, the more expensive the paper. Although white may seem like the most logical paper color to choose, pure white paper can be more difficult to read because of glare. If possible, investigate other subtle colors. Another option is to purchase predesigned newsletter paper from a paper supply company. Predesigned papers come in many colors and designs. They may also have different blocks of color on the page to help separate and organize your text.

After considering paper size, weight, and color, determine the margins of your newsletter pages. Margin size is linked to the number of columns needed, the formality desired, and the amount of text and visual elements to be included. Keep the margins consistent throughout your newsletter.

Figure 120.3 Newsletter Article 3 for Document 120.1

The following are a few general guidelines for margins in newsletters:

A wide right margin is considered formal. This approach positions the text at the left side of the page—the side where most readers tend to look first. If the justification is set at full, the newsletter will appear even more formal.

A wide left margin is less formal. A table of contents or marginal subheads can be placed in the left margin to give the newsletter an airy, open appearance.

Equal margins tend to create an informal look.

Figure 61.3 Print Backstage Area

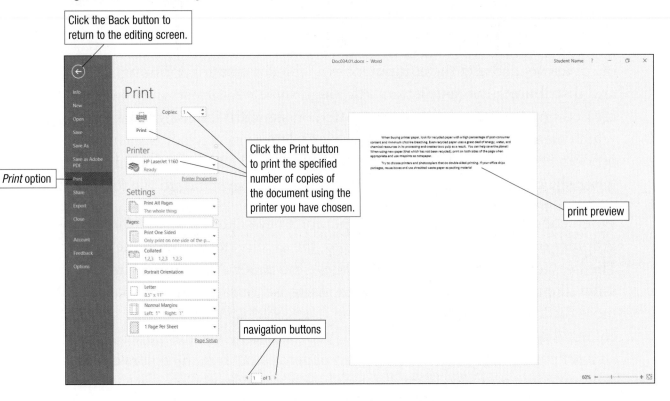

The image of the document on the screen is called a *soft copy*. To print a copy of a document, referred to as a *hard copy*, click the File tab and then click *Print* to display the Print backstage area, shown in Figure 61.3. You can also display the Print backstage area by pressing Ctrl + P.

The Print backstage area displays a preview of how the document will print, and the navigation buttons below the preview image allow you to advance through the document pages (for documents with more than one page). Before clicking the Print button, set the desired number of copies to print in the *Copies* measurement box in the *Print* section. Use the drop-down list in the *Printer* section to select a printer. The drop-down lists in the *Settings* section provide options for specifying how a document is printed, including which pages are to be printed, the orientation, and the paper size.

Using the Online Lab to Complete Document Activities

Sessions 34 through 60 in *Paradigm Keyboarding & Applications I Using Microsoft Word: Sessions 1–60* introduced many of the fundamental features of Microsoft Word. In completing those sessions, you gained experience with these features as you generated and edited a variety of business documents. The sessions in *Paradigm Keyboarding & Applications II* will review some of these basic features and introduce more advanced features. You will apply these skills in producing Word documents while working on improving your keyboarding speed and accuracy. As in *Paradigm Keyboarding & Applications I*, you will complete the document activities using the Online Lab, which will launch Word on your computer. You will start with either a blank document or a document that already contains some text and/or formatting.

For information about the Online Lab, see the "Online Lab Features" and "Getting Started in the Online Lab" sections of this book's Preface. These sections include instructions for downloading and installing the Online Lab application, enrolling in your Keyboarding course, and navigating and using the Online Lab.

Video
61.1

Watch Video 61.1 in the Online Lab. The video shows how to complete document activities.

Document 120.2

Informational Document with Text Converted to a Table

Read all instructions below before starting this document activity.

1 Navigate to the Document 120.2 launch page in the Online Lab and then click the Launch Activity button to open **Doc120.02** in the activity window.

2 Key the text shown in Figure 120.4. Center the title and subtitle.

3 Change the title font to 14-point Copperplate Gothic Bold and the subtitle font to 12-point Copperplate Gothic Light. *Hint: Format the nonprinting paragraph marks following the headings.*

4 Convert the text from the heading *Honesty* through the text *build strong relationships* to a two-column table. Include the period following *relationships*.

5 Select the table and then change the spacing before and after paragraphs to 8 points.

6 Change the width of the first column to 2 inches and the second column to 3.5 inches.

7 Remove the table borders.

8 Center the table horizontally.

9 Proofread the document and correct any errors.

10 Save the document.

11 Click the Check button to upload the document for checking.

12 If errors are reported by the Online Lab, view the results document, correct the errors in the submitted document, save the document, and then click the Check Again button.

Figure 120.4 Informational Document Content for Document 120.2

ABOUT THE BYRON COMMUNITY ASSOCIATION

Core Values

The Byron Community Association (BCA) is a registered community association for homeowners in the Byron community. There are approximately 1,500 members. Our mission is to enhance the daily living of our members by providing opportunities for input into initiatives, community building, and community development. BCA core values are listed in the following table:

Honesty: [Tab] We demonstrate this cornerstone of our community through accountability and high ethical standards.

Respect: [Tab] We create respect within our community and association through listening, understanding, and acknowledging member feedback.

Adaptability: [Tab] We ensure the success of our association by embracing positive change and by nurturing diversity, creativity, and visionary thinking.

Communication: [Tab] We remain approachable at all levels, communicate openly, and build strong relationships.

Figure 61.1 Microsoft Word 2016 Blank Document Screen

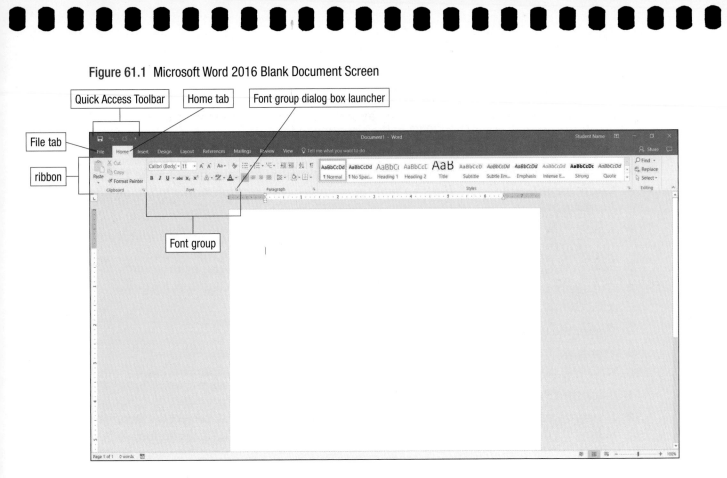

Figure 61.2 Save As Dialog Box

Agenda Template

Read all instructions below before starting this document activity.

1 Navigate to the Document 120.3 launch page in the Online Lab and then click the Launch Activity button to open **Doc120.03** in the activity window.

2 Edit the agenda template so that the final document matches the content shown in Figure 120.5.

3 Save the document.

4 Click the Check button to upload the document for checking.

5 If errors are reported by the Online Lab, view the results document, correct the errors in the submitted document, save the document, and then click the Check Again button.

Figure 120.5 Agenda Content and Format for Document 120.3

AGENDA

Byron Community Association
February 21, 2020
9:30 a.m. – 4:00 p.m.

Meeting called by **Samuel Morrison, Chair**

| **Attendees:** | Julie Jankowski, Katerina Holland, Jackson Sterling |
| **Please bring:** | Minutes of January 13, 2020 Meeting |

9:30 a.m. – 10:00 a.m.	**Introduction** Continental Breakfast Welcome	 Samuel Morrison	Empire Room
10:00 a.m. – noon	**Community Projects 2020 Update** Community Gardens Community Forestry	 Katerina Holland Samuel Morrison	Empire Room
noon – 1:00 p.m.	**Lunch** Working Lunch—Group Discussions		Executive Lounge
1:00 p.m. – 2:30 p.m.	**Accessibility Advisory Committee** Concerns Regarding Parking	 Julie Jankowski	Empire Room
2:30 p.m. – 3:30 p.m.	**Community Safety and Crime Prevention** Pathway Lighting Walk-in-Pairs Promotion	 Julie Jankowski Katerina Holland	Empire Room
3:30 p.m. – 4:00 p.m.	**Wrap-up** Adjournment	 Samuel Morrison	Empire Room

Additional Instructions:
Please remember to bring in your parking ticket for validation.

Timings
61.1–61.2

Visit a wild animal park. A park shows animals roaming freely in settings like their native homelands. Wild animal parks have all gained worldwide recognition for their conservation. View the many animals living together on sweeping plains and in dense forests. You can observe the special behavior of animals living in herds and flocks. There will probably be 14 to 15 shows during your park visit. Be sure to take your camera along with you on your visit to the park. You will want to get lots of shots of all the animals.

Ergonomic Tip

Use two hands for two-key combos. Whenever you use a Shift, Ctrl, or Alt key together with another key, always press one key with one hand and the other key with the opposite hand. Trying to perform these actions with one hand will cause unnecessary muscle strain.

Opening Microsoft Word 2016 and Creating, Saving, and Printing a Word Document

The steps to open Word may vary depending on your operating system setup. At the Windows 10 desktop, click the Start button and then click the Word 2016 tile. At the Word 2016 opening screen, click the *Blank document* template.

When you click the *Blank document* template, a blank document displays, as shown in Figure 61.1. Figure 61.1 also shows some of the commonly used features in the Word 2016 interface. The Word interface features a ribbon that contains several tabs. Each tab provides a different set of formatting commands and buttons. The Home tab is indicated in Figure 61.1.

The content of each tab is presented in different groups. A group contains a set of options that allow you to control related aspects of document preparation and editing. For example, the Font group on the Home tab contains buttons and options that change the way type appears in the document. You can use the buttons and options in this group to increase or decrease the size of the type, make it **bold** or *italic*, and change the color of the text. You can also use the Font group dialog box launcher to display the Font dialog box, where you can make additional formatting changes to the text.

No matter which tab you select, the Quick Access Toolbar is always available. By default, this toolbar appears above the ribbon and provides buttons to save the document, undo a change, and redo or repeat a change. You can customize this toolbar by adding or removing buttons.

There are several ways to save a Word document. The most common are to press Ctrl + S; click the Save button on the Quick Access Toolbar; or click the File tab and then click *Save As*. When you choose one of these options, the Save As backstage area displays. At this backstage area, click the *Browse* option to display the Save As dialog box, as shown in Figure 61.2. At the Save As dialog box, navigate to the desired location in which to save the file, type the name of the file in the *File name* text box and then press Enter or click the Save button. Press the F12 function key to display the Save As dialog box without having to first display the Save As backstage area.

Ending the Session

The Online Lab automatically saved the work you completed for this session. You may exit the Online Lab and continue later.

Session

61

Reviewing Basic Word Processing and Document Production

Session Objectives

- **Review basic word processing features**
- **Review how to access the Online Lab to complete document activities**
- **Use the show or hide nonprinting characters feature and move the insertion point**
- **Insert and delete text**
- **Split and join paragraphs**
- **Review proofreading marks and techniques**
- **Identify and understand the effects of sexist language in documents**
- **Efficiently produce documents in mailable form**

Getting Started

Exercise 61.1

Begin the work for Session 61 by completing Exercise 61.1, a warm-up drill, in the Online Lab.

Continue your session work by completing Exercise 61.2 in the Online Lab. In this timed short drill, you (1) select the drill goal to key for either speed or accuracy, (2) set the desired drill duration at 15 seconds, 30 seconds, or 60 seconds, and (3) identify your personal words per minute (WPM) goal. It is important that you select appropriate goals each time and that you focus intently on meeting those goals. You can repeat this exercise as many times as you like before moving on to the timing assessments.

Exercise 61.2

Assessing Your Speed and Accuracy

Complete Timings 61.1 and 61.2 in the Online Lab using the timing text shown on the next page. Both timings use the same paragraph.

For all timings, once you are on an active timing screen, the timing will start as soon as you begin keying. Press the Tab key at the beginning of each paragraph. Do not press the Enter key at the end of each line but only at the end of the paragraph. If you finish keying the timing passage before the time expires, press Enter, press Tab, and then start keying the timing text again. When time expires, the Online Lab will display your WPM rate and any errors. The results will be saved in your Timings Performance report. *Note: In this book, all 1-minute timings will be taken twice. Both the first and second timing will use the same paragraph or paragraphs. In contrast, all 3-minute and 5-minute timings will be taken once.*

If you do not key at or above the WPM rate identified in the Online Lab on Timing 61.1, concentrate on speed on Timing 61.2. If you meet the Online Lab's WPM goal but make more errors than the goal identified in the Online Lab on Timing 61.1, concentrate on accuracy on Timing 61.2. However, if you meet or exceed both goals for Timing 61.1, push for greater speed on Timing 61.2.

Appendix A

Keyboard Shortcuts in Microsoft Word 2016

Feature	Keyboard Shortcuts
Bold formatting	Ctrl + B
Center align text	Ctrl + E
Copy	Ctrl + C
Cut	Ctrl + X
Find (Navigation pane)	Ctrl + F
Find and Replace	Ctrl + H
Insert line space	Shift + Enter
Insert page break	Ctrl + Enter
Insert tab in a table	Ctrl + Tab
Italic formatting	Ctrl + I
Justify align text	Ctrl + J
Left align text	Ctrl + L
Move insertion point one word to left	Ctrl + ←
Move insertion point one word to right	Ctrl + →
Move insertion point to end of document	Ctrl + End
Move insertion point to end of line	End
Move insertion point to start of line	Home
Move insertion point to top of document	Ctrl + Home
New document	Ctrl + N
Open document	Ctrl + O
Paste	Ctrl + V
Print	Ctrl + P
Right align text	Ctrl + R
Save	Ctrl + S
Select all	Ctrl + A
Show/hide nonprinting characters	Ctrl + Shift + *
Undo	Ctrl + Z
Underline formatting	Ctrl + U

Unit 13   Emails and Memos Part II

Appendix B

Proofreading Marks

Mark	Meaning	Example	Change Implemented
#	insert space	lettertothe	letter to the
ℒ	delete	the commands is	the command is
⌐ or ⓛ𝒸/	lowercase	he is Branch Manager	he is branch manager
ⓒⓐⓟ or UC ≡	uppercase	Margaret simpson	Margaret Simpson
¶	new paragraph	¶ The new product	The new product
no ¶	no paragraph	the meeting. no ¶ Bring the	the meeting. Bring the
⌐	line break	the dog│and cat	the dog and cat
V or ∧	insert	pens,clips (and)	pens, and clips
⌄	insert comma	In addition we	In addition, we
⊙	insert period	a global search	a global search.
⌐	move right	⌐ With the papers	With the papers
⌐	move left	⌐access the code	access the code
⌐⌐	center	⌐Chapter Six⌐	Chapter Six
∪	transpose	It is raesonable	It is reasonable
ⓢⓟ ◯	spell out	ⓢⓟ 475 Mill Ave.	475 Mill Avenue

Session 72: Modifying the Layout of Tables

Exercise 72.1: Warm-Up Drill

Exercise 72.2: Timed Short Drill — Click a link to view the activity.

Timing 72.1: 1 Minute

Timing 72.2: 1 Minute

Timing 72.3: 5 Minutes

Word Tutor: Changing the Table Layout

Document 72.1: Inserting Rows and Columns and Merging Cells in a Table

Document 72.2: Deleting a

Document 72.3: Cutting and

Document 72.4: Using Auto

Document 72.5: Adjusting a

Document 72.6: Creating a

Document 72.7: Designing

Activity list in Online Lab

Click to view the Course Menu page.

Click to go to the next activity.

Click to go to the previous activity.

Click to repeat the activity.

progress counter

Timed short drill settings screen in Online Lab

When you click the Launch button, you will see a screen similar to the one shown above—in this case, a screen where you choose your own settings and goals for a timed short drill.

To move around the Online Lab, you can click the Next button to go to the next activity, click the Previous button to go to the previous activity, or click the Repeat button to return to the beginning of the present activity. To see the list of all activities, grouped by session (as shown in the top image above), click the Course Menu button.

Directions for the activity display at the top of the activity window. If there is text for you to read as you key, it appears below the instructions. (For many activities, the text to key is in the textbook.) The insertion point (blinking vertical line) is positioned in the text box in which you will key text. Some activities are divided into more than one part. You can check how many parts of an activity you have completed by noting the progress counter on the right side of the screen.

Instructor eResources

The Keyboarding Online Lab is a web-based learning management system that lets instructors easily deliver customized keyboarding courses and efficiently communicate with enrolled students. The Online Lab includes extensive reports documenting student activity and a grade book for assigning grades and tracking student progress.

Additional instructor support is available through the Instructor eResources link in the Online Lab and includes a sample syllabus, reference material and instructional support for each session, a theory quiz, general suggestions on teaching keyboarding, a set of PowerPoint presentations with lecture notes, rubrics for evaluating unchecked document activities, as well as content for pretest and posttest timings. The pretest and posttest timings are completed in the Online Lab.

Mark	Meaning	Example	Change Implemented
(stet) ...	stet (Latin for "Let it stand")	(stet) I am ~~very~~ pleased	I am very pleased
⌣	combine or close up	regret fully	regretfully
ss	single-space	The margin top ss is 1 inch.	The margin top is 1 inch.
ds	double-space	ds Paper length is set for 11 inches.	Paper length is set for 11 inches.
ts	triple-space	ts The F8 function key turns on Extend	The F8 function key turns on Extend
bf ∿	boldface	bf Boldface type provides emphasis.	**Boldface** type provides emphasis.
(ital) —	italic	(ital) Use italic for terms to be defined.	Use *italic* for terms to be defined.
(BL)	bulleted list	(BL) Start a bulleted list	• Start a bulleted list.
-- or /m	em dash	Southeast even	Southeast—even
⨍ ⨎	parenthesis	⨍Figure 69.4⨎	(Figure 69.4)
=	insert hyphen	555=1212	555-1212
⟲	move text	12 June, 2013	June 12, 2016
∼	run text in	John Smith, President	John Smith, President

8   At the web page that displays, fill in the fields of the form to create a user account.

　　a   Your email address will already appear in the *Email* field.

　　b   Enter your first and last names.

　　c   Create a password at least 8 characters long, including at least one UPPERCASE letter, one number, and one special character (such as ! or #).

9   Click the CREATE AN ACCOUNT button.

Logging in to the Online Lab

Once the Online Lab application is installed on your computer and you are enrolled in the Paradigm Keyboarding course, follow these steps to log in:

1   Return to the Paradigm Keyboarding Online Lab application by clicking the Online Lab icon on the Windows taskbar or your computer desktop.

2   On the LOGIN tab, enter your email address and password.

3   Click the LOG IN button.

Navigating in the Online Lab

Once enrolled and logged in to your Keyboarding course in the Online Lab, you will see a Course Menu page listing the activities in your course as well as a Navigation pane and additional resources. The image at the top of the next page shows the Activity List within the Course Menu. Click an activity link to go to that activity's View page. Then click the Launch button to bring up that activity.

Index

3 At the Paradigm Keyboarding Online Lab website, click the DOWNLOAD AND INSTALL button to download the desktop installer application.

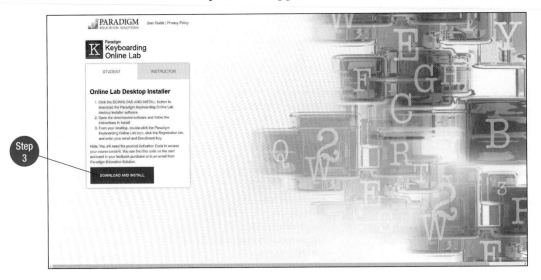

4 Click the Open, Save File, or Run button (this will vary based on your browser), open the downloaded file, and follow the instructions to install the desktop application.

Enrolling in the Online Lab

Once you have installed the Online Lab application, complete the following steps to enroll in the Online Lab for your Keyboarding course.

1 Double-click the Launch Online Lab icon on your computer desktop.

2 Click the REGISTRATION tab.

3 Enter your email address.

4 Enter the Enrollment Key given to you by your instructor for your course.

5 Click the REGISTER button.

6 Check your email for a message welcoming you to the Paradigm Keyboarding Online Lab.

7 In the body of the email message, click the CREATE AN ACCOUNT button.

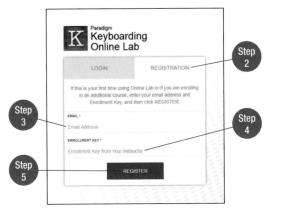

steps continue

Unchecked Document Activities

Unchecked document activities require the student to create a type of document that is either ungradable by the Online Lab or more open-ended than the checked documents. In these types of activities, students compose a document according to the instructions in the textbook. When the student finishes the activity, he or she clicks the Submit button. The document is then sent to the Online Lab, where the instructor can review it.

Word Tutor

The Online Lab includes skills-based tutorials that provide interactive, guided training and measured practice to support Word skills taught in the courseware. Word Tutor content expands the skills training provided in the textbook and applied in the Online Lab activities.

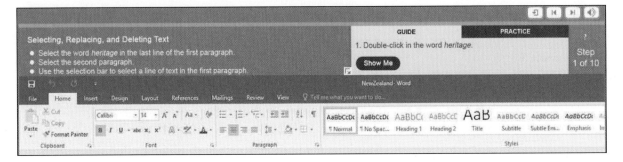

Grade Book and Reports

The Online Lab includes a grade book that automatically documents the grades for all completed timings and checked document activities. Instructors can add other activities to the grade book and then enter grades for those activities. Instructors can also edit grades. All grade data may be easily exported to other learning management systems.

The Online Lab also includes reports designed to allow students and instructors to assess student progress through the courseware. The reports include the Prescriptive Analysis report, the Progress report, the Timings Performance report, the Average Timings Performance report, and the Document Performance report.

Getting Started in the Online Lab

You will be using the Online Lab application along with your textbook to complete session activities that will help you develop your keyboarding skills.

Installing the Online Lab Software

If your computer does not already have the Online Lab application, complete the following steps to install it.

1 Connect to the Internet.
2 Launch your web browser (such as Chrome) and then go to http://key7e .paradigmeducation.com.

steps continue

Document Activities

For each document activity, students launch the activity in the Online Lab, complete the activity as specified by the easy-to-follow, step-by-step instructions in the textbook, and then submit the document for assessment. The launch page for each document activity in the Online Lab includes a textbook icon and a reference to the corresponding textbook page number(s).

The Online Lab automatically manages the files for each document activity. When the student clicks the Launch Activity button, Word opens in the Online Lab window and retrieves the base document used in the activity. The Online Lab also automatically saves all files created in the document activities for future reference.

There are two types of document activities: checked activities and unchecked activities.

Checked Document Activities

For most document activities, the Online Lab will evaluate keying and formatting accuracy. For these types of document activities, when the student has completed the activity and proofread the document, he or she clicks the Check button, which initiates the checking process. While the checking process is occurring, the Results button displays an embedded green progress bar until the results document is ready for review. The results document, accessible by clicking the Results button, visually indicates any differences (that is, errors) between the student's submitted document and the model answer.

After viewing the results document, students can then return to the Word document that they generated by clicking the Submitted button. Alternatively, students can view both their submitted document and the results document by clicking the Show Both button. The Show Both button splits the screen and displays both documents in an over/under format. A student can then make corrections to the submitted document, which can be checked again for errors.

Instructors can adjust the maximum error goals for document activities, schedule multiple document attempts, and specify which attempt's score will be used for the final grade. These options provide opportunities to tailor assessments based on students' needs and abilities.

The results document shows the differences between the student's submitted document and the model answer.

The Online Lab reports WPM rates and number of errors. WPM is reported for the first checked document. *Errors* reflect the most recently submitted document.

Paradigm Keyboarding and Applications II Using Microsoft Word 2016, Sessions 61–120, Seventh Edition, is divided into 10 units. Units 13–19 present a variety of Word features that are used to prepare different types of business documents. The first four sessions of each unit introduce the Word features and their use in business documents. The fifth session of these units provides additional practice and assessments.

The documents and scenarios that the student will encounter in Units 20 and 21 simulate realistic work experiences. Unit 20 is set in a legal office and Unit 21 in a medical center. In the first several sessions of these units, legal and medical document types are introduced. The latter part of these units consists of projects in which students evaluate a set of tasks, establish priorities, and plan necessary actions. Unit 22 provides an opportunity to assess student document production skills developed in preceding units of the courseware.

Each session in Paradigm *Keyboarding and Applications II Using Microsoft Word 2016: Sessions 61–120*, Seventh Edition, is a coherent lesson with specific objectives that focus on particular skills. Students can work at their own pace and can repeat session activities as often as needed. For most sessions, students will complete warm-up drills and timings. Timings are specifically designed to boost keying speed and enhance accuracy. Furthermore, Success Tip and Ergonomic Tip feature boxes provide suggestions to help students work efficiently and effectively.

Online Lab Features

The Paradigm Keyboarding Online Lab is a web-based keyboarding tutor and learning management system (LMS) application. Download and install the Online Lab from http://Key7e .ParadigmEducation.com. The Online Lab gives students access to their course activities from any web-connected, Windows-based computer. Instructors also have access to all student work and scores by launching and logging into the Online Lab.

All Online Lab activities are referenced in the textbook, individually numbered, and clearly identified in the left margin of the text. The activities in the Online Lab include exercises, timings, and documents. In addition, the Online lab includes Word tutorials.

Warm-up drill in Online Lab

Corresponding textbook page for exercises and timings

Exercises

Session work begins with exercises that include warm-up drills and timed short drills. Warm-up drills prepare the student for the document production activities that follow. The timed short drills provide students an opportunity to enhance their keying speed or accuracy.

Timings

Timings are an important tool in assessing keying proficiency, and the Online Lab provides immediate feedback on speed and accuracy for all timings. Sessions include combinations of 1-minute, 3-minute, and 5-minute timings. Instructors can adjust the minimum-error and target-WPM counts for timings as desired.

Results of a 1-minute timing in Online Lab

Preface

Keyboarding and using Microsoft® Word to produce documents are fundamental skills for anyone who plans to work in any type of business environment. To be effective in communicating through email, business correspondence, and other types of documents, a person must be able to think and key simultaneously. Keyboarding and document production are no longer nice-to-know skills—they are now *essential* skills.

Paradigm Keyboarding and Applications II Using Microsoft Word 2016: Sessions 61–120, Seventh Edition, and the accompanying Online Lab provide instruction in the basic and more advanced elements of word processing using Microsoft Word 2016 for document production. Word features are applied to the production of a variety of business documents, including email, memos, business letters, business reports, and manuscripts. To use this textbook and the Online Lab successfully, students should be able to key alphanumeric text at an average rate of 40 words per minute (WPM) with a maximum of one error per minute.

The emphasis of this courseware is to develop a student's keyboarding speed and accuracy skills, a firm command of Word features, and the ability to prepare documents quickly, accurately, and with correct formatting. After successfully completing a course that uses this textbook and the accompanying Online Lab, students will be able to do the following:

- Key straight-copy alphanumeric material using correct touch techniques at an average rate of 55 words per minute (WPM) with a maximum of one error per minute
- Use basic Word features such as inserting and deleting text, changing fonts and line spacing, centering and aligning text, checking spelling and grammar, using tabs, formatting bulleted and numbered lists, inserting and modifying tables, inserting headers and footers, keying footnotes and citations, and others
- Prepare and correctly format common business documents including email, memos, business letters, business reports, and manuscripts
- Compose coherent content at the keyboard at the word, sentence, paragraph, and document levels
- Establish priorities and plan necessary actions when placed in a business setting with a variety of tasks that need to be completed

To assist students with the last course objective, two projects (Unit 20, in a virtual legal office; and Unit 21, in a virtual medical center) are provided to help develop decision-making skills.

Keyboarding Program Overview

Paradigm Keyboarding and Applications II Using Microsoft Word 2016: Sessions 61–120, Seventh Edition, and Online Lab provide a streamlined and contemporary approach to mastering lifelong keyboarding, word processing, and document production skills.

This courseware includes the final 60 of the 120 sessions that comprise the Paradigm Keyboarding Series. For additional keyboarding timing practice and further instruction in word processing using Microsoft Word 2016, as well as instruction and practice in preparing business documents, see *Paradigm Keyboarding and Applications I Using Microsoft Word 2016: Sessions 1–60*, Seventh Edition. For a course that focuses on keyboarding skills without instruction in Microsoft Word, see *Paradigm Keyboarding: Sessions 1–30*, Seventh Edition. These titles are available at ParadigmEducation.com or by calling 800-353-6685.

Unit 19 Business Publications 301

Unit 20 Legal Documents and Legal Office Project 346

Unit 21 Medical Documents and Medical Center Project 433

Unit 22 Productivity Measurement Part II 491

Contents

Division President	Linda Hein
Vice President, Content Management	Christine Hurney
Developmental Editor	Eric Braem
Editorial Support	Jennifer Gehlhar, Melora Pappas, Katie Werdick
Director of Production	Timothy W. Larson
Production Editor	Blaire Wickstrom
Cover Designer and Production Specialist	Jack Ross
Vice President, Digital Solutions	Chuck Bratton
Digital Projects Manager	Tom Modl
Digital Solutions Manager	Gerry Yumul
Vice President Sales and Marketing	Scott Burns
Director of Marketing	Lara Weber McLellan

Special thanks to the following individuals: Janet Blum, Fanshawe College; Rebecca Born, NorQuest College; and Janet Bradley, Conestoga College.

Care has been taken to verify the accuracy of information presented in this book. However, the authors, editors, and publisher cannot accept responsibility for Web, email, newsgroup, or chat room subject matter or content, or for consequences from application of the information in this book, and make no warranty, expressed or implied, with respect to its content.

Trademarks: Microsoft is a trademark or registered trademark of Microsoft Corporation in the United States and/or other countries. Some of the product names and company names included in this book have been used for identification purposes only and may be trademarks or registered trade names of their respective manufacturers and sellers. The authors, editors, and publisher disclaim any affiliation, association, or connection with, or sponsorship or endorsement by, such owners.

Cover image credit: istock.com/-strizh- (semi-opaque squares; modified)

We have made every effort to trace the ownership of all copyrighted material and to secure permission from copyright holders. In the event of any question arising as to the use of any material, we will be pleased to make the necessary corrections in future printings. Thanks are due to the aforementioned authors, publishers, and agents for permission to use the materials indicated.

ISBN 978-0-76387-807-8 (print)
ISBN 978-0-76387-810-8 (digital)
Paradigm Keyboarding Online Lab: Key7e.ParadigmEducation.com

© 2018 by Paradigm Publishing, Inc.
875 Montreal Way
St. Paul, MN 55102
Email: CustomerService@ParadigmEducation.com
Website: ParadigmEducation.com

Printed in the United States of America

26 25 24 23 22 21 20 19 18 17   1 2 3 4 5 6 7 8 9 10

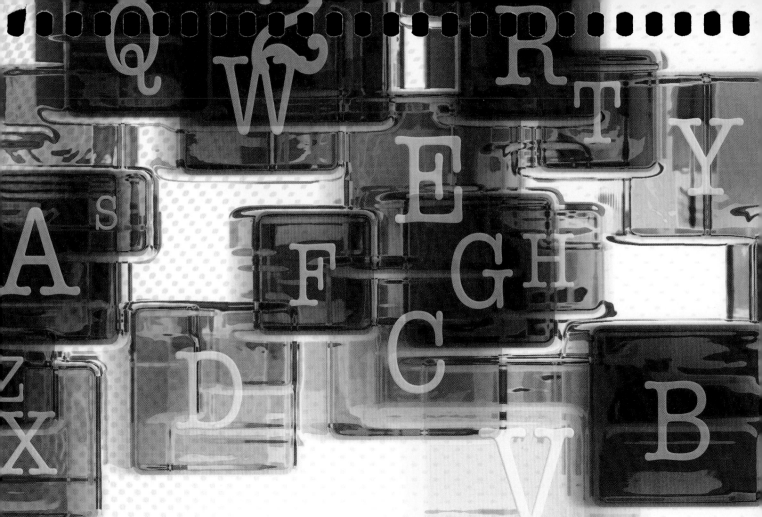

Paradigm

Keyboarding
& Applications II

Using Microsoft® Word 2016

Paradigm

Keyboarding
& Applications II

Using Microsoft® Word 2016

Sessions 61–120

Seventh Edition

William Mitchell ■ **Audrey Roggenkamp** ■ **Patricia King** ■ **Ronald Kapper**

PARADIGM
EDUCATION SOLUTIONS

St. Paul

PARADIGM
EDUCATION SOLUTIONS

Paradigm

Keyboarding

Using Microsoft® Word 2016

& Applications II

Sessions 61–120

ISBN 978-0-76387-807-8

9 780763 878078

ParadigmEducation.com

Seventh Edition

William Mitchell ▪ **Audrey Roggenkamp** ▪ **Patricia King** ▪ **Ronald Kapper**